A HISTORY OF THE
MODERN WORLD

To 1815

TENTH EDITION

A HISTORY OF THE MODERN WORLD

To 1815

 R.R. Palmer   Joel Colton   Lloyd Kramer

Boston   Burr Ridge, IL   Dubuque, IA   Madison, WI   New York
San Francisco   St. Louis   Bangkok   Bogotá   Caracas   Kuala Lumpur
Lisbon   London   Madrid   Mexico City   Milan   Montreal   New Delhi
Santiago   Seoul   Singapore   Sydney   Taipei   Toronto

Higher Education

A HISTORY OF THE MODERN WORLD: TO 1815
Published by McGraw-Hill, a business unit of The McGraw-Hill Companies, Inc., 1221
Avenue of the Americas, New York, NY, 10020. Copyright © 2007, 2002, 1995, 1992, 1984,
1978, 1971, 1965, 1956, 1950 by The McGraw-Hill Companies, Inc. All rights reserved. No
part of this publication may be reproduced or distributed in any form or by any means, or
stored in a database or retrieval system, without the prior written consent of The McGraw-
Hill Companies, Inc., including, but not limited to, in any network or other electronic storage
or transmission, or broadcast for distance learning.

Some ancillaries, including electronic and print components, may not be available to customers outside the United States.

This book is printed on acid-free paper.

5 6 7 8 9 0 DOW/DOW 1 0 9 8 7 6 5 4 3 2

ISBN-13: 978-0-07-310747-9
ISBN-10:   0-07-310747-6

Vice President and Editor-in-Chief: *Emily Barrosse*
Publisher: *Lyn Uhl*
Senior Sponsoring Editor: *Monica Eckman*
Developmental Editor: *Larry Goldberg*
Marketing Manager: *Katherine Bates*
Managing Editor: *Jean Dal Porto*
Lead Project Manager: *Susan Trentacosti*
Manuscript Editor: *Maxine Barber*
Art Director: *Jeanne Schreiber*
Art Editor: *Ayelet Arbel*
Illustrators: *Mapping Specialists and Ayelet Arbel*
Designer: *Marianna Kinigakis*
Photo Research Coordinators: *Nora Agbayani and Sonia Brown*
Photo Researcher: *PhotoSearch, Inc, NY*
Cover Credit: *Réunion des Musées Nationaux/Art Resource, NY*
Senior Supplement Producer: *Louis Swaim*
Lead Media Producer: *Sean Crowley*
Media Project Manager: *Wendy Constantine*
Production Supervisor: *Janean A. Utley*
Composition: *10/12 Times Roman, by TBH Typecast, Inc.*
Printing: *45# New Era Matte, R.R. Donnelley & Sons*

Library of Congress Catalog Number: 2006921641

The Internet addresses listed in the text were accurate at the time of publication. The inclu-
sion of a Web site does not indicate an endorsement by the authors or McGraw-Hill, and
McGraw-Hill does not guarantee the accuracy of the information presented at these sites.

www.mhhe.com

About the Authors

R.R. PALMER was born in Chicago in 1909. After graduating from the University of Chicago he received his Ph.D. from Cornell University in 1934. From 1936 to 1963 he taught at Princeton University, taking leave during World War II to work on historical projects in Washington, D.C. In 1963 he moved to Washington University in St. Louis to serve as dean of arts and sciences but in 1969 resumed his career in teaching and research, this time at Yale. After his retirement in 1977 he lived in Princeton, where he was affiliated with the Institute for Advanced Study, and then in a retirement community in Newtown Pennsylvania. Of the numerous books he wrote, translated, and edited, three of the most important have been his *Catholics and Unbelievers in Eighteenth-Century France* (1939); *Twelve Who Ruled: The Year of the Terror in the French Revolution* (1941, 1989); and his two-volume *Age of the Democratic Revolution* (1959, 1964), the first volume of which won the Bancroft Prize. He served as president of the American Historical Association in 1970, received honorary degrees from universities in the United States and abroad, and was awarded the Antonio Feltrinelli International Prize for History in Rome in 1990. He was a long-time fellow of the American Philosophical Society and of the American Academy of Arts and Sciences. He died in 2002, widely recognized as one of the preeminent historians of his generation.

JOEL COLTON was born in New York City. A graduate of the City College of New York, he served as a military intelligence officer in Europe in World War II, and received his Ph.D. from Columbia University in 1950. Until his retirement in 1989 he served on the faculty of Duke University, chairing the department of history from 1967 to1974 and chairing the university's academic council from 1971 to 1973. On leave from Duke, he served from 1974 to 1981 with the Rockefeller Foundation in New York as director of its research and fellowship program in the humanities. In 1986 Duke voted him a Distinguished Teaching Award. He has received Guggenheim, Rockefeller Foundation, and National Endowment for the Humanities fellowships. He has served on the editorial boards of the *Journal of Modern History, French Historical Studies* and *Historical Abstracts,* and has been co-president of the International Commission on the History of Social Movements and Social Structures. In 1979 he was elected a fellow of the American Academy of Arts and Sciences. His writings include *Compulsory Labor Arbitration in France, 1936–1939* (1951); *Léon Blum: Humanist in Politics* (1966, 1987), for which he received a Mayflower Award; *Twentieth Century* (1968,1980) in *The Time-Life Great Ages of Man Series;* and numerous contributions to journals, encyclopedias, and collaborative volumes. He served as co-author with Professor Palmer of the second to eighth editions of *A History of the Modern World* and with Professor Kramer of the ninth and the current editions.

LLOYD KRAMER was born in Maryville, Tennessee, and graduated from Maryville College. He received his Ph.D. from Cornell University in 1983. Before entering Cornell, he was a teacher in Hong Kong and he traveled widely in Asia. After completing his graduate studies, he taught at Stanford University and Northwestern University. Since 1986 he has been a member of the faculty at the University of North Carolina, Chapel Hill, where he is currently Dean Smith Distinguished Term Professor and Chair of the History Department. He has received two awards for distinguished undergraduate teaching. His writings include *Threshold of a New World: Intellectuals and the Exile Experience in Paris, 1830–1848* (1988); *Lafayette in Two Worlds: Public Cultures and Personal Identities in an Age of Revolutions* (1996), which won the Gilbert Chinard Prize from the Society for French Historical Studies and the Annibel Jenkins Biography Prize from the American Society for Eighteenth-Century Studies; and *Nationalism: Political Cultures in Europe and America* (1998). He has also co-edited several books, including a collection of essays on historical education in America and *A Companion to Western Historical Thought* (2002). He has been a member of the School of Historical Studies at the Institute for Advanced Study and a Fellow at the National Humanities Center; and he served as president of the Society for French Historical Studies.

Brief Contents

List of Illustrations *xi*

List of Chronologies, Maps, Charts, and Tables *xv*

Preface *xvii*

Geography and History *1*

Chapter **1** The Rise of Europe *9*

Chapter **2** The Upheaval in Western Christendom, 1300–1560 *49*

Chapter **3** Economic Renewal and Wars of Religion, 1560–1648 *99*

Chapter **4** The Growing Power of Western Europe, 1640–1715 *145*

Chapter **5** The Transformation of Eastern Europe, 1648–1740 *189*

Chapter **6** The Scientific View of the World *225*

Chapter **7** The Struggle for Wealth and Empire *257*

Chapter **8** The Age of Enlightenment *297*

Chapter **9** The French Revolution *349*

Chapter **10** Napoleonic Europe *395*

Appendix Rulers and Regimes *434*

Suggestions for Further Reading *439*

Index *476*

Contents

List of Illustrations   *xi*
List of Chronologies, Maps, Charts, and Tables   *xv*
Preface   *xvii*
Geography and History   *1*

Chapter   **1**   THE RISE OF EUROPE   *9*

 1. Ancient Times: Greece, Rome, and Christianity   *10*
 2. The Early Middle Ages: The Formation of Europe   *18*
 3. The High Middle Ages: Secular Civilization   *28*
 4. The High Middle Ages: The Church   *37*

Chapter   **2**   THE UPHEAVAL IN WESTERN CHRISTENDOM, 1300–1560   *49*

 5. Disasters of the Fourteenth Century   *50*
 6. The Renaissance in Italy   *56*
 7. The Renaissance outside Italy   *69*
 8. The New Monarchies   *73*
 9. The Protestant Reformation   *77*
 10. Catholicism Reformed and Reorganized   *93*

Chapter   **3**   ECONOMIC RENEWAL AND WARS OF RELIGION, 1560–1648   *99*

 11. The Opening of the Atlantic   *99*
 12. The Commercial Revolution   *106*
 13. Changing Social Structures   *114*
 14. The Wars of Catholic Spain: The Netherlands and England   *121*
 15. The Disintegration and Reconstruction of France   *130*
 16. The Thirty Years' War, 1618–1648: The Disintegration of Germany   *135*

Chapter   **4**   THE GROWING POWER OF WESTERN EUROPE, 1640–1715   *145*

 17. The *Grand Monarque* and the Balance of Power   *146*
 18. The Dutch Republic   *149*

19. Britain: The Civil War   *155*

20. Britain: The Triumph of Parliament   *162*

21. The France of Louis XIV, 1643–1715:
The Triumph of Absolutism   *169*

22. The Wars of Louis XIV: The Peace of Utrecht, 1713   *181*

Chapter   **5**   THE TRANSFORMATION OF EASTERN EUROPE, 1648–1740   *189*

23. Three Aging Empires   *190*

24. The Formation of an Austrian Monarchy   *199*

25. The Formation of Prussia   *203*

26. The "Westernizing" of Russia   *211*

Chapter   **6**   THE SCIENTIFIC VIEW OF THE WORLD   *225*

27. Prophets of a Scientific Civilization: Bacon and Descartes   *226*

28. The Road to Newton: The Law of Universal Gravitation   *231*

29. New Knowledge of Human Beings and Society   *240*

30. Political Theory: The School of Natural Law   *249*

Chapter   **7**   THE STRUGGLE FOR WEALTH AND EMPIRE   *257*

31. Elite and Popular Cultures   *258*

32. The Global Economy of the Eighteenth Century   *265*

33. Western Europe after the Peace of Utrecht, 1713–1740   *274*

34. The Great War of the Mid-Eighteenth Century: The Peace of
Paris, 1763   *282*

Chapter   **8**   THE AGE OF ENLIGHTENMENT   *297*

35. The Philosophes—and Others   *298*

36. Enlightened Despotism: France, Austria, Prussia   *311*

37. Enlightened Despotism: Russia   *320*

38. The Partitions of Poland   *325*

39. New Stirrings: The British Reform Movement   *329*

40. The American Revolution   *338*

Chapter   **9**   THE FRENCH REVOLUTION   *349*

41. Backgrounds   *350*

42. The Revolution and the Reorganization of France   *355*

43. The Revolution and Europe:
The War and the "Second" Revolution, 1792   *370*

44. The Emergency Republic, 1792–1795: The Terror   *374*

45. The Constitutional Republic: The Directory, 1795–1799   *383*

46. The Authoritarian Republic: The Consulate, 1799–1804   *389*

Chapter **10** NAPOLEONIC EUROPE   *395*

47. The Formation of the French Imperial System   *396*

48. The Grand Empire: Spread of the Revolution   *404*

49. The Continental System: Britain and Europe   *409*

50. The National Movements: Germany   *414*

51. The Overthrow of Napoleon: The Congress of Vienna   *421*

Appendix RULERS AND REGIMES   *434*

Suggestions for Further Reading   *439*
Index   *476*

List of Illustrations

Color Insert Following Page *288*

The Masters of the Cloth Guild by Rembrandt van Rijn

Portrait of the Artist with Isabelle Brant by Peter Paul Rubens

The Artist's Studio by Jan Vermeer

Old Woman Cooking Eggs by Diego Velásquez

Self-Portrait by Elisabeth Vigée-Lebrun

Mrs. Philip Thicknesse by Thomas Gainsborough

A Woman of the Revolution by Jacques-Louis David

The Gleaners by Jean-François Millet

Chapter Illustrations

The Parthenon   *12*

Ruins of the Roman Forum   *14*

St. Augustine   *18*

Hagia Sophia   *21*

Medieval Spanish Monastery   *26*

Medieval Peasant   *30*

Symbol of Florentine Wool Guild   *34*

The Meeting of St. Anthony and St. Paul by Sassetta   *43*

Thomas Aquinas by Fra Bartelemo   *44*

European Crusaders at Antioch   *47*

Religious Procession of Medieval Flagellants   *54*

Renaissance Italian Bankers   *57*

Renaissance Italian Wool Merchants   *58*

Procession of the Three Kings to Bethlehem by Benozzo Gozzoli   *59*

Lorenzo de' Medici Examining a Model of His Villa   *60*

Portrait of a Condottiere by Giovanni Bellini   *62*

Detail from *Zacharias in the Temple* by Domenico Ghirlandaio   *64*

Portrait of a Family by Lavinia Fontana   *66*

Florentine Council Debating on War with Pisa by Giorgio Vasari   *68*

Erasmus of Rotterdam by Hans Holbein, the Younger   *74*

Interrogation of the Jews   *77*

Martin Luther and His Wife Catherine by Lucas Cranach the Elder   *80*

Siege of Munster, Germany, in 1534   *82*

John Calvin   *87*

Queen Elizabeth I   *90*

Pierre de Moucheron and Family   *92*

St. Ignatius Loyola by Peter Paul Rubens   *96*

Detail from *An Episode in the Conquest of America* by Jan Mostaert   *103*

European Meeting with an African Council in Guinea   *105*

Slaves Processing Diamonds in Brazil   *105*

The Aztec Language in the Latin Alphabet   *107*

The Silver Mines at Potosí   *108*

Study of Two Black Heads by Rembrandt van Rijn   *110*

The Four Estates of Society: Work by Jean Bourdichon   *112*

The Dutch East India Company Headquarters   *115*

Monk Teaching Students at the University of Salamanca   *119*

King Philip II of Spain by Titian   *123*

The Spanish Armada   *127*

St. Bartholomew's Day Massacre by François Dubois   *133*

"The Hanging Tree" [from] *The Great Miseries of War* by Jacques Callot   *138*

Girl Reading a Letter at an Open Window by Jan Vermeer   *151*

The Geographer by Jan Vermeer   *153*

William Shakespeare   *156*

The Execution of King Charles I   *161*

Woman Speaking at a Quaker Meeting   *164*

Molière Performing in "The School for Wives" by François Delpech   *171*

Inspiration of the Epic Poet by Nicolas Poussin   *173*

Louis XIV by Hyacinthe Rigaud   *176*

The Building of Versailles by Adam François van der Mueleh   *178*

View of the Château of Versailles by Pierre Denis Martin   *178*

The Battle of Blenheim   *185*

Peasant Family in a Room by Louis Le Nain   *186*

Count Stanislas Potocki by Jacques-Louis David   *197*

Turkish Siege of Vienna in 1683   *201*

Frederick William, the Great Elector   *207*

Prussian Army Uniforms   *212*

Stephen Razin painted by Surikow   *216*

Peter the Great   *218*

The Construction of St. Petersburg   *221*

Execution for Witchcraft in the Seventeenth Century   *228*

René Descartes by Frans Hal   *230*

A Scholar Holding a Thesis on Botany by Willem Moreelse   *233*

The Copernican Conception of the Solar System   *235*

Founding of the Academy of Sciences and the Observatory in 1666 by Henri Testelin   *238*

Isaac Newton   *240*

Ambassadors from Siam at Versailles   *242*

Seventeenth-Century Library   *245*

Baruch Spinoza by Samuel Van Hoogstraten   *249*

John Locke by John Greenhill   *254*

Gin Lane by William Hogarth   *261*

Café Frascati by Philibert-Louis Debucourt   *261*

A Carnival on the Feast Day of Saint George by Pieter Bruegel, the Younger   *264*

Women at Work in an Irish Cottage   *266*

Slaves Working on a Plantation in Barbados   *271*

The Duet by Arthur Devis   *273*

M. Bachelier, Director of the Lyons Farms by Jean-Baptiste Oudry   *280*

Frederick the Great of Prussia as a Young Man   *284*

Maria Theresa and Her Family by Martin van Meytens   *286*

Schönbrunn Palace   *288*

The Battle of Quebec   *292*

A British Army Officer's Wife in India   *294*

Reading at the Salon of Mme de Geoffrin by Anicet-Charles-Gabriel Lemonnier   *303*

Voltaire by Maurice-Quentin de La Tour   *304*

Jean-Jacques Rousseau by Allan Ramsay   *309*

The Parlement of Paris   *316*

Catherine the Great by Alexander Roslin   *322*

Emelian Pugachev in an Iron Cage   *323*

The Hon. Mrs. Graham by Thomas Gainsborough   *332*

Edmund Burke   *335*

Mrs. Isaac Smith by John Singleton Copley   *340*

American Militia and British Soldiers at Lexington   *343*

Thomas Paine's *Common Sense*   *345*

Declaration of Independence by John Trumbull   *347*

Eighteenth-Century French Peasants Working in Fields   *351*

Meeting of the French Estates General   *358*

The Tennis Court Oath by Jacques-Louis David   *360*

The Capture of the Bastille   *362*

Frenchmen Creating a New Constitution   *365*

French Paper Money; the "Assignats"   *367*

The Festival of the Federation, 1790   *369*

Parisians Pulling Down a Statue of Louis XIV   *376*

The Battle of Fleurus   *381*

The Execution of Robespierre   *382*

Napoleon Crossing the Alps by Jacques-Louis David   *391*

Toussaint L'Ouverture   *398*

Napoleon and Alexander I Meeting on the Niemen River   *401*

The Third of May 1808 by Francisco de Goya   *403*
Germaine de Staël by François Gérard   *410*
The Arch of Triumph in Paris   *413*
The Madeleine Church in Paris   *414*
Blowing Up the Corsican Bottle Conjurer   *417*
The French Army's Retreat from Russia   *424*
The Congress of Vienna   *427*

List of Chronologies, Maps, Charts, and Tables

Chronologies

Notable Events, 500 B.C.–A.D. 1300   *39*

Notable Events, 1309–1555   *84*

Notable Events, 1492–1648   *128*

Notable Events, 1642–1713   *168*

Notable Events, 1640–1740   *214*

Notable Events, 1543–1697   *247*

Notable Events, 1619–1763   *289*

Notable Events, 1733–1795   *336*

Notable Events, 1789–1804   *386*

Notable Events, 1799–1815   *420*

Maps, Charts, and Tables

Contemporary Europe   *inside front cover*

Europe: Physical   *4–5*

The Mediterranean World about A.D. 400, 800, and 1250   *24*

Crusading Activity, 1100–1259   *45*

Estimated Population of Europe, 1200–1550   *52*

Europe, 1526   *78*

State Religions in Europe about 1560   *89*

European Discoveries, 1450–1600   *101*

The Low Countries, 1648   *126*

Europe, 1648   *142–143*

The Expansion of France, 1661–1713   *147*

England in the Seventeenth Century   *166*

France from the Last Years of Louis XIV to the Revolution of 1789   *180*

The Atlantic World after the Peace of Utrecht, 1713   *187*

Central and Eastern Europe, 1660–1795   *193*

Aging Empires and New Powers   *194*

The Growth of the Austrian Monarchy, 1521–1772   *202*

The Growth of Prussia, 1415–1918   *208–209*

The Growth of Russia in the West   *222–223*

The Growth of Geographical Knowledge   *244*

The World in 1763   *295*

Europe, 1740   *313*

Poland since the Eighteenth Century   *328*

The French Republic and Its Satellites, 1798–1799   *388*

Napoleonic Europe, 1810   *407*
Napoleonic Germany   *409*
Europe, 1815   *430*
Contemporary World   *inside back cover*

Preface

Dramatic events in the contemporary world—wars, revolutions, terrorist attacks, catastrophic natural disasters, economic crises and the endless stream of daily news— often obscure the long historical processes that have created the societies in which we live and the problems with which we cope. The mass media pay little attention to the broader historical patterns and contexts that give deeper meaning to the swiftly moving events of our era. This new edition of *A History of the Modern World* may be seen as the most recent version of a continuing search for historical perspectives on the complex, often bewildering, events of our age. It thus carries a guiding assumption that the events, cultures, and conflicts of the contemporary world are always evolving out of the long, complex histories of diverse peoples, ideas, institutions, social mores, economic exchanges, and struggles for political power.

These multiple levels of human history have created modern societies and exerted wide influence on people and cultures around the world. This book therefore describes the histories of specific nations and people and emphasizes landmark events such as wars and revolutions, but it also stresses broad historical trends that have developed deep below the most prominent historical events and created what we now call "the modern world." Our narrative explores the rise of nation-states and the conflicts that have shaped the world over the last several centuries, yet it links such transitions and events to the wider historical influence of the evolving global economy, the development of science and technology, the rise of industry, the significance of religious traditions, the origin and diffusion of new ideas, the changing mores of family and social life, and the complex relations between Western cultures and other cultures around the world.

The term *modern,* as we use it in this book, refers to the historical evolution of societies and cultures that may be said to have had the greatest influence in shaping the modern world—a phase of human history that began to develop about five or six centuries ago and is now evolving more rapidly in more places than ever before. This book makes no claim to be a world history, valuable as such histories may be. By design it focuses primarily on developments in the West until the spread of distinctively modern economic, social, and political institutions in the recent past leads to an increasing global emphasis in the book's later chapters. Although the narrative stresses the influence of European societies (that is, societies shaped by Europeans or the descendants of Europeans) in the emergence of "modern" institutions and social practices, it also emphasizes the worldwide exchanges, conflicts, and interactions that have contributed to the increasingly global culture of the contemporary era.

ORGANIZATION OF THE BOOK: CHANGES AND CONTINUITIES

As in the past, the book is organized in chapters that carry the narrative across specific chronological eras, moving steadily toward the present. Yet the clearly defined and numbered sections within each chapter often deal with themes, events, or issues that do not develop in simple chronological order. Each chapter focuses on a specific time frame but also on themes and problems of continuing historical importance. The chronological organization gives readers a broad historical framework and also provides opportunities for further analysis and discussion of specific historical themes or problems—discussions that can draw, for example, on other materials which can be found on the companion Online Learning Center Web site (www.mhhe.com/palmer10), which now includes an Interactive Glossary.

Although the history of political institutions, revolutions, and international conflicts remains important in this new edition, some details of national and political history have been reduced to expand the discussion of social, cultural, and intellectual history—all of which have been influential in recent historical scholarship. There are sections on the role of women in various historical contexts and eras; descriptions of cultural and intellectual movements from the early modern to the contemporary period; and new analyses of the political, economic, and cultural interactions that have shaped modern global history. Chapters on the Scientific Revolution and the early global economy have been moved in order to show more clearly the chronological relation of notable cultural and economic developments.

In the earlier chapters readers will find discussions of family life during the Renaissance and Reformation; descriptions of literary debates, salon culture, and the evolving public sphere in the Enlightenment; and insights into the cultural dimensions of the French Revolution. Later chapters of the book (in the second volume of the paperback edition) include sections on the emergence of feminism, cultural debates about science and the idea of progress, and discussions of modernist and postmodernist cultural movements.

The chapters on the world since 1945 have been reorganized and divided into new thematic sections. The two longest chapters in the previous edition's narrative of recent historical events have been divided into four new, more concise chapters that will be easier for students and others to read. The new, shorter chapters have a clearer thematic organization, and they convey key patterns in the development of postcolonial societies in Asia, Africa, and the Middle East, as well as the demise of communism in Europe. These reorganized chapters also include new information on recent international confrontations and on the growing globalization of contemporary economic and cultural life. We believe that specific historical information about such developments is the essential starting point for historical analysis, balanced historical insights, and the comprehension of historical change.

Our intention is to help students and other readers understand the complexities of great events such as the religious wars of earlier centuries, the American, French, and Russian Revolutions, the twentieth-century world wars, the spread of democracy and the challenges it has faced, the creation and collapse of the Western-dominated colonial empires, the emergence of new, postcolonial nation-states, and the continuing search for an international order. Readers will also find updated information on current issues such as terrorism, recent upheavals in the Middle East, and the continuing struggle for economic development in the world's poorest countries.

Other revisions have been introduced to make the book even more accessible for a new generation of readers. The visual component has again been extended through the addition of new illustrations, including new images of important works by modern artists such as Pablo Picasso, Berthe Morisot, Jackson Pollock, and Henry Moore. Like other kinds of documents and sources, the images and artwork from past cultures provide important historical information. Knowing how to read and critically evaluate an illustration, painting, or photograph is an essential form of analytical thought and is invaluable for cross-cultural comparisons. In addition to the many illustrations in each chapter, four-color inserts convey both the artistic creativity and the cultural or social preoccupations of different historical eras. The brief captions that accompany all of the illustrations connect events or issues to the book's narrative.

Other key features of this new edition include newly drawn, easier-to-read maps, presented in sharper color. The wide range of maps and charts shows the changing boundaries, populations, and economies of nations and regions over the years. In addition to the revised maps, new chronological timelines—as suggested by reviewers—have been incorporated into each chapter to give a convenient summary of the notable events and dates in each historical era. The revised, up-to-date entries for the comprehensive Suggestions for Further Reading, long a valued feature of the book, include new listings of useful Web sites as well as the titles of significant new scholarly publications.

The changes in this latest version of *A History of the Modern World* have been introduced to enhance the book's accessibility, but not to replace or weaken the style, content, narrative, and analytical qualities that have appealed to teachers and students over the years. More generally, readers will find that the book in its newest edition expresses again a strong belief in the value of historical knowledge and historical perspectives for anyone who wishes to understand as well as to live in the evolving modern world. It achieves its purpose whenever it helps readers of any age or background gain new perspectives on themselves and their world through the new knowledge or new insights that it may offer.

SUPPLEMENTS FOR THE INSTRUCTOR

Instructor's Manual/Test Bank   The first half of this unique manual offers a chapter-by-chapter guide to some of the best documentaries, educational and feature films, videos, and audio recordings to enhance classroom discussion. Brief overviews help instructors select the films best suited to each course topic. The manual also provides instructors with chapter objectives and points for discussion for each chapter, followed by a test bank containing multiple-choice, essay, and identification test questions.

Computerized Test Bank   This CD-ROM version of the test bank is available for both Macintosh and IBM-compatible computers to allow instructors to customize each test.

Overhead Transparencies   This set of over 150 overhead color transparencies of maps from the text can be used to illuminate classroom lectures.

Slide Set   Available through your local McGraw-Hill sales representative, instructors can choose from a list of hundreds of fine art slides to create a customized slide set that will complement the text and enhance classroom lectures.

Instructor Online Learning Center Web Site (www.mhhe.com/palmer10)   At the home page for this text-specific Web site, instructors will find a downloadable version of the Instructor's Manual. Instructors can also create Web-based homework assignments or classroom activities by linking to the Student Online Learning Center and can create an interactive course syllabus using McGraw-Hill's PageOut site.

PageOut (www.mhhe.com/pageout)   On the PageOut Web site instructors can create their own course Web sites. PageOut requires no prior knowledge of HTML, no long hours of coding, and no design skills on the instructor's part. Instructors need simply to plug the course information into a template and click on one of the 16 designs. The process takes little time and creates a professionally designed Web site. Powerful features include an interactive course syllabus that lets instructors post content and links, an online gradebook, lecture notes, bookmarks, and a discussion board where instructors and students can discuss course-related topics.

Videos   A wide range of videos on classic and contemporary topics in history is available through the Films for the Humanities and Sciences collection. Instructors can illustrate and enhance lectures by selecting from a series of videos correlated to the course. Contact your local McGraw-Hill sales representative for further information.

 ## SUPPLEMENTS FOR THE STUDENT

Student Study Guide   Prepared by Joel Colton and Megan McLean, this user-friendly Study Guide helps students process and master important concepts in the text not through rote memorization but by stimulating reflection and interpretation. For each of the 133 sections of the textbook, the Study Guide provides study questions, key discussion sentences, and identification test questions. Each chapter includes general essay questions and general discussion passages. Selected map exercises are also provided. In addition, questions on the numerous illustrations in the text are included in the sections to which they most closely relate and are designed to encourage interpretation and analysis, specifically on the ways in which the illustrations supplement the discussions in the text.

Student Online Learning Center Web Site (www.mhhe.com/palmer10)   New to this Web site and requested by reviewers is an Interactive Glossary, an important learning tool for students that complements the terms and topics highlighted in the margins of the textbook. At this text-specific Web site, students can link to an interactive study guide, including online essay questions, interactive mapping exercises, Internet exercises, interactive chronologies, and links to online primary source documents. Links to trusted history search engines also make the Online Learning Center an ideal place to begin Web-based research.

PowerWeb   PowerWeb for World History gives students password-protected, course-specific articles with assessments from current research journals and popular press articles, refereed and selected by World History instructors, and especially useful for materials that go beyond the scope of this book.

 ## ACKNOWLEDGMENTS

We again gratefully acknowledge the help of the many people who have assisted with the production of this book. We owe a special debt to the editors and staff of McGraw-Hill, Inc., which has published this book since its seventh edition. We are grateful also to Alfred A. Knopf, Inc., the earlier publisher of the book, and to Ashbel Green and the Knopf staff for continuing to make it available in a trade edition for the general public. The support and assistance of Lyn Uhl, Monica Eckman, Larry Goldberg, Susan Trentacosti, Marianna Kinigakis, Ayelet Arbel, Nora Agbayani, Janean Utley, Sonia Brown, Louis Swaim, Sean Crowley, and Katherine Bates at McGraw-Hill have been invaluable and essential. We also thank Christine Buese and Deborah Bull for their expert assistance on illustrations and Bethany Keenan for her help in identifying useful Web sites.

We have benefited from the expert advice of reviewers who have offered suggestions for the ways in which a new edition of this book might be revised; and we have absorbed many additional ideas from other colleagues who have used earlier editions of the book in their courses. We mention specifically the following reviewers: Marc Baer, Hope College; Robert Brown, University of North Carolina at Pembroke; Nathanael Greene, Wesleyan

University; L. Edward Hicks, Faulkner University; George Marcopoulos, Tufts University; James McSwain, Tuskegee University; Florene Memegalos, Hunter College; Jenny Nicholas, West High School; David J. Proctor, Tufts University; Sarah Rudell, Wayzata High School; Tamas Ungvari, California State University, Northridge; and Michael Zirinsky, Boise State University. Other colleagues who provided feedback also deserve mention: Joseph J. Colistra, LaSalle College High School; Michael Corey, Lincoln Way High School; Virginia Mancini, Pleasantville High School; Henry A. Ploegstra, St. Mark's School of Texas; and Michael Stoll, Hinsdale South High School. None of these individuals are in any way responsible for the book's shortcomings, but all have contributed to its strengths. We wish also to acknowledge the exceptional support and contributions of our colleagues and our families.

Finally, we note with a sense of deep loss that our colleague and co-author Robert R. Palmer (who always published as R. R. Palmer) died in 2002 after a long career of outstanding accomplishments. His superb contributions to the study of the French Revolution and of eighteenth- and early nineteenth-century history on both sides of the Atlantic have deservedly received wide recognition. His far-reaching intellect, searching acuity, historical insights, and broad-gauged interests marked this work from its beginning, and he remains the guiding influence and inspiration behind this book. The scholarly collaboration that has long characterized *A History of the Modern World* meanwhile continues and takes on new forms in this new edition, for which the most recent co-author has assumed the major responsibility.

Joel Colton
Lloyd Kramer

A HISTORY OF THE
MODERN WORLD

To 1815

Geography and History

History is the experience of human beings in time, but that experience takes place also in geographic space. Geography describes and maps the earth, but it also studies the changing interactions between human beings and the environments in which they live.

The universe, of which our planet earth and our solar system form but a small part, is now thought to be at least 12 billion years old. Most scientists believe the earth is about 4.6 billion years old. Yet the entire history (and prehistory) of humankind goes back only 3.5 to 5 million years, or perhaps only 2 million years, depending on how humans are defined. What we call history—the recorded cultures and actions of human beings—began with the invention of early forms of writing only about 5,500 years ago.

Oceans and continents have moved about over time, changing in size, shape, and location. The continents as we know them took on their distinctive forms less than 100 million years ago. Dinosaurs, which became extinct some 60 million years before the first humans even emerged, could walk from North America to Europe (as we now call these continents) on solid land in a warm climate. It is only a few thousand years since the end of the most recent glacial age. That Ice Age, which began about 2 million years ago and reached its coldest point only 20,000 years ago, was caused by a slight shift in the earth's orbit around the sun. Water froze into ice 1–2 inches thick and covered the northern parts of the planet (in North America as far south as present-day Chicago and in Europe across large parts of the British Isles and the nearby mainland). The melting of this ice produced the coastlines, offshore islands, inland seas, straits, bays, and harbors that we know today, as well as some of the large river systems and lakes. The process of change in the earth's surface continues. Niagara Falls, on the border between the United States and Canada, has been receding because the ongoing cascade of water erodes the underlying rock. The ocean's tides and human construction erode our shorelines as well, and many scientists believe current patterns of global warming may eventually change the oceans and coasts in much of the world.

Ice Age

Oceans presently cover more than two-thirds of the earth's surface, and many large land areas in the remaining third are poorly suited for habitation by human beings or most other animal and plant organisms. One-tenth of the land remains under ice, as in Antarctica and Greenland; much is tundra; much is desert, as in the Sahara; and much land lies along the windswept ridges of high mountains. Like the oceans, these regions have been important in human history, often acting as barriers to movement and settlement. Human history has therefore evolved in relatively small, scattered sections of the earth's total surface.

Researchers have found persuasive material evidence to show that human beings originated in Africa. Humans belonging to the species *Homo erectus,* the Latin term used by anthropologists and others to denote the upright, walking predecessors of modern humans, seem to have migrated from Africa about 1.8 million years ago, perhaps because of environmental pressures or perhaps because of simple curiosity. Our own species *Homo sapiens,* the Latin term connoting increased cognitive and judgmental abilities, emerged no more than about 100,000 years ago. When humans went beyond merely utilitarian accomplishments and demonstrated aesthetic and artistic interests as well as advanced toolmaking (about 35,000 years ago),

Origins of human beings

we refer to them as the subspecies *Homo sapiens sapiens*. They were the remaining survivors of a very complex human family tree.

The great Ice Age lowered the seas by hundreds of feet and froze huge quantities of water. The English Channel became dry. Land bridges opened up between Siberia and North America over what we now call the Bering Strait. Hunters seeking game walked from one continent to the other. When the glaciers melted, forests sprang up, and many of the open areas in which humans had hunted disappeared, providing added motivation for movement.

Our human ancestors spread eventually to every continent except Antarctica. In doing so, human groups became isolated from each other for millennia, separated by oceans, deserts, or mountains. Wherever they wandered, they evolved slightly over time, developing superficial physical differences that modern cultures have defined as the characteristics of various racial groups. But "race" is a cultural idea rather than a mark of biologically significant differences. All human beings belong to the *Homo sapiens* species, all derive from the same biological ancestry, and all are mutually fertile. Only a very few human genes are responsible for physical differences such as skin pigmentation, in comparison to the vast number of genes that are shared by all members of the human species.

Race: a cultural concept

The basic anatomy and genetic makeup of modern humans has not changed over the last 100,000 years. Geographic separation accounts for the emergence over shorter time periods of distinctive cultures, which can be seen, for example, in the different historical and cultural development of the pre-Columbian Americas, Africa, China, India, the Middle East, and Europe. On a still smaller time scale, geographic separation also explains differences in languages and dialects.

Geography and culture

Geographic distances and diversity of climate have also produced differences in flora and fauna, and hence in the plants and animals upon which humans are dependent. Wheat became the most usual cereal in the Middle East and Europe, millet and rice in East Asia, sorghum in tropical Africa, maize in pre-Columbian America. The horse, first domesticated in north-central Asia about 4,500 years ago, was for centuries a mainstay of Europe and Asia for muscle power, transportation, and fighting. The somewhat less versatile camel was adopted later and more slowly in the Middle East, and the Americans long had no beasts of burden except the llama. Such differences did not begin to diminish until early modern travelers crossed the oceans, taking plants and animals with them and bringing others back to environments where they had never lived before.

Although much remains obscure about the origins of life, and new discoveries and calculations are always displacing older hypotheses, paleontologists studying plant and animal fossils (including human ones) have used techniques such as radiocarbon dating to transform our knowledge of the earth and of the earliest human beings. In geography, aerial and satellite photography and computer technology have enabled us to refine older conceptions of continents and oceans. And astrophysicists are now studying vast amounts of new data about the universe, which have been sent to them from powerful telescopes mounted on unmanned spaceships.

Cartography, the art and science of mapmaking, has evolved rapidly, but we tend to forget how our maps often remain conventional and even parochial. It was Europeans and descendants of Europeans who designed our most commonly used maps, which are oriented North-South and West-East from fixed points in their horizons, and which therefore reflect their own European cultural assumptions. Similar biases can be found in the maps of other cultures too. The Chinese for centuries defined and visualized their country as the "Middle Kingdom." In the early modern centuries maps drawn in India typically represented South Asia as forming the major part of the world. One such map depicted the European continent as a few marginal areas labeled England, France, and "other hat-wearing islands."

Changing conceptualizations of the globe continue in our day. A map drawn and published in contemporary Australia, demonstrating the Australian perspective from "down under," shows South Africa at the top of the map and Capetown at the very tip, the large expanse of contemporary African nations in the middle, and the various European countries crowded at the bottom, the latter appearing quite insignificant. The European-invented term "Middle East" has been called into question, and this region of the world is perhaps better designated as Western Asia. Even our traditional concept of Europe as one of the seven continents (Africa, Asia, Europe, North America, South America, Australia, and Antarctica) is now questioned. Why, for example, should the Indian peninsula be a "subcontinent" when it roughly matches the size and exceeds the population and diversity of the European "continent" (at least that part of the "continent" that lies west of the former Soviet Union)? Europe itself is, of course, actually a peninsula, in a way that the other continents are not. Some geographers ask us to consider it more properly as part of Asia, the western part of a great "Eurasian landmass." Defined in these terms, Europe becomes more of a cultural conception, arising out of perceived differences from Asia and Africa, than a continent in a strictly geographical sense.

Europe's Influence on Modern History

However we define its place on the globe, Europe has undoubtedly shaped much of modern world history—partly because of its overseas expansion, partly because of what it borrowed from other parts of the world, and partly because of its decisive economic and cultural influence on the emergence of an increasingly global civilization. Europe is of course only one of many important cultural spheres in human history. Its economy, political systems, religious tradi-

Europe and history

tions, and social institutions are not the sole historical path to modernity; indeed, people in other regions of the world have often challenged or rejected European forms of "modernization" as they have built their own modern societies. Yet even the critique or rejection of European institutions has usually required historical analysis of Europe's development and role in the world. Much of the modern global economy, for example, emerged in the international trade that Europe's imperial powers controlled and expanded after the sixteenth century. European political ideas, science, philosophy, cultural mores, and people also spread widely across the world, contributing to both the constructive and destructive patterns of modern political, social, and cultural life. Ideas and people have meanwhile flowed constantly into Europe from other parts of the world, so that European societies remain a vital center for cross-cultural exchanges and conflicts.

It is possible to narrate a "history of the modern world" from widely diverging perspectives and with an emphasis on quite different historical themes. This book, however, begins with the recognition that Europe developed and promoted many of the distinctive "modern" ideas and institutions that have now evolved in various forms throughout the contemporary world. Historical understanding of modernity must therefore include a comprehensive analysis of Europe—though an accurate history of the modern world must also insist that Europe represents only one of the diverse, complex cultures that continue to shape modern global history.

ICELAND

SCANDINAVIAN
PENINSULA

Norwegian Sea

FAROE IS.

SHETLAND IS.

*ALAND
IS.*

HEBRIDES

ORKNEY IS.

Oslo

Stockholm

ATLANTIC OCEAN

BRITISH
ISLES

GRAMPIANS
SCOTTISH
LOWLANDS

Edinburgh

*North
Sea*

Skagerrak

Kattegat

L. Vanern

L. Vattern

Gotland

Öland

Baltic Sea

Gulf of Bothnia

Dal R.

KJÖLEN MOUNTAINS

IRISH
CENTRAL
PLAIN

Dublin

Irish Sea

PENNINE CHAIN

JUTLAND
PENINSULA

Copenhagen

Danzig

Nie

St. George's
Channel

THE
WASH

Helgoland

MIDLAND
PLAIN

FRISIAN IS.

Weser R.

Elbe R.

NORTH GERMAN PLAIN

Warta R.

Vistula R.

Bristol Channel

Thames R.

Amsterdam

Ijsselmeer

Berlin

Warsaw

SCILLY IS.

LAND'S END

London

Scheldt R.

Maas R.

Rhine R.

HARTZ
MTS.

Oder R.

Neisse R.

English Channel

Strait of Dover

ERZ MTS.

SUDETEN MTS.

Ushant I.

BRITTANY
PENINSULA

ARDENNES

Meuse R.

Moselle R.

Main R.

Prague

BOHEMIAN
PLAIN

CARPAT

Marne R.

Paris

Seine R.

VOSGES MTS.

BLACK FOREST

Danube R.

BOHEMIAN FOREST

Vienna

*Bay of
Biscay*

PLAIN OF FRANCE

Loire R.

JURA MTS.

L. Constance

Inn R.

Budapest

PLAIN OF
HUNGARY

Tisz

Cape Finisterre

CANTABRIAN MTS.

Garonne R.

MASSIF
CENTRAL

Rhône R.

L. Geneva

A L P S

PLAIN OF
LOMBARDY

Po R.

Trieste

ISTRIA

L.
Balaton

Drave R.

Save R.

IRON G

Belgrade

IBERIAN
PENINSULA

PYRENEES

CÉVENNES

Adige R.

Arno R.

DALMATIANS

DINARIC ALPS

SPANISH

Douro R.

GUADARRAMAS

Madrid

Ebro R.

Corsica

Elba

Tiber R.

APENNINES

Adriatic Sea

Lisbon

Tagus R.

PLATEAU

Rome

BALK
PENINS

Guadiana R.

SIERRA MORENA

BALEARIC IS.

Minorca

Rome

ITALIAN
PENINSULA

Guadalquivir R.

Iviza

Majorca

Sardinia

Mt. Vesuvius

IONIAN IS.

Cape Trafalgar

SIERRA NEVADA

Gibraltar

*Tyrrhenian
Sea*

*Ionian
Sea*

Strait of Gibraltar

Algiers

Mt. Etna

SICILY

Strait of Messina

Fez

LITLLE ATLAS MOUNTAINS

Tunis

PANTELLERIA

MIDDLE ATLAS MOUNTAINS

SAHARAN ATLAS MOUNTAINS

MALTA

MEDITERRANEAN

GREAT ATLAS MOUNTAINS

Tripoli

ALGERIAN SAHARA

Gulf of
Sidra

0   100   200   300 miles

White Sea

N. Dvina R.

L. Onega

L. Ladoga

St. Petersburg

Peipus

NORTH RUSSIAN PLAIN

Dvina R.

Moscow

Oka R.

Volga R.

Kama R.

Ural R.

URAL MOUNTAINS

KIRGHIZ STEPPE

Syr Darya

VOLGA HEIGHTS

BLACK EARTH REGION

CENTRAL RUSSIAN HIGHLANDS

Pripet R.

PRIPET MARSHES

Kiev

Dnieper R.

Donets R.

DONETS HEIGHTS

Volga R.

CASPIAN DEPRESSION

Aral Sea

TURANIAN PLAIN

Amu Darya

Bug R.

Dniester R.

Pruth R.

Don R.

Odessa

CRIMEA

Sea of Azov

N ALPS

Bucharest

Danube R.

TS.

Black Sea

Sinop

Caspian Sea

CAUCASUS MOUNTAINS

ARMENIAN HIGHLANDS

Araxes R.

itsa R.

DOPE MTS.

Istanbul

Bosporus

Sea of Marmara

Dardanelles

Ankara

Kızılırmak R.

L. Van

L. Urmia

ELBURZ MTS.

Tehran

ASIA MINOR (ANATOLIAN PENINSULA)

DODECANESE IS.

Meander R.

TAURUS MOUNTAIN

Rhodes

CYPRUS

CRETE

MESOPOTAMIAN PLAINS

Tigris R.

Euphrates R.

Baghdad

ZAGROS MTS.

Jordan R.

Jerusalem

Dead Sea

SYRIAN DESERT

Persian Gulf

Alexandria

NILE DELTA

Suez Canal

Cairo

SINAI PENINSULA

Nile R.

Gulf of Aqaba

NEFUD DESERT

Europe exemplifies the perennial interactions between human activity and the natural environment, and the study of its historical evolution should begin with some attention to its geography. The accompanying topographical map shows the main physical features of Europe and its surrounding geographical space. This topography has remained virtually unchanged over historic time, despite the constant political and cultural transformations in European societies. Europe is not large. Even with European Russia, it contains hardly more than 6 percent of the earth's land surface, occupying about the same area as the United States mainland plus Alaska. It is only a little larger than Australia. It is physically separated from Africa by the Mediterranean Sea, although the Mediterranean historically has been as much a passageway as a barrier. A truer barrier emerged when the Sahara Desert dried up only a few thousand years ago, which suggests why northern Africa has often been as connected to southern Europe, or culturally to the Middle East, as to sub-Saharan Africa. The physical separation of Europe from Asia is even less clear. The conventional boundary has been the Ural Mountains in Russia, but they are a low and wide chain that does not stretch far enough to make an adequate boundary. The Russians themselves do not recognize any official distinction between European and Asian Russia.

The Mediterranean Sea

Europe is indeed one of several peninsulas jutting off from Asia, like the Arabian and Indian peninsulas. But there are differences. For one thing, the Mediterranean Sea is unique among the world's bodies of water. Closed in by the Strait of Gibraltar, which is only 8 miles wide, it is more shielded than other seas from the open ocean and is protected from the most violent ocean storms. Though over 2,000 miles long, it is subdivided by islands and peninsulas into lesser seas with identities of their own, such as the Aegean and the Adriatic, and it provides access also to the Black Sea. Because it is possible to travel great distances without being far from land, navigation developed on the Mediterranean from early times and one of the first civilizations appeared on the island of Crete. It is possible also to cross between Europe and Asia at the Bosporus and between Europe and Africa at Gibraltar. Populations became mixed by migration, and various historic empires—the Carthaginian, Roman, Byzantine, Arabic, Spanish, Venetian, and Ottoman—have effectively used the Mediterranean to govern their component parts. After the Suez Canal was built in the nineteenth century, the Mediterranean became an important segment in the "lifeline of empire" for the British Empire in its heyday.

Mountains

In southern Europe, north of the Mediterranean and running for its whole length, is a series of mountains, produced over the geological ages by the pushing of the gigantic mass of Africa against the small Eurasian peninsula. The Pyrenees close off Spain from the north, as the Alps do Italy; the Balkan Mountains are difficult to penetrate. The only place where one can travel at water level from the Mediterranean to the north is by the valley of the Rhone River, so that France is the only country that belongs both to the Mediterranean and northern Europe. North of the mountains is a great plain extending from western France all the way into Russia and on into Asia, passing south of the Urals. If one were to draw a straight line from Amsterdam east through what is called the Caspian Gate, north of the Caspian Sea, as far as western China, one would never in traveling these 3,500 miles be higher than 2,000 feet above sea level. This plain has at various times opened Europe to Mongol and other invasions, enabled the Russians to move east and create a huge empire, and made Poland a troubled battleground.

Rivers

The European rivers are worth particular attention. Most are navigable, and they also give access to the sea. With their valleys, they provided areas where intensive local development could take place. Thus the most important older cities of Europe are on rivers—London on the Thames, Paris on the Seine, Vienna and Budapest on the Danube, Warsaw on the Vistula. In northern Europe it was often possible to move goods from one river to another, and then in the eighteenth century to connect them by canals. The importance of water is shown again by the location of Copenhagen, Stockholm, and St. Petersburg on the Baltic and of Amsterdam and Lisbon, which grew rapidly after Europeans began traversing the Atlantic Ocean.

There are important geographical conditions such as climate that a topographical map cannot show. Climate depends on latitude, ocean currents, *Climate* and winds that bring or withhold rainfall. Europe lies as far north as the northern United States and southern Canada, but the parts of Europe near the sea have less extreme temperatures than the corresponding northerly regions of North America. The Mediterranean countries have more sunshine and less severe winters than either northern Europe or the northern United States. Everywhere the winters are cold enough to suppress infectious pathogens and pests and keep out certain diseases that afflict warmer countries. The warm summers with their growing seasons have produced an annual cycle of agriculture, and rainfall has been adequate but not excessive. Europe is the only continent that has no actual desert. It is also for the most part a region of fertile soil. In short, since the end of the Ice Age, or since humans learned to survive winters, Europe has been one of the most favored places on the globe for human habitation.

If we say that climate and the environment not only set limits but also provide opportunities for what human beings can do, then there is no such thing as geographical determinism. Geography is not destiny. What happens depends *Geographical* on the application of knowledge and abilities in any particular time and *determinism* place and in any particular culture. What constitutes a natural resource varies with the state of technology and the possibilities of economic exchange. Even the disadvantages of distance can be overcome by developing new means of transportation. The oceans that long divided human beings became a highway for the Portuguese, Spanish, Dutch, French, and English, and later for others. Chinese and Arab sailors also used the oceans for trade across Asia and East Africa. For most of human history, however, neither persons, information, nor commands could travel much more than 30 miles a day. Localism prevailed, and large-scale commercial or governmental organizations were hard to create and maintain. Like most other regions of the world, therefore, Europe was long made up of small local units, pockets of territory each with its own customs, way of life, and manner of speech, largely unknown to or ignorant of others, and looking inward upon itself. A "foreigner" might come from a thousand miles away, or from only ten.

Agriculture, like commerce and industry, depends on human invention *Agriculture* and decision making. The state of agriculture obviously depends on natural conditions, but it has also depended historically on the invention of the plow, the planting of appropriate crops, the rotation of fields to prevent soil exhaustion, and the availability of livestock from which manure could be obtained as fertilizer. It benefits from stability and is affected by demographic changes. If population grows, new and less fertile or more distant areas must be brought under cultivation. Nor can agriculture be improved without the building of roads and a division of labor between town and country, in which agrarian workers produce surpluses for those not engaged in agriculture. And for agriculture, as for other productive enterprises, elementary security is essential. Farming cannot proceed, nor food be stored over the winter, unless the men and women who work the fields can be protected from attack.

The maps in the present volume cannot show in detail all of the waterways, mountains, and geographical barriers that have helped to shape the course of human history, but they do point to the role of geography in the evolution of political and economic power, or what has become known as geopolitics. Human beings have always developed their institutions and cultures through a complex relation with the natural world, and maps remind us that all human activities take place in geographical space. Readers can also use their imaginations and the scale of maps to convert space into time, remembering that until the invention of the railroad both people and news traveled far more slowly than today. At a rate of 30 miles a day it would take three weeks to travel from London to Venice, and at least six weeks for an exchange of letters. Communication to places outside Europe took even longer. In our own day, when we travel at supersonic speeds and measure electronic communication in nanoseconds, or one-billionth of a second, the barriers of geographic space have virtually disappeared. Yet human beings remain profoundly dependent on their natural environments, and human history remains firmly embedded in the geography of the planet earth.

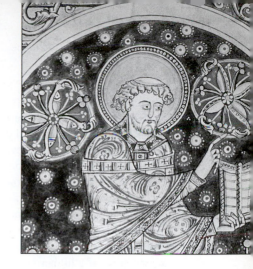

Chapter 1

THE RISE OF EUROPE

1. Ancient Times: Greece, Rome, and Christianity

2. The Early Middle Ages: The Formation of Europe

3. The High Middle Ages: Secular Civilization

4. The High Middle Ages: The Church

It may seem strange for a history of the modern world to begin with the European Middle Ages, for Europe is not the world and the Middle Ages were not modern. But much of what is now meant by "modern" made its first appearance in Europe, and to understand both modern Europe and the wider modern world it is necessary to reach fairly far back in time.

Over the centuries between roughly 1500 and 1900, Europe created the most powerful combination of political, military, economic, technological, and scientific apparatus that the world had ever seen. In doing so, Europe radically transformed itself, and also profoundly affected other societies and cultures in America, Africa, and Asia—sometimes destroying them, sometimes stimulating or enlivening them, and always presenting them with problems of resistance or adaptation. This European ascendancy became apparent about 300 years ago. It reached its zenith with the European colonial empires at the beginning of the twentieth century. Since then, the position of Europe has relatively declined, partly because of conflicts within Europe itself, but mainly because the apparatus which had made Europe so dominant can now be found in other countries. Some, like the United States, are in many ways cultural and political offshoots of Europe. Others have very different and ancient backgrounds. But whatever their backgrounds, and willingly or not, all peoples in the contemporary world have been caught up in processes of "modernization" or "development," which usually turns out to mean acquiring or adapting some of the technical skills and powers first exhibited by Europeans.

There is thus in our time a kind of global modern civilization which overlies or penetrates the diverse, regional cultures of the world. This civilization is an interlocking global system, in that conditions on one side of the globe have repercussions on the other. Communications are almost instantaneous and news travels everywhere. If the air is polluted in one country, neighboring countries are affected; if oil ceases to flow from the Middle East, the life of Europe, North America, and Japan may become very difficult. The modern world depends on elaborate means of transportation; on science, industry, and machines;

Chapter emblem: A medieval representation of Saint Augustine. (Scala/Art Resource, NY) on new sources of energy to meet insatiable demands; on scientific medicine, public hygiene, and methods of raising food. States and nations fight wars by advanced methods, and negotiate or maintain peace by diplomacy. There is an earth-encompassing network of finance and trade, loans and debts, investments and bank accounts, with resulting fluctuations in monetary exchanges and balances of payments. Some 190 very unequal and disunited members compose the United Nations and represent every region of the world, but the very concept of the nation, as represented in that body, is derived largely from Europe.

In most modern countries there have been pressures for increased democracy, and all modern governments, democratic or not, seek to arouse the energies and support of their populations. In a modern society old customs loosen, and ancestral religions are often questioned or transformed. There are usually demands for individual liberation, and an expectation of a higher standard of living. Modern societies typically move toward more equality between sexes and races, between adherents of different religions, or between different parts of the same country; and most modern governments try to reduce the gap between very high and low incomes. Movements for social change may be slow and gradual, or revolutionary and catastrophic, but movement of some kind is universal.

Such are a few of the historical trends of modernity. New "modernizing" forms of technology, culture, or economic organization now emerge in many different regions of the world, but most of the early patterns of modernity appeared first in Europe or in the extension of European societies (including the United States). The present book thus deals mainly with the historical growth of European societies and civilization, with increasing attention in later chapters to the earth as a whole. Antimodern movements and protests have also been part of modern world history. When they occur in Asia or Africa, they are often called anti-Western, as if to show that Europe and the "West" have been at the heart of the problem. Even those movements that most vigorously challenge Western social and cultural systems must confront the institutions, ideas, and legacies of modern European history.

If "modern" refers especially to a certain complicated way of living, it has also another sense, meaning merely what is recent or current. As a time span the word "modern" is purely relative. It depends on what we are talking about. A modern kitchen may be as much as 5 years old, modern physics is about 100 years old, modern science over 300, the modern European languages about 1,000. Modern civilization, the current civilization in which we are living, and which is always changing, is in one sense a product of the last two centuries, but in other senses it is much older. Roughly speaking, it may be said that modern times began in Europe about 1500. Modern times were preceded by a period of 1,000 years called the Middle Ages, which set in about A.D. 500, and which were in turn preceded by about another 1,000 years of classical Greek and Roman civilization. Before that reached the long histories of Egypt and Mesopotamia, and, further east, of the Indus Valley and China. All times prior to the European Middle Ages are commonly called "ancient." But the whole framework—ancient, medieval, and modern—is largely a matter of words and convention, whose meaning developed mainly with reference to Europe. We shall begin our history with a running start, and slow down the pace, surveying the scene more fully in proportion as the times grow more "modern."

1. ANCIENT TIMES: GREECE, ROME, AND CHRISTIANITY

Europeans were by no means the pioneers of human civilization. Half of recorded history had passed before anyone in Europe could read or write. The priests of Egypt began to keep written records between 4000 and 3000 B.C., but 2,000 years later the poems of Homer were still being circulated in the Greek city-states by word of mouth. Shortly after 3000 B.C., while the pharaohs were building the pyramids, Europeans were laboriously setting up the huge, unwrought stones called megaliths, of which Stonehenge is the best-known example. In a word, until after 2000 B.C., Europe was in the Neolithic or New Stone Age. This was in truth a great age in human history, the age in which human beings learned to make and use sharp tools, weave cloth, build living quarters, domesticate animals, plant seeds, harvest crops, and sense the returning cycles of the months and years. But the Middle East—Egypt, the Euphrates and Tigris valley, the island of Crete, and the shores of the Aegean Sea (which belonged more to Asia than to Europe)—had reached its Neolithic Age 2,000 years before Europe. By about 4000 B.C. the Middle East was already moving into the Bronze Age.

After about 2000 B.C., in the dim, dark continent that Europe then was, great changes began that are now difficult to trace. Europeans, too, learned how to smelt and forge metals, with the Bronze Age setting in about 2000 B.C. and the Iron Age about 1000 B.C. There was also a steady infusion of new peoples into Europe. They spoke languages related to languages now spoken in India and Iran, to which similar peoples migrated at about the same time. All these languages (whose interconnection was not known until the nineteenth century) are now referred to as Indo-European, and the people who spoke them became the ancestors both of the classical Greeks and Romans and of the Europeans of modern times. All European languages today are Indo-European with the exceptions of Basque, which is thought to be a survival from before the Indo-European invasion, and of Finnish and Hungarian, which were brought into Europe from Asia some centuries later. It was these invading Indo-Europeans who diffused over Europe the kind of speech from which the Latin, Greek, Germanic, Slavic, Celtic, and Baltic languages were later derived.

Indo-Europeans

The Greek World

The first Indo-Europeans to emerge into the clear light of history, in what is now Europe, were the Greeks. They filtered down through the Balkan peninsula to the shores of the Aegean Sea about 1900 B.C., undermining the older Cretan civilization and occupying most of what has since been called Greece by 1300 B.C. Beginning about 1150 B.C., other Greek-speaking tribes invaded from the north in successive waves. The newcomers included many restless, rough, and warlike tribes, and their coming ushered in several centuries of chaos and unrest before a gradual stabilization and revival began in the ninth century. The *Iliad* and the *Odyssey,* written down about 800 B.C., but composed and recited much earlier, probably refer to wars between the Greeks and other centers of civilization, of which one was at Troy in Asia Minor. The siege of Troy is thought to have occurred about 1200 B.C.

Greek accomplishments

The ancient Greeks proved to be an exceptionally gifted people, achieving supreme heights in thought and letters. They absorbed the knowledge of earlier eastern cultures, the mathematical lore of the ancient Chaldeans, and the arts and crafts that they found in Asia Minor and on voyages to Egypt. They added immediately to everything that they learned. It was the Greeks of the fifth and fourth centuries B.C. who formulated what the Western world long meant by the beautiful, and who first speculated on political freedom.

The Parthenon, constructed in ancient Athens during the fifth century B.C. to honor the goddess Athena, gave architectural form to the Greek respect for balance, order, and symmetry.
(Scala/Art Resource, NY)

As they settled down, the Greeks formed tiny city-states, all independent and often at war with one another, each only a few miles across, and typically including a coastal city and its adjoining farmlands. Athens, Corinth, and Sparta were such city-states. Many were democratic, which meant that all male citizens could congregate in the marketplace to elect officials and discuss their public business. They were not democratic in a modern sense in that slaves, resident noncitizens (called "metics"), and women were excluded from political life.

Politics was turbulent in the small Greek states. Democracy alternated with aristocracy, oligarchy, despotism, and tyranny. From this rich fund of experience was born systematic political science as set forth in the unwritten speculations of Socrates and in the *Republic* of Plato and the *Politics* of Aristotle in the fourth century B.C. The Greeks also were the first to write history as a subject distinct from myth and legend. Herodotus, "the Father of History," traveled throughout the Greek world and far beyond, ferreting out all he could learn of the past; and Thucydides, in his account of the wars between Athens and Sparta, presented history as a guide to enlightened citizenship and constructive statecraft.

The classical virtues

Perhaps because they were a restless and vehement people, the Greeks came to prize the "classical" virtues, which they were the first to define and which would have great influence in the subsequent history of European societies. For them, the ideal lay in moderation, or a golden mean. They valued order, balance, symmetry, clarity, and control. Their statues of idealized males revealed their conception of what humans ought to be—noble creatures, dignified, poised, unterrified by life or death, masters of themselves and their feelings. Their architecture, as in the Parthenon, made use of exactly measured angles and rows of columns. The classical "order," or set of carefully wrought pillars placed in a straight line at specified intervals, represented the firm impress of human reason on the brute materials of nature. The same sense of form was thrown over the torrent of human words. Written language became contrived, carefully planned, organized for effect. The epic poem, the lyric, the drama, the oration, along with history and the philosophical dialogue, each with its own rules and principles of composition, became the "forms" within which, in Western civilization, writers long expressed their thoughts.

Reflecting on the world about them, Greek philosophers concluded that something more fundamental existed beyond the world of appearances, that true reality was not what met the eye. With other peoples, and with the Greeks themselves in earlier times, this same realization had led to the formation of myths, dealing with invisible but mighty beings known as gods and with faraway places on the tops of mountains, beneath the earth, or in a world that followed death. Greek thinkers set to criticizing the web of myth. They looked for rational or natural explanations behind the variety and confusion that they saw. Some, observing human sickness, said that disease was not a demonic possession, but a natural sequence of conditions in the body, which could be identified, understood, and even treated in a natural way. Others, turning to physical nature, said that all matter was in reality composed of a very few things—made up of atoms or elements—which they usually designated as fire, water, earth, and air. Some said that change was a kind of illusion, all basic reality being uniform; some, that only change was real, and that the world was in flux. Some, like Pythagoras, found the enduring reality in "number," or mathematics. The Greeks, in short, laid the foundations for science. Studying also the way in which the mind worked, or ought to work, if it was to reach truthful conclusions, they developed the science of logic. The great codifier of Greek thought on almost all subjects in the classical period was Aristotle, who lived in Athens from 384 to 322 B.C.

Spread of Greek civilization

Greek influence spread widely and rapidly. Hardly were some of the city-states founded when their people, crowded within their narrow bounds, sent off some of their number with equipment and provisions to establish colonies. In this way Greek cities were very early established in south Italy, in Sicily, and even in the western Mediterranean, where Marseilles was founded about 600 B.C. Later the Greek city-states, unable to unite, succumbed to conquest by Philip of Macedon, who came from the relatively crude northern part of the Greek world, and whose son, Alexander the Great (356–323 B.C.), led a phenomenal, conquering march into Asia, across Persia, and on as far as India itself. Alexander's empire did not hold together, but Greek civilization, after having penetrated the western Mediterranean, now began to influence the ancient peoples of Egypt and the Middle East. Greek thought, Greek art, and the Greek language spread far and wide, drawing at the same time on the knowledge and creativity of other ancient cultures. The most famous "Greeks" after the fourth century B.C. and on into the early centuries of the Christian era usually did not come from Greece but from the Hellenized Middle East, and especially from Alexandria in Egypt. Among these later Greeks were the great summarizers or writers of encyclopedias in which ancient science was passed on to later generations—Strabo in geography, Galen in medicine, Ptolemy in astronomy. All three lived in the first and second centuries A.D.

The Roman World

In 146 B.C. the Greeks of Greece were conquered by a new people, the Romans, who kept their own Latin language but rapidly absorbed what they could of the intellectual and artistic culture of the Greeks. Over a period of two or three centuries they assembled an empire

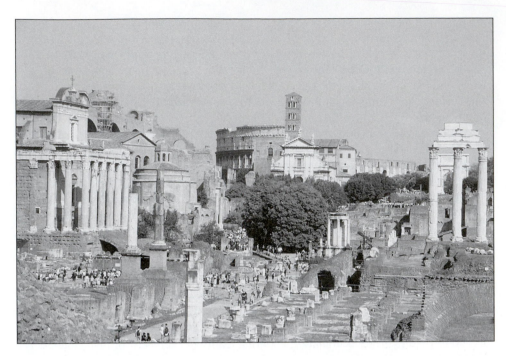

The Forum was the vital center of Roman public life and a symbol of imperial power. Rome's distinctive sense of grandeur and social order can still be discerned in the Forum's ruins, which are pictured here with the famous coliseum in the background.
(Royalty-Free/CORBIS)

in which the whole world of ancient civilization (west of Persia) was included. Egypt, Greece, Asia Minor, Syria all became Roman provinces, but in them the Romans had hardly any deep influence except in a political sense. In the West—in what are now Tunisia, Algeria, Morocco, Spain, Portugal, France, Switzerland, Belgium, and England— the Romans, though ruthless in their methods of conquest, in the long run acted as civilizing agents, transmitting to these hitherto isolated countries the age-old achievements of the East and the more recent culture of Greece and of Rome itself. So thorough was the Romanization that in the West Latin even became the commonly spoken language. It was later displaced by Arabic in Africa but survives to this day, transformed by time, in the Romance languages of France, Italy, Spain, Portugal, and Romania.

The Roman Empire

In the Roman Empire, which lasted with many vicissitudes from about 31 B.C. to the latter part of the fifth century A.D., virtually the entire civilized world of the ancient West was politically united and enjoyed generations of internal peace. Rome was the center, around which in all directions lay the "circle of lands," the *orbis terrarum,* the known world—that is, as known in the West, for the Han Empire at the same time in China (202 B.C. to A.D. 220) was also a highly organized cultural and political entity. The Roman Empire consisted essentially of the coasts of the Mediterranean Sea, which provided the great artery of transport and communication, and from which no part of the empire, except northern Gaul (France), Britain, and the Rhineland, was more than a couple of hundred miles away. Civilization among the elites in this vast empire was remarkably uniform; there were no distinct nationalities, and the most significant cultural difference was that east of Italy the predominant language was Greek;

in Italy and west of it, Latin. Cities grew up everywhere, engaged in a busy commercial life, exchanged ideas with one another, and, like the cities in other ancient cultures, relied on the labor of slaves. There were always more cities in the East, where most of the manufacturing crafts and the densest population were still concentrated, but they sprang up now in the West—indeed, most of the older cities of France, Spain, England, and western and southern Germany boast of some kind of origin under the Romans.

The distinctive aptitude of the Romans lay in organization, administration, government, and law. Never before had armies been so systematically formed, maintained over such long periods, dispatched at a word of command over such distances, or maneuvered so effectively on the field of battle. Never had so many peoples been governed from a single center. The Romans had at first possessed self-governing and republican institutions, but they lost them in the process of conquest, and the governing talents which they displayed in the days of the empire were of an authoritarian character—talents, not for self-government, but for managing, coordinating, and ruling the manifold and scattered parts of one enormous system. Locally, cities and city-states enjoyed a good deal of autonomy. But above them all rose a pyramid of imperial officials and provincial governors, culminating in the emperor at the top. The empire kept peace, the *pax Romana,* and even provided a certain justice for its many peoples. Lawyers worked on the body of principles known ever afterward as Roman law.

The pax Romana

Roman judges had somehow to settle disputes between persons of different regions, with conflicting local customs, for example, two merchants of Spain and Egypt. The Roman law came therefore to hold that no custom is necessarily right, that there is a higher or universal law by which fair decisions may be made, and that this higher, universal, or "natural" law, or "law of nature," will be understandable or acceptable to everyone, since it arises from human nature and reason. Here the lawyers drew on Greek philosophy for support. They held also that law derives its force from being enacted by a proper authority (not merely from custom, usage, or former legal cases); this authority to make law they called *majestas,* or sovereign power, and they attributed it to the emperor. Thus the Romans emancipated the idea of law from mere custom on the one hand and mere caprice on the other; they regarded it as something to be formed by enlightened intelligence, consistent with reason and the nature of things; and they associated it with the solemn action of official power. It must be added that Roman law favored the state, or the public interest as seen by the government, rather than the interests or liberties of individual persons, and it generally provided men with more legal privileges than women. These principles, together with more specific ideas on such matters as property, debt, marriage, and wills were in later centuries to have a great effect in Europe.

The Coming of Christianity

The thousand years during which Greco-Roman civilization arose and flourished were notable in another way even more momentous for all later human history. It was in this period that the great world religions came into being. Within the time bracket 800 B.C.–A.D. 700 the lives of Confucius and Buddha, of the major Jewish prophets, and of Muhammad are all included. At the very midpoint (probably about 4 B.C.), in Palestine in the Roman Empire, a man named Jesus was born, believed by his followers to be the Son of God. Like Jesus, the first Christians were Jews; but both under the impulse of its own doctrine, which held that all people were alike in spirit, and under the strong leadership of Paul, a man of Jewish birth, Roman citizenship, and Greek culture, Christianity began to make converts. The new religion gradually fused the monotheism of Judaism and its ethical teachings with various themes in Greek philosophy, creating a new synthesis of Judeo-Greek thought that would shape much of the later history of ideas in Western cultures. Christianity gained adherents across most of the Roman Empire, and there were certainly a few Christians in Rome by the middle of the first century. Both Paul and the elder apostle, Peter, according to church tradition, died as martyrs at Rome in the time of the Emperor Nero about A.D. 67.[1]

Emergence and spread of Christianity

The Christian teaching spread at first among the poor, the people at the bottom of society, those whom Greek glories and Roman splendors had passed over or enslaved, and who had the least to delight in or to hope for in the existing world. Women were also drawn to the new religion, perhaps in part because early Christianity offered them more autonomy and more opportunities for leadership than they found in the traditional patriarchal order of Roman law and families. Gradually Christian ideas reached the upper classes; a few classically educated and well-to-do people became Christians; in the second century Christian bishops and writers were at work publicly in various parts of the empire. In the third century the Roman government, with the empire falling into turmoil, and blaming the social troubles on the Christians, subjected them to wholesale persecution. In the fourth century (possibly in A.D. 312) the Emperor Constantine accepted Christianity. By the fifth century the entire Roman world was formally Christian; no other religion was officially tolerated; and the deepest thinkers were Christians who combined Christian beliefs with the now thousand-year-old tradition of Greco-Roman thought, philosophy, and social institutions.

It is impossible to exaggerate the importance of the coming of Christianity. It brought with it, for one thing, an altogether new sense of human life. Where the Greeks had demonstrated the powers of the mind, the Christians explored the soul, and they taught that in the sight of God all souls were equal, that every human life was sacrosanct and inviolate, and that all worldly distinctions of greatness, beauty, and brilliancy were in the last analysis superficial. Where the Greeks had identified the beautiful and the good, had thought ugliness to be bad, and had shrunk from disease as an imperfection and from everything misshapen as horrible and repulsive, the Christians resolutely saw a spiritual beauty even in the plainest or most unpleasant exterior and sought out the diseased, the crippled, and the mutilated to give them help. Love, for the ancients, was never quite distinguished from Venus; for the Christians, who held that God was love, it took on deep overtones of sacrifice and compassion. Suffering itself was in a way divine, since God had also suffered on the Cross in human form. A new dignity was thus found for suffering that the world could not cure. At the same time the Christians worked to relieve suffering as none had worked before. They protested against the massacre of prisoners of war, against the mistreatment and degradation of slaves, against the sending of gladiators to kill each other in the arena for another's pleasure. In place of the Greek and pagan self-satisfaction with human accomplishments they taught humility in the face of an almighty Providence, and in place of proud distinctions between high and low, slave and free, civilized and barbarian, they held that all men and women were alike because all were children of the same God.

Christian beliefs

---

[1]The terms B.C. (Before Christ) and A.D. (Annō Domini) are generally used now with little attention to their religious origin. With so many creeds and faiths in the modern world employing this system of calculating dates, readers will increasingly encounter the substitute usage B.C.E. (Before the Common Era) and C.E. (Common Era).

On an intellectual level Christianity also marked a revolution. It was Christianity, not rational philosophy, that dispelled the swarm of greater and lesser gods and goddesses; the blood sacrifices and self-immolation; or the frantic resort to magic, fortune-telling, and divination. The Christians taught that there was only one God. The pagan conception of local, tribal, or national gods disappeared. For all the world there was only one plan of Salvation and one Providence, and all human beings took their origin from one source. The idea of the world as one thing, a "universe," was thus affirmed with a new depth of meaning. The very intolerance of Christianity (which was new to the ancient world) came from this sense of human unity, in which it was thought that all people should have, and deserved to have, the one true and saving religion.

The Christians were often denounced and persecuted for their political ideas. The Roman Empire was a world state; there was no other state but it; no living human being except the emperor was sovereign; no one anywhere on earth was his equal. Between gods and human beings, in the pagan view, there was moreover no clear distinction. Some gods behaved very humanly, and some human creatures were more like gods than others. The emperor was held to be veritably a god. A cult of Caesar was established, regarded as necessary to maintain the state, which was the world itself. All this the Christians firmly refused to accept. It was because they would not worship Caesar that the Roman officials regarded them as social incendiaries who must be persecuted and stamped out.

Persecution

The Christian doctrine on this point went back to the saying gathered from Jesus, that one should render to Caesar the things that were Caesar's, and to God those that were God's. The same dualism was presented more systematically by St. Augustine about A.D. 420 in his *City of God*. Few books have been more influential in shaping the later development of Western civilization.

The "world," the world of Caesar, in the time of St. Augustine, was going to ruin. Rome itself was plundered in 410 by heathen barbarians. Augustine wrote the *City of God* with this event obsessing his imagination. He wrote to show that though the material world could perish there was yet another world that was more enduring and more important.

St. Augustine

There were, he said, really two "cities," the earthly and the heavenly, the temporal and the eternal, the city of man and the City of God. The earthly city was the domain of state and empire, of political authority and political obedience. It was a good thing, as part of God's providential scheme for human life, but it had no inherently divine character of its own. The emperor was human. The state was not absolute; it could be judged, criticized, or corrected from sources outside itself. It was, for all its majesty and splendor, really subordinate in some way to a higher and spiritual power. This power lay in the City of God. By the City of God Augustine meant many things, and readers found all sorts of meanings in later ages. The heavenly city might mean heaven itself, the abode of God and of blessed spirits enjoying life after death. It might mean certain elect spirits of this world, the good people as opposed to the bad. It might, more theoretically, be a system of ideal values or ideal justice, as opposed to the crude approximations of the actual world.

In any case, with this Christian dualism the Western world escaped from what is called Caesaropapism, a political system in which one person holds the powers of ruler and of pontiff. Instead, the spiritual power and the political power were held to be separate and independent. In later times popes and kings often quarreled with each other; the clergy often struggled for political power, and governments have often attempted to dictate what people should believe, or

Caesaropapism

St. Augustine's wisdom and influence on Christian theology were honored throughout the Middle Ages; he appears here in a medieval illustration, dispensing truths from a celestial throne.
(Scala/Art Resource, NY)

love, or hope for. But speaking in general of European history neither side has ever won out, and in the sharp distinction between the spiritual and the temporal has lain the germ of many liberties in later societies. At the same time the idea that no ruler, no government, and no institution is too mighty to rise above moral criticism eventually opened the way to a dynamic and progressive way of living in the West.

2.   THE EARLY MIDDLE AGES: THE FORMATION OF EUROPE

There was really no Europe in ancient times. In the Roman Empire we may see a Mediterranean world, or even a West and an East in the Latin- and Greek-speaking portions. But the West included parts of Africa as well as of Europe, and Europe as we know it was divided by the Rhine-Danube frontier, south and west of which lay the civilized provinces of the empire, and north and east the "barbarians" of whom the Roman world knew almost nothing. To the Romans "Africa" meant Tunisia-Algeria; "Asia" meant the Asia Minor peninsula; and the word "Europe," since it meant little, was scarcely used by them at all. It was in the half-millennium from the fifth to the tenth centuries that Europe as such for the first time emerged with its peoples brought together in a life of their own, clearly set off from Asia or Africa and beginning to create a culture that would become "Western."

The Disintegration of the Roman Empire

The Roman Empire began to fall apart, especially in the West, and the Christianizing of the empire did nothing to impede its decline. The Emperor Constantine, who in embracing Christianity undoubtedly hoped to strengthen the imperial system, also took one other significant step. In A.D. 330 he founded a new capital at the old Greek city of Byzantium, which he renamed Constantinople. (It is now Istanbul.) Thereafter the Roman Empire had two capitals, Rome and Constantinople, and was administered in two halves. Increasingly the center of gravity moved eastward, as if returning to the more ancient centers in the Middle East, as if the experiment of civilizing the West were to be given up as a failure.

Founding of Constantinople

Throughout its long life the empire had been surrounded on almost all sides by people whom the Romans called "barbarians"—wild Celts in Wales and Scotland, Germans in the heart of Europe, Persians or Parthians in the East ("barbarian" only in the ancient sense of speaking neither Greek nor Latin), and, in the southeast, the Arabs. These barbarians, always with the exception of Persia, had never been brought within the pale of ancient Greek or Roman civilization. Somewhat like the Chinese, who about 200 B.C. built several walls to solve the same problem, the Romans simply drew a line beyond which they themselves rarely ventured and would not allow the barbarians to pass. Nevertheless outsiders filtered into the empire. As early as the third century A.D. emperors and generals recruited bands of them to serve in the Roman armies. Their service over, they would receive farmlands, settle down, marry, and mingle with the population. By the fourth and fifth centuries a good many such individuals were even reaching high positions of state.

At the same time, in the West, for reasons that are not fully understood, the activity of the Roman cities began to falter, commerce began to decay, local governments became paralyzed, taxes became more ruinous, and free farmers were bound to the soil. The army seated and unseated emperors. Rival generals fought with each other. Gradually the West fell into decrepitude, and the old line between the Roman provinces and the barbarian world made less and less difference.

Decline in the West

After some centuries of relative stability, the barbarians themselves, pressed by more distant peoples from Asia, rather suddenly began to move. Sometimes they first sought peaceable access to the empire, attracted by the warmer Mediterranean climate, or desiring to share in the advantages of Roman civilization. More often, Germanic tribes moved swiftly and by force, plundering, fighting, and killing as they went. In 476 a barbarian chieftain deposed the last Roman emperor in the West. Sometimes in the general upheaval peoples from Asia rapidly intermixed with other populations in the old Roman Empire. The most famous of these invaders were the Huns, who cut through central Europe and France about 450 under their

Barbarian invasions

leader Attila, the "scourge of God"—and then disappeared. Nor were these invasions all. Two centuries later new irruptions burst upon the Greco-Roman world from the southeast, where hitherto outlying peoples poured in from the Arabian deserts. The Arabs, aroused by the new faith of Islam (Muhammad died in 632), fell as conquerors upon Syria, Mesopotamia, and Persia; occupied Egypt about 640 and the old Roman Africa about 700; and in 711 reached Spain.

Beneath these blows the old unity of the Greco-Roman or Mediterranean world was broken. The "circle of lands" divided into three segments. Three types of civilization now confronted each other across the inland sea.

The Byzantine World, the Arabic World, and the West about 700

Byzantine Empire

The Eastern Roman, Later Roman, Greek, or Byzantine Empire (all names for the same empire) with its capital at Constantinople, and now including only the Asia Minor peninsula, the Balkan peninsula, and parts of Italy, made up one segment of the circle of lands. It represented the most direct continuation of the ancient civilizations of the Middle East. It was Christian in religion and Greek in culture and language. Its people felt themselves to be the truest heirs both of early Christianity and of earlier cultures in Greece. Art and architecture, trades and crafts, commerce and navigation, thought and writing, government and law, while not so creative or flexible as in the classical age, were still carried on actively in the eastern empire, on much the same level as in the closing centuries of ancient times. For all Christians, and for heathen barbarians in Europe, the emperor of the East stood out as the world's supreme ruler, and Constantinople as the world's preeminent and almost fabulous city.

Arabic world

The second segment of the Mediterranean world was the Arabic and Islamic. It became the most dynamic culture in the lands of the old Roman Empire, reaching from the neighborhood of the Pyrenees through Spain and all North Africa into Arabia, Syria, and the East. Arabic was its language; it became, and still remains, the common speech from Morocco to the Persian Gulf. Islam was its religion, and it looked to the prophet Muhammad (c. 570–632) and the Qur'an (or Koran) for its religious truths. Muhammad had spent his early adult years as a merchant in Mecca on the Arabian peninsula, but he began to have a series of intense religious revelations when he was about 40 years old. These revelations led Muhammad to a devout and uncompromising monotheism, which stressed the great power of God—or Allah in Arabic—and the human duty to adhere to God's will. Muhammad saw himself as a prophet in the Jewish and Christian tradition, but he soon came to define his revelations and teachings as the beginning of a new religion. The messages that came to Muhammad through revelation were written down in the sacred book of Islam, the Qur'an, which was organized into 114 chapters (called *suras*). Emphasizing submission to God, the importance of prayer, and an ethical obligation to help others, the Qur'an provided directions for the affairs of daily life as well as a powerful, poetic vision of the grandeur of God.

Muhammad's revelations attracted little early support in Mecca. Indeed, the hostility there forced him to move north in 622 to the city of Medina. This famous flight (the *Hegira*) brought him to a more receptive community, where his teachings quickly gained numerous adherents and from where the first Muslims set out to spread the new faith across all of Arabia, including Mecca. Muhammad died in 632, but the new religion con-

The sixth-century emperor Justinian built the great Hagia Sophia to display his commitment to the Christian religion and the power of his capital city, Constantinople. The church became a mosque after the Byzantine Empire fell to Muslim invaders in the fifteenth century, but it remains the most famous achievement of Byzantine architecture.
(Hirmer Fotoarchiv)

tinued to expand rapidly in all directions. Leadership passed to a series of caliphs who were initially relatives of Muhammad himself. As Muslims conquered new territories and won new converts throughout the Middle East and North Africa, the lands of Islam came under the control of these caliphs. All Muslims were included in the caliphate. The ruling caliph exercised both spiritual and political authority, and he was regarded as the true religious and military successor of Muhammad himself.

Conflicts and lasting divisions nevertheless developed during the era of the third Caliph, Uthman — one of the sons-in-law of Muhammad and a leader of the Umayyad family. Supporters of Ali, a rival leader and also a son-in-law of Muhammad, killed Uthman in 656, and Ali came to power as the fourth caliph. This violence did not resolve the conflict, however, and Ali himself was soon murdered. Ali's followers refused to accept the legitimacy of the Umayyad family, which now regained control of the caliphate. A minority faction, called Shiites, continued to honor Ali and to claim that all true leaders of Islam must descend from him. Although most Muslims supported the Umayyad caliphs, the Shiite minority remained a permanent presence within Islam, sustaining the memory of Ali and challenging the religious legitimacy of the dominant Sunnis (a term that emerged later). Meanwhile, the Umayyad dynasty set up its capital in Damascus, and some members of the family eventually extended their power as far west as Spain.

The Arabic world, like the Byzantine, built upon the heritage of the Greco-Romans. In religion, the early Muslims regarded themselves as successors to the Jewish and Christian traditions. They considered the line of Jewish prophets since Abraham to be spokesmen of the true God, and they put Jesus in this line. But they added that Muhammad was the last and greatest of the prophets, that the Qur'an set forth a revelation replacing that of the Jewish Bible, that the Christian New Testament was mistaken because Christ was not divine, and that the Christian belief in a Trinity was erroneous because there was in the strictest sense only One True God. To the Muslim Arabs, therefore, all Christians were dangerous or misguided infidels.

In mundane matters, the Arabs speedily took over the civilization of the lands they conquered. In the caliphate, as in the Byzantine Empire, the civilization of the ancient world went its way without serious interruption. Huge buildings and magnificent palaces were constructed; ships plied the Mediterranean; Arab merchants ventured over the deserts and traversed the Indian Ocean; holy or learned men corresponded over thousands of miles. The government developed efficient systems to collect taxes, enforce the laws, and keep the provinces in order. In the sciences the Arabs not only learned from but also went beyond the Greeks. They translated Greek scientific literature: we know some of it today only through these medieval Arabic versions. Arab geographers had a wider knowledge of the world than anyone had possessed up to their time. Arab mathematicians developed algebra so far beyond the Greeks as almost to be its creator ("algebra" is an Arabic word), and in introducing the "Arabic" numerals (through their contacts with India) they made arithmetic, which in Roman numerals had been formidably difficult into something that every schoolchild can be taught.

Latin Christendom

The third segment of the ancient Greco-Roman world was Latin Christendom, which about A.D. 700 did not look very promising. It was what was left over from the other two—what the Byzantines were unable to hold and the Arabs were unable to conquer. It included only Italy (shared in part with the Byzantines), France, Belgium, the Rhineland, and Britain. Barbarian kings were doing their best to rule small kingdoms, but in truth all government had fallen to pieces. Usually the invading barbarians remained a minority, eventually to be absorbed. Only in England, and in the region immediately west of the Rhine, did the Germanic element supersede the older Celtic and Latin. But the presence of violent invaders, armed and fierce amid peasants and city dwellers reduced to passivity by Roman rule, together with the disintegration of Roman institutions that had gone on even before the invasions, left this region in chaos.

The Western barbarians, as noted, were Germanic; and the Germanic influence became a distinctive contribution to the making of Europe. Some Germans were Christian by the fourth century, but most were still heathen when they burst into the Roman Empire. Their languages had not been written down, but they possessed an intricate folklore and religion in which fighting and heroic valor were much esteemed. Though now in a migratory phase, they were an agricultural people who knew how to work iron, and they had a rudimentary knowledge of the crafts of the Romans. They were organized in small tribes and had a strong sense of tribal kinship, which (as with many similar peoples) dominated their ideas of leadership and law. They enjoyed more freedom in their affairs than did the citizens of the Roman Empire. Many of the tribes were roughly self-governing in that all free men, those entitled to bear arms, met in open fields to hold council; and often the tribe itself elected its leader or king. They had a strong sense of loyalty to persons, of fealty to the acknowledged king or chief; but they had no sense of loyalty to large or general institutions. They had no sense of the state—of any distant, impersonal, and continuing source of law and rule. Law they regarded as the inflexible custom of each tribe. In the absence of abstract jurisprudence or trained judges, they settled disputes by rough and ready methods. In the ordeal, for example, a person who obstinately floated when thrown into water was adjudged guilty. In trial by battle, the winner of a kind of ritualistic duel was regarded as innocent. The gods, it was thought, would not allow wrong to prevail.

Germanic customs

The Germans who overran the old Roman provinces found it difficult to maintain any political organization at more than a local level. Security and civil order all but disappeared. Peasant communities were at the mercy of wandering bands of habitual fighters. Fighters often captured peasant villages, took them under their protection, guarded them from further marauders, and lived off their produce. Sometimes the same great fighting man came to possess many such villages, moving with his retinue of horsemen from one village to another to support himself throughout the year. Thus originated a new distinction between lord and servant, noble and commoner, martial and menial class. Life became local and self-sufficient. People ate, wore, used, and dwelled in only what they themselves and their neighbors could produce. In contrast to the economies of the Byzantine and Islamic worlds, Western trade died down, the cities became depopulated, money went out of circulation, and almost nothing was bought or sold. The Roman roads fell into neglect; people often used them as quarries for ready-cut building blocks for their own crude purposes. The West not only broke up into localized villages but also ceased to have habitual exchanges across the Mediterranean. It lost contact with the eastern centers from which its former civilization had always been drawn. From roughly A.D. 500 on, Europe fell into what some later historians would call the "Dark Ages."

The Church and the Rise of the Papacy

Only one organized institution maintained a tie with ancient civilization. Only one institution, reaching over the whole West, could receive news or dispatch its agents over the whole area. This institution was the Christian church. Its framework still stood; its network of bishoprics, as built up in late Roman times, remained intact except in places such as England, where the barbarian conquest was complete.

In addition, a new type of religious institution spread rapidly with the growth of monasteries. The serious and the sensitive, both men and women (though not together, to be sure), rejected the savagery about them and retired into communities of their own. Usually they were left unmolested by rough neighbors who held them in religious awe. In a world of violence

Growth of monasteries

they formed islands of quiet, peace, and contemplation. Their prayers, it was believed, were of use to all the world, and their example might at the least arouse pangs of shame in more worldly people. The monastic houses generally adopted the rule of St. Benedict (c. 480–543) and were governed by an abbot. Dedicated to the same ideals, they formed unifying filaments throughout the chaos of the Latin West.

Bishops, abbots, and monks looked with veneration to Rome as the spot where St. Peter, the first apostle, had been martyred. The bishop of Rome corresponded with other bishops, sent out missionaries, gave advice on doctrine when he could, and attempted to keep in mind the situation throughout the Latin world as a whole. Moreover, with no emperor any longer in Rome, the bishop took over the government and public affairs of the city. Thus the bishop of Rome, while claiming a primacy over all Christians, was not dominated by any secular power. In the East the great church functionaries, the patriarchs, fell under the influence of the emperor who continued to rule at Constantinople. A tradition of Caesaropapism grew up in the East; but in the West the independence of the bishop of Rome now confirmed in practice a principle always maintained by the great churchmen of the West—the independence of the spiritual power from the political or temporal.

About A.D. 400
The Roman Empire

About A.D. 800
Latin Christians
Greek Christians
Muslims

About A.D. 1250
Latin Christians
Greek Christians
Muslims

The growing authority of the popes was fortified by various arguments. St. Peter, it was held, had imparted the spiritual authority given to him by Christ himself to the Roman bishops who were his successors. This doctrine of the "Petrine supremacy" was based on two verses in the Bible (Matthew xvi, 18–19), according to which Christ designated Peter as the head of the church, giving him the "power of the keys" to open and close the doors of eternal salvation. As for the pope's temporal rule in Rome, it was affirmed that the Emperor Constantine had endowed the bishop with the government of the city. This "Donation of Constantine" was accepted as historical fact from the eighth century to the fifteenth, when it was proved to be a forgery.

Papal authority

It was the church that incorporated the barbarians into a higher way of life, and when barbarians embraced a more civilized way of living, it was the church that they entered. As early as about A.D. 340, the church sent out Ulfilas to convert the Goths; his translation of the Bible represents the first writing down of any Germanic language. About 496 the king of the Franks, Clovis, was converted to Christianity. A hundred years later, in 597, the king of Kent in southeast England yielded to the persuasions of Augustine of Canterbury, a missionary dispatched from Rome, and the Christianization of the Anglo-Saxons gradually followed. Missionaries from Ireland also, to which Christians of the Roman Empire had fled before the heathen barbarians, now returned to both Britain and the Continent to spread the gospel. By A.D. 700, after three centuries of turmoil, the borders of Christianity in the West were again roughly what they had been in late Roman times. Then in 711, as we have seen, the Arabs entered Spain. They crossed the Pyrenees and raced toward central Europe, but were stopped by a Christian and Frankish army in 732 at Tours on the river Loire. Islam was turned back into Spain, thereby allowing the people of Western Europe to expand their emerging Latin Christian culture.

Conversion of the barbarians

The Empire of Charlemagne, 800–814

Among the Franks, in what is now northern France and the German Rhineland, there had arisen a line of capable rulers of whom the greatest was Charlemagne. The Frankish kings made it their policy to cooperate with the pope. The pope needed a protector against depredations by his barbarian neighbors and against the political claims of the Byzantine Empire upon the city of Rome. The Frankish kings, in return for protection thus offered, won papal support to their side. This made it easier for them to control their own bishops, who were more often seen on horseback than in the episcopal chair, and was of use in pacifying their own domains and in wars of conquest against the heathen. In the year 800, in Rome, the pope crowned Charlemagne as emperor of the West. Frankish king and Roman

THE MEDITERRANEAN WORLD about A.D. 400, 800, and 1250

Greco-Roman civilization, centered about the Mediterranean, was officially Christian and politically unified under the Roman Empire in A.D. 400 but broke apart into three segments in the early Middle Ages. Each segment developed its own type of life. Each segment also expanded beyond the limits of the ancient Mediterranean culture. By 1250 Latin Christendom reached to the Baltic and beyond. Greek Christendom penetrated north of the Black Sea to include the Russians. The Muslim world spread into inner Asia and Africa. In 1250, and until 1492, the Muslims, or Moors, still held the southern tip of Spain. Jews lived in varying numbers in each of the three segments.

This image of a monastery in a medieval Spanish manuscript shows how the early monks became known for their learning as well as their religious contemplation and disciplined labor.
(Pierpont Morgan Library/Art Resource, NY)

bishop both believed that if only the Roman Empire could be restored peace and order might once more reign. Church and empire, religion and the state, were to be as two mighty swords employed in the same holy cause.

Charlemagne

Charlemagne crossed the Pyrenees and won back the northeastern corner of Spain to Christian rule. He overthrew and subordinated the barbarian kings who had set themselves up in northern Italy. He sent forces down the Danube, penetrated into Bohemia, and proceeded against some of the still heathen Germans (the Saxons) who lived along the river Elbe, and whom he either massacred or converted to Christianity. All these regions he brought within his new empire. Except for England and Ireland, which remained outside, the borders of his empire were coextensive with those of the Latin Christian world.

Once more, to a degree, the peoples of Western Europe were united under an empire. But a momentous change had occurred. Its capital did not lie in the ancient world of the Mediterranean. Its capital was now in northern Europe at Aix-la-Chapelle, or Aachen, near the mouth of the Rhine. Its ruler, Charlemagne, was a German of an ethnic group which had remained outside ancient civilization. Its people were Germans, French, and Italians, or, more precisely, the ancestors from whom these nationalities were to emerge. In the Greco-Roman world the north had always been at best provincial. Now the north became a center in its own right. Charlemagne dispatched embassies to the Byzantine emperor at Constantinople and to Harun al-Rashid, the great Muslim caliph at Baghdad. In intellectual matters, too, the north now became a capital. Centuries of violence and confusion had virtually destroyed education and systematic learning, even for the most powerful families in Europe. Charlemagne himself, though he understood Latin, could barely read and never learned to write. He used his

Revival of learning

authority, however, to revive the all but forgotten ancient learning and to spread education at least among the clergy. To his palace school came scholars from England, Germany, France, Italy, Spain. They wrote and spoke in Latin, the only Western language in which complicated ideas could at the time be expressed. Disintegrating ancient manuscripts were copied and recopied to assure a more abundant supply for study—always by hand, but in a more rapid script than had before been used. This so-called "Carolingian minuscule," evolved into the small letters of the modern Western alphabet, only the capital letters being Roman. Meanwhile, Charlemagne sought to foster commerce by creating a new and more reliable coinage, which was based on silver, the gold coins of the Roman Empire having long since vanished.

Ninth-Century Invasions; Europe by 1000

In Charlemagne's empire we first see the shape of Europe as a unit of society and culture distinct from the Mediterranean world of antiquity. The empire did not last. New waves of invaders assailed Western Christendom in the ninth century. The Magyars (called in Latin "Hungarians") terrified various parts of Europe until they settled down on the middle Danube about the year 900. New Germanic tribes uprooted themselves, coming this time *Second wave of invaders* from Scandinavia, and variously known as Norse, Vikings, or Danes. Bursting out in all directions, they reached Kiev in Russia in 864, discovered Iceland in 874, and even touched America in 1000. In the Christian world they assaulted the coasts and pushed up the rivers but settled in considerable numbers only in the Danelaw in England and in Normandy in France. Meanwhile the Arabs raided the shores of France and Italy and occupied Sicily. Nowhere was the power of government strong enough to ward off such attacks. Everywhere the harassed local population found its own means of defense or, that failing, was slaughtered, robbed, or carried off into slavery.

Gradually the second wave of invaders was incorporated as the first had been, by the same process of conversion to Christianity. By the year 1000 this process was nearly complete. In 1001 the pope sent a golden crown to the Magyars to crown St. Stephen as their first king, thus bringing Hungary within the orbit of the Latin West. Poland, Bohemia, and the Scandinavian homelands of the Norse were Christianized during the same era. In older Christian countries, such as France, the last remote and isolated rustics—the "heathen" who lived in the "heath"—were finally ferreted out by missionaries and brought within the Christian fold. In Christian countries Christianity now permeated every corner, and the historic peoples of western Europe had come together within the spreading religious and cultural system of the Latin church.

Meanwhile West and East continued to drift apart. The refusal of *"Great Schism of East and West"* Greek patriarchs at Constantinople to recognize the claims to primacy of the bishop of Rome, whom they regarded as a kind of Western barbarian, and the refusal of the Roman pontiff to acknowledge the political pretensions of the Byzantine Empire, led to the Great Schism of East and West. This schism, after developing for three centuries, became definite in 1054. It divided the Christian world into the Latin or Roman Catholic and the Greek Orthodox churches. It was from Constantinople that Christianity reached the peoples of Russia. The Russians, like the Balkan peoples, remained out of contact with most of Europe during the centuries when spiritual and intellectual contacts were carried through the clergy. They believed, indeed, that the Latin West was evil, heretical, and unholy. The Latin West, at the same time, by the schism, cut one more of its ties with antiquity and emerged more clearly as an independent center of its own civilization.

Emerging Europe

By the year 1000, or soon thereafter, the entity that we call Europe had come into existence. From the turbulence that followed the collapse of the Greco-Roman civilization had issued the peoples and the countries that would evolve into modern Europe. A kingdom of France had emerged, adjoining the great ill-defined bulk of Germany to the east. There were small Christian kingdoms in northern Spain and a number of city-states in the Italian peninsula. In the north there were now a kingdom of England and a kingdom of Scotland; Denmark, Norway, and Sweden had also taken form. In the east rose the three great kingdoms of Poland, Bohemia, and Hungary, the first two predominantly Slavic, Hungary predominantly Magyar, but all were Latin and Catholic in culture and religion, and Western in orientation. The east Slavs, or Russians, and the Slavs and other peoples of the Balkan peninsula also formed kingdoms of their own. Their languages and religion were diverging from the cultures of Western Europe. Christianized by Byzantine missionaries, they were Greek and Orthodox in culture and religion, and oriented toward Constantinople.

The civilization of Western Europeans in the year 1000 was still not much to boast of in the more polished circles of Byzantium or Baghdad. It might still seem that the West would suffer more than the East from their separation. But the West began at this time to experience new social and economic activity, ushering in the European civilization of the High Middle Ages.

3.   THE HIGH MIDDLE AGES: SECULAR CIVILIZATION

Agriculture and the Feudal System after 1000

Some historical periods are so dynamic that a person who lives to a mature age can remember sweeping changes that have come in one's own lifetime. Such a time began in Europe in the eleventh century. People could see new towns rise and grow before their eyes. They could observe new undertakings in commerce or government. Most of the cities that Europe was to know before the modern industrial era sprang up between about 1050 and 1200. The population of western Europe, which had been sparse even in Roman days, and which was even sparser after 500, suddenly began to grow denser about the year 1000, and it expanded steadily for two or three hundred years. The people of the High Middle Ages did not develop the conception of progress because their minds were set upon timeless values and personal salvation in another world, but the period was nevertheless one of rapid progress in nonreligious or "secular" matters. Much was created that remained fundamental far into modern times.

Agriculture and population growth

The new era was made possible by the process of growth in population which went along with agricultural changes. After the Norse and Magyar inroads had stopped, Europe was spared the assaults of other invaders. There came to be more security of life and limb. Farmers could plant with more confidence that they would reap, and people could build houses with the expectation of passing them on to their children. Hence there was more planting and building. Sometime before the year 1000 a heavier plow was invented, which cut a deeper furrow. Better methods of harnessing horses had been found than the ancients had ever known. The Romans had continued simply to throw a yoke over a horse's neck, so that the animal in pulling a weight easily choked. Europeans, before the year 1000, began to use a horse collar that rested on the animal's shoulders. The single horse could pull a greater load, or several horses could now for the first time be hitched in tandem. The amount of available animal power was thus multiplied, at a time when animals were the main source of power other than human muscle. Windmills, unknown to the ancients, were developed in the Low Countries about this time. They too offered a new source of power. Thus at the very beginning of a specifically "European" history, one may detect characteristics of subsequent European civilization—a search for technological invention, a quest for new sources of energy.

With such labor-saving devices people continued to work very hard, but they obtained more results by their efforts. Probably the use of such inventions, together with the influence of the Christian clergy, accounts for the gradual disappearance of slavery from Europe and its replacement by the less-abject and less-degrading status of serfdom. It is true that medieval Christians, when they could, continued to enslave whites as they were later to do with blacks. Usually such slaves were captives in war, taken from tribes not yet converted to Christianity, and sometimes exported as a form of merchandise to the Byzantine and Muslim worlds. As the successive European peoples became Christianized, the supply of slaves dried up. Medieval Christians did not enslave each other, nor was slavery essential to any important form of production.

Not only did population increase, and work become more productive, but also groups of people became less isolated from one another. Communications improved. The roads remained poor or nonexistent, but bridges were built across European rivers, and settlers filled in the wildernesses that had formerly separated the inhabited areas. Trees were felled, land was cleared, and the rural population clustered in village communities. The "nucleated" village gave more security, more contact between families, and readier access to the blacksmith or the priest. It also made possible a communally organized agriculture.

Better ways of using land were introduced in the "three-field" system, *Three-field system* which spread to almost every region where cereal crops were the staple. In this "system" the peasant village divided its arable fields into three parts. In a given year one part was sown with one crop, such as wheat; a second part with another, such as barley; and the third was left to lie fallow. The three parts were rotated from year to year. Thus soil exhaustion was avoided at a time when fertilizers were unknown. Formerly, half or less of the available fields had been cultivated at any one time. With the three-field system two-thirds of the land came into annual use. This change, reinforced by better plowing and more effective employment of animals, led to a huge increase in the supply of food.

The peace and personal security necessary to agriculture were also advanced, in the absence of effective public authority, by the growth of *Feudalism* institutions that we know as "feudalism." Feudalism was intricate and diverse, but in essence it was a means of carrying on some kind of government on a local basis where no organized state existed. After the collapse of Charlemagne's empire the real authority fell into the hands of persons who were most often called "counts." The count was the most important man of a region covering a few hundred square miles. To build up his own position, and strengthen himself for war against other counts, he tried to keep the peace and maintain control over the lesser lords in his county, those whose possessions extended over a few hundred or a few thousand acres. These lesser lords accepted or were forced to accept his protection. They became his vassals, and he became their "lord." The lord and vassal relation was one of reciprocal duties.

Most people in the Middle Ages worked in the fields, coping like the peasant in this late medieval illustration with the seasons, soil, seeds, and animals that shaped agricultural life.
(The British Library)

The lord protected the vassal and assured him justice and firm tenure of his land. If two vassals of the same lord disputed the possession of the same village, the lord decided the case, sitting in council (or "court") with all his vassals assembled and judging according to the common memory or customary law of the district. If a vassal died young, leaving only small children, the lord took the family under his "wardship" or guardianship, guaranteeing that the rightful heirs would inherit in due time. Correspondingly the vassal agreed to serve the lord as a fighting man for a certain number of days in the year. The vassal also owed it to the lord to attend and advise him, to sit in his court in the judging of disputes. Usually he owed no money or material payment; but if the lord had to be ransomed from captivity, or when his children married, the vassal paid a fee. The vassal also paid a fee on inheriting an estate, and the income of estates under wardship went to the lord. Thus the lord collected sporadic revenues with which to finance his somewhat primitive government.

This feudal scheme gradually spread across northern Europe. Lords at the level of counts became in turn the vassals of dukes. In the year 987 the great lords of France chose Hugh Capet as their king and became his vassals. The kings of France enjoyed little real power for another 200 years, but the descendants of Hugh occupied their throne for eight centuries, until the French Revolution. Similarly the magnates of Germany elected a king in 911; in 962 the German king was crowned emperor, as Charlemagne had been before him;

Capetian kings

thus originated the Holy Roman Empire, of which much will be heard in the following chapters.

England in these formative centuries did not choose a king by election. England was conquered in 1066 by the Duke of Normandy, William. The Normans (the Norse reshaped by a century of Christian and French influences) imposed upon England a centralized and efficient type of feudalism which they had developed in Normandy. In England, from an early date, the king and his officials therefore had considerable power, which led to more civil peace and personal security than on the Continent. Within the framework of a strong monarchy self-governing institutions could eventually develop with a minimum of disorder.

The Normans in England

The notable feature of feudalism was its mutual or reciprocal character. In this it differed from the old Roman imperial principle, by which the emperor had been a majestic and all-powerful sovereign. Under feudalism no one was sovereign. King and people, lord and vassal, were joined in a kind of contract. Each owed something to the other. If one defaulted, the obligation ceased. If a vassal refused his due services, the king had the right to enforce compliance. If the king violated the rights of the vassal, the vassals could join together against him. The king was supposed to act with the advice of the vassals, who formed his council or court. If the vassals believed the king to be exceeding his lawful powers, they could impose terms upon him. Although feudalism was always a hierarchical system of lords and vassals, its mutual or contractual character contributed to later European ideas of constitutional government.

Feudalism applied in the strict sense only to the military or noble class. Below the feudal world lay the vast mass of the peasantry. In the village, the lowliest vassal of a higher noble was lord over his own subjects. The village, with its people and surrounding farmlands, constituted a "manor," the estate of a lord. In the eleventh century most people of the manor were serfs. They were "bound to the soil" in that they could not leave the manor without the lord's permission. Few wanted to leave anyway, at a time when the world beyond the village was unknown and dangerous, and filled at best only with other similar manors. The lord, for his part, could not expropriate the villagers or drive them away. He owed them protection and the administration of justice. They in turn worked his fields and gave him part of the produce of their own. No money changed hands, because there was virtually no money in circulation. The manorial system was the agricultural base on which a ruling class was supported. It supported also the clergy, for the church held much land in the form of manors. It gave the protection from physical violence and the framework of communal living without which the peasants could not grow crops or tend livestock.

The manor and serfs

With the rise of agricultural productivity, lords and even a few peasants could produce a surplus, which they might sell if only they could find a market. The country was able to produce enough food for a town population to live on. And since population grew with the increase of the food supply, a surplus of population also began to exist. Restless spirits among the peasants now wanted to get away from the manor. And many went off to the new towns.

The Rise of Towns and Commerce

We have seen how the ancient cities had decayed. In the ninth and tenth centuries, with few exceptions, there were none left in western Europe. Here and there one would find a cluster of population around the headquarters of a bishop, a great count, or a king. But there were no commercial centers. There was no merchant class. The simple crafts—weaving, metalworking, harness making—were carried on locally on the manors. Rarely, an itinerant trader might appear with such semiprecious goods as he could carry for long distances on donkeys—Eastern silks, or a few spices for the wealthy. Among these early traders Jews were often important, because Judaism, part of the Byzantine and Arabic worlds as well as the Western, offered one of the few channels of communication among the different Mediterranean cultures.

Long-distance trade

Long-distance trading was the first to develop. The city of Venice was founded about 570 when refugees fled from invaders and settled in its islands. The Venetians, as time went on, brought Eastern goods up the Adriatic and sold them to traders coming down from central Europe. In Flanders in the north, in what is now Belgium, manufacturers of woolen cloth emerged. Flemish woolens were of a unique quality, owing to peculiarities of the atmosphere and the skill of the weavers. They could not be duplicated elsewhere. Nor could Eastern goods be procured except through the Venetians—or the Genoese or Pisans. Such goods could not possibly be produced locally, yet they were in demand wherever they became known. Merchants traveled in increasing numbers to sell them. Money came back into more general circulation; where it came from is not quite clear, since there was little mining of gold or silver until the end of the Middle Ages. Merchants began to establish permanent headquarters, settling within the deserted walls of ghostly Roman towns or near the seat of a lord or ecclesiastic, whose numerous retainers might become customers. Craftsmen moved from the overpopulated manors to these same growing centers, where they might produce wares that the lords or merchants would wish to buy. The process, once started, tended to snowball: the more people settled in such an agglomeration, the more they needed food brought to them from the country; and the more craftsmen left the villages, the more the country people, lords and serfs, had to obtain clothing and simple tools and utensils from the towns. Hence a busy local trade developed also.

Growth of towns

By 1100, or not long thereafter, such centers existed all over Europe, from the Baltic to Italy, from England as far east as Bohemia. Usually there was one about every 20 or 30 miles. The smallest towns had only a few hundred inhabitants; the larger ones had two or three thousand, or sometimes more. Each carried on a local exchange with its immediate countryside and purveyed goods of more distant origin to local consumers. But their importance was by no means merely economic. What made them "towns" in the full sense of the word was their acquisition of political rights.

The merchants and craftsmen who lived in the towns did not wish to remain, like the country people, subject to neighboring feudal lords. At worst, the feudal lords regarded merchants as a convenient source of ready money; they might hold them up on the road, plunder their mule trains, collect tolls at river crossings, or extort cash by offering "protection." At best, the most well-meaning feudal lord could not supervise the affairs of merchants, for the feudal and customary law knew nothing of commercial problems. The traders in the course of their business developed a "law merchant" of their own, having to do with money and moneychanging, debt and bankruptcy, contracts, invoices, and bills of lading. They wished to have their own means of apprehending thieves, runaway debtors, or sellers of fraudulent goods. They strove, therefore, to get recognition for their own law, their own courts, their own judges and magistrates. They wished, too, to govern their towns themselves and to avoid payment of fees or taxes to nearby nobles.

Everywhere in Latin Christendom, along about 1100, the new towns struggled to free themselves from the encircling feudalism and to set themselves up as self-governing little republics. Where the towns were largest and closest together—along the highly urbanized arteries of the trade routes, in north Italy, on the upper Danube and Rhine rivers, in Flanders, or on the Baltic coast—they emancipated themselves the most fully. Venice, Genoa, Pisa, Florence, Milan became virtually independent city-states, each governing a substantial tract of its surrounding country. In Flanders also, towns like Bruges and Ghent dominated their localities. Along the upper Danube, the Rhine, the North Sea, the Baltic, many towns became imperial free cities within the Holy Roman Empire, each a kind of small republic owing allegiance to no one except the distant and usually ineffectual emperor. Nuremberg, Frankfurt, Augsburg, Strasbourg, Hamburg, and Lübeck were free cities of this kind. In France and England, where the towns in the twelfth century were somewhat less powerful, they obtained less independence but received charters of liberties from the king. By these charters they were assured the right to have their own town governments and officials, their own courts and law, and to pay their own kind of taxes to the king in lieu of ordinary feudal obligations.

Often towns formed leagues or urban federations, joining forces to repress banditry or piracy or to deal with ambitious monarchs or predatory nobles. The most famous such league was the Hanse; it was formed mainly of German towns, fought wars under its own banner, and dominated the commerce of the North Sea and the Baltic until after 1300. Similar tendencies of the towns to form political leagues, or to act independently in war and diplomacy, were suppressed by the kings in England, France, and Spain.

The fact that Italy, Germany, and the Netherlands were commercially more advanced than the Atlantic countries in the Middle Ages, and so had a more intensive town life, was to be one cause (out of many) preventing political unification in the early modern era. Not until 1860 or 1870 were nationwide states created in this region. In the west, where more of a balance was kept between town and country, the towns were absorbed into nationwide monarchies that were arising under the kings. This early difference between central and western Europe would later shape much of Europe's history in modern times.

The liberties won by the towns were corporate liberties. Each town *Corporate liberties* was a collective entity. The people in towns did not possess individual rights, but only the rights which followed from being a resident of a particular town. Among these were personal liberty; no townsman could be a serf, and fugitive serfs who lived over a year in a town were generally deemed to be free. But townspeople did not seek individual liberty in the modern sense. The world was still too unsettled for the individual to act alone. The citizens wanted to join together in a compact body and to protect themselves by all sorts of regulations and controls. The most obvious evidence of this communal solidarity was the wall within which most towns were enclosed. The citizens in time of trouble looked to their own defense. As the towns grew, they built new walls farther out. Today, in Paris or Cologne, one may still see remains of different walls in use from the tenth to the thirteenth centuries.

Economic solidarity was of more day-to-day importance. The towns required neighboring peasants to sell foodstuffs only in the town marketplace. They thus protected their food supply against competition from other towns. Or they forbade the practice of certain trades in the country; this was to oblige peasants to make purchases in town and to protect the jobs and livelihood of the town craftsmen. They put up tariffs and tolls on the goods of other towns brought within their own walls. Or they levied special fees on merchants from outside who did business in the town. In Italy and Germany they often coined their own money; and the typical town fixed the rates at which various moneys should be exchanged. The medieval towns, in short, at the time of their greatest liberty, followed in a local way

The crafts and trade in medieval towns were dominated by the guilds, whose symbols conveyed the meaning of their work. The sheep on this emblem represents the wool guild in Florence.
(Alinari/Art Resource, NY)

the same policies of protectionism and exclusiveness which national governments were often to follow in modern times.

Guilds

Within each town merchants and craftsmen formed associations called "guilds," whose "masters" supervised the affairs of a specific trade or craft. Merchants formed a merchant guild. Stonemasons, carpenters, barbers, dyers, goldsmiths, coppersmiths, weavers, hatters, tailors, shoemakers, grocers, and apothecaries formed craft guilds of their own. The guilds served a public purpose. They provided that work should be done by reliable and experienced persons, thereby protecting people from the pitfalls of shoddy garments, clumsy barbers, poisonous drugs, or defective and poorly built houses. They also provided a means of vocational education and marked out a career for young men. Women also worked in many trades and could belong to guilds; they were particularly numerous in certain guilds of the clothing trades. Women were nevertheless excluded from some of the guilds' social activities, and they were not granted the political privileges that men received as they moved up through the ranks of the guild hierarchy. Typically a boy became an apprentice to some master, learned the trade, and lived with and was supported by the master's family for a term of years, such as seven. Then he became a journeyman, a qualified and recognized worker, who might work for any master at a stated wage. Most workers remained journeymen throughout their lives, especially in the later Middle Ages. The guild system enabled some workers to improve their social position, however; and a lucky young man might eventually become a master, open his own shop, hire journeymen, and take apprentices. So long as the towns were growing, a boy had some chance to become a master; but as early as 1300 many guilds were becoming frozen, and the masters were increasingly chary of admitting new persons to their own status. Although widows often continued to work in the trades or artisanal crafts of their husbands, women almost never became masters. From the beginning, in any case, it was an important function of the guilds to protect their own members. The masters, assembled together, preserved their reputation by regulating the quality of their product. They divided work among themselves and fixed the terms of apprenticeship, the wages to be paid to journeymen, and the prices at which their goods must be sold. Or they took collective steps to meet or keep out the competition of the same trade in nearby towns.

Whether among individuals within the town itself, or as between town and country, or between town and town, the spirit of the medieval economy was to prevent competition. Risk, adventure, and speculation were not wanted. Almost no one thought it proper to work for monetary profit. The few who did, big merchants trading over large areas, met with suspicion and disapproval wherever they went.

The towns tried in many ways to subject the peasants' interests to their own but nevertheless had an emancipating influence on the country. A rustic by settling in town might escape from serfdom. But the town influence was more widespread and far out of proportion to the relatively small number of people who could become town dwellers. The growth of towns increased the demand for food. Lords began to clear new lands. All western

Towns and the decline of serfdom

Europe set about developing a kind of internal frontier. Formerly villages had been separated by dark tracts of roadless woods, in which wolves roamed freely, shadowed by the gnomes, elves, and fairies of popular folklore. Now pioneers with axes cleared farmlands and built villages. The lords who usually supervised such operations (since their serfs were not slaves, and could not be moved at will) offered freer terms to entice peasants to settle on the new lands. It was less easy for the lord of an old village to hold his people in serfdom when in an adjacent village, within a few hours' walk, the people were free.

The peasants, moreover, were now able to obtain a little money by selling produce in town. The lords wanted money because the towns were producing more articles which money could buy. It became common for peasants to obtain personal freedom, holding their own lands, in return for an annual money payment to the lord for an indefinite period into the future. As early as the twelfth century serfdom began to disappear in northern France and southern England, and by the fifteenth century it had disappeared from most of western Europe. The peasant could now, in law, move freely about. But the manorial organization remained; the peasant owed dues and fees to the lord and was still under his legal jurisdiction.

The Growth of Monarchies and Government Institutions

Meanwhile the kings were busy, each trying to build his kingdom into an organized monarchy that would outlast his life. Monarchy became hereditary; the king inherited his position like any other feudal lord or possessor of an estate. Inheritance of the crown made for peace and order, for elections under conditions of the time were usually turbulent and disputed, and where the older Germanic principle of elective monarchy remained alive,

Changes in monarchical rule

as in the Holy Roman Empire, there was periodic commotion. The kings sent out executive officers to supervise their interests throughout their kingdoms. The kings of England, adopting an old Anglo-Saxon practice, had a sheriff in each of the 40 shires; the kings of France created similar officers who were called bailiffs. The kings likewise instituted royal courts, under royal justices, to decide property disputes and repress crime. This assertion of legal jurisdiction, together with the military might necessary to enforce judgments upon obstinate nobles, became a main pillar of the royal power. In England especially, and in lesser degree elsewhere, the kings required local inhabitants to assist royal judges in the discovery of relevant facts in particular cases. They put them on oath to declare what they knew of events in their own neighborhood. It is from this enforced association of private persons with royal officers that the jury developed.

Taxation

The kings needed money to pay for their governmental machinery or to carry on war with other kings. Taxation, as known in the Roman Empire, was quite unknown to the Germanic and feudal tradition. In the feudal scheme each person was responsible only for the customary fees which arose on stated occasions. The king, like other lords, was supposed to live on his own income—on the revenue of manors that he owned himself, the proceeds of estates temporarily under his wardship, or the occasional fees paid to him by his vassals. No king, even for the best of reasons, could simply decree a new tax and collect it. At the same time, as the use of money became more common, the kings had to assure themselves of a money income. As the towns grew up, with a new kind of wealth and a new source of money income, they agreed to make stipulated payments in return for their royal charters.

The royal demands for money and the claims to exercise legal jurisdiction were regarded as innovations. They were constantly growing and sometimes were a source of abuse. They met with frequent resistance in all countries. A famous case historically (though somewhat commonplace in its own day) was that of Magna Carta in England in 1215, when a group of English lords and high churchmen, joined by representatives of the city of London, required King John to confirm and guarantee their historic liberties.

The king, as has been said, like any lord, was supposed to act in council or "court" with his vassals. The royal council became the egg out of which departments of government were hatched—such as the royal judiciary, exchequer, and military command. From it also was hatched the institution of parliaments. The kings had always, in a way, held great parleys or "talks" (the Latin *parliamentum* meant simply a "talking") with their chief retainers. In the twelfth and thirteenth centuries the growth of towns added a new element to European life. To the lords and bishops was now added a burgher class, which, if of far inferior dignity, was too stubborn, free-spirited, and well furnished with money to be overlooked. When representatives of the towns began to be summoned to the king's great "talks," along with lords and clergy, parliaments may be said to have come into being.

Origins of parliaments

Parliaments, in this sense, sprouted all over Europe in the thirteenth century. Nothing shows better the similarity of institutions in Latin Christendom, or the inadequacy of tracing the history of any one country by itself. The new assemblies were called *cortes* in Spain, diets in Germany, Estates General or provincial estates in France, parliaments in the British Isles. Usually they are referred to generically as "estates," the word "parliament" being reserved for Britain, but in origin they were all essentially the same.

The kings called these assemblies as a means of publicizing and strengthening the royal rule. They found it more convenient to explain their policies, or to ask for money, to a large gathering brought together for that purpose than to have a hundred officials make local explanations and strike local bargains in a hundred different places. The kings did not recognize, nor did the assemblies claim, any right of the parliament to dictate to the king and his government. But usually the king invited the parliament to state grievances; his action upon them was the beginning of parliamentary legislation.

The three estates

The parliaments were considered to represent not the "nation" nor "people" nor yet the individual citizen, but the "estates of the realm," the great collective interests of the country. The first and highest estate was the clergy; the second was the landed or noble class; to these older ruling groups were added, as a "third estate," the burghers of the chartered towns. Quite commonly these three types of people sat separately as three distinct chambers. But the pattern varied from country to country. In England, Poland, and Hungary the clergy as a whole ceased to be represented; only the bishops came, sitting with lay magnates in an upper house. Eventually the burghers dropped out in Poland, Bohemia, and Hungary, leaving the landed aristocracy in triumph in eastern Europe. In Castile and Württemberg, on the other hand, the noble estate eventually refused to attend parliament, leaving the townspeople and clergy in the assemblies. In some countries—in Scandinavia, Switzerland, and in the French Estates General—even peasants were allowed to have delegates.

In England the Parliament developed eventually in a distinctive way. After a long period of uncertainty there came to be two houses, known as the Lords and the Commons. The Lords, as in Hungary or Poland, included

England's Parliament

both great prelates and lay magnates. The House of Commons developed features not found on the Continent. Lesser landholders, the people who elsewhere counted as small nobles, sat in the same House of Commons with representatives of the towns. The Commons was made up of "knights and burgesses," or gentry and townsmen together, a fact which greatly added to its strength, for the middle class of the towns long remained too weak to act alone. The mingling of classes in England, the willingness of townsmen to follow the leadership of the gentry, and of the gentry to respect the interests of townsmen, helped to root representative institutions in England more deeply than in other countries during the medieval era. Moreover, England was a small country in the Middle Ages. There were no provincial or local parliamentary bodies (as in France, the Holy Roman Empire, or Poland) which might jealously cut into the powers of the central body or with which the king could make local arrangements without violating the principle of representative government. And finally, as a reason for the strength of Parliament in England, the elected members of the House of Commons very early obtained the power to *commit* their constituents. If they voted a tax, those who elected them had to pay it. The king, in order to get matters decided, insisted that the votes be binding. Constituents were not allowed to repudiate the vote of their deputies, nor to punish or harass them when they came home, as often happened in other countries. Parliament thus exercised power as well as rights.

In summary, the three centuries of the High Middle Ages laid foundations both for order and for freedom. Slavery was defunct and serfdom was expiring. Politically, the multitude of free chartered towns, the growth of juries in some places, and the rise of parliaments everywhere provided means by which peoples could take some part in their governments. The ancient civilizations had never created a free political unit larger than the city-state. The Greeks had never carried democracy beyond the confines within which people could meet in person, nor had the Romans devised means by which, in a large state, the governed could share any responsibilities with an official bureaucracy. The ancients had never developed the idea of representative government, or of government by duly elected and authorized representatives acting at a distance from home. The idea is by no means as obvious or simple as it looks. It first appeared in the medieval monarchies of the West, and, after much subsequent development, it would become a fundamental principle for political systems in most of the modern world.

4. THE HIGH MIDDLE AGES: THE CHURCH

So far in our account of the High Middle Ages we have told the story of Hamlet without speaking of the Prince of Denmark, for we have left aside the church, except, indeed, when some mention of it could not be avoided. In the real life of the time the church was omnipresent. Religion permeated political and social life. In feudalism the mutual duties of lord and vassal were confirmed by religious oaths, and bishops and abbots, as holders of lands, became feudal personages themselves. In the monarchies, the king was crowned by the chief churchman of his kingdom, adjured to rule with justice and piety, and anointed with holy oils. In the towns, guilds served as lay religious brotherhoods; each guild chose a patron saint and marched in the streets on holy days. For amusement the townspeople watched religious dramas, the morality and miracle plays in which religious themes were enacted. The rising town, if it harbored a bishop, took especial care to erect a new cathedral. Years of effort and of religious fervor produced the Gothic cathedrals which still stand as the best-known memorials of medieval civilization.

The Development of the Medieval Church and Papacy

If, however, we turn back to the tenth century, the troubled years before 1000, we find the church in as dubious a condition as everything else. It was fragmented and localized. Every bishop went his own way. Though the clergy was the only literate class, many of the clergy themselves could not read and write.

The church in crisis

Christian belief was mixed with the old pagan magic and superstition, and most Christians knew nothing about the theology that had shaped the traditions of the Catholic church. The monasteries were in decay. Priests often lived in a concubinage that was generally condoned. It was customary for them to marry, so that they had recognized children, to whom they intrigued to pass on their churchly position. Powerful laymen often dominated their ecclesiastical neighbors, with the big lords appointing the bishops and the little ones appointing the parish priests. When people thought about Rome at all, they sensed a vague respect for something legendary and far away; but the bishop of Rome, or pope, had no influence and was treated in unseemly fashion by nobles in his own city.

The Roman Catholic church is in fact unrecognizable in the jumble of the tenth century. So far at least as human effort was concerned, it was virtually created in the eleventh century along with the other institutions of the High Middle Ages.

Reform efforts

The impulse to reform came from many quarters. Sometimes a secular ruler undertook to correct conditions in his own domains. For this purpose he asserted a strict control over his clergy. In 962 the Holy Roman Empire was proclaimed. This Empire, like the Carolingian and Roman empires which it was supposed to continue, was in theory coterminous with Latin Christendom itself and endowed with a special mission to preserve and extend the Christian faith. Neither in France nor in England (nor, when they became Christian states, in Spain, Hungary, Poland, or Scandinavia) was this claim of the Holy Roman Empire ever acknowledged. But the Empire did for a time embrace Italy as well as Germany. The first emperors, in the tenth and eleventh centuries, denouncing the conditions of the church in Rome, strove to make the pope their appointee.

At the same time a reform movement arose from spiritual sources. Serious Christians took matters into their own hands. They founded a new monastery at Cluny in France, which soon had many affiliated houses. It was their purpose to purify monastic life and to set a higher Christian ideal to which all clergy and laity might aspire. To rid themselves of immediate local pressures, the greed, narrowness, ignorance, family ambition, and self-satisfied inertia that were the main causes of corruption, the Cluniacs refused to recognize any authority except that of Rome itself. Thus, at the very time when conditions in Rome were at their worst, Christians throughout Europe built up the prestige of Rome, of the idea of Rome, as a means to raise all Latin Christendom from its depths.

CHRONOLOGY OF NOTABLE EVENTS, 500 B.C.–A.D. 1300

500–300 B.C.	Creative era of Classical Greek Civilization: Plato, Aristotle
46 B.C.	Roman Republic conquers Greece
45–31 B.C.	Roman Republic evolves into the Roman Empire
c. A.D. 26–29	Jesus is active in Palestine; beginnings of Christianity
306–337	Roman Emperor Constantine: toleration of Christianity
c. 420	St. Augustine writes *City of God*
476	End of Roman Empire in the West
450–750	Roman Catholic Church gains converts and influence in Western Europe
610–632	Prophet Muhammad teaches the new religion of Islam
635–750	Islam spreads across Middle East, North Africa, and Spain
800	Coronation of Emperor Charlemagne; the Carolingian Empire
1000–1200	Improvements in European agriculture and rise of towns
1054	Schism of Roman Catholic Church and Orthodox Eastern Church
1095–1099	First Christian Crusade in Palestine
1100–1200	Arabic and Greek science enters European Culture
1147–1221	Second-Fifth Christian Crusades
1198–1216	Pope Innocent III: height of Medieval Papacy
1100–1300	Development of Universities and Scholasticism
1267–1273	Thomas Aquinas writes the *Summa Theologica*

As for the popes in Rome, those who preserved any independence of judgment or respect for their own office, it was their general plan to free themselves from the Roman mobs and aristocrats without falling into dependence upon the Holy Roman Emperor. In 1059 Pope Nicholas II issued a decree providing that future popes should be elected by the cardinals. The cardinals, at that time, were the priests of churches in the city of Rome or bishops of neighboring dioceses. By entrusting the choice of future popes to them, Pope Nicholas hoped to exclude all influence from outside the clergy itself. Popes have been elected by cardinals ever since, though not always without influence from outside.

One of the first popes so elected was Gregory VII, known also as *Gregory VII* Hildebrand, a dynamic and strong-willed man who was pope from 1073 to 1085. He had been in touch with the Cluniac reformers, and dreamed of a reformed and reinvigorated Europe under the universal guidance of the Roman pontiff. Gregory believed that the church should stand apart from worldly society, that it should judge and guide all human actions, and that a pope had the supreme power to judge and punish kings and emperors if he deemed them sinful. His ideal was not a "world state," but its spiritual counterpart, a world church officered by a single-minded and disciplined clergy, centralized under a single authority. He began by insisting that the clergy free itself of worldly involvements. He required married priests to put aside their wives and families.

Celibacy of the clergy, never generally established in the Greek Orthodox church, and later rejected by Protestants in the West, became the rule for the Roman Catholic priesthood. Gregory insisted also that no ecclesiastic might receive office through appointment by a layman. In his view only clergy might institute or influence clergy, for the clergy must be independent and self-contained.

Gregory soon faced a battle with that other aspirant to universal supremacy and a sacred mission, the Holy Roman Emperor, who at this time was Henry IV. In Germany the bishops and abbots possessed a great deal of the land, which they held and governed under the emperor as feudal magnates in their own right. To the emperor it was vitally important to have his own men, as reliable vassals, in these great positions. Hence in Germany "lay investiture" had become very common. "Lay investiture" meant the practice by which a layman, the emperor, conferred upon the new bishop the signs of his spiritual authority, the ring and the staff. Gregory prohibited lay investiture. He supported the German bishops and nobles when they rebelled against Henry, but the emperor remained obstinate. Gregory then excommunicated him, that is, outlawed him from Christian society by forbidding any priest to give him the sacraments. Henry, baffled, sought out the pope at Canossa in Italy to do penance. "To go to Canossa" in later times became a byword for submission to the will of Rome.

Lay investiture

In 1122, after both original contenders had died, a compromise on the matter of lay investiture was effected by which bishops recognized the emperor as their feudal head but looked to Rome for spiritual authority. But the struggle between popes and emperors went on unabated. The magnates of Germany, lay lords as well as bishops, often allied with the pope to preserve their own feudal liberties from the emperor. The emperor in Germany was never able to consolidate his domains as did the kings in England and France. The unwillingness of lords and churchmen (and of towns also, as we have seen) to let the emperors build up an effective government left its mark permanently upon Europe in two ways. It contributed to the centralization of Latin Christendom under Rome, while it blocked the development of a more unified monarchical state in central Europe.

Innocent III

The height of the medieval papacy came with Innocent III, whose pontificate lasted from 1198 to 1216. Innocent virtually realized Gregory's dream of a unified Christian world. He intervened in politics everywhere. He was recognized as a supreme arbiter. At his word, a king of France took a wife, a king of England accepted an unwanted archbishop, a king of León put aside the cousin whom he had married, and a claimant to the crown of Hungary deferred to his rival. The kings of England, Aragon, and Portugal acknowledged him as feudal overlord within their realms. Huge revenues now flowed to Rome from all over Latin Christendom, and an enormous bureaucracy worked there to dispatch the voluminous business of the papal court. As kings struggled to repress civil rebellion, so Innocent and his successors struggled to repress heresy, which, defined as doctrine at variance with that of the church at large, was becoming alarmingly common among the Albigensians of southern France.

In 1215 Innocent called a great church council, the greatest since antiquity, attended by 500 bishops and even by the patriarchs of Constantinople and Jerusalem. The council labored at the perplexing task of keeping the clergy from worldly temptations. By forbidding priests to officiate at ordeals or trials by battle, it virtually ended these survivals of barbarism. It attempted to regularize belief in the supernatural by controlling the superstitious traffic in relics. It declared the sacraments to be the channel of God's saving grace and defined them authoritatively.[2] In the chief sacrament, the Eucharist or Mass, it promulgated the dogma of transubstantiation, which held that, in the Mass, the priest converts the substance of bread and wine into the substance of Christ's body and blood. Except for heretics, who were suppressed, the reforms and doctrines of Innocent's council were accepted with satisfaction throughout Latin Europe.

Intellectual Life: The Universities, Scholasticism

Under the auspices of the church, as rising governments gave more civil security, and as the economy of town and country became able to support people devoted to a life of thought, the intellectual horizon of Europeans began to open. The twelfth and thirteenth centuries saw the founding of the first universities. These originated in the natural and spontaneous coming together of teachers and students which had never wholly disappeared even in the most chaotic era of the early Middle Ages. By 1200 there was a center of medical studies at Salerno in south Italy, of legal studies at Bologna in north Italy, of theological studies at Paris. Oxford was founded about 1200 by a secession of disgruntled students and professors from Paris; Cambridge, shortly thereafter. By 1300 there were a dozen such universities in Latin Europe; by 1500 there were almost a hundred.

The founding of universities

As the early agglomerations of traders developed into organized towns and guilds, so the informal concourses of students and teachers developed into organized institutions of learning, receiving the sharp corporate stamp that was characteristic of the High Middle Ages. It was in having this corporate identity that medieval universities resemble our own and differed from the schools of Athens or Alexandria in ancient times. A university, the University of Paris, for example, was a body of individuals, young and old, interested in learning and endowed by law with a communal name and existence. It possessed definite liberties under some kind of charter, regulated its own affairs through its own officials, and kept its own order among its often boisterous population. It gave, and even advertised, courses and lectures, and it decided collectively which professors were the best qualified to teach. It might consist of distinct schools or "faculties"—the combination of theology, law, and medicine, as at Paris, was the most usual. It held examinations and awarded degrees, whose meaning and value were recognized throughout the Latin West. The degree, which originated as a license to teach, admitted its holder to certain honors or privileges in the same way that members of other guilds were authorized to practice a specific craft. With such degrees, professors might readily move from one university to another. Students moved easily also because all universities used the Latin language and offered a similar curriculum. The university, moreover, though typically beginning in poverty, was a corporate body capable of holding property; and the benefactions of pious donors often built up substantial endowments in lands and manors. So organized, free from outside control, and enjoying an income from property, the university lived on as a permanent institution, through good times and bad.

---

[2]A sacrament is understood to be the outward sign of an inward grace. In Catholic doctrine the sacraments were and are seven in number: baptism, confirmation, penance, the Eucharist, extreme unction, marriage, and holy orders. Except for baptism, a sacrament may be administered only by a priest. A dogma is the common belief of the church, in which all the faithful share and must share so long as they are members of the church. Dogmas are regarded as implicitly the same in all ages; they cannot be invented or developed, but may from time to time be clarified, defined, promulgated, or proclaimed.

Theology

The queen of the sciences was theology, the intellectual study of religion. Many in Europe, by the eleventh century, were beginning to reflect upon their beliefs. They continued to believe in God but could no longer believe with unthinking acceptance. It was accepted as a fact, for example, that the Son of God had been incarnated as a man in Jesus Christ. But in the eleventh century an Italian named Anselm, who became archbishop of Canterbury, wrote a treatise called *Cur Deus Homo?*—"Why Did God Become Man?"—giving reasoned explanations to show why God had taken human form to save sinful human beings. Anselm argued that reason strongly supported the Christian faith in God. Soon afterward Abelard, who taught at Paris, wrote his *Sic et Non*—"Yes and No" or "Pro and Con"—a collection of inconsistent statements made by St. Augustine and other Fathers of the Church. Abelard's purpose was to apply logic to the inherited mass of patristic writings, show wherein the truth of Christian doctrine really lay, and so make the faith consistent with reason and reflection.

Meanwhile, in the twelfth century a great stream of new knowledge poured into Europe, bringing about a veritable intellectual revolution. It was derived from the Arabs, with whom Christians were in contact in Sicily and Spain. The Arabs, as has been seen, had taken over the ancient Greek science, translated Greek writings into Arabic, and in many ways added further refinements of their own. Bilingual Christians (assisted by numerous learned Jews who traveled readily between the Christian and Muslim worlds) translated these works into Latin. Above all, they translated Aristotle, the great codifier of Greek knowledge who had lived and written in the fourth century B.C. The Europeans, drawing on the commentaries of Muslim scholars such as Averroës (1126–1198), were overwhelmed by this sudden disclosure of an undreamed universe of knowledge. Aristotle became The Philosopher, the unparalleled authority on all branches of knowledge other than religious.

Arabic and Greek learning

The great problem for Europeans was how to digest the gigantic bulk of Aristotle, or, in more general terms, how to assimilate or reconcile the body of Greek and Arabic learning to the Christian faith. The universities, with their "scholastic" philosophers or "schoolmen," performed this function. Most eminent of scholastics was Thomas Aquinas (1225–1274), the Angelic Doctor, known also to his own contemporaries as the Dumb Ox from the slow deliberation of his speech. His chief work, appropriately called the *Summa Theologica,* was a survey of all knowledge.

Thomas Aquinas

The chief accomplishment of Thomas Aquinas was his demonstration that faith and reason could not be in conflict. By reason he meant a severely logical method, with exact definition of words and concepts, deducing step by step what follows and must follow if certain premises are accepted. His philosophy is classified as a form of moderate "realism," a term whose medieval meaning differed from its common usage today. For medieval philosophers "realism" meant that the general idea is more "real" than the particular—that "man" or "woman" is more real than this or that man or woman, that "law" as such is more real and binding than this or that particular law. He derived his philosophy from what he took to be the nature of God, of law, of reason, of human life, and of beings in general. Thomas taught a hierarchic view of the universe and of society, of which God was the apex. All things and all people were subordinated to God in a descending order, each bound to fulfill the role set by its own place and nature. It was the emphasis on the superior reality of abstractions that enabled people in the Middle Ages to believe steadfastly in the church while freely

THE MEETING OF ST. ANTHONY AND ST. PAUL
by Sassetta (Italian, 1392–1450)

This picture conveys the abstractness of medieval thought. There is no attempt to portray the figures as unique individuals; they are typical saints with the halos designating sacred persons. St. Anthony appears in three places—walking alone, converting a centaur, and embracing St. Paul. The forest and hills represent the idea of trees or mounds of earth, but there is no physical specificity in these representations of nature.

THOMAS AQUINAS
by Fra Bartelemo (Italian, 1472–1517)

Thomas Aquinas combined Aristotelian knowledge with Christian faith in his scholastic theology, thus gaining permanent respect (and sainthood) from the Catholic Church and artistic recognition from painters such as Fra Bartelemo.
(Nicolo Orsi Battaglini/Art Resource, NY)

attacking individual churchmen, to have faith in the papacy while denouncing the popes as scoundrels—or to accept without difficulty the mystery of transubstantiation, which declared that what admittedly looked and tasted like bread and wine was, in real inner substance, the body of Christ.

Scholasticism

The scholastic philosophy, as perfected by Thomas Aquinas, was not very favorable to the growth of natural science, because its emphasis on an inner reality drew attention away from the actual details and behavior of concrete things. On the other hand, the scholastic philosophy laid foundations on which later European thought was to be reared. It habituated Europeans to great exactness, to careful distinctions, even to the splitting of hairs. It called for disciplined thinking. And it made the world safe for reason. If any historical generalization may be made safely, it may be said that any society that believes reason to threaten its foundations will suppress reason. In Thomas's time, there were some who said that Aristotle and the Arabs were infidels, dangerous influences that must be silenced. Any reasoning about the faith, they warned, was a form of weakness. Thomas's doctrine that faith could not be endangered by reason gave a freedom to thinkers to go on thinking.

The Crusades; New Invasions; Europe by 1300

Meanwhile, the West was beginning to expand. Europe in the eleventh century launched a military offensive against Islam. All Latin Christendom went on the Crusades. War itself was subordinated to the purposes of religion.

Finns Converted
by Swedes c. 1150

LIVONIA

BALTIC SEA

PRUSSIA
POMERANIA

Teutonic Knights 1100–125

Eastern Limit of Latin Christianity

London

Paris

c. 1250

1000–125

CASTILLE
AND LEÓN

NAVARRE ALBIGENSIANS

Venice

PORTUGAL   1000–
1250 ARAGON

SPAIN
c. 1250   VALENCIA

Rome

1070–
1100

Byzantium (Constantinople)

GRANADA

MEDITERRANEAN SEA

Antioch

Tripoli
Tyre Damascus
Acre HOLY
Jaffa LAND
Jerusalem

0   200   400 miles

Regions Christianized after about A.D. 900

Muslims in Granada, North Africa, and the Holy Land

CRUSADING ACTIVITY, 1100–1250

Medieval Christendom expanded geographically until about 1250. Darker regions are those christianized shortly before and after 1000. Arrows indicate organized military-religious expeditions, which by 1250 had recovered most of Spain from Muslim control, but had failed to do so in the Holy Land. Dates are rounded and very rough.

The most ambitious, best remembered, and least successful of such expeditions were the Crusades to win back the Holy Land. The First Crusade was preached in 1095 by Pope Urban II, who hoped thereby to advance the peace of God by draining off bellicose nobles to fight the infidels and to build up the pope's leadership in Europe. Crusades to the Holy Land, with varying success, and sometimes departing woefully from their religious aims, went on intermittently for 200 years. It was the growth of Italian shipping in the Mediterranean, the rise of more orderly feudal monarchies, the increasing sense of a Europe-wide common purpose that made possible the assembly and transport of considerable forces over a great distance. But the motivation for such Crusades, especially in the beginning, came mostly from a wave of religious fervor that brought nobles and commoners alike into the Crusader armies. This fervor contributed to brutal, deadly attacks on Jewish communities within Europe as well as to the extraordinary violence against entire Muslim populations in cities such as Antioch and Jerusalem. At the same time, however, the Crusades

Crusades to the Holy Land

gave Europeans a new awareness of the world beyond their own local realms of religion and small-town economies. Historians have argued that the Crusaders' contacts with Arab societies in the Middle East stimulated subsequent European economic development and a new cultural identity among "Western" peoples. Although this argument points to important consequences of the Crusades, it is also true that the campaigns against Islam grew out of Europe's own growing political and military strength. For a century the Latin Christians occupied parts of Palestine and Syria. But military defeats forced them to withdraw in the thirteenth century, and the Muslims remained in possession.

Other crusades

Other crusades (for such they were) had more lasting results. A party of Normans won Sicily from the Arabs about 1100. Iberian Christians, descending from the mountains of northern Spain, carried on a *reconquista* of two centuries against the Moors. By 1250 they had staked out the Christian kingdoms of Portugal, León, Castile, Aragon, and Valencia, leaving the Muslims only Granada in the extreme south, which was conquered much later, in 1492. In southern France, an Albigensian crusade in the thirteenth century put down the heretics, those born in the Christian faith but erring from the reigning interpretations of it. Crusading expeditions were also launched against a few remaining "heathen" populations in northeastern Europe. The Teutonic Order, a military-religious society of knights founded originally to fight in the Holy Land, transferred its operations to the north. Christianity was brought by the sword to primitive Prussia and the east Baltic regions.

About the year 1250 there developed a new threat of invasion from Asia. As the Huns had burst out of Asia in the fifth century, and the Magyars in the ninth, so now the Tartars appeared in the thirteenth century, to be followed in the fourteenth by the Ottoman Turks. We shall see how the Turks long continued to press upon central Europe. But, on the whole, by the thirteenth century, Europe was capable of resistance. Always until then it had been vulnerable as an outlying, backward, thinly populated protuberance from the Eurasian land mass. It had lain open in the remote past to wandering Indo-Europeans, then to Roman imperial conquerors, to Germanic barbarians, to Huns, Magyars, and, in part, the Arabs. All these were gradually assimilated by the Roman church, the Latin language, the common institutions of feudalism, monarchy, a free town life, parliamentary assemblies, and scholastic learning. An increasingly connected and coherent culture ran from England to Sicily and from Portugal to Poland.

The "rise of Europe"

By 1300 the "rise of Europe" was an accomplished fact. The third of the three segments into which the Greco-Roman world had divided, the one which in A.D. 700 had been the most isolated and fragmented, now some 600 years later had a civilization of its own. It was still only one among the several great cultures of the world, such as the Islamic, Byzantine, Indian, and Chinese. It enjoyed no preeminence. The Chinese empire, for example, in the thirteenth century, had cities whose population reached into millions. It had an affluent merchant class, great textile manufacturers, and an iron industry that produced over 100,000 tons a year. The arts and sciences were assiduously pursued. Government was centralized and complex; it issued paper money and employed a civil service recruited by competitive examinations. Books on religious, technical, and agricultural subjects, including whole multivolume encyclopedias, were printed in enormous numbers, even though the lack of an alphabet and the thousands of Chinese characters made it difficult for literacy to become widely spread. The Venetian Marco Polo was dazzled by the China that he lived in from 1275 to 1292.

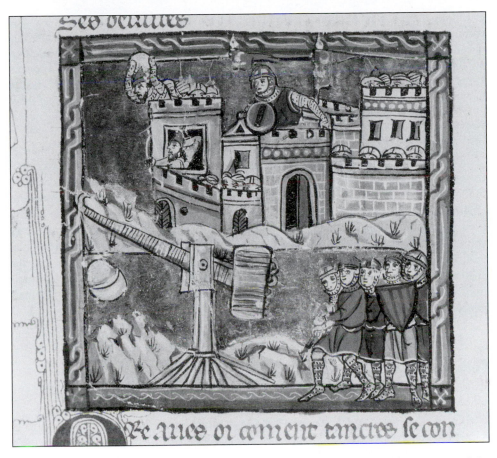

Europeans took pride in their crusading armies, represented here in a medieval image of the conquest of Antioch in 1098 during the First Crusade.
(Art Resource, NY)

Many have asked why China did not generate, as Europe did in these centuries, the forces that ultimately led to the modern scientific and industrial world. One answer is suggested by the fact that it was Europeans such as Marco Polo who went to China, not Chinese who went to Europe. It was the Chinese who invented printing, but it was Europe that was revolutionized by printed books. The Chinese knew of gunpowder, but the Europeans developed more effective guns. Chinese merchant vessels also traded with India but did not pursue the advantage. In the fifteenth century, over the years 1405 to 1433, a Ming emperor launched a large-scale series of long-range naval expeditions, seven in all, headed by his admiral Cheng Ho. The expeditions sailed to ports in Southeast Asia, India, the Persian Gulf, and East Africa, exchanging gifts in transactions that recognized the emperor's power and prestige. But the emperor and his advisers ultimately terminated the entire venture. China turned its back on overseas commercial opportunities and turned inward to the protection and expansion of its land frontiers. Never again (until the recent past) did it embark on similar expeditions or send its ships to distant, unknown seas. It was the Europeans who pursued the development of trade in India and also crossed the Atlantic to discover America. Somehow Europe became more enterprising and restless, perhaps because in Europe there was no all-embracing empire as in China, but kings, lords, and towns that competed with each other. With religion and the church kept distinct from the state, the questions of what one should do with one's life were less dependent on the political powers than in China. Europe was disorderly and full of conflict—rivalries and wars between kings, quarrels between kings and their barons, disputes between church and state, clashes between lords and their peasant workers. Much of this conflict was destructive, yet there was also a kind of freedom in such disorder and a dynamism which promoted change.

European civilization in 1300

European civilization in 1300 was by no means a "modern" society, yet the ancient and medieval cultures on European lands had created institutions and traditions that remained influential even in the most recent eras of modern world history. By 1300 people in Europe had developed separate (at times contending) institutions of church and state to control a growing population, economic institutions to promote urban commerce and long-distance trade, judicial and parliamentary councils to codify or revise the law, and universities to teach or redefine their intellectual traditions. These traditions included a pervasive, enduring faith in Christianity, but the ancient Christian beliefs were challenged, revised, and extended by other ancient traditions of rhetoric, philosophy, and rational inquiry—all of which contributed to the emergence of what is now called early modern history.

For interactive exercises, glossary, chronologies, and more, go to the *Online Learning Center* at **www.mhhe.com/palmer10.**

Chapter 2

THE UPHEAVAL IN WESTERN CHRISTENDOM, 1300–1560

5. Disasters of the Fourteenth Century

6. The Renaissance in Italy

7. The Renaissance outside Italy

8. The New Monarchies

9. The Protestant Reformation

10. Catholicism Reformed and Reorganized

In the transition from traditional to more modern forms of society all the old civilizations have had to reexamine their religious base. Today we can observe this process at work everywhere: the Chinese reconsider the age-old teachings of Confucius, the Muslims enter into wider activities than those known to the Qur'an, and the peoples of India are rapidly expanding an economy in which historic Hindu practices no longer form the dominant pattern. People in modern societies do not necessarily reject their ancestral religion. In fact, they may strongly reaffirm it, but they usually try also to adapt it to modern economic and political conditions and to make room for new and nonreligious interests. The process of developing a variety of activities outside the sphere of religion is called "secularization."

Latin Christendom was the first of the world's major religious cultures to become "secularized." In the very long run it was those aspects of European civilization that were least associated with Christianity, such as natural science and industrial technology, or military and economic power, that the non-European world proved to be most willing to adopt. If in our own time there has come to be such a thing as a global civilization, it is because all the world's great traditional cultures have been increasingly secularized. This secularization of human cultures, although often challenged by popular religious movements in the contemporary world, remains one of the decisive trends in modern world history, and it is a trend that began to appear in Europe at the end of the Middle Ages.

The Europe which had become both expansive and more prosperous by the thirteenth century soon entered upon a series of disasters. The Mongols after about 1240 held Russia in subjugation for 200 years. The Ottoman Turks, who had originated in central Asia, penetrated the Byzantine Empire, crushed the medieval Serbian kingdom at the battle of Kosovo in 1389, and spread over the Balkans. They took Constantinople itself in 1453. Eastern Christianity continued to exist, but under alien political domination. Latin Christianity,

Chapter emblem: Detail from *A Portrait of a Family* by Lavinia Fontana (1552–1614). (Scala/Art Resource, NY)

reaching from Poland and Hungary to the Atlantic, remained independent but was beset with troubles. The authority of the papacy and of the Roman Catholic church was called into question. Eventually the Protestant churches emerged, and the religious unity of medieval civilization disappeared. Yet new forces also asserted themselves alongside or outside the religious tradition. Government, law, philosophy, science, the arts, material and economic activities were pursued with less regard for Christian values. Power, order, beauty, wealth, knowledge, and control of nature were regarded as desirable in themselves.

In this mixture of decline and revival, of religious revolution and secularization, medieval Christendom evolved into the social, political, and cultural world of early modern Europe.

5.   DISASTERS OF THE FOURTEENTH CENTURY

The Black Death and Its Consequences

During the fourteenth century, and quite abruptly, almost half the population of Europe was wiped out. Although it is impossible to know exactly how many people lived in medieval Europe, the total population probably fell from roughly 70 million in 1300 to about 45 million in 1400. Some died in sporadic local famines that began to appear after 1300. The great killer, however, was the plague, or Black Death, which first struck Europe in 1348. The precise medical cause of the plague is still debated. Most modern historians believe that the disease was carried by rats, but this theory may not explain how the contagion moved so quickly across Europe or why so many humans became vulnerable to a bacillus that normally lives in rodents. Despite the uncertainty about its physiological origins, historians agree that the plague had decisive effects on European social life. Since the plague returned at irregular and unpredictable intervals, and killed off the young as well as the old, it disrupted marriage and family life and made it impossible for many years for Europe to regain the former level of population. In some places whole villages disappeared. Cultivated fields were abandoned for want of able-bodied men and women to work them. The towns were especially vulnerable, because the contagion spread quickly through populations crowded within town walls. Trade and exchange were obstructed; prices, wages, and incomes moved erratically; famine made its victims more susceptible to disease; and deaths from the plague contributed to famine. The living were preoccupied with the burial of the dead and with fears for their own future.

The Black Death

There were immediate social and political repercussions. In some cases, survivors benefited because the scarcity of labor led to higher wages. On the other hand, in the general disorganization, and with landowners and urban employers decimated also, many of the poor could find no work or took to vagabondage and begging. The upper classes, acting through governments, attempted to control wages and prices. Rebellions of workers broke out in various towns, especially in Flanders, and there were massive insurrections of peasants in many parts of Europe. In France these were called "jacqueries" (from "Jacques," a nickname for a peasant), of which the first was in 1358. In England a similar large-scale uprising in 1381 came to be known as Wat Tyler's rebellion. Sometimes the spokesmen for these movements went beyond their immediate grievances to raise broader social questions about why some should be rich and others poor. Governments and the upper classes replied to this menace with ferocious repression. The peasants generally returned to their

Revolts and repression

usual labors. Yet something was gained for the rural workers, at least in the long run, as underlying economic and demographic forces continued to assert themselves. The landowners, or feudal class, in order to get the work done on their manors and assure their own incomes, had to offer more favorable terms. These included, for example, the giving of lifetime tenures to peasant families, in return for fixed payment of sums of money. Over the years many of these peasant holdings became hereditary and the value of money decreased, so that payment of a shilling, for example, which in 1400 represented a significant amount, became much less burdensome for the rural worker by 1600. In effect, a class of small peasant property owners began to emerge in much of Europe.

The kings also, who had been building up their position against the church and the feudal lords since the eleventh century, found their problems complicated by the disasters of the fourteenth. They still had their governments to maintain, and their ambitions to satisfy, even if death removed large fractions of their subjects. They even had to increase their incomes, as it became usual for kings to employ royal armies of foot soldiers against the recurring possibility of feudal resistance. Various means of increasing the royal spending power were devised. Currency was debased; that is, the king ordered a given weight of gold or silver to represent a larger number of monetary units. Thus he temporarily had more money, but the result was inflation and higher prices, that is, the declining value of money already mentioned. New taxes were introduced. About 1300 the kings of both England and France undertook to tax the clergy of their respective kingdoms, in both of which the clergy were substantial owners of land. The kings made increasing demands as well on great noble landholders and urban merchants. These demands were resisted, or made subject to bargains by the representative bodies whose origin was described in the last chapter, so that the fourteenth century, and still more the fifteenth, has been called the "golden age" of the medieval parliaments.

In 1337 the Hundred Years' War began between England and France. The battles all took place in France, which was internally divided, some parts, like Aquitaine, having long belonged to the English crown. France was ravaged by marauding bands of English soldiers and their French *The Hundred Years' War* adherents, until French forces began to achieve military victories under the inspired leadership of Joan of Arc, the young woman whom the English burned at the stake in Rouen in 1431 after she was convicted by the church of heresy and witchcraft. In England the effects of the long and intermittent war were less divisive. As English soldiers with their longbows defeated the mounted French knights, a kind of early patriotism arose in England. Parliament widened its powers as the kings needed money for their campaigns. But the great English barons also became more unruly. They deposed Richard II in 1399, then quarreled among themselves, in a confusion punctuated by invasion from Scotland and revolt in Wales. Disorder became worse in the fifteenth century. Dukes and earls and their followers formed private armies and fought with each other; they defied the royal law courts and intimidated juries, used Parliament and government for their own purposes, and exploited their peasants. From about 1450 until 1485 England was beset by upper-class turmoil that came to be called the Wars of the Roses, because the opposing noble factions adopted red and white roses as their symbols.

Troubles of the Medieval Church

Meanwhile similar calamities afflicted the church. In 1300, the church of the High Middle Ages, centralized in the papacy, stood at its zenith. But the church was weakened by its

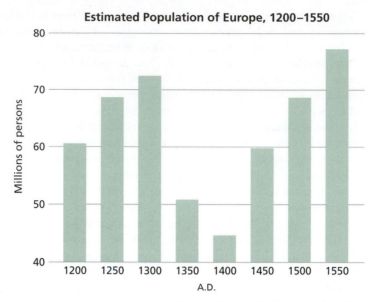

Estimated Population of Europe, 1200–1550

Source: M. K. Bennett, *The World's Food* (New York: Harper, 1954).

This graph shows the growth of Europe's population after 1200, the catastrophic impact of the Black Death in the fourteenth century, and the revival of the European population after the early 1400s.

very successes. It faced the danger that besets every successful institution—a form of government or a university, to choose modern examples—the danger of believing that the institution exists for the benefit of those who conduct its affairs. The papacy, being at the top, was the most liable to this danger. It became "corrupt," set in its ways, out of touch with public opinion, and controlled by a self-perpetuating bureaucracy. It was unable to reform itself, and unwilling to let anyone else reform it.

Both Edward I of England and Philip the Fair of France, in the 1290s, assessed taxes on the landed estates belonging to the great abbeys, bishoprics, and other components of the church. The pope, Boniface VIII, prohibited the taxation of clergy by the civil ruler. In the ensuing altercation, in 1302, he issued the famous bull, *Unam Sanctam,* the most extreme of all assertions of papal supremacy, which declared that outside the Roman church there was no salvation, and that "every human creature" was "subject to the Roman pontiff."[1] The French king sent soldiers to arrest Boniface, who soon died. French influence in the College of Cardinals brought about the election of a pope who was expected to be subservient to

The "Babylonian Captivity"

Philip, and who took up his residence, with his court and officials, at Avignon on the lower Rhone river, on what were then the borders of France. Thus began the "Babylonian Captivity" of the church. The rest of Europe regarded the popes at Avignon throughout the century as tools of France. The papacy lost much of its prestige as a universal institution.

---

[1]Bulls, so-called from the Latin word for their seal, are known by their first one or two Latin words, which in this case mean "one holy (church)"; a "bull," while the most solemn form of papal edict, does not as such embody a dogma; and it is not Catholic practice today to affirm this policy of Boniface VIII.

Attempts to correct the situation made matters worse. In 1378 the College of Cardinals, torn by French and anti-French factions within it, elected two popes. Both were equally legitimate, being chosen by cardinals, but one lived at Rome, one at Avignon, and neither would resign. The French and their supporters recognized the Avignon pope; England and most of Germany, the Roman. For forty years both lines were perpetuated. There were now two papacies, estranged by the Great Schism of the West.

The Great Schism

Never had the papacy been so externally magnificent as in the days of the Captivity and the Schism. The papal court at Avignon surpassed the courts of kings in splendor. The papal officialdom grew in numbers, ignoring the deeper problems while busily transacting each day's business. Papal revenues mounted, and new papal taxes were devised, for example, the "annates," by which every bishop or abbot in Christendom had to transmit to Rome most of the first year's income of his office. In the continuing movement of funds from all over Europe to the papal court, from the thirteenth century on, a new class of international bankers rose and prospered.

But the papacy, never so sumptuous, had never since the tenth century rested on such shaky foundations. People pay willingly for institutions in which they believe, and admire magnificence in leaders whom they respect. But before 1378, with the pope submissive to France, and after 1378, with two popes and two papacies to support, there was growing complaint at the extravagance and worldliness of papal rule. It must be remembered that all this happened in a Europe traumatized by the plague, and with a declining number of people expected to bear increasing financial burdens. The most pious Christians were the most shocked. They recognized the vital necessity of obtaining God's grace, but with two churches under two popes, each claiming to hold the keys of Peter, how could they be certain that their church gave true salvation? In a society that was still primarily a religious community, this sense of religious insecurity was a source of uneasiness and dread.

The old moorings were weakened, the wrath of God seemed to be raining upon the earth, and no one had the slightest notion of how the world was going to turn out. Symptoms of mass neurosis appeared. Some people sought refuge in a hectic merriment or luxury and self-indulgence. Others

Responses to crisis

became preoccupied with grisly subjects. Some frantically performed the Dance of Death in the cemeteries, while others furtively celebrated the Black Mass, parodying religion in a mad desire to appease the devil. The Order of Flagellants grew up; its members went through the streets, two by two, beating each other with chains and whips. Religious anxieties and fearful religious rumors contributed also to waves of anti-Jewish violence, murder, and expulsion that spread across parts of France and Germany in the fourteenth century. And it was at this time that people first became obsessed with the fear of witches, a delusion that would ultimately cause thousands of persons (often older women) to be tortured and executed over the following three centuries.

Disaffection with the church, or the thought that it might not be the true or the only way to salvation, spread in all ranks of society. It was not only kings who disputed the claims of the clergy but also obscure parish priests, close to the distress of ordinary people, who began to doubt the powers of their ecclesiastical superiors. One of these humble clerics was William Langland, who in his *Piers Plowman,* in the 1360s, contrasted the sufferings of the honest poor with the hypocrisy and corruption in high places. Such unsettling ideas spread very widely; in England those who held them were known as Lollards. Since the actual poor left no records, it is hard to say exactly what they thought, but some of their ideas were probably

Lollards and Hussites

Extreme expressions of religious anxiety appeared in the later Middle Ages among the flagellants who wandered through towns beating themselves to appease the wrath of God. They are portrayed here in a later sixteenth-century engraving of their processions.
(Giraudon/Art Resource, NY)

expressed by John Wyclif, who taught at Oxford. About 1380, Wyclif was saying that the true church could do without elaborate possessions, and even that an organized church might not be necessary for salvation, since ordinary, devout persons could do without priests and obtain salvation by reading the Bible, which he translated into English. Similar ideas appeared in Bohemia in central Europe, with John Huss as their spokesman. Here they became a national movement, for the Hussites were both a religious party and at the same time a Slavic or Czech party protesting against the supremacy of the Germans who lived in Bohemia. The Hussite wars ravaged central Europe for decades in the fifteenth century. The ideas of the Lollards and of Huss and Wyclif were branded as heresy, or unacceptable deviations from the true doctrine of the church.

Influential and established persons did not yet turn to heresy, and still less to witchcraft or flagellation. Their answer to the needs of the day was to assemble a great Europewide or general council of the church, in which reforms could be pressed by the whole body of Christians upon the reluctant and rival popes.

The Conciliar Movement

In 1409 such a church council met at Pisa. All parts of the Latin West were represented. The council declared both reigning popes deposed and obtained the due election of another, but since the first two refused to resign there were now three. In 1414 an even greater and more fully attended council met at Constance. Its aims were three: to end the now threefold schism, to extirpate heresy, and to reform the church "in head and members," or from top to bottom. Not much was accomplished in reform. To discourage heresy, John Huss was interrogated, condemned, and burned at the stake. The schism was ended. All three popes were at last persuaded or compelled to withdraw, and another, Martin V, was elected. The unity of the church, under the papacy, was at last restored.

The majority of the Council of Constance wished to make general councils part of the permanent apparatus of the church for all time in the future. Martin V, however, soon reaffirmed the prerogatives of the papal office, dissolved the Council of Constance, and repudiated its decrees. The next 30 years saw a continuing contest of wills between successive popes and successive councils.

General councils

In this battle for jurisdiction few reforms could be adopted, and fewer still could be enforced. Increasingly the life of the church was corrupted by money. No one believed in bribery, but everyone knew that many high churchmen (like many high civil officials of the day) could be bribed. To buy or sell a church office was a crime in the canon law known as "simony," but it was a crime which in the fifteenth century could not be suppressed. For churchmen to live with mistresses was considered understandable, if unseemly; the standards of laymen in such matters were not high; but for a bishop or other ecclesiastic to give lucrative church positions to his own children (or other relatives) was the abuse known as nepotism, and it, too, could not be eradicated. To sell divine grace for money, all agreed, was not only wrong but also impossible. But in 1300 Boniface VIII had given encouragement to the practice of "indulgences." A person, if properly confessed, absolved, and truly repentant, might, by obtaining an indulgence, be spared certain of the temporal punishments of purgatory. One usually obtained such an indulgence in return for a donation of money. The practice proved to be a fatally easy method of fund raising, despite complaints against the sale of indulgences simply for money.

Church corruption and indulgences

Gradually the popes prevailed over the councils. The conciliar movement was greatly weakened for Christendom as a whole when the powerful French element secured its aims by a local national arrangement. In the Pragmatic Sanction of Bourges, in 1438, the Gallican (or French) church affirmed the supremacy of councils over popes, declared its administrative independence from the Holy See, suppressed the payment of annates to Rome, and forbade papal intervention in the appointment of French prelates. The papacy thus lost influence in France, but the popes remained preeminent in Europe as a whole. In 1449, with the dissolution of the Council of Basel, the conciliar movement came to an end. In 1450 a great Jubilee was held to celebrate the papal triumph.

The papacy, its prestige and freedom of action thus secured, now passed into the hands of a series of cultivated gentlemen, men of the world, men of "modern" outlook in tune with their times—the famous popes of the Renaissance. Some, like Nicholas V (1447–1455) or Pius II (1458–1464), were accomplished scholars and connoisseurs of books. Some were like Innocent VIII (1484–1492), a pleasant man who was the first pope to dine in public with ladies. Alexander VI (1492–1503), of the Spanish Borgia family, exploited his office for the benefit of his relatives, trying to make his son Cesare Borgia the ruler of all Italy, while his daughter, Lucretia Borgia, became duchess of Ferrara and gathered literary men and artists at her famous Renaissance court. Alexander VI's successor, Julius II (1503–1513), was a capable general, and Leo X (1513–1521) was a superb patron of architects and painters. But we must now describe the Italian Renaissance, in which worthies of this kind were elevated to the Holy See.

The Renaissance popes

6.   THE RENAISSANCE IN ITALY

In Italy in the fifteenth century, and especially at Florence, we observe not merely a decay of medieval certainties but the appearance of a new and invigorating attitude toward the world. The Renaissance, a French word meaning "rebirth," first received its name from those who thought of the Middle Ages as a dark time from which the human spirit had to be awakened. It was called a *re*birth in the belief that people now, after a long interruption, had taken up and resumed a civilization like that of the Greco-Romans. Medieval people had thought of the times of Aristotle or Cicero as not sharply distinct from their own. In the Renaissance, with a new historical sense, arose the conception of "modern" and "ancient" times, separated by a long period with a different lifestyle and appropriately called the Middle Ages.

The basic institutions of Europe, the distinctive languages and national cultures, the great frameworks of collective action in law, government, and economic production—all originated in the Middle Ages. But the Renaissance marked a new era in thought and feeling, by which Europe and its institutions were in the long run to be transformed. The origins of modern natural science can be traced more to the medieval universities than to the Renaissance thinkers. But it was in the Italy of the Quattrocento (as Italians call the fif-

The Italian influence

teenth century) that other fields of thought and expression were first cultivated. The Italian influence in other countries, in these respects, remained very strong for at least 200 years. It pertained to high culture, and hence to a limited number of persons, but extended over the whole area represented by literature and the arts—literature meaning all kinds of writing and the arts including all products of human skill. The effects of the Italian Renaissance, though much modified with the passage of time, were evident in the books and art galleries of Europe and America, and in the architecture of their cities, even after the revolution of "modern" art in the early twentieth century. They involved the whole area of culture which was neither theological nor scientific but concerned with moral and civic questions about what human beings ought to be or ought to do, with the answers reflected in matters of taste, style, propriety, decorum, personal character, and education. In particular, it was in Renaissance Italy that an almost purely secular attitude first appeared, in which life was no longer seen by leading thinkers as a brief preparation for the hereafter.

The Italian Cities and the New Conception of Life

The towns of Italy, so long as trade converged in the Mediterranean, were the biggest and most bustling of all the towns that rose in Europe in the Middle Ages. The crafts of Italy included many refined trades such as those of the goldsmith or stonecarver, which were so zealously pursued that artisanship turned into art, and a delight in the beautiful became common among all classes. Merchants made fortunes in commerce: they lent their money to popes or princes and so made further fortunes as bankers. They bought the wares of the craftsmen-artists. They rejoiced, not so much in money or the making of money, as in the beautiful things and psychological satisfactions that money could buy; and if they forgot the things that money could not buy, this is only to say again that their outlook was becoming more "secular."

The Italian city-states

The towns were independent city-states. There was no king to build up a government for Italy as a whole, and for several generations the popes were either absent at Avignon or engaged in disputes arising from the Great Schism, so that the influence of Rome was unimportant. The merchant oli-

The wealthiest persons in Italian towns were often bankers who made money from the kind of financial exchange that appears in this fifteenth-century illustration.
(Scala/Art Resource, NY)

garchies, each in its own city, enjoyed an unhampered stage on which to pursue interests other than those of business. In some, as at Milan, they succumbed to or worked with a local prince or despot. In others, as at Florence, Venice, and Genoa, they continued to govern themselves as republics. They had the experience of contending for public office, of suppressing popular revolt or winning popular favor, of producing works of public munificence, of making alliances, hiring armies, outwitting rivals, and conducting affairs of state. In short, Italy offered an environment in which many facets of human personality could be developed.

All this was most especially true in Florence, the chief city of Tuscany, which had grown wealthy in the later Middle Ages from the production of woolens. In the fifteenth century it had a population of about 60,000, which made it only moderately large as Italian cities went. Yet, like ancient Athens, Florence produced an extraordinary sequence of gifted individuals. From the years of Dante, Petrarch, and Boccaccio, who all died before 1375, to those of Machiavelli, who lived until 1527, an amazing number of the leading figures of the Italian Renaissance were Florentines. Like Athens also, Florence lost its republican liberty as well as its creative powers. Its history *The Medici family* can be summarized in that of the Medici family. The founder of the family fortunes was Giovanni (1360–1429), a merchant and banker of Florence. His son, Cosimo de' Medici (1389–1464), allying himself with the popular element against some of the leading families of the republic, soon became unofficial ruler himself.

Two wool merchants display their goods and bags of wool. This illustration, which is from a 1492 book on arithmetic, shows the use of both Arabic and Roman numerals.
(Biblioteca Riccardiana, Florence)

Cosimo's grandson, Lorenzo the Magnificent (1449–1492), also used his great wealth to govern but is chiefly remembered as a poet, connoisseur, and lavish benefactor of art and learning. In the next century Tuscany became a grand duchy, of which the Medici were hereditary grand dukes until the family died out in 1737. Thus established, they furnished numerous cardinals and two popes to the church, and two Medici women became queens of France.

A secular conception of life

What arose in Italy, in these surroundings, was no less than a new secular conception of life. It seemed very doubtful whether a quiet, cloistered, or celibate life was on a higher plane than an active gregarious life, or family life, or even a life of promiscuity and adventure. It was hard to believe that clergy were any better than laity or that life led to a stern divine judgment in the end. That human will and intelligence might prove misleading seemed a gloomy doctrine. The belief that human beings were frail creatures, in need of God's grace and salvation, though perhaps said with the lips, seemed to evoke less feeling in the heart. Instead, what captivated the Italians of the Renaissance was a sense of the vast range of human powers.

Formerly, the ideal behavior had been seen in renunciation, in a certain disdain for the concerns of this world. Now a life of involvement was also prized. Formerly, poverty had been greatly respected, at least in Christian doctrine. Now there was more praise for a proper enjoyment of wealth. Medieval Europeans had admired a life of contemplation, or meditative withdrawal. Now the humanist Leonardo Bruni could write, in 1433, "The whole glory of man lies in activity." Often, to be sure, the two attitudes existed in the same person. Sometimes they divided different groups within the same city. As always, the old persisted along with the new. The result might be psychological stress and civil conflict.

Individualism

The new esteem for human activity took both a social and an individualistic turn. In cities maintaining their republican forms, as at Florence in the early fifteenth century, a new civic consciousness or sense of public duty was expressed. For this purpose the writings of Cicero and other

This procession is part of a fresco that Benozzo Gozzoli executed in 1469 for a Medici chapel. Although its title refers to the three kings on their way to Bethlehem, it actually represents important personages in fifteenth-century Florence. Cosimo de' Medici is on a white horse, followed by a throng of supporters.
(Scala/Art Resource, NY)

ancients were found to be highly relevant, since they provided an ethics independent of the Christian and medieval tradition. There was also a kind of cult of the great individual, hardly known to the ancients, and one which gave little attention to collective responsibility. Renaissance individualism emphasized the outstanding attainments of extraordinary men (women, by contrast, were usually expected to pursue the ordinary tasks of domestic life). The great man shaped his own destiny in a world governed by fortune. He had *virtù,* the quality of being a man (*vir,* "man"), and although a few women might also exhibit *virtù,* it was a quality which in the society of the day was more to be expected in the most aggressive adult males. It meant the successful demonstration of human powers. A man of *virtù,* in the arts, in war, or in statecraft, was a man who knew what he was doing, who, from resources within himself, made the best use of his opportunities, hewing his way through the world and excelling in all that he did. For the arts, such a spirit is preserved in the autobiography of Benvenuto Cellini.

The growing preoccupation with things human can be traced in new forms of painting, sculpture, and architecture that arose in Italy at this time. These arts likewise reflected

Lorenzo de' Medici, known as the Magnificent, examines a model for a villa that was built for him about 1480 on the outskirts of Florence.
(Scala/Art Resource, NY)

an increasing this-worldliness, a new sense of reality and a new sense of space, of a kind different from that of the Middle Ages, and which was to underlie much European thought until the early twentieth century. Space was no longer indeterminate, unknowable, or divine; it was a zone occupied by physical human beings, or one in which human beings might at least imagine themselves moving about. Reality meant visible and tangible persons or objects in this space, "objective" in the sense that they looked or felt the same to all normal persons who perceived them. It was a function of the arts to convey this reality, however idealized or suffused by the artist's individual feeling, in such a way that observers could recognize in the image the identity of the subject portrayed.

Architecture reflected the new tendencies. Though the Gothic cathedral at Milan was built as late as 1386, at Florence and elsewhere architects preferred to adapt Greco-Roman principles of design, such as symmetrical arrangements of doors and windows, the classical column, the arch and the dome. More public buildings of a nonreligious character were built, and more substantial town houses were put up by wealthy merchants, in styles meant to represent grandeur, or civic importance, or availability and convenience for human use. Gardens and terraces were added to many such buildings.

Realism in sculpture and painting

Sculpture, confined in the Middle Ages to the niches and portals of cathedrals, now emerged as an independent and free-standing art. Its favored subjects were human beings, now presented so that the viewer could walk around the object and see it from all directions. The difference from the religious figures carved on medieval churches was very great. Like the architects, the sculptors in parting from the immediate past found much in the Greek and Roman tradition that was modern and useful to their purpose. They produced portrait busts of eminent contemporaries, or figures of great leaders, sometimes on horseback, or statues depicting characters from Greco-Roman history and mythology. The use of the nude, in mythological or allegorical subjects, likewise showed a conception of humanity that was more in keeping with the Greek than with the Christian tradition.

Painting was less influenced by the ancients, since the little of ancient painting that had survived was unknown during the Renaissance. The invention of painting in oils opened new pathways for the art. Merchants, ecclesiastics, and princes provided a mounting demand. In subject matter painting remained conservative, dealing most often with religious themes. It was the conception and presentation that were new. The new feeling for space became evident. With the discovery of the mathematics of perspective, space was presented in exact relation to the beholder's eye. The viewer, in a sense, entered into the world of the painting. A three-dimensional effect was achieved, with careful representation of distance through variation of size, and techniques of shading or chiaroscuro added to the illusion of physical volume. Human figures were often placed in a setting of painted architecture, or against a background of landscape or scenery, showing castles or hills, which though supposedly far away yet framed the composition with a knowable boundary. In such a painting everything was localized in place and time; a part of the real world was caught and put in the picture. The idea was not to suggest eternity, as in earlier religious painting, nor yet to express private fantasy or the workings of the unconscious, as in much "modern" art, but to present a familiar theme in an understandable setting, often with a narrative content, that is, by the telling of a story.

Painters were able also, like the sculptors, by a close study of human anatomy, to show people in distinctive and living attitudes. Faces took on more expression as artists sought to depict individual personalities. Painting became less symbolic, less an intimation of general or abstract truths, more a portrayal of concrete realities as they met the eye. In the portrait by Bellini of a *condottiere* the reader can see how a strong, real, and vivid personality looks out from the canvas. Similarly, the great religious paintings were peopled with human beings. In Leonardo da Vinci's *Last Supper* Christ and his disciples are seen as a group of men each with his own characteristics. Raphael's Madonnas seem to be young Italian women, and in the mighty figures of Michelangelo the attributes of humanity invade heaven itself.

Humanism: The Birth of "Literature"

The literary movement in Renaissance Italy is called humanism because of the rising interest in humane letters, *litterae humaniores*. There had indeed been much writing in the later Middle Ages. Much of it had been of a technical character, as in theology, philosophy, or law; some of it had been meant to convey information, as in chronicles, histories, and descriptions of the physical world. Great hymns had been composed, lively student songs had been sung at the universities, plays had been performed in cathedrals, the old legends of King Arthur and Roland had been written down, and occasionally a monk would try his hand at a long narrative poem. Yet a new kind of literature and literary culture began to appear in the fourteenth and fifteenth centuries in Italy. A new class of writers looked upon literature as their main life's work, wrote for each other and for a somewhat larger public, and used writing to deal with general questions, or to examine their own states of mind, or resolve their own difficulties, or used words to achieve artistic effects, or simply to please and amuse their readers. Almost all of the writers were men, but a few women also entered the new literary culture of the era. The writings of Christine de Pisan, for example, helped

**PORTRAIT
OF A CONDOTTIERE
by Giovanni Bellini (Italian,
1430–1516)**

**This portrait provides an em-
phatic statement of Renaissance individualism. The artist
represents here a concrete,
strong-willed human being
rather than an abstract type,
stressing his subject's independence and self-sufficiency by
placing him against a dark and
entirely vacant background.**
(Giovanni Bellini, *Giovanni Emo,*
Samuel H. Kress Collection, © 2000
Board of Trustees, National Gallery
of Art, Washington, D.C.)

to spread humanist themes in France during the early fifteenth century (her family had
moved to France from Italy) and also demonstrated that women could participate in the
debates of European intellectual life.

Humanists and Latin

The Italian humanists, like their predecessors, wrote a good deal in
Latin. They differed from earlier literate persons in that they were not, for
the most part, members of the clergy. They complained that Latin had
become monkish, barbaric, and "scholastic," a jargon of the schools and universities, and
they greatly preferred the classic style of a Cicero or a Livy. Medieval Latin was a vigorous living language that used words in new senses, many of which have passed into
English and the Romance languages as perfectly normal expressions. Yet in the ancient
writers the humanists found qualities that medieval writing did not have. They discovered
a new range of interests, a new sensibility, discussion of political and civic questions, a
world presented without the overarching framework of religious belief. In addition, the
Greeks and Romans unquestionably had style—a sense of form, a taste for the elegant and
the epigrammatic. They had often also written for practical ends, in dialogues, orations, or
treatises that were designed for purposes of persuasion.

If the humanists therefore made a cult of antiquity, it was because they saw kindred
spirits in ancient cultures. They sensed a relevancy for their own time. The classical influence, never wholly absent in the Middle Ages, now reentered as a main force in the higher
civilization of Europe. The humanists polished their Latin, and increasingly they learned

Greek. They searched assiduously for classical texts hitherto unknown. Many were found; they had of course been copied and preserved by the monks of preceding times.

But while a special dignity attached to writing in Latin, known throughout Europe, most of the humanists wrote in Italian also. Or rather, they used the mode of speech current in Florence. This had also been the language of Dante in the *Divine Comedy*. To this vast poem the humanists now added many writings in Florentine or Tuscan prose. The result was that Florentine became the standard form of modern Italian. It was the first time that a European vernacular—that is, the com- *The vernacular* mon spoken tongue as opposed to Latin—became thus standardized amid the variety of its dialects and adapted in structure and vocabulary to the more complex requirements of a written language. French and English soon followed, and most of the other European languages somewhat later.

The Florentine exile, Francesco Petrarca, or Petrarch, has been called the first man of letters. The son of a merchant, he spent his life in travel *Petrarch* throughout France and Italy. Trained for the law, and an ordained clergy- man, he became a somewhat rootless critic of these two esteemed professions, which he denounced for their "scholasticism." He lived in the generation after Dante, dying in 1374, and he anticipated the more fully developed humanism that was to come. His voluminous writings show the complex, contradictory attitudes of early Renaissance thought. Attracted by life, love, beauty, travel, and connections with people of importance in church and state, he could also spurn all these things as ephemeral and deceptive. He loved Cicero for his common sense and his commitment to political liberty; indeed, he discovered a manuscript of Cicero's letters in 1345. He loved St. Augustine for his otherworldly vision of the City of God. But in Cicero's writings he also found a deep religious concern, and in St. Augus- tine he esteemed the active man who had been a bishop, a writer heavily engaged in the controversies of his time, and one who taught that for true Christians the world is not evil.

Petrarch wrote sonnets in Italian, an epic in Latin, an introspective study of himself, and a great many letters which he clearly meant to be literary productions. He aspired to literary fame. In all this we see a new kind of writer, who uses language not merely as a practical tool but as a medium of more subtle expression, to commune with himself, to convey moods of discouragement or satisfaction, to clarify doubts, to improve his own understanding of the choices and options that life affords. With Petrarch, in short, literature became a kind of calling, and also a consideration of moral philosophy, still related but no longer subordinate to religion. It was moral philosophy in the widest sense, raising ques- tions of how human beings should adjust to the world, what a good life could be or ought to be, or where the genuine and ultimate rewards of living were to be found.

Petrarch was an indication of things to come. Boccaccio, his contemporary and also a Florentine, wrote the *Decameron* in Italian, a series of tales designed both to entertain and to impart a certain wisdom about human character and behavior. They were followed by the main group of humanists, far more numerous but less well remembered. Men of letters began to take part in public life, to gather stu- *The humanists* dents and found schools, to serve as secretaries to governing bodies or princes, and even to occupy office themselves. Thus the humanist Coluccio Salutati became chancellor of Florence in 1375. During the following decades Florence was threat- ened by the expansive ambitions of Milan, where the princely despotism of the Visconti family had established itself. Against such dangers a new and intense civic consciousness asserted itself. Salutati, in addition to the usual duties of chancellor, served the state with his pen, glorifying Florentine liberty and identifying it with the liberties of ancient repub- lican Rome before they were undermined by the Caesars. He was succeeded as chancellor

The three men in this painting were Florentine humanists around 1490. They appear in a larger work that the artist Domenico Ghirlandaio painted for a chapel. Ghirlandaio followed the typical Renaissance practice of using religious stories or events to convey secular subjects and ideas.
(Alinari/Art Resource, NY)

by two other humanists, Bruni and Poggio. Bruni wrote a history of Florence which marked a new achievement in historical writing, when compared with the annals and chronicles of the Middle Ages. He saw the past as clearly past, different from but relevant to the present; and he introduced a new division of historical periods. On the model of such ancient writers as Livy, he adopted a flowing narrative form. And he used history for a practical political purpose, to show that Florence had a long tradition of liberty and possessed values and attainments worth fighting for against menacing neighbors. History took on a utility that it had had for the Greeks and Romans and was to retain in the future in Europe and eventually in other parts of the world: the function of heightening a sentiment, not yet of nationalism, but of collective civic consciousness or group identity. It was meant to arouse its readers to a life of commitment and participation.

All this literary activity was of a scholarly type, in which authors broadened their understanding as much by reading as by personal experience of the world. And scholarly activity, the habit of attending closely to what a page really said, had consequences that went beyond either pure literature or local patriotism. A new critical attitude developed. Bruni, in his history, showed a new sense of the need for authentic sources. Lorenzo Valla became one of the founders of textual criticism. Studying the Latin language historically, he observed that its characteristic words and expressions varied from one time to another. He put this knowledge to the service of the king of Naples in a dispute with the pope. Valla showed, by analysis of the language used in the document, that the Donation of Constantine, on which the papacy then based its temporal claims, could not have been written in Constantine's time in the fourth century, and so was a forgery. Such scholarship helped establish modern methods for assessing the truth of written texts, and it contributed also to humanist optimism about the range and utility of human knowledge. Pico della Mirandola

Modern critical methods

and others looked for aspects of truth not revealed in the Christian scriptures. In 1486, the enthusiastic and very learned Pico, for example, claimed at the age of 23 that he could summarize all human knowledge in 900 theses, which he had drawn from "the Chaldaic, Arabic, Hebrew, Grecian, Egyptian, and Latin sages."

Schooling, Manners, and Family Life

While Italian humanism thus contributed much to literature and scholarship, to classical learning, and to the formation of modern national languages, it also had tangible and lasting effects in education. Here its impact persisted in all regions of European civilization down to the present. The medieval universities were essentially places for professional training in theology, medicine, and law. Except in England this continued to be their primary function. What came to be known as secondary education, the preparation of young men either for the universities or for "life," owes more to the Renaissance. The organized education of women came much later; some girls learned to read at home or in one of the few female primary schools, but young women were excluded from humanist academies and Renaissance universities.

Medieval schooling had been chaotic and repetitious. Youngsters of all ages sat together with a teacher, each absorbing from the confusion whatever could be understood of Latin rules and vocabulary. The Renaissance launched the idea of putting different age groups or levels of accomplishment into separate classes, in separate rooms, each with its own teacher, with periodic promotion of the pupil from one level to the next. Latin remained the principal subject, with Greek now added. But many new purposes were seen in the study of Latin.

Renaissance education

It was intended to give skill in the use of language, including the pupil's native tongue. Rhetoric was the art of using language to influence others. It heightened communication. Knowledge alone was not enough, said the historian and chancellor Bruni, who also wrote a short work on education—"to make effectual use of what we know we must add the power of expression." Nor was Latin merely the necessary professional tool for the priest, the physician, the lawyer, or the government servant. The student learned Latin (and Greek) in order to read the ancient writings—epics, lyrics, orations, letters, histories, dialogues, and philosophical treatises—and it was assumed that such writings offered practical lessons for the educated elites of every generation. Readers therefore learned how to find relevant historical models or failures in the rise and decline of the Roman republic and the troubles of the Greek city-states. The classics were meant also to have a moral impact, to produce a balanced personality, and to form character. Not everyone could be important or gifted, said the humanist Vittorino, but we all face a life of "social duty" and are responsible for our "personal influence" on others. These aims became permanent themes in the educational systems that trained the young men of early modern Europe.

Young people were trained also for a more civilized deportment in everyday social living. Personal style in the upper classes became somewhat more studied. Hitherto Europeans had generally acted like big children; they spat, belched, and blew their noses without inhibition, snatched at food with their fingers, bawled at each other when aroused, or sulked when their feelings were offended. It was Italians of the Renaissance who first taught more polite habits. Books of etiquette began to appear, of which the most successful was Castiglione's *Book of the Courtier* (1528). The "courtier" was ancestor to the "gentleman"; "courtesy" was originally the kind of behavior suited to princely courts.

This painting by the Italian artist Lavinia Fontana (1552–1614) portrays an appreciation for the generations and social roles that constituted late Renaissance family life. The people are arranged by age and gender, thus suggesting a different identity and destiny for each person and each group.
(Scala/Art Resource, NY)

The "courtier"

The "courtier," according to Castiglione, should be a man of good birth but is chiefly the product of training. His education in youth, and his efforts in mature years, should be directed toward mixing agreeably in the company of his equals. His clothes should be neat, his movements graceful, his approach to other people perfectly poised. He must converse with facility, be proficient in sports and arms, and know how to dance and appreciate music. He should know Latin and Greek. With literary and other subjects he should show a certain familiarity but never become too engrossed. For the well-bred man speaks with "a certain carelessness, to hide his art, and show that what he says or does comes from him without effort or deliberation." Pedantry and heaviness must yield to an air of effortless superiority, so that even if the "courtier" knows or does something seriously, he must treat it lightly as one of many accomplishments. At its best, the code taught a consideration for the feelings of others and incorporated some of the moral ideas of the humanists, aiming at a creditable life in active society. Castiglione's book was translated into numerous languages, and a hundred editions were printed before 1600.

Castiglione's ideal court also included women, whose civilizing influence was supposed to encourage the good manners, polite conversation, and cultural graces that rough-edged men might otherwise ignore. Expressing views of men and women that shaped much of Renaissance culture, Castiglione expected men to cultivate a "robust and sturdy manliness," which would be balanced in court society by the "soft and delicate tenderness" of women. Such distinctions suggested also the gender divisions in Renaissance families and households, including those that were far removed from the courts of princes.

The marriages that created Renaissance households grew out of careful negotiations in which the families of prospective brides and grooms sought to enhance their respective social positions. In Florence, for example, parents typically arranged for their daughters to be married by age 18 to older men whose economic or political connections would be advantageous to the young woman's own family. Florentine husbands, who had usually reached age 30 before their first marriage, were well advanced in trades or professions before they established their new households, which depended also on the dowries that they received through their marriage contracts. The different ages of husbands and wives reinforced the gender divisions in Renaissance families; men pursued their public careers with their professional peers while their much younger wives raised children in the home. The high mortality rates in Renaissance cities, however, meant that women often outlived their older husbands, and, as young widows were forced to raise the children and manage the household. The young men who attended the new Renaissance schools therefore came from families in which mothers usually provided the most important training during their early years. Renaissance education and manners, as taught in the new schools and academies of the era, thus developed within the distinctive patterns of family life in the Italian cities.

Renaissance marriages

Politics and the Italian Renaissance

The Italian Renaissance, for all its accomplishments, produced no institution or great idea by which masses of people living in society could be held together. Indeed, the greatest of Europe's institutions, the Roman church, in which Europeans had lived for centuries, and without which they did not see how they could live at all, fell into neglect under the Renaissance popes. Nor did Italy develop any effective political institutions. Florence during the fifteenth century passed from a high-spirited republicanism to acceptance of one-man rule. Throughout the peninsula the merchants, bankers, connoisseurs, and courtly classes who controlled the city-states could not fight for themselves, nor arouse their citizens to fight for them. They therefore hired professional fighting men, *condottieri,* private leaders of armed bands, who contracted with the various city-states to carry on warfare and often raised their price or changed sides during hostilities. Italian politics became a tangled web, a labyrinth of subterfuge and conspiracy, a platform on which powerful individuals might exhibit their *virtù.* "Italian cunning" became a byword throughout Europe. Dictators rose and fell. The Medici became dukes in Florence, the Sforza in Milan, while in Venice and Genoa, where the republics survived, narrow oligarchies held tight control. These states, along with the states of the church, jockeyed about like pugilists in a ring, held within an intricate, shifting, and purely local balance of power.

Italy was the despair of its patriots, or of such few as remained. One of these was Niccolò Machiavelli, who, in *The Prince* (1513), wrote the most lasting work of the Italian Renaissance. He dreamed of the day when the citizens of his native Florence, or indeed of all Italy, should behave like early Romans—show virility in their politics, fight in citizen armies for patriotic causes, and uphold their

Machiavelli

The governing council in Florence deliberates on going to war against Pisa during a brief period of republican revival after the Medici were expelled in 1494. A nemesis, or omen of failure and retribution, floats over the councilors' heads and represents the challenge of making political decisions in a Renaissance Italian state.
(Alinari/Art Resource, NY)

dignity before Europe. It was outside Italy, in kings Ferdinand of Aragon, Louis XI of France, and Henry VII of England, that Machiavelli was obliged to find his heroes. He admired them because they knew how to exercise power and how to build strong states. In *The Prince* he produced a handbook of statecraft which he hoped Italy might find useful. He produced also the first purely secular treatise on politics.

Medieval writings on politics, those of Thomas Aquinas or Marsiglio of Padua, for example, had always talked of God's will for the government of people, with such accompanying matters as justice and right, or divine and natural law. All this Machiavelli put aside. He "emancipated" politics from theology and moral philosophy. He undertook to describe simply what rulers actually did. What really happens, said Machiavelli, is that effective rulers and governments act only in their own political interest. They keep faith or break it, observe treaties or repudiate them, are merciful or ruthless, forthright or sly, peaceable or aggressive, according to their estimates of their political needs. Machiavelli was prepared to admit that such behavior was bad; he only insisted that it was in this way, however regrettably, that successful rulers behaved. He was thought unduly cynical even in an age that lacked political delicacy. He had nevertheless diagnosed the new era with considerable insight. It was an age when politics was in fact breaking off from religion, with the building up of states and state authority emerging as goals that required no other justification.

But the most successful states of the time, as Machiavelli saw, were not in Italy. They were what history knows as the New Monarchies, and they owed their strength to something more than princely craft, for they enjoyed a measure of loyalty from the people they governed. The city-states in Renaissance Italy failed to sustain even this limited sense of loyalty between governments and their people. Italian politics became an affair of individual or elite *virtù;* and, as outsiders began to realize, the people of Italy lost interest in both the politics and the wars of their own city-states.

So Italy, the sunny land of balmy Mediterranean skies, rich in the busy life of its cities, its moneyed wealth, its gorgeous works of art, became vulnerable to the depredations of less easygoing peoples, from Spain and the *Italian vulnerability* north, who possessed institutions in which men could act together in large numbers. In a new age of rising national monarchies the city-states of Italy were too small to compete. In 1494 a French army crossed the Alps. Italy became a bone of contention between France and Spain. In 1527 a horde of undisciplined Spanish and German mercenaries, joined by footloose Italians, fell upon Rome itself. Never, not even from the barbarian Goths of the fifth century, had Rome experienced anything so horrible and degrading. The city was sacked, thousands were killed, soldiers milled about in an orgy of rape and loot, the pope was imprisoned, and cardinals were mockingly paraded through the streets facing backward on the backs of mules.

After the sack of Rome the Italian Renaissance faded away. Politically, for over three hundred years, Italy remained divided, the passive object of the ambitions of outside powers. Meanwhile its culture permeated the rest of Europe.

7.   THE RENAISSANCE OUTSIDE ITALY

Outside Italy people were much less conscious of any sudden break with the Middle Ages. Developments north of the Alps, and in Spain, were more an outgrowth of what had gone before. There was indeed a Renaissance in the Italian sense. In some of the innovations in painting the Flemish masters preceded those of Italy. In the north also, as in Italy, writers favored a revival of classical Latin, but the modern written languages also began to develop.

The northern Renaissance was more a blend of the old and the new. In it, above all, the religious element was stronger than in Italy. The most important northern humanists were writers like Thomas More in England and Erasmus in Holland. The French humanism that produced the earthy François Rabelais also produced the austere John Calvin.

Religious Scholarship and Science

Christian humanists

Historians like to distinguish between the "pagan" humanism of Italy and the Christian humanism of the north. In the north, Christian humanists studied the Hebrew and Greek texts of the Bible and read the Church Fathers, both Latin and Greek, in order to deepen their understanding of Christianity and to restore its moral vitality. Among people without pretense to humanistic learning, religion also remained a force. Medieval intellectual interests persisted. This is apparent from the continuing foundation of universities. The humanists generally regarded universities as centers of a pedantic, monkish, and "scholastic" learning. Concentrating upon theology, or upon medicine and law, the universities gave little encouragement to experimental science and still less to purely literary studies. In Italy in the fifteenth century no new universities were established. But in Spain, in France, in Scotland, in Scandinavia, and above all in Germany, new universities continued to develop. Between 1386 and 1506 no less than 14 universities were established in Germany. At one of the newest, Wittenberg, founded in 1502, Martin Luther was to launch the Protestant Reformation.

Germany at this time, on the eve of the great religious upheaval, and before the shift of the principal commercial arteries from central Europe to the Atlantic seaboard, was a main center of European life. Politically, the German-speaking world was an ill-defined and ill-organized region, composed of many diverse parts, from which the Netherlands and Switzerland were not yet differentiated. Economically, nevertheless, western and southern Germany enjoyed a lead over most of Western Europe; the towns traded busily, and German banking families, like the famous Fugger, controlled more capital than any others in Europe. Technical inventiveness was alive; mining was developing; and it was in the Rhineland, at Mainz, that Gutenberg, about 1450, produced the first European books printed with movable type. In painting, the western fringe of the Germanic world produced the Flemish masters, and south Germany gave birth to Albrecht Dürer and the Holbeins.

Intellectually, Germany shared in the Latin culture of Europe, a fact often obscured by the Latin names that German authors used in the early modern era. Regiomontanus (the Latin name of Johann Müller) laid the foundations during his short lifetime (1436–1476)

German contributions to early modern science

for a mathematical conception of the universe. He was probably the most influential scientific worker of the fifteenth century, especially since Leonardo da Vinci's scientific labors remained unknown. Nicholas of Cusa (1401?–1464), a Rhinelander, was a churchman whose mystical philosophy entered into the later development of mathematics and science. From such a background of mathematical interests came Copernicus (Niklas Koppernigk, 1473–1543), who believed that the earth moved about the sun; he was indeed a Pole, but he originated in the mixed German-Polish region of East Prussia. Fortified by the same mathematical interests, Europe's best-known cartographers were also Germans, such as Behaim and Schöner, whose world maps represented the most advanced geographical knowledge of the time. Paracelsus (Latin for Hohenheim) undertook to revolutionize medicine at the University of Basel. His wild prophecies made him a mixture of scientist and charlatan; but, in truth, science was not yet clearly distinguished from the occult, with which it shared the idea of control over natural forces. A similar figure, remembered in literature and the arts, was the celebrated Dr. Faustus. In real life, Faust, or Faustus, was perhaps a learned German of the first part of the sixteenth century. He was rumored to have sold his soul to the devil in return for knowledge and power, The Faust story was dramatized in England as early as 1593 by Christopher Marlowe, and, much later, by Goethe in German poetry. In the legend of Faust later generations were to see a symbol of the inordinate ambitions of modern people.

The idea of human powers to understand and control physical nature, as developed most especially north of the Alps, corresponded in many ways to the more purely Italian and humanistic idea of the infinite richness of human personality. Together, they constituted the new Renaissance spirit, for both emphasized the emancipation of humanity's limitless potentialities. The two ideas constantly interacted; in fact, most of the scientific workers just mentioned—Regiomontanus, Nicholas of Cusa, Copernicus—spent many years in Italy, receiving the stimulus of Italian thought.

Mysticism and Lay Religion

In the north a genuine religious impulse, in addition to religious humanistic scholarship, also remained alive. Where in Italy the religious sense, if not extinct, seemed to pass into a joyous and public cult in which God was glorified by works of art, in the north it took on a more mystical and soberly moral tone. Germany in the fourteenth century produced a series of mystics. The mystic tendencies of Nicholas of Cusa have been mentioned. More typical mystics were Meister Eckhart (d. 1327) and Thomas à Kempis (d. 1471), author of the *Imitation of Christ*. The essence of mysticism lay in the belief, or experience, that the individual soul could in perfect solitude commune directly with God. The mystic had no need of reason, nor of words, nor of joining with other people in open worship, nor of the sacraments administered by the priests—nor even of the church. The mystics did not rebel against the church; they accepted its pattern of salvation; but at bottom they offered, to those who could follow, a deeper religion in which the church as a social institution had no place. All social institutions, in fact, were transcended in mysticism by the individual soul; and on this doctrine, both profound and socially disruptive, Martin Luther was later to draw.

Mysticism and the individual soul

For the church, it was significant also that religion was felt deeply outside the clergy. Persons stirred by religion, who in the Middle Ages would have taken holy orders, now frequently remained laymen. In the past the church had often needed reform. But in the past, in the bad times of the tenth century, for example, the clergy had found reformers within their own ranks. The church had thus been repeatedly reformed and renewed without revolution. Now, in the fifteenth and early sixteenth centuries an ominous line seemed to be increasingly drawn: between the clergy as an established interest, inert and set in its ways, merely living, and living well, off the church; and groups of people outside the clergy—religious laypersons, religiously inclined humanists and writers, impatient and headstrong rulers—who were more influential than ever before and more critical of ecclesiastical abuses.

Lay religion was especially active in the Netherlands. A lay preacher, Gerard Groote, attracted followers by his sermons on spiritual regeneration. In 1374 he founded a religious sisterhood, which was followed by establishments for religiously minded men. They

The Sisters and Brothers of the Common Life

called themselves, respectively, the Sisters and the Brothers of the Common Life, and they eventually received papal approval. They lived communally, but not as monks and nuns, for they took no vows, wore ordinary clothing, and were free to leave at will. They worked at relieving the poor and in teaching. The schools of the Brothers, since some of them came to have as many as a thousand boys, were the first to be organized in separate classes, each with its own room and its own teacher, according to the pupil's age or level of advancement. The Sisters maintained similar though less elaborate schools for girls. Reading and writing were of course taught, but the emphasis was on a Christian ideal of character and conduct, to instill such qualities as humility, tolerance, reverence, love of one's neighbor, and the conscientious performance of duty. This Modern Devotion, as it was called, spread widely in the Netherlands and adjoining parts of Germany.

Erasmus of Rotterdam

Erasmus of Rotterdam

In this atmosphere grew up the greatest of all the northern humanists, and indeed the most notable figure of the entire humanist movement, Erasmus of Rotterdam (1466–1536). Like all the humanists, Erasmus chose to write in a "purified" and usually intricate Latin style. He regarded the Middle Ages as benighted, ridiculed the scholastic philosophers, and studied deeply the classical writers of antiquity. He had the strength and the limitations of the pure man of letters. To the hard questions of serious philosophy he was largely indifferent; he feared the unenlightened excitability of the common people, and he was almost wholly unpolitical in his outlook. He rarely thought in terms of worldly power or advantage and made too little allowance for those who did. An exact contemporary to the most worldly Renaissance popes, Erasmus was keenly aware of the need for reform of the clergy. He put his faith in education, enlightened discussion, and gradual moral improvement. He led no burning crusade and counseled against all violence or fanaticism. He prepared new Greek and Latin editions of the New Testament. Urging people to read the New Testament in the vernacular languages, he hoped that a better understanding of Christ's teaching might turn them from their evil ways. In his *Praise of Folly* he satirized all worldly pretensions and ambitions, those of the clergy most emphatically. In his *Handbook of a Christian Knight* he showed how a man might take part in the affairs of the world while remaining a devout Christian, and in his influential treatise *On Civility in Children* he offered guidance for proper behavior in the social situations of daily life. Tolerance, restraint, good manners, scholarly understanding, a love of peace, a critical and reforming zeal, and a reasonable tone from which shouting and bad temper were always excluded—such were the Erasmian virtues.

Erasmus achieved an international eminence such as no one of purely intellectual attainments had ever enjoyed. He corresponded with the great of Europe. He lectured at Cambridge and edited books for a publisher at Basel. The king of Spain named him a councilor, the king of France called him to Paris, and Pope Leo X assisted him when he was in trouble. Theologians found fault with Erasmus's ideas (in which, indeed, the supernatural had little importance), but among the leaders of the church, the popes and prelates, he had many admirers. Erasmus, it must be noted, attacked only the abuses in the church, the ignorance or sloth of the clergy, and the moral or financial corruption of their lives. The essence and principle of the Roman Catholic church he never called into question. Whether the Erasmian spirit, so widely diffused about 1520, would have sufficed to restore the church without the revolutionary impact of Protestantism is one of the many unanswerable questions of history.

✑ 8.   THE NEW MONARCHIES

Meanwhile, in Europe outside Italy, kings were actively building the institutions of the modern state. It was these states, more than any other single factor, that were to determine the course of the religious revolution. Whether a country turned Protestant, remained Catholic, or divided into separate religious communities was to depend very largely upon political considerations.

War, civil war, class war, feudal rebellion, and plain banditry afflicted a good deal of Europe in the middle of the fifteenth century. In this formless violence central governments had become very weak. Various rulers now tried to impose a kind of civil peace. They have been conveniently called the New Monarchs, but they were not really very new because they resumed the interrupted labors of kings in the High Middle Ages. They thus laid foundations for later national, or at least territorial, states.

The New Monarchs offered the institution of monarchy as a guarantee of law and order. Arousing latent sentiments of loyalty to the reigning dynasty, they proclaimed that hereditary monarchy was the legitimate form of public power, which all should accept without turmoil or resistance. They especially enlisted the support of middle-class people in the towns, who were tired of the private wars and marauding habits of the feudal nobles. Townspeople were willing to let parliaments be dominated or even ignored by the king, for parliaments had proved too often to be strongholds of unruly barons, or had merely accentuated class conflict. The king, receiving money in taxes, was able to organize armies with which to control the nobles. The use of the pike and the longbow, which enabled the foot soldier to stand against the horseman, was here of great potential value. The king, if only he could get his monarchy sufficiently organized and his finances into reliable order, could hire large numbers of foot soldiers, who generally came from the growing population of commoners, unlike the knightly horsemen. But to organize his monarchy, the king had to break down the mass of feudal, inherited, customary, or "common" law in which the rights of the feudal classes were entrenched. For this purpose, at least on the Continent, the New Monarch made use of Roman law, which was now actively studied in the universities. He called himself a "sovereign"—it was at this time that kings began to be addressed as "majesty." The king, said the experts in Roman law, incorporated the will and welfare of the people in his own person. He could therefore *make* law by his own authority, regardless of previous custom or even of historic liberties—and they quoted Latin phrases to argue that "what pleases the prince has the force of law."

The New Monarchy in England, France, and Spain

The New Monarchy came to England with the dynasty of the Tudors (1485–1603), whose first king, Henry VII (1485–1509), after gaining the throne by force, put an end to the civil turbulence of the Wars of the Roses.

The Tudors

In these wars the great English baronial families had seriously weakened each other, to the great convenience of the king and the bulk of the citizenry. Henry VII passed laws against "livery and maintenance," the practice by which great lords maintained private armies wearing their own livery or insignia, and he used his royal council as a new court to deal with property disputes and infractions of the public peace. It met in a room decorated with stars, whence its name, the Star Chamber. It represented the authority of the king and his council, and it operated without a jury. Later denounced as an instrument of despotism, it was popular enough at first, because it preserved order and rendered substantial justice.

ERASMUS OF ROTTERDAM
by Hans Holbein, the Younger (German,
1497–1543)

This portrait was painted in 1523, when
Erasmus was 56, and the Lutheran
Reformation had begun in Germany. A
classic portrayal of humanism at its best,
the painting captures the life of thought
and emphasizes the only weapon that
Erasmus could use—the pen.
(Alinari/Art Resource, NY)

Henry VII, though miserly and unpleasant in person, was accepted as a good ruler. National feeling in England consolidated around the house of Tudor.

The Valois

In France the New Monarchy was represented by Louis XI (1461–1483), of the Valois line, and his successors. In the five centuries since the first French king had been crowned, the royal domain had steadily expanded from its original small nucleus around Paris through a combination of inheritance, marriage, war, intrigue, and conquest. Louis XI continued to round out the French borders. Internally, he built up a royal army, suppressed brigands, and subdued rebellious nobles. He acquired far greater powers than the English Tudors to raise taxation without parliamentary consent. The French monarchy also enlarged its powers over the clergy. We have seen how, by the Pragmatic Sanction of 1438, the Gallican church had won considerable independence to manage its own administrative affairs. In 1516 King Francis I reached an agreement with Pope Leo X in the Concordat of Bologna, which rescinded the Pragmatic Sanction. The pope henceforth received his "annates," or money income, from French ecclesiastics, but the king appointed the French bishops and abbots. The fact that, after 1516, the kings of France already controlled their own national clergy was one reason why, in later years, they were never tempted to turn Protestant.

Aragon and Castile

Strictly speaking, there was no kingdom of Spain. Various Spanish kingdoms had combined into two, Aragon and Castile. To Aragon, which lay along the Mediterranean side of the peninsula, belonged the Balearic Islands, Sardinia, Sicily, and the south Italian kingdom of Naples. To Castile, after 1492, belonged the newly discovered Americas. The two were joined in a personal union by the marriage of Ferdinand of Aragon and Isabella of Castile in 1469. The union was personal only; that is, both kingdoms recognized the two monarchs, but they had no common political, judicial, or administrative institutions. There was little or no Spanish national feeling; indeed, the Catalans in northern Aragon spoke a language quite different from Castilian Spanish. The most significant common feeling throughout

Spain came from the sense of belonging to the Spanish Catholic church. The common memory was that of the Christian crusade against the Moors. The one common institution, whose officials had equal authority and equal access to all the kingdoms, was a church court, the Inquisition. Meanwhile, the *reconquista* was at last completed when the southern tip of Spain, Granada, was conquered from the Moors in 1492. Its annexation added to the heterogeneous character of the Spanish dominions.

In these circumstances the New Monarchy in Spain followed a religious bent. Unification took place around the church. The rulers, though they made efforts at political centralization, worked largely through facilities offered by the church, and the early sense of "Spanishness" was linked to a sense of Catholicity. Formerly the Spanish had been among the most tolerant of Europeans; Christians, Muslims, and Jews had managed to live together. But in the wave of religious excitement that accompanied the conquest of Granada both the Jews and the Moors were expelled. The expulsion of the Jews by a decree of 1492 was actually a sign of former toleration in Spain, for the Jews had been earlier expelled from England in 1290 and from France in 1306. They were not again legally allowed in England until the mid-seventeenth century, nor in France (with great exceptions) until the French Revolution. In Spain, as in the history of many European peoples, the emergence of an early "national" consciousness seemed to produce a feeling against Jews as "outsiders."[2]

All persons in Spain were now supposed to be Christians. In fact, however, Spain was one of the places in Europe where a person's Christianity could not be taken for granted, because many Spanish families had been Jewish or Muslim for centuries and had only accepted Christianity to avoid expulsion. Hence arose a fear of false Christians, of an unassimilated element secretly hostile to the foundations of Spanish life. It was feared that Moriscos (Christians of Moorish background) and Marranos (Christians of Jewish background) retained a clandestine sympathy for the religion of their forebears. Thousands of such persons were brought before the Inquisition, where, as in the civil courts under Roman procedure, torture could be employed to extort confessions. It was thus safest to be profuse in one's external religious devotions because adherence to the Catholic Church became the way of proving oneself to be a good Spaniard.

Fusing the national and the Catholic

The life of Spain carried forward some of the long-existing commitment to a crusade—which had now evolved into a campaign within Spain against Moriscos and Marranos, and a new campaign against the Moors in Africa itself, which the Spanish invaded immediately after the conquest of Granada. The Spanish also extended their religious energies into the Americas, where the Spanish church set about gathering the Indians into the Christian fold. And Spain's strong religious identity would soon contribute to its growing role in the wider political and religious conflicts of sixteenth-century Europe. Spanish history had prepared the country (before Protestantism ever appeared) to become a leading defender of Roman Catholic traditions as well as an advocate for Catholic renewal and internal reforms.

---

[2]The Jews who left Spain (the Sephardic Jews) went to North Africa and the Middle East, and in smaller numbers to the Dutch Netherlands and even to southwestern France (one of the exceptions noted above). Those who left England two centuries earlier generally went to Germany, the great center of Ashkenazic Jewry in the Middle Ages. Driven from Germany in the fourteenth century they concentrated in Poland, which remained the great center of European Jews until the Nazi massacres of the 1940s.

The Holy Roman Empire and the Habsburg Supremacy

Ideas of the New Monarchy were at work even in Germany, which is to say, in the Holy Roman Empire. There were three kinds of states in the Empire. There were the princely states—duchies, margraviates, etc.—each a little hereditary dynastic monarchy in itself, such as Saxony, Brandenburg, or Bavaria. There were ecclesiastical states—bishoprics, abbacies, etc.—in which the bishop or abbot, whose rule was of course not hereditary, conducted the government. A large portion of the area of the Empire consisted of these church-states. Third, there were the imperial free cities, some 50 in number; their collective area was not large, but they dominated the commercial and financial life of the country.

The German states, over the centuries, had prevented the emperor from infringing upon their local liberties. They had taken care to keep the emperorship an elective office, so that with each election local liberties could be reaffirmed. After 1356 the right of electing an emperor was vested in seven electors—namely, four of the princely lords, the Count Palatine, Duke of Saxony, Margrave of Brandenburg, and King of Bohemia (the one king in the Empire), and in three ecclesiastical lords, the archbishops of Mainz, Trier, and Cologne. In 1452 the electors chose the Archduke of Austria to be emperor.

The Habsburgs

His family name was Habsburg. The Habsburgs, by using the resources of their hereditary possessions in Austria (and later elsewhere) and by delicately balancing and bribing the numerous political forces within Germany, managed to get themselves consistently reelected to the Holy Roman emperorship in every generation, with one exception, from 1452 until 1806. The Habsburg emperors also tried to introduce the centralizing principles of the New Monarchy into an empire that lacked institutions for the exercise of centralized power.

Under Maximilian I (1493–1519) there seemed to be progress in that direction: the Empire was divided into administrative "circles," and an Imperial Chamber and Council were created, but they were all doomed to failure before the immovable obstacle of states' rights. Maximilian was also the author of the Habsburg family fortunes through his strategic use of royal marriages, which brought the Habsburgs into control of a vast empire. Maximilian's grandson, Charles, thus inherited from his four grandparents the lands of Austria, the Netherlands, and part of Burgundy; Castile and Aragon in Spain; the whole of Spanish America; and scattered possessions in Italy and the Mediterranean. In addition, in 1519, Charles was elected Holy Roman Emperor and so became the symbolic head of all Germany.

Charles V

Charles V of the Empire (he was known as Charles I in Spain) was thus beyond all comparison the most powerful ruler of his day. But still other fortunes awaited the house of Habsburg. The Turks, who had occupied Constantinople in 1453, were at this time pushing through Hungary and menacing central Europe. In 1526 they defeated the Hungarians at the battle of Mohacs. The parliaments of Hungary, and of the adjoining kingdom of Bohemia, hoping to gain allies in the face of the Turkish threat, thereupon elected Charles V's brother Ferdinand as their king. Ferdinand soon lost much of Hungary to the Turkish Sultan, Sulayman I, but he retained his royal crown and gradually expanded Habsburg influence in central Europe. No royal family since Charlemagne had stood so far above all rivals. Contemporaries cried that Europe was threatened with "universal monarchy," with a kind of imperial system in which no people could preserve its independence from the Habsburgs.

The reader who wishes to understand the religious revolution, and the consequent emergence of Protestantism must bear in mind the intricate interplay of the factors that have now been outlined: the decline of the church; the growth of secular and humanistic feeling; the spread of lay religion outside the official clergy; the rise of monarchs who

This painting entitled *Interrogation of the Jews*, by an unknown artist in the 1480s, suggests the dangers that non-Christian people faced in late fifteenth-century Spain. Influential, wealthy interrogators questioned the beliefs or behavior of persons whose religion made them "suspicious" and vulnerable to the powerful people who distrusted them.
(Museo de Bellas Artes, Zaragoza, Spain)

wished to control everything in their kingdoms, including the church; the resistance of feudal elements to these same monarchs; the lassitude of the popes and their fear of church councils; the division of Germany; the Turkish entry into central Europe; the zeal of Spain; the preeminence of Charles V; and the fears felt in other countries, especially in France, of absorption by the amazing empire of the Habsburgs.

 ## 9.   THE PROTESTANT REFORMATION

Three streams contributed to the religious upheaval in sixteenth-century Europe. First, among common people, or the laboring poor, who might find their spokesmen among local priests, there was an endemic dissatisfaction with all the grand apparatus of the church, or a belief that its bishops and abbots were part of a wealthy and oppressive ruling class. For such people, religious ideas were mixed with protest against the whole social order. They found expression in the great peasant rebellion in Germany in the 1520s. The sects which emerged from these social groups are known historically as Anabaptists, and the modern Baptists, Mennonites, and Moravian Brothers are among their descendants. Second, and forming a

Political and social discontents

EUROPE, 1526

The main feature of the political map of Europe about 1526 is the predominance of the house of Habsburg. Much of Europe was ruled by the Habsburg Emperor Charles V, who was at the same time King Charles I of Spain. Charles left his possessions in Austria, Hungary, and Bohemia to his brother and those in Spain, the Netherlands, Italy, and America to his son, thereby establishing the Austrian and Spanish branches of the Habsburg dynasty. France was nearly encircled by Habsburg dominions and habitually formed alliances to oppose the Habsburg kings.

group generally more educated and with broader views of the world, were the middle classes of various European cities, especially of cities that were almost autonomous little republics, as in Germany, Switzerland, and the Netherlands. They might wish to manage their own religious affairs as they did their other business, believing that the church hierarchy was too much embedded in a feudal, baronial, and monarchical system with which they had little in common. The modern churches of Calvinist origin came in large part from this stream. Third, there were the ruling sovereigns and princes, who had long disputed with the church on matters of property, taxes, legal jurisdiction, and political influence. All such rulers wanted to be masters in their own territory. In the end it was the power of such rulers that determined which form of religion should officially prevail. The Lutheran and Anglican churches were in this tradition, and to some extent the Gallican church, as the French branch of the Roman Catholic church was called. As it turned out, by 1600, the second and third streams had won many successes, but the first was suppressed. Socio-religious radicalism was reduced to an undercurrent in countries where Anglican, Lutheran, Calvinist, or Roman Catholic churches were established during the sixteenth century.

Since northern Europe became Protestant while the south remained Catholic, it may look as if the north had broken off in a body from a once solid Roman church. The reality was not so simple. Let us for a moment put aside the term "Protestant," and think of the adherents of the new religion as religious revolutionaries.[3] Their ideas were revolutionary because they held, not merely that "abuses" in the church must be corrected, but also that the Roman church itself was wrong in principle. Even so, there were many who hoped, for years, that old and new ideas of the church might be combined. Many deplored the extremes but gradually in the heat of struggle had to choose one side or the other. The issues became drawn, and each side aspired to destroy its adversary. For over a century the revolutionaries maintained the hope that "popery" would everywhere fall. For over a century the upholders of the old order worked to annihilate or reconvert "heretics." Only slowly did Catholics and Protestants come to accept each other's existence as an established fact of European society. Though the religious frontier that was to prove permanent appeared as early as 1560, it was not generally accepted until after the Thirty Years' War, which ended in 1648.

Luther and Lutheranism

The first who successfully defied the older church authorities was Martin Luther. He was a monk, and an earnest one, until he was almost 40 years old. A vehement and spiritually uneasy man, with many dark and introspective recesses in his personality, Luther was terrified by the thought of the awful omnipotence of God, distressed by his own littleness, apprehensive of the devil, and suffering from the chronic conviction that he was damned. The means offered by the church to allay such spiritual anguish—the sacraments, prayer, attendance at Mass—gave him no satisfaction. From a reading and pondering of St. Paul (Romans i, 17)—"the just shall live by faith"—there dawned upon him a new realization and sense of peace. He developed the doctrine of justification by faith alone. This held that what "justifies" a person is not what the church knew as "works" (prayer, alms, the sacraments, holy living) but "faith alone," an inward bent of spirit given to each soul directly by God. Good works, Luther thought, were the consequence and external evidence of this inner

Luther's "justification by faith"

---

[3] The word "Protestant" arose as an incident in the struggle, at first denoting certain Lutherans who drew up a formal protest against an action of the diet of the Empire in 1529. Only very gradually did the various groups of anti-Roman reformers think of themselves as collectively Protestant.

Martin Luther and his wife Catherine, portrayed here by the artist Lucas Cranach the Elder, represent the acceptance of marriage among the clergy and religious leaders of the new Protestant churches. Catherine had lived in a convent before she married Luther and took on the new tasks of a religious wife in a Protestant minister's household.
(Scala/Art Resource, NY)

grace, but in no way its cause. People did not "earn" grace by doing good; they did the good because they possessed the grace of God. With this idea Luther for some years lived content. Even years later some high-placed churchmen believed that in Luther's doctrine of justification by faith there was nothing contrary to the teachings of the Catholic church.

Luther, now a professor at Wittenberg, was brought out of seclusion by an incident of 1517. A friar named Tetzel was traveling through Germany distributing indulgences, authorized by the pope to finance the building of St. Peter's in Rome. Tetzel claimed that indulgences would free people from some of the punishments of purgatory, and in return for the indulgences the faithful paid certain stipulated sums of money. Luther thought that people were being deluded, that no one could obtain grace in this way, or ease the pains of relatives in purgatory, as was officially claimed. In the usual academic manner of the day, he posted 95 theses on the door of the castle church at Wittenberg. Reviewing the Catholic sacrament of penance, Luther held in these theses that, after confession, the sinner is freed of sinful burdens not by the priest's absolution but by inner grace and faith alone. Increasingly, it seemed that the priesthood performed no necessary function in the spiritual relation between human beings and God.

Luther at first appealed to the pope, Leo X, to correct the abuse of indulgences in Germany. When the pope refused action Luther (like many before him) urged the assembly of a general church council as an authority higher even than the pope. He was obliged, however, to admit in public debate that even the decision of a general council might be mistaken. The Council of Constance, he said, had in fact erred in its condemnation of John Huss. But if neither the pope, nor yet a council, had authority to define true Christian belief, where was such authority to be found? Luther's answer was, in effect: there is no such authority. He held that individuals might read the Bible and freely make their own interpretations according to their own conscience. This idea was as revolutionary for the church as would be the assertion today that neither the Supreme Court nor any other body may authoritatively interpret or enforce the Constitution of the United States, since each citizen may interpret the Constitution in his or her own way.

From his first public appearance Luther won ardent supporters, for there was a good deal of resentment in Germany against Rome. In 1519 and 1520 he rallied public opinion in a series of tracts, setting forth his main beliefs. He declared that the claim of the clergy to be different from the laity was an imposture. He urged people to find Christian truth in the Bible for themselves, and in the Bible only. He denounced the reliance on fasts, pilgrimages, saints, and Masses. He rejected the belief in purgatory. He reduced the seven sacraments to two—baptism and the communion, as he called the Mass. In the latter he repudiated the new and "modern" doctrine of transubstantiation, while affirming that God was still somehow mysteriously present in the bread and wine. He declared that the clergy should marry, upbraided the prelates for their luxury, and demanded that monasticism be eliminated. To drive through such reforms, while depriving the clergy of their pretensions, he called upon the temporal power, the princes of Germany. He thus issued an invitation to the state to assume control over religion, an invitation which, in the days of the New Monarchy, a good many rulers were enthusiastically willing to accept.

Luther's criticisms of the Church

Threatened by a papal bull with excommunication unless he recanted, Luther solemnly and publicly burned the bull. Excommunication followed. To the emperor, Charles V, now fell the duty of apprehending the heretic and repressing the heresy. Luther was summoned to appear before a diet of the Empire, held at Worms in the Rhineland. He declared that he could be convinced only by Scripture or right reason; otherwise "I neither can nor will recant anything, since it is neither right nor safe to act against conscience. God help me! Amen." He was placed under the ban of the Empire. But the Elector of Saxony and other north German princes took him under their protection. In safe seclusion, he began to translate the Bible into German.

Lutheranism, or at least anti-Romanism, quickly swept over Germany, assuming the proportions of a national upheaval. It became mixed with all sorts of political and social revolution. A league of imperial knights, adopting Lutheranism, attacked their neighbors, the church-states of the Rhineland, hoping by annexations to enlarge their own meager territories. In 1524 the peasants of a large part of Germany revolted. They were stirred by new religious ideas, worked upon by preachers who went beyond Luther in asserting that each individual could readily understand what was right or wrong. Their aims, however, were social and economic; they demanded a regulation of rents and security of common village rights and complained of exorbitant exactions and oppressive rule by their manorial overlords. Luther repudiated all connection with the peasants, called them filthy swine, and urged the princes to suppress them by the sword. The peasants were unmercifully put down, but popular unrest continued to stir the country, expressing itself, in a religious age, in various forms of extreme religious frenzy.

Social revolution

The radical Anabaptist movement in Münster was severely repressed after the city's former rulers regained control in early 1536. This illustration depicts the public torture and death of John of Leyden, whose punishment served as a vivid warning to other revolutionary Protestants throughout Germany.
(akg-images)

Various religious leaders attracted devout followers, who came to be known collectively as Anabaptists. Some said that all the world needed was love, some that Christ would soon come again, some that they were saints and could do no wrong, and some that infant baptism was useless, immersion of full-grown adults being required, as described in the Bible. The roads of Germany were alive with religious radicals, of whom some tens of thousands converged in 1534 on the city of Münster. There they proclaimed the reign of the saints, abolished property, and introduced polygamy as sanctioned in the Old Testament. A Dutch tailor, John of Leyden, claimed that authority came to him directly from God. Hemmed in by besieging armies, he ruled Münster by a revolutionary terror. Luther advised his followers to join even with Catholics to repress such a dangerous religious and social menace. After a full year Münster fell to the forces of its former rulers. The "saints" were pitilessly rooted out; John of Leyden died in torture.

Luther's reaction

Luther, horrified at the way in which religious revolution became confused with social revolution, defined his own position more conservatively. He restricted, while never denying, the right of private judgment in matters of conscience, and he made a larger place for an established clergy, Lutheranized, to be sure, but still established as teachers over the laity. Always well disposed to temporal rulers, having called upon the princes to act as religious reformers, he was thrown by the peasant and Anabaptist uprisings into an even closer alliance with them.

Lutheranism became more submissive to the state. Christian liberty, Luther insisted, was an internal freedom, purely spiritual, known only to God. In worldly matters, he said, the good Christian owed obedience to established authority. Lutheranism thus came to view the state with more deference and respect than governments usually received from either Roman Catholicism or the Calvinism which soon arose.

In the revolution that was rocking Germany it was not the uprising of imperial knights, nor that of peasants or tailors and journeymen, that was successful, but the rebellion of the higher orders of the Empire against the emperor. Charles V, as Holy Roman Emperor, was bound to uphold Catholicism because only in a Catholic world did the Holy Empire have any meaning. The states of the *Political rebellion* Empire, always fearing the loss of local liberty, saw in Charles's efforts to repress Luther a threat to their own freedom. Many imperial free cities, and most of the dynastic states of north Germany, now insisted on adding to their other rights and liberties the right, or liberty, to determine their own religion. The right or power to reform, they said, belonged to member states, not to the Empire itself. They became Lutheran, locally, introducing Lutheran bishops, doctrines, and forms of worship. Where a state turned Lutheran it usually confiscated the church properties within its borders, a process which considerably enriched some of the Lutheran princes and gave them a strong material interest in the success of the Lutheran movement. In most of the church-states, since the Catholic archbishop or bishop was himself the government, Catholicism prevailed. But a few church-states turned Lutheran. A good example of the secularization of a church-state was afforded in East Prussia, just outside the Empire. This territory belonged to the Teutonic Order, a Catholic organization of which the grand commander, an elective official, was at this time Albert of Brandenburg. In 1525 Albert declared for Luther and converted East Prussia into a secular duchy, of which he and his descendants became hereditary dukes.

Against the emperor, a group of Lutheran princes and free cities formed the League of Schmalkald. The king of France, Francis I, though a Catholic in good standing, allied with and supported the League. Political interests overrode religious ones. Against the "universal monarchy" of the swollen Habsburgs the French found alliances where they could, allying with the Turks as with the Lutherans, building up a balance of power against their mighty foe. It became the studied policy of Catholic France to maintain the religious division of Germany.

Threatened by French and Turkish armies and challenged by the resistance of German princes within his own empire, Charles appealed to the pope, urging him to assemble a Europe-wide council in which all disputed *Charles's appeals to* matters could be considered, the Protestants could be heard, compromises *the papacy* could be effected, and church unity and German unity (such as it was) could be restored. The king of France schemed at Rome to prevent the pope from calling any such council. The kings of both France and England urged national councils instead, in which religious questions could be settled on a national basis. Pope after pope delayed. The papacy feared that a council of all Latin Christendom might get out of control, since Catholics as much as Protestants demanded reform. To the papacy, remembering the Council of Constance, nothing was more upsetting than the thought of a council, not even the Protestants, not even the Turks. So the popes procrastinated, no council met, years passed, and a new generation grew up in Lutheranism. Meanwhile the Schmalkaldic League, allied with France, actually went to war with the emperor in 1546. Germany fell into an anarchy of civil struggle between Catholic and Protestant states, the latter aided by France. The war was ended by the Peace of Augsburg of 1555.

CHRONOLOGY OF NOTABLE EVENTS, 1309–1555

1309–1378	"Babylonian Captivity": Papacy in Avignon
1337–1453	Hundred Years' War between England and France
1348–1350	Black Death decimates European population
c. 1350–1500	Renaissance Humanism and Art
1378–1417	Schism of Roman Catholic Church: Popes in Avignon and Rome
1454	Johann Gutenberg begins printing books with movable type
1494	French invasion of Italy destroys independence of city-states
1513	Niccolò Machiavelli writes *The Prince*
1517	Martin Luther posts his "95 theses"; beginning of Protestant Reformation
1545–1563	Roman Catholic Council meets at Trent; promotes Catholic reforms
1555	Peace of Augsburg recognizes Protestant and Catholic states in Germany

The terms set at Augsburg signified a complete victory for the cause of Lutheranism and states' rights. Each state of the Empire received the liberty to be either Lutheran or Catholic as it chose. No individual freedom of religion was permitted; if a ruler or a free city decided for Lutheranism, then all persons had to be Lutheran. Similarly in Catholic states all had to be Catholic. The Peace of Augsburg provided also, by the so-called Ecclesiastical Reservation, that any Catholic bishop or other churchman who turned Lutheran in the future (or who had turned Lutheran as recently as 1552) should not carry his territory with him, but should turn Lutheran as an individual and move away, leaving his land and its inhabitants Catholic. Since the issues in Germany were still far from stabilized, this proviso was often disregarded in later years.

The Peace of Augsburg

The Peace of Augsburg was thus, in religion, a great victory for Protestantism, and at the same time, in German politics and constitutional matters, a step in the disintegration of Germany into a mosaic of increasingly separate states. Lutheranism prevailed in the north and in the south in the duchy of Württemberg and various detached islands formed by Lutheranized free cities. Catholicism prevailed in the south (except in Württemberg and certain cities), in the Rhine valley, and in the direct possessions of the house of Habsburg, which in 1555 reached as far north as the Netherlands. The Germans, because of conditions in the Holy Roman Empire, were the one large European people to emerge from the religious conflict almost evenly divided between Catholic and Protestant.

No rights were granted by the Peace of Augsburg to another group of religious revolutionaries which neither Lutherans nor Catholics were willing to tolerate, namely, the followers of John Calvin.

Lutheranism, it must be pointed out, was adopted by the kings of Denmark and Sweden as early as the 1520s. Since Denmark controlled Norway, and Sweden ruled Finland and the eastern Baltic, all Scandinavia and the Baltic regions became, like north Germany, Lutheran. Beyond this area Lutheranism failed to take root. Like Anglicanism in England (to be described shortly), Lutheranism was too closely associated with established states to spread easily as an international movement. The most successful international form of the Protestant movement was Calvinism.

Calvin and Calvinism

John Calvin was a Frenchman, born Jean Cauvin, who called himself Calvinus in Latin. Born in 1509, he was a full generation younger than Luther. He was trained both as a priest and as a lawyer and had a humanist's knowledge of Latin and Greek, as well as Hebrew. At the age of 24, experiencing a sudden conversion, or fresh insight into the meaning of Christianity, he joined forces with the religious revolutionaries of whom the best known was then Luther. Three years later, in 1536, he published, in *Calvin's Doctrines* the international language, Latin, his *Institutes of the Christian Religion*. Where Luther had aimed much of his writing either at the existing rulers of Germany, or at the German national feeling against Rome, Calvin addressed his *Institutes* to all the world. He seemed to appeal to human reason itself; he wrote in the severe, logical style of the trained lawyer; he dealt firmly, lucidly, and convincingly with the most basic theological issues. In the *Institutes* people in all countries, if dissatisfied with the existing Roman church, could find cogent expression of universal propositions, which they could apply to their own local circumstances as they required.

With Luther's criticisms of the Roman church, and with most of Luther's fundamental religious ideas, such as justification by faith and not by works, Calvin agreed. In what they retained of the Catholic Mass, the communion or Lord's Supper as they called it, Luther and Calvin developed certain doctrinal differences. Both rejected transubstantiation, but where Luther insisted that God was somehow actually present in the bread and wine used in the service ("consubstantiation"), Calvin and his followers tended more to regard it as a pious act of symbolic or commemorative character.

The chief differences between Calvin and Luther were two. Calvin made far more of the idea of predestination. Both, drawing heavily on St. *Predestination* Augustine, held that human beings could never earn salvation by their own actions, that any grace which anyone possessed came from the free action of God alone. God, being Almighty, knew and willed in advance all things that happened, including the way in which every life would turn out. God thus knew and willed, from all eternity, that some were saved and some were damned. Calvin, a severe critic of human nature, felt that those who had grace were relatively few. They were the "elect," the "godly," the small group chosen without merit of their own, from all eternity, for salvation. People could feel in their own minds that they were among the saved, God's chosen few, if throughout all trials and temptations they persisted in pursuing a saintly life. Thus the idea of predestination, of God's omnipotence, instead of turning to fatalism and resignation, became a challenge to unrelenting effort, a sense of burning conviction, a conviction of being on the side of that Almighty Power which must in the end be everlastingly triumphant. It was the most resolute spirits that were attracted to Calvinism. Calvinists, in all countries, were militant, uncompromising, perfectionist—or Puritan, as they were called first in England and later in America.

The second way in which Calvinism differed from Lutheranism was in its attitude to society and to the state. Calvinists refused to recognize the subordination of church to state, or the right of any government—king, parliament, or civic magistracy—to lay down laws for religion. On the contrary, they insisted that true Christians, the elect or godly, should Christianize the state. They wished to remake society itself into the image of a religious community. They rejected the institution of bishops (which both the Lutheran and Anglican churches retained) and provided instead that the church should be governed by presbyteries, elected bodies made up of ministers and devout laymen. By thus bringing an element of lay control into church affairs, they broke the monopoly of priestly power and so promoted secularization. On the other hand, they were the reverse of secular, for they wished to Christianize all society.

Calvin's Geneva

Calvin, called in by earlier reformers who had driven out their bishop, was able to set up his model Christian community at Geneva in Switzerland. A body of ministers ruled the church; a consistory of ministers and elders ruled the town. The rule was strict; all loose, light, or frivolous living was suppressed; disaffected persons were driven into exile. The form of worship was severe and favored the intellectual rather than the emotional or the aesthetic. The service was devoted largely to long sermons elucidating Christian doctrine, and all appeals to the senses—color, music, incense—were rigidly subdued. The black gown of Geneva replaced brighter clerical vestments. Images, representing the saints, Mary, or Christ, were taken down and destroyed. Candles went the way of incense. Chanting was replaced by the singing of hymns. Instrumental music was frowned upon, and many Calvinists thought even bells to be a survival of "popery." In all things Calvin undertook to regulate his church by the Bible. Nor was he more willing than Luther to countenance any doctrine more radical than his own. When a Spanish refugee, Michael Servetus, who denied the Trinity, that is, the divinity of Christ, sought asylum at Geneva, Calvin pronounced him a heretic and had him burned at the stake.

The spread of Calvinism

Reformers of all nationalities flocked to Geneva to see and study a true scriptural community so that they might reproduce it in their own countries. Geneva became the Protestant Rome, the one great international center of Reformed doctrine. Everywhere Calvinists made their teachings heard (even in Spain and Italy in isolated cases), and everywhere, or almost everywhere, little groups which had locally and spontaneously broken with the old church found in Calvin's *Institutes* a reasoned statement of doctrine and a suggested method of organization. Thus Calvinism spread very widely. In Hungary and Bohemia large elements turned Protestant, and usually Calvinist, partly as a way of opposing the Habsburg rule. In Poland there were many Calvinists, along with less-organized Anabaptists and Unitarians, or Socinians, as those who denied the Trinity were then called. Calvinists spread in Germany, where, opposing both Lutheran and Catholic churches as ungodly impositions of worldly power, they were disliked equally by both. In France the Huguenots were Calvinist, as were the Protestants of the Netherlands. John Knox in the 1550s brought Calvinism to Scotland, where Presbyterianism became and remained the established religion. At the same time Calvinism began to penetrate England, from which it was later to reach British America, giving birth to the Presbyterian and Congregationalist churches of the United States.

Calvinism and democracy

Calvinism was far from democratic in any modern sense. It carried an almost aristocratic outlook, in that those who sensed themselves to be God's chosen few felt free to dictate to the wider population of lost souls. Yet in many ways Calvinism entered into the development of what became democracy. For one thing, Calvinists never venerated the state; they always held that the sphere of the state and of public life was subject to moral judgment. For another, the Calvinist doctrine of the "calling" taught that a person's labor had a religious dignity and that any form of honest work was pleasing in the sight of God. In the conduct of their own affairs Calvinists developed a type of self-government. They formed "covenants" with one another and devised machinery for the election of presbyteries. They refused to believe that authority was transmitted downward through bishops or through kings. They were inclined also to a democratic outlook by the circumstance that in most countries they remained an unofficial minority. Only at Geneva, in the Dutch Netherlands, in Scotland,

This image of John Calvin suggests that his influence among Protestants came from his intellectual rigor as well as his disciplined leadership of the religious reformers in Geneva.
(Snark/Art Resource, NY)

and in New England (and for a few years in England in the seventeenth century) were Calvinists ever able to prescribe the mode of life and religion of a whole country. In England, France, and Germany, Calvinists remained in opposition to the established authorities of church and state and hence were disposed to favor limitations upon established power. In Poland and Hungary many Calvinists were nobles who disliked royal authority.

The Reformation in England

England was peculiar in that its government broke with the Roman church before adopting any Protestant principles. Henry VIII (1509–1547) in fact prided himself on his orthodoxy. When a few obscure persons, about 1520, began to whisper Luther's ideas in England, Henry himself wrote a *Defense of the Seven Sacraments* in refutation, for which a grateful pope conferred

Henry VIII

upon him the title "Defender of the Faith." But the king had no male heir. Recalling the violent anarchy from which the Tudor dynasty had extricated England, and determined as a New Monarch to build up a durable monarchy, he decided that he must remarry in order to have a son. He therefore requested the pope, Clement VII, to annul his existing marriage to Catherine of Aragon. Popes in the past had obliged monarchs in similar situations. The pope now, however, was embarrassed by the fact that Catherine, who objected, was the aunt of the Emperor Charles V, whom the pope was in no position to offend. Henry, not a patient man, drove matters forward. He appointed a new archbishop of Canterbury, repudiated the Roman connection, secured the annulment of his earlier marriage, and married the youthful Anne Boleyn. The fact that only three years later he put to death the unfortunate Anne, and thereafter in quick succession married four more wives, for a total of six, threw considerable doubt on the original character of his motives.

Henry acted through Parliament, believing, as he said, that a king was never stronger than when united with representatives of his kingdom. In 1534 Parliament passed the Act of Supremacy, which declared the English king to be the "Protector and Only Supreme Head of the Church and Clergy of England." All subjects were required, if asked, to take the oath of supremacy acknowledging the religious headship of Henry and rejecting that of the pope. For refusing this oath Sir Thomas More, a statesman and humanist best known as the author of *Utopia,* was executed for treason. He received a somewhat delayed reward four centuries later when the Roman church pronounced him to be a saint. Henry, in the next few years, closed all the monasteries in England, seized the extensive monastic lands, and passed them out to numerous followers. He thus strengthened and reconstituted a landed aristocracy which had been seriously weakened in the Wars of the Roses. The new landed gentry remained firm supporters of the house of Tudor and the English national church, whatever its doctrines.

The Act of Supremacy

It was Henry's intent not to change the doctrines at all. He simply wished to be the supreme head of an English Catholic church. On the one hand, in 1536, he forcibly suppressed a predominantly Catholic rebellion, and, on the other, in 1539, through the Six Articles, required everybody to believe in transubstantiation, the celibacy of the clergy, the need of confession, and a few other test items of Catholic faith and practice. But it proved impossible to maintain this position, for a great many people in England began to favor one or another of the ideas of Continental Reformers, and a small minority were willing to accept the entire Protestant position.

For three decades the government veered about. Henry died in 1547 and was succeeded by his 10-year-old son, Edward VI, the child of his third wife, Jane Seymour. The Protestant party now came to the fore. But Edward died in 1553 and was succeeded by his much older half-sister, Mary, the daughter of Catherine of Aragon and a devout Roman Catholic whose whole life had been embittered by the break with Rome. Mary tried to re-Catholicize England, but she actually made Catholicism more unpopular with the English. In 1554 she married Philip of Spain, who became king of England, though only in name. The English did not like Philip, nor the Spanish, nor the intense Spanish Catholicism that Philip represented. Under Mary, moreover, some three hundred persons were burned at the stake, as heretics, in public mass executions. It was the first (and last) time that such a thing had happened in England, and it set up a wave of horror. In any event, Mary did not live long. She was succeeded in 1558 by Henry's younger daughter, Elizabeth, the child of Anne Boleyn. Whatever Elizabeth's real views in religion might be (she concealed them successfully and was rumored to have none), she could not be a Roman Catholic. For Catholics she was illegitimate and so unable to be queen.

The Church of England

Under Elizabeth the English became Protestant, gradually and in their own way. The Church of England took on a form of its own. Organizationally, it resembled a Lutheran church. It was a state church, for its existence and doctrines were determined by the temporal power, in this case the monarch acting through Parliament. All English subjects were obliged to belong to it, and laws were passed against "recusants," a term used to cover both the Roman Catholics and the more advanced Calvinists who refused to acknowledge it. With the exception of monasteries and certain other church foundations, the Church of England retained the physical possessions, buildings, and internal organization of the medieval church—the bishops and the archbishops, who continued to sit in the House of Lords, the episcopal

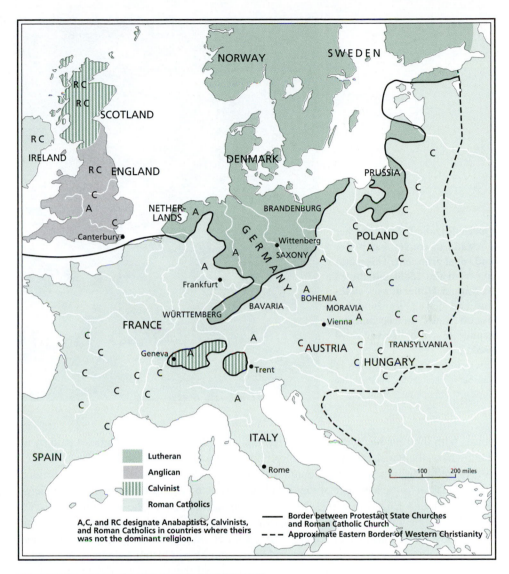

STATE RELIGIONS IN EUROPE ABOUT 1560

This map shows the legally authorized, established churches about 1560, but it does not show the precise distributions of religious communities. Many Catholics lived north of the heavy line, and many Protestants south of it. Most widely dispersed were the Calvinists and the more radical Protestants or Anabaptists. In Germany, under the Holy Roman Empire, each principality and free city chose its own religion; hence, the Germans were the only large European nationality to emerge from the Reformation almost evenly divided between Catholics and Protestants.

Queen Elizabeth I wanted her portraits to convey her power and royal grandeur. This painting from the 1580s, attributed to Nathan Hilliard, uses clothing and jewels to show her wealth and an ornamental ermine to symbolize her royal rank.

(By permission of the Marquess of Salisbury. Photograph: Photographic Survey, Courtauld Institute of Art)

courts with their jurisdiction over marriage and wills, the tithes or church taxes paid by all landowners, the parish structure, the universities of Oxford and Cambridge.

In religious practice, the Church of England was definitely Protestant: English replaced Latin as the language of the liturgy, there was no cult of the saints, and the clergy married, though Elizabeth confessed to some embarrassment at the thought of an archbishop having a wife. In doctrine, it was Elizabeth's policy to make the dogmas broad and ambiguous, so that persons of all shades of belief could be more readily accommodated. The Thirty-nine Articles (1563), composed by a committee of bishops, defined the creed of the Anglican church. In the light of the burning issues of the day many of the articles were evasive, though Protestant in tone. All but one of the Anglican bishops had been newly appointed by Elizabeth at her accession; many had lived in exile among Continental Protestants in the reign of Mary Tudor; and except on the matter of church government through bishops (known as episcopacy) a strong Calvinist impress was set upon Anglican belief in the time of Elizabeth.

The same ecclesiastical settlement was prescribed for Ireland, where English or rather Anglo-Norman conquerors had settled since the twelfth century, shortly after the Norman conquest of England. A replica of the Church of England was now established, called the Church of Ireland, which took over the properties and position of the Roman church. The native Irish, however, remained almost solidly Roman Catholic. As in Hungary or Bohemia people who resented the Habsburgs were likely to turn Protestant rather than share in the ruler's religion, so in Ireland the fact that the ruling English were Protestant only confirmed the Irish in their attachment to the Roman church. The Catholic priests, deprived of status, income, and church buildings, and often in hiding, became national leaders of a discontented people.

The Consolidation of Protestantism by 1560

Neither in England, nor in Germany, nor in international Calvinism were the religious issues regarded as settled in 1560. Nor had the Roman church accepted the new situation. But by 1560 the chief Protestant doctrines had been affirmed, and geographically Protestantism had made many conquests. The institutional unity of Latin Christendom had been broken. A world of separate churches, states, and nations was taking its place.

Protestants differed with one another, yet there was much that all had in common. All rejected the papal authority. None participated in any effective international organization; the ascendancy of Geneva was spiritual only and proved to be temporary. All Protestants rejected the special, sacerdotal, or supernatural character of the priesthood; indeed, the movement was perhaps most fundamentally a revolt against the medieval position of the clergy. Protestants generally called their clergy ministers, not priests. All Protestant clergy could marry. There were no Protestant monks, nuns, or friars. All Protestant churches replaced Latin with the vernacular in religious services—English, French, German, Czech, as the case might be. All Protestants reduced the number of sacraments, usually to two or three; such sacraments as they retained they regarded more as symbols than as actual carriers of divine grace; all believed, in one way or another, in justification by faith. All denied transubstantiation, or the miracle of the Mass. All gave up the obligatory confessional, and with it priestly absolution. All gave up the idea of purgatory as a kind of temporal zone between heaven and hell and hence abandoned the practice of saying prayers and Masses for the dead. It need hardly be added that nothing like indulgences remained. All gave up the cult of the saints and of the Virgin Mary, whose intercession in heaven was no longer expected. All declared that the one true source of Christian belief was the Holy Scripture. And while all established Protestant churches in the sixteenth century insisted on conformity to their own doctrines, allowing no individual freedom, all Protestants still had some small spark of the spirit first ignited by Luther, so that none flatly repudiated the right of private judgment in matters of conscience.

What Protestants held in common

It has sometimes been maintained that one of the motivations in Protestantism was economic—that a new acquisitive, dynamic, capitalistic impulse shook off the restrictions imposed by medieval religion. The fact that Protestant England and Holland soon underwent a rapid capitalistic development gives added credibility to this idea. The alacrity with which Protestant governments confiscated church lands shows a keen material interest; but in truth, both before and after the Reformation, governments confiscated church properties without breaking with the Roman church. That profound economic changes were occurring at the time will become apparent in the following chapter. Yet it seems that economic conditions were far less decisive than religious convictions and political circumstances. Calvinism won followers not only in cities but also in agrarian countries such as Scotland, Poland, and Hungary. Lutheranism spread more successfully in the economically retarded north Germany than in the busy south. The English were for years no more inclined to Protestantism than the French, and in France, while many lords and peasants turned Protestant, Paris and many other towns remained as steadfastly Catholic. It is possible that Protestantism, by casting a glow of religious righteousness over a person's daily business and material prosperity, later contributed to

The ideal Protestant household is represented by an unknown artist in this sixteenth-century Dutch painting of the family of a successful merchant. There are clear divisions between the men, women, and children, but everyone expresses the sobriety and wealth of a prosperous Calvinist community.

(© Rijksmuseum Foundation)

the economic success of Protestant peoples, but it does not seem that the Protestant work ethic or any other economic factors were of any distinctive importance in the first stages of Protestantism.

Protestants and family life

The new religious movements had a more immediate influence on attitudes about marriage and the family. In contrast to medieval Catholicism, which had praised sexual abstinence and celibacy as key traits of the most exalted religious persons, Protestantism strongly promoted marriage as the ideal social institution for clergy and lay people alike. Parenthood became honorable for even the most pious Protestant leaders. Although women sometimes wrote hymns or preached in the more radical Protestant churches, the model Protestant woman was the conscientious mother in a devout, religious household. The opportunities, even if limited, that some women had found in medieval convents and religious communities disappeared in Protestant societies, which may explain why nuns in Protestant territories were often among the last persons to accept the new religious ideas.

Apart from the new emphasis on marriage, however, Protestants did little to change the role of women in Christian churches or in the wider social order. The pastors in Protestant communities were all men, and though more women may have become literate in order to read the Bible, they became less visible in Protestant rituals as the long venerated female saints vanished from prayers, religious writings, and charitable institutions. Meanwhile, women in the convents of Catholic countries were more strictly cloistered and controlled as Catholicism developed its own powerful movements for reform and reorganization.

ꙮ 10.   CATHOLICISM REFORMED AND REORGANIZED

The Catholic movement corresponding to the rise of Protestantism is known as the Catholic Reformation or the Counter Reformation, the former term being preferred by Catholics; the latter by Protestants. Both are applicable. On the one hand the Catholic church underwent a genuine reform, which might have worked itself out in one way or another even if the stimulus of revolutionary Protestantism had been absent. On the other hand the character of the reform, the decisions made, and the measures adopted were shaped by the need of responding explicitly to the Protestant challenge; and certainly, also, there was a good deal of purely "counter" activity aimed at the elimination of Protestantism as such.

The demand for reform was as old as the abuses against which it was directed. Characteristically, it had expressed itself in the demand for a general or ecumenical church council. The conciliar movement, defeated by the popes about 1450, showed signs of revival after 1500. The Lutheran upheaval thus provoked new calls for a general council of the church, and we have seen how Charles V, in the interests of German unity, sought to persuade the pope to assemble an adequately empowered council, which might remove some of the abuses in the church and take away the grounds upon which many Germans were turning to Lutheranism. But meanwhile the king of France found reason to favor the pope and to oppose the emperor. The French king, Francis I (1515–1547), could support the pope because he had obtained from the papacy what he wanted, namely, control over the Gallican church, as acquired in the Concordat of Bologna of 1516. And he had reason to oppose Charles V, because Charles V ruled not only in Germany but also in the Netherlands, Spain, and much of Italy, thus encircling France and threatening Europe with what contemporaries called "universal monarchy." Francis I therefore actively encouraged the Protestants of Germany, as a means of maintaining dissension there, and used his influence at Rome against the calling of a council by which the troubles of the Catholic world might be relieved.

The call for reform

Gradually, in the curia, there arose a party of reforming cardinals who concluded that the need for reform was so urgent that all dangers of a council must be risked. Pope Paul III summoned a council to meet in 1537, but the wars between France and the Empire forced its abandonment. Finally, in 1545, a council assembled and began deliberations. It met at Trent, on the Alpine borders of Germany and Italy. The Council of Trent, which shaped the destiny of modern Catholicism, sat at irregular intervals for almost 20 years. It was not until the Second Vatican Council in the 1960s that some of the main decisions made at Trent were substantially modified.

The Council of Trent

The council was beset by difficulties of a political nature, which seemed to show that under troubled conditions an international council was no longer a suitable means of regulating Catholic affairs. Significantly, it was not well attended. Whereas earlier councils of the church had assembled as many as 500 prelates, the attendance at Trent was never nearly so great; it sometimes fell as low as 20 or 30, and the important decree on "justification," the prime issue raised by Luther, and one on which some good Catholics had until then believed a compromise to be possible, was passed at a session where only 60 prelates were present. Even with the small attendance, the old conciliar issue was raised. A party of bishops believed that the bishops of the Catholic church, when assembled in council from all parts of the Catholic world, collectively constituted an authority superior to that of the pope. To stave off this "episcopal" movement was one of the chief duties of the cardinal legates deputed by the pope to preside over the sessions.

Preserving papal authority

The popes managed successfully to resist the idea of limiting the papal power. In the end they triumphed, through a final ruling voted by the council, that no act of the council should be valid unless accepted by the Holy See. It is possible that had the conciliar theory won out, the Catholic church might have become as disunited in modern times as the Protestant. It was clear, at Trent, that the various bishops tended to see matters in a national way, in the light of their own problems at home, and to be frequently under strong influence from their respective secular monarchs. In any case, the papal party prevailed, which is to say that the centralizing element, not the national, triumphed. The Council of Trent thus preserved the papacy as a center of unity for the Catholic church and helped prevent the very real threat of its dissolution into state churches. Even so, the council's success was not immediate, for in every important country the secular rulers at first accepted only what they chose of its work, and only gradually did its influence prevail.

Questions of national politics and of church politics apart, the Council of Trent addressed itself to two kinds of labors—to a statement of Catholic doctrine and to a reform of abuses in the church. When the council began to meet in 1545, the Protestant movement had already gone so far that any reconciliation was probably impossible: Protestants, especially Calvinists, simply did not wish to belong to the church of Rome under any conditions. In any case, the Council of Trent made no concessions.

The Council of Trent: defining Catholic doctrine

It declared justification to be by works and faith combined. It enumerated and defined the seven sacraments, which were held to be vehicles of grace independent of the spiritual state of those who received them. The priesthood was declared to be a special estate set apart from the laity by the sacrament of holy orders. The procedures of the confessional and of absolution were clarified. Transubstantiation was reaffirmed. As sources of Catholic faith, the council put Scripture and tradition on an equal footing. It thus rejected the Protestant claim to find true faith in the Bible alone and reasserted the validity of church development since New Testament times. The Vulgate, a translation of the Bible into Latin made by St. Jerome in the fourth century, was declared to be the only version on which authoritative teaching could be based. The right of individuals to believe that their own interpretation of Scripture was more true than that of church authorities (private judgment) was denied. Latin, as against the national languages, was prescribed as the language of religious worship—a requirement abolished by the Second Vatican Council in the 1960s. Celibacy of the clergy was maintained. Monasticism was upheld. The existence of purgatory was reaffirmed. The theory and correct practice of indulgences were restated. The veneration of saints, the cult of the Virgin, and the use of images, relics, and pilgrimages were approved as spiritually useful and pious actions.

It was easier for a council to define doctrines than to reform abuses, since the latter consisted in the rooted habits of people's lives. The council decreed, however, a drastic reform of the monastic orders. It acted against the abuse of indulgences while upholding the principle. It ruled that bishops should reside habitually in their dioceses, attend more carefully to their proper duties, and exercise more administrative control over clergy in their own dioceses. The abuse by which one man had held numerous church offices at the same time (pluralism) was checked, and steps were taken to assure that church officials should be competent. To provide an educated clergy, the council ordered that a seminary should be set up in each diocese for the training of priests.

The Counter Crusade

As laws in general have little force unless sustained by opinion, so the reform decrees of the Council of Trent would have remained ineffectual had not a renewed sense of religious seriousness been growing at the same time. Herein lay the inner force of the Catholic Reform. In Italy, as the Renaissance became more undeniably pagan, and as the sack of Rome in 1527 showed the depths of hatred felt even by many Catholics toward the Roman clergy, the *Catholic religious renewal* voices of moralists began to be heeded. The line of Renaissance popes was succeeded by a line of reforming popes, of whom the first was Paul III (1534–1549). The reforming popes insisted on the primacy of the papal office, but they regarded this office, unlike their predecessors, as a moral and religious force. In many dioceses the bishops began on their own initiative to be stricter. The new Catholic religious sense, more than the Protestant, centered in a reverence for the sacraments and a mystical awe for the church itself as a divine institution. Both men and women founded many new religious orders, of which the Jesuits became the most famous. Others were the Oratorians for men and the Ursulines for women. The new orders dedicated themselves to a variety of educational and philanthropic activities. Missionary fervor for a long time was more characteristic of Catholics than of Protestants. It reached into Asia and the Americas, and in Europe expressed itself as an intense desire for the reconversion of Protestants. It showed itself, too, in missions among the poor, as in the work of St. Vincent de Paul among the human wreckage of Paris, for which the established Protestant churches failed to produce anything comparable. In America, as colonies developed in the sixteenth and seventeenth centuries, the Protestant clergy tended to take the layman's view of the Indians, while Catholic clergy labored to convert and protect them; and the Catholic church generally worked to mitigate the brutal treatment of enslaved Africans, to which the pastors in English and Dutch colonies, perhaps because they were more dependent upon the laity, remained largely indifferent.

We have seen how in Spain, where the Renaissance had never taken much hold, the very life of the country was connected to a kind of ongoing Christian crusade. It was in Spain that much of the new Catholic feeling first developed, and from Spain that much of the missionary spirit first went out. Spanish writers produced the most influential sixteenth-century accounts of Catholic mysticism, including Teresa of Avila's famous descriptions of her encounters with Christ. It was also Spain that produced St. Ignatius Loyola (1491–1556). A soldier in youth, he too, like Luther and Calvin, had a religious "experience" or "conversion," which occurred in 1521, before he had heard of Luther and while Calvin was still a boy. Loyola resolved to become a soldier of the church, a militant crusader for the pope and the Holy See. On this principle he established the Society of Jesus, commonly known as the Jesuits. Authorized by Pope Paul III in 1540, the Jesuits constituted a monastic order of a *The Jesuits* new type, less attached to the cloister, more directed toward active participation in the affairs of the world. Only men of proven strength of character and intellectual force were admitted. Each Jesuit had to undergo an arduous and even horrifying mystical training, set forth by Loyola in his *Spiritual Exercises*. The order was ruled by an iron discipline, which required each member to see in his immediate superior the infallibility of the Holy Church.

St. Ignatius Loyola's religious inspiration is portrayed in this painting by Peter Paul Rubens, whose work often represented the religious and political leaders of Catholic countries.
(Giraudon/Art Resource)

If, said Loyola, the church teaches to be black what the eye sees as white, the mind must believe it to be black.

For two hundred years the Jesuits were the most famous schoolmasters of Catholic Europe, eventually conducting some 500 schools for boys of the upper and middle classes. In them they taught, besides the faith, the principles of gentlemanly deportment (their teaching of dancing and dramatics became a scandal to more puritanical Catholics), and they carried over the Renaissance and humanist idea of the Latin classics as the main substance of adolescent education. The Jesuits made a specialty of work among the ruling classes. They became confessors to kings and hence involved in political intrigue. In an age when Protestants subordinated an organized church either to the state or to an individual conscience, and when even Catholics frequently thought of the church within a national framework, the Jesuits seemed almost to worship the church itself as a divine institution, the Church Militant and the Church Universal, internationally organized and governed by the Roman pontiff. All full-fledged Jesuits took a special vow of obedience to the pope. Jesuits in the later sessions of the Council of Trent fought obstinately, and successfully, to uphold the position of Rome against that of the national bishops.

By 1560 the Catholic church, renewed by a deepening of its religious life and by an uncompromising restatement of its dogmas and discipline, had devised also the practical machinery for a counteroffensive against Protestantism. The Jesuits acted as an international missionary force. They recruited members from all countries, including those in which the governments had turned Protestant. English Catholics, for example, trained as Jesuits on the Continent, returned to England to attempt to overthrow the heretic usurper, Elizabeth, seeing in the universal church a higher cause than national independence in religion. Jesuits poured also into the most hotly disputed regions where the religious issue still swayed in the balance—France, Germany, Bohemia, Poland, Hungary. As after every great revolution, many people after an initial burst of Protestantism were inclined to turn back to the old order, especially as the more crying evils within the Catholic church were corrected. The Jesuits reconverted many who thus hesitated.

For the more recalcitrant other machinery was provided. All countries censored books; Protestant authorities labored to keep "papist" works from the eyes of the faithful, and Catholic authorities took the same pains to suppress all knowledge of "heretics." All bishops, Anglican, Lutheran, and Catholic, regulated reading matter within their dioceses. In the Catholic world, with the trend toward centralization under the pope, a special importance attached to the list published by the bishop of Rome, the papal Index of Prohibited Books. Only with special permission, granted to reliable persons for special study, could Catholics read books listed on the Index, which was not abandoned until the 1960s.

All countries, Protestant and Catholic, also set up judicial and police machinery to enforce conformity to the accepted church. In England, for example, Elizabeth established the High Commission to bring "recusants" into the Church of England. All bishops, Protestant and Catholic, likewise possessed machinery of enforcement in their episcopal courts. But no court made itself so dreaded as the Inquisition. In reality two distinct organizations went under this name, the word itself being simply an old term of the Roman law, signifying a court of inquest or inquiry. One was the Spanish Inquisition, established originally, about 1480, to ferret out Jewish and Muslim survivals in Spain. It was then introduced into all countries ruled by the Spanish crown and employed against Protestantism, particularly in the Spanish Netherlands, which was an important center of Calvinism. The other was the Roman or papal Inquisition, established at Rome in 1542 under a permanent committee of cardinals called the Holy Office; it was in a sense a revival of the famous medieval tribunal established in the thirteenth century for the detection and repression of heresy. Both the Spanish and the Roman Inquisitions employed torture, for heresy was regarded as the supreme crime, and all persons charged with crime could be tortured, in civil as well as ecclesiastical courts, under the existing laws. In the use of torture, as in the imposition of the harshest sentence, burning alive, the Roman Inquisition was less severe than the Spanish. The Roman Inquisition in principle offered a court to protect purity of faith in all parts of the Catholic world. But the national resistance of Catholic countries proved too strong; few Catholics wished the agents of Rome inquiring locally into their opinions; and the Roman Inquisition never functioned for any length of time outside of Italy.

Enforcing religious conformity

In the "machinery" of enforcing religious belief, however, no engine was to be so powerful as the apparatus of state. Where Protestants won control of government, people became Protestant. Where Catholics retained control of governments, Protestants became in time small minorities. And it was in the clash of governments, which is to say in war, for about a century after 1560, that the fate of European religion was worked out. In 1560 the strongest powers of Europe—Spain, France, Austria—were all officially Catholic. The Protestant states were all small or at most middle-sized. The Lutheran states of Germany, like all German states, were individually of little weight. The Scandinavian monarchies were far away. England, the most considerable of Protestant kingdoms, was a country of only four million people, with an independent and hostile Scotland to the north, and with no sign of colonial empire yet in existence. In the precedence of monarchs, as arranged in the earlier part of the century, the king of England ranked just below the king of Portugal, and next above the king of Sicily. Clearly, had a great combined Catholic crusade ever developed, Protestantism could have been wiped out. Yet such a crusade, partially launched on various fronts by the king of Spain, never succeeded. Religious divisions became a permanent reality in European culture, contributing eventually, like Renaissance humanism and the new European monarchies, to a gradual secularization of modern societies.

For interactive exercises, glossary, chronologies, and more, go to the *Online Learning Center* at **www.mhhe.com/palmer10.**

Chapter 3

ECONOMIC RENEWAL AND WARS OF RELIGION, 1560–1648

11. The Opening
    of the Atlantic

12. The Commercial
    Revolution

13. Changing Social Structures

14. The Wars of Catholic
    Spain: The Netherlands
    and England

15. The Disintegration and
    Reconstruction of France

16. The Thirty Years' War,
    1618–1648:
    The Disintegration
    of Germany

It is convenient to think of European history in the period following 1560 as the age of the Wars of Religion, which may be said to have ended with the Peace of Westphalia in 1648. France, England, the Netherlands, and the Holy Roman Empire fell into internal and international struggles in which religion was often the most burning issue, but in which political, constitutional, economic, and social questions were also involved. The time of the long, drawn-out conflicts between Catholics and Protestants was also a time of economic renewal. From the beginning of the sixteenth century European society was transformed by contacts with a newly discovered overseas world, by expanded trade routes, an emergent capitalism, and the formation of new social classes.

This was the era in which the modern global economic system began to develop. The effects of these profound changes, however, were obscured and delayed by the politico-religious struggles. In the present chapter we must first examine the geographical discoveries, then survey the broad new economic and social developments under way, and finally trace the impact of the religious wars on various parts of Europe. The wars, as we shall see, left Spain and Germany very much weakened, and opened the way for the English, Dutch, and French to profit from the economic changes and play leading roles in the drama of early modern times.

11. THE OPENING OF THE ATLANTIC

Always until about 1500 the Atlantic Ocean had been a barrier, an end. About 1500 it became a bridge, a starting place. The consequences were enormous for all concerned. In

Chapter emblem: Detail from Jean Bourdichon (1457–1521), *The Four Estates of Society: Work,* which shows a carpenter working with the tools of his craft. (Giraudon/Art Resource, NY)

general, they were favorable for Europeans but devastating for peoples elsewhere—in America through massive depopulation by diseases such as smallpox brought from Europe, in Africa through the transatlantic slave trade, and ultimately in places as far away as Australia through the destruction of long-existing cultures or languages. Older, celebratory accounts of Europe's "overseas discoveries" have therefore been widely challenged in recent decades by historians who approach the story of European expansion from the perspective of Native Americans or African Americans. Viewed from these perspectives, Columbus's first voyage to America in 1492 launched a history of terrible losses rather than a story of heroic European explorations and conquests.

But few would deny that the new, complex association of the Old and New Worlds, as Europeans called them, became a momentous event in human history. The endless migration of people, the worldwide movement of trade, and the disorienting experiences of cross-cultural encounters marked the true beginning of modern global history. Europeans transformed or even destroyed numerous other cultures, but their own culture was also transformed through steadily expanding contacts with other peoples, social traditions, and religions in every part of the world. A new wealthy commercial class grew up in cities along Europe's Atlantic coast. Naval power became decisive. European populations grew with the adoption of the American potato, and people in Europe became dependent on imported commodities such as sugar and tobacco. European writers took increasing pride in their understanding of the world and in what they regarded as the superiority of their own cultural or religious traditions. There was also much speculation on the diversity of the human races and cultures, which sometimes led to a new kind of race consciousness on the part of Europeans and sometimes to a cultural relativism in which European customs were seen as only one variant of human behavior as a whole. Meanwhile, people in the Americas and Africa struggled to defend their own evolving cultures and institutions as European soldiers, traders, and missionaries entered the various civilizations of an increasingly interconnected transatlantic economic system.

Cultural transformation and destruction

The Portuguese in the East

Europeans had skirted their Atlantic coast since prehistoric times. Vikings had settled in Iceland in the ninth century and had even reached North America soon thereafter. In 1317 Venetians had established the Flanders galleys, commercial flotillas that regularly made the passage between the Adriatic and North seas. In the fifteenth century, improvements in shipbuilding, the rigging of sails, and the adoption of the mariner's compass made it feasible to sail on the open ocean out of sight of land. When the Portuguese about 1450 settled in the Azores Islands, in the mid-Atlantic, they found steady westerly winds to assure a safe return to Europe. It seemed that the ocean might even lead to Asia.

For centuries Asia had been a source for Europe of many highly valued commodities, partly manufactures in which Europe could not compete, such as silk and cotton fabrics, rugs, jewelry, porcelains, and fine steel, and partly raw or semimanufactured drugs and foodstuffs, such as sugar and, above all, spices. Europeans had never themselves gone to the sources of supply of Eastern goods. Somewhere, east of Suez, barely known to Europeans, was another world of other merchants who moved the wares of China, India, and the East Indies Spice Islands by caravan over land and by boat through the Red Sea or Persian Gulf to the markets of the eastern Mediterranean. Traders of the two worlds met and did business at such thriving centers as Alexandria or Beirut or Constantinople.

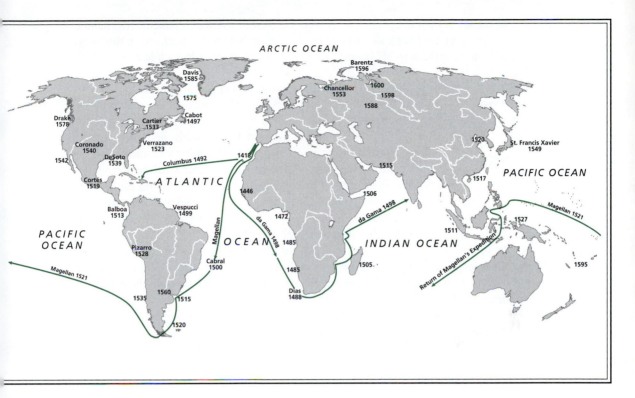

EUROPEAN DISCOVERIES, 1450–1600

Discovery means the bringing of newly found countries within the habitual knowledge or permanent commercial activity of the society from which the discoverer comes. Although sailors and travelers from Asia had long made voyages to distant places and engaged in trade across the Indian Ocean or South Pacific, it was the Europeans who discovered much of the world in the sense indicated here. They did so in the period between 1450 and 1600, using maritime skills and geographical knowledge developed in the Mediterranean and off the Atlantic coast. Dates on the map show the years of first significant European arrival at the points indicated.

In 1498 the Portuguese navigator Vasco da Gama, having rounded Africa in the wake of other intrepid explorers, found himself in the midst of the unknown world of Arab commerce. He landed on the Malabar Coast (the southwest coast of India), where he found a busy commercial population of heterogeneous religious background. These people knew at least as much about Europe as Europeans did about India (one Jew was able to act as da Gama's interpreter), and they realized that the coming of the Portuguese would disturb their established channels of commerce. Da Gama, playing upon local rivalries, was able to load his ships with the coveted wares, but on his second voyage, in 1502, he came better prepared, bringing a fighting fleet of no less than 21 vessels. A ferocious war broke out between the Portuguese and Arab merchants, the latter supported in one way or another by the Egyptians, the Turks, and even the distant Venetians, all of whom had an interest in maintaining the old routes of trade. For the Portuguese, trained like the Spaniards in long wars against the Moors at home, no atrocities were too horrible to commit against the infidel competitors whom they found at the end of their heroic quest. Cities were devastated, ships were burned at their docks, prisoners were butchered, and their dismembered hands, noses, and ears were sent back as derisive trophies. One Brahmin, mutilated in this way, was left alive to bear them to his people. Such, unfortunately, was India's introduction to the West.

In the following years the Portuguese built permanent fortified stations at Goa on the Malabar Coast, at Aden near the mouth of the Red Sea, at Hormuz near the mouth of the Persian Gulf, and in East Africa. In 1509 they reached Malacca, near modern Singapore, from which they passed northward into China itself and eastward to Amboina, the heart of the Spice Islands, just west of New Guinea. Thus an empire was created, the first of Europe's commercial-colonial empires, maintained by superiority of firearms and sea power and with trade alternating with war and plunder. The early European traders were soon followed by bold Jesuits, including St. Francis Xavier, who, by 1550, had baptized thousands of souls in India, Indonesia, and even Japan.

Portuguese trading empire

By the new route the cost of Eastern goods for Europeans was much reduced, for the old route had involved many transshipments, unloadings, and reloadings, movements by sea and by land, through the hands of many merchants. In 1504 spices could be bought in Lisbon for only a fifth of the price demanded in Venice. The Venetians (who in their desperation even talked of digging a Suez canal) were hopelessly undersold: their trade thereafter was confined to products of the Middle East. As for the Portuguese, never was a commercial monopoly built so fast. The lower prices added enormously to European demand and consumption. Beginning in 1504, only five years after da Gama's first return, an average of 12 ships a year left Lisbon for the East.

The Discovery of America

Meanwhile, the same quest for a route to the East had led to the somewhat disappointing discovery of America. Like most such discoveries, this was no chance hit of an isolated genius. Behaim's globe, constructed in 1492, the very year of Columbus's first voyage, suggested that China could be reached by crossing the Atlantic and thus supported the idea of sailing westward to arrive in the East. Nevertheless, it was Christopher Columbus who had the persistence and daring to undertake the unprecedented westward voyage. Before the invention of sufficiently accurate clocks (in the eighteenth century) mariners had no way of determining longitude, that is, their east-west position, and learned geographers greatly underestimated the probable distance from Europe westward to Asia. When Columbus struck land, he naturally supposed it to be an outlying part of the Indies. The people were soon called Indians, and the islands where Columbus landed, the West Indies.

Columbus had sailed with the backing of Queen Isabella of Castile, and the new lands became part of the composite dominions of the crown of Spain. The Spaniards, hoping to beat the Portuguese to the East (which da Gama had not yet reached), received Columbus's first reports with enthusiasm. For his second voyage they gave him 17 ships, filled with 1,500 workmen and artisans. Columbus himself, until his death in 1506, kept probing about in the Caribbean, baffled and frustrated, still believing he had discovered a route to Asia and hoping to find something that looked like the fabulous East. Others were more willing to accept the new land for what it was. Churchmen, powerful in Spain, regarded it as a new field for crusading and conversion. The government saw it as a source of gold and silver for the royal exchequer. Footloose gentry of warlike habits, left

An Episode in the Conquest of America **was painted by the Dutch artist Jan Mostaert about 1545. In this detail from an early European visualization of the New World, the American Indians are seen as naked, helpless, confused, and very different from Europeans.**
(Foto Marburg/Art Resource, NY)

idle by the end of war with the Moors in Iberia, turned to America to make their fortunes. The *conquistadores* fell upon the new lands. Cortés conquered the Aztecs in Mexico; Pizarro, the Incas in Peru. They despoiled the native empires. Mines for precious metals were opened almost immediately. The Indians were put to forced labor, in which many died. The rapid decline in the Indian population, the attempts of the church to protect its Indian converts, and the restrictions set by royal authorities on their exploitation led almost immediately to the importation of African slaves, of whom, it was estimated, 100,000 had been brought to America by 1560. This massive, forced migration of Africans continued for more than two centuries; indeed, the number of enslaved Africans reaching America, including the two continents and the West Indies, was far greater than the number of Europeans who settled there before 1800.

Conquest begins in the Americas

Meanwhile, explorers began to feel their way along the vast American continent that barred them from Asia. A Spanish expedition, led by Magellan, found a southwestern passage in 1520, sailed from the Atlantic into the Pacific, crossed the Pacific, discovered the Philippine Islands, and fought its way through hostile Portuguese across the Indian Ocean back to Spain. The globe was thus

Further explorations

circumnavigated for the first time, and an idea of the true size and interconnection of the oceans was brought back to Europe. Geographical experts immediately incorporated the new knowledge. Europeans still knew little about the vast, newly discovered continents, however, and other explorers sailing for Spain, the Cabots sailing for England, Jacques Cartier for France, began the long and fruitless search for a northwest passage to the Pacific. An English expedition, looking for a northeast passage, discovered the White Sea in 1553. English merchants immediately began to take the ocean route to Russia. Archangel became an ocean port.

For a century it was only the Spanish and Portuguese who followed up the new ocean routes to America and the East. These two peoples, in a treaty of 1494, divided the globe between them by an imaginary north-and-south line that ran from a point in the middle of the North Atlantic Ocean through the north pole and across eastern Asia. Spain claimed all the Americas by this treaty, and Portugal, all rights of trade in Africa, Asia, and the East Indies. But when Brazil was discovered in 1500 by Pedro Cabral, it was found to be far enough east to lie within the Portuguese area, and when the Philippine Islands were discovered by Magellan in 1521, they were claimed to be in the Spanish zone.

In the populous, long-established civilizations of the East the Portuguese were never more than a handful of outsiders who could not impose their language, their religion, or their way of life. It was otherwise in the Americas, where previously unknown diseases such as smallpox decimated the native populations, and where Spanish invaders set about imposing European culture on the weakened and demoralized survivors.

The Spanish Empire in America

In South America, Mexico, and the Caribbean, after the first ferocity of the *conquista,* the Spanish established their own civilization. In Protestant countries, and also in France, as the years went on there arose an extremely unfavorable idea of the Spanish regime in America, where, it was noted, the Inquisition was presently established and the native peoples were reduced to servitude by the conquerors. The Spanish themselves came to dismiss this grim picture as a false legend concocted by their rivals. The true character of the Spanish empire in America is not easy to portray. The Spanish government (like the home governments of all colonial empires) regarded its empire as existing primarily for the benefit of the mother country. The Indians were put into servitude, to work in mines or in agriculture. They also died in large numbers from infections brought by Europeans to which Europeans over past centuries had developed immunities but against which the native American peoples had no such protection. The same was true farther north in what later became the United States. The Spanish government made efforts to moderate the exploitation of Indian labor. It introduced the encomienda, by which Indians were required to work for an owner a certain number of days in the week, while retaining parcels of land on which to work for themselves. How much the royal regulations were enforced on remote encomiendas is another question, to which answers vary. Black African slavery became less important in most of Spanish America than it later became in some of the Dutch, French, and English colonies or in Portuguese Brazil. But the white population remained relatively small. Castilian Spaniards looked down on American-born whites, called Creoles. Since fewer women than men emigrated from Spain, there arose a large class of mestizos, of mixed white and Indian descent.

The mestizos, along with many pure Indians, adopted to a considerable degree the Spanish language and the faith of the Spanish church. The Indians, while unfree, had

Spanish colonial rule

Europeans negotiate with an African chief and his council on the Guinea coast, perhaps for the purchase of slaves. The Europeans have guns while the Africans have only spears, but in contrast to early European images of American Indians the Africans are fully clothed and seated in a dignified manner.
(Photographs and Prints Division, Schomburg Center for Research in Black Culture, The New York Public Library, Astor, Lenox and Tilden Foundations)

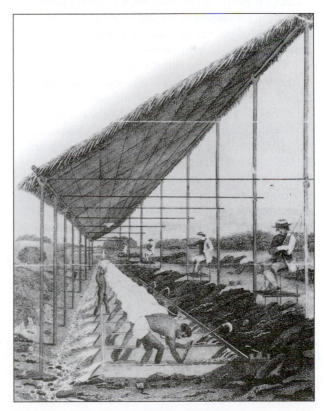

Black slaves are stooped over in a diamond-processing operation in Brazil, while white overseers watch with whips.
(Photographs and Prints Division, Schomburg Center for Research in Black Culture, The New York Public Library, Astor, Lenox and Tilden Foundations)

usually lacked freedom under their own tribal chiefs; they were spared from tribal war; and the rigors of the Inquisition were mild compared with the physical cruelty that many faced under the Aztecs or Incas. The printing press was brought to Mexico in 1544. By the middle of the sixteenth century Spanish America consisted of two great viceroyalties, those of Mexico and Peru, with 22 bishoprics, and with a university in each viceroyalty; the University of Lima was established in 1551, that of Mexico in 1553.

The Potosí silver mines

When Harvard College was founded in New England (in 1636), there were five universities on the European model in Spanish America.

In 1545 a great discovery was made, the prodigiously rich silver deposits at Potosí in Peru. (It is now in Bolivia.) Almost simultaneously, better methods of extracting silver from the ore by the use of mercury were developed. American production of precious metals shot up suddenly and portentously. For years, after the mid-century, 500,000 pounds of silver and 10,000 pounds of gold flowed annually from America to Spain. The riches of Potosí financed the European projects of the king of Spain. Peruvian ores, Indian labor, and Spanish management combined to make possible the militant, anti-Protestant phase of the Counter Reformation.

Meanwhile, beginning in 1565, the Spanish also established a lucrative trade route between their colonies in Mexico and the Philippines. Large ships called the "Manila Galleons" carried vast cargoes of silver from Acapulco to Manila, where the silver was traded for Chinese luxury goods—spices, porcelain, silks, and ivory—all of which were transported back to Mexico and on to Europe. This valuable trade continued until the early nineteenth century. It carried perhaps a third of all the silver extracted from Spain's American colonies off to Asia; and it helped to create the first modern global network for commercial exchange, in part because it brought Chinese consumers the only commodity that they wanted to buy from Europeans during this era. Silver from New World mines therefore sustained the whole Asian-American-European trading system and enabled Spain to control much of the burgeoning global market for Chinese products.

The opening of the Atlantic thus reoriented Europe. In an age of oceanic communications Europe became a center from which America, Africa, and Asia could all be reached. In Europe itself, the Atlantic coast enjoyed great advantages over the center. No sooner did the Portuguese begin to bring spices from the East Indies than Antwerp began to flourish as the point of redistribution for northern Europe. But for a century after the Spanish and Portuguese began to build their empires, the northern peoples did not take to the oceans. French corsairs did indeed put out from Bayonne or Saint-Malo, and Dutch prowlers and English "sea dogs" followed at the close of the century, all bent upon plundering the Iberian treasure ships. Still the Spanish and Portuguese kept their monopoly. No organized effort, backed by governments, came from the north until about 1600. For it is by no means geography alone that determines economic development; the English, Dutch, and French could not make use of the opportunities with which the opening of the Atlantic provided them until they had cleared up their domestic troubles and survived the perils and hazards of the Wars of Religion.

12.   THE COMMERCIAL REVOLUTION

Population growth

In the great economic readjustment that was taking place in Europe, the opening of ocean trade routes was important, but it was by no means the only factor. Two others were the growth of population and a long, gradual rise in prices, or a slow inflation.

The Spaniards stamped out much of the Indian religion as idolatrous, yet it is to Spanish priests that we owe the preservation of much of our knowledge of the pre-Conquest culture. This page is from a book in which a Spaniard wrote down the Aztec language in the Latin alphabet. A human sacrifice is also depicted.
(Scala/Art Resource, NY)

European population again grew rapidly, as in the High Middle Ages, reaching about 90 million in 1600, of which 20 million represented the growth during the sixteenth century. The increase took place in all countries, though the distribution was quite different from the population increases in more recent times. England in 1600 had no more than five million inhabitants. France had almost four times as many, and the German states altogether about as many as France. Italy and Spain had fewer than France, and distant Russia, within its then boundaries, may have had no more than 10 million people. Some cities grew substantially, with London and Paris approaching 200,000; Antwerp, Lisbon, and Seville, thanks to the ocean trade, jumped to 100,000 by 1600. But smaller towns remained much the same; Europe as a whole was probably no more urbanized than in the later Middle Ages. Most of the population growth represented increasing density in the rural regions.

The steady rise in prices, which is to say the steady decline in value of a given unit of money (such as a shilling), constituted a gradual inflation. It has been called a "price revolution," but it was so slow as to be hardly comparable to the kinds of inflation known in some modern societies. One cause seems to have emerged from the growth of population itself, which set up an increasing demand for food. This meant that new land was brought under cultivation, land that was less fertile, more inaccessible or more difficult to work than the fields that had been cultivated previously. With increasing costs of production, agricultural prices

The price revolution

The silver mines at Potosí, portrayed here in a late sixteenth-century illustration, sent over 500,000 pounds of silver to Spain every year. American precious metals and the labor of American Indians enabled the Spanish government to wage its costly European wars and to maintain a lucrative trade with Chinese merchants in Asia.
(Courtesy of The Hispanic Society of America, New York)

rose; in England, for example, they about quadrupled during the sixteenth century. Prices were also pushed upward by the increase in the volume of money. The royal habit of debasing the currency brought a larger amount of money into circulation, since larger numbers of florins, *reals,* or *livres* were obtained from the same amount of bullion. The flow of gold and silver from America also made money more plentiful, but the impact of Peruvian and Mexican mines can easily be exaggerated. Even before the discovery of America, the development of gold and silver mines had augmented the European money supply. Although the expansion of both population and commerce checked the inflationary forces, the long trend of prices was upward. It affected all prices, including rents and other payments that were set in money values, but the price of hired labor, that is, wages, rose the least. The price changes thus had different effects on the well-being of social classes.

Commercial undertakings were favored by the rising prices and growing population. Merchants could count on increasing numbers of customers, new people could enter trade with hope of success, stocks of goods rose in value with the passage of time, and borrowed money could more easily be repaid. Governments benefited also, so far as kings could count on having more taxpayers and more soldiers.

The economic changes in Europe in the early modern period have been called the "Commercial Revolution," signifying the rise of a capitalistic economy and the transition from a town-centered to a nation-centered economic system. This "revolution" was an exceptionally slow and protracted one; it began at least as early as the fourteenth century and lasted until machine industry began to overshadow commerce in the early nineteenth century.

Changes in Commerce and Production

In the Middle Ages the town and its adjoining country formed an economic unit. Craftsmen, organized in guilds, produced common articles for local use. Peasants and lords sold their agricultural products to the local town, from which they bought what the craftsmen produced. The town protected itself by its own tariffs and regulations. In the workshop the master both owned his "capital"—his house, workbench, tools, and materials—and acted as a workman himself along with half a dozen journeymen and apprentices. The masters owned a modest capital, but they were hardly capitalists. They produced only upon order, or at least for customers whose tastes and number were known in advance. There was little profit, little risk of loss, and not much innovation.

All this changed with the widening of the trading area, or market. Even in the Middle Ages, as we have seen, there was a certain amount of long-distance trading in articles that could not be produced as well in one place as in another. Gradually more articles came within this category. Where goods were produced to be sold at some time in the future, in faraway places, to persons unknown, the local guildmaster could not manage the operation. He lacked the money (or "capital") to tie up in stocks of unsold wares; he lacked the knowledge of what distant customers wanted, or where, in what quantities, and at what price people would buy. In this new type of long-distance business, new kinds of entrepreneurs became prominent in European commercial life. They usually started out as merchants working *New entrepreneurs* in an extensive market and ended up as bankers. The Italian Medici family has been mentioned as important in Renaissance banking and culture. Equally typical were the German Fuggers.

The first of this family, Johann Fugger, a small-town weaver, came to Augsburg in 1368. He established a business in a new kind of cloth, called fustian, in which cotton was mixed, and which had certain advantages over the woolens and linens in which people then clothed themselves. He thus enjoyed a more than local market. Gradually the family began to deal also in spices, silks, and other Eastern goods obtained at Venice. They invested their large profits in other enterprises, notably mining. They lent money to the Renaissance popes. They lent Charles V the money which he spent to obtain election as Holy Roman Emperor in 1519. They became bankers to the Habsburgs in both Germany and Spain. Together with other German and Flemish bankers, the Fuggers financed the Portuguese trade with Asia, either by outright loans or by providing in advance, on credit, the cargoes which the Portuguese traded for spices. The wealth of the Fuggers became proverbial and declined only through repeated Habsburg bankruptcies and with the general economic decline that beset Germany in the sixteenth century.

Other dealers in cloth, less spectacular than the first Fugger, broke away from the town-and-guild framework in other ways. England until the fifteenth century was an exporter of raw wool and an importer of finished woolens from Flanders. In the fifteenth century certain English entrepreneurs began to develop the spinning, weaving, and dyeing of wool in England. To avoid the restrictive practices of the towns and guilds they "put out" the work to people in the country, providing them with looms and other equipment for the purpose, of which they generally *The "putting out"* retained the ownership themselves. This "putting out" or "domestic" sys- *system* tem spread very widely outside the guild system, and, by the early modern period, typically depended on a gendered division of labor. Women usually did the work of spinning wool into thread (hence the later English term for an unmarried woman, "spinster"); men usually wove the thread into cloth. In France the cloth dealers of Rouen, feeling the competition of the new silk trade, developed a lighter, cheaper, and more simply made type of woolen cloth. Various guild regulations in Rouen, to protect the workers there, prohibited the manufacture of this cheaper cloth. The Rouen dealers, in 1496, took the industry into the country, installed looms in peasant cottages, and farmed out the work to the peasants.

STUDY OF TWO BLACK HEADS
by Rembrandt van Rijn (Dutch, 1606–1669)

One consequence of the new international trade was the transportation of enslaved black Africans to the Americas. Some Africans appeared also in Europe, where their presence contributed to the growing speculation on the diversity of the human races. Rembrandt, though he never traveled more than 20 miles from his native Leyden, painted all types of people who streamed into the Netherlands, including these two men who had to cope with the strange European world into which they had been cast.

(Maurithshuis, The Hague)

Capital and Labor

The system of rural household industry remained typical of production in many lines (cloth, hardware, etc.) in western Europe until the introduction of factories in the late eighteenth century. It signified a new divergence between capital and labor. On the one hand were the workers, men and women who worked as the employer needed them, received wages for what they did, and had little interest in or knowledge of more than their own task. Living both by agriculture and by cottage industry, they formed an expansible labor force, available when labor was needed, left to live by farming or local charity when times were bad. On the other hand was the manager or entrepreneur (almost always a man) who directed the whole affair. He had no personal acquaintance with the workers. Estimating how much of his product, let us say woolens, he could sell in a national or even international market, he purchased the needed raw materials, passed out wool to be spun by one group of peasants, took the yarn to another group for weaving, collected the cloth and took it still elsewhere to be dyed, paying wages on all sides for services rendered, while retaining ownership of the materials and the equipment and keeping the coordination and management of the whole enterprise in his own head. Much larger business enterprises could be established in this way than within the municipal framework of guild and town. Indeed, the very master weavers of the guilds often sank to the status of subcontractors, hardly different from wage employees, of the great "clothiers" and "drapers" by whom the business was dominated. The latter, with the widening market, became personages of national or even international repute. And, of course, the bigger the business the more of a capital investment it represented.

Divergence between capital and labor

Certain other industries, new or virtually new in the fifteenth and sixteenth centuries, could by their nature never fit into a town-centered system and were capitalistic from the start, in that they required a large initial outlay before any income could be received. One such was mining. Another was printing and the book trade. Books had a national and even international market, being mainly in Latin; and no ordinary craftsman could afford the outlay required for a printing press, for fonts of type, supplies of paper, and stocks of books on hand. Printers therefore borrowed from capitalists or shared with them an interest in business. Shipbuilding was so stimulated by the shift to the oceans as almost to be a new industry, and still another was the manufacture of cannons and muskets. For the latter the chief demand came from the state, from the New Monarchies which were organizing national armies. In the rise of capitalism the needs of the military were in fact fundamentally important. Armies, which started out by requiring thousands of weapons, in the seventeenth century required thousands of uniforms, and in the eighteenth century many new barracks and fortifications. These heavy demands were the first to require mass production. Where governments themselves did not take the initiative, private middlemen stepped in as links to the many small handicraft workers and families who before the industrial age still manufactured the actual product.

New industries

The new sea route to the East and the discovery of America brought a vast increase in trade not only of luxury items but of bulk commodities like rice, sugar, tea, and other consumer goods. Older commercial activities were transformed by the widening of markets. Spain increasingly drew cereals from Sicily. The Netherlands were fed from Poland; the French wine districts lived on food brought from northern France. With the growth of shipping, the timber, tar, pitch, and other "naval stores" of Russia and the Baltic entered the commercial scene. There was thus an ever-growing movement of heavy staple commodities, in which again only persons controlling large funds of capital could normally take part.

The growing production of cloth in early modern Europe depended on the labor of families in rural cottage industries. Spinning thread became an important economic activity for many women, as Jean Bourdichon (1457–1521) demonstrates in this illustration of a family at work. The man is apparently a skilled woodworker, and the child is gathering wood chips that can be used for cooking food or heating the house. The solid walls and ceiling show that this is a prosperous, hard-working family.
(Giraudon/Art Resource, NY)

Not all capital was invested; some was simply lent to the church, to governments, to impecunious nobles, or, though perhaps this was the least common type of lending in the sixteenth century, to persons engaged in trade and commerce. Bankers and others who lent money expected to receive back, after a time, a larger sum than that of the loan. They expected "interest"; and they sometimes received as much as 30 percent a year. In the Middle Ages the taking of interest had been frowned upon as usury, denounced as avarice, and forbidden in the canon law. It was still frowned upon in the sixteenth century by almost all but the lenders themselves. The Catholic church maintained its prohibitions. The theologians of the University of Paris also ruled against it in 1530. Luther, who hated bankers like the Fuggers, continued to preach against usury. Calvin made allowances, but as late as 1640, in capitalist Holland itself, the stricter Calvinist ministers still denounced lending at interest.

New banking practices

Nothing could stop the practice. Borrowers compounded with lenders to evade prohibitions, and theologians of all churches began to distinguish between "usury" and a "legitimate return." Gradually, as interest rates fell, as banking became more established, and as loans were made for economically productive uses rather than to sustain ecclesiastics, princes, and nobles in their personal habits, the feeling against a "reasonable" interest died down and interest became an accepted feature of capitalism. The Bank of Amsterdam, for example, attracted depositors because they knew their money was safe, would earn interest, and could be withdrawn at will. Deposits thus flowed into the bank from all countries and enabled it to make low-interest loans that financed new commercial activities.

The net effect of all these developments was a "commercialization of industry." The dynamic, entrepreneurial persons in commercial life were the merchants. Industry, the actual processes of production, still in an essentially handicraft stage, was subordinate to the buyers and sellers. Pro- *Commercial capitalism* ducers—spinners, weavers, hatters, metalworkers, gunsmiths, glasswork- ers—worked to fill the orders of the merchants, and often with capital which the merchants supplied and owned. The entrepreneur who knew where the article could be sold prevailed over the person who simply knew how to produce it. This commercial capitalism remained the typical form of capitalism until after 1800, when, with the introduction of power machinery, it yielded to industrial capitalism, and merchants became dependent on indus- trialists who owned, understood, and organized the machines.

Mercantilism

There was still another aspect of the commercial revolution, namely, the various govern- ment policies that go historically under the name of "mercantilism." Rulers, as we have seen, were hard pressed for money and needed more of it as it fell in value. The desire of kings and their advisers to force gold and silver to flow into their own kingdoms was one of the first impulses leading to mercantilist regulation. Gradually this "bullionist" idea was replaced by the more general idea of building up a strong and self-sufficient economy. The means adopted, in either case, was to "set the poor on work," as they said in England, to turn the country into a hive of industry, to discourage idleness, begging, vagabondage, and unemployment. New crafts and manufactures were introduced, and favors were given to merchants who provided work for "the poor" and who sold the country's products abroad. It was thought desirable to raise the export of finished goods and reduce the export of unprocessed raw materials, to curtail all imports except of needed raw materials, and thus obtain a "favorable" balance of trade so that other countries would have to pay their debts in bullion. Since all this was done by a royal or nationwide system of regulations, mercan- tilism became in the economic sphere what the state building of the New Monarchies was in the political, signifying the transition from town to national units of social living.

Mercantilists frowned upon the localistic and conservative outlook of *Opposition to guilds* the guilds. In England the guilds ceased to have importance. Parliament, in the time of Elizabeth, did on a national scale what guilds had once done locally when it enacted the Statute of Artificers of 1563, regulating the admission to apprenticeship and level of wages in various trades. In France the royal government main- tained the legal existence of the guilds, because they were convenient bodies to tax, but it deprived them of most of their old independence and used them as organizations through which royal control of industry could be enforced. In both countries the government assisted merchants who wished to set up domestic or cottage industry in the country, against the protests of the town guilds, which in their heyday had forbidden rural people to engage in crafts. Governments generally tried to suppress idleness. The famous English Poor Law of 1601 (which remained in effect, with amendments, until 1834) was designed both to force people to work and to relieve absolute destitution.

Governments likewise took steps to introduce new industries. The silk industry was brought from Italy to France under royal protection, to the dismay of French woolen and linen interests. The English government assisted in turning England from a producer of raw wool into a producer of finished woolens, supervising the immigration of skilled Flemish weavers and even fetching from faraway Turkey, about 1582, two youths who understood the more advanced dyeing arts of the Middle East. Generally, under mercantilism, governments fought to steal skilled workers from each other while prohibiting or discouraging the emigration of their own skilled workers, who might take their trade secrets and "mysteries" to foreign parts.

National markets

By such means governments helped to create a national market and an industrious nationwide labor supply for their great merchants. Without such government support the great merchants, such as the drapers or clothiers, could never have risen and prospered. The same help was given to merchants operating in foreign markets. Henry VII of England in 1496 negotiated a commercial treaty with Flanders; and in the next century the kings of France signed treaties with the Ottoman Empire by which French merchants obtained privileges in the Middle East. A merchant backed by a national monarchy was in a much stronger position than one backed merely by a city, such as Augsburg or Venice. This backing on a national scale was again given when national governments subsidized exports, paying bounties for goods whose production they wished to encourage, or when they erected tariff barriers against imports to protect their own producers from competition. Thus a national tariff system was superimposed on the old network of provincial and municipal tariffs. These latter were now thought of as "internal tariffs," and mercantilists usually wished to abolish them to create an area of free trade within the state as a whole. But local interests were so strong that for centuries they were unable to get rid of local tariffs except in England.

In distant parts of the world, or in less accessible regions nearer home, such as the Muslim lands or Russia, it was not possible for individual European merchants to act by merely private initiative. Merchants trading with such countries needed a good deal of capital, they often had to obtain special privileges and protection from native rulers, and they had to arm their ships against Barbary or Malay pirates or against hostile Europeans. Merchants and their respective governments came together to found official companies for the transocean trade. In England, soon after the English discovery of the White Sea in 1553, a Russia Company was established. A Turkey Company soon followed. Shortly after 1600 a great many such companies were operating out of England, Holland, and France. The most famous of all were the East India Companies, which the English founded in 1600, the Dutch in 1602, the French not until 1664. Each of these companies was a state-supported organization with special rights. Each was a monopoly in that only merchants who belonged to the company could legally engage in trade in the region for which the company had a charter. Each was expected to find markets for the national manufactures, and most of them were expected to bring home gold or silver. With these companies the northern European peoples began to encroach on the Spanish and Portuguese monopoly in America and the East. With them new commercial-colonial empires were to be launched. But, as has been already observed, before this could happen it was necessary for certain domestic and purely European conflicts and controversies to be settled.

13.   CHANGING SOCIAL STRUCTURES

Social structure, for present purposes, refers to the composition, functions, and interrelationships of social classes. Because changes in social structure are slow, they are hard to identify with any particular period of time. In general, however, with the effects of the commercial revolution, population growth, and the falling value of money, the classes of

The headquarters of the Dutch East India Company in Bengal in 1665, long before the British gained predominance there. It is wholly walled off from the Indian life around it, with offices, living quarters, and spacious gardens for employees of the company.
(© Rijksmuseum, Amsterdam)

Europe, broadly defined, took on forms that were to last until the industrial era of the nineteenth and twentieth centuries. These classes were the landed aristocracy, the peasantry or mass of agricultural workers, the miscellaneous middle classes, and the urban poor.

While all prices rose in the sixteenth century, it was agricultural prices that rose the most. Anyone who had agricultural products to sell was likely to benefit. Among such beneficiaries were peasants who held bits of land in return for payments to a manorial lord set in unchangeable sums of money, in the old values of the fourteenth or even thirteenth century. The price inflation of the sixteenth century enabled such peasants in effect to pay much less to the lord than in the past. Other rural workers, however, either held no land of their own or produced only at a subsistence level with nothing to sell in the market. Such peasants, and hired hands dependent on wages, found their situation worsened. Village life became less egalitarian than it had been in the Middle Ages. In England a class of small freeholders (the "yeomanry") developed between the landed gentry and the rural poor. On the Continent, at least in France, western Germany, and the Netherlands, some peasants acquired more secure property rights, resembling those of small freeholders in England. But both in England and on the Continent a large class of unpropertied rural workers remained in poverty.

Small freeholders

Land rents went up as agricultural prices rose, and inflation and population growth drove up rentals for housing in the towns. Owners of real property (that is, land and buildings) were favored by such changes, but within the former class of feudal lords the effects were mixed. If one's great-grandfather had let out land in earlier times in exchange for fixed sums of money, the value of the income received had actually declined. But those who received payments in kind from their tenants, for example, in bushels of wheat or barley, or who managed their estates themselves, could sell their actual agricultural products at current prices and so increase their money income.

Social Classes

The former feudal class, or nobles, thus turned into a more modern kind of aristocracy. If income from their estates declined, they sought service in the king's army or government or appointment to the more prestigious offices in the church. If landed income increased, they were more wealthy. In either case they became more concerned with civilian pursuits and were likely to develop more refined tastes and pay more attention to the education of their children. Like the peasants, the landowning class became more heterogeneous, ranging from the small gentry to the great peers of England and from small or impoverished nobles to the *grands seigneurs* of France. Some led a life of leisure; others were eager to work in the higher reaches of organized government. The most impoverished nobles sometimes had the longest pedigrees. As their social functions changed, and as persons of more recent family background competed for education, government employment, and even military service, there came to be an increasing importance set upon ancestry as a badge of status. Among the upper class, there was more insistence on high birth and distinguished forebears in the seventeenth and eighteenth centuries than there had been before. But many nobles also claimed that they deserved special privileges because they contributed meritorious service to kings or the expanding national governments.

The bourgeoisie

Below the aristocracy were the "middle classes," or "bourgeoisie." *Bourgeois* was a French word, which, like the English "burgher," originally meant a person living in a chartered town or borough and enjoying its liberties. The bourgeoisie was the whole social class made up of individual bourgeois. In a much later sense of the word, derived from Karl Marx, the term "bourgeoisie" was applied to the class of owners of capital. This Marxist concept of the bourgeoisie must be kept distinct from the meaning of the word in an earlier era. "Bourgeoisie" referred in preindustrial times to the middle levels of society between the aristocracy, which drew its income from land, and the laboring poor, who depended on wages or charity, or who often went hungry. Class lines tended to blur as aristocratic families formed the habit of living in towns and middle-class burghers began to buy land in the country. Some bourgeois thus came to live on landed rents, while some of the gentry and aristocracy, most notably in England, bought shares in the great overseas trading companies or engaged in other forms of business enterprise. Aristocrats possessing large agricultural estates, timberlands, or mines increasingly brought their products to market to be sold at a profit. But even when aristocrat and bourgeois became economically more alike, a consciousness of social difference between them remained.

Middle class growth and diversity

The middle class became more numerous in the sixteenth century, and increasingly so thereafter. It was an indefinite category, since the countries of Europe were very different in the size and importance of their middle classes, in the kinds of persons who belonged to them, and in the types of occupations pursued. Near the top were the urban elites who governed the towns; they might draw their incomes from rural property, from commerce, or from the emoluments of government itself, and they sometimes intermarried with persons of noble status. Especially where the towns were strong or royal government was weak, as in the Netherlands, the German free cities, or north Italy, such urban patriciates formed virtual aristocracies in themselves. But in a larger perspective the families of merchants, bankers, and shipowners were middle-class, as were those of the traditional learned professions, law and medicine. So in general were judges, tax officials, and other employees of governments, except in the highest ranks. In the professions and in government service the younger sons of the aristocracy might be found alongside the offspring of the middle classes, most commonly in England, less so in France, and even less as one moved into Germany or Spain.

The clergy was drawn from all classes; there were poor parish priests, who might be the sons of peasants, and noblemen among the bishops and abbots; but the bulk of the clergy was recruited from middle-class families. In Protestant countries, where the clergy married, their sons and daughters became an important element in the middle class. Members of trade guilds were middle class, though the guilds differed widely in social status, from those of the great wholesale merchants or the goldsmiths, down through the guilds of such humble occupations as the tanners and barrel makers. At the bottom the middle class faded into the world of small retail shopkeepers, innkeepers, owners of workshops in which ordinary articles were manufactured by hand, the lesser skilled tradespeople, and their employees, journeymen, and apprentices.

The mass of the population in all countries was composed of the work-ing poor. These included not only the unskilled wage laborers but the unemployed, unemployable, and paupers, with a large fringe that turned to *The working class poor* vagabondage and begging. They were unable to read or write and were often given to irregular habits which distressed both middle-class persons and government officials. The efforts of mercantilist governments to put the poor to work, or make them contribute to the wealth of the country, have already been mentioned. Charitable relief also developed toward the end of the sixteenth century, as shown in the English Poor Law of 1601 and in similar efforts on the Continent. The idea gained ground that begging was a public nuisance and that the poor should be segregated in workhouses or hospices from the rest of society. Most of the poor were of course not recipients of such relief. They were the people who tilled the fields, tended the livestock, dug in the mines, or went to sea as fishermen and common sailors. They also found work in the towns as casual laborers, porters, water carriers, or removers of excrement; or they entered the domestic service of noble and upper middle-class families, whose rising standard of living required a growing number of chambermaids, cooks, washerwomen, footmen, lackeys, coachmen, and stable boys. Domestic service was in fact the most common job for women during the entire period of early modern history, and the pay for such work remained extremely low. Wages rose less than prices in the sixteenth century. The poor, if not positively worse off than in former times, gained the least from the great commercial developments with which economic history is usually concerned. The very growth of social differentiation, the fact that the middle and upper classes made such advances, left the condition of the poor correspondingly worse.

Social Roles of Education and Government

Education in the latter part of the sixteenth century took on an altogether new importance for the social system. One consequence of the Reformation, in both Protestant and

Catholic countries, was the attempt to put a serious and effective pastor in each parish. This set up a demand for a more educated clergy. The growth of commerce made it necessary to have literate clerks and agents. Governments wanted men from both the noble and middle classes who could cooperate in large organizations, be reliable, understand finance, keep records, and draft proposals. There was also a widespread need for lawyers.

New schools and universities

The new demand for education was met by an outburst of philanthropy, which reached a high point in both England and France between about 1580 and 1640. Many endowed scholarships were established. At what would now be called a secondary level, hundreds of "grammar schools" were founded at this time in England. In France the *collèges* combined the work of the English grammar school with what corresponded to the first year or two of university work at Oxford or Cambridge. Of the 167 most important French colleges still existing at the time of the Revolution in 1789, only 36 had been founded in the centuries before 1560, and 92 were established in the years between 1560 and 1650. Provision for girls' schools was more sporadic, but the Ursuline sisters, for example, founded in Italy in 1535, had established about 350 convents by the year 1700 in Catholic Europe and even in Canada, in most of which the education of girls was a principal occupation of the sisters.

Dutch and Swiss Protestants founded the universities of Leyden and Geneva. New universities, both Protestant and Catholic, appeared in Germany. In Spain the multiplication of universities was phenomenal. Castile, with only 2 universities dating from the Middle Ages, had 20 by the early seventeenth century; Salamanca was enrolling over 5,000 students a year. Five universities also existed in Spanish America by 1600. In England, new colleges were founded at Oxford and Cambridge, and it was especially in these years that some of the Oxford and Cambridge colleges became very wealthy. Annual freshman admissions at Oxford, barely 100 in 1550, rose to over 500 in the 1630s, a figure not exceeded, or even equaled, during the following two hundred years.

Wider access to education

The schools, colleges, and universities drew their students from a wide range of social classes. For girls less organized schooling was offered, but an intelligent and lucky boy of poor family had perhaps a better chance for education than at any time in Europe until very recently. In Spain most of the students seem to have been lesser nobles, or "hidalgos," aspiring to positions in the church or government; but hidalgos were very numerous in Spain, overlapping with what might be called the middle class in other countries. The French colleges, including those operated by the Jesuits, recruited their students very widely, taking in the sons of nobles, merchants, shopkeepers, artisans, and even, more rarely, of peasants. English grammar schools did likewise; it was in later times that a few of them, like Eton and Harrow, became more exclusive Public Schools. As for universities, we have detailed knowledge for Oxford, which recorded the status of its students at matriculation, classifying them as "esquires," "gentlemen," "clergy," and "plebeians." From 1560 to 1660 about half of the Oxford students were "plebeians," which in the language of that time could embrace the whole middle class from big merchants down to quite modest levels. It seems certain that Oxford and Cambridge were more widely representative of the English people in 1660 than in 1900.

Government and social classes

Social classes were formed not only by economic forces, and not only by education, but also by the action of governments. Government could inhibit economic growth, as in Spain, or promote it, as in England. Kings contributed to the rise of capitalism and a business class by granting

A seventeenth-century monk is teaching in Spain at the University of Salamanca, one of the largest European universities of the time and an example of how such institutions expanded in both Catholic and Protestant countries during the century after the Protestant Reformation.
(Index/Bridgeman Art Library)

monopolies, borrowing from bankers, and issuing charters to trading companies. In many countries, and notably in France, many families owed their middle-class position to the holding of government offices, some of which might become a form of inheritable property. It might also be the action of governments, as much as economic conditions, that defined or promoted distinctions between nobles and commoners, or "privileged" and "unprivileged" classes. Where peasants suffered heavily from royal taxes, it was more from political than from economic causes. The king, by "making" nobles—that is, by conferring titles of nobility on persons who did not inherit them—could raise a few in the middle class to higher status. Tax exemption could be a sign of high social standing. The king was also the fountain of honor, at the top of "society." The royal court formed the apex of a pyramid of social rank, in which each class looked up to or down upon the others. Those favored with the royal presence disdained the plain country nobility, who sniffed at the middle classes, who patronized or disparaged the hired servants, day laborers, and the poor. Looking upward, people were expected to show deference for their betters.

Eastern and Western Europe

One other remark may be made on social structure. It was in the sixteenth century that important social differences developed between eastern and western Europe. In the west, the changes brought by the commercial revolution were advantageous to the middle class and to many of the peasantry for whom the old burdens of the manorial system were lightened. In eastern Europe, it was the lords who benefited from rising prices and the growing market for grain and forest products. Here too the institution of the manor existed; but the peasants' land tenures were more precarious than in the west, more dependent on accidents of death or on the wishes of the lord, and the lord worked a larger part of the manor with his own workforce for his own use or profit.

The rise of prices and expansion of Baltic shipping gave the lord the incentive to increase his output. In northeast Germany (where such lords were called Junkers), in Poland, and as time went on in Russia, Bohemia, and Hungary, beginning in the sixteenth century and continuing into the eighteenth, a vast process set in by which the mass of the

Serfdom in eastern Europe

peasantry sank into serfdom. It was hastened in many regions by the violence and insecurity engendered by the religious wars. Typically, peasants lost their individual parcels of land or received them back on condition that they render unpaid labor services to the lord. Usually peasants owed three or four days a week of such forced labor (called *robot* in Bohemia and adjoining territories), remaining free to work during the remainder of the week on their own parcels. Often the number of days of *robot* exacted by the lord was greater, since in eastern Europe, where central monarchy was weak and centralized legal systems were almost unknown, the lord himself was the final court of appeal for his people. His people were in fact his "subjects."

Serfdom in Germany was not called serfdom, but "hereditary subjection." By whatever name they were known throughout eastern Europe, serfs, or hereditary subjects of the manorial lord, could not leave the manor, marry, or learn a trade without the lord's express permission. The lord, drawing on this large reserve of compulsory labor, using most of it for agriculture but teaching some quick-minded youths the various handicrafts that were needed on the estate, worked the land as his own venture, sold the produce, and retained the profit.

Thus, in eastern Europe at the beginning of modern times, the rural masses lost personal freedom and lived in a poverty unknown among the peasants to the west, poor as the latter were. In western Europe there were peasants who were already on the way to becoming small proprietors. They were free people under the law. They could migrate, marry, and learn trades as opportunity offered. Those who held land could defend it in the royal courts and raise crops and take part in the market economy on their own account. They owed the lord no forced labor—or virtually none, for the ten days a year of corvée still found in parts of France hardly compared with the almost full-time *robot* of the peasant of eastern Europe.

The landlord in the east, from the sixteenth century onward, was solidly entrenched in his own domain, monarch of all he surveyed, with no troublesome bourgeoisie to annoy him (for towns were few), and with kings and territorial rulers solicitous of his wishes. Travelers from the west were impressed with the wealth of great Polish and Lithuanian magnates, with their palatial homes, private art galleries, well-stocked libraries, collections of jewels, gargantuan dinners, and lavish hospitality. The Junkers of northeast Germany lived more modestly, but enjoyed the same kind of independence and social superiority.

The growing power of wealthy landlords and the weakening position of impoverished peasants would have decisive social and political consequences for the later history of Prussia, Poland, Russia, and the Austrian world. But meanwhile, amidst all the economic growth, social development, and overseas conquests that have been described in the preceding pages, Europe was torn by the destructive ferocity of the Wars of Religion.

14.   THE WARS OF CATHOLIC SPAIN: THE NETHERLANDS AND ENGLAND

The Ambitions of Philip II

Charles V, having tried in vain for 35 years to preserve religious unity in Germany, abdicated his many crowns and retired to a monastery in 1556, the year after the Peace of Augsburg had given the ruler of each German state the right to choose its own religion. He left Austria, Bohemia, and Hungary (or the small part of it not occupied by the Turks) to his brother Ferdinand, who was soon elected Holy Roman Emperor (see map, p. 78). All his other possessions Charles left to his son Philip, who became Philip II of Spain. The Habsburg dynasty remained thereafter divided into two branches, the Austrian and the Spanish. The two cooperated in European affairs. The Spanish branch for a century was the more important. Philip II (1556–1598) not only possessed the Spanish kingdoms but in 1580 inherited Portugal, so that the whole Iberian peninsula was brought under his rule. He possessed the 17 provinces of the Netherlands and the Free County of Burgundy, which were member states of the Holy Roman Empire, lying on its western border, adjacent to France. Milan in north Italy and Naples in the south belonged to Philip, and since he also held the chief islands, as well as Tunis, he enjoyed a naval ascendancy in the western Mediterranean which was threatened only by the Turks. For five years, until 1558, he was titular king of England, and in 1589, in the name of his daughter, he laid claim to the throne of France. All America belonged to Philip II, and after 1580 all the Portuguese empire as well, so that except for a few nautical daredevils all ships plying the open ocean were the Spanish king's.

Philip II therefore naturally regarded himself as an international figure, and the more so because he combined the organizing methods of a new monarchy with a profound interest in the political and religious issues that were dividing post-Reformation Europe. He saw Spain as a leader of European Catholicism, and he believed that the advance of Spanish power in Europe served the cause of the universal church as well as the interests of his own monarchy and the people of Spain. Yet his attempts to protect and enhance Spanish power in Italy sometimes led to conflicts with the popes, and much of his foreign policy was directed against the Ottoman Empire in   *Philip's goals* a continuing struggle for control of the Mediterranean Sea. European Protestantism was thus only one of Philip's many international concerns.

Philip's active participation in Europe's religious wars should therefore be seen as part of his wider military and political campaigns to protect Spanish and Habsburg interests rather than a single-minded crusade for Catholicism. In his personal life, he was serious, devout, and hardworking. He gave the most detailed attention to the management of his far-flung territories. The wealth that flowed to his country from Potosí and other mines in South America enabled Philip to pursue his goals throughout Europe and the Mediterranean. Meanwhile, Spain also entered upon the Golden Age of its early modern culture.

In this period, the *siglo de oro,* running in round dates from 1550 to 1650, Cervantes wrote his *Don Quixote* (in two parts, 1605, 1615) and Lope de Vega wrote his 200 dramas, while El Greco, Murillo, and Velázquez painted their pictures, and the Jesuit Suarez composed works on philosophy and law that were read even in Protestant countries. As Cervantes showed in *Don Quixote,* many Spaniards were highly aware of the enduring tensions between high ideals and the difficult realities of social, political, and religious life. But Catholic traditions and the Catholic Church remained a powerful force in Spanish culture. The church was vitally present at every social level, from the archbishop of Toledo, who ranked above grandees and could address the king as an equal, down to a host of penniless and mendicant friars, who mixed with the poorest and most disinherited of the people.

The Escorial

Philip II built himself a new royal residence, the Escorial, which well expressed in solid stone its creator's political and religious determination.

Madrid itself was a new town, merely a government center, far from the worldly distractions of Toledo or Valladolid. But it was 30 miles from Madrid, on the bleak arid plateau of central Castile, overlooked by the jagged Sierra, that Philip chose to erect the Escorial. He built it in honor of St. Lawrence, on whose feast day he had won a battle against the French. The connecting buildings were laid out in the shape of a grill, since, according to martyrologists, St. Lawrence, in the year 258, had been burned alive on a grill over burning coals. Somber and vast, made of blocks of granite meant to last forever, and with its highest spire rising three hundred feet from the ground, the Escorial was designed not only as a palace but as a center for religious life and the efficient management of a vast empire. Working constantly in this somber setting, Philip II dispatched his couriers to Mexico, to Manila, to Vienna, and to Milan. He sent his troops off to Italy and the Netherlands, his diplomats to all the royal courts of Europe, and his spies wherever they were needed—seeking to extend the influence of his powerful state and (when possible) to promote the Catholicism in which he devoutly believed.

The first years of Philip's reign were also the first years of Elizabeth's reign in England, where the religious issue was still in flux; they were years in which Calvinism agitated the Netherlands, and when France, ruled by teenaged boys, fell apart into implacable civil war. Religious loyalties that knew no frontiers overlapped all political boundaries. Everywhere there were people who looked for guidance outside their own countries. Fervent Calvinists in England, France, and the Netherlands felt closer to one another than to their own monarchs or their own neighbors. Fervent Catholics, in all three countries, welcomed the support of international Catholic forces—the Jesuits, the king of Spain, the pope. National unity threatened to dissolve or was not yet formed. The sense of mutual trust between people who lived side by side was eaten away; and people who lived not only in the same country, but in the same town, on the same street, or even in the same house, turned against each other in the name of a higher cause.

The Catholic offensive

For about five years, beginning in 1567, it seemed that a resurgent Catholicism might prevail. Catholic forces took the offensive on all fronts. In 1567 Philip sent a new and firmer governor general to the Netherlands, the Duke of Alva, with 20,000 Spanish soldiers; the duke proceeded to suppress religious and political dissidents by establishing a Council of Troubles. In 1569 Philip, who was preparing for a new war with the Ottoman Turks, put down a revolt of the Moriscos (converted Muslims) in Spain. In the same year the Catholics of northern England, led by the Duke of Norfolk and sewing the cross of crusaders on their garments, rose in armed rebellion against their heretic queen. In the next year, 1570, the pope excommunicated Elizabeth and absolved her subjects from allegiance to her, so that English Catholics, if they wished, could henceforth in good conscience conspire to overthrow her. In 1571 the Spanish joined with the Venetians and others to win a great naval battle against the Turks, at Lepanto off the coast of Greece. Although this battle was part of the ongoing military struggle for political and economic control of the Mediterranean, some Spanish sailors wove a cross on their sails and portrayed their war with the Ottomans as a new Christian resistance to Islam. In the next year, 1572, the Catholic leaders of France, with the advice of the pope and of Philip II, decided to make an end of the Huguenots, or French Protestants. Over 3,000 were seized and put to death on the eve of

KING PHILIP II
By Titian (Italian, 1488–1576)
This portrait of the Spanish king suggests the highly focused political, religious, and military purpose in this devout Catholic monarch.
(Alinari/Art Resource, NY)

St. Bartholomew's Day in Paris alone; and this massacre was followed by lesser liquidations throughout the provinces.

But none of these victories proved enduring. The Turks soon recovered from their defeat at Lepanto and built a new fleet. In fact, they took Tunis from Philip two years later. The Moriscos were not assimilated (they would be expelled from Spain in 1609). The English Catholic rebellion was stamped out; 800 persons were put to death by Elizabeth's government. The revolt in the Netherlands remained very much alive, as did the French Huguenots. Twenty years later England was Protestant, the Dutch were winning independence, a Huguenot had become king of France, and the Spanish fleet had gone to ruin in northern waters.

The Revolt of the Netherlands

The Netherlands, or Low Countries, roughly comprised the area of the modern kingdoms of the Netherlands and Belgium and the grand duchy of Luxembourg. They consisted of 17 provinces, which in the fifteenth century, one by one, had been inherited, purchased, or conquered by the dukes of Burgundy, from whom they were inherited by Charles V and his son,

The Netherlands provinces

Philip II. In the mid-sixteenth century neither a Dutch nor a Belgian nationality yet existed. In the northern provinces the people spoke German dialects; in the southern provinces they spoke dialects of French; but neither here, nor elsewhere in Europe, was it felt that language boundaries had anything to do with political borders. The southern provinces had for centuries been busy commercial centers, and we have seen how Antwerp, having once flourished in trade with Venice, now flourished in trade with Lisbon. The northern provinces that were most open to the sea, the counties of Holland and Zeeland, had developed rapidly in the fifteenth century. They had a popular literature of their own, written in their own kind of German, which came to be called Dutch. The wealth of the northern provinces was drawn from deep-sea fishing. Amsterdam was said to be built on herring bones, and the Dutch, when they added trading to fishing, still lived by the sea.

The northern provinces felt no tie with each other and no sense of difference from the southern provinces. Each of the 17 provinces was a small state or country in itself, and each enjoyed typical medieval liberties and privileges. The only common bond of all 17 provinces was simply that beginning with the dukes of Burgundy they had the same ruler; but since they had the same ruler, they were called upon from time to time to send delegates to an estates general, and so developed an embryonic sense of federal collaboration. The feeling of Netherlandish identity was heightened with the accession of Philip II, for Philip, unlike his father, was thought of as foreign, a Spaniard who lived in Spain; and after 1560 Spanish governors general, Spanish officials, and Spanish troops were seen more frequently in the Netherlands. Moreover, since the Netherlands was the crossroads of Europe, with a tradition of earnestness in religion, Protestant ideas took root very early, and after 1560, when the religious wars began in France, a great many French Calvinists fled across the borders. At first, there were probably more Calvinists in the southern provinces than in the northern, more among the people whom we now call Belgians than among those whom we now call Dutch.

The revolt against Philip II was inextricably political and religious at the same time, and it became increasingly an economic struggle as the years went by. It began in 1566, when some 200 nobles of the various provinces founded a league to check the "foreign" or Spanish influence in the Netherlands. The league, to which both Catholic and Protestant nobles belonged, petitioned Philip II not to employ the Spanish Inquisition in the Netherlands. They feared the trouble it would stir up; they feared it as a foreign court; they feared that in the enforcement of its rulings the liberties of their provinces would be crushed. Philip's agents in the Netherlands refused the petition. A mass revolt now broke out. Within a week fanatical Calvinists pillaged 400 churches, pulling down images, breaking stained-glass windows, defacing paintings and tapestries, making off with gold chalices, destroying with a fierce contempt the symbols of "popery"— and "idolatry." The rank and file for these anti-Catholic and anti-Spanish demonstrations consisted chiefly of journeymen wage earners, whose fury was driven by social and economic grievances as well as religious belief. Before such vandalism many of the petitioning nobles recoiled; the Catholics among them, as well as less militant Protestants, unable to control their revolutionary followers, began to look upon the Spanish authorities with less disfavor.

Revolt of the Netherlands

Philip II, appalled at the sacrilege, forthwith sent in the Inquisition, the Duke of Alva, and reinforcements of Spanish troops. Alva's Council of Troubles, nicknamed the Council of Blood, sentenced some thousands to death, levied new taxes, and confiscated the estates of a number of important nobles. These measures united people of all classes in opposition. What might have been primarily a class conflict now took on the character of a national opposition. At its head emerged one of the noblemen whose estates had been confiscated, William of Orange (called William the Silent), Philip II's "stadholder" or lieutenant in the County of Holland. Beginning to claim the authority of a sovereign, he authorized ship captains to make war at sea. Fishing crews, "sea dogs," and downright pirates began to raid the small port towns of the Netherlands and France, descending upon them without warning, desecrating the churches, looting, torturing, and killing, in a wild combination of religious rage, political hatred, and lust for booty. The Spanish reciprocated by renewing their confiscations, their inquisitorial tortures, and their burnings and hangings. The Netherlands was torn by anarchy, revolution, and civil war. No lines were clear, either political or religious. But in 1576 the anti-Spanish feeling prevailed over religious difference. Representatives of all 17 provinces, putting aside the religious question, formed a union to drive out the Spanish at any cost.

The Involvement of England

But the Netherlands revolution, though it was a national revolution with political independence as its first aim, was only part of the international politico-religious struggle. All sorts of other interests became involved in it. Queen Elizabeth of England lent aid to the Netherlands, though for many years surreptitiously, not wishing to provoke a war with Spain, in which it was feared that English Catholics might side with the Spaniards. Elizabeth was troubled by having on her hands an unwanted guest, Mary Queen of Scots. Mary had remained a Catholic and had been queen of France until her husband's premature death, and queen of Scotland until driven out by irate Calvinist lords, and who—if the pope, the king of Spain, the Society of Jesus, and many English Catholics were to have their way—would also be queen of England instead of the usurper Elizabeth.[1] Elizabeth under these circumstances kept Mary Stuart imprisoned. Many intrigues were afoot to put Mary on the English throne, some with and some without Mary's knowledge.

> *England lends support to the Dutch*

In 1576 Don Juan, hero of the Spanish naval victory at Lepanto and half-brother of Philip II, became governor general of the embattled Netherlands. He developed a grandiose plan to subdue the Netherlands and then to use that country as a base for an invasion of England. After overthrowing Elizabeth with Spanish troops, he would put Mary Stuart on the throne, marry her himself, and so become king of a re-Catholicized England. Thus the security of Elizabethan and Protestant England was coming to depend on the outcome of fighting in the Netherlands. Elizabeth signed an alliance with the Netherlands patriots.

Don Juan died in 1578 and was succeeded as governor general of the Netherlands by the prince of Parma. A diplomat as well as a soldier, Parma broke the solid front of the 17 provinces by a mixture of force and persuasion. He promised that the historic liberties of the provinces would be respected, and he appealed not only to the more zealous Catholics but also to moderates who were wearying of the struggle and repelled by mob violence and religious vandalism. On this basis he rallied the southernmost provinces to his side. The seven northern provinces, led by Holland and Zeeland, responded by forming the Union of

---

[1]Mary Stuart, a great-granddaughter of Henry VII, was the next lawful heir to the English throne after Elizabeth, since Elizabeth had no children.

THE LOW COUNTRIES, 1648

This group of towns and provinces, along the lower reaches of the Rhine, Meuse, and Scheldt rivers, originated in the Middle Ages as part of the Holy Roman Empire. The northern or Dutch provinces were recognized as independent of the Empire in 1648. Early in the seventeenth century a political frontier emerged between the "Dutch" and "Belgian" parts, but the word "Belgium" was not used until much later, the southern or Habsburg provinces being called the Spanish Netherlands in the seventeenth century and the Austrian Netherlands in the eighteenth. The large bishopric of Liège remained a separate church-state until the French Revolution. The language frontier, then as now, ran roughly east and west somewhat south of Brussels, with French to the south and Flemish (a form of Dutch, and hence Germanic) to the north of the line.

The Union of Utrecht

Utrecht in 1579. In 1581 they formally declared their independence from the king of Spain, calling themselves the United Provinces of the Netherlands. Thus originated what was more commonly called the Dutch Republic, or simply "Holland" in view of the predominance of that county among the seven. The great Flemish towns—Antwerp, Ghent, and Bruges—at first sided with the Union.

Where formerly all had been turmoil, a geographical line was now drawn. The south rallying to Philip II now faced a still rebellious north. But neither side accepted any such partition. Parma still fought to reconquer the north, and the Dutch, led by William the Silent, still struggled to clear the Spanish out of all 17 provinces. Meanwhile the two sides fought to capture the intermediate Flemish cities. When Parma moved upon Antwerp, still the leading port of the North Sea, and one from which an invasion of England could best be mounted, Elizabeth at last openly entered the war on the side of the rebels, sending 6,000 English troops to the Netherlands under the Earl of Leicester in 1585.

The vast size of the Spanish naval armada and the English opposition to it are suggested in this illustration by an unknown artist. Both navies had crosses on the flags of their ships, thereby claiming divine support for their cause and indicating the religious and national stakes in this epic conflict.
(National Maritime Museum, London)

England was now clearly emerging as the chief bulwark of Protestantism and of anti-Spanish feeling in northwestern Europe. In England itself, the popular fears of Spain, the popular resentment against Catholic plots revolving about Mary Stuart, and the popular indignation at "foreign" and "outside" meddling in English matters produced an unprecedented sense of national solidarity. The country rallied to Protestantism and to Elizabeth, and even the Catholic minority for the most part disowned the conspiracies against her. The English were now openly and defiantly allied with the Protestant Dutch. Not only were they fighting together in the Netherlands, but both English and Dutch sea raiders also fell upon Spanish shipping, captured the treasure ships, and even pillaged the mainland coast of northern South America. The Dutch were beginning to penetrate East Indian waters. Elizabeth was negotiating with Scotland, with German Calvinists, and with French Huguenots. At the Escorial it was said that the Netherlands could only be rewon by an invasion of England, that the queen of the heretics must be dethroned, that it was cheaper to launch a gigantic attack upon England than to pay the cost of protecting Spanish galleons year after year against the depredations of piratical sea dogs.

England as bulwark of Protestantism

Philip II therefore prepared to invade England. The English retorted with vigor. Mary Stuart, after almost 20 years of imprisonment, was executed in 1587; an aroused Parliament, more than Elizabeth herself, demanded her life on the eve of foreign attack. Sir Francis Drake, most spectacular of the sea dogs, sailed into the port of Cádiz and burnt the very ships assembling there to join the Armada. This was jocosely described as singeing the beard of the king of Spain.

The great Armada, the *armada católica,* was ready early in 1588. With crosses on the sails and banners bearing the image of the Holy Virgin, it went forth as to a new Lepanto against the Turks of the north. It consisted of 130 ships, weighing 58,000 tons, carrying 30,000 men and 2,400 pieces of artillery—the most prodigious assemblage of naval power that the world had ever seen. The plan was for the fleet to sail to the Netherlands, from which it was to escort the prince of Parma's army across the straits to the English coast.

The Spanish Armada

But the Armada never reached the Spanish army. It was met in the English Channel by some 200 English vessels, which encircled the Spanish fleet near Calais. The English

CHRONOLOGY OF NOTABLE EVENTS, 1492–1648

1492	Christopher Columbus reaches America
1519–1522	Ferdinand Magellan circumnavigates the globe
1519–1533	Spanish conquests of Native American empires in the Americas
1556–1598	Reign of King Philip II in Spain
1562–1598	Religious and civil wars in France
1565	"Manila Galleons" open Spanish trade route between Asia and America
1566	Revolt against Spanish control begins in the Netherlands
1588	Spanish Armada is destroyed off the coast of England and Scotland
1598	King Henry IV issues Edict of Nantes; grants religious rights to French Protestants
1618–1648	The Thirty Years' War in Germany
1648	Peace of Westphalia recognizes system of sovereign European states

craft—lighter, smaller, and faster, though well furnished with guns—harried the lumbering mass of the Armada, broke up its formations, and attacked its great vessels one by one. It found no refuge at Calais, and English fireships drove it out again to sea. Then arose a great storm, which the English would later call the "Protestant wind." The storm blew the broken Armada northward around the tip of Scotland, the Orkneys, the Hebrides, and northern Ireland—forbidding coasts which the Spaniards had to skirt without charts or pilots or adequate provisions, and which they strewed with their wreckage and their bones.

The Results of the Struggle

The war for control of the Netherlands went on for several years, even after Philip died in 1598. In the wars with Spain the English had, above all else, assured their national independence. They had acquired an intense national spirit, a love of "this other Eden, demi-paradise," "this precious stone set in the silver sea," as Shakespeare wrote; and they had become more solidly Protestant, almost unanimously set against "popery." With the ruin of the Armada, they were more free to take to the sea; we have seen how the English East India Company was founded in 1600.

In the Netherlands, the battle lines swayed back and forth until 1609. In that year a Twelve Years' Truce was agreed to. By this truce the Netherlands were partitioned. The line of partition ran somewhat farther north than it had in Parma's time, for the Spaniards had retaken Antwerp and other cities in the middle zone. The seven provinces north of the line, those that had formed the Union of Utrecht in 1579, were henceforth known as Dutch. The ten provinces south of the line were known as the Spanish Netherlands. Protestants in the south either became Catholics or fled to the north, so that the south (the modern Belgium) became solidly Catholic, while the number of Protestants in the north was increased. Even so, the Dutch were not a completely Protestant people, for probably as many as a third of them remained Catholic. Calvinism was the religion of most Dutch burghers and the religion favored by the state; but in the face of an exceptionally large religious minority the Dutch Netherlands adopted a policy of toleration.

Partition of the Netherlands

The southern Netherlands were ruined by almost 40 years of war. The Dutch, moreover, occupied the mouth of the Scheldt River and refused to allow oceangoing vessels to proceed upstream to Antwerp or to Ghent. The Scheldt remained "closed" for two centuries, and the Flemish cities never recovered their old position. Amsterdam became the commercial and financial center of northern Europe; it retained its commercial supremacy for a century and its financial supremacy for two centuries. For the Dutch, as for the English, the weakening of Spanish naval power opened the way to the sea. The Dutch East India Company was organized in 1602. Both Dutch and English began to found overseas colonies. The English settled in Virginia in 1607, the Dutch at New York in 1612.

As for Spain, while it remained the most formidable military power of Europe for another half-century, its political and economic decline had already begun. At the death of Philip II the monarchy was living from hand to mouth, habitually depending on the next arrival of treasure from the Indies. The productive forces of the country were weakened by inflation, by taxation, by emigration, by depopulation. At Seville, for example, only 400 looms were in operation in 1621, where there had been 16,000 a century earlier. Spain suffered from the very circumstances that made it great. Qualities that developed in the centuries of religious war and in the reliance upon imported gold or silver from America were not those on which a more modern economy and society could easily be built. The long history of campaigns against infidels and heretics had produced an exceptionally large number of minor aristocrats who often saw their class status as a reason to avoid various forms of mundane work. Their relative indifference to the newer, expanding institutions of European commercial activity may have influenced the country as a whole. In any case, many of the ablest Spaniards continued to enter the church, and there were few innovations in Spain's political and economic life.

The beginnings of Spanish decline

The very unity accomplished under Ferdinand and Isabella threatened to dissolve. After more than a century of the Inquisition people were still afraid of false Christians and crypto-Muslims. The question of the Moriscos rose again in 1608. The Moriscos included some of the best farmers and most skilled artisans in the country. They lived in almost all parts of Spain and were in no sense a "foreign" element, since they were simply the descendants of those Spaniards who, in the Muslim period, which had begun 900 years before, had adopted the Muslim religion and Arabic language and culture. They were now supposedly Christian, but the true and pure Christians accused them of preserving in secret the rites of Islam and of sympathy for the Barbary pirates. They were thought to be clannish, marrying among themselves; and they were so efficient, sober, and hardworking that they outdistanced other Spaniards in competition. In 1609 some 150,000 Moriscos were driven out of Valencia; in 1610 some 64,000 were driven from Aragon; in 1611 an unknown number were expelled from Castile. All were simply put on boats and sent off with what they could carry. Spain, whose total population was rapidly falling in any case, thus lost one of the most socially valuable, if not religiously orthodox, of all its minorities.

The Moriscos

Nor could the Christian kingdoms hold peaceably together, despite the centralizing projects of the main government minister, the Count of Olivares. Coming to power under King Philip IV in 1621, Olivares sought to curb the independence of the church, increase the king's revenues, control the aristocracy, and send the Spanish army into both the Netherlands and the religious wars in Germany. His policies provoked strong opposition throughout Spain. In 1640 Portugal, which had been joined to the Spanish crown since 1580 when its own ruling line had run out, reestablished its independence. That same year Catalonia rose in open rebellion. The Catalan war, in which the French streamed across the

Pyrenees to aid the rebels, lasted for almost 20 years. Catalonia was at last reconquered, but it managed to preserve its old privileges and separate identity. Catalan and Castilian viewed each other with increased repugnance. The Spanish kingdoms were almost as disunited, in spirit and in institutions, as in the days of Isabella and Ferdinand. They suffered, too, during the seventeenth century from a line of kings whose mental peculiarities reached the point of positive imbecility. Meanwhile, however, the might of Spain was still to be felt in both Germany and France.

15.   THE DISINTEGRATION AND RECONSTRUCTION OF FRANCE

Both France and Germany, in the so-called Wars of Religion, fell into an advanced state of decomposition. France was torn apart by almost 40 years of civil war between 1562 and 1598, while Germany entered a long period of civil troubles that culminated in the Thirty Years' War between 1618 and 1648. From this decomposition France recovered in the seventeenth century, but Germany did not.

Political and Religious Disunity

The Wars of Religion in France, despite the religious savagery shown by partisans of both sides, were no more religious than they were political. They were essentially a new form of the old phenomenon of feudal rebellion against a higher central authority. "Feudal," in this postmedieval sense, generally refers not to nobles only, but to all sorts of groups having rights within the state, and so includes towns and provinces, and even craft guilds and courts of law, in addition to the church and the noble class. It remained to be seen whether all these elements could be welded into one body politic.

In France the New Monarchy, resuming the work of medieval kings, had imposed a certain unity on the country. Normally the country acted as a unit in foreign affairs. The king alone made treaties, and in war his subjects all fought on his side, if they fought at all. Internally, the royal centralization was largely administrative; that is, the king and those who worked for him dealt with subordinate bodies of all kinds, while these subordinate bodies remained in existence with their own functions and personnel. France by the ideas of the time was a very large country. It was three times as large as England and five times as populous—roughly 18 million in the sixteenth century. At a time when the traveler could move hardly 30 miles a day, it took three weeks of steady plodding to cross the kingdom. Local influence was therefore very strong. Beneath the platform of royalty there was almost as little substantial unity in France as in the Holy Roman Empire. When the Empire had 300 "states," France had some 300 areas with their own legal systems. Where the Empire had free cities, France had *bonnes villes,* the king's "good towns," each with its stubbornly defended corporate rights. Where the Empire had middle-sized states like Bavaria, France had provinces as great as some European kingdoms—Brittany, Burgundy, Provence, Languedoc—each ruled by the French king, to be sure, but each with its own identity, autonomy, laws, courts, tariffs, taxes, and parliament or provincial estates. To all this diversity, in France as in Germany, was now added diversity of religion. Calvin himself was by birth and upbringing a Frenchman. Calvinism spread in France very rapidly.

Nor was France much attached to a papal or international Catholicism. The French clergy had long struggled for its national or Gallican liberties; the French kings had dealt

Centralization vs. localism

rudely with popes, ignored the Council of Trent, and allied for political reasons with both the Lutherans and the Turks. Since 1516 the king of France had the right to nominate the French bishops. The fact that both the monarchy and the clergy already felt independent of Rome held them back from the revolutionary solutions of Protestantism. The Protestantism which did spread in France therefore developed without government support and embraced the most radical theological wing of the Reformation, namely Calvinism, which preached at kings, attacked bishops, smashed religious images, and desecrated the churches. Within the main countries that became Protestant—England, north Germany, even the Netherlands—this extreme Protestantism was the doctrine of a minority. In France there was no middle-of-the-road Protestantism, no broad and comfortable Anglicanism, no halfway Lutheranism inspired by governments; and in the long run, as will be seen, the middle of the road was occupied by Catholics.

At first, however, the Huguenots, as the French Calvinists were called, though always a minority, were neither a small group nor modest in their demands. In a class analysis, it is clear that it was chiefly the nobility that was attracted to Protestantism, though of course it does not follow that most French Protestants were nobles, since the nobility was a small class. More than a third, and possibly almost a half, of the French nobility was Protestant in the 1560s or 1570s. Frequently the seigneur, or lord of one or more manors, believed that he should have the right to regulate religion on his own estates, as the princes of Germany decided the religion of their own territories. It thus happened that a lord might defy the local bishop, put a Calvinist minister in his village church, throw out the images, simplify the sacraments, and have the service conducted in French. In this way peasants also became Huguenots. Occasionally peasants turned Huguenot without encouragement by the lord. It was chiefly in southwestern France that Protestantism spread as a general movement affecting whole areas. But in all parts of the country, north as well as south, many towns converted to Protestantism. Usually this meant that the bourgeois oligarchy, into whose hands town government had generally fallen, went over to Calvinism and thereupon banned Catholic services. The journeymen wage earners might follow along; or estranged by class differences arising from within the local economy, they might remain attached to their old priests. In general, the unskilled laboring population probably remained the least touched of all classes by Calvinist doctrine.

The Huguenots

Both Francis I and Henry II opposed the spread of Calvinism—as did Lutheran and Anglican rulers—for Calvinism, a kind of grassroots movement in religion, rising spontaneously among laity and reforming ministers, seemed to threaten not only the powers of monarchy but also the very idea of a nationally established church. The fact that in France the nobility, a traditionally ungovernable class, figured prominently in the movement only made it look the more like political or feudal rebellion. Persecution of Huguenots, with burnings at the stake, began in the 1550s.

Opposition to Calvinism

Then in 1559 King Henry II was accidentally killed in a tournament. He left three sons, of whom the eldest in 1559 was only 15. Their mother, Henry's widow, was Catherine de' Medici, an Italian woman who brought to France some of the polish of Renaissance Italy, along with some of its taste for political intrigue, with which she attempted to govern the country for her royal sons. (Their names were Francis II, who died in 1560, Charles IX, who died in 1574, and Henry III, who lasted until 1589.) With no firm hand in control of the monarchy, the country fell apart; and in the ensuing chaos various powerful factions tried to get control of the youthful monarchs for their own purposes. Among these factions were both Huguenots and Catholics. The Huguenots, under persecution, were too strong a minority to go into hiding. Counting among their number a third or more of the professional warrior class, the nobles, they took naturally and aggressively to arms.

The Civil and Religious Wars

The civil wars in sixteenth-century France were not wars in which one region of a country takes up arms against another, each retaining some apparatus of government, as in the American Civil War or the civil wars of the seventeenth century in England. They were civil wars of the kind fought in the absence of government. Roving bands of armed men, without territorial base or regular means of subsistence, wandered about the country, fighting and plundering, joining or separating from other similar bands, in shifting hosts that were quickly formed or quickly dissolved. The changing economic and social conditions of the era detached many people from their old routines and threw them into a life of adventure. The more prominent leaders could thus easily obtain followers, and at the coming of such cohorts the peasants usually took to the woods, while bourgeois would lock the gates of their cities. Peasants would form protective leagues, like vigilantes; and even small towns maintained diminutive armies.

The Huguenots were led by various personages of rank, such as Admiral de Coligny and Henry of Bourbon, king of Navarre, a small independent kingdom at the foot of the Pyrenees between Spain and France. A pronounced Catholic party arose under the Guise family, headed by the Duke of Guise and the Cardinal of Lorraine. Catherine de' Medici was left in the middle, opposed like all monarchs to Calvinism but unwilling to fall under the domination of the Guises. While the Guises wished to extirpate heresy, they wished even more to govern France. Among the Huguenots some fought for local liberties in religion, while the more ardent spirits hoped to drive "idolatry" and "popery" out of all France, and indeed out of the world itself. Catherine de' Medici for a time tried to play the two parties against each other. But in 1572, fearing the growing influence of Coligny over the king, and taking advantage of a great concourse of leading Huguenots in Paris to celebrate the marriage of Henry of Navarre, she decided to rid herself of the heads of the

St. Bartholomew's Day massacre

Huguenot party at a single blow. In the resulting massacre of St. Bartholomew's Day some thousands of Huguenots were dragged from their beds after midnight and unceremoniously murdered. Coligny was killed; Henry of Navarre escaped by temporarily changing his religion.

This outrage only aroused Huguenot fury and led to a renewal of civil war, with mounting atrocities committed by both sides. The armed bands slaughtered each other and terrorized noncombatants. Both parties hired companies of mercenary soldiers, mainly from Germany. Spanish troops invaded France at the invitation of the Guises. Protestant towns, such as Rouen and La Rochelle, appealed for armed support from Elizabeth of England, reminding her that kings of England had once reigned over their parts of France; but Elizabeth was too preoccupied with her own problems to give more than very sporadic and insignificant assistance. Neither side could subdue the other, and hence there were numerous truces, during which fighting still flared up, since no one had the power to impose peace.

The Politiques

Gradually, mainly among the more perfunctory Catholics, but also among moderate Protestants, there developed still another group who thought of themselves as the "politicals" or *politiques*. The *politiques* concluded that too much was being made of religion, that no doctrine was important enough to justify everlasting war, that perhaps after all there might be room for

The St. Bartholomew's Day Massacre, in which thousands of Protestants were massacred in Paris in 1572, sparked waves of further atrocities by both sides in France's religious wars. As this image of the massacre suggests, it also became an enduring symbol of the brutal conflicts that divided the nation throughout the late sixteenth century.
(Musée Cantonal de Beaux Arts, Lausanne)

two churches, and that what the country needed above all else was civil order. Theirs was a secular rather than a religious view. They believed that people lived primarily in the state, not in the church. They were willing to overlook the religious ideas of people in different churches if such persons would simply obey the king and go peaceably about their business. To escape anarchy they put their hopes in the institution of monarchy. Henry of Navarre, now again a Protestant, was at heart a *politique*. Another was the political philosopher Jean Bodin (1530–1596), the first thinker to develop the modern theory of sovereignty. He held that in every society there must be one power strong enough to give law to all others, with their consent if possible, without their consent if necessary. Thus from the disorders of the religious wars in France was germinated the idea of royal absolutism and of the sovereign state.

The End of the Wars: Reconstruction under Henry IV

In 1589 both Henry III, the reigning king, and Henry of Guise, the Catholic party chief who was trying to depose him, were assassinated, each by a partisan of the other. The throne now came by legal inheritance to the third of the three Henrys, Henry of Navarre, the Huguenot chieftain. He reigned as Henry IV. Most popular and most amiably remembered of all French kings, except for medieval St. Louis, he was the first of the Bourbon dynasty, which was to last until the French Revolution.

The civil wars did not end with the accession of Henry IV. The Catholic party refused to recognize him, set up a pretender against him, and called in the Spaniards. Henry, the *politique,* sensed that the majority of the French people were still Catholic and that the Huguenots were not only a minority but, after 30 years of civil strife, an increasingly unpopular minority. Paris especially, Catholic throughout the wars, refused to admit the heretic king within its gates. Supposedly remarking that "Paris is well worth a Mass," Henry IV in 1593 abjured the Calvinist faith, and subjected himself to the elaborate processes of papal absolution. Thereupon the *politiques* and less excitable Catholics consented to work with him. The Huguenots, at first elated that their leader should become king, were now not only outraged by Henry's abjuration but also alarmed for their own safety. They demanded positive guarantees for their personal security as well as protection of their religious liberty.

Henry IV accepts Catholicism

The Edict of Nantes

Henry IV in 1598 responded by issuing the Edict of Nantes. The Edict granted to every seigneur, or noble who was also a manorial lord, the right to hold Protestant services in his own household. It allowed Protestantism in towns where it was in fact the prevailing form of worship, and in any case in one town of each *bailliage* (a unit corresponding somewhat to the English shire) throughout the country; but it barred Protestant churches from Catholic episcopal towns and from a zone surrounding and including the city of Paris. It promised that Protestants should enjoy the same civil rights as Catholics, the same chance for public office, and access to the Catholic universities. In certain of the superior law courts it created "mixed chambers" of both Protestants and Catholics—somewhat as if a stated minority representation were to be legally required in United States federal courts today. The Edict also gave Protestants their own means of defense, granting them about 100 fortified towns to be held by Protestant garrisons under Protestant command.

The Huguenot minority, reassured by the Edict of Nantes, became less of a rebellious element within the state. The majority of the French people viewed the Edict with suspicion. The parlements, or supreme law courts, of Paris, Bordeaux, Toulouse, Aix, and Rennes all refused to recognize it as the law of the land. It was the king who forced toleration upon the country. He silenced the parlements and subdued Catholic opposition by doing favors for the Jesuits. France's chief minority was thus protected by the central government, not by popular wishes. Where in England the Catholic minority had no rights at all, and in Germany the religious question was settled only by cutting the country into small and hostile fragments, in France a compromise was effected, by which the Protestant minority had both individual and territorial rights. A considerable number of French statesmen, generals, and other important persons in the seventeenth century were Protestants.

Henry IV, having appeased the religious controversy, did everything that he could to let the country gradually recover from its decades of civil war. His ideal, as he breezily put it, was a "chicken in the pot" for every Frenchman. He worked also to restore the ruined government, to collect taxes, pay officials, discipline the army, and supervise the administration of justice. Roads and bridges were repaired and new manufactures were introduced under mercantilist principles. Never throughout his reign of 21 years did he summon the Estates General. A country that had just hacked itself to pieces in civil war was scarcely able to govern itself, and so, under Henry IV, the foundations of the later royal absolutism of the Bourbons were laid down.

The foundations of absolutism

Henry IV was assassinated in 1610 by a crazed fanatic who believed him a menace to the Catholic church. Under his widow, Marie de' Medici, the nobility and upper Catholic clergy again grew restless and forced the summoning of the Estates General, in which so many conflicting and mutually distrustful interests were represented that no program could be adopted. Marie dismissed them in 1615 to the general relief of all concerned. No Estates General of the kingdom as a whole thereafter met until the French Revolution. National government was to be conducted by and through the king.

Cardinal Richelieu

In the name of Marie de' Medici and her young son, Louis XIII, the control of affairs gradually came into the hands of an ecclesiastic, Cardinal Richelieu. In the preceding generation Richelieu might have been called a *politique*. It was the state, not the church, whose interests he worked to further. He tried to strengthen the state economically by mercantilist edicts. He attempted to draw impoverished gentlemen into trade by allowing them to engage in maritime commerce without loss of noble status. For wholesale merchants, as an incentive, he made it possible to become nobles, in return for payments into the royal exchequer. He founded and supported many commercial companies on the Anglo-Dutch model.

For a time it seemed that civil war might break out again. Nobles still feuded with each other and evaded the royal jurisdiction. Richelieu prohibited private warfare and ordered the destruction of all fortified castles not manned and needed by the king himself. He even prohibited dueling, a custom much favored by the nobles of the day, but regarded by Richelieu as a mere remnant of private war. The Huguenots, too, with their own towns and their own armed forces under the Edict of Nantes, had become something of a state within the state. In 1627 the Duke of Rohan led a Huguenot rebellion, based in the city of La Rochelle, which received military support from the English. Richelieu after a year suppressed the rebellion and in 1629, by the Peace of Alais, amended the Edict of Nantes. For this highly secularized cardinal of the Catholic church it was agreeable for the Protestants to keep their religion but not for them to share in the instruments of political power. The Huguenots lost, in 1629, their fortified cities, their Protestant armies, and all their military and territorial rights, but in their religious and civil rights they were not officially disturbed for another 50 years.

Renewed threat of civil war

The French monarchy no sooner reestablished itself after the civil wars than it began to return to the old foreign policy of Francis I, who had opposed on every front the European supremacy of the house of Habsburg. The Spanish power still encircled France at the Pyrenees, in the Mediterranean, in the Free County of Burgundy (the Franche-Comté), and in Belgium. The Austrian branch had pretensions to supremacy in Germany and all central Europe. Richelieu found his opportunity to assail the Habsburgs in the civil and religious struggles which now began to afflict Germany.

16.   THE THIRTY YEARS' WAR, 1618–1648: THE DISINTEGRATION OF GERMANY

The Holy Roman Empire extended from France on the west to Poland and Hungary on the east. It included the Czechs of Bohemia and sizable French-speaking populations in what are now Belgium, Lorraine, eastern Burgundy, and western Switzerland; but with these exceptions the Empire was made up of Germans (see maps, pp. 78, 142–143). Language, however, was far less important than religion as the tie which people felt to be basic to a community; and in religion the Empire was almost evenly divided. Where in England, after stabilization set in, Roman Catholics sank to a minority of some 3 percent, and in France the Huguenots fell to not much over 5 percent, in Germany there was no true minority, and hence no majority, and religion gave no ground for national concentration. Possibly there were more Protestants than Catholics in the Empire in 1600, for not only was Protestantism the state religion in many of the 300 states, but individual Protestants were also numerous in the legally Catholic states of the Austrian Habsburgs. Bohemia had a Protestant majority, rooted in the Czech people. Farther east, outside the Holy Roman Empire, the Hungarian nobles were mainly Protestant, and Transylvania, in the elbow of the Carpathian Mountains, was an active center of Calvinism.

German decline

In 1500 Germany had led in the life of Europe, but by 1600 it had lost much of its former cultural creativity and leadership. Where both Catholics and Calvinists recognized international affiliations, Lutherans were suspicious of the world outside the Lutheran states of Germany and Scandinavia, and hence suffered from a cultural isolation. The German universities, both Lutheran and Catholic, attracted fewer students than formerly, and their intellectual effort was consumed in combative dogmatics, each side demonstrating the truth of its own ideas. Many of the most deadly, large-scale campaigns against witchcraft took place in the small German states, and more women were burned as witches in Germany than in other countries in Western Europe. The commerce of south Germany and the Rhineland was in decay, both because of the shift of trade to the Atlantic and because the Dutch controlled the mouth of the Rhine in their own interests. German bankers, such as the Fuggers, were of slight importance after 1600. Capital was now being formed in the centers of maritime trade.

Background of the Thirty Years' War

The Peace of Augsburg in 1555 had provided that in each state the government could prescribe the religion of its subjects. In general, in the decades following the Peace of Augsburg, the Lutherans made considerable gains, putting Lutheran administrators into the church states, or "secularizing" them and converting them into lay principalities. In addition, Calvinism spread into Germany. Though Calvinists had no rights under the Peace of Augsburg, a number of states became Calvinist. One of these was the Palatinate, important because it was strategically placed across the middle Rhine, and because its ruler, the Elector Palatine, was one of the seven persons who elected the Holy Roman Emperor. In 1608 the Protestant states, urged on by the Elector Palatine, formed a Protestant union to defend their gains. To obtain support, they negotiated with the Dutch, with the English, and with Henry IV of France. In 1609 a league of Catholic German states was organized by Bavaria. It looked for help from Spain.

Lutheran gains

The Germans were thus falling apart, or rather coming together, into two parties in anticipation of a religious war, and each party solicited foreign assistance against the other. Other issues were also maturing. The Twelve Years' Truce between Spain and the Dutch, signed in 1609, was due to expire in 1621. The Spanish (whose military power was still unaffected by internal decline) were again preparing to crush the Dutch Republic. Since the Dutch insisted on independence, a renewal of the Dutch-Spanish war appeared to be inevitable. The Spanish also wished to consolidate the Habsburg position in central Europe and enhance their access to the Netherlands by gaining control of new territories along the Rhine River and in various Swiss cantons (see map, pp. 142–143).

These Spanish designs in the Rhineland and Switzerland naturally aroused the opposition of France. Moreover, the Austrian branch of the Habsburg family was slowly bestirring itself to eradicate Protestantism in its own domains and to turn the Holy Roman Empire into a more modern type of state. The idea of a strong power in Germany was abhorrent to the French. Through opposition to the Habsburgs, France was again put in the position of chief protector of Protestantism. France was a giant of Europe, five times as populous as England, over ten times as populous as Sweden or the Dutch Republic, incomparably more populous than any single German state. And France after 1600 was at last unified within—at least relatively. As a French writer has observed, speaking of these years, the appearance of the fleur-de-lis upon the Rhine would tumble to the ground the vast projects of the Counter Reformation.

The Thirty Years' War, resulting from all these pressures, was therefore exceedingly complex. It was a German civil war fought over the Catholic-Protestant issue. It was also a German civil war fought over constitutional issues, between the emperor striving to build up the central

The complexity of the Thirty Years' War

power of the Empire and the member states struggling to maintain independence. These two civil wars by no means coincided, for Catholic and Protestant states were alike in objecting to imperial control. It was also an international war, between France and the Habsburgs, between Spain and the Dutch, with the kings of Denmark and Sweden and the prince of Transylvania becoming involved, and with all these outsiders finding allies within Germany, on whose soil most of the battles were fought. The wars were further complicated by the fact that many of the generals were soldiers of fortune who aspired to create principalities of their own and who fought or refused to fight to suit their own convenience.

The Four Phases of the War

The fighting began in Bohemia. It is in fact customary to divide the war into four phases, the Bohemian (1618–1625), the Danish (1625–1629), the Swedish (1630–1635), and the Swedish-French (1635–1648).

The Bohemian war

In 1618 the Bohemians, or Czechs, fearing the loss of their Protestant liberties, dealt with two emissaries from the Habsburg Holy Roman Emperor, Matthias (who was also their king), by a method occasionally used in that country—throwing them out of the window. After this "defenestration of Prague" the king-emperor sent troops to restore his authority, whereupon the Bohemians deposed him and elected a new king. In order to obtain Protestant assistance, they chose the Calvinist Elector Palatine, the head of the Protestant Union, who assumed the title of Frederick V. He brought aid to the Bohemians from the Protestant Union, the Dutch, and the prince of Transylvania. The Emperor Ferdinand, Matthias's successor, assisted by money from the pope, by Spanish troops sent from Milan, and by the forces of Catholic Bavaria, managed to overwhelm the Bohemians at the battle of the White Mountain in 1620. Frederick fled, jeered or pitied as the "winter king." His ancestral domains in the Palatinate were overrun by the Spaniards.

The Habsburgs now set out to reconquer and revolutionize Bohemia. The Emperor Ferdinand got himself elected as king and soon confiscated the estates of almost half the Bohemian nobles. He granted these lands as endowments for Catholic churches and monasteries or as gifts to adventurers of all nationalities who had entered his service and who became the new landed aristocracy of Bohemia.

With Protestant fortunes at a low ebb, and the Protestant Union itself dissolved in 1621, the lead in Protestant affairs was now taken by the king of Denmark, who was also

Ifrael ex. Cum Priuil. Reg.

A la fin ces Voleurs infames et perdus ,   Monftrent bien que le crime (horrible et noire engeance)   Et que ceft le Deftin des hommes vicieux
Comme fruits malheureux a cet arbre pendus   Eft luy mefme inftrument de honte et de vengeance ,   Defprouuer toft ou tard la iuftice des Cieu

The violence of the Thirty Years' War in Germany, depicted here in a vivid illustration by Jacques Callot entitled simply *The Hanging Tree* (1633), produced terror, bitter memories, and political divisions in central Europe that lasted long after the fighting finally ended in 1648.
(Anne S.K. Brown Military Collection, Brown University Library)

Duke of Holstein, a state of the Holy Roman Empire. With a little aid from the Dutch and English, and with promises from Richelieu, he entered the fray. Against him the Emperor Ferdinand raised another army, or, rather, commissioned Albert of Wallenstein to raise one on his own private initiative. Wallenstein assembled a force of professional fighters, of all nationalities, who lived by pillage rather than by pay. His army was his personal instrument, not the emperor's, and he therefore followed a policy of his own, which was so tortuous and well concealed that the name of Wallenstein has always remained an enigma. Wallenstein and other imperial generals soon defeated the king of Denmark, reached the Baltic coast, and even invaded the Danish peninsula.

The full tide of the Counter Reformation now flowed over Germany. Not only was Catholicism again seeping into the Palatinate, and again flooding Bohemia, but it also rolled northward into the inner recesses of the Lutheran states. By the Edict of Restitution, in 1629, the emperor declared all church territories secularized since 1552 automatically restored to the Catholic church. Some of these territories had been Protestant since the oldest person could remember. Terror swept over Protestant Germany. It seemed that the whole Protestant Reformation, now a century old, might be undone.

French and Swedish alarm

Among those to be alarmed were the French and the Swedes. Richelieu, however, was still putting down fractious nobles and Huguenots. He had not yet consolidated France to his satisfaction and believed that France, without fighting itself, could counter the Habsburg ambitions through the use of allies. He sent diplomats to help extricate the king of Sweden from a war with Poland, and he promised him financial assistance, which soon rose to a million livres a year in return for the maintenance in Germany of 40,000 Swedish troops. The Dutch subsidized the Swedes with some 50,000 florins a month.

The king of Sweden was Gustavus Adolphus, a ruler of superlative ability, who had conciliated all parties in Sweden and had extended Swedish holdings on the east shore of the Baltic. Using Dutch and other military experts, he had created the most modern army of the time, noted for its firm discipline, high courage, and mobile cannon. Himself a religious man, he had his troops march to battle singing Lutheran hymns. He was ideally suited to be the Protestant champion, a role he now willingly took up, landing in Germany in 1630. Richelieu, besides giving financial help, negotiated with the Catholic states of Germany, playing on their fears of imperial centralization and seeking to isolate the emperor, against whom the Swedish war machine was now hurled.

Gustavus Adolphus

The Swedes, with military aid from Saxony, won a number of spectacular victories, at Breitenfeld in 1631 and Lützen in 1632, where, however, Gustavus Adolphus was killed. His chancellor, Oxenstierna, carried on. The Swedish army penetrated into Bohemia and as far south as the Danube. What those in the higher counsels of Sweden were aiming at is not clear. Perhaps they dreamed of a great federal Protestant empire, to include Scandinavia and north Germany, a Lutheran empire confronting a Catholic and Habsburg empire in the south. But the brilliant Swedish victories came to little. Both sides were weakened by disagreement. Wallenstein, who disliked the Spanish influence in Germany, virtually ceased to fight the Swedes and Saxons, with whom he even entered into private talks hoping to create an independent position for himself. He was finally disgraced by the emperor and assassinated by one of his own staff. On the Swedish-Saxon side, the Saxons decided to make a separate peace. Saxony therefore signed with the emperor the Peace of Prague of 1635. The other German Protestant states concurred in it and withdrew their support from the Swedes. The emperor, by largely annulling the Edict of Restitution, allayed Protestant apprehensions. The Swedes were left isolated in Germany. It seemed that the German states were coming together, that the religious wars might be nearing an end. But, in fact, in 1635, the Thirty Years' War was only well begun. Neither France nor Spain wished peace or reconciliation in Germany.

Richelieu renewed his assurances to the Swedes, paid subsidies even to the wealthy Dutch, hired a German princeling, Bernard of Saxe-Weimar, to maintain an army of Germans in the French service, and at last brought Catholic France into open support of the German Protestants.

So the fleur-de-lis finally moved toward the Rhine, though not at first with the success for which the French or Protestants might hope. The Spanish, from their bases in Belgium and Franche-Comté, drove instead deep into France. Champagne and Burgundy were ravaged, and Paris itself was seized with panic. The Spanish also raided the south. The French had a taste of the plunder, murder, burnings, and stealing of cattle by which Germany had been afflicted. But the French soon turned the tables. When Portugal and Catalonia rebelled against Philip IV, France immediately recognized the independence of Portugal under the new royal house of Braganza—as did England, Holland, and Sweden with equal alacrity. French troops streamed over the Pyrenees into Catalonia, spreading the usual devastation. Richelieu even recognized a Catalan republic.

European involvement

In Germany the last or Swedish-French phase of the war was not so much a civil war among Germans as an international struggle on German soil. Few German states now sided with the French and Swedes. A feeling of national resentment against foreign invasion even seemed to develop.

The Peace of Westphalia, 1648

Peace talks began in 1644 in Westphalia, at the two towns of Münster and Osnabrück. The German states were crying for peace, for a final religious settlement, and for "reform" of the Holy Roman Empire. France and Sweden insisted that the German states should individually take part in the negotiations, a disintegrating principle that the German princes eagerly welcomed and which the emperor vainly resisted. To Westphalia, therefore, hundreds of diplomats and negotiators now repaired, representing the Empire, its member states, Spain, France, Sweden, the Dutch, the Swiss, the Portuguese, the Venetians, many other Italians, and the pope. There had been no such European congress since the Council of Constance, and the fact that a European assemblage had in 1415 dealt with affairs of the church, and now in the 1640s dealt with affairs of the state, war, and power, was a measure of the secularization that had come over Europe.

Lengthy peace negotiations

The negotiations dragged on, because the armies were still fighting, and after each battle one side or the other raised its terms. France and Spain refused to make peace with each other at all and in fact remained at war until 1659. But for the Holy Roman Empire a settlement was agreed to, incorporated in 1648 in the two treaties of Münster and Osnabrück, and commonly known as the Peace of Westphalia.

The Peace of Westphalia represented a general checkmate to the Counter Reformation in Germany. It not only renewed the terms of the Peace of Augsburg, granting each German state the right to determine its own religion, but it also added Calvinism to Lutheranism and Catholicism as an acceptable faith. On the controversial issue of church territories secularized after 1552 the Protestants won a complete victory; Catholic claims to the territories were abandoned.

Dissolution of the Holy Roman Empire

The dissolution of the Holy Roman Empire, which had been advanced by the drawing of internal religious frontiers in the days of Luther, was now confirmed in politics and international law. Borderlands of the Empire fell away. The Dutch and Swiss ceased to belong to it, and both the United Provinces and Swiss cantons (or Helvetic Body) were recognized as sovereign and independent. From the disintegrating western frontier of the Holy Roman Empire the French cut off small pieces, receiving sovereignty over three Lorraine bishoprics, which they had occupied for a century, and certain rights in Alsace which were so confused that they later led to trouble. The king of Sweden received new territories in northern Germany, thus adding to Sweden's trans-Baltic possessions.

It was in the new constitution of the Empire itself, not in territorial changes, that the greatest victory of the French and their Swedish and Dutch allies was to be found. The German states, over 300 in number, became virtually sovereign.

Germany fragmented

Each received the right to conduct diplomacy and make treaties with foreign powers. The Peace of Westphalia further stipulated that no laws could be made by the Empire, no taxes could be raised, no soldiers could be recruited, no war could be declared or peace terms ratified except with the consent of the imperial estates — the 300-odd princes, ecclesiastics, and free cities in the Reichstag assembled. Since it was well known that agreement on any such matters was impossible, the principle of self-government, or of medieval constitutional liberties, was used to destroy the Empire itself as an effective political entity. While most other European countries were consolidating under royal absolutism, Germany sank back into fragmentation and localism.

The Peace of Westphalia blocked the Counter Reformation, frustrated the Austrian Habsburgs, and forestalled for almost two centuries any movement toward German national unification. Within Europe as a whole, however, it marked the advent in international law of the modern system of sovereign states. The diplomats who assembled at Westphalia represented independent powers which recognized no superior or common tie. No one any longer pretended that Europe had any significant religious or political unity. Statesmen delighted in the absence of any such unity, in which they sensed the menace of "universal monarchy." Europe was understood to consist of a large number of unconnected sovereignties, free and detached atoms, or states, which acted according to their own laws, following their own political interests, forming and dissolving alliances, exchanging embassies and legations, alternating between war and peace, shifting position with a shifting balance of power.

System of sovereign states

Physically Germany was wrecked by the Thirty Years' War. Cities were sacked by mercenary soldiers with a rapacity that their commanders could not control; or the commanders themselves, drawing no supplies from their home governments, systematically looted whole areas to maintain their armies. Magdeburg was besieged ten times; Leipzig, five. In one woolen town of Bohemia, with a population of 6,000 before the wars, the citizens fled and disappeared, the houses collapsed, and eight years after the peace only 850 persons were found there. The peasants, murdered, put to flight, or tortured by soldiers to reveal their few valuables, ceased to farm; agriculture was ruined; starvation followed, and with it came pestilence. Even revised modern estimates allow that in many extensive parts of Germany as much as a third of the population may have perished. The effects of fire, disease, undernourishment, homelessness, and exposure in the seventeenth century were the more terrible because of the lack of means to combat them. The horrors of modern war for civilians are not wholly different from horrors that men and women have experienced in the past.

Germany as such, physically wrecked and politically cut into small pieces, ceased for a long time to play any significant part in European affairs. A kind of political and cultural vacuum existed in central Europe. On the one hand, the western or Atlantic peoples— French, English, Dutch—began in the seventeenth century to take the lead in European politics, trade, and culture. On the other hand, in eastern Germany, around Berlin and Vienna, new and only half-German centers of power began to form. These themes will be traced in the two following chapters.

With the close of the Thirty Years' War the Wars of Religion came to an end. While religion remained an issue in some later conflicts, it was never again an important cause of conflicts in the political affairs of Europe as a whole. In general, by the close of the seventeenth century, the division between Protestant and Catholic had become stabilized. Neither side any longer expected to make territorial gains at the expense of the other. Both the Protestant and the Catholic reformations were accomplished facts. The political struggle for territory, wealth, and strategic alliances had become secularized in that "reasons of state" now prevailed over religious allegiances in shaping both the foreign policies of governments and the military conflicts of sovereign powers.

Austrian Habsburgs

Spanish Habsburgs

Swedish Dominions

Brandenburg-Prussia

Church Lands

Ottoman Empire controlled lands

Boundary of the Holy Roman Empire

0   100   200   300 miles

SHETLAND I.

ORKNEY I.

SCOTLAND

Edinburgh

Belfast

IRELAND

Dublin   Liverpool

ENGLAND
(COMMONWEALTH 1649–1660
UNITED KINGDOM 1707)

Bristol

London

ENGLISH CHANNEL

ATLANTIC OCEAN

North Sea

NORWAY

Bergen

KINGDOM OF
DENMARK AND NORWAY

DENMARK

(TO SWEDEN, 1658)
Copenhagen

SWEDISH
POMERANIA

SCHLESWIG

HOLSTEIN

Hamburg   Lübeck   Stralsund

Bremen   Stettin

UNITED
PROVINCES

Amsterdam   HANOVER   POMERALIA

Ryswick   Verden   BRANDENBURG   Berlin

Utrecht   Osnabrück   Magdeburg   GREAT
POLAND

Brussels   Münster

SPANISH   Cologne   MINOR   Leipzig   Breslau

NETH.   GERMAN STATES   SAXONY   Dresden

Rouen   Trier   Manz   SILESIA

Paris   Metz   PALATINATE   Prague

Rennes   Nantes   Orléans   Strasbourg   BOHEMIA   MORAVIA

FRANCE   Augsburg   BAVARIA   Vienna   HUNGARY

FRANCHE-   SWISS CANTONS   AUSTRIA

Bordeaux   Lyon   COMTE   SLAVONIA

SAVOY   Milan   Venice

La Coruña   Montauban   PIEDMONT   Parma   REPUBLIC   BOSNIA

León   Avignon   Genoa   OF VENICE   Zara

Oporto   Marseille   Florence   Adriatic Sea

PORTUGAL   Valladolid   TUSCANY   PAPAL

(TO SPAIN   NAVARRE   STATES

1580–1640)   SPAIN   Saragossa   CORSICA   Rome   Aquila

Lisbon   Escorial   Madrid   ARAGON   CATALONIA   (Genoa)   Bari

Mérida   CASTILE   Toledo   Barcelona   Naples   NAPLES

Valencia   SARDINIA   KINGDOM OF THE

BALEARIC I.   MINORCA   TWO SICILIES

Seville   Murcia   MAJORCA   Palermo

Cadiz   Malaga   Mediterranean   SICILY

Tangier   Ceuta   MALTA

(Spain)   Algiers   (Knights of St. John)

Oran (Spain)   Tunis

FEZ AND MOROCCO   ALGERIA   TUNISIA   Sea

B A R B A R Y   S T A T E S

PYRENEES

LORRAINE

ALSACE

EUROPE, 1648

This map shows the European states at the time of the Peace of Westphalia. A plurality of independent sovereign states was henceforth considered normal. The plurality of religions was also henceforth taken for granted within Europe as a whole, though each state continued to require or favor religious uniformity within its borders. By weakening the Habsburgs and furthering the disintegration of Germany, the Peace of Westphalia opened the way for the political ascendancy of France.

Chapter 4

THE GROWING POWER OF WESTERN EUROPE, 1640–1715

17. The *Grand Monarque* and the Balance of Power

18. The Dutch Republic

19. Britain: The Civil War

20. Britain: The Triumph of Parliament

21. The France of Louis XIV, 1643–1715: The Triumph of Absolutism

22. The Wars of Louis XIV: The Peace of Utrecht, 1713

If the reader were to take a map of Europe, set a compass on the city of Paris, and draw a circle with a radius of 500 miles, a zone would be marked out from which much of modern "Western" civilization radiated after about 1640. It was within this zone that a secular society, modern natural science, a developed capitalism, the modern state, parliamentary government, democratic ideas, machine industry, and much else either originated or received their first full expression. The extreme western parts of Europe—Ireland, Portugal, and Spain—were somewhat outside the zone in which the most rapid changes occurred. But within it were England, southern Scotland, France, the Low Countries, Switzerland, western and central Germany, and northern Italy. This area, for over two hundred years beginning in the seventeenth century, was the earth's principal center of what anthropologists might call cultural diffusion. Although the economy and culture of Western Europe were deeply influenced by the expanding trade and contacts with people outside Europe, the growing power of western European states, trading companies, science, and cultural institutions had a profound and spreading impact on the rest of Europe, the Americas, and ultimately the whole world.

This western European influence grew steadily in the half-century following the Peace of Westphalia. The fading out of the Italian Renaissance, the subsiding of religious wars, the ruin of the Holy Roman Empire, and the decline of Spain all cleared the stage on which the Dutch, English, and French were to be the principal actors. But the Dutch were few in number, and the English during most of the seventeenth century were weakened by domestic discord. It was France that for a time played the most imposing

Chapter emblem: Detail from a portrait of King Louis XIV by Hyacinthe Rigaud (1659–1743). (Giraudon/Art Resource, NY)

role. The whole half-century following the Peace of Westphalia is in fact often called the Age of Louis XIV.

17.   THE *GRAND MONARQUE* AND THE BALANCE OF POWER

This king of France inherited his throne in 1643 at the age of 5, assumed the personal direction of affairs in 1661 at the age of 23, and reigned for 72 years until his death in 1715. No one else in modern history has held so powerful a position for so long a time. Louis XIV was more than a figurehead. For over half a century, during his whole adult life, he was the actual and working head of the French government. Inheriting the state institutions that Richelieu had developed earlier in the seventeenth century, he made France the strongest country in Europe. Using French money, by bribes or other inducements, he built up a pro-French interest in virtually every country from England to Turkey. His policies and the counterpolicies that others adopted against him set the pace of public events, and his methods of government and administration, war and diplomacy, became a model for other rulers to copy. During this time the French language, French thought and literature, French architecture and landscape gardens, and French styles in clothes, cooking, and etiquette became the accepted standard for Europe. Louis XIV was called by his fascinated admirers Louis the Great, the *Grand Monarque,* and the Sun King.

Internationally, the consuming political question of the last decades of the seventeenth century (at least in western Europe—eastern Europe we reserve for the next chapter) was

The weakness of Spain

the fate of the still vast possessions of the Spanish crown. Spain was what Turkey was later called, "the sick man of Europe." To its social and economic decline was added hereditary physical deterioration of its rulers. In 1665 the Spanish throne was inherited by Charles II, an unfortunate afflicted by many ills of mind and body, impotent, even imbecile, the pitiable product of generations of inbreeding in the Habsburg house. His rule was irresolute and feeble. It was known from the moment of his accession that he could have no children and that the Spanish branch of the Habsburg family would die out with his death. The whole future not only of Spain but also of the Spanish Netherlands, the Spanish holdings in Italy, and all Spanish America was therefore in question. Charles II dragged out his miserable days until 1700, the object of jealousy and outright assault during his lifetime, and precipitating a new European war by his death.

The ambitions of Louis XIV

Louis XIV, who in his youth married a sister of Charles II, intended to benefit from the debility of his royal brother-in-law. His expansionist policies followed two main lines. One was to push the French borders eastward to the Rhine, annexing the Spanish Netherlands (or Belgium) and the Franche-Comté or Free County of Burgundy, a French-speaking region lying between ducal Burgundy and Switzerland (see maps, pp. 142–143, 147). Such a policy involved the further dismemberment of the Holy Roman Empire. The other line of Louis XIV's ambitions, increasingly clear as time went on, was his hope of obtaining the entire Spanish inheritance for himself. By combining the resources of France and Spain he would make France supreme in Europe, in America, and on the sea. To promote these ends Louis XIV intrigued with the smaller and middle-sized powers of Europe and also contacted dissidents (i.e., potential allies) in all the countries whose governments opposed him.

THE EXPANSION OF FRANCE, 1661–1713

The map shows how the foreign policy and wars of King Louis XIV gradually extended France's borders toward the east and northeast, bringing the Franche-Comté and new lands in both Alsace and Lorraine under French control. Louis also gained other territories in the Spanish Netherlands and expanded French holdings in the south along the frontier with Savoy. In addition to the expansion shown here, Louis XIV's other great ambition was to obtain control of Spain and the Spanish Empire in the Americas.

Were Louis XIV to succeed in his aims, he would create the "universal monarchy" dreaded by diplomats, that is to say, a political situation in which one state might subordinate all others to its will. The technique used against universal monarchy was the balance of power. Universal monarchy had formerly been almost achieved by the Austro-Spanish Habsburgs. The Habsburg supremacy had been blocked mainly by a balance of power headed by France, of which the Thirty Years' War and the Peace of Westphalia were the outstanding triumphs. Now the danger of universal monarchy came from France, and it was against France that the balance of power was directed.

The Idea of the Balance of Power

Motives for alliances

The aim of statesmen pursuing policies of balance of power in the seventeenth and eighteenth centuries was generally to preserve their own independence of action to the utmost. Hence the basic rule was to ally against any state threatening domination. If one state seemed to dictate too much, others would shun alliance with it unless they were willing (from ideological sympathy or other reasons) to become its puppets. They would seek alliance with the other weaker states instead. They would thus create a balance or counterweight, or "restore the balance," against the state whose ascendancy they feared. Another more subtle reason for preferring alliance with the weak rather than with the strong was that in such an alliance the leaders of each state could believe their own contribution to be necessary and valued, and by threatening to withdraw their support could win consideration of their own policies. Indeed, the balance of power may be defined as a system in which each state tends to throw its weight where it is most needed, so that its own importance may be enhanced.

Balance-of-power politics

The purpose of balance-of-power politics was not to preserve peace but to preserve the sovereignty and independence of the states of Europe, or the "liberties of Europe," as they were called, against potential aggressors. The system was effective as a means to this end in the seventeenth and eighteenth centuries. Combinations were intricate, and alliances were readily made and unmade to deal with emerging situations. One reason for the effectiveness of the system lay in the great number of states capable of pursuing an independent foreign policy. These included not only the greater and middle-sized states of Austria, Spain, France, England, Holland, Sweden, and Bavaria, but a great number of small independent states, such as Denmark, the German principalities, Portugal after 1640, and Savoy, Venice, Genoa, and Tuscany. States moved easily from one alliance to another or from one side of the balance to another. They were held back by no ideologies or sympathies, especially after the religious wars subsided, but could freely choose or reject allies, aiming only to protect their own independence or enlarge their own interests. Moreover, owing to the military technology of the day, small states might count as important military partners in an alliance. By controlling a strategic location, like the king of Denmark, or by making a contribution of ships or money, like the Dutch Republic, they might add just enough strength to an alliance to balance and overbalance the opposing great power and its allies.

As the ambitions of Louis XIV became bolder, and as the capacity of Spain to resist them withered away, the prevention of universal monarchy under France depended increasingly on combining the states of Europe into a balance of power against him. The balance against Louis XIV was engineered mainly by the Dutch. The most tireless of his enemies, and the one who did more than any other to checkmate him, was the Dutchman William III, the prince of Orange, who in his later years was king of England and Scotland as well.

Let us, after first surveying the Dutch in the seventeenth century, turn to the British Isles, where a momentous conflict occurred between Parliament and king. We shall then examine the French absolute monarchy under Louis XIV and conclude the present chapter with the wars of Louis XIV, particularly the War of the Spanish Succession, in which the resistance to French ambitions ultimately restored the European balance of power.

18. THE DUTCH REPUBLIC

Dutch Civilization and Government

The ambassadors of kings, strolling beside a canal at The Hague, might on occasion observe a number of burghers in plain black garments step out of a boat and proceed to make a meal of cheese and herring on the lawn, and they would recognize in these portly figures the provincial delegates of the Estates General of the United Provinces, as the Dutch government was known in the diplomatic language of the day. Though noblemen lived in the country, the Dutch were the most bourgeois of all peoples. They were not the only republicans in Europe, since the Swiss cantons, Venice, Genoa, and even England for a few years were republics, but of all republics the United Provinces was by far the most wealthy, the most flourishing, and the most important in international diplomacy and culture.

The Dutch acquired a nationality of their own in the long struggle against Spain, and with it a pride in their own freedom and independence. In the later phases of the war with Spain, notably during the Thirty Years' War, they were able to rely more on their wealth and diplomacy than on actual fighting, so that during the whole seventeenth century they enjoyed a degree of comfort, and of intellectual, artistic, and commercial achievement unexcelled in Europe. The classic Dutch poets and dramatists wrote at this time, making a literary language of what had formerly been a dialect of Low German. Hugo Grotius produced, in his *Law of War and Peace*, a pioneering treatise on international law. Baruch Spinoza, of a family of refugee Portuguese Jews, quietly turned out works of philosophy, examining the nature of reality, of human conduct, and of church and state. Spinoza made his living by grinding lenses; there were many other lens grinders in Holland; some of them developed the microscope, and some of these, in turn—Leeuwenhoek, Swammerdam, and others—peering through their microscopes and beholding for the first time the world of microscopic life, became founders of modern biological science. The greatest Dutch scientist was Christian Huyghens (1629–1695), who worked mainly in physics and mathematics; he improved the telescope (a Dutch invention), made clocks move with pendulums, discovered the rings of Saturn, and launched the wave theory of light. A less famous writer, Balthasar Bekker, in his *World Bewitched* (1691) delivered a decisive blow against the expiring superstition of witchcraft. Meanwhile, the extraordinarily learned scholar and artist Anna Maria van Schurman (1607–1678) developed an important seventeenth-century argument for the education of women in her influential treatise *The Learned Maid or Whether a Maid May Be Called a Scholar* (1638).

Dutch achievements

But the most eternally fresh of the Dutch creations, suffering from no barrier of time or language, were the superb canvases of the painters. Frans Hals produced bluff portraits of the common people. Jan Vermeer threw a spell of magic and quiet dignity over men, and especially women, of the burgher class, many of whom he portrayed in typical domestic scenes. Rembrandt conveyed the mystery of human consciousness itself. In Rembrandt's *Masters of the Cloth Guild* (see color illustrations following p. 288) we face a group of six men who seem about to speak from the canvas, inclined slightly forward, as intent on their business as judges on the proceedings in a courtroom. Such men conducted the affairs of Holland, in both commerce and government; intelligent and calculating but not cunning, honest but determined to drive a hard bargain; the sober black cloaks, with the clean white collars, set against the carved woodwork and rich table covering of the Cloth Hall, seem to suggest that personal vanity must yield to collective undertakings and that personal simplicity must be maintained in the midst of material opulence. And in

Vermeer's *Geographer* (see p. 153), painted in 1669, there appears not only an immaculately scrubbed and dusted Dutch interior, but something of a symbol of the modern world in its youth—the pale northern sunlight streaming through the window, the globe and the map, the dividers in the scholar's right hand, instrument of science and mathematics, the tapestry flung over the table (or is it an Oriental rug brought from the East?), the head lifted in thought, and eyes resting on an invisible world of fresh discoveries and opening horizons. The same interest in the complexities of human character and the details of household objects appears in Vermeer's *Girl Reading a Letter at an Open Window,* which he painted in the late 1650s (see p. 151), and *The Artist's Studio,* which dates from about 1665 (see color illustrations following p. 288).

Dutch paintings in this era showed certain characteristics of the wider seventeenth-century artistic style that came to be known as Baroque. The fascination with lighting, the representation of interior spaces, the use of distinctive colors or subtle hues, and a more naturalistic image of human beings often shaped the distinctive appearance of Baroque paintings. In contrast to most Dutch artists, however, many of the best-known Baroque painters identified with the Catholic Church or the Counter Reformation. The Flemish painter Peter Paul Rubens was one prominent example of this identification with Catholicism in the Low Countries (see his *Portrait of the Artist with Isabelle Brant,* c. 1610, in the color illustrations following p. 000); but art in the Netherlands tended to portray scenes of everyday life rather than the passion of religious ecstasy.

In religion, after initial disputes, the Dutch Republic adopted toleration. Early in the seventeenth century the Dutch Calvinists divided. One group favored a modification of Calvinism, with a toning down of the doctrine of absolute and unconditional predestination. This more moderate Calvinism drew its main support from the comfortable burghers and its

Religious toleration

doctrines from a theologian of Leyden named Arminius, whose ideas were condemned at an international Calvinist synod in 1618. But beginning in 1632 the Arminians were tolerated. Rights were granted to the large Catholic minority. Jews had long been welcomed in the republic; and Christian sects despised everywhere else, such as the Mennonites, found a refuge in it. Although none of these people had as many political or economic rights as the Calvinists, the resulting mixture stimulated both the intellectual life and the commercial enterprise of the country.

Dutch explorations and settlements

The Dutch as early as 1600 had 10,000 ships, and throughout the seventeenth century they owned most of the shipping of northern Europe. They were the carriers between Spain, France, England, and the Baltic. They also settled in Bordeaux to buy wines, lent money to vintners, and soon owned many vineyards in France itself. They sailed on every sea. They entered the Pacific by way of South America, where they rounded Cape Horn and named it after Hoorn in Holland. Organized in the East India Company of 1602, their merchants increasingly replaced the Portuguese in India and the Far East. In Java, in 1619, they founded the city of Batavia—the Latin name for Holland. (The city is now called Jakarta.)

Not long after 1600 the Dutch reached Japan. But the Japanese, fearing the political consequences of Christian penetration, in 1641 expelled all other Europeans and confined the Dutch to limited operations on an island near Nagasaki. The Dutch remained for over two centuries the sole link of the West with Japan. In 1612 the Dutch founded their first settlement on Manhattan Island, and in 1621 they established a Dutch West India Company to exploit the loosely held riches of Spanish and Portuguese America. They founded colonies at Pernambuco and Bahia in Brazil (lost soon thereafter) and at Caracas, Curaçao, and in Guiana in the Caribbean. In 1652 the Dutch captured the Cape of Good Hope in

GIRL READING A LETTER AT AN OPEN WINDOW
by Jan Vermeer (Dutch, 1632–1675)

Vermeer's characteristic interest in the mysteries of human character, the subtle shades of light, and the complex folds of a curtain appear in this painting of a young woman who seems to have received a disconcerting message or perhaps long anticipated news from afar.

(Erich Lessing/Art Resource, NY)

South Africa from the Portuguese. Dutch settlers soon appeared. Moving inland, they occupied the territory of the Khoikhoi and displaced or enslaved the people whose ancestors had lived there for centuries. From these Dutch settlers and from French Huguenots and others have come the modern Afrikaner people, whose language and religion still reflect their mainly Dutch origins.

The Bank of Amsterdam

In 1609 the Dutch founded the Bank of Amsterdam. European money was a chaos; coins were minted not only by great monarchs but also by small states and cities in Germany and Italy, and even by private persons. In addition, under inflationary pressures, kings and others habitually debased their coins by adding more alloy, while leaving the old coins in circulation along with the new. Anyone handling money thus accumulated a miscellany of uncertain value. The Bank of Amsterdam accepted deposits of such mixed money from all persons and from all countries, assessed the gold and silver content, and, at rates of exchange fixed by itself, allowed depositors to withdraw equivalent values in gold florins minted by the Bank of Amsterdam. These were of known and unchanging weight and purity. They thus became an internationally sought money, an international measure of value, acceptable everywhere. Depositors were also allowed to draw checks against their accounts. These conveniences, plus a safety of deposits guaranteed by the Dutch government, attracted capital from all quarters and made possible loans for a wide range of purposes. Amsterdam remained the financial center of Europe until the French Revolution.

Under their republican government the Dutch enjoyed great freedom, but it can hardly be said that their form of government met all the requirements of a state. The seven provinces that sent representatives to the Estates General of the United Provinces were all jealous of their own independence. Each province had, as its executive, an elected stadholder, but there was no stadholder for the United Provinces as a whole. This difficulty was overcome by the fact that most of the various provinces usually elected the head of the house of Orange as stadholder. This family had enjoyed exceptional prestige in the republic since the days of William the Silent and the wars for independence, but the prince of Orange, apart from being stadholder, was simply one of the feudal noblemen of the country. In general, however, the commercial class had more wealth than the older noble families, and affairs were usually managed by the burghers.

Politics in the Dutch Republic was a seesaw between the burghers, pacifistic and absorbed with business, and the princes of Orange, to whom the country owed most of its military security. When foreigners threatened invasion, the power of the stadholder increased. When all was calm, the stadholder could do little. The Peace of Westphalia produced a mood of confidence in the burghers, followed by a constitutional crisis, in the course of which the stadholder William II died, in 1650. No new stadholder was elected for 22 years. The burgher, civilian, and decentralizing tendencies prevailed.

William of Orange

In 1650, eight days after his father's death, the third William was born in the house of Orange, seemingly fated never to be stadholder and to pass his life as a private nobleman on his own estates. William III grew up to be a grave and reserved young man, small and rather stocky, with thin, compressed lips and a determined spirit. He learned to speak Dutch, German, English, and French with equal facility and to understand Italian, Spanish, and Latin. He observed the requirements of his religion, which was Dutch Calvinism, with sober regularity. He had a strong dislike for everything magnificent or pompous; he lived plainly, hated flattery, and took no pleasure in social conversation. In these respects he was the opposite of his life-long enemy the Sun King, whom he resembled only in his diligent preoccupation with affairs. In 1677 he married the king of England's niece, Mary Stuart.

THE GEOGRAPHER
by Jan Vermeer (Dutch, 1632–1675)

The impact on Europe of the opening of the Atlantic may be seen in this painting. For the first time in human history it had become possible to understand with some accuracy the relationships of the oceans and continents throughout the globe. The Dutch built up a large ocean-growing trade, and many of the leading cartographers lived in the Netherlands.

(Städelsches Kunstinstitut, Frankfurt)

Foreign Affairs: Conflict with the English and French

Meanwhile matters were not going favorably for the Dutch Republic. In 1651 the revolutionary government then ruling England passed a Navigation Act. This act may be considered the first of a long series of political measures by which the British colonial empire was built up. It was aimed against the Dutch carrying trade. It provided that goods imported into England and its dependencies must be transported on English ships or on

Threats by sea and land

ships belonging to the country exporting the goods. Since the Dutch were too small a people to be great producers and exporters themselves, and lived largely by carrying the goods of others, they saw in the new English policy a threat to their economic existence. The Dutch and English soon entered into a series of three wars, running with interruptions from 1652 to 1674 and generally indecisive, though in 1664 the English annexed New Amsterdam and renamed it New York.

While thus assaulted at sea by the English, the Dutch were menaced on land by the French. Louis XIV made his first aggressive move in 1667, claiming the Spanish Netherlands and Franche-Comté by alleging certain rights of his Spanish wife, and overrunning the Spanish Netherlands with his army. The Dutch, to whom the Spanish Netherlands were a buffer against France, set into motion the mechanism of the balance of power. Dropping temporarily their disputes with the English, they allied with them instead; and since they were able also to secure the adherence of Sweden, the resulting Triple Alliance was sufficient to give pause to Louis XIV, who withdrew from the Spanish Netherlands. But in 1672 Louis XIV again rapidly crossed the Spanish Netherlands, attacked with forces five times as large as the Dutch, and occupied three of the seven Dutch provinces.

The election of William as stadholder

A popular clamor now arose among the Dutch for William of Orange, demanding that the young prince, who was 22 years of age, be installed in the old office of stadholder, in which his ancestors had defended them against Spain. He was duly elected stadholder in six provinces. In 1673 these six provinces voted to make the stadholderate hereditary in the house of Orange. William, during his whole "reign" in the Netherlands, attempted to centralize and consolidate his government, put down the feudal liberties of the provinces, and free himself from constitutional checks, moving generally in the direction of absolute monarchy. He was unable, however, to go far in this course, and the United Provinces remained a decentralized patrician republic until 1795.

Meanwhile, to stave off the immediate menace of Louis XIV, William resorted to a new manipulation of the balance of power. He formed an alliance this time with the minor powers of Denmark and Brandenburg (the small German state around Berlin) and with the Austrian and Spanish Habsburgs. Nothing could indicate more clearly the new balance of power precipitated by the rise of France than this coming over of the Dutch to the Habsburg side. This alliance presented a forceful new challenge to Louis XIV and pushed him into negotiations that ended this phase of his expansionist wars. Peace was signed in 1678 (by the treaty of Nimwegen), but only at the expense of Spain and the Holy Roman Empire, from which Louis XIV took the long coveted Franche-Comté, together with another batch of towns in Flanders (see map, p. 147). The Dutch preserved their territory intact.

William comes to the English throne

In the next ten years came the great windfall of William's life. In 1689 he became king of England. He was now able to bring the British Isles into his perpetual combinations against France. Since the real impact of France was yet to be felt, and the real bid of Louis XIV for universal monarchy was yet to be made, and since the English at this time were rapidly gaining in strength, the entrance of England was a decisive addition to the balance formed against French expansion. In this way the constitutional troubles of England, by bringing a determined Dutchman to the English throne, entered into the general stream of European affairs and helped to assure that western Europe and its overseas offshoots should not be dominated totally by France.

19.   BRITAIN: THE CIVIL WAR

After the defeat of the Spanish Armada and recession of the Spanish threat the English were for a time less closely involved with the affairs of the Continent. They played no significant part in the Thirty Years' War and were almost the only European people west of Poland who were not represented at the Congress of Westphalia. At the time of the Westphalia negotiations in the 1640s they were in fact engaged in a civil war of their own. This English civil war was a milder variant of the Wars of Religion which desolated France, Germany, and the Netherlands. It was fought not between Protestants and Catholics as on the Continent, but between the more extreme or Calvinistic Protestants called Puritans and the more moderate Protestants, who adhered to the established Church of England. As in the wars on the Continent, religious differences were mixed indistinguishably with political and constitutional issues. As the Huguenots represented to some extent feudal rebelliousness against the French monarchy, as German Protestants fought for states' rights against imperial centralization, and the Calvinists of the Netherlands for provincial liberties against the king of Spain, so the Puritans asserted the rights of Parliament against the mounting claims of royalty in England.

The civil war in England took many lives, but was less destructive than most such wars on the Continent; and England escaped the worst horrors of the Wars of Religion. The same was not true of the British Isles as a whole. After 1603 the kingdoms of England and Scotland, while otherwise separate, were ruled by the same king; the kingdom of Ireland remained, as before, a dependency of the English crown. Between England and Presbyterian Scotland there was constant friction, but the worst trouble was between England and Catholic Ireland, which was the scene of religious warfare as savage as that on the Continent.

England in the Seventeenth Century

For the English the seventeenth century was an age of great achievement, during which they made their debut as one of the chief peoples of modern Europe. In 1600 only four or five million persons, in England and Lowland Scotland, spoke the English language. The number did not rise rapidly for another century and a half. But the population began to spread. Religious discontents, reinforced by economic pressures, led to considerable emigration. Twenty thousand Puritans settled in New England between 1630 and 1640, and about the same number went to Barbados and other West India islands during the same years. A third stream, again roughly of the same size, but made up mainly of Scottish Presbyterians, settled in northern Ireland under government auspices, driving away or expropriating the native Celts. English Catholics were allowed by the home government to settle in Maryland. A great many members of the Church of England went to Virginia during and after the mid-century civil war, adding to the small settlement made at Jamestown in 1607. Except for the movement to northern Ireland, called the "plantation of Ulster," these

English emigration to North America

The English playwright William Shakespeare helped to shape the modern English language as well as much of the later history of English theater and literature. This image of the famous author appeared on an early seventeenth-century edition of his collected works.
(Getty Images)

migrations took place without much attention on the part of the government, through private initiative organized in commercial companies. After the middle of the century the government began deliberately to build an empire. New York was conquered from the Dutch, Jamaica from the Spanish, and Pennsylvania and the Carolinas were established. All the thirteen colonies except Georgia were founded before 1700, but there were at that time still less than half a million people in British North America.

The English also, like the Dutch, French, and Spanish at the time, were creating their national culture. Throughout western Europe the national languages, encroaching upon international Latin on the one hand and local dialects on the other, were becoming adequate vehicles for the expression of thought and feeling. William Shakespeare helped to shape the evolving English language through the enduring influence of his great plays, including the famous tragedies *Hamlet, Macbeth,* and *King Lear* — all of which were first performed and published in the early years of the seventeenth century. John Milton published his influential epic poems *Paradise Lost* and *Paradise Regained* later in this same century, after the bitter conflicts of the English Civil War. Shakespeare and Milton projected their mighty conceptions of human experience, aspirations, and tragedy with the imaginative power of both new and old words. The English classical literature, rugged in form but deep in content, vigorous yet subtle in insight, majestic, abundant, and sonorous in expression, was almost the reverse of French classical writing, with its virtues of order, economy, propriety, and graceful precision. Proud of their literary culture and their own great writers, the English could never thereafter quite yield to French standards, nor be dazzled or dumbfounded, as some peoples were, by the cultural glories of the Age of Louis XIV. There were no seventeenth-century painters comparable to those on the Continent, but in music it was the age of Thomas Campion and Henry Purcell, and in architecture the century closed with the great buildings of Christopher Wren.

Economic activity

Economically the English were enterprising and affluent, though in 1600 far outdistanced by the Dutch. They had a larger and more productive country than the Dutch, and were therefore not as limited to purely mercantile and seafaring occupations. Coal was mined around Newcastle and was increasingly used, but was not yet a leading source of English wealth. The great industry was the growing of sheep and manufacture of woolens, which were the main export. Spinning and weaving were done mostly by workers in the country, under the putting-out system, and organized by merchants according to the methods of commercial capitalism. Since 1553 the English had traded with Russia by way of the White Sea; they were increasingly active in the Baltic and eastern Mediterranean; and with the founding of the East India Company, in 1600, they competed with the Dutch in assaulting the old Portuguese monopoly in India and East Asia. But profitable as such overseas operations were, the main wealth of England was still in the land. The richest men were not merchants but landlords, and the landed aristocracy formed the richest class.

Background to the Civil War: Parliament and the Stuart Kings

In England, as elsewhere in the seventeenth century, the kings clashed with their old medieval representative institutions. In England the old institution, Parliament, won out against the king. But this was not the unique feature in the English development. In Germany the estates of the Holy Roman Empire triumphed against the emperor, and much the same thing, as will be seen, occurred in Poland. But on the Continent the triumph of the old representative institutions generally meant political dissolution or even anarchy. Successful governments were generally those in which kingly powers increased; this was the strong tendency of the time, evident even in the Dutch Republic after 1672 under William of Orange. The unique thing about England was that Parliament, in defeating the king, arrived at a workable form of government. Government remained strong but came under parliamentary control. This determined the character of modern England and launched into the history of Europe and of the world the great movement of liberalism and representative institutions.

The violent struggles that ultimately produced England's new political order emerged from the conflicting ambitions of the Stuart kings and the most powerful social groups in the English Parliament. In 1603, on the death of Queen Elizabeth, the English crown was inherited by the son of Mary Stuart, James VI of Scotland. As a descendant of Henry VII he became king of England also, taking there the title of James I. James was a philosopher of royal absolutism. He had even written a book on the subject, *The True Law of Free Monarchy*. By a "free" monarchy James meant a monarchy free from control by Parliament, churchmen, or laws and customs of the past. It was a monarchy in which the king, as father to his people, looked after their welfare as he saw fit, standing above all parties, private interests, and pressure groups. He even declared that kings drew their authority from God and were responsible to God alone, a doctrine known as the divine right of kings.

The Stuarts and Parliament

Probably any ruler succeeding Elizabeth would have had trouble with Parliament, which had shown signs of restlessness in the last years of her reign but had deferred to her as an aging woman and a national symbol. She had maintained peace within the country and fought off the Spaniards, but these very accomplishments persuaded many people that they could safely bring their grievances into the open. James I was a foreigner, a Scot, who lacked the touch for dealing with the English and who was moreover a royal pedant, the "wisest fool in Christendom," as he was uncharitably called. Not content with the actualities of control, as Elizabeth had been, he read the Parliament tiresome lectures on the royal rights. He also was in constant need of money. The wars against Spain had left a considerable debt. James was far from economical, and, in any case, in an age of rising prices, he could not live within the fixed and customary revenues of the English crown. These were of medieval character, increasingly quaint under the new national and international conditions.

Neither to James I nor to his son Charles I, who succeeded him in 1625, would Parliament grant adequate revenue, because it distrusted them both. Many members of Parliament were Puritans, whose Calvinist beliefs made them dissatisfied with the organization and doctrine of the Church of England. Elizabeth had tried to hush up religious troubles, but James threatened to "harry the Puritans out of the land," and Charles supported the Church hierarchy which, under Archbishop Laud, sought to enforce religious conformity. Many members of Parliament were also lawyers, who feared that the common law of England, the historic or customary law, was in danger. They disliked the prerogative courts—the Star Chamber set up by Henry VII to settle disputes without the deliberations of a jury and the High Commission set up by Elizabeth to ensure conformity to the theology of the Church of England. They heard with trepidation the new doctrine that the sovereign king could make laws and decide cases at his own discretion. Last but not least, practically all members of Parliament were property owners. Landowners, supported by the merchants, feared that if the king succeeded in raising taxes on his own authority, their wealth would be insecure. Hence there were strong grounds for resistance.

Parliamentary resistance

In England the Parliament was so organized as to make resistance effective. There was only one Parliament for the whole country. There were no provincial or local estates, as in the Dutch Republic, Spain, France, Germany, and Poland. Hence all parliamentary opposition was concentrated in one place. In this one and only Parliament, there were only two houses, the House of Lords and the House of Commons. The landed interest dominated in both houses, the noblemen in the Lords and the gentry in the Commons. In the Commons the gentry, who formed the bulk of the aristocracy, mixed with representatives of the merchants and the towns. Indeed the towns frequently chose country gentlemen to represent them. Hence the houses of Parliament did not accentuate, as did the estates on the Continent, the class division within the country.

Nor was the church present in Parliament as a separate force. Before Henry VIII's break with Rome the bishops and abbots together had formed a large majority in the House of Lords. Now there were no abbots left, for there were no monasteries. The House of Lords was now predominantly secular; in the first Parliament of James I there were 82 lay peers and 26 bishops. The great landowners had captured the House of Lords. The smaller landowners of the Commons had been enriched by receiving former monastic lands and had prospered by raising wool. The merchants had likewise grown up under mercantilistic protection. Parliament was strong not only in organization but also in the social interests and wealth that it represented. No king could long govern against its will.

In 1629 king and Parliament came to a deadlock. Charles I attempted to rule without Parliament, which could legally meet only at the royal summons. He intended to give England a good and efficient government. Had he succeeded, the course of English constitutional development would have paralleled that of France. But by certain reforms in Ireland he antagonized the English landlords who had interests in that country. By supporting the leadership and theology of the Church of England he made enemies of the Puritans. By attempting to modernize the navy with funds raised without parliamentary consent (called "ship money") he alarmed all property owners, who feared that they would be forced to pay for policies they opposed.

The ship-money dispute illustrates the best arguments of both sides. It was the old custom in England for coastal towns to provide ships for the king's service in time of war. More recently, these coastal towns had provided money instead. Charles I wished to maintain a navy in time of *The ship-money dispute* peace and to have ship money paid by the country as a whole, including the inland counties. In the old or medieval view it was the function of the towns which were directly affected to maintain a fleet. In the new view, sponsored by the king, the whole nation was the unit on which a navy should be based. The country gentlemen whom Parliament mainly represented, and most of whom lived in inland counties, had less interest in the navy, and in any case were unwilling to pay for it unless they could control the foreign policies for which a navy might be used. The parliamentary class represented the idea, derived from the Middle Ages, that taxes should be authorized by Parliament. The king represented the newer ideas of monarchy that were developing on the Continent, which included a belief in the king's right to collect revenues that were needed by the state. The politically significant classes in England would not accept such ideas. Until the king could govern with the confidence of Parliament, or until Parliament itself was willing, not merely to keep down taxes but to assume the financial responsibilities of government under modern conditions, neither a navy nor any effectual government could be maintained.

The Scots were the first to rebel. In 1637 they rioted in Edinburgh against attempts to impose the Church of England's prayer book and episcopal organization in Scotland. Charles, to raise funds to put down the Scottish rebellion, convoked the English Parliament in 1640, for the first time in 11 years. When it proved hostile to him, he dissolved it and called for new elections. The same men were returned. The resulting body, since it sat theoretically for 20 years without new elections, from 1640 to 1660, is known historically as the Long Parliament. Its principal *The Long Parliament* leaders were small or moderately well-to-do landowning gentry. The merchant class, while furnishing no leaders, lent its support.

The Long Parliament, far from assisting the king against the Scots, used the Scottish rebellion as a means of pressing its own demands. These were revolutionary from the outset. Parliament insisted that the chief royal advisers be not merely removed but impeached and put to death. It abolished the Star Chamber and the High Commission. The most extreme Calvinist element, the "root and branch" men or "radicals," drove through a bill for the abolition of bishops, revolutionizing the Church of England. In 1642 Parliament and king came to open war: the king drawing followers mainly from the north and west; the Parliament, from the commercially and agriculturally more advanced counties of the south and east (see map, p. 166). A series of bloody battles steadily weakened the king's position, and his army dissolved in 1646. During the war, as the price of support from the Scottish army, Parliament adopted the Solemn League and Covenant. This prescribed that religion in England, Scotland, and Ireland should be made uniform "according to the word of God and the example of the best reformed churches." Thus Presbyterianism became the established legal religion of the three kingdoms.

The Emergence of Cromwell

The parliamentary forces, called Roundheads from the close haircuts favored by Puritans, gained their major military victories with an efficient new army, the New Model Army, and a highly competent commander, Thomas Fairfax. The wars also brought a hitherto unknown gentleman named Oliver Cromwell to the foreground. A devout Protestant, he organized a new and especially effective regiment in the New Model Army, the Ironsides, in which extreme Protestant exaltation provided the basis for morale, discipline, and the will to fight. By the late 1640s Cromwell had become the most powerful political and military leader of the parliamentary forces. The army, in which a more popular class was represented than in the Parliament, became the center of advanced democratic ideas. Many of the soldiers objected to Presbyterianism as much as to the Church of England. They favored a free toleration for all "godly" forms of religion, with no superior church organization above local groups of like-minded spirits.

Cromwell concluded that the defeated king, Charles I, could not be trusted, that "ungodly" persons of all kinds put their hopes in him (what later ages would call counterrevolution), and that he must be put to death. Since Parliament hesitated, Cromwell with the support of the army moved against Parliament. The Long Parliament, having started in 1640 with some 500 members, had sunk by 1649 to about 150 (for this

Pride's Purge

revolution, like others, was pushed through by a minority); of these Cromwell now drove out almost 100, leaving a Rump of 50 or 60. This operation was called Pride's Purge, after Colonel Pride who commanded the soldiers by whom Parliament was intimidated; and in subsequent revolutions such excisions have been commonly known as purges, and the residues, sometimes, as rumps. The Rump condemned King Charles for "treason" and sent him to death on the scaffold in 1649.

England, or rather the whole British Isles, was now declared a republic. It was named the Commonwealth. Cromwell tried to govern as best he could. Religious toleration was decreed except for Unitarians and atheists on the one hand, and except for Roman Catholics and the most obstinate supporters of the Church of England on the other. Cromwell had to subdue both Scotland and Ireland by force. In Scotland the execution of the king, violating the ancient national Scottish monarchy of the Stuarts, had

Religious violence in the Commonwealth

swung the country back into the royalist camp. Cromwell crushed the Scots in 1650.

Meanwhile the Protestant and Calvinist fury swept over Ireland. A massacre of newly settled Protestants in Ulster in 1641 had left bitter memories which were now avenged. The Irish garrisons of Drogheda and Wexford were defeated and massacred. Thousands of Catholics were killed; priests were put to the sword, and women and small children were dispatched in cold blood. Where formerly, in the "plantation" of Ulster, a whole Protestant population had been settled in northern Ireland, bodily replacing the native Irish, now Protestant landlords were scattered over the country as a whole, replacing the Catholic landlords and retaining the Catholic peasantry as their tenants. Ireland's native religion and clergy were driven underground, a foreign and detested church was established, and a new and foreign landed aristocracy, originally recruited in large measure from military adventurers, was settled upon the country, in which it ceased to reside as soon as it assured the payment of its rents.

In England itself Cromwell ruled with great difficulty. His regime was more successful in pursuing English interests abroad, for he not only completed the subjugation of Ireland, but in the Navigation Act of 1651, which barred Dutch ships from carrying goods between other countries and England or its colonies, he also opened the English attack on the Dutch maritime supremacy. He further waged a war with Spain in which England acquired Jamaica, thereby enhancing the English commercial position in the Caribbean and launching an English campaign for some of the vast inheritance of the Spanish Habsburgs. But he failed to gain the support of a majority of the English. The Puritan Revolu-

The execution of King Charles I marked the dramatic triumph of the radical, parliamentary forces in 1649, but the king's death—portrayed here in a seventeenth-century engraving—raised unprecedented questions about the proper limits for political authority and religious radicalism in English society.
(The Granger Collection, NY)

tion, like others, produced its extremists. It failed to satisfy the most ardent and could not win over the truly conservative, so that Cromwell found himself reluctantly more autocratic, and more alone.

A party arose called the Levellers, who were in fact what later times would call radical political democrats. They were numerous in the Puritan army, though their chief spokesman, John Lilburne, was a civilian. Appealing to natural rights and to the rights of Englishmen, they asked for a nearly universal manhood suffrage, equality of representation, a written constitution, and subordination of Parliament to a reformed body of voters. They thus anticipated many ideas of the American and French revolutions over a century later. There were others in whom religious and social radicalism were indistinguishably mixed. George Fox, going beyond Calvinism or Presbyterianism, founded the Society of Friends, or "Quakers." The Quakers caused much consternation by insisting that all believers could have new revelations of spiritual truth, by rejecting various social and religious hierarchies, and by allowing or even encouraging women to preach at their meetings. A more ephemeral group, the "Diggers," proceeded to occupy and cultivate common lands, or lands privately owned, in a general repudiation of property. The Fifth Monarchy Men were a millennial group who felt that the end of the world was at hand. They were so called from their belief, as they read the Bible, that history has seen four empires, those of Assyria, Persia, Alexander, and Caesar; and that the existing world was still "Caesar's" but would soon give way to the fifth monarchy, of Christ, in which justice would at last rule.

Religious and social radicalism

Cromwell opposed such movements by which all established persons in society felt threatened. As a regicide and a Puritan, however, he could not turn to the royalists or the former leaders of the Church of England. Unable to agree even with the Rump, he abolished it also in 1653, and thereafter vainly attempted to govern, as Lord Protector, through representative bodies devised by himself and his followers, under a written constitution, the Instrument of Government. Actually, he was driven to place England under military rule, the regime of the "major generals." These officials, each in his district, repressed malcontents, vagabonds, and "bandits," closed ale houses, and prohibited cockfighting, in a mixture of moral puritanism and political dictatorship. Cromwell died in 1658; and his son was unable to maintain the Protectorate. Two years later, with all but universal assent, royalty was restored. Charles II, son of the dead Charles I, became king of England and of Scotland.

Cromwell, by beheading a king and keeping his successor off the throne for eleven years, had left a lesson which was not forgotten. Though he favored constitutional and parliamentary government and had granted a measure of religious toleration, he had in fact

Legacy of the revolution

ruled as a dictator in behalf of a stern Puritan minority. The English people now began to blot from their memories the fact that they had ever had a real revolution. The fervid dream of a "godly" England was dissipated forever. What was remembered was a nightmare of standing armies and major generals, of grim Puritans and overwrought religious enthusiasts. The English lower classes ceased to have any political role or consciousness for over a century, except in sporadic rioting over food shortages or outbursts against the dangers of "popery." Democratic ideas were rejected as "levelling." They were generally abandoned in England after 1660 or were cherished by obscure individuals and religious radicals who could not make themselves heard. Such ideas, indeed, had a more continuous history in the English colonies in America, where some leaders of the discredited revolution took refuge.

20.   BRITAIN: THE TRIUMPH OF PARLIAMENT

The Restoration, 1660–1688: The Later Stuarts

What was restored in 1660 was not only the monarchy, in the person of Charles II, but also the Church of England and the Parliament. Everything, legally, was supposed to be as it had been in 1640. The difference was that Charles II, knowing the fate of his father, was careful not to provoke Parliament to extremes and that the classes represented in Parliament, frightened by the disturbances of the past 20 years, were more warmly loyal to the king than they had been before 1640 and more willing to uphold the established church.

New legislation

Parliament during the Restoration enacted some far-reaching legislation. It changed the legal basis of land tenure, abolishing certain old feudal payments owed by landholders to the king. The possession of land thus came to resemble private property of modern type, and the landowning class became more definitely a propertied aristocracy. In place of the feudal dues to the king, which had been automatically payable, Parliament arranged for the king to receive income in the form of taxation, which Parliament could raise or reduce in amount. This gave a new power to Parliament and a new flexibility to government. The aristocracy thus cleared their property of customary restrictions and obligations, and at the same time undertook to support the state by imposing taxes on themselves. The English aristocracy proved more willing than the corresponding classes on the Continent to pay a large share of the expenses of government. Its reward was that, for a century and a half, it virtually ran the government to the exclusion of everyone else. Landowners in this period directed not only national affairs through Parliament but also local affairs as justices of the peace. The justices, drawn from the gentry of each county, decided small lawsuits, punished misdemeanors, and supervised the parish officials charged with poor relief and care of the roads. The regime of the landlord-justices came to be called the "squirearchy."

Other classes drew less immediate advantage from the Restoration. The Navigation Act of 1651 was renewed and even added to, so that commercial, shipping, and manufacturing interests were well protected. But in other ways the landed classes now in power showed themselves unsympathetic to the business classes of the towns. Many people in the towns were Dissenters, of the element formerly called Puritan and now refusing to accept the restored Church of England. Parliament excluded Dissenters from the town "corporations," or governing bodies, forbade any dissenting clergymen to teach school or come within five miles of an incorporated town, and prohibited all religious meetings, called "conventicles," not held according to the forms and by the authority of the Church of England. The *Exclusion of Dissenters* effect was that many middle-class townspeople found it difficult or impossible to follow their preferred religion, to obtain an education for their children, either elementary or advanced (for Oxford and Cambridge were a part of the established church), to take part in local affairs through the town corporations, or to sit in the House of Commons, since the corporations in many cases chose the burgesses who represented the towns. The lowest classes, the very poor, were discouraged by the same laws from following sectarian and visionary preachers. Another enactment fell upon them alone, the Act of Settlement of 1662, which decentralized the administration of the Poor Law, making each parish responsible only for its own paupers. Poor people, who were very numerous, were condemned to remain in the parishes where they lived. A large section of the English population was immobilized.

But it was not long after the Restoration that Parliament and king were again at odds. The main issue was again religion. Many Protestants throughout Europe at this time were returning voluntarily to Roman Catholicism, a tendency naturally dreaded by the Protestant churches. It was most conspicuously illustrated when the daughter of Gustavus Adolphus himself, Queen Christina of Sweden, to the consternation of the Protestant world, abdicated her throne and was received into the Roman church. In England the national feeling was excitedly anti-Catholic. No measures were more popular than those against "popery"; and the squires in Parliament, stiffly loyal to the Church of England, dreaded papists even more than Dissenters. The king, Charles II, was personally inclined to Catholicism. He admired the magnificent monarchy of Louis XIV, which he would have liked to duplicate, so far as possible, in England. At odds with his Parliament, Charles II made overtures to Louis XIV. The secret treaty of Dover of 1670 was the outcome. Charles thereby agreed to join Louis XIV in his expected war against the Dutch; and Louis agreed to pay the king of England three million livres a year during the war. He hoped also that Charles II would soon find it opportune to rejoin the Roman church.

While these arrangements were unknown in detail in England, it was known that Charles II was well disposed to the French and to Roman Catholicism. England went to war again with the Dutch. The king's brother and heir, James, Duke of York, publicly announced his conversion to Rome. Charles II, in a "declaration of indulgence," announced the nonenforcement of laws against Dissenters. The king declared that he

COACRES ET COACRESSE
DANS LEURS ASSEMBLÉES.

Among the many religious groups that rose to prominence during the English Revolution, the Quakers became especially notorious for their critique of religious hierarchies and their willingness to let women speak at their meetings. The novelty of the group is suggested in this seventeenth-century French illustration of a woman addressing a Quaker assembly.
(Fotomas Index/Bridgeman Art Library)

Charles II and the Test Act

favored general toleration, but it was rightly feared that his real aim was to promote Roman Catholicism in England. Parliament retorted in 1673 by passing the Test Act, which required all officeholders to take communion in the Church of England. The Test Act renewed the legislation against Dissenters and also made it impossible for Catholics to serve in the government or in the army and navy. The Test Act remained on the statute books until 1828.

While Charles's pro-French and pro-Catholic policies were extremely unpopular, both among the country gentry who disliked the French from prejudice and the merchants who found them increasingly pressing competitors, the situation might not have come to a head except for the avowed Catholicism and French orientation of Charles's brother James, due to be the next king since Charles had no legitimate children. A strong movement developed in Parliament to exclude James by law from the throne. The exclusionists—and those generally who were most suspicious of the king, Catholics, and the French—received the nickname of Whigs. The king's supporters were popularly called Tories. The Whigs, while backed by the middle class and merchants of London, drew their main strength from the upper aristocracy, especially certain great noblemen who might expect, if the king's power were weakened, to play a prominent part in ruling the country themselves. The Tories were the party of the lesser aristocracy and gentry, those who were suspicious of the "moneyed interest" of London, and felt a strong loyalty to church and king. These two parties, or at least their names, became permanently established in English public life. But all the Whigs and Tories together, at this time, did not number more than a few thousand persons.

The Revolution of 1688

James II, despite Whig vexation, became king in 1685. He soon antagonized even the Tories, who strongly supported the Church of England. As landowners they appointed most of the parish clergy, who imparted Tory sentiments to the rural population, and from their ranks were drawn the bishops, archdeacons, university functionaries, and other high personnel of the church. The laws keeping Dissenters and Catholics from office had given Anglicans (i.e., members of the Church of England) a monopoly in local and national government and in the army and navy. James II acted as if there were no Test Act, claiming the right to suspend its operation in individual cases, and appointed a good many Catholics to influential and lucrative positions. He offered a program, as his brother had done, of general religious toleration, to allow Protestant Dissenters as well as Roman Catholics to participate in public life.

Such a program, whether frankly meant as a secularizing of politics or indirectly intended as favoritism to Catholics, was repugnant to the Church of England. Seven bishops refused to endorse it. They were prosecuted for disobedience to the king but were acquitted by the jury. James, by these actions, violated the liberties of the established church, threatened the Anglican monopoly of church and state, and aroused the popular terrors of "popery." He was also forced to take the position philosophically set forth by his grandfather James I, that a king of England could make and unmake the law by his own will. The Tories joined the Whigs in opposition. In 1688, a son was born to James II and baptized into the Catholic faith. The prospect now opened up of an indefinite line of Catholic rulers in England. Leading men of both parties thereupon abandoned James II. They offered the throne to his grown daughter Mary, born and brought up a Protestant before her father's conversion to Rome.

Whigs and Tories in opposition to the crown

Mary was the wife of William of Orange. William, it will be recalled, had spent his adult life blocking the ambitions of the king of France, who likewise had threatened Europe with a "universal monarchy" by absorbing or inheriting the world of Spain. To William III it would be a mere distraction to be husband to a queen of England, or even to be king in his own name, unless England could be brought to serve his own purposes. He was immutably Dutch; his purpose was to save Holland and hence to ruin Louis XIV. His chief interest in England was to bring the English into his balance of power against France. Since the English were generally anti-French, and had chafed under the pro-French tendencies of their kings, William without difficulty reached an understanding with the discontented Whigs and Tories. Protected by a written invitation from prominent Englishmen, he invaded England with a considerable army. James II fled, and William was proclaimed co-ruler with Mary over

William invades England

ENGLAND IN THE SEVENTEENTH CENTURY

The maps show the principal seventeenth-century English towns and the rough division of the country into royalist and parliamentary regions during the English Civil War. King Charles I drew his strongest support from the north and west; Parliament drew its strongest support from the southeast and from London. Similar regional political patterns emerged in later conflicts between the Royalist "Tories" and the Parliamentary "Whigs." The Whigs were generally supported by the upper aristocracy and the commercial classes of London, who opposed the pro-French, pro-Catholic policies of the Stuart kings Charles II and James II.

England and Scotland. In the next year, 1690, at the Boyne River in Ireland, a motley army of Dutchmen, Germans, Scots, and French Huguenots under William III defeated a French and Irish force led by James II. Thus the constitutional liberties of England were saved and Anglican Protestantism remained the official religion of the English nation. James II fled to France.

Louis XIV of course refused to recognize his inveterate enemy as ruler of England. He maintained James at the French court with all the honors due the English king. It was thereafter one of his principal war aims to restore the Catholic and Stuart dynasty across the Channel. The English, contrariwise, had added reason to fight the French. A French victory would mean counterrevolution and royal absolutism in England. The whole Revolution of 1688 was at stake in the French wars.

In 1689, Parliament enacted a Bill of Rights, stipulating that no law could be suspended by the king (as the Test Act had been), no taxes could be raised or army maintained except by parliamentary consent, and no subject (however poor) could be arrested and detained without legal process. *Bill of Rights and the Toleration Act*
William III accepted these articles as conditions to receiving the crown. Thereafter the relation between king and people was a kind of contract. It was further provided, by the Act of Settlement of 1701, that no Catholic could be king of England; this excluded the descendants of James II, known in the following century as the Pretenders. Parliament also passed the Toleration Act of 1689, which allowed Protestant Dissenters to practice their religion but still excluded them from political life and public service. Since ways of evading these restrictions were soon found, and since even Catholics were not molested unless they supported the Pretenders, there was thereafter no serious trouble over religion in England and Lowland Scotland.

The English Parliament could make no laws for Scotland, and it was to be feared that James II might someday be restored in his northern kingdom. The securing of the parliamentary revolution in England, and of the island's defenses against France, required that the two kingdoms be organically joined. There was little sentiment in Scotland, however, for a merger with the English. The English tempted the Scots with economic advantages. The Scots still had no rights in the English East India Company, nor in the English colonies, nor within the English system of mercantilism and Navigation Acts. They obtained such rights by consenting to a union. In 1707 the United Kingdom of Great Britain was created. The Scots retained their own legal system and established Presbyterian church, but their government and parliament were merged with those of England. The term "British" came into use to refer to both English and Scots.

As for Ireland, it was now feared as a center of Stuart and French intrigue. The Revolution of 1688 marked the climax of a long record of trouble. Ireland had never been simply "conquered" by England, though certain English or rather Anglo-Norman families had carved out estates there since the twelfth century. By the end of the Middle Ages Ireland was organized as a separate kingdom with its own parliament, subordinate to the English crown. During *The Irish threat to the Revolution of 1688*
the Reformation the Irish remained Catholic while England turned Protestant, but the monasteries were dissolved in Ireland as in England; and the organized church as such, the established Church of Ireland, with its apparatus of bishoprics, parishes, and tithes, became an Anglican communion in which the mass of native Irish had no interest. Next came the plantation of Ulster, already mentioned, in which a mass of newcomers, mainly Scottish and Presbyterian, settled in the northern part of the island. Then in Cromwell's time, as just seen, English landlords spread through the rest of the country; or rather, a new Anglo-Irish upper class developed, in which English landowning families, residing most often in England, added the income from Irish estates to their miscellaneous revenues.

Ireland therefore by the close of the seventeenth century was a very mixed country. Probably two-thirds of its population was Catholic, of generally Celtic ethnic background; perhaps a fifth was Presbyterian, with recent Scottish connections; the small remainder was made up of Anglicans, largely Anglo-Irish of recent or distant origin in England, who controlled most of the land, manned the official church, and were influential in the Irish

CHRONOLOGY OF NOTABLE EVENTS, 1642–1713

1642–1648	Civil War in England
1649	Execution of King Charles I in London
1649–1658	Oliver Cromwell leads the English "Commonwealth" and "Protectorate"
1660	Restoration of English Monarchy, King Charles II
1661	King Louis XIV takes personal control of French government; reign continues to 1715
1685	Revocation of Edict of Nantes; persecution of French Protestants
1688	"Glorious Revolution" brings William and Mary to English throne and strengthens power of Parliament
1702–1713	War of Spanish Succession; "balance of power" limits French expansion
1713	Peace of Utrecht

parliament. It was essentially a landlord and peasant society, in which the Presbyterian as well as the Catholic mass was overwhelmingly agricultural; towns were small, and the middle class scarcely developed.

After the Revolution of 1688, in which the final overthrow of James II took place at the Boyne River, the English feared Ireland as a source of danger to the postrevolutionary arrangements in England. Resistance of the subjugated Catholics had also to be prevented. English elites who were defending their own liberties at home thus set about destroying the religious, political, and social liberties of Irish Catholics. In addition to the burden of an alien church and absentee landlordism, the Irish were now subjected to a new "penal code." Catholic clergy were banished, and Catholics were forbidden to vote or to sit in the Irish parliament. Catholic teachers were forbidden to teach, and Catholic parents were forbidden to send children overseas to be educated in Catholic schools. No Catholic could take a degree at Trinity College (Dublin University), an Anglican institution. Catholic Irishmen were forbidden to purchase land, to lease it for more than 31 years, to inherit it from a Protestant, or to own a horse worth more than £5. A Catholic whose son turned Protestant found his own property rights limited in his son's favor. Catholics were forbidden to be attorneys, to serve as constables, or, in most trades, to have more than two apprentices. Some disabilities fell on the Protestant Irish also. Thus Irish shipping was excluded from the British colonies, nor could the Irish import colonial goods except through England. Export of Irish woolens and glass manufactures was prohibited. No import tariff on English manufactures could be levied by the Irish parliament. About all that was left to the Irish, in international trade, was the export of agricultural produce; and the foreign exchange acquired in this way went very largely to pay the rents to absentee landlords.

Restrictions for Catholics

The purpose of the penal code was in part strategic, to weaken Ireland as a potentially hostile country during a long period of English wars with France. In part it was commercial, to favor English manufactures by removing Irish competition. And in part it was social, to confirm the position of the Anglican interest, or "ascendancy" as it came to be called. Parts of the code were removed piecemeal in the following decades, and a Catholic merchant class grew up in the eighteenth century; but much remained in effect for a long time, so that, for example, a Catholic could not vote for members of the Irish parliament until 1793, and even then could not be elected to it. In general, the Irish emerged from the seventeenth century as the most repressed people of western Europe.

England, immediately after the expulsion of James II, joined William III's coalition against France. To the alliance England brought a highly competent naval force, together with very considerable wealth. William's government, to finance the war, borrowed £1,200,000 from a syndicate of private lenders, who in return for holding government bonds were given the privilege of operating a bank. Thus originated, in 1694, both the Bank of England and the British national debt. Owners of liquid assets, merchants of London and Whig aristocrats with fat rent rolls, having lent their money to the new regime, had a compelling reason to defend it against the French and James II. And having at last a government whose policies they could control, they were willing to entrust it with money in large amounts. The national debt rapidly rose, while the credit of the government held consistently good; and for many years the Continent was astonished at the wealth that the British government could tap at will and the quantities of money that it could pour into the wars of Europe.

Coalition against France

The events of 1688 came to be known to the English as the Glorious Revolution. The Revolution was portrayed as vindicating the principles of parliamentary government, the rule of law, and even the right of rebellion against tyranny (though, as noted above, England's governing classes denied all such rights in Ireland). The overthrow of James II and the enactment of new parliamentary restrictions on the power of English kings have often been depicted as the climax in the growth of English constitutional self-government. Political writers like John Locke, shortly after the events, helped to give wide currency to these ideas. There was in truth some justification for these views even though in more recent times some writers have "deglorified" the Revolution of 1688. They point out that it was a class movement, promoted and maintained by the landed aristocracy. The Parliament which boldly asserted itself against the king was at the same time closing itself to large segments of the people. Where in the Middle Ages members of the House of Commons had usually received pay for their services, this custom disappeared in the seventeenth century, so that thereafter only men with independent incomes could sit. After the parliamentary triumph of 1688 this tendency became a matter of law. An act of 1710 required members of the House of Commons to possess private incomes at such a level that only a few thousand persons could legally qualify. This income had to come from the ownership of land. England from 1688 to 1832 was the best example in modern times of a true aristocracy, that is, of a country in which the men of the aristocratic landowning class not only enjoyed privileges but also conducted the government. But the landowning interest was then the only class sufficiently wealthy, numerous, educated, and self-conscious to stand on its own feet. The rule of the "gentlemen of England" was within its strict social limits a regime of political liberty.

The Glorious Revolution

21. THE FRANCE OF LOUIS XIV, 1643–1715: THE TRIUMPH OF ABSOLUTISM

French Civilization in the Seventeenth Century

Having traveled in the outer orbits of the European political system, we come now to its radiant and mighty center, the domain of the Sun King himself, the France against which the rest of Europe felt obliged to combine because its power threatened the interests of so many other countries—the future of the Spanish possessions, the independence of Holland, the maintenance in England of the parliamentary revolution. The France of Louis XIV owed much of its ascendancy to the quantity and quality of its people. Population was stabilized or possibly even falling in the seventeenth century, the last century in which France was seriously disturbed by famine, pestilence, and peasant rebellion. With 19 million inhabitants in 1700 France was still over three times as populous as England and twice as populous as Spain. Its fertile soil, in an agricultural age, made it a wealthy country, though the wealth was very unevenly distributed.

The contradictions of French society

France was big enough to harbor many contradictions. Millions of its people lived in poverty, yet the number in comfortable or even luxurious circumstances was very large. There were both modest country nobles and cosmopolitan *grands seigneurs*. The middle class included an inordinate number of lawyers, officeholders, and bureaucrats. The country was less commercial than Holland or England, yet in sheer numbers there may have been more merchants in France than in either of the other two countries. Protestants were a declining minority, yet in the mid-seventeenth century there were still more French Huguenots than Dutch Calvinists. It was a self-sufficient country, yet the French in this century began trading in India and Madagascar, founded colonial settlements in Canada, penetrated the Great Lakes and the Mississippi valley, set up plantations in the West Indies, expanded their ancient commerce with the Levant, enlarged their mercantile marine, and for a time had the leading navy of Europe.

The dominance of France meant the dominance not merely of power but of a people whom most Europeans viewed as the forefront of seventeenth-century civilization. They carried over the versatility of the Italy of the Renaissance. In Nicholas Poussin and Claude Lorrain they produced a notable school of painters, their architecture was emulated throughout Europe, and they excelled in military fortification and engineering. Much of their literature, though often written by bourgeois writers, was designed for an aristocratic and courtly audience, which had put aside the uncouth manners of an earlier day and prided itself on the refinement of its tastes and perceptions. Corneille and Racine wrote austere tragedies on the personal conflicts and social relations of human life. Molière, in his comedies, ridiculed bumbling doctors, new-rich bourgeois, and foppish aristocrats, making the word "marquis" almost a joke in the French language. La Fontaine gave the world his animal fables, and La Rochefoucauld, in his witty and sardonic maxims, a nobleman's candid judgment on human nature. In Descartes the French produced a great mathematician and scientific thinker; in Pascal, a scientist who was also a profound spokesman for Christianity; in Bayle, the father of modern skeptics. It was French thought and the French language, not merely the armies of Louis XIV, which in the seventeenth century were sweeping the European world.

Patronage of the arts by Louis XIV

Louis XIV understood that France's dominant position in Europe required more than large armies and that a flourishing cultural life greatly enhanced the international prestige of even the wealthiest or most powerful sovereign state. He therefore gave generous financial support to his favorite writers and artists, especially those who produced works for his new palace at Versailles. He also brought the arts and sciences into the state's administrative system by establishing royal academies in which various theorists taught the correct principles for art, literature, music, dance, and scientific knowledge. The favored or official aesthetic theory in these academies was called classicism, a theory that emphasized order, harmony, and the artistic achievements of antiquity. Following the example of painters

The French playwright Molière often performed in his own plays, including some that were staged at the court of Louis XIV. He is portrayed here as a character in _The School for Wives_, a popular comedy about conflicts and deceptions in the relations between women and men.

(Giraudon/Art Resource, NY)

such as Poussin, young artists learned to portray scenes from classical Roman history or mythology with harmonious and almost geometric precision. The great literary theorist of the day, Nicolas Boileau, urged writers to emulate the poetic works of ancient writers who had shown how literature addresses the timeless themes of human knowledge rather than the frivolities of daily life. The classicism of French artists and writers thus fit comfortably with the Sun King's appreciation for order, harmony, and hierarchy in every sphere of social, political, and cultural life.

Yet neither the king nor his official academies could control all of France's artistic and intellectual activity. Some literary critics, soon known as the "Moderns," began to argue that modern literature and knowledge had in fact surpassed the achievements of antiquity and that Boileau's academic writers, soon called the "Ancients," deferred much too rigidly to ancient authorities. Meanwhile, other centers of intellectual life emerged outside the royal academies in the new salons of Paris. Developing rapidly in the second half of the seventeenth century, the salons became the unofficial gathering places for Parisian nobles, wealthy professional persons, and creative writers or artists. They were organized by upper-class women who invited people into their homes to discuss philosophy, literature, and art—all of which could be debated without the formal constraints and solemnity of the academies. The salons attracted criticism and even ridicule from some people in the government and academies, partly because

Salons

they were created by energetic women and partly because they flourished outside the official cultural institutions of the state. But the Parisian salons, like the royal academies, became an enduring, distinctive institution in French cultural life. They also welcomed distinguished foreign visitors, thus contributing to the spread of French ideas and social mores throughout Europe. Parisian-style salons eventually appeared in other European cities, along with French fashion, French manners, and the French language.

The Development of Absolutism in France

This ascendancy of French culture went along with a regime in which political liberties were at a discount. The culture embellished what historians have often called the "absolute monarchy" of Louis XIV, though the king's power was never as far-reaching as the term "absolutism" suggests. The Sun King had to secure the cooperation of the nobility and other social classes; and his power was constrained in various ways by regional institutions, French legal traditions, and a fragmented system of local economies. France had a tradition of political freedom in the feudal sense. It had the same kind of background of feudal liberties as did the other countries of Europe. It had an Estates General, which had not met since 1615 but was not legally abolished. In some regions Provincial Estates, still

The "parlements"

meeting frequently, retained a measure of self-government and of power over taxation. There were about a dozen bodies known as parlements,[1] which, unlike the English Parliament, had developed as courts of law, each being the supreme court for a certain area of the country. The parlements upheld certain "fundamental laws" which they said the king could not overstep, and they often refused to enforce royal edicts that they declared to be unconstitutional. France, beneath the surface, was almost as diverse as Germany (see map, p. 180). French towns had won charters of acknowledged rights, and many of the great provinces enjoyed liberties written into old agreements with the crown. These local liberties were the main reason for a good deal of institutional complication. There were some 300 "customs" or regional systems of law; it was observed that travelers sometimes changed laws more often than they changed horses. Internal tariffs ran along the old provincial borders. Tolls were levied by manorial lords. The king's taxes fell less heavily on some regions than on others. Neither coinage nor weights and measures were uniform throughout the country. France was a bundle of territories held together by allegiance to the king.

This older kind of feudal freedom discredited itself in France at the very time when by triumphing in Germany it pulled the Holy Roman Empire to pieces, and when in England it successfully made the transition to a more modern form of political liberty, embodied in the parliamentary though aristocratic state. In France the old medieval or local type of liberty became associated with disorder. It has already been related how after the disorders of the sixteenth-century religious wars people had turned with relief to the monarchy and how Henry IV and then Richelieu had begun to make the monarchy strong. The troubles of

The Fronde

the Fronde provided additional incentive for the centralization of political power in France.

The Fronde broke out immediately after the Peace of Westphalia, while Louis XIV was still a child, and was directed against Cardinal Mazarin, who was governing in his name. It was an abortive revolution, led by the same elements, the parlements and the nobility, which were to initiate the great French Revolution in 1789. The parlements, especially the Parlement of Paris, insisted in 1648 on their

---

[1]Spelled *parlements* in French, to distinguish from the English Parliament.

INSPIRATION OF THE EPIC POET
by Nicolas Poussin (French, 1594–1665)

Poussin's interest in both the themes and forms of classicism appear in this image of a poet who yearns for the honor of a laurel crown as he meditates on the Greek god Apollo (with his lyre) and Calliope, the muse of epic poetry. The painting shows the careful symmetry and balance of much seventeenth-century French art.

(Scala/Art Resource, NY)

right to pronounce certain edicts unconstitutional. Barricades were thrown up and street fighting broke out in Paris. The nobility rebelled, as it had often in the past. Leadership was assumed by certain prominent noblemen who had enough wealth and influence to believe that, if the king's power were contained, they might govern the country themselves. The nobility demanded a calling of the Estates General, expecting to dominate over the bourgeoisie and the clergy in that body. Armed bands of soldiers, unemployed since the Peace of Westphalia and led by nobles, roamed about the country terrorizing the peasants. If the nobles had their way, it was probable that the manorial system would fall on the peasants more heavily, as in eastern Europe, where triumphant lords were at this very time exacting increased labor services from the peasants. Finally the rebellious nobles called in Spanish troops, though France was at war with Spain. By this time the bourgeoisie, together with the parlements, had withdrawn support from the rebellious nobles. The agitation subsided in total failure. Bourgeoisie and aristocracy could not work together; the nobles outraged people throughout France by bringing Spanish soldiers into their rebellion; and the *frondeurs,* especially after the parlements deserted them, had no systematic or constructive program, aiming only at the overthrow of the unpopular Cardinal Mazarin and at obtaining offices and favors for themselves.

After the Fronde, as after the religious wars, the bourgeoisie and peasantry of France, to protect themselves against the claims of the aristocracy, were in a mood to welcome the exercise of strong power by the kings. And in the young Louis XIV they had a man more than willing to grasp all the power he could get. Louis, at age 23, on Mazarin's death in 1661, announced that he would govern the country himself. He was the third king of the Bourbon line. It was the Bourbon tradition, established by Henry IV and by Richelieu, to draw the teeth from independent aristocrats, and this tradition Louis XIV followed. He was not a man of any transcendent abilities, though he had the capacity, often found among successful executives, of learning a good deal from conversation with experts. His education was not very good, having been made purposely easy; but he had the ability to see and stick to definite lines of policy, and he was extremely methodical and industrious in his daily habits, scrupulously loading himself with administrative business throughout his reign. He was extremely fond of himself and his position of kingship, with an insatiable appetite for admiration and flattery; he loved magnificent display and elaborate etiquette, though to some extent he simply adopted them as instruments of policy rather than as a personal whim.

With the reign of Louis XIV the "state" in its modern form took a long step forward. The state in the abstract has always seemed somewhat theoretical to the English-speaking world. Let us say, for simplicity, that the state represents a fusion of justice and power. A sovereign state possesses, within its territory, a monopoly over the administration of justice and the use of force. Private persons neither pass legal judgments on others nor control private armies of their own. For private and unauthorized persons to do so, in an orderly state, constitutes rebellion. This was in contrast to the older feudal practice, by which feudal lords maintained manorial courts and led their own followers into battle. Against these feudal practices Louis XIV energetically worked, though not with complete success, claiming to possess in his own person, a sovereign ruler, a monopoly over the lawmaking processes and the armed forces of the kingdom. This is the deeper meaning of his reputed boast, *L'état, c'est moi*—"the state is myself." In the France of the seventeenth century, divided by classes and by regions, there was in fact no practical means of consolidating the powers of state except in the shared deference to one individual.

"L'etat, c'est moi"

The state, however, while representing law and order within its borders, has generally stood in a lawless and disorderly relation to other states, since no higher monopoly of law and force has existed. Louis XIV, personifying the French state, had no particular regard for the claims of other states or rulers. He was constantly either at war or prepared for war with his neighbors. The modern state, indeed, was created by the needs of peace at home and war abroad. Machinery of government, as devised by Louis XIV and others, was a means of giving order and security within the territory of the state, and of raising, supporting, and controlling armies for use against other states.

The idea that law and force within a country should be monopolized by the lawful king was the essence of the seventeenth-century doctrine of absolutism. Its principal theorist in the time of Louis XIV was Bishop Bossuet. Bossuet advanced the old Christian teaching that all power comes from God and that all who hold power are responsible to God for the way they use it. He held that kings were God's representatives in the political affairs of earth. Royal power, according to Bossuet, was absolute but not arbitrary: not arbitrary because it must be reasonable and just, like the will of God which it reflected; absolute in that it was free from dictation by parlements, estates, or other subordinate elements within the country. Law, therefore, was the will of the sovereign king, so long as it conformed to the higher law which was the will of God.

This doctrine, affirming the divine right of kings, was popularly held in France at the time and was taught in the churches. "Absolutism" and "absolute monarchy" became the prevailing concepts of government on much of the European continent in the seventeenth and eighteenth centuries. It must be remembered, however, that these terms referred more to legal theories than to facts. A ruler was "absolute" because he was not legally bound by any other persons or institutions in the country. In reality he became dependent upon a host of advisers and bureaucrats; he often had to compromise with vested interests; and he could be thwarted by the sheer weight of local custom or meet resistance from lawyers, ecclesiastics, nobles, grandees, hereditary officeholders, and miscellaneous dignitaries. And the slow pace of both transportation and communication prevented early modern "absolutist" rulers from controlling their subjects as quickly or as efficiently as governments have controlled their people in modern nation-states.

Absolutism

Government and Administration

Possibly the most fundamental step taken by Louis XIV was to assure himself of control of the army. Armed forces had formerly been almost a private enterprise. Specialists in fighting, leading their own troops, worked for governments more or less as they chose, either in return for money or to pursue political aims of their own. This was especially common in central Europe, but even in France great noblemen had strong private influence over the troops, and in times of disorder nobles led armed retainers about the country. Colonels were virtually on their own. Provided with a general commission and with funds by some government, they recruited, trained, and equipped their own regiments, and likewise fed and supplied them, often by preying upon bourgeois and peasants in the vicinity. In these circumstances it was often difficult to say on whose side soldiers were fighting. It was hard for governments to set armies into motion and equally hard to make them stop fighting, for commanders fought for their own interests and on their own momentum. War was not a "continuation of policy"; it was not an act of the state; it easily degenerated, as in the Thirty Years' War, into a kind of aimless and perpetual violence.

War: a state activity

Louis XIV made war an activity of state. He saw to it that all armed persons in France fought only for him. This produced peace and order in France, while strengthening the fighting power of France against other states. Under the older conditions there was also little integration among different units and arms of the army. Infantry regiments and cavalry went largely their own way, and the artillery was supplied by civilian technicians under contract. Louis XIV created a stronger unity of control, put the artillery organically into the army, systematized the military ranks and grades, and clarified the chain of command, placing himself at the top. The government supervised recruiting, required colonels to prove that they were maintaining the proper number of soldiers, and assumed most of the responsibility for equipping, provisioning, clothing, and housing the troops. Higher officers, thus becoming dependent on the government, could be subjected to discipline. The soldiers were put into uniforms, taught to march in step, and housed in barracks; thus they too became more susceptible to discipline and control.

LOUIS XIV
by Hyacinthe Rigaud
(French, 1659–1743)

The grandeur of the Sun King is conveyed in this portrait by Rigaud. He uses the king's clothing, stance, and royal emblems to express the power of the French monarchy.
(Giraudon/Art Resource, NY)

    Armed forces became less of a terror to their own people and a more effective weapon in the hands of government. They were employed usually against other governments but sometimes to suppress rebellion at home. Louis XIV also increased the French army in size, raising it from about 100,000 to about 400,000. These changes, both in size and in degree of government control, were made possible by the growth of a large civilian administration, the heads of which under Louis XIV were civilians. They were in effect the first ministers of war, and their assistants, officials, inspectors, and clerks constituted the first organized war ministry.

    Louis XIV was not only a vain man, but made it a political principle to overawe the country with his own grandeur. He built himself a whole new city at the old village of Versailles about ten miles from Paris. Where the Escorial in Spain had the atmosphere of a monastery, Versailles was a monument to worldly splendor. Tremendous in size, fitted out with polished mirrors, gleaming chandeliers, and magnificent tapestries, opening on to a formal park with fountains and shaded walks, the palace of Versailles became the marvel of Europe and the envy of lesser kings. It was virtually a public building, much of it used for government offices, with nobles, churchmen, notable bourgeois, and servants milling about on the king's affairs. The more exclusive honors of the château were reserved for the higher aristocrats. The king surrounded his daily routine of rising, eating, and going to bed (known as the *lever, dîner,* and *coucher*) with an infinite series of ceremonial acts, so minute and so formalized that there were, for example, six different entries of persons at the *lever,* and a certain gentleman at a specified moment held the right sleeve of the king's nightshirt as he took it off. The most exalted persons thought themselves the greater for thus waiting on so august a being. With such honors, and by more material favors, many great lords were induced to live habitually at court. Here, under the royal eye, they might

The splendor of Versailles

engage in palace intrigue but were kept away from real political mischief. Versailles had a debilitating effect on the French aristocracy.

For most positions in the government, as distinguished from his personal entourage, Louis XIV preferred to use men whose upper-class status was recent. Such men, unlike hereditary nobles, could aspire to no independent political influence of their own. He never called the Estates General, which in any case no one except some of the nobility wanted. Some of the Provincial Estates, because of local and aristocratic pressures, he allowed to remain functioning. He temporarily destroyed the independence of the parlements, commanding them to accept his orders, as Henry IV had commanded them to accept the Edict of Nantes. He developed a strong system of administrative coordination, centering in a number of councils of state, which he attended in person, and in "intendants" who represented these councils throughout the country. Councilors of state and intendants were generally of bourgeois origin or newly ennobled. Each intendant, within his district, embodied all aspects of the royal government—supervising the flow of taxes and recruiting of soldiers, keeping an eye on the local nobility, dealing with towns and guilds, controlling the more or less hereditary officeholders, policing the marketplaces, relieving famine, watching and often participating in the local law courts. A firm and uniform administration was superimposed upon the heterogeneous mass of the old France. In contrast to England, many local questions were handled by agents of the central government, usually honest and often efficient, but essentially bureaucrats constantly instructed by, and referring back to, their superiors at Versailles.

Administrative tactics of Louis XIV

Economic and Financial Policies: Colbert

To support the reorganized and enlarged army, the panoply of Versailles, and the growing civil administration, the king needed a good deal of money. Finance was always the weak spot in the French monarchy. Methods of collecting taxes were costly and inefficient. Direct taxes passed through the hands of many intermediate officials; indirect taxes were collected by private concessionaries called tax farmers, who made a substantial profit. The state always received far less than what the taxpayers actually paid. But the main weakness arose from an old bargain between the French crown and nobility; the king might raise taxes without consent only if he refrained from taxing the nobles. Only the "unprivileged" classes paid direct taxes, and these came almost to mean the peasants only, since many bourgeois in one way or another obtained exemptions. The system was outrageously unjust in throwing a heavy tax burden on the poor and helpless. Louis XIV was willing enough to tax the nobles but was unwilling to fall under their control, and only toward the close of his reign, under extreme stress of war, was he able, for the first time in French history, to impose direct taxes on the aristocratic elements of the population. This was a step toward equality before the law and toward sound public finance, but so many concessions and exemptions were won by nobles and bourgeois that the reform lost much of its value.

Taxation

Like his predecessors, Louis resorted to all manner of expedients to increase his revenues. He raised the tax rates, always with disappointing results. He devalued the currency. He sold patents of nobility to ambitious bourgeois. He sold government offices, judgeships, and commissions in the army and navy. For both financial and political reasons the king used his sovereign authority to annul the town charters, then sold back reduced rights at a price; this produced a little income but demoralized local government and civic spirit. The need for money arose from the fundamental inability to tax the wealthy. This problem reflected the weakness and limitations of absolutism because the government's

refusal to share its rule with the propertied classes corrupted much of French public life and undermined the political aptitude of the French people.

Louis XIV wished, if only for his own purposes, to make France economically powerful. His great minister Colbert worked for 20 years to do so. Colbert went beyond Richelieu in the application of mercantilism, aiming to make France a self-sufficing economic unit, to expand the export of French goods, and to increase the wealth from which government income was drawn. There was not much that he could do for agriculture, the principal industry of the kingdom, which remained less developed than in England and the Netherlands. But he managed to reduce internal tariffs in a large part of central France, where he set up a tariff union oddly entitled the Five Great Farms (since the remaining tolls were collected by tax farmers); and although vested interests and provincial liberties remained too strong for him to do away with all internal tariffs, the area of the Five Great Farms was in itself one of the largest free-trade areas in Europe, being about the size of England.

The Five Great Farms

For the convenience of business Colbert promulgated a Commercial Code, replacing much of the local customary law with a new model of business practice and regulation. He improved communications by building roads and canals. Working through the guilds, he required the handicraft manufacturers to produce goods of specified kind and quality, believing that foreigners, if assured of quality by the government, would purchase French products. He gave subsidies, tax exemptions, and monopolies to expand the manufacture of silks, tapestries, glassware, and woolens. He helped to found colonies, built up the navy, and established the French East India Company. Export of some goods, notably foodstuffs, was forbidden, for the government wished to keep the populace quiet by holding down the price of bread. Export of other goods, mainly manufactures, was encouraged, partly as a means of bringing money into the country, where it could be funneled into the royal treasury. The growth of the army, and the fact that under Louis XIV the government clothed and equipped the soldiers and hence placed unprecedentedly large orders for uniforms, overcoats, weapons, and ammunition, greatly stimulated the employment of weavers, tailors, and gunsmiths and advanced the commercial capitalism by which such labors were organized. Trade and manufacture thus developed in France under more direct government guidance than in England. They long gave the English an extremely brisk competition. Not until the age of iron and coal did France begin economically to lag.

Colbert's Commercial Code

In general, the system elaborated in the two centuries of Bourbon rule, known in retrospect as the Old Regime, was a society in which groups of many kinds could identify their own special interests with those of the "absolute" monarchy. But it rested on a precarious inconsistency. On the one hand, the royal government, through its intendants and bureaucracy, worked to restrict the privileges of provinces, nobles, and others. On the other hand, it multiplied and protected these and other privileges in its perpetual need for money. The inconsistency was not resolved until the Revolution of 1789, when the principle of equality of rights replaced the regime of privilege.

Thirty thousand workers were employed at one time in the building of the great royal château at Versailles. The seventeenth-century painting (upper) illustrates the complex labor and planning that were required during the process of construction; the lower painting dates from the early eighteenth century, and it shows the activity that surrounded Versailles when the king, government ministers, and nobles were assembled in the vast buildings and gardens. The grandeur and scale of these buildings were designed to symbolize the king's power and to create a sense of awe in the foreign visitors who came to meet Louis XIV or his advisers.

(Réunion des Musées Nationaux/Art Resource, NY; and The Royal Collection © 2000, Her Majesty Queen Elizabeth II)

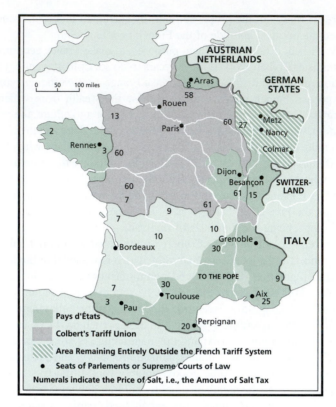

AUSTRIAN NETHERLANDS

GERMAN STATES

0 50 100 miles

Arras 8
58
Rouen

13

60 27 Metz
Paris 60 Nancy

2

Rennes 3 60
Colmar

Dijon
Besançon 61 15 SWITZER-LAND

60
7

61

9

7

10

7 10
Grenoble ITALY
Bordeaux 30

TO THE POPE 9

7 30
Toulouse Aix 25

3 Pau

20 Perpignan

Pays d'États

Colbert's Tariff Union

Area Remaining Entirely Outside the French Tariff System

• Seats of Parlements or Supreme Courts of Law

Numerals indicate the Price of Salt, i.e., the Amount of Salt Tax

FRANCE FROM THE LAST YEARS OF LOUIS XIV TO THE REVOLUTION OF 1789

The map gives an idea of the diversity of law and administration before the Revolution. Dark areas are "pays d'etats," provinces in which representative bodies ("estates") continued to meet. Cities named are the seats of what the French called parlements (see p. 172). The key indicates Colbert's tariff union, the Five Great Farms. The area marked with hatching remained outside the French tariff system entirely; it continued to trade with the states of the Holy Roman Empire (from which it had been annexed) without interference by the French government. Numerals indicate the price of salt, i.e., the varying burden of the salt tax, in various regions. In general, it will be seen that regions farthest from Paris enjoyed the most "privileges" or "liberties," preserving their legal and judicial identity, Provincial Estates, local tariffs, and a favored position in national taxation.

Religion: The Revocation of the Edict of Nantes, 1685

The consolidation of France under Louis XIV reached its high point in his policies toward religion. For the Catholics, Louis backed the old claims of the Gallican church to enjoy a certain national independence from Rome. He repressed the movement known as Jansenism, a kind of Calvinism within the Catholic church, which persisted for almost two centuries. Jansenists criticized moral laxity in high places as well as the religious influence of the Jesuits, so there was wide support at Versailles when the king moved against all the main centers of Jansenist theology. But it was the Protestants who suffered most in a new wave of religious persecutions.

France, in the early years of Louis XIV's reign, still allowed more religious toleration than any other large state in Europe. The Huguenots had lost their separate political status under Richelieu, but they continued to live in relative security, protected by the Edict of Nantes of 1598. From the beginning, however, toleration had been a royal rather than a popular policy, and under Louis XIV the royal policy changed. The fate of Catholics at the hands of a triumphant Parliament in England suggests that the Protestants in France would have been no better off under more popular institutions.

Bending all else to his will, Louis XIV resented the presence of heretics among his subjects. He considered religious unity necessary to the strength and dignity of his rule. He fell under the influence of certain Catholic advisers, who, not content with the attrition by which some

Louis XIV seeks religious unity

Protestants were turning back to Catholicism in any case, wished to hasten the process to the greater glory of themselves. Systematic conversion of Huguenots was begun. Life for Protestant families was gradually made unbearable. Finally they were literally "dragooned," mounted infantrymen being quartered in Huguenot homes to reinforce the persuasions of missionaries. In 1685 Louis revoked the Edict of Nantes. During the persecutions hundreds of thousands of Protestants left France, migrating to Holland, Germany, and America. Their loss was a severe blow to French economic life, for although Protestants were found in all levels of French society, those of the commercial and industrial classes were the most mobile. With the revocation of the Edict of Nantes France embarked on a century of official intolerance (slowly mitigated in practice), under which Protestants in France were in much the same position as Catholics in the British Isles. The fact that 100 years later, when Protestants were again tolerated, many of them were found to be both commercially prosperous and politically loyal indicates that they fared far better than the Catholic Irish.

All things considered, the reign of Louis XIV brought considerable advantages to the French middle and lower classes. His most bitter critics, with the natural exception of Protestants, were disgruntled nobles such as the duke of Saint-Simon, who thought that he showed too many favors to

Accomplishments of Louis XIV

persons of inferior social rank. Since Protestants were an unpopular minority, his repression of them won much approval. Colbert's system of economic regulation, and perpetuation of the guilds, meant that innovation and private enterprise developed less fully than in England, but France was economically stronger in 1700 than in 1650. Peasants were heavily taxed to pay for Louis XIV's wars, and they suffered through devastating famines after 1690 (also caused partly by the wars). But they did not sink into the serfdom that was rising in eastern Europe. Compared to later times, France was still a hodgepodge of competing jurisdictions, special privilege, and bureaucratic ineptitude. The king was in truth far from "absolute" but France was nevertheless the best organized of the large monarchies on the Continent. Louis XIV, in turning both high and low into dutiful subjects, ended civil war and even advanced the cause of civil equality. For a long time he was generally popular. What finally turned his people against him in his last years was the strain of his incessant wars.

22.   THE WARS OF LOUIS XIV: THE PEACE OF UTRECHT, 1713

Before 1700

From the outset of his reign Louis pursued a vigorous foreign policy. The quarrel between the house of France and the house of Habsburg had gone on for more than a century. When

Louis XIV assumed his personal rule in 1661, Spanish territories still faced France on three sides (northeast, east, and south), but so weakened was Spain that this fact was no longer a menace to France so much as a temptation to French expansion. Louis XIV could count on popular support in France, for the dream of a frontier on the Rhine and the Alps was captivating to Frenchmen. He struck first in 1667 by sending a large army into the Spanish Netherlands. He was blocked, as noted earlier, by the Triple Alliance of the Dutch, the English, and the Swedes. With strength renewed by reforms at home, and in alliance now with Charles II of England, he struck again in 1672 (the "Dutch War"), invading the Dutch provinces on the lower Rhine, and this time raising up against him his great adversary and inveterate enemy, the prince of Orange. William III, bringing the Austrian and Spanish Habsburgs, Brandenburg, and Denmark into alliance with the Dutch Republic, forced Louis to sign the treaty of Nimwegen in 1678. The French gave up their ambitions against Holland but took from Spain the rich province of Franche-Comté, which outflanked Alsace on the south and brought French power to the borders of Switzerland (see map, p. 147).

French incursions into the Holy Roman Empire

In the very next year, Louis further infiltrated the dissolving frontier of the Holy Roman Empire, this time in Lorraine and Alsace. By the Peace of Westphalia the French king had rights in this region, but the terms of that treaty were so ambiguous, and the local feudal law so confusing, that claims could be made in contrary directions. French troops thereupon moved in. In 1681 French troops occupied the city of Strasbourg, which, as a free city of the Holy Roman Empire, regarded itself as an independent little republic. A protest went up throughout Germany against this undeclared invasion. But Germany was not a political unity. Since 1648 each German state conducted its own foreign policy, and at this very moment, in 1681, Louis XIV had an ally in the Elector of Brandenburg (forerunner of the kings of Prussia). The diet of the Holy Roman Empire was divided between an anti-French and a pro-French party. The emperor, Leopold I, was distracted by developments in the East. The Hungarians, incited and financed by Louis XIV, were again rebelling against the Habsburgs. They appealed to the Turks, and the Turks in 1683 moved up the Danube and besieged Vienna. Louis XIV, if he did not on this occasion positively assist the Turks, ostentatiously declined to join the proposed crusade against them.

The emperor, with Polish assistance, succeeded in getting the Turkish army out of Austria. Returning to western problems and observing the western border of the Empire crumbling, Franche-Comté already lost, the Spanish Netherlands threatened, and Lorraine and Alsace absorbed bit by bit, the Emperor Leopold gathered the Catholic powers into a combination against the French. The Protestant states at the same time, aroused by the French revocation of the Edict of Nantes in 1685 and by Huguenot émigrés who called down the wrath of God on the perfidious Sun King, began to ally the more readily with William of Orange. Catholic and Protestant enemies of Louis XIV came together in 1686 in the League of Augsburg, which comprised the Holy Roman Emperor, the kings of Spain and of Sweden, the electors of Bavaria, Saxony, and the Palatinate, and the Dutch Republic. In 1686 the king of England was still a protégé of France, but three years later, when William became king in England, that country too joined the League.

The War of the League of Augsburg

The War of the League of Augsburg broke out in 1688. The French armies won battles but could not drive so many enemies from the field. The French navy could not overpower the combined fleets of the Dutch and English. Louis XIV found himself badly strained (it was at this time that he first imposed direct taxes on the French nobles) and finally made peace at Ryswick in the Netherlands in 1697, leaving matters about where they had been when the war began.

In all the warring and negotiating the question had not been merely the fate of this or that piece of territory, nor even the French thrust to the east, but the eventual disposition of the whole empire of Spain. The Spanish king, Charles II, prematurely senile, momentarily expected to die, yet lived on year after year. He was still alive at the time of the Peace of Ryswick. The greatest diplomatic issue of the day was still unsettled.

The War of the Spanish Succession

The War of the Spanish Succession lasted 11 years, from 1702 to 1713. It was less destructive than the Thirty Years' War, for armies were now supplied in more orderly fashion, subject to more orderly discipline and command, and could be stopped from fighting at the will of their governments. Except for the effects of civil war in Spain and of deadly famines in France, the civilian populations were generally spared from violence and destruction. In this respect the war foreshadowed the typical warfare of the eighteenth century, fought by professional armies rather than by whole peoples. Among wars of the largest scale, the War of the Spanish Succession was the first in which religion counted for little, the first in which commerce and sea power were the principal stakes, and the first in which English money was liberally used in Continental politics. It was also the first that can be called a "world war," because it involved the overseas world together with the leading powers of Europe. Wars within Europe were becoming linked to the global competition for colonies and trade.

The struggle had long been foreseen. The two main aspirants to the Spanish inheritance were the king of France and the Holy Roman Emperor. Each had married a sister of the perpetually moribund Charles II, and each could hope to place a younger member of his family on the throne of Spain. During the last decades of the seventeenth century the powers had made various treaties agreeing to "partition" the Spanish possessions. The idea was, by dividing the Spanish heritage between the two claimants, to preserve the balance of power in Europe. But when Charles II finally died in 1700, it was found that he had made a will, which stipulated that the empire of Spain should be kept intact, that all Spanish territories throughout the world should go to the grandson of Louis XIV, and that if Louis XIV refused to accept in the name of his 17-year-old grandson, the entire inheritance should pass to the son of the Habsburg emperor in Vienna. Louis XIV decided to accept. With Bourbons reigning in Versailles and Madrid, even if the two thrones were never united, French influence would run from Belgium to the Straits of Gibraltar, and from Milan to Mexico and Manila. At Versailles the word went out: "The Pyrenees exist no longer."

"The Pyrenees exist no longer"

Never, at least in almost two centuries, had the political balance within Europe been so threatened. Never had the other states faced such a prospect of relegation to the sidelines. William III acted at once; he gathered the stunned or hesitant diplomats into the last of his coalitions, the Grand Alliance of 1701. He died the next year, before hostilities began, and with Louis XIV at the seeming apex of his grandeur, but he had in fact launched the engine that was to crush the Sun King. The Grand Alliance included England, Holland, and the Austrian emperor, supported by Brandenburg and eventually by Portugal and the Italian duchy of Savoy. Louis XIV could count on Spain, which was generally loyal to the late king's will. Otherwise his only ally was Bavaria, whose rivalry with Austria made it a habitual satellite of France. The Bavarian alliance gave the French armies an advanced position toward Vienna and

Threats to political balance

maintained that internal division within Germany which was fundamental to the politics of the time, and of a long time to come.

The war was long, mainly because each side no sooner gained a temporary advantage than it raised its demands on the other. The English, though they sent relatively few troops to the Continent, produced in John Churchill, Duke of Marlborough, a preeminent military commander for the Allied forces. The Austrians were led by Prince Eugene of Savoy. The Allies won notable battles at Blenheim in Bavaria (1704), and at Ramillies (1706), Oudenarde (1708), and Malplaquet (1709) in the Spanish Netherlands. The French were routed; Louis XIV asked for peace but would not agree to it because the Allied terms were so enormous. Louis fought to hold the two crowns, to conquer Belgium, to get French merchants into Spanish America, and at the worst in self-defense. After minor successes in 1710 he again insisted on controlling the crown of Spain. The Spanish fought to uphold the will of the deceased king, the unity of the Spanish possessions, and even the integrity of Spain itself—for the English moved in at Gibraltar and made a menacing treaty with Portugal. Meanwhile, the Austrians landed at Barcelona and invaded Catalonia, which (as in 1640) again rose in rebellion, recognizing the Austrian claimant, so that all Spain fell into civil war.

Motives of the warring states

The Austrians fought to keep Spain in the Habsburg family, to crush Bavaria, and to carry Austrian influence across the Alps into Italy. The Dutch fought as always for their security, to keep the French out of Belgium, and to control access to the river Scheldt. The English fought for these same reasons and also to keep the French-supported Catholic Stuarts out of England and preserve the Revolution of 1688. It was to be expected that the Stuarts, if they returned, would ruin the Bank of England and repudiate the national debt. Both maritime powers, England and Holland, fought to keep French merchants out of Spanish America and to advance their own commercial position in America and the Mediterranean. These being the war aims, the Whigs were the implacable war party in England, the vaguely pro-Stuart and anticommercial Tories being quite willing to make peace at an early date. As for the minor allies, Brandenburg and Savoy, their rulers had simply entered the alliance to gain such advantages as might turn up.

The Peace of Utrecht

The partition of Spain's holdings

Peace was finally made at the treaties of Utrecht and Rastadt of 1713 and 1714. The treaty of Utrecht, with its allied instruments, in fact partitioned the world of Spain. But it did not divide it between the two legal claimants only. The British remained at Gibraltar, to the great irritation of the Spaniards, and likewise annexed the island of Minorca. The Duke of Savoy eventually gained the former Spanish island of Sardinia in return for his contribution to the Allied cause. The rest of the Spanish Mediterranean holdings—Milan, Naples, and Sicily —passed to the Austrian Habsburgs, as did the Spanish Netherlands (or Belgium), subsequently referred to as the Austrian Netherlands. In Spain itself, shorn of its European possessions but retaining America, the grandson of Louis XIV was confirmed as king (Philip V of Spain), on the understanding that the French and Spanish thrones should never be inherited by the same person. The Bourbons reigned in Spain, with interruptions, from Philip V to the republican revolution of 1931. French influence was strong in the eighteenth century, for a good many French courtiers, advisers, administrators, and businessmen crossed the Pyrenees with Philip V. They helped somewhat to revive the Spanish

The battle of Blenheim, fought in Bavaria in 1704, was a great victory for the English and the Allied forces that joined to oppose the French in the War of the Spanish Succession. Blenheim brought fame and honors to the British commander, John Churchill, Duke of Marlborough; for the French, it was the first in a series of devastating military defeats that steadily weakened the power of Louis XIV.
(Fotomas Index/Bridgeman Art Library)

monarchy by applying the methods of Louis XIV, and they passed a swelling volume of French manufactures through Seville into Spanish America.

The old objective of William III, to prevent domination by France, was realized at last. The war itself was the main cause of French loss of strength. It produced poverty, misery, and depopulation, and it exposed Louis XIV to severe criticism at home. Recurring famines and tax increases

Consequences of the war for France

provoked peasant uprisings, which were brutally repressed. Dissatisfaction with the war led also to a revival of aristocratic and parliamentary opposition. By the peace treaties the French abandoned, for the time being, their efforts to conquer Belgium. They ceased to recognize the Stuart pretender as king of Great Britain. They surrendered to the British two of their colonies, Newfoundland and Nova Scotia (called Acadia), and recognized British sovereignty in the disputed American Northwest, known as the Hudson Bay territory. But the French were only checked, not downed. They retained the conquests of Louis XIV in

PEASANT FAMILY IN A ROOM
by Louis Le Nain (French, 1593–1648)
Although Le Nain portrayed a family in the early half of the seventeenth century, the people in this painting do not differ much from the peasants who later suffered through wars, famines, and tax increases in the last decades of the long reign of Louis XIV.
(Erich Lessing/Art Resource, NY)

Alsace and the Franche-Comté. Their influence was strong in Spain. Their deeper strength and capacity for recovery were soon evident in renewed economic expansion. Their language and civilization continued to spread throughout Europe.

The Dutch received guarantees of their security. They were granted the right to garrison the "Dutch Barrier," a string of forts in Belgium on the side toward France. But the Dutch, strained by the war and outdistanced by England, never again played a primary role in European political affairs. Two other small states ascended over the diplomatic horizon, Savoy (or Piedmont) and Brandenburg. The rulers of both, for having sided with the victors, were recognized as "kings" by the treaty of Utrecht. Savoy came to be known as "Sardinia," and Brandenburg as "Prussia." More is said of Prussia in the next chapter.

Britain becomes a great power

The greatest winners were the British. Great Britain made its appearance as a great power. Union of England and Scotland had taken place during the war. Based at Gibraltar and Minorca, Britain was now a power in the Mediterranean. Belgium, the "pistol pointed at the heart of England," was in the innocuous hands of the Austrians. The British added to their American holdings, but far more valuable than Newfoundland and Nova Scotia was the *asiento* extorted from Spain. The *asiento* granted the lucrative privilege (which the French had sought) of providing Spanish America with African slaves. Much of the wealth of Bristol and Liverpool

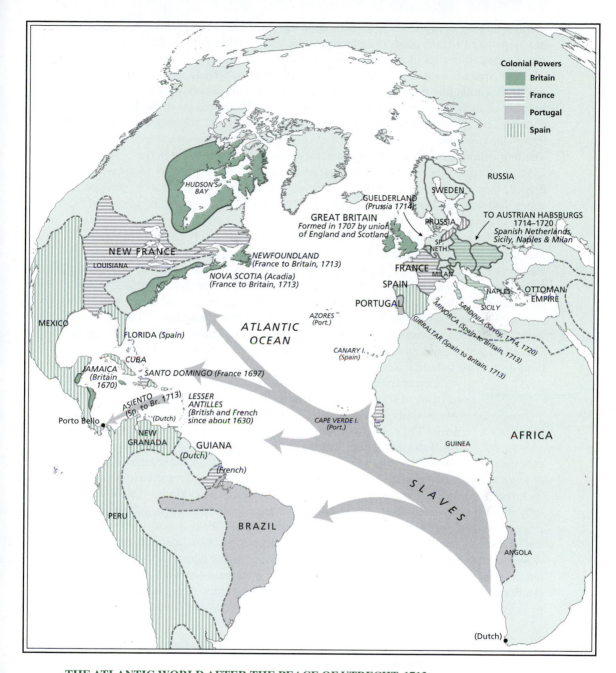

Colonial Powers

- Britain
- France
- Portugal
- Spain

RUSSIA

SWEDEN

GUELDERLAND
(Prussia 1714)

GREAT BRITAIN
Formed in 1707 by union
of England and Scotland

PRUSSIA

TO AUSTRIAN HABSBURGS
1714–1720
*Spanish Netherlands,
Sicily, Naples & Milan*

HUDSON'S
BAY

NEW FRANCE

LOUISIANA

NEWFOUNDLAND
(France to Britain, 1713)

NOVA SCOTIA *(Acadia)*
(France to Britain, 1713)

SP.
NETH.

FRANCE

SPAIN

MILAN

PORTUGAL

NAPLES   OTTOMAN
EMPIRE

SARDINIA *(Savoy, 1714, 1720)*

SICILY

MINORCA *(Spain to Britain, 1714, 1720)*

GIBRALTAR *(Spain to Britain, 1713)*

MEXICO

FLORIDA *(Spain)*

ATLANTIC
OCEAN

AZORES
(Port.)

CANARY I.
(Spain)

CUBA

JAMAICA
*(Britain
1670)*

SANTO DOMINGO *(France 1697)*

ASIENTO
(Sp. to Br. 1713)

(Dutch)

LESSER
ANTILLES
*(British and French
since about 1630)*

CAPE VERDE I.
(Port.)

AFRICA

GUINEA

Porto Bello

NEW
GRANADA

GUIANA

(Dutch)

(French)

PERU

BRAZIL

S L A V E S

ANGOLA

(Dutch)

THE ATLANTIC WORLD AFTER THE PEACE OF UTRECHT, 1713

The map shows the partitioning of the Spanish empire and the rise of the British. Spain and its American possessions went to the Bourbon Philip V; the European possessions of Spain—the Netherlands, Milan, Naples and Sicily—went to the Austrian Habsburgs. Britain meanwhile was strengthened by the union of England and Scotland, the acquisition of Minorca, Gibraltar, and the commercial privilege of the "asiento" from Spain, and of Newfoundland and Nova Scotia from France.

in the following decades was to be built upon the slave trade. The *asiento,* by permitting one shipload of British goods to be brought each year to Porto Bello in Panama, also provided opportunities for illicit trade in nonhuman cargoes.

The Spanish empire was pried open, and British merchants entered on an era of wholesale smuggling into Spanish America, competing strenuously with the French, who because of their favored position in Spain were usually able to go through more legal channels. Moreover, the British, by defeating France, assured themselves of a line of Protestant kings and of the maintenance of constitutional and parliamentary government. The ratification of the Peace of Utrecht actually marked a further step in the evolution of English constitutional history. The Whigs, who were the main supporters of the war with France, thought the treaty insufficiently favorable to England. The Tories, pledged to peace, had won the House of Commons in 1710, but the Whigs continued to control the House of Lords. Queen Anne, at the request of Tory leaders and in the interests of peace, raised 12 Tory commoners to the peerage in order to create a Tory majority in the Lords and hence to obtain ratification of the treaty. This established itself as a precedent; it became an unwritten article of the British constitution that when the Lords blocked the Commons on an important issue, the monarch could create enough new lords to make a new majority in that House. After 1713, the Lords never again allowed themselves to be swamped by newcomers and thus acceded in all future disputes to the will of the Commons. The landed aristocracy and their merchant allies could now govern as they saw fit. The result was a rapid increase of wealth in England, precipitating within a few generations a veritable Industrial Revolution.

Confirmation of the European system

Except for the addition of England, the same powers were parties to the treaty of Utrecht in 1713 as to the Peace of Westphalia in 1648, and they now confirmed the system of international relations established by Westphalia. The powers accepted each other as members of the European system; recognized each other as sovereign states connected only by free negotiation, war, and treaty; and adjusted their differences through rather facile exchanges of territory, made in the interests of a balance of power, and without regard to the nationality or presumed wishes of the peoples affected. With Germany still in its "feudal chaos," Italy divided into minor states or controlled by foreign kings, and Spain subordinated to France, the treaty of Utrecht left France and Great Britain as the two most vigorous imperial powers of Europe. These countries soon became the two principal carriers and exporters of the European civilization that would spread its institutions and ideas throughout the modern world. In the next chapter we look at how the societies of central and eastern Europe, developed along lines of their own, even when they were strongly influenced by the growing power and wealth of the western European states.

For interactive exercises, glossary, chronologies, and more, go to the *Online Learning Center* at **www.mhhe.com/palmer10.**

Chapter 5

THE TRANSFORMATION OF EASTERN EUROPE, 1648–1740

23. Three Aging Empires

24. The Formation of an Austrian Monarchy

25. The Formation of Prussia

26. The "Westernizing" of Russia

In Eastern Europe, in the century after the Peace of Westphalia of 1648, it became apparent that political systems that failed to become more "modern" might be in danger of going out of existence. In the mid–seventeenth century most parts of Eastern Europe belonged to one or another of three old-fashioned political organizations—the Holy Roman Empire, the Republic of Poland, and the empire of the Ottoman Turks (see maps, pp. 193, 194). All three were loose, decentralized, and increasingly ineffective. They were superseded by three new and stronger powers—Prussia, Austria, and Russia. These three, by overrunning the intermediate ground of Poland, came to adjoin one another and cover all Eastern Europe except the Balkans. It was in this same period that Russia expanded territorially, adopted some of the technical and administrative apparatus of western Europe, and became an active participant in European affairs.

East and West are of course relative terms. For the Russians Germany and even Poland were "western." But for Europe as a whole a significant though indefinite social and economic line ran along the Elbe and the Bohemian Mountains to the head of the Adriatic Sea. East of this line towns were fewer than in the West, human labor was less productive, and the middle classes were less strong. Above all, the peasants were governed by their landlords. From the sixteenth to the eighteenth century, in eastern Europe in contrast to what happened in the West, the peasant mass increasingly lost its freedom. The commercial revolution and widening of the market created a strong merchant class in western Europe and tended to turn working people into a legally free and mobile labor force. In eastern Europe these changes strengthened the great landlords who produced for export and who secured their labor force by the institutions of serfdom and "hereditary subjection." The main social unit was the agricultural estate, which the lord exploited with uncompensated compulsory labor (or *robot*) furnished by his people, who could neither migrate, marry, nor learn a trade except as he permitted, and who, until the eighteenth

Chapter emblem: Russian workers building the new city of St. Petersburg during the reign of Tsar Peter I (1689–1725). (Tass/Sovfoto)

century, had no legal protector or court of appeal other than himself. In the East, therefore, the landlords were exceedingly powerful. They were the only significant political class. And the three new states that grew up—Prussia, Austria, Russia—were alike in being landlord states.

23.   THREE AGING EMPIRES

In 1648 the whole mainland of Europe from the French border almost to Moscow was occupied by the three large and loosely built structures that have been mentioned—the Holy Roman Empire, the Republic of Poland, and the empire of the Ottoman Turks. The Turkish power reached to about 50 miles from Vienna, and it extended over what is now Romania and over the Tartars on the north shore of the Black Sea. Even so, its European holdings were but a projection from the main mass of the Ottoman Empire in Asia and Africa. Poland extended from roughly 100 miles east of Berlin to a hundred miles west of Moscow and virtually from "sea to sea" in the old phrase of its patriots, from the Baltic around Riga almost to the Black Sea coast. The Holy Roman Empire extended from Poland and Hungary to the North Sea.

These three empires were by no means alike. The Holy Roman Empire bore some of the oldest traditions of Christendom. Poland too had old connections with western Europe and Christian religious institutions. Turkey was a Muslim power, closely connected to the Islamic civilization of the Middle East and filled with peoples who generally lived outside European cultural traditions (despite a long history of Mediterranean trade and commerce). Yet in some ways the three resembled each other. In all of them central authority had become weak, consisting largely of understandings between a nominal head and outlying dignitaries or potentates. All lacked efficient systems of administration and government. All were being made obsolete by newer centralizing states of which France was the leading example. All, but especially Poland and Turkey, were made up of diverse ethnic or language groups. The whole immense area was therefore politically weak. It was malleable in the hands of kings or ruling elites who might become a little stronger than their neighbors. We must try to see in what this weakness consisted, and how newer, stronger state forms were created.

Weaknesses of the empires

The Holy Roman Empire after 1648

With the Holy Roman Empire the reader is already familiar. It was an empire, especially after the Peace of Westphalia, with next to no army, revenues, or working organs of a central government. Voltaire called it neither holy, Roman, nor an empire. Created in the Middle Ages, it was Roman in that it was believed to continue the imperial sway of the Rome of antiquity, and it was holy in being the secular counterpart to the spiritual empire of the pope. It had been ruined by the Reformation, which left the Germans divided almost evenly between Protestant and Catholic, with each side thereafter demanding special safeguards against the other. The Empire continued, however, to be universal in principle, having no relation to nationality and theoretically being a form of government suitable to all peoples, although it had never lived up to this theoretical claim and had shown no expansionist tendency since the Middle Ages. In actuality, the Empire was roughly coterminous with the German states and the region of the German language, except that it excluded after 1648 the Dutch and Swiss, who no longer considered themselves German; and it likewise excluded those Germans who since the fourteenth century had settled along the eastern shores of the Baltic.

Large parts of the Empire had suffered repeatedly from the Thirty Years' War. Yet the war, and the peace terms that followed it, only accentuated a situation that had long been unfavorable. Postwar revival was difficult; the breakup of commercial connections and the wartime losses of savings and capital were hard to overcome. Germany fell increasingly out of step with the economic expansion and cultural changes in western Europe. The burgher class, its ambitions blocked, lost much of its old vitality. No overseas colonies could be founded, for want of strong enough government backing, as was shown when a colonial venture of Brandenburg came to nothing. There was no stock exchange in Germany until one was established at Vienna in 1771, half a century after those of London, Paris, and Amsterdam. Laws, tariffs, tolls, and coinage were more diverse than in France. Even the calendar varied. It varied, indeed, throughout Europe as a whole, since Protestant states long declined to accept the corrected calendar issued by Pope Gregory XIII in 1582; in parts of divided Germany the holidays, the date of the month, and the day of the week changed every few miles. The arts and letters, flourishing in western Europe as never before, were at a low ebb in Germany in the seventeenth century. In science the Germans during and after the Thirty Years' War accomplished less than the English, Dutch, French, or Italians, despite the great mathematician and philosopher Leibniz, one of the great minds of the age. Only in music, as in the work of the Bach family, did the Germans at this time excel. But music was not then much heard beyond the place of its origin. Germany for the rest of the world was a byway in the higher civilization of Europe.

Effects of the Thirty Years' War

After the Thirty Years' War each German state had sovereign rights. These "states" numbered some 300 or 2,000, depending on how they were counted. The higher figure included the "knights of the Empire," found in south Germany and the Rhineland. They were persons who acknowledged no overlordship except that of the emperor himself. The knights had tiny estates of their own, averaging not over 100 acres apiece, consisting of a castle and a manor or two, enclosed by the territory of a larger state but not forming a part of it. But even without the knights there were about 300 states capable of some independence of action—free cities, abbots without subjects, archbishops and bishops ruling with temporal power, landgraves, margraves and dukes, and one king, the king of Bohemia.

All these states were intent on preserving what were called the "Germanic liberties." They were gladly assisted by outside powers, notably but not exclusively France. The Germanic liberties meant freedom of the member states from control by emperor or Empire. The rulers of the most important states within the empire elected the emperor (there were nine electors by the end of the seventeenth century), and they always required the successful candidate to accept certain "capitulations," in which he promised to safeguard all the privileges and immunities of the states. The Habsburgs, though consistently elected after 1438, had none of the advantages of hereditary rulers, each having to bargain away in turn any gains made by his predecessor. The elective principle meant that imperial power could not be accumulated and transmitted from one generation to the next. It opened the doors to foreign intrigue, since the electors were willing to consider whichever candidate would promise them most. The French repeatedly supported a rival candidate to the Habsburgs. After 1648 they had supporters in the electoral college, Bavaria and Cologne being the most consistently pro-French. In 1742

The "Germanic liberties"

the French obtained the elevation of their Bavarian ally to the imperial throne. The office of emperor became a political football for Germans and non-Germans.

Nor would the German states, after the Thirty Years' War, allow any authority to the imperial diet. The diet possessed the power to raise troops and taxes for the whole Empire, but the power remained unused because the various states feared that any such action would diminish their own authority and independence. Meanwhile, the states which insisted with such obstinacy on their liberties from the Empire gave few liberties to their subjects. The free cities were closed oligarchies, as indeed were most cities in other countries, but in Germany the burgher oligarchs of the free cities were virtually sovereign also. Most of the other states, large or small, developed in the direction of absolutism. Absolutism was checked for Germany as a whole, only to reappear in miniature in hundreds of different places. Each ruler thought himself a little Louis XIV, each court a small Versailles. Subjects became attached by ties of sentiment to their rulers, who almost always lived in the neighborhood and could be readily seen by passers-by. People liked the little courts, the little armies, the gossipy politics, and the familiar officials of their tiny states; and despite all its flaws, the Empire had the merit of holding this conglomeration of states in a lawful relation to one another. It was a kind of miniature league of nations. For a century and a half after the Peace of Westphalia small states existed alongside larger ones, or often totally enclosed within them, without serious fear for their security and without losing their independence.

Yet there were many ambitious rulers in Germany after the Peace of Westphalia. They had won recognition of their sovereignty in 1648. They were busily building absolutist monarchies. They aspired also to extend their dominions and cut a greater figure in the world. There were other ways of doing this than by devouring their smaller neighbors outright. One was by marriage and inheritance. The Empire in this respect was a paradise for fortune hunters; the variety of possible marriages was enormous because of the great number of ruling families. Another outlet for ambition lay in the high politics of the Empire. The Wittelsbach family, which ruled in Bavaria, managed to win an electorate in the Thirty Years' War; they consistently placed members of the family as archbishop of Cologne, and in ecclesiastical posts elsewhere in the Rhineland. With the interest thus built up, they were able to sell their influence to France, which in turn backed them against the Habsburgs. The Guelph family, ruling in Hanover, schemed for years to obtain an electorate, which they finally extorted from the emperor in 1692; in 1714 they inherited the throne of Great Britain with King George I, preferred by the British as Protestants to their Catholic Stuart cousins. The Hohenzollerns, electors of Brandenburg, inherited territories as far apart as the Rhine and the Vistula.

The half-century after the Peace of Westphalia was thus a highly critical period in central Europe. The situation in Germany was fluid. No one could tell which, if any, of the half-dozen chief German states would emerge in the lead. Nothing was crystallized; anything

CENTRAL AND EASTERN EUROPE, 1660–1795

This complex area is shown in simplified form on p. 194. The upper panel of the map indicates boundaries as of 1660; the lower panel those of 1795. Both panels show the border between the eastern and western agrarian zones, running from the mouth of the Elbe River into central Germany and down to Trieste. East of this line, from the sixteenth to the eighteenth centuries, the mass of people sank into a kind of serfdom in which they rendered forced labor to their lords on large farms. West of the line the peasants owed little or no forced labor and tilled small farms which they owned or rented. This line marks a somewhat imprecise but significant social boundary that would also have an important influence on the political and economic history of modern Europe.

1660
—— Boundary of Holy Roman Empire
╌╌ Boundary Between Agrarian Zones
▨ Church Lands

0   100   200 miles

SWEDEN
Baltic Sea
DENMARK
Riga
Moscow
RUSSIA
BRANDENBURG-PRUSSIA
Elbe R.
Berlin
Minsk
Cologne
SAXONY
SILESIA
Vistula R.
REPUBLIC OF POLAND
FRANCE
Warsaw
Prague
BOHEMIA
MORAVIA
Rhine R.
GALICIA
Kiev
BAVARIA
AUSTRIA
Vienna
Lemberg
SWISS
CONFED.
KINGDOM OF HUNGARY
Budapest
MOLDAVIA
PIEDMONT
VENICE
Trieste
HUNGARY
SLAVONIA
TRANSYLVANIA
TUSCANY
PAPAL
STATES
BOSNIA
OTTOMAN EMPIRE
Adriatic Sea
SERBIA
Danube R.
Black Sea
Rome
BULGARIA

1795
—— Boundary of Holy Roman Empire
╌╌ Boundary Between Agrarian Zones
▨ Church Lands

0   100   200 miles

SWEDEN
Baltic Sea
DENMARK
Riga
Moscow
HANOVER
Elbe R.
Berlin
PRUSSIA
Minsk
RUSSIAN EMPIRE
Cologne
SAXONY
SILESIA
Vistula R.
Warsaw
FRANCE
Prague
BOHEMIA
GALICIA
Kiev
Rhine R.
BAVARIA
AUSTRIA
Lemberg
Vienna
SWISS
CONFED.
AUSTRIAN MONARCHY
Budapest
MOLDAVIA
PIEDMONT
VENICE
Trieste
HUNGARY
TRANSYLVANIA
TUSCANY
PAPAL
STATES
BOSNIA
Adriatic Sea
SERBIA
Danube R.
Black Sea
Rome
OTTOMAN EMPIRE
BULGARIA

AGING EMPIRES AND NEW POWERS

The left panel shows the "three aging empires" which occupied much of central and eastern Europe in the seventeenth century. Though maintaining themselves with growing difficulty under modern conditions, the Polish Republic lasted until 1795, the Holy Roman Empire until 1806, the Ottoman Empire until 1923. Meanwhile, beginning in the seventeenth century, the political leadership in this area was assumed by three states of more modern type, organized around the institutions of monarchy, the standing army, and the professional bureaucracy or civil service—the reorganized Austrian Empire of the Habsburgs, the Hohenzollern kingdom of Prussia, and the Russian Empire of the Romanovs. These are shown in the right panel. All three figured prominently in the affairs of Europe for over 200 years; all perished in the First World War, 1914–1918.

Austria and Prussia

might happen. Two states definitely came forward after 1700, built by the skill and persistence of their rulers—Austria and Prussia. It is a curious and revealing fact that neither really had a name of its own. They were for a long time known most commonly as "houses"—the house of Austria or Habsburg and the house of Brandenburg or Hohenzollern. Each house put together a certain combination of territories. Each would have been as willing to possess any other combination had the course of events been different. By extension of meaning, one came to be called "Austria," which for centuries had been simply an archduchy on the upper Danube. The other, "Prussia," for centuries had meant only a certain stretch of the Baltic coast. To these two states we shall shortly turn.

The Republic of Poland about 1650

Running almost 1,000 miles eastward from the Holy Roman Empire in the middle of the seventeenth century lay the vast tract of the Republic of Poland, called a republic because its king was elected and because the political classes took pride in their constitutional liberties. Its vast size was one cause of its internal peculiarities. No administrative system could have kept up with the expansion of its frontiers, so that a large degree of freedom had always been left to outlying lords. In addition, the population was heterogeneous.

The Polish state was a far more recent and less substantial creation than the Holy Roman Empire. It was made up of two main parts, Poland proper (the Kingdom of Poland) in the west and the Grand Duchy of Lithuania in the east. They had been joined by a union of their crowns (see maps, pp. 193, 194). Only in the west was there a mass of Polish population. The Duchy of Prussia, a fief of the Polish crown, was peopled mainly by Germans. Further east a Byelorussian and Ukrainian peasantry was subject to a scattering of Polish and Lithuanian landlords. Even in Poland itself the town population was not generally Polish, being largely Germans and Jews. The latter spoke Yiddish, derived from German, and were very numerous because a king of Poland in the later Middle Ages had welcomed Jewish refugees fleeing from anti-Jewish violence in Germany. They lived in separate communities with their own law, language, and religion, forming large islands of Orthodox Jewish life in the Gentile ocean. The Germans too held aloof, resisting assimilation to their less-advanced surroundings. An unsurpassable barrier thus existed between town and country. There was no national middle class. The official and political language was Latin. Roman Catholicism was the leading religion.

Poland and Lithuania

Poland is interesting as the region in which the landed aristocracy won over all other groups in the country, neither allowing the consolidation of the state on absolutist lines, nor yet creating an effective constitutional or parliamentary government. The Polish aristocracy, or *szlachta,* made up some eight percent of the population, a far higher proportion than the aristocracy of any country of western Europe. On this ground the old Polish kingdom has sometimes been considered, especially by later Polish nationalists, as the possessor of an early form of democracy. The aristocracy were sticklers for their liberties, called the "Polish liberties," which resembled the German liberties in that they consisted largely of a fierce suspicion of central authority and were a perpetual invitation to foreign interference. As in the Holy Roman Empire, the monarchy was elective, and the king upon election had to accept certain contractual agreements, which, like the German "capitulations," prevented the accumulation of authority by the crown. The Poles were too politically divided to accept one of their own number as king, so from 1572 to the extinction of Poland over two centuries later there were only two native Polish kings who reigned for any length of time. One of these kings was the national hero John Sobieski, who led a decisive campaign against the Turks in the 1680s.

As in Germany, the central diet was ineffective and the centers of political action were local. The aristocracy met in 50 or 60 regional diets, turbulent assemblages of warlike gentry, in which the great lords used the lesser lords for their own purposes. The central diet, from which the towns were excluded, was a periodic meeting of emissaries, under binding instructions from the regional diets. It came to be recognized, as one of the liberties of the country, that the central diet could take no action to which any member objected. Any member, by stating his unalterable opposition, could oblige a diet to disband. This was the famous *liberum veto,* the free veto, and to use it to break up a diet was called "exploding" the diet. The first diet was exploded in 1652. Of 55 diets held from that year to 1764, 48 were exploded.

Weakness of central government

Government became a fiasco. The monopoly of law and force, characteristic of the modern state, failed to develop in Poland. The king of Poland had practically no army, no law courts, no officials, and no income. The nobility paid no taxes. By 1750 the revenues of the king of Poland were about one-thirteenth those of the tsar of Russia and one seventy-fifth those of the king of France. Armed force was in the hands of a dozen or so aristocratic leaders, who also conducted their individual foreign policies, pursuing their own adventures against the Turks, or bringing in Russians, French, or Swedes to help them against other Poles. The landlords became local monarchs on their manorial estates. The mass of the rural population fell deeper into a serfdom scarcely different from slavery, bound to compulsory labor on estates resembling plantations, with police and disciplinary powers in the hands of the lords and with no outside legal or administrative system to set the limits of exploitation.

Pressures on Poland

The huge expanse comprised under the name of Poland was, in short, a power vacuum; and as more powerful centers developed, notably around Berlin and Moscow, the push against the Polish frontiers became steadily stronger. It was facilitated by the Poles themselves. As early as 1660 the East Prussian fief became independent of the Polish crown. As early as 1667 the Muscovites reconquered Smolensk and Kiev. Already there was confidential talk of partitioning Poland, which, however, was deferred for a century. Much of the history of the modern world would have been different had the Poland of the seventeenth century held together. There would have been no kingdom of Prussia and no Prussian influence in Germany; nor would Russia have become the chief Slavic power or reached so far into central Europe.

The Ottoman Empire about 1650

The Ottoman state, the third of the three empires which together spread over so much of Europe, was larger than either of the others, and in the seventeenth century it was more solidly organized and powerful. In 1529 the Turks had attacked Vienna and seemed about to burst into Germany. To most people in the Christian world the Turks were a mystery as well as a terror. They had formerly been among the rougher of the Muslim peoples, who had migrated from central Asia only a few centuries before and owed most of their higher civilization to the Arabs and the Persians. Their dominions extended, about 1650, from the Hungarian plain and the south Russian steppes as far as Algeria, the upper Nile, and the Persian Gulf. The empire was based to a large degree on military proficiency.

Long before Europe the Turks had a standing army, of which the janissaries were the main striking force. The janissaries were originally recruited from Christian children taken from their families in early childhood, brought up as Muslims, reared in military surroundings, and forbidden to marry; without background or ties, interests, or ambition outside the military organization to which they belonged, they were ideal fighting material in the hands of political leaders. The Turkish forces were long as well equipped as the Christian, being especially strong in heavy artillery. But by the mid-seventeenth century they were falling behind. They had changed little, or for the worse, since the days of Suleiman the Magnificent a century before, whereas in the better-organized Christian states discipline and military administration had been improved, and firearms, land mines, and siegecraft had become more effective.

The Turks cared little about assimilating subject peoples to their language or institutions. Local populations within the empire thus retained most of their cultural traditions and autonomy. Law was religious law derived from the Qur'an. Law courts and judges were hard to distinguish from religious authorities, for there was no separation between religious and secular spheres. The sultan was also the caliph, the commander of the faithful; while on the one hand there was no clergy in the European sense, on the other hand religious influences affected all aspects of life. The Turks, for the most part, applied the Muslim law only to Muslims; and the overall administration of imperial policies was controlled by a powerful government official called the grand vizier.

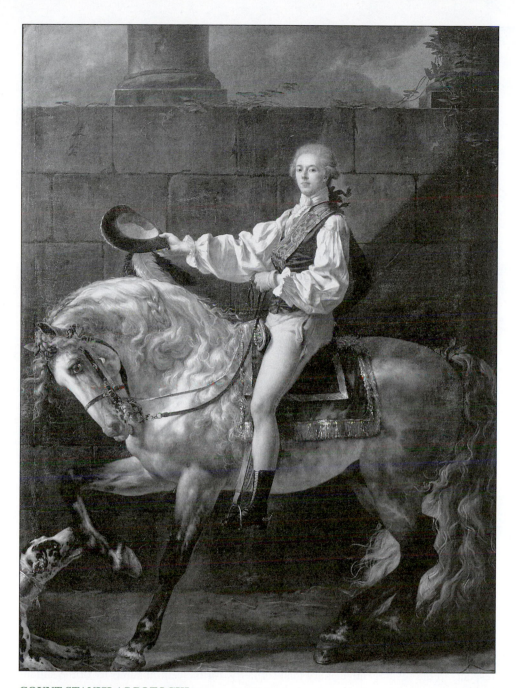

COUNT STANISLAS POTOCKI
by Jacques-Louis David (French, 1748–1825)
This portrait of a well-known eighteenth-century Polish nobleman—painted by David in
1781—expresses the sense of independent grandeur that characterized the Polish aristocracy
for several centuries in the early modern era.

(Erich Lessing/Art Resource, NY)

Tolerance of non-Muslim subjects

The Ottoman government left its non-Muslim subjects to settle their own affairs in their own way, not according to nationality, which was generally indistinguishable, but according to religious groupings. The Greek Orthodox church, to which most Christians in the empire belonged, thus became an almost autonomous intermediary between the sultan and a large fraction of its subjects. Armenian Christians and Jews formed other separate bodies. Except in the western Balkans (Albania and Bosnia) there was no general conversion of Christians to Islam during the Turkish rule, although there were many individual cases of Christians turning Muslim to obtain the privileges of the ruling faith. North of the Danube the Christian princes of Transylvania, Wallachia, and Moldavia (later combined into modern Romania) continued to rule over Christian subjects. They were kept in office for that purpose by the sultan, to whom they paid tribute. In general, since their subjects were more profitable to them as Christians, the Turks were not eager to proselytize for Islam.

The Ottoman Empire was therefore a relatively tolerant empire, far more so than the states of Europe. Christians in the Turkish empire fared better than Muslims would have fared in Christendom or than the Moors had in fact fared in Spain. Christians were less disturbed in Turkey than were Protestants in France, after 1685, or Catholics in Ireland. The empire was tolerant because it was composite, an aggregation of peoples, religions, and laws, having no drive, as did the Western states, toward internal unity and complete legal sovereignty. The same tolerance was evident in the attitude toward foreign merchants, who were active throughout most of the empire.

The king of France had had treaty arrangements with Turkey since 1535, and many traders from Marseilles had spread over the port towns of the Middle East. They were exempted by treaty from the laws of the Ottoman Empire and were liable to trial only by their own judges, who though residing in Turkey were appointed by the king of France. They were free to exercise their Roman Catholic religion, and if disputes with Muslims arose, they appeared in special courts where the word of an infidel received equal weight with that of a follower of the prophet. Similar rights in Turkey were obtained by other European states. Thus began "extraterritorial" privileges of the kind obtained by Europeans in later centuries in China and elsewhere, wherever the local laws were regarded as "backward," or hostile to Europeans. To the Turks of the seventeenth century there was nothing exceptional about such arrangements. Only much later, under Western influence, did the Turks come to resent these "capitulations" as impairments of their own sovereignty.

"Extraterritorial" privileges

Yet the Turkish rule was oppressive, and the "terrible Turk" was with reason the nightmare of eastern Europe. Ottoman rule was oppressive to Christians if only because it relegated them to a despised position and because everything they held holy was viewed by the Turks with contempt. But it was oppressive also in that it was often arbitrary and brutal even by the none too sensitive standards of Europeans. It was worse in these respects in the seventeenth century than formerly, for the central authority of the sultans had become corrupt, and the outlying governors, or pashas, had a virtual free hand with their subjects.

Disputed regions

Those parts of the Ottoman Empire which adjoined the Christian states were among the least firmly attached to Constantinople. The Tartar Khans of south Russia, like the Christian princes of the Danubian principalities, were simply protégés who paid tribute. Hungary was occupied but was more a battlefield than a province. These regions were disputed by Germans, Poles, and

Russians. It seemed in the middle of the seventeenth century as if the grip of the Turks might be relaxing. But a series of capable grand viziers, of the Köprülü family, came to power and retained it contrary to Turkish customs for 50 years. Under them the empire again launched a military campaign to expand into the Habsburg lands in central Europe. By 1663 the janissaries were again mobilizing in Hungary. Tartar horsemen were on the move. Central Europe again felt the old terror. The pope feared that the dreaded enemy might break into Italy. Throughout Germany by the emperor's order special "Turk bells" sounded the alarm. The states of the Empire voted to raise a small imperial army. The Holy Roman Empire thus bestirred itself temporarily against the historic enemy of European Christians. However, it was not under the auspices of the Holy Roman Empire, but by the house of Austria that the Turks were repelled.

24.   THE FORMATION OF AN AUSTRIAN MONARCHY

The Recovery and Growth of Habsburg Power, 1648–1740

The Austria which appeared by 1700 was actually a new creation, though not as obviously so as the two other rising states in Prussia and Russia. The Austrian Habsburgs had long enjoyed an eminent role. Formerly their position had rested on their headship of the Holy Roman Empire and on their family connection with the wealthy Habsburgs of Spain. In the seventeenth century these two supports collapsed. The hope for an effective Habsburg empire in Germany disappeared in the Thirty Years' War. The connection with Spain lost its value as Spain declined, and it vanished when in 1700 Spain passed to the house of France. The Austrian family in the latter half of the seventeenth century stood at the great turning point of its fortunes. It successfully made a difficult transition, emerging from the husk of the Holy Roman Empire and building an empire of its own. At the same time the Habsburgs continued to be Holy Roman Emperors and remained active in German affairs, using resources drawn from outside Germany to maintain their influence over the German princes. The relation of Austria to the rest of Germany remained a political conundrum down to the twentieth century.

The dominions considered by the house of Austria to be its direct possessions were in three parts. The oldest were the "hereditary provinces"— *Dominions of Austria* Upper and Lower Austria, with the adjoining Tyrol, Styria, Carinthia, and Carniola. Second, there was the kingdom of Bohemia—Bohemia, Moravia, and Silesia joined under the crown of St. Wenceslas. Third, there was the kingdom of Hungary—Hungary, Transylvania, and Croatia joined under the crown of St. Stephen. Nothing held all these regions together except the fact that the Austrian Habsburg dynasty, in the seventeenth century, reaffirmed its grip upon them all. During the Thirty Years' War the dynasty rooted Protestantism and feudal rebelliousness out of Austria and the hereditary provinces and reconquered and re-Catholicized Bohemia. And in the following decades it conquered Hungary also.

Since 1526 most of Hungary had been occupied by the Turks. For generations the Hungarian plain was a theater of intermittent warfare between the armies of Vienna and Constantinople. The struggle flared up again in 1663, when Turkish armies began to move up the Danube. A mixed force, assembled from the Empire and its various European allies, obliged the Turks in 1664 to accept a 20-year truce. But Louis XIV, who in these years was busily dismembering the western frontier of the Empire, stood to profit greatly from a diversion on the Danube. He incited the Turks (old allies of France through common hostility to the Habsburgs) to resume their assaults, which they did as the 20-year truce came to a close.

Vienna besieged by the Turks

In 1683 a vast Turkish army reached the city of Vienna and besieged it. The Turks again, as in 1529, peered into the very inner chambers of Europe. The garrison and people of Vienna, greatly outnumbered, held off the besiegers for two months, enough time for a defending force to arrive. Both sides showed the "international" character of the conflict. The Turkish army included Christians—Romanian and Hungarian—the latter in rebellion against Habsburg rule in Hungary. The anti-Turkish force was composed mainly of Poles, Austrian dynastic troops, and Germans from various states of the Empire. It was financed largely by Pope Innocent XI; it was commanded in the field by the Habsburg general, Duke Charles of Lorraine, who hoped to protect his inheritance from annexation by France; and its higher command was entrusted to John Sobieski, king of Poland. Sobieski contributed greatly to the relief of Vienna, and his bold action represented the last great military effort of the moribund Republic of Poland. When the Turks abandoned the siege, a general anti-Turkish counteroffensive developed. Armed forces of the pope, Poland, Russia, and the republic of Venice joined with the Habsburgs. It was in this war, in fighting between Turks and Venetians, that the Parthenon at Athens, which had survived for 2,000 years but was now used as an ammunition dump by the Turks, was severely damaged.

Prince Eugene of Savoy

The Habsburgs had the good fortune to obtain the services of a man of remarkable talent, Prince Eugene of Savoy. Eugene, like many other servants of the Austrian house, was not Austrian at all; he was in fact French by origin and education but like many aristocrats of the time he was an international personage. More than anyone else he was the founder of the modern Austrian state. Distinguished both as a military administrator and as a commander in the field, he reformed the supply, equipment, training, and command of the Habsburg forces, along lines laid out by Louis XIV; and in 1697 he won the battle of Zenta, driving the Turks out of Hungary. At the Peace of Karlowitz (1699) the Turks yielded most of Hungary, together with Transylvania and Croatia, to the Habsburg house; and the Ottoman Empire was pushed back permanently into Romania and the Balkans.

The Habsburgs were now free to pursue their designs in the west. They entered the War of the Spanish Succession to win the Spanish crown, but they had to content themselves by the treaty of Rastadt in 1714 with the annexation of the old Spanish Netherlands and with Milan and Naples. Prince Eugene, freed now in the west, again turned eastward. Never before or afterward were the Austrians so brilliantly successful. Eugene captured Belgrade and pushed through the Iron Gate into Wallachia. But the Turks were not yet helpless; and by the Peace of Belgrade (1739) a frontier was drawn which on the Austrian side remained unchanged until the twentieth century. The Turks continued to hold Romania and the whole Balkan peninsula except Catholic Croatia, which was incorporated into the Habsburg empire. The Habsburg government, to open a window on the Mediterranean, developed a seaport at Trieste.

The Austrian Monarchy by 1740

Thus the house of Austria, in two or three generations after its humiliation at the Peace of Westphalia, acquired a new empire of considerable proportions. Though installed in Bel-

The Austrian Habsburgs mobilized a large force of military alllies, including Polish troops under King John Sobieski, to repel the Turkish army that besieged Vienna in 1683. This painting by Franz Geffels (1635–c. 1699) portrays the final, decisive clash that forced the Turks to abandon their siege of the city.
(Erich Lessing/Art Resource, NY (*The Relief of Vienna, 1683* by Franz Geffels (1635/6–c. 1699)))

gium and Italy, it was essentially an empire of the middle Danube, with its headquarters at Vienna in Austria proper, but possessing the sizable kingdoms of Hungary and Bohemia. Though German influence was strong, the empire was international—or nonnational. At the Habsburg court, and in the Habsburg government and army, the names of Czech, Hungarian, Croatian, and Italian noblemen were common. When the nationalist movements swept over Europe in the nineteenth century, the empire was denounced as tyrannical by Hungarians, Croats, Serbs, Romanians, Czechs, Poles, Italians, and even by some Germans, whose national ambitions were blocked by its existence. Later, disillusioned by nationalism in central and eastern Europe, some tended to romanticize unduly the old Habsburg monarchy, noting that it had at least the merit of holding many discordant peoples together.

The empire was from the beginning international, based on a cosmopolitan aristocracy of landowners who felt closer to each other, despite differences of language, than to the laboring masses who worked on their estates. Not for many years, until after 1848, did the Habsburg government really touch these rural masses; it dealt with the landed class and with the relatively few cities, but it left the landlords to control the peasants. The old diets, or assemblies, survived in Bohemia, Hungary, and the Austrian provinces. No diet was created for the empire as a whole. The diets were essentially assemblages of landlords; and though they no longer enjoyed their medieval freedom, they retained powers over taxation and administration and a sense of constitutional liberty against the crown. So long as they

An international empire

THE GROWTH OF THE AUSTRIAN MONARCHY, 1521–1772

The map shows the main body of the Austrian monarchy as it evolved in the eighteenth century and endured until the collapse of the empire in 1918. There were three main parts: (1) a nucleus, composed of Austria and adjoining duchies, often called the "hereditary provinces"; (2) the lands of the Bohemian crown, which became Habsburg in 1526 and where the Habsburgs reasserted their power during the Thirty Years' War; and (3) the lands of the Hungarian crown, where at first the Habsburgs held only the segment called Imperial Hungary, the rest remaining Turkish until reconquered by the Habsburgs in 1699. In the first partition of Poland (1772) the Habsburgs annexed Galicia. Silesia was lost to Prussia in 1740.

produced taxes and soldiers as needed, and accepted the wars and foreign policy of the ruling house, no questions were asked at Vienna. Religion was a different matter, however, for the Habsburgs forcefully repressed the Protestantism that had spread widely across both Bohemia and Hungary. Many of the estates of Protestant nobles and rebels were confiscated, giving the Habsburgs valuable lands with which to reward soldiers and supporters from all parts of Europe. An increasingly heterogeneous population of Germans, Croats, and Serbs settled in Habsburg territories, especially in Hungary. Meanwhile, the peasants remained in, or reverted to, serfdom.

Despite the concerted political, religious, and military policies of the Habsburg rulers, the Austrian monarchy remained a collection of territories held together by a personal union. Inhabitants of Austria proper considered their ruler as archduke, Bohemians saw in him the king of Bohemia; Magyars, the apostolic king of Hungary. Each country retained its own law, diet, and political life, all of which made it difficult or impossible for the Habsburgs to establish laws and institutions that would be accepted in all the territories they ruled. No feeling in the people held these regions together, and even the several aristocracies were joined only by common service to the Habsburgs. For the empire to exist, all crowns had to be inherited by the same person.

After the reconquest of Hungary the king-archduke, Charles VI (1711–1740), devised a form of insurance to guarantee such an undivided succession. This took the form of a document called the Pragmatic Sanction, first issued in 1713. By it every diet in the empire and the various archdukes of the Habsburg family were to agree to regard the Habsburg territories as indivisible and to recognize only the Habsburg line of heirs. The matter became urgent when it developed that Charles would have no male heir. The direct male line of the Austrian Habsburgs, as of the Spanish a few years before, was about to become extinct. But Charles did have a daughter, Maria Theresa, and he gradually won acceptance of the "Pragmatic Sanction" by all parts of his empire and all members of his family. This agreement recognized Maria Theresa's right to the Habsburg throne and to the inheritance of all Habsburg territories. He then set about having foreign powers guarantee it, knowing that Bavaria, Prussia, or others might well put in claims for this or that part of the inheritance. This process took years, and was accomplished at the cost of many damaging concessions. Charles VI had attempted, for example, to revive Belgium commercially by founding an overseas trading company at Ostend. The British government, before agreeing to guarantee the Pragmatic Sanction, demanded and obtained the renunciation of this commercial project. Finally all powers signed. Charles VI died in 1740, having done all that could be done, by domestic law and international treaty, to assure the continuation of the Austrian empire.

Charles VI and the Pragmatic Sanction

He was scarcely dead when armed "heirs" presented themselves. A great war broke out to partition the Austrian empire, as the Spanish empire had been partitioned shortly before. Bohemia threw off its allegiance. Hungary almost did the same. But these events belong later in the story. At the moment it is enough to know that by 1740 a populous empire of great military strength existed on the Danube.

25. THE FORMATION OF PRUSSIA

It was characteristic of the seventeenth century that very small states were able to play an influential part in European affairs, seemingly out of all proportion to their size. The main reason why small states could act as great powers was that armies were small and weapons were simple. Difficulties of supply and communications, the poor condition of the roads, the lack of maps, the absence of general staffs, together with many other administrative and technical difficulties, reduced the number of soldiers who could be successfully managed in a campaign. The battles of the Thirty Years' War, on the average, were fought by armies of less than 20,000 men. And while Louis XIV, by the last years of his reign, built up a military establishment aggregating some 400,000, the actual field armies in the wars of Louis XIV did not exceed, on the average, 40,000. Armies of this size were well within the reach of smaller powers. If especially well trained, disciplined, and equipped, and if ably commanded, the armies of small powers could defeat those of much larger neighbors. On this fact, fundamentally, the German state of Prussia was to be built.

But Prussia was not the first to exploit the opportunity with spectacular consequences. The first was Sweden.

Sweden's Short-Lived Empire

Sweden almost, but not quite, formed an empire in central and eastern Europe in the seventeenth century. The population of Sweden at the time was not over a million; it was smaller than that of the Dutch Republic. But the Swedes produced a line of extraordinary rulers, ranging from genius in Gustavus Adolphus (1611–1632) through the brilliantly erratic Queen Christina (1632–1654) to the amazing military exploits of Charles XII (1697–1718). The elective Swedish kingship was made hereditary, the royal power freed from control by the estates. Craftsmen and experts were brought from the west, notably Holland; war industries were subsidized by the government; and an army was created with many novel features in weapons, organization, and tactics.

Swedish territorial victories

With this army Gustavus Adolphus crossed the Baltic in the Thirty Years' War, made alliances with Protestant German princes, cut through the Holy Roman Empire, and helped to ward off unification of Germany by the Habsburgs. The Swedish crown, by the Peace of Westphalia, received certain coastal regions of Germany. Subsequently, in a confused series of wars, in which a Polish king claimed to be king of Sweden and a Swedish king claimed to be king of Poland, the Swedes won control of virtually all the shores and cities of the Baltic. Only Denmark at the mouth of that sea and the territories of the house of Brandenburg, which had almost no ports, remained independent. For a time the Baltic was a Swedish lake. The Russians were shut off from it, and the Poles and even the Germans, who lived on its shores, could reach it only on Swedish terms.

Charles XII

The final Swedish campaign for imperial expansion took place during the meteoric reign of Charles XII. As a young man he found his dominions attacked by Denmark, Poland, and Russia; he won remarkable victories over them but would not make peace; he then led an army back and forth across the East European plain, only to be crushed by the Russians. He fled to Turkey and spent long years as a guest and protégé of the Turks. By 1718 the Swedish sphere had contracted to Sweden itself, except that Finland and reduced holdings in northern Germany remained Swedish for a century more. The Swedes in time proved themselves exceptional among European peoples in not harping on their former greatness. They successfully and peaceably made the transition from the role of a great power to that of a small one.

The Territorial Growth of Brandenburg-Prussia

In the long run it was to be Prussia that dominated this part of Europe. Prussia became famous for its "militarism," which may be said to exist when military needs and military values permeate all other spheres of life. Through its influence on Germany over a period of two centuries it played a momentous part in the modern world. The south coast of the Baltic, where Prussia was to arise, was an unpromising site for the creation of a strong political power. It was an uninviting country, thinly populated, with poor soil and without mineral resources, more backward than Saxony or Bohemia, not to mention the busy centers of south Germany and western Europe. It was a flat open plain, merging imperceptibly into Poland, without prominent physical features or natural frontiers (see maps, pp. 4–5,

193, 194, 208–209). The coastal region directly south from Sweden was known as Pomerania. Inland from it, shut off from the sea, was Brandenburg, centering about Berlin. Brandenburg had been founded in the Middle Ages as a border state, a "mark" or "march" of the Holy Roman Empire, to fight the battles of the empire against the then heathen Slavs. Its ruler, the margrave, was one of the seven princes who, after 1356, elected the Holy Roman Emperor. Hence he was commonly called the Elector of Brandenburg. After 1415 the electors were always of the Hohenzollern family.

All Germany east of the Elbe, including Brandenburg, represented a medieval conquest by the German-speaking peoples—the German *Drang nach Osten,* or drive to the East. From the Elbe to Poland, German conquerors and settlers had replaced the Slavs, eliminating them or absorbing them by intermarriage. Eastward from Brandenburg, and outside the Holy Roman Empire, stretched a region inhabited by Slavic peoples. Next to the east came "Prussia," which eventually was to give its name to all territories of the Hohenzollern monarchy. This original Prussia formed part of the lands of the Teutonic Knights, a military crusading order which had conquered and Christianized the native peoples in the thirteenth century. Except for its seacoast along the Baltic, the duchy of Prussia was totally enclosed by the Polish kingdom. To the north, along the Baltic, as far as the Gulf of Finland, German minorities lived among Lithuanians, Latvians (or Letts), and Estonians. The towns were German, founded as German commercial colonies in the Middle Ages, and many of the landlords were German also, descendants of the Teutonic Knights, and later known as the "Baltic barons."

Germans expand eastward

Modern Prussia began to appear in the seventeenth century when a number of territories came into the hands of the Hohenzollerns of Brandenburg, who, we have noted, had ruled in Brandenburg since 1415. In 1618 the Elector of Brandenburg inherited the duchy of Prussia. Another important development occurred when the old ruling line in Pomerania expired during the Thirty Years' War. Although the Swedes succeeded in taking the better part of Pomerania, including the city of Stettin, the Elector of Brandenburg received at the Peace of Westphalia eastern Pomerania. Barren, rural, and harborless though it was, it at least had the advantage of connecting Brandenburg with the Baltic. The Hohenzollerns no sooner obtained it than they began to dream of joining it to the duchy of Prussia, a task which required the absorption of an intermediate and predominantly Slavic area, which was part of Poland, a task not accomplished until 1772.

Territorial acquisitions of the Hohenzollerns

Had the duchy of Prussia and eastern Pomerania been the only acquisitions of the Hohenzollerns, their state would have been oriented almost exclusively toward eastern Europe. But at the Peace of Westphalia they received, in addition to eastern Pomerania, new territories on the west bank of the Elbe. Moreover, through the play of inheritance common in the Holy Roman Empire, the Hohenzollerns had earlier fallen heir, in 1614, to the small state of Cleves on the Rhine at the Dutch border and a few other small territories also in western Germany. These were separated from the main mass around Brandenburg by many intermediate German principalities. But they gave the Hohenzollerns a direct contact with the more advanced regions of western Europe and a base from which larger holdings in the Rhineland were eventually to be built up.

In the seventeenth century, meanwhile, the dominions of the house of Brandenburg were in three disconnected territories. The main one was Brandenburg, with adjoining Pomerania and territories along the Elbe. There was a detached eastern territory in ducal Prussia and another small detached western territory on and near the Rhine. To connect and unify these three territorial possessions became the long-range policy of the Brandenburg house.

In the midst of the Thirty Years' War, in 1640, a young man of 20, named Frederick William, succeeded to these diverse possessions. Known later as the Great Elector, he was the first of the men who shaped modern Prussia. He had grown up under trying conditions. Brandenburg was one of the parts of Germany to suffer most heavily from the war. Its location made it the stamping ground of Swedish and Habsburg armies. In 1640, in the 22 years since the beginning of the war, the population of Berlin had fallen from about 14,000 to about 6,000. Hundreds of villages had been wiped out. Wolves roamed over the countryside.

The Great Elector

Frederick William concluded that in his position, ruling a small and open territory, without natural frontiers or possibility of defense in depth, he must put his main reliance on a competent army. With an effective army, even if small, he could oblige the stronger states to take him into their calculations and so could enter with some hope of advantage into the politics of the balance of power. This long remained the program of the Brandenburgers— to have an army but not to use it, to conserve it with loving and even miserly care, to keep an "army in being," and to gain their ends by diplomatic maneuver. They did so by siding with France against the Habsburgs, or with Sweden against Poland. They aspired also to the title not merely of margrave or elector, but king. The opportunity came in 1701, when the Habsburg emperor was preparing to enter the War of the Spanish Succession. The emperor requested the elector of Brandenburg, who was then Frederick III, to support him with 8,000 troops. The elector named his price: recognition of himself, by the emperor, as king "in Prussia." The emperor yielded; the title, at first explicitly limited to the less honorable king *in* Prussia, soon became king *of* Prussia. The elector Frederick III of Brandenburg became King Frederick I of Prussia. Another rent was made in the old fabric of the Holy Roman Empire. There was now a German king above all the other German princes.

The Prussian Military State

The preoccupation of Prussia with its army was unquestionably defensive in origin, arising from the horrors of the Thirty Years' War. But it outlasted its cause and became the settled habit and character of the country. Prussia was not unique in the attention it paid to its armed forces. The unique thing about Prussia was the disproportion between the size of the army and the size of the resources on which the army was based. The government, to maintain the army, had to direct and plan the life of the country for this purpose. Nor was Prussia the originator of the "standing" army, kept active in time of peace and always preparing for war. Most governments imitated Louis XIV in establishing standing armies, not merely to promote foreign ambitions but to keep armed forces out of the hands of nobles and military adventurers and under control by the state.

The Prussian army

But Prussia was unique in that, more than in any other country, the army developed a life of its own, almost independent of the life of the state. It was older than the Prussian state. In 1657 the Great Elector fought a great battle at Warsaw with soldiers from all parts of his dominions. It was the first time that men from Cleves, Brandenburg, and ducal Prussia had ever done anything together. The army was the first "all Prussian" institution. Institutions of civilian government developed later and largely to meet the needs of the army. And in later generations the army proved more durable than the state. When Prussia collapsed before Napoleon in 1806, the spirit and morale of the Prussian army carried on; and when the Hohenzollern empire finally

Frederick William, who became known as the Great Elector, governed Prussia for almost 50 years (1640–1688) and set his country on a course toward new power and military influence in central Europe.
(Foto Marburg/Art Resource, NY)

crashed in 1918, the army still maintained its life and traditions on into the Weimar Republic, which again it survived. Not until the defeat of Adolf Hitler in the Second World War and the establishment of a new republican regime was the army totally subordinated to civilian authority.

In all countries, to some extent, the machinery of the modern state developed as a means of supporting armed forces, but in Prussia the process was exceptionally clear and simple. In Prussia the rulers drew roughly half their income from the crown domain and only about half from taxes. The crown domain, consisting of manors and other productive enterprises owned directly by the ruler as lord, was in effect a kind of government property, for the Prussian rulers used their income almost entirely for state purposes, being personally simple and even Spartan in their habits. The rulers of Prussia, until a century after the accession of the Great Elector, were able to pay the whole cost of their civil government from their own income, the proceeds of the crown domain. But to maintain an army they had to make the domain more productive and also find new income derived from taxes. To develop the domain and account for and transfer the funds, they created a large body of civilian officials. The domain bulked so large that much of the economy of the country was not in private hands but consisted of enterprises owned and administered by the state. For additional income the Great Elector introduced taxes of the kind used in France, such as excise taxes on consumers' goods and a government monopoly on the sale of salt. All taxes, for a century after the accession of the Great Elector, were levied for the use of the army.

Maintaining the army

Economic life grew up under government sponsorship, rather than through the enterprise of a venturesome business class. This was because, for a rural country to maintain an organized army, productive and technical skills had to be imported, mainly from the West. The Great Elector in his youth spent a number of years in Holland, where he was impressed by the wealth and prosperity that he saw. After becoming elector he settled Swiss and Frisians in Brandenburg (the Frisians were akin to the Dutch); he welcomed Jews from Poland; and when Louis XIV began to persecute the French Protestants, he provided funds and special officials to assist the immigration of 20,000 Huguenots to Brandenburg. French immigrants for a time formed a sixth of the population of Berlin and were

THE GROWTH OF PRUSSIA, 1415–1918

The maps shown here, going well beyond the scope of this chapter, give a conspectus of Prussian history from the time when Brandenburg began to expand in the seventeenth century. One may see, by looking at all the panels together, how Prussia was really an east-European state until 1815; its center of gravity shifted westward, in significant degree, only in the nineteenth century. Panel 2 shows the early formation of three unconnected territories; Panel 3, the huge bulk of Silesia relative to the small kingdom that annexed it; Panel 4, the fruits of the partitions of Poland; Panel 5, Napoleon pared Prussia down. The main crisis at the Congress of Vienna, and its resolution, are shown in Panels 6 and 7. Bismarck's enlargement of Prussia appears in Panel 8. The boundaries established by Bismarck remained unchanged until the fall of the monarchy in 1918.

the most advanced commercial element of that comparatively primitive city. The government, as in France under Colbert, initiated and helped to finance various industries; but the importance of such government participation was greater than in France, because the amount of privately owned capital available for investment was incomparably less. Military needs, more than elsewhere, dominated the market for goods, because civilian demand in so poor a country was relatively low; the army, in its requirements for food, uniforms, and weapons became a strong force in shaping the economic growth of the country.

The army had a profound effect also on the social development and class structure of Prussia. The civilian middle class remained submissive, and it became the policy of the rulers to absorb practically the whole landed aristocracy, the Junkers, into military service. They used the army, with conscious purpose, as a means of implementing an "all Prussian" psychology in the landed families of Cleves, Brandenburg, Pomerania, and the former dominions of the Teutonic Knights. The fact that Prussia was a very recent and artificial combination

The army and Prussian society

of territories, so that identification with it was not a natural sentiment, made it all the more necessary to instill loyalty by martial means. Emphasis fell on duty, obedience, service, and sacrifice. That military virtues became characteristic of the whole male Prussian aristocracy was also due, like so much else, to the small size of the population. In France, for example, with perhaps 50,000 male adult nobles, only a small minority served as army officers. In Prussia there were few Junker families that did not have some of their members in uniform.

The Great Elector and his successors, like all absolutist rulers of the era, repressed the estates or parliamentary assemblages in which the landed aristocracy was the main element. To mollify the squires, the rulers promised commissions in the army to men of their class. They promised them also a free hand over their peasants. The Prussian monarchy was largely based on an understanding between the ruler and the landlord gentry—the latter agreed to accept the ruler's government and to serve in his army, in return for holding their own peasants in hereditary subjection. Serfdom spread in Prussia as elsewhere in eastern Europe. In East Prussia the condition of the peasants became as deplorable as in Poland.

The Prussian rulers believed that the Junkers made better army officers because they were brought up in the habit of commanding their own peasants. To preserve the officer class, legislation forbade the sale of "noble" lands, that is, manors, to persons not noble. In France, again by way of contrast, where manorial rights had become simply a form of property, bourgeois and even peasants could legally acquire manors and enjoy a lordly or "seigneurial" income. In Prussia this was not possible; classes were frozen by owning nonexchangeable forms of property. It was thus harder for middle-class persons to enter the aristocracy by setting up as landed gentry. The bourgeois class in any case had little spirit of independence. Few of the old towns of Germany were in Prussia. The Prussian middle class was not wealthy. It was not strong through the possession of private property. The typical middle-class man was an official who worked for the government as an employee of the large crown domain or in an enterprise subsidized by the state. The civil service in Prussia, from the days of the Great Elector, became notable for its honesty and efficiency. But the middle class, more than elsewhere, deferred to the nobles, served the state, and stood in awe of the army.

Limited social mobility

Frederick William I

These peculiar features of Prussia developed especially under Frederick William I, who was king from 1713 to 1740. He was an earthy, uncouth man, who disdained whatever savored of "culture," to which his father, his grandfather (the Great Elector), and also his son (Frederick the Great) were all strongly attracted. He begrudged every penny not spent on the army. He cut the expense of the royal household by three-fourths. On his coronation journey to Königsberg he spent 2,547 thalers, where his father had spent five million. He ruled the country in a fatherly German way, supervising it like a private estate, prowling the streets of Berlin in an old seedy uniform, and disciplining negligent citizens with blows of his walking stick. He worked all the time and expected everyone else to do likewise.

He loved the army, which all his policies were designed to serve. He was the first Prussian king to appear always in uniform. He rearranged the order of courtly precedence, moving army officers up and civilians down. His love of tall soldiers is famous; he collected a special unit, men between 6 and 7 feet tall, from all over Europe, and indeed the Russian Tsar Peter the Great sent him some from Asia. He devised new forms of discipline and maneuver, founded a cadet corps to train the sons of the Junkers, and invented a new system of recruiting (the canton system, long the most effective in Europe), by which each regiment had a particular district or canton assigned to it as a source of soldiers. He raised the size of the army from 40,000 at his accession to 83,000 at his death. During his reign Berlin grew to be a city of 100,000, of whom 20,000 were soldiers, a proportion probably matched in no other city of Europe. He likewise left to his successor (for he fought practically no wars himself) a war chest of 7,000,000 thalers.

With this army and war chest Frederick II, later called the Great, who became king in 1740, startled Europe. Charles VI of Austria had just died. His daughter Maria Theresa entered upon her manifold inheritance. All Europe was hedging on its guarantee of the Pragmatic Sanction. While others waited, Frederick struck. Serving no notice, he moved his forces into Silesia, to which the Hohenzollerns had an old though doubtful claim. Silesia was a part of the kingdom of Bohemia on the side toward Poland, lying in the upper valley of the Oder River and adjoining Brandenburg on the north. The addition of Silesia to the kingdom of Prussia almost doubled the population and added valuable industries, so that Prussia now, with 6,000,000 people and an army which Frederick raised to 200,000, at last established itself as a great power. It must be added that, judged simply as a human accomplishment, Prussia was a remarkable creation, a state made on a shoestring, a triumph of work and duty.

The advances of Frederick the Great

26. THE "WESTERNIZING" OF RUSSIA

The affairs of central and eastern Europe, from Sweden to Turkey and from Germany to the Caspian Sea, were profoundly interconnected. The underlying theme of the present chapter, it may be recalled, is that this whole great area was fluid, occupied by the weak political bodies of the Holy Roman Empire, Poland, and Turkey, and that in this fluid area three new powers gradually developed—the modern Austrian monarchy, the kingdom of Prussia, and the Russian empire. All, too, in varying degree, became modern eighteenth-century states by borrowing various ideas and administrative systems from the West, though each of these new eastern states also retained its own distinctive political, social, and cultural characteristics.

In the century after 1650 the old tsardom of Muscovy turned into modern Russia. Moving out from the region around Moscow, the Russians not only established themselves across northern Asia, reaching the Bering Sea about 1700, but also entered into closer relations with Europe, undergoing especially in the time of Tsar Peter the Great (1682–1725) a rapid process of Europeanization. To what extent Russia became truly European has always been an open question, disputed both by western Europeans and by Russians themselves. In some ways the Russians have been European from as far back as Europe itself can be said to have existed, that is, from the early Middle Ages. Ancient Russia had been colonized by Vikings, and the Russians had become Christian long before the Swedes, the Lithuanians, or the Finns.

Europeanization

Yet Russia had not been part of the general development of Europe for a number of reasons. Russia had been converted to the Greek Orthodox branch of Christianity; therefore, the religious and cultural influence of Constantinople, not of Rome, had predominated. Second, the Mongol invasions and conquest about 1240 had kept Russia under Asian domination for about 250 years, until 1480 when a grand duke of Muscovy, Ivan III (1462–1505), was able to throw off the Mongol overlordship and cease payment of tribute. Last, Russian geography, especially the lack of warm-water or ice-free seaports, had made commerce and communication with the West difficult. Russia had therefore not shared in the general European development after about 1100, and the changes that took place in the

The uniforms of these Prussian soldiers in the era of King Frederick II (1740–1786) represent the status and importance of the military class in Prussian society during the eighteenth century. (akg-images)

seventeenth and eighteenth centuries may accurately be called Europeanization, or at least a wholesale borrowing of the new knowledge and institutions that had developed in the early modern European states. The Europeanizing or westernizing of Russia was by no means a unique thing. It was a step in the expansion of the modern European type of civilization or social organization and hence in the formation of the modern world as we have known it in recent centuries.

Parallels with Prussia

In some ways the new Russian empire resembled the new kingdom of Prussia. Both took form in the great plain which runs uninterruptedly from the North Sea into inner Asia. Both lacked natural frontiers and grew by addition of territories to an original nucleus. In both countries the state arose primarily as a means of supporting a modern army. In both the government developed autocratically, in conjunction with a landlord class which was impressed into state service and which in turn held the peasantry in serfdom. Neither Russia nor Prussia had a native commercial class of any political importance. In neither country could the modern state and army have been created without the importation of new skills from western Europe. Yet Prussia, with its German connections, its Protestant religion, its universities, and its nearness to the busy commercial artery of the Baltic, was far more "European" than

Russia, and the Europeanization of Russia may perhaps better be compared with the later "westernization" of Japan. In the Russia of 1700, as in the Japan of 1870, the main purpose of the westernizers was to obtain scientific, technical, and military knowledge from the West, in part with a view to strengthening their own countries against penetration or conquest by Europeans. Yet here too the parallel must not be pushed too far. In time, the Russian upper classes intermarried with Europeans, and Russian music and literature became part of the culture of Europe. Russia developed a unique blend of European and non-European traits.

Russia before Peter the Great

The Russians in the seventeenth century, as today, were a medley of peoples distinguished by their language, which was of the Slavic family, of the great Indo-European language group. The Great Russians or Muscovites lived around Moscow. Moving out from that area, they had penetrated the northern forests and had also settled in the southern steppes and along the Volga, where they had assimilated various Asian peoples known as Tartars. After two centuries of expansion, from roughly 1450 to 1650, the Russians had almost but not quite reached the Baltic and the Black seas. The Baltic shore was held by Sweden. The Black Sea coast was still held by Tartar Khans under the protection of Turkey. In the rough borderlands between Tartar and Russia lived the semi-independent cowboy-like Cossacks, largely recruited from migratory Russians. West of Muscovy were the White Russians (or Byelorussians) and southwest of Muscovy the Little Russians (Ruthenians or Ukrainians), both in the seventeenth century under the rule of Poland, which was then the leading Slavic power.

The energies of the Great Russians were directed principally eastward. They conquered the Volga Tartars in the sixteenth century and reached the Ural Mountains, which they immediately crossed. Muscovite pioneers, settlers, and townbuilders streamed along the river systems of Siberia, felling timber and trading in furs as they went. In the 1630s, while the English were building Boston and the Dutch New York, the Russians were establishing towns in the vast Asian stretches of Siberia, reaching to the Pacific itself. A whole string of settlements, remote, small, and isolated—Tomsk and Tobolsk, Irkutsk and Yakutsk—extended for 5,000 miles across northern Asia.

It was toward the vast heartland of central Asia that Muscovy really faced, looking out upon Persia and China across the deserts. The bazaars of Moscow and Astrakhan were frequented by Persians, Afghans, Indians, and Chinese. The Caspian Sea, into which flowed the Volga, the greatest of Russian rivers, was better known than was the Baltic. Europe as sensed from Moscow was in the rear. During most of the seventeenth century even Smolensk and Kiev belonged to Poland. Yet the Russians were not totally shut off from Europe. In 1552, when Ivan the Terrible conquered Kazan from the Tartars, he had a German engineer in his army. In the next year, 1553, Richard Chancellor arrived in Moscow from England by the roundabout way of Archangel on the White Sea. Thereafter trade between England and Muscovy was continuous. The tsars valued Archangel as their only inlet from the West through which military materials could be imported. The English valued it as a means of reaching the wares of Persia.

Russia in the seventeenth century reflected its long estrangement from the culture and social mores that had been developing in Europe. Women of the upper classes were secluded and often wore veils. Men wore beards and skirted garments that seemed exotic to Europeans. Customs were crude, wild drunkenness and revelry alternating with spasms of repentance and religious prostration.

Russian estrangement from Europe

CHRONOLOGY OF NOTABLE EVENTS, 1640–1740

1640–1688	Frederick William, the Great Elector, develops state and military power in Prussia
1663	Ottoman Empire begins new phase of expansion in Central Europe
1667–1671	Stephen Razin leads rebellion of rural population in Russia
1683	Ottoman imperial army is forced to abandon siege of Vienna
1698–1725	Tsar Peter the Great introduces "westernizing" reforms in Russia
1711–1740	Habsburg Charles VI builds the Austrian Empire
1713–1740	Frederick William I expands the army and wealth of the Prussian state

Superstition infected the highest classes of church and state. Life counted for little; murder, kidnapping, torture, and elaborate physical cruelty were common. The Russian church supported no such educational or charitable institutions as did the Catholic and Protestant churches of Europe. Churchmen feared the incipient Western influences. "Abhorred of God," declared a Russian bishop, "is any who loves geometry; it is a spiritual sin." Even arithmetic was hardly understood in Russia. Arabic numerals were not used, and merchants computed with the abacus. The calendar was dated from the creation of the world. Ability to predict an eclipse seemed a form of magic. Clocks, brought in by Europeans, seemed as wonderful in Russia as they did in China, where they were brought in by Jesuits at about the same time.

Yet this great, non-European Russia, which fronted on inner Asia, was European in some of its fundamental social institutions. It possessed a variant of the manorial and feudal systems. It felt the same wave of constitutional crises that was sweeping over Europe at the same time. Russia had a duma or council of retainers and advisers to the tsar, and the rudiments of a national assembly corresponding to meetings of the estates in western Europe. In Russia as in Europe the question was whether power should remain in the hands of these bodies or become concentrated in the hands of the ruler. Ivan the Terrible, who ruled from 1533 to 1584 and was the first grand duke of Muscovy to assume the title of tsar,[1] was a shrewd observer of contemporary events in Poland. He saw the dissolution that was overtaking the Polish state and was determined to avoid it in Muscovy. His ferocity toward those who opposed him made him literally terrible, but though his methods differed from the methods commonly used in Europe, his aims were the aims of his European contemporaries. Not long after his death Russia passed into a period known as the Time of Troubles (1604–1613), during which the Russian nobles elected a series of tsars and demanded certain assurances of their own liberties. But the country was racked by contending factions and a civil war in which the violence resembled the religious wars in France or the Thirty Years' War in central Europe.

The Romanovs

In 1613 a national assembly, hoping to settle the troubles, elected a 17-year-old boy as tsar, or emperor, believing him young enough to have no connection with any of the warring factions. The new boy tsar was Michael Romanov, of a gentry family, related by marriage to the old line of Ivan the

---

[1]The Slavic word *tsar,* like the German *Kaiser,* derives from *Caesar,* a title used as a synonym for *emperor* in the Roman, the Holy Roman, and the Byzantine (or Eastern Roman) empires. The spelling *czar,* also common in English, reveals the etymology and the current English-language pronunciation, *zar.*

Terrible. Thus was established, by vote of the political classes of the day, the Romanov dynasty which ruled in Russia until 1917. The early Romanovs, aware of the fate of elective monarchy in Poland and elsewhere, soon began to repress the representative institutions of Russia and set up as absolute monarchs. Here again, though they were more lawless and violent than any European king, they followed the general pattern of contemporary Europe.

Nor can it be said that the main social development of the seventeenth century in Russia, the sinking of the peasantry into an abyss of helpless serfdom, was exclusively a Russian phenomenon. The same process generally took place in eastern Europe. Serfdom had long been overtaking the older free peasantry of Russia. In Russia, as in the American colonies, land was abundant and labor was scarce. The natural tendency of labor was to migrate over the great Russian plain. In the Time of Troubles, especially, there was a good deal of movement. The landlords, wishing to assure themselves of their labor force, obtained the support of the Romanov tsars.

Serfdom in Russia

The manor, or what corresponded to it in Russia, came to resemble the slave plantation of the New World. Laws against fugitive serfs were strengthened; lords won the right to recover fugitives up to 15 years after their flight, and finally the time limit was abolished altogether. Peasants came to be so little regarded that a law of 1625 authorized anyone killing another man's peasant simply to give him another peasant in return. Lords exercised police and judicial powers. By a law of 1646 landowners were required to enter the names of all their peasants in government registers; peasants once so entered, together with their descendants, were regarded as attached to the estate on which they were registered. Thus the peasants lost the freedom to move at their own will. For a time they were supposed to have secure tenure of their land; but a law of 1675 allowed the lords to sell peasants without the land, and thus to move peasants like chattels at the will of the owner. This sale of serfs without land, which made their condition more like slavery as then practiced in America, became indeed a distinctive feature of serfdom in Russia, since in Poland, Prussia, Bohemia, and other regions of serfdom, the serf was generally regarded as "bound to the soil," inseparable from the land.

Against the loss of their freedom the rural population of Russia protested as best it could, murdering landlords, fleeing to the Cossacks, taking refuge in a vagrant existence, countered by wholesale government-organized manhunts and by renewed and more stringent legislation. A tremendous uprising was led in 1667 by Stephen Razin, who gathered a host of fugitive serfs, Cossacks, and adventurers, outfitted a fleet on the Caspian Sea, plundered Russian vessels, defeated a Persian squadron, and invaded Persia itself. He then turned back, ascended the Volga, killing and burning as he went and proclaiming a war against landlords, nobles, and priests. Cities opened their gates to him; an army sent against him went over to his side. He was finally captured and put to death in 1671. The consequence of the rebellion, for over a century, was that serfdom was clamped on the country more firmly than ever.

Even from the church the increasingly wretched rural people drew little comfort. The Russian Orthodox church at this time went through a great internal crisis, and ended up as hardly more than a department of the tsardom, useful to the government in instilling a superstitious reverence for Holy Russia. The Russian church had historically looked to the Patriarch of Constantinople as its head. But the conquest of Constantinople by the Turks made the head of the Greek Orthodox church a merely tolerated inferior to the Muslim sultan-caliph, so that the Russians in 1589 set up an independent Russian patriarch of their own. In the following generations the Russian patriarchate first became dependent on, then was abolished by, the tsarist government.

The Russian Orthodox church

Stephen Razin became an almost mythic figure in Russian popular memory after leading a vast peasant rebellion in the late 1660s. This painting by Wassili Iwanowitsch Suriow (1848–1916) suggests Razin's later prominence in Russian culture and his symbolic status in modern social and political movements.
(akg-images (*Stepan Rasin,* 1906 by Wassili Iwanowitsch Surikow (1848–1916)))

In the 1650s the Russian patriarch undertook certain church reforms, mainly to correct mistranslations in Russian versions of the Bible and other sacred writings. The changes aroused the horror and indignation of the general body of believers. Superstitiously attached to the mere form of the written word, believing the faith itself to depend on the customary spelling of the name of Jesus, the malcontents saw in the reformers a band of cunning Greek scholars perpetrating the work of Antichrist and the devil. The patriarch and higher church officials forced through the reforms but only with the help of the government and the army. Those who rejected the reforms came be called Old Believers. More ignorant and fanatical than the established church, agitated by visionary preachers, dividing into innumerable sects, the Old Believers became very numerous, especially among the peasants. Old Believers were active in Stephen Razin's rebellion and in all the sporadic peasant uprisings that followed. The peasants, already placed by serfdom outside the protection of law, were also estranged from the established religion. A distrust of all organized authority settled over the Russian masses, to whom both church and government seemed mere engines of repression.

Old Believers

But while willing enough to modernize to the extent of correcting mistranslations from the Greek, the church officials resisted the kind of modernization that was coming in from western Europe. They therefore opposed Peter the Great at the end of the century. After 1700 no new patriarch was appointed. Peter put the church under a committee of bishops called the Holy Synod, and to the Synod he attached a civil official called the Procurator of the Holy Synod. The Procurator was not a churchman but head of a government bureau whose task was to see that the church did nothing displeasing to the tsar. Peter thus secularized the church, making himself in effect its head. But while the consequences were more extreme in Russia than elsewhere, it must again be noted that this action of Peter's followed the general pattern of Europe. Secular supervision of religion had become the rule almost everywhere, especially in Protestant countries. Indeed an Englishman of the time thought that Peter the Great, in doing away with the patriarchate and putting the church under his own control, was wisely imitating England, which he had visited in his youth.

Peter the Great: Foreign Affairs and Territorial Expansion

The Russia in which Peter the Great became tsar in 1682 was thus already "European" in some ways and had in any case been in contact with Westerners for over a century. Without Peter, Russia would have developed its European connections more gradually. Peter, by his tempo and methods, made the process a social revolution.

Peter obtained his first knowledge of the West in Moscow itself, where a part of the city known as the German quarter was inhabited by Europeans of various nationalities, whom Peter often visited as a boy. Peter also in his early years mixed with Westerners at Archangel, still Russia's only port, for *Exposure to the West* he was fascinated by the sea and took lessons in navigation on the White Sea from Dutch and English ship captains. Like the Great Elector of Brandenburg, Peter as a young man spent over a year in western Europe, especially Holland and England, where he became profoundly aware of the commercial and technical backwardness of his own country. He had considerable talents as a mechanic and organizer. He labored with his own hands as a ship's carpenter in Amsterdam and talked with political and business leaders on means of introducing Western organization and technology into Russia. He visited workshops, mines, commercial offices, art galleries, hospitals, and forts. Europeans saw him as a barbarian of genius, a giant of a man standing a head above most others, bursting with physical vitality and plying all he met with interminable questions on their manner of working and living. He had neither the refinement nor the pretension of Western monarchs; he mixed easily with workmen and technical people, dressed cheaply and carelessly, loved horseplay and crude practical jokes, and dismayed his hosts by the squalid disorder in which he and his companions left the rooms put at their disposal. A man of acute practical mind, he was as little troubled by appearances as by moral scruples.

Peter on his visit to Europe in 1697–1698 recruited almost 1,000 experts for service in Russia, and many more followed later. He cared nothing for the civilization of Europe except as a means to an end, and this end was to create an army and a state which could stand against those of the West. His aim from the beginning was in part defensive, to ward off the Poles, Swedes, and Turks who had long pushed against Russia; and in part expansionist, to obtain warm-water seaports on the Baltic and Black seas, which would offer year-round access to trade with Europe. For all but two years of his long reign Peter was at war.

The Poles were a receding threat to Peter's ambitions. A Polish prince *Polish threat recedes* had indeed been elected tsar of Muscovy during the Time of Troubles, and for a while the Poles aspired to conquer and Catholicize the Great Russians. But in 1667 the Russians had regained Smolensk and Kiev, and the growing anarchy in Poland made that country no longer a menace, except as the Swedes or others might install themselves in it. The Turks and their Tartar dependencies, though no longer expanding, were still obstinate foes. Peter before going to Europe managed in 1696 to capture Azov at the mouth of the Don, but he was unable to hold any of the Black Sea coast; and he came to recognize the inferiority of the Russian army during these campaigns. The Swedes were the main enemy of Russia. Their army, for its size, was still probably the best in Europe.

The aspirations of Peter the Great are suggested in this formal portrait of a monarch whose clothing and appearance resemble the style of Western European elites in the early eighteenth century.
(Scala/Art Resource, NY)

They controlled the whole eastern shore of the Baltic including the Gulf of Finland. In 1697, the Swedish king having died, Peter entered into an alliance with Poland and Denmark to partition the overseas possessions of the Swedish house.

The Swedes

The new king of Sweden, the youthful Charles XII, was in some ways as crude as Peter (as an adolescent he had sheep driven into his rooms in the palace in order to enjoy the warlike pleasure of killing them), but he proved also to have remarkable aptitude as a general. In 1700, at the battle of Narva, with an army of 8,000 men, he routed Peter's 40,000 Russians. The tsar thus learned another lesson on the need of westernizing his state and army. Fortunately for the Russians Charles XII, instead of immediately pressing his advantage in Russia, spent the following years in furthering Swedish interests in Poland, where he forced the Poles to elect the Swedish candidate as their king. Peter meanwhile, with his imported officers and technicians, reformed the training, discipline, and weapons of the Russian army.

Eventually, Charles XII invaded Russia with a large and well-prepared force. Peter used against him the strategy later used by the Russians against Napoleon and Adolf Hitler; he drew the Swedes into the endless plains, exposing them to the Russian winter, which happened to be an exceptionally severe one, and in 1709, at Poltava in south Russia, he met and overwhelmed the demoralized remainder. The entire Swedish army was destroyed at Poltava, only the king and a few hundred fugitives managing to escape across the Turkish frontier. Peter in the next years conquered Livonia and part of eastern Finland. He landed troops near Stockholm itself. He campaigned in Pomerania almost as far west as the Elbe. Never before had Russian influence reached so deeply into Europe.

The imperial day of Sweden was now over, terminated by Russia. Peter had won for Russia a piece of the Baltic shore and with it warm-water outlets. These significant developments ending the great Northern War (1700–1721) were confirmed in the treaty of Nystadt in 1721.

War is surely not the father of all things, as has been sometimes claimed, but these wars did a good deal to shape imperial Russia. The undisciplined, poorly organized Russian army was transformed into a professional force of the kind maintained by Sweden, France, or Prussia. The *War and imperial Russia* elite of the old army had been the *streltsi,* a kind of Moscow guard, composed of nobles and constantly active in politics. A rebellion of the *streltsi* in 1698 had cut short Peter's tour of Europe; he had returned and quelled the mutiny by ferocious use of torture and execution, killing five of the rebels with his own hands. The *streltsi* were liquidated only two years before the great Russian defeat at Narva. Peter then rebuilt the army from the ground up. He employed European officers of many nationalities, paying them half again as much as native Russians of the same grades. He filled his ranks with soldiers supplied by districts on a territorial basis, somewhat as in Prussia. He put the troops into uniforms resembling those of the West and organized them in regiments of standardized composition. He armed them with muskets and artillery of the kind used in Europe and tried to create a service of supply.

With this army he not only drove the Swedes back into Sweden but also dominated Russia itself. At the very time of the Swedish invasion large parts of the country were in rebellion, as in the days of Stephen Razin, for the whole middle and lower Volga, together with the Cossacks of the Don and Dnieper, rose against the tsar and rallied behind slogans of class war and hatred of the tsar's foreign experts. Peter crushed these disturbances with the usual ruthlessness. The Russian empire, loose and heterogeneous, was held together by military might.

While the war was still in progress, even before the decisive battle of Poltava, Peter laid the foundations of a wholly new city in territory conquered from the Swedes and inhabited not by Russians but by various Baltic peoples. Peter named it St. Petersburg after himself and his patron saint. From the beginning it was more truly a city than Louis's spectacular creation at Versailles *The founding of St. Petersburg* established at almost the same time. Standing at the head of the Gulf of Finland, it was Peter's chief window on the West. Here he established the offices of government, required noblemen to build town houses, and gave favorable terms to foreign merchants and craftsmen to settle. Peter meant to make St. Petersburg a symbol of the new Russia. It was a new city facing toward Europe and drawing the minds of the Russians westward, replacing the old capital, Moscow, which faced toward Asia and was the stronghold of opposition to his westernizing program. St. Petersburg soon became one of the leading cities of northern Europe. It remained the capital of Russia (renamed Petrograd in 1914) until the Revolution of 1917, when Moscow resumed its old role. After the Revolution Petrograd became Leningrad. Its name reverted to St. Petersburg on the eve of the dissolution of the Soviet Union in 1991.

Internal Changes under Peter the Great

The new army, the new city, the new and expanding government offices all required money, which in Russia was very scarce. Taxes were imposed on an inconceivable variety of objects—on heads, as poll taxes; on land; on inns, mills, hats, leather, cellars, and coffins; on the right to marry, sell meat, wear a beard, or be an Old Believer. The tax burden fell mainly on the peasants; and to assure the payment of taxes the mobility of peasants was further restricted, and borderline individuals were classified as peasants in the government records, so that serfdom became both more onerous and more nearly universal. To raise government revenues and to stimulate production Peter adopted the mercantilist policies exemplified by Colbert in France. He encouraged exports, built a fleet on the Baltic, and developed mining, metallurgy, and textiles, which were indispensable to the army. He organized mixed groups of Russians and foreigners into commercial companies, provided them with capital from government funds (little private capital being available), and gave them a labor supply by assigning them the use of serfs in a given locality.

Mercantilism encouraged

Serfdom, in origin mainly an agricultural institution, began to spread in Russia as an industrial institution also. The fact that serf owners obtained the right to sell serfs without land, or to move them from landed estates into mines or towns, made it easier for industry in Russia to develop on the basis of unfree labor. Nor were the employers of serfs, in these government enterprises, free to modify or abandon their projects at will. They too were simply in the tsar's service. The economic system rested largely on impressment of both management and labor, not on private profit and wages as in the increasingly capitalistic West. In this way Peter's efforts to force Russia to a European level of material productivity widened the social differences between Russia and western Europe.

Serfs in industry

To oversee and operate this system of tax collecting, recruiting, economic controls, serf hunting, and repression of internal rebellion Peter created a new administrative system. The old organs of local self-government wasted away. The duma and the national assembly, decadent anyway in that they could not function without disorder, disappeared. In their place Peter put a "senate" dependent on himself, and 10 territorial areas called "governments," or *gubernii*. The church he ruled through his Procurator of the Holy Synod. At the top of the whole structure was the tsar himself, an absolute ruler and autocrat of all the Russias. Before his death, dissatisfied with his son, he abolished the rule of hereditary succession to the tsardom, claiming the right for each tsar to name his own successor. Transmission of supreme power was thus put outside the domain of law, and in the following century the accession of tsars and tsarinas was marked by strife, conspiracy, and assassination. The whole system of centralized absolutism, while in form resembling that of the West, notably France, was in fact significantly different, for it lacked legal regularity, was handicapped by the poor education of many officials, and was imposed on a turbulent and largely unwilling population. The empire of the Romanovs has been called a state without a people.

New administrative system

Peter sought to assure the success of his reforms by developing what was called "state service," which had been begun by his predecessors. Virtually all landowning and serf-owning aristocrats were required to serve in the army or civil administration. Offices were multiplied to provide places for all. In the state service birth counted for nothing. Peter used men of all classes; Prince Dolgoruky was of the most ancient nobility, Prince Menshikov had been a cook, the tax administrator Kurbatov was an ex-serf, and many others were foreigners of unknown background. Status in Peter's Russia depended not on inherited rank which Peter could not control, but on rank in his state service. "History," wrote a Scot serving in Peter's army, "scarcely affords an example where so many people of low birth have been raised to such dignities as in tsar Peter's reign, or where so many of the highest birth and fortune have been leveled to the lowest ranks of life."

The construction of the city of St. Petersburg became the most important architectural project in Peter the Great's long-term campaign to westernize Russian society. This new city was designed to be a western-looking capital and a new center for commercial contacts with Western Europe; like the construction of the French palace at Versailles, the Russian tsar's architectural goals required the labor of thousands of poor workers and peasants.
(Tass/Sovfoto)

In this respect especially, Peter's program resembled a true social revolution. It created a new governing element in place of the old, almost what in modern terms would be called a party, a body of men working zealously for the new system with a personal interest in its preservation. These men, *Peter's social revolution* during Peter's lifetime and after his death, were the bulwarks against an anti-Western reaction, the main agents in making Peter's revolution stick. In time the new families became hereditary themselves. The priority of state service over personal position was abandoned a generation after Peter's death. Offices in the army and government were filled by men of property and birth. After Peter's revolution, as after some others, the new upper class became merged with the old.

Revolutionary also, suggesting the great French Revolution or the Russian Revolution of 1917, were Peter's unconcealed contempt for everything reminiscent of the old Russia and his zeal to reeducate his people in the new ways. He required all gentry to put their sons in school. He sent many abroad to study. He simplified the Russian alphabet. He edited the first newspaper to appear in Russia. He ordered the preparation of the first Russian book of etiquette, teaching his subjects not to spit on the floor, scratch themselves, or gnaw bones at dinner, to mix socially with women, take off their hats, converse pleasantly, and look at people while talking. The beard he took as a symbol of Muscovite backwardness; he forbade it in Russia, and himself shaved a number of men at his court. He forced people to attend evening parties to teach them manners. He had no respect for hereditary

THE GROWTH OF RUSSIA IN THE WEST

At the accession of Peter the Great in 1682 the Russian empire, expanding from the old grand duchy of Muscovy, had almost reached the Black and Baltic seas. Most of Peter's conquests were in the Baltic region where he pushed back the Swedes and built St. Petersburg. Under Catherine the Great (1762–1796) Russia took part in the three partitions of Poland and also reached the Black Sea. Tsar Alexander I (1801–1825), thanks largely to the Napoleonic wars, was able to acquire still more of Poland and annex Finland and Bessarabia; he also made conquests in the Caucasus. In the nineteenth century the western boundary of Russia remained stabilized, but additional gains were made in the Caucasus. Russia also spread over northern Asia in the seventeenth century, first reaching the Pacific as early as 1630.

aristocracy, torturing or executing the highborn as readily as the peasants. As for religion, we are told that he was a pious man and enjoyed singing in church, but he was contemptuous of ecclesiastical dignity, and in one wild revel paraded publicly with drunken companions clothed in religious vestments and mocking the priests. Like many revolutionists since his time he was aggressively secular.

The Results of Peter's Revolution

Peter's tactics provoked a strong reaction. Some adhered strictly to the old ways; others simply thought that Peter was moving too fast and too indiscriminately toward the new.

Resistance to reforms

Many Russians resented the inescapable presence of foreigners, who often looked down on Russians and who enjoyed special privileges such as the right of free exit from Russia and higher pay for similar employment. One center around which malcontents rallied was the church. Another was Peter's son Alexis, who declared that when he became tsar he would put a stop to the innovations and restore respect for the customs of old Russia. Peter, after some hesitation, finally put his own son to death. He ruled that each tsar should choose his own successor. He would stop at nothing to remake Russia in his own fashion.

Peter died in 1725, proclaimed "the Great" in his own lifetime by his admiring Senate. Few persons in all history have exerted so strong an individual influence, which indirectly became more far-reaching as the stature of Russia itself grew in later centuries. Though the years after Peter's death were years of turmoil and vacillation, his revolutionary changes held firm against those who would undo them. It is not simply that he Europeanized Russia and conquered a place on the Baltic; these developments might have come about in any case. It is by the methods he used, his impatient forcing of a new culture on Russia, that he set the future character of his empire. His methods fastened autocracy, serfdom, and bureaucracy more firmly upon the country. Yet he was able to reach only the upper classes. Many of these became more Europeanized than he could dream, habitually speaking French and living spiritually in France or in Italy. But as time went on many upper-class Russians, because of their very knowledge of Europe, became impatient of the stolid immovability of the peasants around them, sensed themselves as strangers in their own country, or were troubled by a guilty feeling that their position rested on the degradation and enslavement of human beings. Russian psychology, often mysterious to people in the West, could perhaps be explained in part by the violent paradoxes set up by rapid Europeanization. As for the peasant masses, they remained outside the system, egregiously

Exclusion of peasants exploited, estranged from their rulers and their social superiors, regarded by them as brutes or children, never sharing in any comparable way in their increasingly Europeanized civilization. Much of this worked itself out in the social conflicts of later times. As for Peter's own time, Russia by his efforts came clearly out of its isolation, its vast bulk was now organized to play a part in international affairs, and its history thenceforward was a part of the history of Europe and increasingly of the world. Russia, like Prussia and the Austrian monarchy, was to be counted among the powers of Europe.

The rising influence of these three monarchies depended in part on their ability to acquire modern weaponry, organize more efficient bureaucracies, and bring new forms of European knowledge into their government institutions. By the beginning of the eighteenth century, European science and technologies often gave European states a comparative advantage in their economic, political, and military encounters with other peoples or governments—as the ruling elites in Austria, Prussia, and Russia had learned from their own struggles for power in central Europe. Indeed, the new science would ultimately become one of the most distinctive and significant forces in modern world history. Science helped to transform economic production, military strategies, and traditional cultures as well as imperial conflicts in Europe and around the world. We must therefore look more closely at the ways in which the development of modern scientific thought increasingly influenced the knowledge and control of both nature and human beings.

For interactive exercises, glossary, chronologies, and more, go to the *Online Learning Center* at **www.mhhe.com/palmer10.**

Chapter 6

THE SCIENTIFIC VIEW OF THE WORLD

27. Prophets of a Scientific Civilization: Bacon and Descartes

28. The Road to Newton: The Law of Universal Gravitation

29. New Knowledge of Human Beings and Society

30. Political Theory: The School of Natural Law

The seventeenth century has been called the century of genius. One reason is that it was the age when science became "modern." It was the great age of Galileo and Sir Isaac Newton, whose combined lifetimes spanned the century, with Galileo dying and Newton being born in the same year, 1642. When Galileo was young, those who probed into the secrets of nature still labored largely in the dark, isolated from one another and from the general public, working oftentimes by methods of trial and error, not altogether clear on what they were trying to do, with their thinking still complicated by ideas not nowadays considered scientific. They had never-theless accomplished a good deal, without which the intellectual revolution of the seventeenth century would not have occurred. But in a way all scientific investigators before Galileo seem to be precursors, patient workers destined never to enter into the world toward which they labored. In 1727, when Newton died, all was changed. Scientists were in continual touch with one another, and science was recognized as one of the principal enterprises of European society. Scientific methods of inquiry had been defined. The store of factual knowledge had become very large. The first modern scientific synthesis, or coherent theory of the physical universe, had been presented by Newton. Scientific knowledge was applied increasingly to navigation, mining, agriculture, and many branches of manufacture. Science and invention were joining hands. Science was accepted as the main force in the advancement of civilization and progress. And science was becoming popularized; many people who were not themselves scientists "believed" in science and attempted to apply scientific habits of thought to diverse problems of social and political life.

The history of science is too complex a story to be told in this book, but there are a few ideas about it which even a book of this kind must attempt to make clear. First, science, purely as a form of thought, is one of

Science

Chapter emblem: Detail from a portrait of Isaac Newton by an anonymous artist. (Bettmann/Corbis)

the supreme achievements of the human mind, and to have a historical understanding of human intellectual powers one must sense the importance of science, as of philosophy, literature, or the arts. Second, science has increasingly affected practical affairs, entering into the health, wealth, and happiness of humankind. It has changed the size of populations and the use of raw materials, revolutionized methods of production, transport, business, and war, and so helped to relieve some human problems while aggravating others. This is especially true of modern civilization since the seventeenth century. Third, in the modern world ideas have had a way of passing over from science into other domains of thought. Many people today, for example, in their notions of themselves, their neighbors, or the meaning of life, are influenced by ideas which they believe to be those of Freud or Einstein—they talk of repressions or relativity without necessarily knowing much about them. Ideas derived from biology and from Darwin—such as evolution and the struggle for existence—have likewise spread far and wide. Similarly the scientific revolution of the seventeenth century had repercussions far beyond the realm of pure science. It changed ideas of religion and of God and human beings. And it helped to spread certain very deep-seated beliefs, such as that the physical universe is essentially orderly and harmonious, that human reason is capable of understanding and dealing with it, and that human affairs can be conducted by methods of peaceable exchange of ideas and rational discussion. Thus was laid a foundation for belief in free and democratic institutions.

The historical influence of modern science therefore extended far beyond the specific knowledge that transformed the human understanding and use of nature. Scientific methods for establishing truth or defining progress shaped a wide range of modern social institutions, including armies, hospitals, universities, trading companies, government bureaucracies, law courts, and even literary journals. The meaning of the word "modern" became linked to the intellectual prestige of science, and scientific knowledge became the most important intellectual force in the history of the modern world. The purpose of this chapter is to sketch the rise of modern science in the seventeenth century and the emergence of the scientific view of the world and of human affairs. The chapters that follow will describe the increasing application of this new knowledge in the expanding global economy and the influence of scientific thought in eighteenth-century European culture, which is generally known as the Age of Enlightenment.

27.   PROPHETS OF A SCIENTIFIC CIVILIZATION: BACON AND DESCARTES

Science before the Seventeenth Century

The scientific view became characteristic of elite European society about the middle of the seventeenth century. There had, indeed, been a few in earlier times who caught glimpses of a whole civilization reared upon science. To us today the most famous of these is Leonardo da Vinci (1452–1519), the universal genius of the Italian Renaissance, who had been artist, engineer, and scientific thinker all in one.

Leonardo da Vinci

Leonardo, by actual dissection of dead bodies, had obtained an accurate knowledge of human anatomy; he had conceived of the circulation of the blood and the movement of the earth about the sun; and he had drawn designs for submarines and airplanes and speculated on the use of parachutes and poison gases. But Leonardo had not published his scientific ideas. He was known almost exclusively as an artist. His work in science remained outside the stream of scientific thought, without influence on its course.

It was not even known until the discovery of his private notebooks in the twentieth century. Leonardo thus figures in the history of science as an isolated genius, a man of brilliant insights and audacious theories, which died with their author's death, whereas science depends on a transmission of ideas in which investigators build upon one another's discoveries, test one another's experiments, and fill in the gaps in one another's knowledge. Modern science evolved as a kind of new cultural system, more dependent on communications and widely shared cultural beliefs than on the brilliance of isolated thinkers. Leonardo's scientific work, remaining unpublished, never entered the cultural institutions in which new scientific knowledge would be produced, challenged, and revised.

A century after the death of Leonardo da Vinci educated Europeans were by no means scientifically minded. Among thoughtful persons many currents were stirring. On the one hand there was a great deal of skepticism, a constantly doubting frame of mind, which held that no certain knowledge is possible for human beings at all, that all beliefs are essentially only customs, that some people believe one thing and some another, and that there is no sound way of choosing between them. This attitude was best expressed by the French essayist Michel de Montaigne (1533–1592), whose thought distilled itself into an eternal question, *Que sais-je?* "What do I know?" with the always implied answer, "Nothing." Montaigne's philosophy led to a tolerant, humane, and broad-minded outlook, but as a system of thought it was not otherwise very constructive. On the other hand, there was also a tendency to over-believe in mysterious, supernatural powers, arising from the same inability to distinguish between true and false. There was no accepted line between chemistry and alchemy or between astronomy and astrology; all alike were regarded as ways of penetrating the "secrets" of nature. The sixteenth century had been a great age of charlatans, such as Nostradamus and Paracelsus, some of whom, notably Paracelsus, mixed magic and valid science in a way hardly understandable to later or modern scientists. As late as the seventeenth century, especially in central Europe where the Thirty Years' War produced chaos and terror, kings and generals kept private astrologers to divine the future.

Witchcraft panic

The two centuries from about 1450 to about 1650 were also the period when fear of witches was at its height. The great campaign against witches thus coincided with Europe's brutal religious wars and with the early development of the new scientific culture among members of Europe's educated elite, but even highly educated persons often believed that witches actually existed. Witches were blamed for all kinds of natural disasters and personal tragedies—bad harvests, epidemics, the mysterious deaths of children. Although most of the persons prosecuted for witchcraft were women, men were also imprisoned or executed for various crimes of "sorcery." The witchcraft panic lasted longest in Germany and central Europe, probably kept alive by the insecurities engendered by the Thirty Years' War. But about 20 persons were hanged as witches in Massachusetts as late as 1692, for the English colonies, as a remote and outlying part of the European world, were among the last to feel some of the intellectual currents originating in Europe. The last known execution for witchcraft took place in 1722 in Scotland.

It was by no means clear, in the early part of the seventeenth century, which way Europe was going to develop. It might conceivably have fallen into a kind of political chaos, as India did at about this time. We have seen how much of Europe was racked by chronic and marauding violence, which was ended by the consolidation of the modern state and the conversion of armed bands into organized and disciplined armies. Similarly, in matters of the mind, there was no settled order. Doubt went with superstition,

Women were executed on charges of witchcraft from the later Middle Ages down through the seventeenth century, when a new fear of witches happened to coincide with the early modern scientific revolution. This mid-seventeenth-century English illustration shows a typical pattern of persecution in which several women were put to death at the same time for the alleged crime of "sorcery" or conspiring with "witches."
(Topham/The Image Works)

indifference with persecution. Science in time provided Europe with a new faith in itself. The rise of science in the seventeenth century possibly saved European civilization from petering out in a long postmedieval afterglow or from wandering off into the diverse paths of a genial skepticism, ineffectual philosophizing, desultory magic, or mad fear of the unknown.

Bacon and Descartes

Two men stand out as prophets of a world reconstructed by science. One was the Englishman Francis Bacon (1561–1626); the other was the Frenchman René Descartes (1596–1650). Both published their most influential books between 1620 and 1640. Both addressed themselves to the problem of knowledge. Both asked themselves how it is possible for human beings to know anything with certainty or to have a reliable, truthful, and usable knowledge of the world of nature. Both shared in the doubts of their day. They branded virtually all beliefs of preceding generations (outside religion) as worthless. Both ridiculed the tendency to put faith in ancient books, to cite the writings of Aristotle or others, on questions having to do with the workings of nature. Both attacked earlier methods of seeking knowledge; they rejected the methods of the "schoolmen" or "scholastics," the thinkers in the academic tradition of the universities founded in the Middle Ages. On the whole, medieval philosophy had been deductive. That is, its characteristic procedure was to start with definitions and general propositions and then discover what further knowledge could be logically deduced from the definitions thus accepted. Or it proceeded by affirming the nature of an object to be such-and-such (e.g., that "man is a political animal") and then described how objects of such a nature do or should behave. These methods, which owed much to Aristotle and other ancient codifiers of human thought, had generally ceased to be fruitful in producing new knowledge of nature. Bacon and Descartes held that the medieval (or Aristotelian) methods were backward. They held that truth is not something that we postulate at the beginning and then explore in all its ramifications, but that it is something which we find at the end, after a long process of investigation, experiment, and intermediate thought.

Bacon and Descartes thus went beyond mere doubt. They offered a constructive program, and though their programs were different, they both became heralds or philosophers of a scientific view. They maintained that there was a true and reliable method of knowledge. And they maintained in addition that once this true method was known and practiced, once the real workings of nature were understood, people would be able to use this knowledge for their own purposes, control nature in their own interests, make undreamed of useful inventions, improve their mechanical arts, and add generally to human wealth and comfort. Bacon and Descartes thus announced the advent of a scientific civilization.

Francis Bacon and empiricism

Francis Bacon planned a great work in many volumes, to be known as the *Instauratio Magna* or "Great Renewal," calling for a complete new start in science and civilization. He completed only two parts. One, published in 1620, was the *Novum Organum* or new method of acquiring knowledge. Here he insisted on *inductive* method. In the inductive method we proceed from the particular to the general, from the concrete to the abstract. For example, in the study of leaves, if we examine millions of actual leaves of all sizes and shapes and if we assemble, observe, and compare them with minute scrutiny, we are using an *inductive* method in the sense meant by Bacon; if successful, we may arrive at a knowledge, based on observed facts, of the general nature of a leaf as such. If, on the other hand, we begin with a general idea of what we think all leaves are like, that is, all leaves have stems, and then proceed to describe an individual leaf on that basis, we are following the *deductive* method; we draw logical implications from what we already know, but we learn no more of the nature of a leaf than what we knew or thought we knew at the beginning. Bacon advised his readers to put aside all traditional ideas, to rid themselves of prejudices and preconceptions, to look at the world with fresh eyes, to observe and study the innumerable things that are actually perceived by the senses. Thinkers before Bacon used the inductive method, but he formalized it as a method and became a leading philosopher of empiricism, the founding of knowledge on observation and experience. This philosophy has always proved a useful safeguard against fitting facts into preconceived patterns. It demands that we let the patterns of our thought be shaped by actual facts as we observe them. Scientific knowledge thus links particular facts to general principles and typically combines inductive method with the broader claims of deductive thought.

The other completed part of Bacon's great work, published in 1623, was called in its English translation *The Advancement of Learning*. Here Bacon developed the same ideas and insisted also that true knowledge was useful knowledge. In *The New Atlantis* (1627), he portrayed a scientific utopia whose inhabitants enjoyed a perfect society through their knowledge and command of nature. The usefulness of knowledge became the other main element in the Baconian tradition. In this view there was no sharp difference between pure science and applied science or between the work of the purely scientific investigators and that of the inventors who in their own way probed into nature and devised instruments or machines for putting natural forces to work. The fact that knowledge could be used for

**RENÉ DESCARTES
by Frans Hals (1584–1666)**

Descartes worked for many years in Amsterdam, where he developed his work in mathematics, described his philosophical methods of systematic doubt, and sat for this famous portrait by Frans Hals.
(Eric Lessing/Art Resource, NY)

practical purposes became a sign or proof that it was true knowledge. For example, the fact that soldiers could aim their cannon and hit their targets more accurately in the seventeenth century became a proof of the theory of ballistics which had been scientifically worked out. Enthusiastic Baconians believed that knowledge was power. True knowledge could be put to work, if not immediately at least in the long run, after more knowledge was discovered. It was useful to mankind, unlike the "delicate learning" of the misguided scholastics. In this coming together of knowledge and power arose the far-reaching modern idea of progress. And in it arose many modern problems, since the power given by scientific knowledge can be used for either good or evil.

But Bacon, though a force in redirecting the European mind, never had much influence on the development of actual science. Kept busy as Lord Chancellor of England and in other government duties, he was not even fully abreast of the most advanced scientific thought of his day. Bacon's greatest weakness was his failure to understand the role of mathematics. Mathematics, dealing with pure abstractions and proceeding deductively from axioms to theorems, was not an empirical or inductive method of thought such as Bacon demanded. Yet science in the seventeenth century went forward most successfully in subjects where mathematics could be applied. Even today the degree to which a subject is truly scientific depends on the degree to which it can be made mathematical. We have pure science where we have formulas and equations, and the scientific method itself is both inductive and deductive.

René Descartes

Descartes was a great mathematician in his own right. He is considered the inventor of coordinate geometry. He showed that by use of coordinates (or graph paper, in simple language) any algebraic formula could be plotted as a curve in space, and contrariwise that any curve in space, however complex, could be converted into algebraic terms and thus dealt with by methods of calculation. One effect of his general philosophy was to create belief in a vast world of nature that could be reduced to mathematical form.

Descartes set forth his ideas in his *Discourse on Method* in 1637 and in many more technical writings. He advanced the principle of systematic doubt. He began by trying to doubt everything that could reasonably be doubted, thus sweeping away past ideas and clearing the ground for his own "great renewal," to use Bacon's phrase. He held that he could not doubt his own existence as a thinking and doubting being (*cogito ergo sum,* "I think, therefore I exist"); he then deduced, by systematic reasoning, the existence of God and much else. He arrived at a philosophy of dualism, the famous "Cartesian dualism," which held that God has created two kinds of fundamental reality in the universe. One was "thinking substance"— mind, spirit, consciousness, subjective experience. The other was "extended substance"— everything outside the mind and hence objective. Of everything except the mind itself the most fundamental and universal quality was that it occupied a portion of space, minute or vast. Space itself was conceived as infinite and everywhere geometric.

This philosophy had profound and long-lasting effects. For one thing, the seemingly most real elements in human experience, color and sound, joy and grief, seemed somehow to be shadowy and unreal, or at least illusive, with no existence outside the mind itself. But all else was quantitative, measurable, reducible to formulas or equations. Over all else, over the whole universe or half-universe of "extended substance," the most powerful instrument available to the human understanding, namely, mathematics, reigned supreme. "Give me motion and extension," said Descartes, "and I will build you the world."

Descartes also shared Bacon's belief in useful knowledge and human progress. Instead of the "speculative philosophy of the schools," he wrote in the *Discourse on Method,* one might discover a "practical philosophy by which, understanding the forces and action of fire, water, air, the stars and heavens and all other bodies that surround us, as distinctly as we understand the mechanical arts of our craftsmen, we can use these forces in the same way for all purposes for which they are appropriate, and so make ourselves the masters and possessors of nature. And this is desirable not only for the invention of innumerable devices by which we may enjoy without trouble the fruits of the earth and the conveniences it affords, but mainly also for the preservation of health, which is undoubtedly the principal good and foundation of all other good things in this life." Science, in short, opened the way to a better life that philosophy alone could never produce.

28.   THE ROAD TO NEWTON: THE LAW OF UNIVERSAL GRAVITATION

Scientific Advances

Meanwhile actual scientific discovery was advancing on many fronts. It did not advance on all with equal speed. Some of the sciences were, and long remained, dependent mainly on the collection of specimens. Botany was one of these; Europe's knowledge of plants expanded enormously with the explorations overseas, and botanical gardens and herb collections in Europe became far more extensive than ever before, bringing important enlargements in the stock of medicinal drugs. Other sciences drew their impetus from intensive and open-minded observation. The Flemish Vesalius, by a book published in 1543, *The Structure of the Human Body,* renewed and modernized the study of anatomy. Formerly anatomists had generally held

Botany, anatomy, and physiology

that the writings of Galen, dating from the second century A.D., contained an authoritative description of all human muscles and tissues. They had indeed dissected cadavers but had dismissed those not conforming to Galen's description as somehow abnormal or not typical. Vesalius put Galen behind him and based his general description of the human frame on actual bodies as he found them.

In physiology also, dealing with the functioning rather than the structure of living bodies, there was considerable progress. Here the method of laboratory experiment could be profitably used. William Harvey, after years of laboratory work, including the vivisection of animals, published in 1628 a book *On the Movement of the Heart and Blood* which set forth the doctrine of the continual circulation of the blood through arteries and veins. The Italian Malpighi, using the newly invented microscope, confirmed Harvey's findings by the discovery of capillaries in 1661. The Dutch Leeuwenhoek, also by use of the microscope, was the first to see blood corpuscles, spermatozoa, and bacteria, of which he left published drawings. Another seventeenth-century Dutch scientist, Régnier de Graaf, published the first description of the female ovaries, thus challenging Galen's ancient theories of human sexuality and the long-accepted idea that women contributed less than men to the biological processes of reproduction.

Astronomy and physics

These sciences, and also chemistry, although work in them went forward continually, did not come fully into their own until after 1800. They were long overshadowed by astronomy and physics. Here mathematics could be most fully applied, and mathematics underwent a rapid development in the seventeenth century. Decimals came into use to express fractions, the symbols used in algebra were improved and standardized, and in 1614 logarithms were invented by the Scot John Napier. Coordinate geometry was mapped out by Descartes, the theory of probabilities was developed by Pascal, and calculus was invented simultaneously in England by Newton and in Germany by Leibniz. These advances made it more generally possible to think about nature in purely quantitative terms, to measure with greater precision, and to perform complex and laborious computations. Physics and astronomy were remarkably stimulated, and it was in this field that the most astonishing scientific revolution of the seventeenth century took place.

The Scientific Revolution: Copernicus to Galileo

Ever since the Greek Ptolemy had codified ancient astronomy in the second century A.D., educated Europeans had held a conception of the cosmos which we call Ptolemaic. The cosmos in this view was a group of concentric spheres, a series of balls within balls each having the same center. The innermost ball was the earth, made up of hard, solid, earthy substance such as people were familiar with underfoot. The other spheres, encompassing the earth in series, were all transparent. They were the "crystalline spheres" made known to us by the poets; their harmony was the "music of the spheres." These spheres all revolved about the earth, each sphere containing, set in it as a jewel, a luminous heavenly body or orb which moved about the earth with the movement of its transparent sphere. Nearest to the earth was the sphere of the moon; then, in turn, the spheres of Mercury and Venus, then the sphere of the sun, then those of the outer planets. Last came the outermost sphere containing all the fixed stars studded in it, all moving majestically about the earth in daily motion, but motionless with respect to each other because they were held firmly in the same sphere. Beyond the sphere of the fixed stars, in general belief, lay the "empyrean," the home of angels and immortal spirits; but this was not a matter of natural science.

The Ptolemaic system

A SCHOLAR HOLDING A THESIS ON BOTANY by Willem Moreelse (Dutch, before 1630–1666)

This scholar may be a new doctor of the University of Utrecht, where the little-known painter Willem Moreelse worked in the seventeenth century. Crowned with the laurel, the successful candidate proudly displays his thesis, on which the Latin words announce "any plant shows the presence of God"— an example of the growing scientific interest in hitherto unknown plants that reached Europe from other parts of the world in this era.

(Toledo Museum of Art. Purchased with funds from the Libbey Endowment, Gift of Edward Drumond Libbey. (1962.70))

Persons standing on the earth and looking up into the sky thus felt themselves to be enclosed by a dome of which their own position was the center. In the blue sky of day they could literally see the crystalline spheres; in the stars at night they could behold the orbs which these spheres carried with them. All revolved about the observer, presumably at no very alarming distance. The celestial bodies were commonly supposed to be of different material and quality from the earth. The earth was of heavy dross; the stars and planets and the sun and moon seemed made of pure and gleaming light, or at least of a bright ethereal substance almost as tenuous as the crystal spheres in which they moved. The cosmos was a hierarchy of ascending perfection. The heavens were purer than the earth.

This system corresponded to actual appearances, and except for scientific knowledge would be highly believable today. It was formulated also in rigorous mathematical terms. Ever since the Greeks, and becoming increasingly intricate in the Middle Ages, a complex geometry had grown up to explain the observed motion of the heavenly bodies. The Ptolemaic system was a mathematical system. And it was for purely mathematical reasons that it first came to be reconsidered. There was a marked revival of mathematical interest at the close of the Middle Ages, in the fourteenth and fifteenth centuries, a renewed concentration on the philosophical traditions of Pythagoras and Plato. In these philosophies could be found the doctrine that numbers might be the final key to the mysteries of nature. With them went a metaphysical belief that simplicity was more likely to be a sign of truth than complexity and that a simpler mathematical formulation was better than a more complicated one.

These ideas motivated Nicholas Copernicus (1473–1543), born in Poland of German and Polish background, who, after study in Italy, wrote his epochal work *On the Revolutions of the Heavenly Orbs*. In this book,

Nicholas Copernicus

published in 1543 after his death, he held the sun to be the center of the solar system and of the whole universe; the earth, he argued, was one of the planets revolving in space around it. This view had been entertained by a few isolated thinkers before. Copernicus gave a mathematical demonstration. To him it was a purely mathematical problem. With increasingly detailed knowledge of the actual movement of the heavenly bodies it had become necessary, as the years passed, to make the Ptolemaic system more intricate by the addition of new "cycles" and "epicycles," until, as John Milton expressed it later, the cosmos was

> *With Centric and Concentric scribbled o'er,*
> *Cycle and Epicycle, Orb in Orb.*

Copernicus needed fewer such hypothetical constructions to explain the known movements of the heavenly bodies. The heliocentric or sun-centered theory was mathematically simpler than the geocentric or earth-centered theory hitherto held.

The Copernican doctrine long remained a hypothesis known only to experts. Most astronomers for a time hesitated to accept it, seeing no need, from the evidence yet produced, to make such a radical readjustment of current ideas. Tycho Brahe (1546–1601), the greatest authority on the actual positions and movements of the heavenly bodies in the generations immediately after Copernicus, never accepted the Copernican system in full. But his assistant and follower, Johannes Kepler (1571–1630), building on Tycho's exact observations, not only accepted the Copernican theory but carried it further.

Johannes Kepler

Kepler, a German, was a kind of mathematical mystic, part-time astrologer, and scientific genius. Copernicus had believed the orbits of the planets about the sun to be perfect circles. Tycho showed that this belief did not fit the observable facts. It was Kepler who discovered that the orbits of the planets were ellipses. The ellipse, like the circle, is an abstract mathematical figure with knowable properties. Kepler demonstrated that the closer a planet is to the sun in its elliptical orbit, the faster it moves; and he showed that the length of time in which the several planets revolve about the sun varies proportionately with their distance from the sun.

It is not possible for most people to understand the mathematics involved, but it is possible to realize the astounding implications of Kepler's laws of planetary motion. Kepler showed that the actual world of stubborn facts, as observed by Tycho, and the purely rational world of mathematical harmony, as surmised by Copernicus, were not really in any contradiction to each other—that they really corresponded exactly. Why they should he did not know; it was the mystery of numbers. He digested an overwhelming amount of hitherto unexplained information into a few brief statements. He showed a cosmic mathematical relationship between space and time. And he described the movement of the planets in explicit formulas, which any competent person could verify at will.

Galileo

The next scientific step was taken by Galileo (1564–1642). So far the question of what the heavenly bodies were made of had hardly been affected. Indeed, they were not thought of as bodies at all, but rather as orbs. Only the sun and moon had any dimension; stars and planets were only points of light; and the theories of Copernicus and Kepler, like those of Ptolemy, might apply to insubstantial luminous objects in motion. In 1609 Galileo built a telescope. Turning it to the sky, he perceived that the moon had a rough and apparently mountainous surface, as if made of the same kind of material as the earth. Seeing clearly the dark part of the moon in its various phases, and

The Copernican conception of a solar system revolving around the sun was long unknown outside a small circle of experts, and few persons understood the mathematics upon which it was based. But the meaning of the Copernican theories later spread in visual images that depicted the new astronomical view of the sun, earth, and other planets.

noting that in every position it only reflected the light of the sun, he concluded that the moon was not itself a luminous object, another indication that it might be made of earth-like substance. He saw spots on the sun, as if the sun were not pure and perfect. He found that the planets had visible breadth when seen in the telescope but that the fixed stars remained only points of light, as if incalculably further away. He discovered also that Jupiter had satellites, moons moving around it like the moon around the earth. These discoveries reassured him of the validity of the Copernican theory, which he had in any case already accepted. They suggested also that the heavenly bodies might be of the same substance as the earth, masses of matter moving in space. Contrariwise, it became easier to think of the earth itself as a kind of heavenly body revolving about the sun. The difference between the earth and the heavens was disappearing. This struck a terrifying blow at all earlier philosophy and theology. Some professors were afraid to look through the telescope, and Galileo was condemned and forced to an ostensible recantation by his church.

Moreover, where Kepler had found mathematical laws describing the movement of planets, Galileo now found mathematical laws describing the movement of bodies on the earth. Formerly it had been thought that some bodies were by nature heavier than others and that heavier bodies fell to the ground faster than light ones. Galileo in 1591, according to the story, dropped a 10-pound and a 1-pound weight simultaneously from the top of the Leaning Tower of Pisa. The truth of this story has been questioned, but in any case Galileo showed that despite all previous speculation on the subject two bodies of different weights, when allowance was made for differences in air resistance due to differences of size or shape, struck the ground at the same time. His further work in dynamics, or the science of motion of bodies, took many years to accomplish. He had to devise more refined means for measuring small intervals of time, find means of estimating the air resistance, friction, and other impediments which always occur in nature, and conceive of pure or absolute motion, and of force and velocity, in abstract mathematical terms. He made use of a new conception of inertia, in which only *change* in motion, not the origination of motion, had to be explained. This dispensed with the need of an Unmoved Mover felt in the older philosophy.

The Achievement of Newton: The Promise of Science

It was the supreme achievement of Isaac Newton (1642–1727) to bring Kepler and Galileo together, that is, to show that Kepler's laws of planetary motion and Galileo's laws of terrestrial motion were two aspects of the same laws. Galileo's discovery that moving bodies move uniformly in a straight line unless deflected by a definite force made it necessary to explain why the planets, instead of flying off in straight lines, tend to fall toward the sun, the result being their elliptical orbits—and why the moon, similarly, tends to fall toward the earth. Newton seems early to have suspected that the answer would be related to Galileo's laws of falling bodies—that is, that gravity, or the pull of the earth upon objects on earth, might be a form of a universal gravitation, or a similar pull characterizing all bodies in the solar system. Great technical difficulties stood in the way, but finally, after inventing calculus, and using a new measurement of the size of the earth made by a Frenchman and experiments with circular motion made by the Dutch Huyghens on the pendulum, Newton was able to bring his calculations to fruition, and to publish, in 1687, his *Mathematical Principles of Natural Philosophy*.

Universal gravitation

This stupendous book showed that all motion that could be timed and measured, whether on the earth or in the solar system, could be described by the same mathematical formulas. All matter moved as if every particle attracted every other particle with a force proportionate to the product of the two masses and inversely proportionate to the square of the distance between them. This "force" was universal gravitation. What it was Newton did not pretend to explain. For 200 years the law stood unshaken, always verified by every new relevant discovery. Only in the past century were its limitations found; it does not hold good in the infinitesimal world of subatomic structure or in the macrocosm of the whole physical universe as now conceived.

It was in Newton's time that the pursuit of natural knowledge became institutionalized. Organized institutions, possessing equipment and funds, were engaged in scientific study, most notably the Royal Society of London, founded in 1662, and the Royal Academy of Sciences in France, founded in 1666. Both originated when earlier and informal groups, usually gentlemen of the landed class, received charters from their governments to pursue scientific interests. Scientific periodicals began to be published. Scientific societies provided the medium for prompt interchange of ideas indispensable to the growth of scientific knowledge. They held meetings, proposed projects for research, and published articles not only on the natural sciences and mathematics, but also on paleography, numismatics, chronology, legal history, and natural law. The work of the learned had not yet yielded to specialization.

In all these activities the promise of science seemed fulfilled. Even in practical affairs conveniences followed, as anticipated by the Baconians. The tides could now be understood and predicted by the gravitational interplay of earth, moon, and sun. Exact mathematical knowledge of the celestial bodies, together with the invention of more accurate timepieces, was of great help to navigation and mapmaking. Measures of latitude, or of north-south distances on the spherical earth, had been known to the ancient Greeks. But longitude, or east-west distances, could not be measured until the eighteenth century, when it became possible to determine it by use of a chronometer and observation of heavenly bodies at a known time. Merchant ships and naval squadrons could thus operate with more assurance. Places on land could be located and mapped more exactly. Eighteenth-century Europeans were the first human beings to have a fairly accurate idea of the shapes and sizes of all the continents and oceans. Better local and regional maps of places in Europe also became available.

Scientific improvements

Mathematical advance, including the development of calculus, which allowed an exact treatment of curves and trajectories, reinforced by technical discoveries in the working of metals, led to an increased use of artillery. Armies in 1750 used twice as many cannon per soldier as in 1650. Naval ordnance also improved. These items made armed forces more expensive to maintain, requiring governments to increase their taxes, and hence producing constitutional crises. Improved firearms heightened the advantage of armies over insurrectionists or private fighting bands, thus strengthening the sovereignty of the state. They also gave Europeans the military advantage over other peoples, in America, India, or elsewhere, on which the world ascendancy of Europe was built in the eighteenth century.

The instance of the steam engine may also be cited. Steam power was eventually almost literally to move the world. In 1700 it was only in its earliest stages, but it was in sight on the horizon. A Frenchman, Denis Papin, in 1681 invented a device in which steam moved a piston, but it produced so little power that it was used only in cooking. British scientists turned their minds to it. Robert Boyle, discoverer of "Boyle's Law" on the pressure of gases, studied the problem; scientists, mechanics, and instrument makers collaborated. In 1702 Thomas Newcomen, a man without scientific training but associated with scientists, produced the steam engine known thereafter as Newcomen's engine, from which, as will be seen, James Watt developed the steam engine as we know it. Newcomen's engine was primitive according to later ideas. It burned so much fuel that it could be used only in coal mines. But it was used. Not long after 1700 it was widely employed to pump water from the coal pits. It saved labor, cheapened production, and opened hitherto unusable deposits to exploitation. It was the first application of steam to an economic purpose.

No distinction was yet felt between pure and applied science. The modern sense of the word hardly existed; what we call "science" was called natural philosophy or "useful knowledge." Traveling public lecturers, in explaining the laws of force and motion, showed their application in devices such as pulleys, scales, levers, cogwheels, waterwheels, and pumps. Such lectures were attended, especially in England, by a mixed audience of philosophers, experimenters, inventors, artisans, landed gentlemen who wished to develop their estates, and small businessmen wishing to enlarge their markets. The scientific movement thus opened the way to agricultural and industrial improvements in Great Britain and other places where the new knowledge was brought into economic activities.

FOUNDING OF THE ACADEMY OF SCIENCES AND THE OBSERVATORY IN 1666
by Henri Testelin (1616–1695)

Testelin was an instructor at the Royal Academy of Painting and a strong defender of the academic traditions in French art. He portrayed King Louis XIV visiting the new Royal Academy of Sciences in this painting, which expresses his respect for both the king and the new scientific knowledge. But Testelin's life also exemplified another side of life in late seventeenth-century France. He was a Protestant who eventually had to give up his academic position and move to the Netherlands to practice his religion.

(Giraudon/Art Resource, NY)

The Scientific Revolution and the World of Thought

It was perhaps in the world of thought that the revolution accomplished from Copernicus to Newton was most profound. It has been called the greatest spiritual readjustment that human beings have been required to make. The old heavens were exploded. Humans were no longer the center of creation. The luminaries of the sky no longer shone to light their way or to give them beauty. The sky itself was an illusion, its color a thing in the mind only, for anyone looking upward was really looking only into the darkness of endless space. The old cosmos, comfortably enclosed and ranked in an ascending order of purity, gave way to a new cosmos which seemed to consist of an infinite emptiness through which particles of matter were distributed. Humans were the puny denizens of a material object swinging in space along with other very distant material objects of the same kind. About the physical universe there was nothing especially Christian, nothing that the God portrayed in the Hebrew or the Christian Bible would be likely to have made. The gap between religion and natural science, always present yet always bridged in the Middle Ages, now opened wider than ever. It was felt with anguish by some in the seventeenth century, notably by the Frenchman Blaise Pascal, a considerable scientist, preeminent mathematician, and deep and troubled Christian believer. He left a record of his state of mind in his *Pensées,* or *Thoughts,* jottings from which he hoped some day to write a great book on the Christian faith. "I am terrified," he said in one of these jottings, "by the eternal silence of these infinite spaces."

But on the whole the reaction was more optimistic. Man might be merely a reed, as Pascal said, but Pascal added, he was "a thinking reed." Human beings might be no longer the physical center of the world. But it was the human mind that had penetrated the world's laws. The Newtonian system, as it became popularized, a process which took about 50 years, led to a great intellectual complacency. Never had confidence in human powers been so high. As the English poet Alexander Pope put it,

The Newtonian system

> Nature and nature's laws lay hid in night;
> God said, "Let Newton be," and all was light.

Or, according to another epigram on the subject, there was only one universe to discover, and this universe had been discovered by Newton. Everything seemed possible to human reason. Although Newton and most other scientists continued to believe in the existence of God, the old feeling of dependency on divine powers and judgments lost much of its force or became something to be discussed by clergymen in church on Sunday. Human beings were not really little creatures, wayfarers in a world that was alien, yearning for the reunion with God that would bring peace. They were creatures of great capacity in their own right, living in a world that was understandable and manageable. These ideas contributed greatly to the secularizing of European society, gradually pushing religion and churches to the sidelines of European political power and many of the era's new intellectual debates.

The scientific discoveries also reinforced the old philosophy of natural law. This philosophy, developed by the Greeks and renewed in the Middle Ages, held that the universe is fundamentally orderly and that there is a natural rightness or justice, universally the same for all people and knowable by reason. It was very important in political theory, where it stood out against arbitrariness and the mere claims of power. The laws of nature as discovered by science were somewhat different, but they taught the same lesson, namely, the orderliness and minute regularity of the world. It was reassuring to feel that everywhere throughout an infinite space every particle of matter was quietly attracting every other particle by a force proportionate to the product of the masses and inversely proportionate to the square of the distance. The physical universe laid bare by science—orderly, rational, balanced, smoothly running, without strife or rivalry or contention—became a model on which many thinkers, as time went on, hoped to refashion human society. They hoped to make society also fulfill the rule of law.

In some ways it would be possible to exaggerate the impact of pure science. Scientists themselves did not usually apply their scientific ideas to religion and society. Few suffered the spiritual torment of Pascal. Both Descartes and Newton wrote earnest tracts arguing for the truth of certain religious doctrines. Bacon and Harvey were conservative politically,

Isaac Newton became the famous public symbol of the new scientific knowledge and the new scientific researcher. This portrait by an anonymous artist emphasizes the focused brilliance that made Newton an icon in the expanding institutions of scientific culture and in the wider development of eighteenth-century intellectual life.
(Bettmann/Corbis)

upholders of king against Parliament. The Englishman Joseph Glanvill, in the 1660s, used the Cartesian dualism to demonstrate the probable existence of witches. Descartes, despite his systematic doubt, held that the customs of one's country should usually be accepted without question. Natural science, in the pure sense, was not inherently revolutionary or even upsetting. If Europeans in the seventeenth century began to waver in many old beliefs, it was not only because of the stimulus of pure science but also because of an increasing knowledge and study of humanity itself.

29. NEW KNOWLEDGE OF HUMAN BEINGS AND SOCIETY

The discovery and exploration of the world overseas became a decisive new influence on European views of human cultures and the nature of human beings. Europe was already becoming part of the world as a whole and could henceforth understand itself only by comparison with non-European regions. Great reciprocal influences were at work. The influences of European expansion on other parts of the world are easily seen: the Indian societies of America were modified or extinguished; the indigenous societies of Africa were dislocated and many of their members were enslaved and transported; in the long run even the ancient societies of Asia were to be disrupted or undermined. From the beginning the counterinfluence of the rest of the world upon Europe was equally great. It took the form of new medicines, new diseases, new foods, new and exotic manufactures brought to Europe, and the growth of material wealth in west-European countries, but it also affected European thinking. New questions were raised about the diversity of religious traditions, the history of languages, and the origins of human civilizations. The growing involvement with other cultures undermined the old Europe and its ideas, just as Europe was undermining the old cultures beyond the oceans. Vast new horizons opened before Europeans in the sixteenth and seventeenth centuries. Europeans of this period were the first people to know the globe as a whole, to establish colonial outposts around most of the world, or to realize the variety of the human race and its multifarious manners and customs.

The Current of Skepticism

This realization was very unsettling. The realization of human differences had the effect, in Europe, of breaking what has been called the "cake of custom." A new sense of the relative nature of social institutions developed. It became harder to believe in any absolute rightness of one's own ways. Montaigne, already mentioned, expressed the relativist outlook clearly, and nowhere more clearly than in his famous essay on cannibals. The cannibals, he said humorously, did in fact eat human flesh; that was their custom, and they have their customs as we have ours; they would think some of our ways odd or inhuman; peoples differ, and who are we to judge? Travelers' books spread the same message increasingly through the seventeenth century. As one of them observed (whether or not rightly), in Turkey it was the custom to shave the hair and wear the beard, in Europe to shave the beard and wear the hair; *Travelers' tales*
what difference does it really make? That the ways of non-Europeans might be good ways was emphasized by Jesuit missionaries. Writing from the depths of the Mississippi Valley or from China, the Jesuit fathers often dwelt on the natural goodness and mental alertness of the native peoples they encountered, perhaps hoping in this way to gain support in Europe for their missionary labors. People from the American wilderness or from Asia sometimes appeared in Europe itself. In 1684 a delegation of aristocratic Siamese arrived in Paris, followed by another in 1686. The Parisians went through a fad for Siam (now Thailand); they recounted how the king of Siam, when asked by a missionary to turn Christian, replied that divine Providence, had it wished a single religion to prevail in the world, could easily have so arranged it. The philosophical Siamese seemed civilized and wise; they allowed Christians to preach in their own country, whereas it was well known what would happen to a Siamese missionary who undertook to preach in Paris. China also was seen at this time as a civilized center of learning, tolerance, and wise ethical traditions. By 1700 there were even professors of Arabic, at Paris, Oxford, and Utrecht, who said that Islam was a religion to be respected, as good for Muslims as Christianity was for Christians.   *Skepticism*

Thus was created a strong current of skepticism, holding that all beliefs are relative, varying with time and place. Its greatest spokesman at the end of the century was Pierre Bayle (1647–1706). Bayle was influenced by the scientific discoveries also; not exactly that he understood them, for he was an almost purely literary scholar, but he realized that many popular beliefs were without scientific foundation. Between 1680 and 1682 a number of comets were seen. The one of 1682 was studied by a friend of Newton's, Edmond Halley, the first man to predict the return of a comet. He identified the comet of 1682 with the one observed in 1302, 1456, 1531, and 1607, and predicted its reappearance in 1757 (it appeared in 1759); it was seen again in 1910 and 1986

AMBASSADEURS DE SIAM

The arrival of ambassadors from Siam at Versailles in 1684 made a vivid impression on a French generation that was fascinated by reports on distant lands and peoples. Although the bowing ambassadors show the requisite respect for the Sun King, their presence in France contributed to the growing speculation on cultural differences and the relativism of cultural customs.

(Musées Versailles, Reunion des Musées Nationaux/Art Resource, NY)

and is still called Halley's Comet. In the 1680s people were talking excitedly about the significance of comets. Some said that comets emitted poisonous exhalations; others, that they were supernatural omens of future events.

Bayle, in his *Thoughts on the Comet,* argued at great length that there was no basis for any such beliefs except human credulity. In 1697 he published his *Historical and Critical Dictionary,* a tremendous repository of miscellaneous lore, conveying the message that what is called truth is often mere opinion, that most people are amazingly gullible, that many things firmly believed are really ridiculous, and that it is very foolish to hold too strongly to one's own views. Bayle's *Dictionary* remained a reservoir on which skeptical writers continued to draw for generations. Bayle himself, having no firm basis in his own mind for settled judgment, mixed skepticism with an impulse to faith. Born a Protestant, he was converted to Rome, then returned to his Calvinist background. In any case his views made for toleration in religion. For Bayle, as for Montaigne, no opinion was worth burning your neighbor for.

The New Sense of Evidence

But in the study of humankind, as in the study of physical nature, Europeans of the seven-teenth century were not generally content with skepticism. They were not possessed by a mere negative and doubting mood, important and salutary as such an attitude was. In the subjects collectively called the humanities, as in pure science, they were looking not for disbelief but for understanding. They wanted new means of telling the true from the false, a new method for arriving at some degree of certainty of conviction. And here, too, a kind of scientific view of the world arose, if that term is understood in a general sense. It took the form of a new sense of evidence. Evidence is that which allows one to believe a thing to be true, or at least truer than something else for which the evidence is weaker. And if to believe without evidence is the sign of primitive or irrational thinking, to require evidence before believing is in a way to be scientific, or at least to trust and use the power of human intelligence.

The new sense of evidence, and of the need of evidence, revealed itself in many ways. One of the clearest was in the law. The English law of evidence, for example, began to take on its modern form at the close of the seventeenth century. It was long believed that less evidence should be necessary in arriving at a verdict of guilty in trials for the most atrocious crimes; this was thought necessary to protect society from the more hideous offenses.

English law of evidence

From the end of the seventeenth century, in English law, the judge lost his power of dis-cretion in deciding what should constitute evidence, and the same rules of evidence were applied in all forms of accusation, the essential question being recognized as always the same—did such-and-such a fact (however outrageous) occur or did it not? After 1650 mere hearsay evidence, long vaguely distrusted, was ruled definitely out of court. After 1696 even persons charged with felony were allowed legal counsel.

The new sense of evidence was probably the main force in putting an end to the delusions of witchcraft. What made witchcraft so credible and so fearsome was that many persons confessed themselves to be witches, admitting to supernatural powers and to evil designs upon their neighbors.

Evidence and witchcraft

Many or most such confessions were extracted under torture. Reformers urged that confes-sions obtained under torture were not evidence, that people would say anything to escape unbearable pain, so that no such confessions offered the slightest ground for believing in witches. As for the voluntary confessions, and even the boastings of some people of their diabolical powers, it was noted that such statements often came from persons who would today be called hysterical or psychotic. Witches came to be regarded as self-deluded. Their ideas of themselves were no longer accepted as evidence. But it must be added that, except in England, the use of legal torture lasted through most of the eighteenth century in crimi-nal cases in which the judge believed the accused to be guilty.

History and Historical Scholarship

What are called the historical sciences also developed rapidly at this time. History, like the law, depends on the finding and using of evidence. The historian and the judge must answer the same kind of question—did such-and-such a fact really occur? All knowledge of history, so far as it disengages itself from legend and wishful thinking, rests ultimately on pieces of evidence, written records, and other works created in the past and surviving in some form or other in the present. On this mass of material the vast picture of the past is

THE GROWTH OF GEOGRAPHICAL KNOWLEDGE

The four maps show the best scientific knowledge at their respective dates. Behaim has no inkling of the existence of America and has filled in the hemisphere opposite to Europe with a mass of islands, representing what he has heard of the East Indies and Japan. He knows pretty well the limits of Africa. Schöner in 1523 fills in America and even distinguishes two American continents. He knows of the Gulf of Mexico but fails to realize the narrowness of the Isthmus of Panama. He knows of the Straits of Magellan (but not Cape Horn) and hopefully fills in a corresponding Northwest Passage in the north. His conception of the Indian Ocean is quite accurate. To Homan, two centuries later, the size and shapes of oceans and continents are well known, but he believes New Guinea joined to Australia and is frankly ignorant of the northwest coast of North America, representing it by a straight line. The Great Lakes and the interior of North America have become known to Europe. D'Anville in 1761 has no island of Tasmania, does not understand that Alaska is a peninsula, and believes the American polar regions to be impassable by sea. Otherwise his map is indistinguishable from one on the same scale today.

built, and without it people would be ignorant of their own antecedents or would have only folktales and oral traditions.

There was much skepticism about history in the seventeenth century. Some said that history was not a form of true knowledge because it was not mathematical. Others said that it was useless because Adam, the perfect man, neither had nor needed any history. Many felt that what passed for history was only a mass of fables. History was distrusted also because historians were often pretentious, claiming to be high-flying men of letters, writing for rhetorical or inspirational appeal or for argumentative reasons, disdaining the hard labor of actual study. History was losing the confidence of thinking people who came to view science as the model for reliable knowledge. How was it possible, they asked, to feel even a modicum of certainty about alleged events that had happened long before any living person had been born?

This doubting attitude itself arose from a stricter sense of evidence, or from a realization that there was really no proof for much of what was said about the past. But scholars set to work to assemble what evidence there was. They hoped to create a new history, one that should contain only reliable statements. Europe was littered with old papers and parchments. Abbeys, manor houses, and royal archives were full of written documents, many of them of unknown age or unknown origin, often written in a handwriting that people could no longer read. Learned and laborious enthusiasts set to work to explore this accumulation. They added so much to the efforts of their predecessors as virtually to create modern critical scholarship and erudition. The French Benedictine monk Jean Mabillon, in 1681, in his book *On Diplomatics* (referring to ancient charters and "diplomas") established the science of paleography, which deals with the deciphering, reading, dating, and authentication of manuscripts. The Frenchman DuCange in 1678 published a dictionary of medieval Latin which is still used. Others, like the Italian Muratori, spent whole lifetimes exploring archives, collecting, editing, or publishing masses of documents, comparing manuscript copies of the same text and trying to discover what the author had really written, rejecting some as fabrications or forgeries, pronouncing others to be genuine pieces of

New historical scholarship

The early modern interest in the preservation and study of historical materials led to a systematic organization of the libraries and sources that careful scholarship would require. This seventeenth-century engraving of a library in Leiden shows the subjects that scholars studied and the tables at which they stood to read the books.
(Corbis)

historical evidence. Others made themselves experts in ancient coins, many of which were far more ancient than the oldest manuscripts; they founded the science of numismatics. Still others, or indeed the same persons, turned to a critical examination of the inscriptions on old buildings and ruins.

Another important but little-known historical "science," namely, chronology, was greatly stimulated also. Chronology deals with the age of the world and with finding a common denominator between the dating systems of various peoples. Probably it is not natural for the human mind to think in terms of dates at all. For simple or nonhistorically minded people it is enough to know that some things happened "long ago." In the seventeenth century the new interest in numbers, evident in physical science, turned also to the human past. Archbishop James Usher, an Anglican prelate of Ireland, after much study of the Bible, announced the date of 4004 B.C. as that of the creation of the world. His chronological system was later printed in the margins of the Authorized Version of the English Bible and is still adhered to by some fundamentalists as if part of the Bible itself. But Usher's system was not accepted by scholars even in his own time. Geographical knowledge was revealing China and its dynasties to Europe; historical knowledge was beginning to discover ancient Egypt. The Chinese and Egyptian records claimed a greater antiquity for their countries than the Old Testament seemed to allow for the human race. There was much erudite conjecture; one scholar about 1700 counted 70 estimates of the age of the world, ranging as high as 170,000 years, a figure which then seemed fantastic and appalling.

The difficulty was not only in the language of the Old Testament. It was in finding the correspondence between the chronological systems of different peoples. A Chinese system of dating by dynasties might be coherent within itself, but how could it be equated with the European system of dating from the birth of Christ, a date as little known to the Chinese as the date of Wu Wang was to Europeans? Even European records presented the same difficulty; the Romans counted by consulships, or from the supposed year of the founding of Rome; many medieval documents told only the year of some obscure ruler's reign. Only infinite patience, interminable research, and endless calculation could reduce such a jumble to the simple system of modern textbooks. This is of more importance than may be at first thought. A common system of dating is a great aid to thinking of human history as an interconnected whole. An overall conception of the human race is made easier by the dating of all events according to the Christian era. This itself, it may be pointed out, is an arbitrary and conventional scale, since Christ is now thought to have been born not in A.D. 1, but in 4 B.C.

A common system of dating

Common dating was of importance in practical affairs as well as in historical knowledge. Europe was disunited even on the Christian calendar. Protestant and some Orthodox countries followed the old or Julian calendar; Catholic countries, the corrected or Gregorian calendar issued in the sixteenth century under authority of Pope Gregory XIII. The two calendars varied in the seventeenth century by 10 days. Only gradually was the Gregorian calendar accepted, by England in 1752, by Russia in 1918. Most other peoples today, in China, India, the Arabic world, and elsewhere, use or recognize the Gregorian calendar. Without a uniform way of specifying days and years it would be difficult to transact international affairs, hold international conferences, make plans, or pay and receive money; a global system for defining time and dates thus became essential for global economic exchanges and communications. This common dating, easily taken for granted, was a consequence of the predominance of Europe in modern times. It is a sign of growing unity in world civilization.

CHRONOLOGY OF NOTABLE EVENTS, 1543–1697

1543	Publication of Copernicus's *On the Revolution of the Heavenly Orbs* and Vesalius's *The Structure of the Human Body*
1609	Galileo builds a telescope
1620–1627	Francis Bacon argues for empirical method to advance knowledge
1637	René Descartes publishes *Discourse on Method*
1651	Thomas Hobbes publishes *Leviathan*
1662	Royal Society is founded in London
1666	Royal Academy of Sciences is founded in Paris
1687	Isaac Newton publishes *Mathematical Principles of Natural Philosophy*
1690	John Locke publishes *Essay Concerning Human Understanding* and *Two Treatises on government*
1697	Pierre Bayle publishes *Historical Critical Dictionary*

The Questioning of Traditional Beliefs

The historical sciences provided a foundation on which a knowledge of human activities in the past could be built, and the growing geographical knowledge spread a panorama of human diversity in the present. This new knowledge shared with natural science the view that many traditional ideas were erroneous but that much could be known by a disciplined use of the human mind. The humanities and the sciences were alike in demanding evidence for belief and in trusting to the power of reason. In their impact on the old certainties of European life, the studies of human cultures exerted possibly a greater direct force than those of nature. Pascal, in his attempt to defend the Christian faith, feared the spirit of Montaigne, the mood of skepticism and denial, which he felt himself, more than he feared the findings of mathematical and physical science. And the movement of historical thought, with its insistence on textual criticism, threw doubt on much of the Christian religion, or at least on the sacred history related in the Bible, which was considered to be part and parcel of religion itself.

Biblical scholarship and criticism

In 1678 a French priest, Richard Simon, published a pioneering work in Biblical criticism, his *Critical History of the Old Testament*. Although his book was condemned both by the church and by the government of Louis XIV, Richard Simon always felt himself to be orthodox; Catholic faith, he insisted, depended more on church tradition than on the literal statements of the Bible. He simply applied to the Old Testament the methods of textual criticism which others were applying to secular documents. He concluded that the Old Testament, as known, rested on medieval manuscripts, many of which were of unknown or doubtful origin, that monkish copyists had introduced errors and corruptions, and that the books thought to have been written by Moses could not have been written by him, since they contained obvious contradictions and matter clearly inserted after his death. Others went further, questioning not merely the evidence of the Biblical text, but the very possibility of some events that it related. From the scientific idea of the absolute regularity of nature on the one hand, and from a strong sense of human credulity on the other, they denied that miracles had ever occurred and looked upon oracles and prophecies among either the Greeks or the Hebrews with a dubious eye.

The most profoundly disturbing of all thinkers of the time was Baruch Spinoza (1632–1677), the lens grinder of Amsterdam, a Jew who was excommunicated by his own synagogue and who refused a professorship at the University of Heidelberg, craving only the quiet to think in peace. Spinoza drew on both the scientific and humanistic thought of his day. He arrived at a philosophy holding that God had no existence apart from the world, that everything was itself an aspect of God—a philosophy technically called pantheism but considered by many to be really atheistic. He denied the inspiration of the Bible, disbelieved in miracles and the supernatural, rejected all revelation and revealed religion, Jewish or Christian, and held that few if any governments of the day were really just. He taught a pure, stern, and intellectual ethical code, and one which had few consolations for the average person. His name became a byword for impiety and horrendous unbelief. People were literally afraid to read his works, even when they could find them, which was not often because of the censorship. His influence spread slowly, through the mediation of other writers, contributing to the later development of rationalist philosophy.

Baruch Spinoza

More widely read, less abstruse, were the writings of the Englishman John Locke (1632–1704), who summarized many of the intellectual trends of his lifetime and exerted a strong influence for the following hundred years. He combined practical experience and theoretical interests in a philosophy that dwelled on the merits of common sense. Educated in medicine, he kept in touch with the sciences and was acquainted with Newton. He was associated with the great Whig noblemen who were the main authors of the English revolution in 1688. For political reasons he spent several years in the 1680s in the Netherlands, where he became familiar with thought on the Continent. He wrote on many subjects—finance, economics, education, religious policy, political theory, general philosophy—always with an engaging directness and sober air of the sensible man of the world. In his *Letter on Toleration* (1689) he advocated an established church but with toleration of all except Roman Catholics and atheists; these he held to be dangerous to society: the former because of a foreign allegiance; the latter because they lacked a basis of moral responsibility. In his *Reasonableness of Christianity* he argued that Christianity, rightly considered, is after all a reasonable form of religion; this softened the friction between religion and natural knowledge but tended to shut out the supernatural and merge religious feeling into an unruffled common sense.

Locke's deepest book was his *Essay Concerning the Human Understanding* (1690). Here he faced the great problem of the day, the problem of knowledge; he asked if it was possible to know anything with certainty, and how certain knowledge was arrived at. His answer was that true or certain knowledge is derived from experience—from perceptions by the sense organs and reflection of the mind on these perceptions. Locke at the end of the century thus echoes Bacon at the beginning; they became the two great pillars of empirical philosophy, insisting on experience and observation as the source of truth. Locke denied Descartes's doctrine of innate ideas, or inevitable disposition of the human mind to think in certain ways. He held that the mind at birth is a blank tablet or *tabula rasa* and that the social environment shapes what people think or believe. Locke's environmentalist philosophy became fundamental to liberal and reforming thought in later years. It seemed that false ideas or superstitions were the result of bad environment and bad education. It seemed that the evil in human actions was due to bad social institutions and that an improvement in human society would improve human behavior. This philosophy, whether or not wholly true in the final analysis, was largely true with respect to many practical conditions. It gave confidence in the possibility of social progress and turned attention to a

The Dutch, Jewish philosopher Baruch Spinoza (1632–1677), portrayed here in a painting by Samuel Van Hoogstraten, developed a materialist or pantheistic philosophy that provoked strong opposition from many of his contemporaries; but Spinoza became an influential thinker for later writers who expressed skepticism about traditional religious beliefs.
(Bettmann/CORBIS)

sphere in which planned and constructive action was possible, namely, the sphere of government, public policy, and legislation. Here we touch on political theory, to which Locke contributed *Two Treatises of Government* (these works are discussed later in this chapter).

30. POLITICAL THEORY: THE SCHOOL OF NATURAL LAW

Political theory can never be strictly scientific. Science deals with what does exist or has existed. It does not tell what ought to exist. To describe what society and government ought to be like, in view of human nature and the capacity to be miserable or contented, is a main purpose of political theory. Political theory is in a sense more practical than science. It is the scientists and scholars who are most content to observe facts as they are. Practical people, and scientists and scholars insofar as they have practical interests, must always ask themselves what ought to be done, what policies ought to be adopted, what measures ought to be taken, what state of affairs ought to be maintained or brought about. Conservatives and radicals, traditionalists and innovators, are alike in this respect. It is impossible in human affairs to escape the word "ought."

But political theory was affected by the scientific view. The Renaissance Italian, Niccolò Machiavelli (1469–1527), whom we have discussed earlier, had opened the way in this direction. Machiavelli too had his "ought"; he preferred a republican form of government in which citizens felt a patriotic attachment to their state. But in his book *The Prince* he disregarded the question of the best form of government, a favorite question of Christian and scholastic philosophers of the Middle Ages. He separated the study of politics from theology and moral philosophy. He undertook to describe how governments and rulers actually behaved. He observed that successful rulers behaved as if holding or increasing power

Niccolò Machiavelli

were their only object, that they regarded all else as means to this end. Princes, said Machiavelli, kept their promises or broke them, told the truth or distorted or colored it, sought popularity or ignored it, advanced public welfare or disrupted it, conciliated their neighbors or destroyed them—depending merely on which course of action seemed the best means of advancing their political interests. All this was bad, said Machiavelli; but that was not the question, for the question was to find out what rulers really did. Drawing his conclusions from the evidence of history, Machiavelli chose to be nonmoral in order to be scientific. To most readers he seemed to be simply immoral. Nor was it possible to draw the line between *The Prince* as a scientific description of fact and *The Prince* as a book of maxims of conduct. In telling how successful rulers obtained their successes, Machiavelli also suggested how rulers *ought* to proceed. And though governments did in fact continue to behave for the most part as Machiavelli said, most people refused to admit that they ought to.

Natural Right and Natural Law

Political theory in the seventeenth century did not embrace the cynicism attributed to Machiavelli. Nor did it fall into the skepticism of those who said that the customs of one's country should be passively accepted or that one form of government was about as good as another. It directly faced the question, What is right? The seventeenth century was the classic age of the philosophy of natural right or of natural law.

"Natural law" and "natural right"

The idea of natural law underlies a good deal of modern democratic development, and its decline in the last century has been closely connected with many of the troubles of recent times. It is not easy to say in what the philosophy of natural law essentially consisted. It held that there is, somehow, in the structure of the world, a law that distinguishes right from wrong. It held that right is "natural," not a mere human invention. This right is not determined, for any country, by its heritage, tradition, or customs, nor yet by its actual laws (called "positive" laws) of the kind that are enforced in the law courts. All these may be unfair or unjust. We detect unfairness or injustice in them by comparing them with natural law as we understand it; thus we have a basis for saying that cannibalism is bad or that a law requiring forced labor from orphan children is unjust. Nor is natural law, or the real rightness of something, determined by the authority of any person or people. No king can make right that which is wrong. No people, by its will as a people, can make just that which is unjust. Right and law, in the ultimate sense, exist outside and above all peoples. They are universal, the same for all. No one can make them up to suit themselves. A good king or a just people is a king or people whose actions correspond to the objective standard. But how, if we cannot trust our own positive laws or customs, or our leaders, or even our collective selves, can we know what is naturally right? How do we discover natural law?

The answer, in the natural law philosophy, is that we discover it by reason. Philosophers of natural law said that human beings are rational animals. And they assumed that all human beings have, at least potentially and when better enlightened, the same powers of reason and understanding—Germans or English, Asians, Africans or Europeans. This view favored a cosmopolitan outlook and made international agreement and general world progress seem realizable goals. As time went on, the premises of this philosophy came to be questioned. By the twentieth century it was widely thought that the human mind was not especially rational but was motivated by unconscious drives or urges or instincts and that human cultural differences were so fundamental that people of different nationalities or classes could never expect to see things in the same way. Challenged by such theories of human irrationality and cultural difference (which could be promoted with much ancient and modern evidence), the older philosophy of a universal natural law lost its hold on many minds.

In the seventeenth and eighteenth centuries, however, it was generally accepted. Some, carrying over the philosophy of the Middle Ages, thought of natural law as an aspect of the law of God. Others, more secular in spirit, held that the natural law stood of itself. These included even some churchmen; a group of theologians, mainly Jesuits, were condemned by the pope in 1690 for holding that universal right and wrong might exist by reason only, whether God existed or not. The idea of natural law and the faith in human reason went side by side, and both were fundamental in the thought of the time. They were to be found everywhere in Europe, in their religious or their secular form.

On the basis of natural law some thinkers tried to create an international law or "law of nations," to bring order into the maze of sovereign territorial states, great and small, that was developing in Europe. Hugo Grotius, in 1625, published the first great book devoted exclusively to this subject, his *Law of War and Peace*. Samuel Pufendorf followed with his *Law of Nature and of Nations* in 1672. Both held that sovereign states, though bound by no positive law or author-ity, should work together for the common good, that there was a community of nations as of individuals, and that in the absence of a higher international sovereignty they were all still subordinate to natural reason and justice. Certain concrete doctrines, such as the free-dom of the seas or the immunity of ambassadors, were put forward. The principles of international law remained those of natural law. The content came to include specific agreements between governments, certain kinds of admiralty and maritime law, and the terms of treaties such as the treaties of Westphalia, Utrecht, and others. The means of enforcement, to be sure, remained weak or nonexistent in crises.

"Law of nations"

Hobbes and Locke

In domestic affairs the philosophy of natural law, though it rather favored constitutional-ism, was used to justify both constitutional and absolutist governments. Right itself was held to be in the nature of things, beyond human power to change. But forms of govern-ment were held to be means to an end. No philosopher at the time thought the state to have an absolute value in itself. The state had to be "justified," made acceptable to the moral consciousness or to reason. There were, indeed, important competing philosophies. On the side of absolutism was the doctrine of the divine right of kings. On the side of constitution-alism were arguments based on heritage or custom, emphasizing the charters, bulls, or compacts of former times and the historic powers of parliaments and estates. But neither the supernatural argument of the divine right of kings nor the historical argument pointing back to liberties of the Middle Ages was entirely satisfactory in the scientific atmosphere of the seventeenth century. Neither carried complete conviction to the reason or moral sense of the most acute thinkers. Both were reinforced by arguments of natural law. Two Englishmen stand out above all others in this connection. Absolutism was philosophically justified by Thomas Hobbes; constitutionalism, by John Locke.

Hobbes (1588–1679) followed the scientific and mathematical discov-eries of his time with more than an amateur interest. In philosophy he held to a materialistic and even atheistic system. In English politics he sided with king against Parliament; he disliked the disorder and violence of the civil war of the 1640s and the unstable conditions of the English republic of the 1650s. He concluded that humans have no capacity for self-government. His opinion of human

Absolutism and Thomas Hobbes

nature was low; he held that people in the "state of nature," or as imagined to exist without government, were quarrelsome and turbulent, forever locked in a war of all against all. In his famous phrase, life in the state of nature was "solitary, poor, nasty, brutish and short." From fear of each other, to obtain order and enjoy the advantages of law and right, people came to a kind of agreement or "contract" by which they surrendered their freedom of action into the hands of a ruler. It was necessary for this ruler to have unrestricted or absolute power. Only thus could he maintain order. It was intolerably dangerous, according to Hobbes, for anyone to question the actions of government, for such questioning might reopen the way to chaos. Government must therefore be a kind of Leviathan (the monster mentioned in the Bible, Job 41); and Hobbes in fact used the word *Leviathan* for the title of his principal book, published in 1651, two years after the execution of King Charles I.

By this book Hobbes became the leading secular exponent of absolutism and one of the principal theorists of the unlimited sovereignty of the state. His influence on later thinkers was very great. He accustomed political theorists to the use of purely natural arguments. He quoted freely from the Bible, but the Bible had no influence on his thought. After Hobbes, all advanced political theorists regarded government as a device created by human purpose. It was no longer considered, except popularly and except by professional theologians, as part of God's divine dispensation to human history. Hobbes also affected later theorists by his arguments for a sovereign authority and, more negatively, by obliging them to refute his idea of an unlimited personal sovereign. But he was never a popular writer. In England the cause which he favored was lost. In those continental countries where royal absolutism prevailed his arguments were received with secret gratification, but his irreligion was too dangerous to make public, and the absolutist argument, on the popular level, remained that of the divine right of kings. In any case Hobbes's arguments were in some ways insufficient for real monarchs. Hobbes abhorred struggle and violence. He believed that absolutism would produce civil peace, individual security, and a rule of law. He also held that absolute power depended on, or had at least originated in, a free and rational agreement by which people accepted it. An absolute monarchy that flagrantly violated these conditions could with difficulty be justified even by the doctrines of Hobbes. It is in these respects that Hobbes differs from totalitarian theorists of more recent times. For Hobbes, in the final analysis, absolute power was an expedient to promote individual welfare. It was a means necessary to the realization of natural law.

John Locke

John Locke (1632–1704), as has been seen, also stood in the main current of scientific thought and discovery. But in his political philosophy he carried over many ideas of the Middle Ages, as formulated in the thirteenth century by St. Thomas Aquinas and kept alive in England by successive thinkers of the Anglican church. Medieval philosophy had never favored an absolute power. With Hobbes, Locke shared the idea that good government is an expedient of human purpose, neither provided by divine Providence nor inherited by a national tradition. He held, too, like Hobbes and the whole school of natural law, that government was based on a kind of contract, or rational and conscious agreement upon which authority was based. In contrast to Hobbes, he sided with Parliament against king in the practical struggles of politics. About 1680, in the course of these disputes, he wrote *Two Treatises of Government,* which, however, were not published until shortly after the parliamentary revolution of 1688–1689.

Locke took a more genial view of human nature than Hobbes. As he showed in his other books, he believed that a moderate religion was a good thing and above all that people could learn from experience and hence could be educated to an enlightened way of life.

These ideas favored a belief in self-government. Locke declared (in contradiction to Hobbes) that people in the "state of nature" were reasonable and well disposed, willing to get along with one another though handicapped by the absence of public authority. They likewise had a moral sense, quite independently of government; and they also possessed by nature certain rights, quite apart from the state. These rights were the rights to life, liberty, and property.

Locke placed heavy emphasis on the right of property, by which he usually meant the possession of land. His philosophy can in fact be regarded as an expression of the landed classes of England, who challenged the power of kings by defending the political and social rights of private property. Individuals in the state of nature are not altogether able, according to Locke, to win general respect for their individual natural rights. They cannot by their own efforts protect what is "proper" to them, that is, their property. They agree to set up government to enforce observance of the rights of all. Government is thus created by a contract, but the contract is not unconditional, as claimed by Hobbes. It imposes mutual obligations. The people must be reasonable; only rational beings can be politically free. Liberty is not an anarchy of undisciplined will; it is the freedom to act without compulsion by another. Only rational and responsible creatures can exercise true freedom; but adult human beings, according to Locke, are or can be educated to be rational and responsible. They therefore can and should be free. On government, also, certain conditions and obligations are imposed. If a government breaks the contract, if it threatens the natural rights which it is the sole purpose of government to protect, if, for example, it takes away a man's property without his consent, then the governed have a right to reconsider what they have done in creating the government and may even in the last extremity rebel against it. The right to resist government, Locke admits, is very dangerous, but it is less dangerous than its opposite, which would lead to the loss of all liberty; and in any case we are talking about reasonable and responsible people.

If Locke's ideas seem familiar, especially to Americans, it is because of the wide popularizing of his philosophy in the century after his death. Nowhere was his influence greater than in the British colonies. The authors of the American Declaration of Independence and of the Constitution of the United States knew the writings of Locke very thoroughly. Some phrases of the Declaration of Independence echo his very language. In Great Britain also, and in France *Locke's influence* and elsewhere, in the course of time, Locke's influence was immense. But it should be noted that his ideas did not always mean the same thing for all people or in all places. Locke did not extend his ideas of human liberty to enslaved Africans, apparently because he viewed slavery as a legitimate form of private property. Locke himself invested in the slave-trading Royal African Company and endorsed the development of slavery in the American colonies. The growing influence of Locke's political theories may also have contributed indirectly to the emergence of new racist ideas in the eighteenth century. New justifications for slavery became necessary when the political classes of England and America began to believe that human beings possessed natural rights to life, liberty, and property. How could slavery be reconciled with such beliefs? The answer appeared in new forms of racism, which justified the enslavement of Africans by arguing that the African "race" lacked certain rational human traits of the European "race" and that black people could be denied fundamental human rights because they differed from other human beings.

In general, however, Locke's ideas of natural rights and human liberty were later used to challenge absolutist or repressive institutions, including also the institutions of slavery. What Locke did was to convert an episode in English history into an event of universal

**JOHN LOCKE
by John Greenhill (English,
1642–1676)**
**Locke's writings on govern-
ment and natural rights summarized the arguments against
royal power in England and
also won adherents wherever
political theorists challenged
monarchical absolutism.**
(Snark/Art Resource, NY)

political meaning. In England, in 1688, certain great lords, winning the support of the established church, gentry, and merchants, deposed one king and brought in another. On the new king they imposed certain obligations—specified in the Bill of Rights of 1689 and all dealing with legal or technical interpretations of the English constitution. The Revolution of 1688 was a very English affair. England in 1688 was still little known to the rest of Europe. The proceedings in England, so far as known, might seem no different from a rebellion of the magnates of Hungary. Locke, in arguing that Parliament had been right to eject James II, put the whole affair on a level of reason, natural right, and human nature. It thus came to have meaning for people who had no connection with the specific problems of English political history.

Locke on the English revolution

At the same time, Locke made the English revolution a sign of progress rather than reaction. The new and modern form of government in 1690 was royal absolutism, with its professional bureaucracy and corps of paid officials. Almost everywhere there was resistance to the kings, led by landed interests and harking back to earlier freedoms. Such resistance seemed to many Europeans to be feudal and medieval. Locke made the resistance in England, namely, the Revolution of 1688 against James II, into a modern and forward-looking move. He checked the prestige of absolutism. He gave new prestige to constitutional principles. He carried over, in modified form, many ideas from the scholastic philosophers of the Middle Ages, who had generally maintained that kings had only a relative and restricted power and were responsible to their peoples. To these ideas he added the force of the newer scientific view of the world. He did not rest his case on supernatural or providential arguments. He did not say that constitutional government was the will of God. He said that it rested on experience and observation of human nature, on recognition of certain individual rights and especially the right of property, and on the existence of a purely natural law of reason and justice. He was an almost entirely secular thinker, and, as such, he developed ideas that could be drawn into the political and social conflicts of most modern nations.

One must not claim too much for Locke, or for any writer. England was in fact, in 1688, more modern in many ways than other countries in Europe. The Glorious Revolution was in fact not exactly like uprisings of the landed and propertied classes elsewhere. England in the following century did in fact create a form of parliamentary government that was unique. But facts go together with the theories that give them an understandable meaning. Events in England, as explained by Locke, and as seen in other countries and even in England and its colonies through Locke's eyes, launched into the mainstream of modern history the superb tradition of constitutional government, which has been one of the principal themes in the history of the modern world ever since.

By 1700, at the close of the "century of genius," some beliefs that were to become characteristic of modern times had clearly taken form, notably a faith in science, in human reason, in natural human rights, and in progress. The new scientific knowledge was beginning to transform the global economy, the culture of European elites, and the conflicts within or among European empires. Meanwhile, the cultural institutions of modern science were spreading across Europe, and new scientific theories in physics, astronomy, and physiology were challenging both the theology and thought systems of earlier generations. The following period, generally known as the Age of Enlightenment, was to be a time of clarifying and popularizing ideas which the more creative seventeenth century had produced. These ideas were eventually to revolutionize Europe, America, and the world. They were also in subsequent years to be modified, amended, challenged, and even denied. But they are still very much alive today.

For interactive exercises, glossary, chronologies, and more, go to the *Online Learning Center* at **www.mhhe.com/palmer10.**

Chapter 7

THE STRUGGLE
FOR WEALTH
AND EMPIRE

31. Elite and Popular Cultures

32. The Global Economy
    of the Eighteenth Century

33. Western Europe after
    the Peace of Utrecht,
    1713–1740

34. The Great War
    of the Mid–Eighteenth
    Century: The Peace of
    Paris, 1763

In earlier chapters we have seen how western Europe, and especially England and France, by about the year 1700 came to occupy a position of power and influence in Europe as a whole. We have traced the political history of western Europe through the War of the Spanish Succession, terminated in 1713–1714 by the treaties of Utrecht and Rastadt. Affairs of central Europe and Germany have been carried to 1740. In that year a new kingdom of Prussia and a new or renovated Austrian monarchy, each passing into the hands of a new ruler, stood on the eve of a struggle for ascendancy in central Europe. As for eastern Europe, we have observed the Europeanizing and expansion of the Russian empire.

More important in the long run than these political events, and continuing through the seventeenth and eighteenth centuries, was the cumulative expansion of all forms of knowledge, which we saw in the rapid development of seventeenth-century science and to which we turn again in the next chapter. Equally important was the growing wealth of Europe, or at least of the Atlantic region north of Spain. The new wealth, in the widest sense, meaning conveniences of every kind, resulted partly from the new technical and scientific knowledge, which in turn it helped to produce; and the two together, more wealth and more knowledge, helped to form one of the most far-reaching ideas of modern times, the idea of progress. This idea challenged the traditional deference to ancient authorities and fostered critical inquiry, creative innovations, and remarkable optimism in most spheres of social and intellectual life. Although the world wars and environmental problems of more recent times would eventually provoke widespread anxieties about the historical consequences of new technologies, a belief in progress, even if somewhat chastened, remains a powerful cultural force in all modern societies.

Chapter emblem: Detail from an Indian miniature (c. 1785), showing an Englishwoman and one of her servants in India. (Werner Forman Archive/Art Resource, NY)

The new wealth of Europe was not like the age-old wealth of the great empires in the East, said by Milton to "shower on her kings barbaric pearl and gold." It consisted of gold, to be sure, but even more of bank deposits and facilities for credit, of more and better devices for mining coal, casting iron, and spinning thread, more productive agriculture, better and more comfortable houses, a wider variety of diet on the table, more and improved sailing ships, warehouses, and docks; more books, more newspapers, more medical instruments, more scientific equipment; greater government revenues, larger armies, and more numerous government employees. In the wealthy European countries, and because of the growing wealth, more people were freed from the necessity of toiling for food, clothing, and shelter, and were enabled to devote themselves to all sorts of specialized callings in government, management, finance, war, teaching, writing, inventing, exploring, and researching, and in producing the amenities rather than the barest necessities of life. These new forms of mechanical production, social organization, and specialized knowledge also began to spread to European colonies around the world, thus contributing to the expanding systems of global trade and to the growing belief in human progress.

31.   ELITE AND POPULAR CULTURES

The accumulation of wealth and knowledge was not evenly distributed among the various social classes. There had always been differences between rich and poor, with many gradations between the extremes, but at the time we are now considering, as the seventeenth century turned into the eighteenth, there came to be a more obvious distinction between elite and popular cultures. The terms are hard to define. The elite culture was not exactly the culture of the rich and well-to-do, nor was the popular culture limited to the poor and lower economic classes. The word "elite" suggests a minority within a given range of interests; thus there are elites not only of wealth, but of social position and of power; elites of fashion, of patronage and connoisseurship in the arts, and of artists themselves; elites of education, of special training as in medicine and law, and of discovery and accomplishment in technology and the sciences. In general, persons taking part in an elite culture could share at will in the popular culture by attending public amusements or simply by talking familiarly with their servants. But the relation was asymmetric. Those born in popular culture could not easily share in the intellectual or social culture of the elites, at least not without transforming themselves, through education or marriage, which could occur only in exceptional cases.

A main difference was simply one of language. At the popular level people generally used a local form of speech, varying from one place to another, with a distinctive accent, and with words that had become obsolete elsewhere or that might not be understood even a few miles away. In the Middle Ages this variety had been overcome by the use of Latin. Since the invention of printing and the rise of national literatures, and with the spreading influence of schools, of which we have seen that many were founded between 1550 and 1650, there came to be standard forms of English, French, Italian, and other languages, employed by all educated persons. Grammar and spelling became regularized. Virtually all printing was in a national language when it was not in Latin. Since only a minority were able to get the necessary education, the mass of the people continued to speak as they did before. Their way of talking was now considered a dialect, a peasant language, or what was called *patois* in French

National languages

or *Volkssprache* in German. And while it may be true, as some scientific philologists have said, that no form of speech is "better" than another, it is also true that facility in the national language was a sign of elite culture until the spread of universal elementary schooling in the nineteenth century. It gave access to at least certain segments of the elite culture, as it continues to do today, and it enabled educated persons to participate in the elite institutions of government, commerce, and the professions.

The elite culture was transmitted largely by way of books, although acquired also by word of mouth within favored families and social circles. The popular culture was predominantly oral, although also expressed in cheaply printed almanacs, chapbooks, woodcuts, and broadsides. Since it was so largely oral, and left so few written records, popular culture is difficult for historians to reconstruct, although it made up the daily lives, interests, and activities of the great majority in all countries. It must always be remembered that what we read as history, in this as in most other books, is mostly an account of the work of a small minority, either of power-wielders, decision-makers, and innovators whose actions nevertheless affected whole peoples, or of writers and thinkers whose ideas appealed to a limited audience. Persons who were illiterate or barely literate changed their ideas more slowly than the more mobile and more informed members of the elite. Cultural changes initiated by such elites spread slowly, generation after generation, to wider social classes, so that what was characteristic of popular culture at a given moment, such as a belief in magic, had often been common to all classes a century or two before. All people and social classes make history and participate in the processes of historical change, but the new knowledge, education, and wealth in early modern societies also created new forms of social distinctions and new hierarchies of cultural power.

Oral vs. print culture

The humanism of the Renaissance, being transmitted so largely through books and the study of Greek and Latin, remained limited to the elite culture. The strength of the Protestant Reformation lay in combining the efforts of highly educated persons, such as Luther and Calvin, with the anger, distress, disillusionment, and hopes of many very ordinary people. The new science and the ensuing eighteenth-century Enlightenment emerged in the work of small numbers of experimenters and writers but slowly reshaped the thinking of others. The process of diffusion might be slow and uncertain. Astrology, for example, was in the Middle Ages a branch of scientific inquiry; in the seventeenth century astrologers were still consulted by emperors and kings; then divination by the stars was denounced by both the clergy and secular thinkers as a superstition, and astrology was expelled from astronomy, but horoscopes still appear in American and European newspapers in our own time.

The differences of wealth, if not wholly decisive, were of great importance. Culture in the broader or anthropologist's sense of the word includes material circumstances of food, drink, and shelter. In some respects the lot of the poor in the seventeenth century was worse than in the Middle Ages. Less meat was eaten in Europe, because as population grew there was less land available for the raising of livestock. With the growth of a market economy many peasants raised wheat, but ate bread made of rye, barley, or oats, or even looked for acorns and roots in times of famine. The consumption of bread by working people in France in the eighteenth century was about a pound per day per person, because little else except cabbages and beans was eaten on ordinary days; after 1750 the use of white bread became more usual. Meanwhile the rich, or the merely affluent, developed more delicate menus prepared by professional cooks, one of whom is said to have committed suicide when his soufflé fell.

Living standards

In the towns the poor lived in crowded and unwholesome buildings, and in the country they lived in dark and shabby cabins where stoves only gradually replaced holes in the roof for the escape of smoke. The poor had no glass in their windows, the middle classes had some, and the rich had glass windows and mirrors in profusion. In humble homes the dishes were wooden bowls, slowly replaced by pewter, while china plates began to appear on the tables of the more well-to-do. Table forks, with one for each diner, originating in Italy, were brought to France in the sixteenth century by Catherine de Medici along with other items of Italian culture, and soon spread among those able to afford them, though Louis XIV still preferred to use his fingers. Silver bowls and pitchers were ancient but became more elaborate and more often seen in upper-class circles. The poor had no furniture, or only a few benches and a mat to sleep on; the middle classes had chairs and beds; the rich not only had substantial furniture but were becoming more conscious of style. Among persons of adequate income it became usual to have houses with specialized rooms, such as separate bedrooms, and a dining room. The prominent and the fashionable fitted out rooms for social receptions and entertainments, called salons in France, with walls of wood paneling, lighted by chandeliers reflected in mirrors, and provided with sofas and armchairs, which the invention of upholstery made more comfortable. The poor, after dark, huddled on chests or on the floor by a single candle.

Housing conditions

In the use of beverages the seventeenth century saw progress, if that is the right word. Coffee and tea, along with sugar and tobacco, all imported from overseas, were exotic rarities in 1600, more widely enjoyed in 1700, and available to all but the very destitute by the time of the French Revolution. Coffee shops developed and taverns multiplied. Cheap wines became more plentiful in southern Europe, as did beer in the north. The distillation of alcohol had been developed in the Middle Ages, when brandy, a distilled wine, was used as a medicine; by the seventeenth century it was a familiar drink. Whisky and gin also came into use at about this time. The taverns and coffee shops offered a place for neighborly gatherings for the middling and lower social classes. Drunkenness became a more visible problem in European cities, especially among workers who could not drink in domestic privacy and who were therefore often seen in the streets, as shown by Hogarth's pictures of "Gin Lane" in London about 1750. Arising from all this poverty and disorganization, especially in the large cities, was an increase in out-of-wedlock births and abandonment of children. It was calculated that in Paris in 1780 there were 7,000 abandoned children for 30,000 births, but many of these infants were brought from the country to be deposited in the foundling hospitals of the city, which were overwhelmed.

There was much that persons of all classes and cultures shared. Most important, in principle, was religion. The refined and the rude, the learned and the untutored, heard the same sermons in church, were baptized, married, and buried by the same sacraments, often by the same priest, and were subject to religious and moral obligations that transcended the boundaries of social class. Such was most likely to be the case in small communities of unmixed religion or where the lord and lady of the manor attended the same church as the villagers. Where different churches existed in fact, whether or not officially tolerated, religion played less of a role in social cohesion. In England, for example, the Nonconformists, who succeeded the old Puritans after the Stuart Restoration, developed a kind of middle-class culture that was noticeably different from the culture of the Anglican gentry. Rich families in both Protestant and Catholic countries might have their own private chaplains and build chapels of their own. In towns that were big enough for neighborhood diversification some churches

Religion

GIN LANE
by William Hogarth (English, 1697–1764)

Hogarth showed both the popularity and dangers of alcohol in the lives of Britain's working classes, as in this illustration of drunkenness in the streets of London.

(Metropolitan Museum of Art, Harris Brisbane Dick Fund, 1932)

The popularity of coffee and tea in the eighteenth century made the coffeehouse a popular meeting place in large cities such as London and Paris. The establishment portrayed here attracted a fashionable, wealthy clientele, but many coffeehouses also catered to the lower classes.

(The Metropolitan Museum of Art, Harris Brisbane Dick Fund, 1935 (35.100.31))

became fashionable and others merely popular. In any case some people in the seventeenth century were not very religious at all; these would include those in inaccessible rural areas as well as some of the poorest in the larger towns, who were often uprooted and homeless migrants from an overcrowded countryside. Reforming bishops, especially in France, undertook to ameliorate the situation, so that the seventeenth century was a great age of internal missionary work, and it may be that in the following century, as skepticism began to pervade the elite culture, the popular culture became more Christianized than it had been in the past.

Health

Rich and poor were subject to the same diseases, the same dangers of tainted food and polluted water, and the same smells and filth in noisy streets littered with horse droppings, puddles, and garbage. Not of course equally: in the elite culture people called on the service of doctors, who had been trained in the universities, while ordinary sufferers sought out popular healers, who were often women and whose remedies consisted of strange herbs or mysterious potions (women did not become doctors because they could not attend universities); and it made a difference whether one rode through the streets in a coach, as the affluent did, or picked one's way on foot with the common people. Congestion was worst in rapidly growing cities, such as London, Paris, Amsterdam, and Naples, where the differences between wealth and poverty were both more extreme and more shockingly visible. There were recurrent fears of short-age of food, as crop failure or local famine struck this or that region, in which case some starved and some ate less, while those able to do so simply paid higher prices. In some towns charitable organizations developed, often on the initiative of upper-class women, to finance and assist religious sisters in relief of the poor. Hunger and the fear of hunger sometimes produced riots, which however had little political significance except insofar as upper-class people tried to make use of them for their own purposes.

It was also in less material aspects that the elite and popular cultures increasingly diverged. The upper strata set a new importance on polite manners, in which the French now set the tone, with much bowing, doffing of hats, and exchange of compliments, beside which the manners of ordinary people now seemed uncouth. The etiquette of princely courts became more formal, the court fools and jesters disappeared, and royalty surrounded itself not with rough retainers but with ladies and gentlemen. About 1600 the plays of Shakespeare were staged in public theaters where all classes mixed and enjoyed the same performance, but in the following century it became usual for the upper classes to have private theaters. People of higher social position took to stylish dancing, which their children had to learn from dancing teachers, while plain people continued to cavort more spontaneously in country dances and jigs. For evening parties, the polite world met in salons to engage in the art of cultured conversation, while working people, especially in the country, met in a neighbor's house after the day's labors were over, and there, while the men mended their implements and the women mended the clothes, engaged in local gossip, listened to story-tellers, or sat by while someone read aloud from one of the cheaply printed books that were now widely circulated.

Politeness, etiquette, entertainment

Enough of these books have survived, along with popular almanacs, to make it possi-ble to form some ideas of the mental horizons of the nonliterate and inarticulate classes. They were often written by printers or their employees or by others who were in effect intermediaries between the elite and popular cultures and who purposely addressed them-selves to what they knew of popular interests. The almanacs purveyed astrological obser-vations, advice on the weather, proverbs, and scraps of what had once been science but was now offered as occult wisdom. Other little books undertook to teach the ABCs or told how to behave in church; how to approach persons of the other sex; how to show respect for superiors; or how to compose a proper letter of love, thanks, or condolence, or have such a letter written by the professional letter writers to whose services illiterate persons resorted. Still others put into print the stories that had long circulated in the oral tradition, fairy tales, saints' lives, or accounts of outlaws such as Robin Hood. Miracles, prodigies, witches, ogres, angels, and the devil figured prominently in such narratives.

It is a curious fact that where educated persons were now schooled in Greek mythology and admired the heroes of ancient Rome, the plain people were still engrossed by tales of medieval chivalry, knights errant, and holy hermits that had once been told in baronial halls. Memories of the times of King Arthur and Charlemagne lingered in the popular consciousness. There were many long and complex tales of the exploits of Roland and other paladins who had fought for Christianity against the infidels, all set in a world of faraway adventure without definite location in time or place. Saracens, Moors, Turks, and Muslims, and at times Jews, were generally portrayed in such stories as menacing figures.

Belief in witchcraft and magic was to be found in 1600 in all social classes. The witches in *Macbeth* were perfectly believable to Shakespeare's audience. Learned books were still written on these subjects, and indeed it may be that learned writers and the judges in law courts had stirred up more anxiety about witches and magicians than ordinary people would otherwise have felt. By 1700 a great change was evident: witches, magicians, and miscellaneous enchantments were disappearing from the elite culture, but they still figured in the popular mind. Unaffected as yet by either science or doubt, most ordinary people inclined to think that there was something true about magic, which they distinguished as good and bad. Good magic unlocked the "secrets" of nature; popular writings on alchemy told of famous sages of the past who knew how to turn base metals into gold; there were special formulas that added to the efficacy of prayer. Some old women had a secret knowledge of medicinal herbs, in which indeed there might be some pragmatic value but which was blended with the mysterious and the occult. Bad magic was used to cause harm; it taught the black arts; it gave force to curses; it often involved a compact with the devil; it was what made witches so fearsome. By 1700 such ideas were subsiding. Judges no longer believed that such powers existed, and so would no longer preside at witchcraft trials. The same may be said of belief in prophecies and oracles: in the elite culture only those recorded in the Bible retained any credibility, but there was still a popular acceptance of recent prophecies and foretellings of the future.

Witchcraft and magic

Popular culture continued to express itself also in fairs and carnivals. For men and women who lived limited lives these were exciting events that occurred only at certain times of the year and to which people flocked from miles around. At the fairs one could buy things that local shops and wandering peddlers could not supply. There would be puppet shows, jugglers, and acrobats. There were conjurers who refused to admit like modern magicians that they were using merely natural means. A mountebank was someone who mounted a platform (*banco* in Italian) where he sold questionable remedies for various ills while keeping up a patter of jokes and stories, often accompanied by a clown. Blind singers and traveling musicians entertained the throngs, and for the tougher minded there were cockfights and bear baiting. In such a hubbub itinerant preachers might denounce the vanities of this world or throw doubt on the wisdom of bishops and lawyers.

Carnival went on for several weeks preceding Lent. The word itself, from the Italian *carne vale,* meant "farewell to meat," from which good Christians were to abstain during the 40-day Lenten fast; in France it climaxed in the Mardi Gras ("fat Tuesday"). It persisted in Protestant countries also. It was a time for big eating and heavy drinking and for general merrymaking and foolery. Comical processions marched through the streets. Farces were performed and mock sermons were delivered. Young men showed their strength in tugs-of-war, footraces,

Carnival

A CARNIVAL ON THE FEAST DAY OF SAINT GEORGE
by Pieter Bruegel, the Younger (Flemish, 1564–1638)
Carnivals broke the normal patterns of daily life in towns and villages throughout the early
modern era. This painting shows an early seventeenth-century carnival near the Flemish city
of Antwerp, but the games, eating, drinking, dancing, and banners were typical of the carni-
vals in almost every European village during this era.
(Christie's Images/Bridgeman Art Library)

and a rough-and-tumble kind of football. A common theme was what was called in
England "the world turned upside down." Men and women put on each other's clothing.
Horses were made to move backward with the rider facing the tail. Little street dramas
showed the servant giving orders to the master, the judge sitting in the stocks, the pupil
beating the teacher, or the husband holding the baby while the wife clutched a gun. In general, the carnival was a time for defying custom and ridiculing authority. It is hard to know
how much such outbursts were expressions of genuine resentments and how much they
were only a form of play. They could, indeed, be both.

In 1600 people of all classes took part in these festive activities. In the following century, as both the Protestant and the Catholic Reformations extended their influences, the
clergy undertook to purge such public events of what they considered excesses, and with
the growth of the state the civil authorities began to frown on them as incitements to sub-
version. By 1700 the people of elite culture, the wealthy, the fashionable, and the educated,

were more inclined to stay away or attended only as spectators to be amused at the simple pleasures of the common people. In the eighteenth century, as the various elites took to more formal manners and to neoclassicism in literature and the arts, the gulf between the elite and popular cultures widened. The clergy campaigned against necromancy and tried to restrain the faithful in the matter of pilgrimages and veneration of dubious local saints. As the medical profession developed, the popular healers and venders of nostrums were seen as charlatans and quacks. As scientific and other knowledge increased among educated elites, those who lacked such knowledge appeared to be simply superstitious or ignorant. It may be said both that the elites withdrew from the popular culture and that the people as a whole had not yet been brought into the pale of higher civilization. In any case, class distinctions became sharper than ever. But nothing ever stands still, and before the year 1800 there were persons in the elite culture who were beginning to "rediscover" the people, to collect ballads and fairy tales, and to lay a foundation for what in the nineteenth century was called "folklore."

32. THE GLOBAL ECONOMY OF THE EIGHTEENTH CENTURY

The opening of the Atlantic in the sixteenth century, it will be recalled, had reoriented Europe. In an age of oceanic communications western Europe became a center from which America, Asia, and Africa could all be reached. A global economy had been created. The first to profit from it had been the Portuguese and Spanish, and they retained their monopoly through most of the sixteenth century; but the decline of the Portuguese and Spanish paved the way for the triumph of the British, the French, and the Dutch. In the eighteenth century the outstanding economic development was the expansion of the global economy and the fact that Europe became incomparably wealthier than any other part of the world.

Commerce and Industry in the Eighteenth Century

The increase of wealth was brought about by the methods of commercial capitalism and handicraft industry. Though the Industrial Revolution in England is usually dated from 1760 or 1780, it was not until the nineteenth century that the use of steam engines and power-driven machinery, and the growth of large factories and great manufacturing cities, brought about the conditions of modern industrialism. The economic system of the eighteenth century, while it contained within itself the seeds of later industrialism, represented the flowering of the older merchant capitalism, domestic industry, and mercantilist government policies which had grown up since the sixteenth century.

Most people in the eighteenth century lived in the country. Agriculture was the greatest single industry and source of wealth. Cities remained small. London and Paris, the largest of Europe, each had a population of

Rural industry

600,000 or 700,000, but the next largest cities did not much exceed 200,000, and in all Europe at the time of the French Revolution in 1789 there were only 50 cities with as many as 50,000 people. Urbanization, however, was no sign of economic advancement. Spain, Italy, and even the Balkan peninsula, according to an estimate made in the 1780s, each had more large cities (over 50,000) than did Great Britain. Urbanization did not equate with industry because most industry was carried on in the country, by peasants and part-time agricultural workers who worked for the merchant capitalists of the towns. Thus, while it is true to say that most people still lived in the country, it would be false to say that their lives and labors were devoted to agriculture exclusively. One English estimate, made

Most people who were "engaged in manufactures" in eighteenth-century Europe still worked in their own rural homes. This engraving from the early 1780s shows three women at work in an Irish cottage, where they are spinning and winding thread while another woman prepares a meal and watches a child.

(SSPL/The Image Works)

in 1739, held that there were 4,250,000 persons "engaged in manufactures" in the British Isles, a figure that included women and children and comprised almost half the entire population. These people worked characteristically in their own cottages, employed as wage earners by merchant capitalists under the "domestic" system. Almost half of them were engaged in the weaving and processing of woolens. Others were in the copper, iron, lead, and tin manufactures; others in leather goods; much smaller were the paper, glass, porcelain, silk, and linen trades; and smallest of all, in 1739, was the manufacture of cotton cloth, which accounted for only about 100,000 workers. The list suggests the importance of nonagricultural occupations in the preindustrial age.

England, even with half its population engaged at least part of the time in manufactures, was not yet the unrivaled manufacturing country that it was to become after 1800. England in the eighteenth century produced no more iron than Russia and no more manufactures than France. The population of England was still small; it began to grow rapidly about 1760, but as late as 1800 France was still twice as populous as England and Scotland together. France, though less intensively developed than England, with probably far less than half its people "engaged in manufactures," nevertheless, because of its greater size, remained the chief industrial center of Europe.

Although foreign and colonial trade grew rapidly in the eighteenth century, it is probable that, in both Great Britain and France, the domestic or internal trade was greater in volume and occupied more people. Great Britain, with no internal tariffs, with an insignificant guild system, and with no monopolies allowed within the country except to inventors, was the largest area of internal free trade in Europe. France, or at least Colbert's Five Great Farms, offered an almost equal-sized free-trading internal market. A great deal of economic activity was therefore domestic, consisting of exchange between town and town or between region and region. The proportions between domestic and international trade cannot be known. But foreign trade was increasingly important for the largest business enterprises. International trade created the greatest commercial fortunes and the main accumulations of new capital. And it was the foreign trade that led to international rivalry and war.

The World Economy: The Dutch, British, and French

On the international economic scene a great part was still played by the Dutch. After the Peace of Utrecht the Dutch ceased to be a great political power; but their role in commerce, shipping, and finance remained undiminished, or diminished only when compared to the continuing commercial growth of France and Great Britain. They were still the middlemen and common carriers for other peoples. Their freight rates remained the lowest of Europe. They continued to grow rich on imports from the East Indies. To a large extent also, in the eighteenth century, the Dutch lived on their investments. The capital they had accumulated over 200 years they now lent out to French or British or other entrepreneurs. Dutch capital was to be found in every large commercial venture of Europe and was lent to governments far and wide. A third of the capital of the Bank of England in the mid–eighteenth century belonged to Dutch shareholders. The Bank of Amsterdam remained the chief clearinghouse and financial center of Europe. Its supremacy ended only with the invasion of Holland by a French Revolutionary army in 1795.

Trade

The Atlantic trade routes, leading to America, to Africa, and to Asia, attracted the merchants of many nationalities in Europe. A great many East India companies were established—usually to do business in America as well as the East, for the "Indies" at the beginning of the eighteenth century was still a general term for the vast regions overseas. Both the English and the French East India companies were reorganized, with an increased investment of capital, shortly after 1700. A number of others were established—by the Scots, the Swedes, the Danes, the imperial free city of Hamburg, the republic of Venice, Prussia, and the Austrian monarchy. But, with the exception of the Danish company that lasted some 60 years, they all failed after only a few years, either for insufficiency of capital or because they lacked strong diplomatic, military, and naval support. Their failure showed that, in the transocean trade, unassisted business enterprise was not enough. Merchants needed strong national backing to succeed in this sphere. Neither free city, nor small kingdom, nor tiny republic, nor the amorphous Austrian empire provided a firm enough base.

East India companies

It was the British and French who won out in the commercial rivalry of the eighteenth century. Britain and France were alike in having, besides a high level of industrial production at home, governments organized on a national scale and able to protect and advance, under mercantilist principles, the interests of their merchants in distant countries. For both peoples the eighteenth century—or the three-quarters of a century between the end of the War of the Spanish Succession in 1713 and the beginning of the French Revolution in 1789—was an age of spectacular enrichment and commercial expansion.

Commercial rivalry

Although the trade figures are difficult to arrive at, French foreign and colonial trade may well have grown even more rapidly than the British in the years between the 1720s and the 1780s. In any event, by the 1780s, the two countries were about equal in their total foreign and colonial trade. The British in the 1780s enjoyed proportionately more of the trade with America and Asia; the French, more of the trade with the rest of Europe and the Middle East. The contest for markets played an important part in the colonial and commercial wars between Britain and France all through the eighteenth century and on into the final and climactic struggle, and British triumph, in the time of Napoleon.

Asia, America, and Africa in the Global Economy

In the expanding global economy of the eighteenth century each continent played its special part. The European trade with Asia was subject to an ancient limitation. Asia was almost useless as a market for European manufactures. There was much that Europeans wanted from Asia but almost nothing that Asians wanted from Europe. The peoples of Chinese, Indian, and Malay culture had elaborate civilizations with which they were content; Asian elites in this era lacked the dynamic restlessness of European entrepreneurs, and the masses were so impoverished (more so even than in Europe) that they could buy nothing anyway. Europeans found that they could send little to Asia except gold. The trade of gold from Europe to Asia had gone on since ancient times, and even more gold and silver flowed to east Asia from European colonies in the Americas after the sixteenth century. Accumulating over time, the wealth from this trade became one source of the fabulous treasures of Eastern princes. To finance the swelling demand for Asian products it was necessary for Europeans constantly to replenish their stocks of gold. The British found an important new supply in Africa along the Gulf of Guinea, where one region (the present Ghana) was long called the Gold Coast. The word "guinea" became the name of a gold coin minted in England from 1663 to 1813 and long remained a fashionable way of saying 21 shillings.

Spices and Eastern manufactures

What Europeans sought from Asia was still in part spices—pepper and ginger, cinnamon and cloves—now brought in mainly by the Dutch from their East India islands. But they wanted manufactured goods also. Asia was still in some lines superior to Europe in technical skill. It is enough to mention rugs, chinaware, and cotton cloth. The very names by which cotton fabrics are known in English and other European languages reveal the places from which they were thought to come. "Madras" and "calico" refer to the Indian cities of Madras and Calicut; "muslin," to the Arabic city of Mosul. "Gingham" comes from a Malay word meaning "striped"; "chintz," from a Hindustani word meaning "spotted." Most of the Eastern manufactures were increasingly imitated in the eighteenth century in Europe. Axminster and Aubusson carpets competed with Oriental rugs. In 1709 a German named Boettcher discovered a formula for making a vitreous and translucent substance comparable to the porcelain of China; this European "china," made at Sèvres, Dresden, and in England, soon competed successfully with the imported original.

Cotton fabrics were never produced in Europe at a price to compete with India until after the introduction of power machinery, which began in England about 1780. Before that date the demand for Indian cotton goods was so heavy that the woolen, linen, and silk interests became alarmed. They could produce nothing like the sheer muslins and bright calico prints which caught the public fancy, and many governments, to protect the jobs and capital involved in the old European textile industries, simply forbade the import of Indian cottons altogether. But it was a time of many laws and little enforcement, the forbidden fabrics continued to come in, and Daniel Defoe observed in 1708 that, despite the laws, cottons were not only sought as clothing by all classes, but "crept into our houses, our closets and bedchambers; curtains, cushions, chairs and at last beds themselves were nothing but calicoes or Indian stuffs." Gradually, in the face of tariff protection for "infant industries" in Europe, and the rapid growth of European cotton manufactures, import of cottons and other manufactures from Asia declined. After about 1770 most of the imports of the British East India Company consisted of tea, which was brought from China.

The Americas, including the West Indies, bulked larger than Asia in the eighteenth-century trade of western Europe. The American trade was based mainly on one commodity—sugar. Sugar had long been known in the East, and in the European Middle Ages little bits of it had trickled through to delight the palates of lords and prelates. About 1650 sugar cane was brought in quantities from the East and planted in the West Indies by Europeans. A whole new economic system arose in a few decades. It was based on the "plantation." A plantation was an economic unit consisting of a considerable tract of land, a sizable investment of capital, often owned by absentees in France or England, and a force of impressed labor, supplied by black workers brought from Africa as slaves. Sugar, produced in quantity with cheap labor at low cost, proved to have an inexhaustible market.

Sugar and the plantation system

The eighteenth century was the golden age, economically speaking, of the West Indies. From its own islands alone, during the 80 years from 1713 to 1792, Great Britain imported a total of £162,000,000 worth of goods, almost all sugar; imports from India and China, in the same 80 years, amounted to only £104,000,000. The little islands of Jamaica, Barbados, St. Kitts, and others, as suppliers of Europe, not only dwarfed the whole mainland of British America but the whole mainland of Asia as well. For France, less well established than Britain on the American mainland and in Asia, the same holds with greater force. The richest of all the sugar colonies, Santo Domingo (now divided between Haiti and the Dominican Republic) belonged to France.

The plantation economy, first established in sugar and later in cotton (after 1800), brought Africa into the foreground. Slaves had been obtained from Black Africa from time immemorial, both by the Roman Empire and by the Muslim world, both of which, however, enslaved blacks and whites indiscriminately. After the European discovery of America, blacks were taken across the Atlantic by the Spanish and Portuguese. Dutch slavetraders also took them to Virginia in 1619, a year before the arrival of the Pilgrim Fathers in Massachusetts. But slavery in the Americas before 1650 may be described as occasional. With the rise of the plantation economy after 1650, and especially after 1700, it became a fundamental economic institution. Slavery now formed the labor supply of a very substantial and heavily capitalized branch of world production. About 610,000 blacks were landed from Africa in the island of Jamaica alone between 1700 and 1786. Total figures are hard to give, but it is certain that, until well after 1800, far more Africans than Europeans made the voyage to the Americas.

Slave trade

The transatlantic slave trade in the eighteenth century was conducted mainly by English-speaking interests, principally in England but also in New England, followed as closely as they could manage it by the French. Yearly export of merchandise from Great Britain to Africa, used chiefly in exchange for slaves, increased tenfold between 1713 and 1792. As for merchandise coming into Britain from the British West Indies, virtually all produced by slaves, in 1790 it constituted almost a fourth of all British imports. If we add British imports from the American mainland, including what after 1776 became the United

States, the importance of black labor to the British economic system will appear still greater, since a great part of exports from the mainland consisted of agricultural products, such as tobacco and indigo, produced partly by slaves. The rapid growth of trade within the British empire and the phenomenal rise of British capitalism in the eighteenth century were therefore based to a considerable extent on the enslavement of Africans. The town of Liverpool, an insignificant place on the Irish Sea in 1700, built itself up by the slave trade and the trade in slave-produced commodities to a busy transatlantic commercial center, which in turn, as will be seen later, stimulated the "industrial revolution" in Manchester and other neighboring towns.

Slavery and British capitalism

The west-European merchants, British, French, and Dutch, sold the products of America and Asia to their own peoples and those of central and eastern Europe. Trade with Germany and Italy was fairly stable. With Russia it enormously increased. To cite the British record only, Britain imported 15 times as much goods from Russia in 1790 as in 1700, and sold the Russians 6 times as much. The Russian landlords, as they became Europeanized, desired Western manufactures and the colonial products such as sugar, tobacco, and tea which could be purchased only from western Europeans. They had grain, timber, and naval stores to offer in return. Similarly, landlords of Poland and north Germany, in the seventeenth and eighteenth centuries, found themselves increasingly able to move their agricultural products out through the Baltic and hence increasingly able to buy the products of western Europe, America, and Asia in return. Landlords of eastern Europe thus had an incentive to make their estates more productive. "Big" agriculture spread, developing in eastern Europe a system not unlike the plantation economy of the New World. It had many effects. It contributed, along with political causes, to reducing the bulk of the east-European population to serfdom. It helped to bring western European culture to the upper classes of eastern Europe. And it helped to enrich the cities and merchants of western Europe.

The Wealth of Western Europe: Social Consequences

The wealth which accumulated along the Atlantic seaboard of Europe was, in short, by no means produced by the efforts of western Europeans only. All the world contributed to its formation. The natural resources of the Americas, the gold and people of Africa, the labor of enslaved workers on Caribbean islands, the resources and manufacturing skills of Asia, all alike went into producing the vastly increased volume of goods moving in world commerce. Europeans directed the movement. They supplied capital; they contributed technical and organizing abilities; and it was the demand of Europeans, at home in Europe and as traders abroad, that set increasing numbers of Indians to spinning cotton, Chinese to raising tea, Malays to gathering spices, and Africans to the tending of sugar cane. A few non-Europeans might benefit in the process—Indian or Chinese merchants "subsidized" by the East Indian companies, African chiefs who captured slaves from neighboring tribes and sold them to Europeans. But the profits of the world economy really went to Europe. The new wealth, over and above what was necessary to keep the far-flung and polyglot labor force in being, and to pay other expenses, piled up in Britain, Holland, and France.

Private property

Here it was owned by private persons. It accumulated within the system of private property and as part of the institutions of private enterprise or private capitalism. Governments were dependent on these private owners of property, for governments, in western Europe, had no important sources of revenue except loans and taxes derived from their peoples. When the owners of

The Earliest Known Illustration Showing An American Tobacco-Factory. From the HISTOIRE GENERALE DES ANTILLES, by Father Jean Baptiste Du Tertre, Paris, 1667-1671.

European traders and merchants gained much of their new wealth in the seventeenth and eighteenth centuries from commodities produced on plantations in the Americas and the Caribbean. This plantation economy depended on the labor of enslaved African workers such as the people in this seventeenth century illustration, who are preparing tobacco for export from one of the Caribbean islands.

(Rare Books and Manuscripts Division, New York Public Library, Astor, Lenox and Tilden Foundations)

wealth gave their support, the government was strong and successful, as in England. When they withdrew support, the government collapsed, as it was to collapse in France in the Revolution of 1789.

In a technical sense there were many "capitalists" in western Europe, persons who had a little savings which they used to buy a parcel of land or a loom or entrusted to some other person to invest at interest. And in a general sense the new wealth was widely distributed; the standard of living rose in western Europe in the eighteenth century. Tea, for example, which cost as much as £10 a pound when introduced into England about 1650, was an article of common consumption a hundred years later. But wealth used to produce more wealth, that is, capital, was owned or controlled in significant amounts by relatively few persons. In the eighteenth century some people became unprecedentedly rich (including some who started quite poor, for it was a time of open opportunity); the great intermediate layers of society became noticeably more comfortable; and the people at the bottom, such as the serfs of eastern Europe, the Irish peasantry, the dispossessed farm workers in England, the poorest peasants and workers of France, were worse off than they had been before. The poor continued to live in hovels. The prosperous created for themselves that pleasant, comfortable world of the eighteenth century that connoisseurs still admire, a world of well-ordered Georgian homes, closely cropped lawns and shrubs, furniture by Chippendale or à la Louis XV, coach-and-four, family portraits, high chandeliers, books bound in morocco, and a staff of servants "below stairs."

The merging of bourgeois and aristocratic wealth

Families enriched by commerce, and especially the daughters, mixed and intermarried with the old families who owned land. Women thus played an essential economic role in the carefully arranged marriages that both protected and increased the wealth of upper-class families. Landowners needed the capital that could be acquired through marriages with the daughters of wealthy traders; prosperous entrepreneurs sought the landed properties that might come into their families through marriages with women of the old aristocracy. But marriage was only one of the ways in which the old and new wealth of Europe came together. The merchant in England or France no sooner became prosperous than he bought himself a landed estate. In France he might also purchase a government office or patent of nobility. Contrariwise, the landowning gentleman, especially in England, no sooner increased his landed income than he invested the proceeds in commercial enterprise or government bonds. The two forms of property, bourgeois and aristocratic, tended to merge. Until toward the end of the century the various propertied interests worked harmoniously together, and the unpropertied classes, the vast majority, could influence the government only by riot and tumult. The eighteenth century, though an era of rapid commercial expansion, was on the whole an age of considerable social stability in western Europe. It was the upheavals of the French Revolution that would disrupt and transform much of the social and political order in European societies after 1789.

The foregoing might be illustrated from the lives of thousands of men and women. Two examples are enough, one English and one French. They show the working of the world economic system, the rise of the commercial class in western Europe, and the role of that class in the political life of the Western countries.

Thomas Pitt

Thomas Pitt, called "Diamond" Pitt, was born in 1653, the son of a parish clergyman in the Church of England. He went to India in 1674. Here he operated as an "interloper," trading in defiance of the legal monopoly of the East India Company. Returning to England, he was prosecuted by the company and fined £400 but was rich enough to buy the manor of Stratford and with it the borough of Old Sarum, a rotten borough which gave him a seat in the House of Commons without the trouble of an election. He soon returned to India, again as an interloper, where he competed so successfully with the company that it finally took him into its own employment. He traded on his own account, as well as for the company, sent back some new chintzes to England, and defended Madras against the local ruler of the Carnatic, the coastal area around Madras, buying him off with money. In 1702, though his salary was only £300 a year, he purchased a 410-carat uncut diamond for £20,400. He bought it from an Indian merchant who had himself bought it from an English skipper, who in turn had stolen it from the slave who had found it in the mines and who had concealed it in a wound in his leg. Back in Europe, Pitt had his diamond cut at Amsterdam and sold it in 1717 to the regent of France for £135,000. The regent put it in the French crown; it was appraised at the time of the French Revolution at £480,000. "Diamond" Pitt died in 1726. One of his daughters became the Countess of Stanhope and one of his sons became the Earl of Londonderry. Another son became father to the William Pitt who guided Britain through the

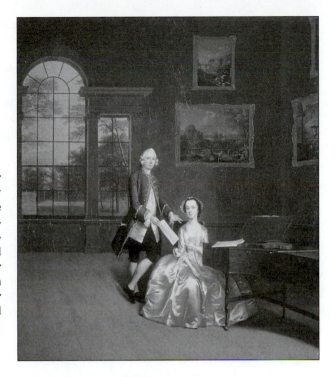

THE DUET
by Arthur Devis (English, 1711–1787)

The prosperity of the upper classes in eighteenth-century England supported the culture and comforts that are represented in this painting. Expanding global trade provided a pleasant, comfortable life for increasingly wealthy European elites and a new market for good furniture, fine art, and talented gardeners.
(Victoria & Albert Museum/Art Resource, NY)

Seven Years' War with France and who was raised to the peerage as the Earl of Chatham. After this Pitt the city of Pittsburgh was named, so that a fortune gained in the East gave its name to a frontier settlement in the interior of America. Chatham's younger son, the second William Pitt, became prime minister at 24. The younger Pitt guided Britain through its wars with revolutionary France and Napoleon, until his death in 1806 during the high tide of the Napoleonic empire.

Jean-Joseph Laborde

Jean-Joseph Laborde was born in 1724, of a bourgeois family of southern France. He went to work for an uncle who had a business at Bayonne trading with Spain and the East. From the profits he built up vast plantations and slaveholdings in Santo Domingo. His ships brought sugar to Europe and returned with prefabricated building materials, each piece carefully numbered, for his plantations and refineries in the West Indies. He became one of the leading bankers in Paris. His daughter became the Countess de Noailles. He himself received the title of marquis, which he did not use. He bought a number of manors and châteaux near Paris. As a real estate operator he developed that part of Paris, then suburban, now called the Chaussée d'Antin. During the Seven Years' War he was sent by the French government to borrow money in Spain, where he was told that Spain would lend nothing to Louis XV but would gladly lend him personally 20,000,000 reals. In the War of American Independence Laborde raised 12,000,000 livres in gold for the government to help pay the French army and navy, thus contributing to the success of the American Revolution. He acted as investment agent for Voltaire, gave 24,000 livres a year to charity, and subscribed 400,000 livres in 1788 toward building new hospitals in Paris. In July 1789 he helped to finance the insurrection which led to the fall of the Bastille and the Revolution. His son, in June 1789, took the Oath of the Tennis Court, swearing to write a constitution for France. He himself was guillotined in 1794. His children turned to scholarship and the arts.

33.   WESTERN EUROPE AFTER THE PEACE OF UTRECHT, 1713–1740

The Peace of Utrecht registered the defeat of French ambitions in the wars of Louis XIV. The French move toward "universal monarchy" had been blocked. The European state system had been preserved. Europe was to consist of independent and sovereign states, all legally free and equal, continuously entering or leaving alliances along the principles of the balance of power. The peace settlement of 1713–1714 placed the Bourbon Philip V on the Spanish throne but gave most of Spain's European possessions, outside Spain itself, to the Austrian Habsburgs (see maps, pp. 187, 313). Great Britain, which had been consolidated during the wars as a combined kingdom of England and Scotland, took Newfoundland, Nova Scotia, and the Hudson Bay region from France and, taking Gibraltar and Minorca from Spain, became a naval power in the Mediterranean. The British also received trading rights in Spanish America, thus enhancing their position as the most dynamic power in the rapidly developing transatlantic economic system.

Repairing the damages of war

Governments now turned to repairing the damages of war. Spain was somewhat rejuvenated by the French influence under its new Bourbon house. The drift and decadence that had set in under the last Habsburgs were at least halted. The Spanish monarchy was administratively strengthened. Its officials followed the absolutist government of Louis XIV as a model. The estates of the east-Spanish kingdoms, Aragon and Valencia, ceased to meet, going like the Estates General of France into the limbo of obsolete institutions. On the whole the French influence in eighteenth-century Spain was intangible. Nothing was changed in substance, but the old machinery functioned with more precision. Administrators were better trained and took a more constructive attitude toward government work; they became more aware of the world north of the Pyrenees and recovered confidence in their country's future. They tried also to tighten up the administration of their American empire. More revenue officers and coast guards were introduced in the Caribbean, whose zeal led to repeated clashes with smugglers, mainly British. Friction on the Spanish Main, reinforced by Spanish dislike for British occupation of Gibraltar, kept Spain and Britain in a continual ferment of potential hostility.

The Dutch after Utrecht receded from the political stage, though their alliance was always sought because of the huge shipping and financial resources they controlled. The Swiss also became important in banking and financial circles. The Belgians founded an overseas trading company in 1723 on the authority of their new Austrian ruler; this "Ostend Company" sent out six voyages to China, which were highly profitable, but the commercial jealousy of the Dutch and British obliged the Austrian emperor to withdraw his support, so that the enterprise soon came to an end. The Scots began at about this time to play their remarkable role of energizing business affairs in many countries. Union with England gave them access to the British empire and to the numerous commercial advantages won by the English. John Law, the financial wizard of France, was a Scot, as was William Paterson, one of the chief founders of the Bank of England.

France and Britain after 1713

Our main attention falls on Britain and France. Though one was the victor and the other the vanquished in the wars that ended in 1713, and though one stood for absolutism and the other for constitutionalism in government, their development in the years after Utrecht was in some ways surprisingly parallel. In both countries for some years the king was personally ineffective, and in both the various propertied interests therefore gained many advantages. Both enjoyed the commercial expansion described above. Both went through a short period of financial experimentation and frantic speculation in stocks, the bubble bursting in each case in 1720. Each was thereafter governed by a statesman, Cardinal Fleury in France and Robert Walpole in England, whose policy was to keep peace abroad and conciliate all interests at home. Fleury and Walpole held office for about two decades, toward the end of which the two countries again went to war. But the differences are at least as instructive as the parallels.

In France the new king was a child, Louis XV, the great-grandson of Louis XIV, and only five years old when his reign began in 1715. The government was entrusted to a regent, the Duke of Orleans, an elder cousin of the young king. Orleans, lacking the authority of a monarch, had to admit the aristocracy to a greater share of the power that nobles had lost during the long reign of Louis XIV. Most of the nobles had never liked the absolutist policies of Louis XIV, and there was much dissatisfaction with absolutism among all classes, because of the ruin and suffering brought by Louis XIV's wars.

The higher nobles, ousted by Louis XIV, now reappeared in the government. For a time Orleans worked through committees of noblemen, roughly corresponding to ministries, a system lauded by its backers as a revival of political freedom; but the committees proved so incompetent that they were soon abandoned. The old parlements of France, and especially *Aristocratic resurgence* the Parlement of Paris, which Louis XIV had reduced to silence, vigorously reasserted themselves after his death. The parlements were primarily law courts, originally composed of bourgeois judges. But Louis XIV and his predecessors, to raise money, had made the judgeships into offices to be sold; and they attached titles of nobility to increase the price. Hence in the time of the Regency the judges of the parlements had bought or inherited their seats and were almost all nobles. Because they had property rights in their offices, they could not be removed by the king. The Regent conceded much influence to the Parlement of Paris, utilizing it to modify the will of Louis XIV. The parlements broadened their position, claiming the right to assent to legislation and taxes, through refusing to enforce government measures that they considered contrary to the unwritten constitution or fundamental laws of France. They managed to exercise this right, off and on, from the days of the Regency until the great Revolution of 1789. The eighteenth century, for France, was a period of absolutism checked and balanced by organized privileged groups. It was an age of aristocratic resurgence, in which the nobles won back many of the powers that Louis XIV had taken from them.

In Great Britain the Parliament was very different from the French parlements, and the British aristocracy was more politically competent than the *noblesse* of France. Parliament proved an effective machine for the conduct of public business. The House of Lords was hereditary, with the large *The English Parliament* exception of the bishops, who were appointed by the government and made up about a quarter of the active members of the upper house. The House of Commons was not at all representative of the country according to modern ideas. Only the wealthy, or those patronized by the wealthy, could sit in it, and they were chosen by diverse and eccentric methods, in counties and towns, almost without regard to the size or wishes of the population. Some boroughs were owned outright, like the Old Sarum of the Pitt family. But through the machinations of bosses, or purchase of seats, all kinds of interests managed to get representatives into the Commons. Some members spoke for the "landed interest";

others for the "funded interest" (mainly government creditors); others for the "London interest," the "West India interest," the "East India interest," and others. All politically significant groups could expect to have their desires heeded in Parliament, and all therefore were willing to go through parliamentary channels. Parliament was corrupt, slow, and expensive, but it was effective. For Parliament was not only a roughly representative body; it had also acquired, in practice, the power to legislate.

Queen Anne, the last reigning Stuart, died in 1714. She was succeeded by George I, Elector of Hanover, as provided for by Parliament in the Act of Settlement of 1701. George I was the nearest relative of the Stuarts who was also a Protestant. A heavy middle-aged German who spoke no English, he continued to spend much of his time in Germany, and he brought with him to England a retinue of German ministers and mistresses. He was never popular in England, where he was regarded as at best a political convenience. He was in no position to play a strong hand in English public life, and during his reign Parliament gained considerable independence from the crown.

The main problem was still whether the principles of the Revolution of 1688 should be maintained. The agreement which had made that revolution relatively bloodless proved to be temporary. The Whigs, who considered the revolution as their work, long remained a minority made up of a few great landowning noblemen, wealthy London merchants, lesser businesspeople, and nonconformists in religion. The Whigs generally controlled the House of Lords, but the House of Commons was more uncertain; at the time of the Peace of Utrecht its majority was Tory. We have already noted the significance for English constitutional development of the conflict at that time between the prowar Whig majority in the House of Lords and the Tory majority in Commons and how the conflict was resolved to help establish the primacy of the House of Commons.

Whigs and Tories

After 1714 the two parties tended to dissolve, and the terms "Whig" and "Tory" ceased to have much definite meaning. In general the government, and the Anglican bishops who were close to the government, remained "Whig." Men who were remote from the central government, or suspicious of its activities, formed a kind of country party quite different from the earlier Tories. Gentry and yeomen of the shires and byways were easily aroused against the great noblemen and men of money who led the Whigs. In the established church the lesser clergy were sometimes critical of the Whig bishops. Outside the official church were a group of Anglican clergy who refused the oath of loyalty after 1688 and were called Non-Jurors; they kept alive a shadow church until 1805. In Scotland also, the ancestral home of the Stuarts, many were disaffected with the new regime.

Tories, Non-Jurors, and Scots made up a milieu after 1688 in which what would now be called counterrevolution might develop. Never enthusiastic for the "Whig wars" against France, critical of the mounting national debt which the wars created, distrustful of the business and moneyed interests, they began to look wistfully to the exiled Stuarts. After 1701, when James died in France, the Stuart claims devolved upon his son, who lived until 1766, scheming time and again to make himself king of England. His partisans were known as Jacobites, from *Jacobus,* the Latin for James. They claimed that he had a divine

"James III"

right to the monarchy and regarded him as "James III," whereas others called him the Pretender. The Jacobites felt that if he would give up his Catholic religion, he should be accepted as Britain's rightful king.

The Whigs could not tolerate a return of the Stuarts. The restoration of "James III" and his divine-right partisans would undo the principles of the Glorious Revolution—limited monarchy, constitutionalism, parliamentary supremacy, the rule of law, the toleration of dissenting Protestants, in short all that was summarized and defended in the political writings of John Locke. Moreover, those who held stock in the Bank of England or who had lent their money to the government would be ruined, since "James III" would surely repudiate a debt contracted by his foes. The Whigs were bound to support the Hanoverian George I. And George I was bound to look for support in a strange country among the Whigs.

George lacked personal appeal even for his English friends. To his enemies he was ridiculous and repulsive. The successful establishment of his dynasty would ruin the hopes of Tories and Jacobites. In 1715 the Pretender landed in Scotland, gathered followers from the Highlands, and proclaimed a rebellion against George I. Civil war seemed to threaten. But the Jacobite leaders bungled, and many of their followers proved to be undecided. They were willing enough to toast the "king over the water" in protest against the Whigs but not willing in a showdown to see the Stuarts, with all that went with them, again in possession of the crown of England. The Fifteen, as the revolt came to be called, petered out. But 30 years later came the Forty-five. In 1745, during war with France, the Pretender's son, "Bonnie Prince Charlie" or the "Young Pretender," again landed in Scotland and again proclaimed rebellion. This time, though almost no one in England rallied, the uprising was more successful. A Scottish force penetrated to within 80 miles of London and was driven back and crushed with the help of Hanoverian regiments rushed over from Germany. The government set out to destroy Jacobitism in the Scottish Highlands. The social system of the Highlands was wiped out, the clans were broken up, and their lands were forcibly reorganized according to modern notions of property and of landlord and tenant.

Threats of civil war

The Jacobite uprisings confirmed the old reputation of England in the eyes of Europe, namely, as Voltaire said, that its government was as stormy as the seas that surrounded it. To partisans of monarchy on the Continent they illustrated the weaknesses of parliamentary government. But their ignominious collapse actually strengthened the parliamentary regime in England. They left little permanent mark and soon passed into romantic legend.

The "Bubbles"

Meanwhile, immediately after the Peace of Utrecht, the problem of dealing with a large postwar government debt had to be faced in both England and France. Organized permanent public debt was new at the time. The possibilities and limitations of large-scale banking, paper money, and credit were not clearly seen. In France there was much amazement at the way in which England and Holland, though smaller and less wealthy than France, had been able to maximize their resources through banking and credit and even to finance the alliance which had eclipsed the Sun King. In addition there was much private demand for both lending and borrowing money. Private persons all over western Europe were looking for enterprises in which to invest their savings. And promoters and organizers, anticipating a profit in this or that line of business, were looking for capital with which to work. Out of this whole situation grew the "South Sea bubble" in England and the "Mississippi bubble" in France. Both bubbles broke in 1720, and both had important long-range effects.

A close tie between government finance and private enterprise was usual at the time, under mercantilist ideas of government guidance of trade. In England, for example, a good deal of the government debt was held by companies organized for that purpose. The government would charter a company, strengthen it with a monopoly in a given line of

Ties between government and private enterprise

business, and then receive from the company, after the stockholders had bought up the shares, a large sum of cash as a loan. Much of the British debt, contracted in the wars from 1689 to 1713, was held in this way by the Bank of England, founded in 1694; by the East India Company, reorganized in 1708 in such a way as to provide funds for the government; and by the South Sea Company, founded in 1711. The Bank enjoyed a legal monopoly over certain banking operations in London, the East India Company over trade with the East, the South Sea Company for exploiting the *asiento* and other commercial privileges extorted from Spain. The companies were owned by private investors. Savings drawn from trade and agriculture, put into shares in these companies, became available both for economic reinvestment and for use of the government in defraying the costs of war.

John Law

In 1716 the Prince Regent of France was attracted to a Scottish financier, John Law, reputedly by Law's remarkable mathematical system in gambling at cards. Law founded a much-needed French central bank. In the next year, 1717, he organized a *Compagnie d'Occident,* popularly called the Mississippi Company, which obtained a monopoly of trade with Louisiana, where it founded New Orleans in 1718. This company, under Law's management, soon absorbed the French East India, China, Senegal, and African companies. It now enjoyed a legal monopoly of all French colonial trade. Seeing this trade as a means to solve France's financial problems, the Regent authorized Law to assume the entire government debt. The Mississippi Company received from individuals their certificates of royal indebtedness or "bonds" and gave them shares of company stock in return. It proposed to pay dividends on these shares and to extinguish the debt from profits in the colonial trade and from a monopoly over the collection of all indirect taxes in France. The project carried with it a plan for drastic reform of the whole taxation system, to make taxes both more fair to the taxpayer and more lucrative to the government. Shares in the Mississippi Company were gobbled up by the public. There was a frenzy of speculation, a wild fear of not buying soon enough. Quotations rose to 18,000 livres a share. But the company rested only on unrealized projects. Shareholders began to fear for their money. They began to unload. The market broke sharply. Many found their life savings gone. Others lost ancestral estates on which they had borrowed in the hope of getting rich. Those, however, who had owned shares in the company before the rise, and who had resisted the speculative fever, lost nothing by the bursting of inflated prices and later enjoyed a gilt-edged commercial investment.

Much the same thing happened in England, where it was thought by many that Law was about to provide a panacea for France. The South Sea Company, outbidding the Bank of England, took over a large fraction of the public debt by receiving government "bonds" from their owners in return for shares of its stock. The size and speed of profits to be made in Spanish America were greatly exaggerated, and the market value of South Sea shares rose rapidly for a time, reaching £1,050 for a share of £100 par value. Other schemes abounded in the passion for easy money. Promoters organized mining and textile companies, as well as others of more fanciful or bolder design—a company to bring live fish to market in tanks, an insurance company to insure female chastity, a company "for an undertaking which shall in due time be revealed." Shares in such enterprises were snatched at mounting prices. But in September 1720 the South Sea stockholders began to sell, doubting whether operations would pay dividends commensurate to £1,000 a share. They dragged down the whole unstable structure. As in France, many people found that their savings or their inheritances had disappeared.

Indignation in both countries was extreme. Both governments were implicated in the scandal. John Law fled to Brussels. The Regent was discredited; he resigned in 1723, and French affairs were afterward conducted by Cardinal Fleury. In England there was a change of ministers. Robert Walpole, a country gentleman of Whig persuasion who had long sat in the Commons and who had warned against the South Sea scheme from the beginning, became the principal minister to George I.

Britain recovered from the crisis more successfully than France. Law's bank, a useful institution, was dissolved in the reaction against him, and France lacked an adequate banking system during the rest of the century. French investors developed a morbid fear of paper securities and a marked preference for putting their savings into land. Commercial capitalism and the growth of credit institutions in France were retarded. In England the same fears were felt. Parliament passed the "Bubble Act," forbidding all companies except those specifically chartered by the government to raise capital by the sale of stock. In both countries the development of joint-stock financing along the lines of the modern corporation was slowed down for over a century. Business enterprises continued to be typically owned by individuals and partnerships, which expanded by reinvestment of their own profits and so had another reason to keep profits up and wages down. But in England Walpole managed to save the South Sea Company, the East India Company, and the Bank, all of which were temporarily discredited in the eyes of the public. England continued to perfect its financial machinery.

The "Bubble Act"

The credit of the two governments was also shaken by the "bubbles." Much of the French war debt was repudiated in one way or another. Repudiation was in many cases morally justifiable, for many government creditors were unscrupulous war profiteers, but financially it was disastrous, for it discouraged honest people from lending their money to the state. Nor was much accomplished toward reform of the taxes. The nobles continued to evade taxes imposed on them by Louis XIV, John Law's plans for taxation evaporated with the rest of his project, and when in 1726 a finance minister tried to levy a two percent tax on all property, the vested interests, led by the Parlement of Paris, demolished this proposal also. Lacking an adequate revenue, and repudiating its debts, the French monarchy had little credit. The conception of the public or national debt hardly developed in France in the eighteenth century. The debt was considered to be the king's debt, for which no one except a few ministers felt any responsibility. The Bourbon government in fact often borrowed through the church, the Provincial Estates, or the city of Paris, which lenders considered to be better financial risks than the king himself. The government was severely handicapped in its foreign policy and its wars. It could not fully tap the wealth of its own subjects.

Credit and the National Debt

In England none of the debt was repudiated. Walpole managed to launch and keep going the system of the sinking fund, by which the government regularly set aside the wherewithal to pay interest and principal on its obligations. The credit of the British government became absolutely firm. The debt was considered a national debt, for which the British people themselves assumed the responsibility. Parliamentary government made this development possible. In France no one could tell what the king or his ministers might do, and hence the French were reluctant to trust them with their money. In England the people who had the money could also, through Parliament, determine the policies of state, decide what the money should be spent for, and levy enough taxes to maintain confidence in the debt. Similarities to France there were; the landowners who controlled the British Parliament, like those who controlled the Parlement of Paris, resisted direct taxation, so that the British government drew two-thirds or more of its revenues from indirect taxes

M. BACHELIER, DIRECTOR OF THE LYONS FARMS
by Jean-Baptiste Oudry (French, 1686–1755)
The "farms" of which M. Bachelier was a director were the semiprivate syndicates to which
the French monarchy delegated or farmed out the collection of its indirect taxes. Tax farmers
were generally hated, and many became very rich. Nothing is known of the man in this picture,
but with his huge wig, his lace cuffs, and his left hand politely extended, he typifies the ruling
elite at the close of the reign of Louis XIV.
(University of Michigan Museum of Art (1968/1.76))

paid by the mass of the population. Yet landowners, even dukes, did pay important amounts of taxes. There were no exemptions by class or rank, as in France. All propertied interests had a stake in the government. The wealth of the country stood behind the national debt. The national credit seemed inexhaustible. This was the supreme trump card of the British in their wars with France from the founding of the Bank of England in 1694 to the fall of Napoleon 120 years later. And it was the political freedom and power of Parliament that gave Britain's government its economic strength.

Fleury in France; Walpole in England

Fleury was 73 years old when he took office in 1726 and 90 when he left it. He was not one to initiate programs for the distant future. Louis XV, as he came of age, proved to be indolent and selfish. Public affairs drifted, while France grew privately more wealthy, especially the commercial and bourgeois classes. Walpole likewise kept out of controversies. His motto was *quieta non movere,* "let sleeping dogs lie." It was to win over the Tory squires to the Hanoverian and Whig regime that Walpole kept down the land taxes; this policy was successful, and Jacobitism quieted down. Walpole supported the Bank, the trading companies, and the financial interests, and they in turn supported him. It was a time of political calm, in which the lower classes were quiet and the upper classes were not quarreling, favorable therefore to the development of parliamentary institutions.

Walpole has been called the first prime minister and the architect of cabinet government, a system in which the prime minister and the ministers who head the cabinet departments are also members of the legislative body. He saw to it, by careful rigging, that a majority in the Commons always supported him. He avoided issues on which his majority might be lost. He thus began to acknowledge the principle of cabinet responsibility to a majority in Parliament, which was to become an important characteristic of cabinet government. And by selecting colleagues who agreed with him, and getting rid of those who did not, he advanced the idea of the cabinet as a body of ministers bound to each other and to the prime minister, obligated to follow the same policies and to stand or fall as a group. Thus Parliament was not only a representative or deliberative body, but also one that developed an effective executive organ, without which neither representative government nor any government could survive.

Cabinet government

To assure peace and quiet in domestic politics the best means was to avoid raising taxes. And the best way to avoid taxes was to avoid war. Fleury and Walpole both tried to keep at peace. They were not in the long run successful. Fleury was drawn into the War of the Polish Succession in 1733. Walpole kept England out of war until 1739. He always had a war party to contend with, and the most bellicose were those interested in the American trade—the slave trade, the sugar plantations, and the illicit sale of goods in the Spanish empire. The British official figures show that while trade with Europe in the eighteenth century was always less in war than in peace, trade with America always increased during war, except, indeed, during the War of American Independence.

In the 1730s there were constant complaints of indignities suffered by Britons on the Spanish Main. The war party produced a Captain Jenkins, who carried with him a small box containing a withered ear, which he said had been cut from his head by the outrageous Spaniards. Testifying in the House of Commons, where he "commended his soul to God and his cause to his country," he stirred up a commotion which led to war. So in 1739, after 25 years of peace, England plunged with wild enthusiasm into the War of Jenkins's Ear.

"They are ringing the bells now," said Walpole; "they will soon be wringing their hands." The war soon merged into a conflict involving Europeans and others in all parts of the world. European wars could no longer be contained within Europe. The global economic and colonial systems that produced the expanding global trade also produced a series of global wars in which the European powers extended their conflicts across all of the distant territories and seas they sought to control.

34.   THE GREAT WAR OF THE MID-EIGHTEENTH CENTURY: THE PEACE OF PARIS, 1763

The fighting lasted until 1763, with an uneasy interlude between 1748 and 1756. It went by many names. The opening hostilities between England and Spain were called, by the English, the War of Jenkins's Ear. The struggle on the Continent in the 1740s over the Habsburg inheritance was often known as the War of the Pragmatic Sanction. The Prussians spoke of the three "Silesian" wars. British colonials in America called the fighting of the 1740s King George's War, or used the term "French and Indian Wars," for the whole sporadic conflict. Disorganized and nameless struggles at the same time shook the peoples of India. Eventually these wars came to be called the War of the Austrian Succession (for hostilities between 1740 and 1748) and the Seven Years' War (for the conflicts between 1756 and 1763). The two wars were really one. They involved the same two principal issues: the global duel of Britain and France for colonies, trade, and sea power, and the European duel of Prussia and Austria for territory and military power in central Europe.

Eighteenth-Century Warfare

Warfare at the time was in a kind of classical phase, which strongly affected the development of events. It was somewhat slow, formal, elaborate, and indecisive. The enlisted ranks of armies and navies were filled with men considered economically useless, picked up by recruiting officers among unwary loungers in taverns or on the wharves. All governments protected their productive population, peasants, mechanics, and bourgeois, preferring to keep them at home, at work, and paying taxes. Soldiers became a class apart, enrolled for long terms, paid wages, professional in their outlook, and highly trained. They lived in barracks or great forts and were dressed in bright uniforms (like the British "redcoats"), which, since camouflage was unnecessary, they wore even in battle. Weapons were not powerful; infantry was predominant and was armed with the smooth-bore musket to which the bayonet could be attached. In war the troops depended on great supply depots built up beforehand, which were practically immovable with the transportation available, so that armies, at least in central and western Europe, rarely operated more than a few days' march from their bases. Soldiers fought methodically for pay. Generals hesitated to risk their troops, which took years to train and equip and were very expensive. Strategy took the form not of seeking out the enemy's main force to destroy it in battle but of maneuvering for advantages of position, applying a cumulative and subtle pressure somewhat as in a game of chess.

Little national feeling

There was little national feeling, or feeling of any kind. The Prussian army recruited half or more of its enlisted personnel outside Prussia; the British army was largely made up of Hanoverian or other German regiments; even the French army had German units incorporated in it. Deserters from one side were enlisted by the other. War was between governments, or between the oligarchies and aristocracies which governments represented, not between whole peoples. It was fought for power, prestige, or calculated practical interests, not for ideologies, moral principles, world conquest, national survival, or ways of life. Popular nationalism had developed farthest in England, where "Rule Britannia" and "God Save the King," both breathing a low opinion of foreigners, became popular songs during these mid-eighteenth-century wars.

Civilians were little affected, except in India or the American wilderness where European conditions did not prevail. In Europe, a government aspiring to conquer a neighboring province did not wish to ruin or antagonize it beforehand. The fact that the west-European struggle was largely naval kept it well outside civilian experience. Never had war been so harmless, certainly not in the religious wars of earlier times or in the national wars initiated later. This was one reason why governments went to war so lightly. On the other hand governments also withdrew from war much more readily than in later times. Their treasuries might be exhausted, their trained soldiers used up; only practical or rational questions were at stake; there was no war hysteria or pressure of mass opinion; the enemy of today might be the ally of tomorrow. Peace was almost as easy to make as war. Peace treaties were negotiated, not imposed. So the eighteenth century saw a series of wars and treaties and rearrangements of alliances, all arising over much the same issues and with exactly the same powers present at the end as at the beginning.

The War of the Austrian Succession, 1740–1748

The War of the Austrian Succession was started by the king of Prussia. Frederick II, or the "Great," was a young man of 28 when he became king in 1740. His youth had not been happy; he was temperamentally incompatible with his father. His tastes as a prince had run to playing the flute, corresponding with French authors, and writing prose and verse in the French language. His father, the sober, military-minded Frederick William I, thought him frivolous and effeminate and dealt with him so clumsily that at the age of 18 he tried to escape from the kingdom. Caught and brought back, he was forced to witness the execution, by his father's order, of the friend and companion who had shared in his attempted flight. Frederick changed as the years passed from a jaunty youth to an aged cynic, equally undeceived by himself, his friends, or his enemies, and seeing no reason to expect much from human nature. Though his greatest reputation was made as a soldier, he retained his literary interests all his life, became a historian of merit, and is perhaps of all modern monarchs the only one who would have a respectable standing if considered only as a writer. An unabashed freethinker, like many others of his day, he considered all religions ridiculous and laughed at the divine right of kings; but he would have no nonsense about the rights of the house of Brandenburg, and he took a solemn view of the majesty of the state.

Frederick II

Frederick lost no time in showing a boldness which his father would have surely dreaded. He decided to conquer Silesia, and on December 16, 1740, he invaded that province, a region adjoining Prussia, lying in the upper valley of the Oder, and belonging to the kingdom of Bohemia and hence to the Danubian empire of the Habsburgs (see map, p. 208, panel 3). The Pragmatic Sanction, a general agreement signed by the European powers, including Prussia, had stipulated that all domains of the Austrian Habsburgs should be inherited integrally by the new heiress, Maria Theresa. The issue was between law and force. Frederick in attacking Silesia could invoke nothing better than "reason of state," the welfare and expansion of the state of which he was ruler.

The young Frederick II of Prussia, who would later be called Frederick the Great, was more interested in music and literature than in the military and political tasks of a monarch—which he nevertheless pursued boldly after becoming king in 1740. This painting by Antoine Pesne portrays the "Crown Prince" in the year before he inherited the Prussian throne.
(Bettmann/CORBIS)

The Pragmatic Sanction was universally disregarded. All turned against Maria Theresa. Bavaria and Saxony put in claims. Spain, still hoping to revise the Peace of Utrecht, saw another chance to win back former Spanish holdings in Italy. The decisive intervention was that of France. It was the fate of France to be torn between ambitions on the European continent and ambitions on the sea and beyond the seas. Economic and commercial advantage might dictate concentration on the impending struggle with Britain. But the French nobles were less interested than the British aristocrats in commercial considerations. They were influential because they furnished practically all the army officers and diplomats. They saw in Austria the traditional enemy, in Europe the traditional field of valor, and in Belgium, which now belonged to the Austrians, the traditional object for annexation to France. Cardinal Fleury, much against his will and judgment, found himself forced into war against the Habsburgs.

Maria Theresa

Maria Theresa was at this time a young woman of 23. She proved to be one of the most capable rulers ever produced by the house of Habsburg. She bore 16 children, and set a model of conscientious family living at a time of much indifference to such matters among the upper classes. She was as devout and as earnest as Frederick of Prussia was irreligious and seemingly flip. She dominated her husband and her grown sons as she did her kingdoms and her duchies. With a good deal of practical sense, she reconstructed her empire without having any doctrinaire program, and she accomplished more in her methodical way than more brilliant contemporaries with more spectacular projects of reform.

Soon after Frederick invaded Silesia, she gave birth to her first son, the future emperor Joseph II, in March 1741. She was preoccupied at the same time by the political crisis. Her dominions were assailed by half a dozen outside powers and her two kingdoms of Hungary and Bohemia (both of which had accepted the Pragmatic Sanction) were waiting to see which way their advantage lay. She betook herself to Hungary to be crowned with the crown of St. Stephen—and to rally support. She made a carefully arranged and dramatic appearance before the Hungarian political elite, implored them to defend her, and swore to uphold the liberties of the Hungarian nobles and the separate constitution of the kingdom of Hungary. All Europe told how the young queen, by raising aloft the infant Joseph, who was to be heir to the throne, at a session of the Hungarian parliament, had thrown the dour Magyars into paroxysms of chivalrous resolve. The story was not quite true, but it is true that she made an eloquent address to the Magyars and that she took her baby with her and proudly exhibited him. The Hungarian magnates pledged their "blood and life" and delivered 100,000 soldiers.

The war, as it worked out in Europe, was reminiscent of the struggles of the time of Louis XIV, or even of the Thirty Years' War now a century in the past. It was, again, a kind of civil struggle within the Holy Roman Empire, in which a league of German princes banded together against the monarchy of Vienna. This time they included the new kingdom of Prussia. It was, again, a collision of Bourbons and Habsburgs, in which the French pursued their old policy of maintaining division in Germany by supporting the German princes against the Habsburgs. The basic aim of French policy, according to instructions given by the French foreign office to its ambassador in Vienna in 1725, was to keep the Empire divided, preventing the union of German powers into "one and the same body, which would in fact become formidable to all the other powers of Europe." This time France had Spain on its side. Maria Theresa was supported only by Britain and Holland, which subsidized her financially but had inadequate land forces. The Franco-German-Spanish combination was highly successful. In 1742 Maria Theresa, hard pressed, accepted the proposals of Frederick for a separate peace. She temporarily granted him Silesia, and he temporarily slipped out of the war which he had been the first to enter. The French and Bavarians moved into Bohemia and almost organized a puppet kingdom with the aid of Bohemian nobles. The French obtained the election of their Bavarian satellite as Holy Roman Emperor, Charles VII. In 1745 the French won the battle of Fontenoy in Belgium, the greatest battle of the war; they dominated Belgium, which neither the Dutch nor British were able to defend. In the same year they fomented the Jacobite rebellion in Scotland to weaken or overthrow the British monarch.

Parallels with past wars

But the situation overseas offset the situation in Europe. It was America that tilted the balance. The French fortress of Louisburg on Cape Breton Island was captured by an expedition of New Englanders in conjunction with the British navy. British warships drove French and Spanish shipping from the seas. The French West Indies were blockaded. The French government, in danger of losing the wealth and taxes drawn from the sugar and slave trades, announced its willingness to negotiate.

Peace was made at Aix-la-Chapelle in 1748. It was based on an Anglo-French agreement in which Maria Theresa was obliged to concur. Britain and France arranged their differences by a return to the prewar *status quo*. The British returned Louisburg despite the protests of the Americans and relaxed their stranglehold on the Caribbean. The French returned Madras, which they had captured, and gave up their hold on Belgium. The Atlantic powers recognized Frederick's annexation of Silesia and required Maria Theresa to cede some Italian duchies to a Spanish Bourbon. Belgium was returned to Maria Theresa at the insistence of Britain and the Dutch. She and her ministers were very dissatisfied. They would infinitely have preferred to lose Belgium and keep Silesia. They were required, in the interest of a European or even intercontinental balance of power, to give up Silesia and to hold Belgium for the benefit of the Dutch against the French.

Peace of Aix-la-Chapelle

MARIA THERESA AND HER FAMILY
by Martin van Meytens (Austrian, 1695–1770)

Maria Theresa had an imposing public image in her dual roles as Queen in the Austrian house of Habsburg and mother in a large household of 16 children. This portrait of the Queen with her husband and many of her children shows her devotion to family life as well as the power she exercised in governing her empire.

(Scala/Art Resource, NY)

The war had been more decisive than the few readjustments of the map seemed to show. It proved the weakness of the French position, straddled as it was between Europe and the overseas world. Maintaining a huge army for use in Europe, the French could not, like Britain, concentrate upon the sea. On the other hand, because they were vulnerable on the sea, they could not hold their gains in Europe or conquer Belgium. The Austrians, though bitter, had reason for satisfaction. The war had been a war to partition the Habsburg empire. The Habsburg empire still stood. Hungary had thrown in its lot with Vienna, a fact of much subsequent importance. Bohemia was won back. In 1745 Maria Theresa got her husband elected Holy Roman Emperor as Francis I, a position for which, as a woman, she could not qualify. But the loss of Silesia was momentous. Silesia was as populous as the Dutch Republic, heavily German, and industrially the most advanced region east of the Elbe. Prussia by acquiring it doubled its population and more than doubled its resources. Prussia with Silesia was unquestionably a great power. Since Austria was still a great power, there were henceforth two great powers in the vague world known as "Germany," a situation which came to be known as the German dualism. But the transfer of Silesia, which doubled the number of Germans ruled by the king of Prussia, made the Habsburg empire less German, more Slavic and Hungarian, more Danubian and international. Silesia was the keystone of Germany. Frederick was determined to hold it; Maria Theresa was determined to win it back. A new war was therefore foreseeable in central Europe. As for Britain and France, the peace of Aix-la-Chapelle was clearly only a truce.

The next years passed in a busy diplomacy, leading to what is known as the "reversal of alliances" and Diplomatic Revolution of 1756. The Austrians set themselves to checking the growth of Prussia. Maria Theresa's foreign minister, Count Kaunitz, perhaps the most artful diplomat of the century, concluded that the rise of Prussia had revolutionized the balance of power. Kaunitz, dramatically reversing traditional policy, proposed an alliance between Austria and France—between the Habsburgs and the Bourbons. He encouraged French aspirations for Belgium in return for French support in the destruction of Prussia. The overtures between Austria and France obliged Britain, Austria's former ally, to reconsider its position in Europe; the British had Hanover to protect and were favorably impressed by the Prussian army. An alliance of Great Britain and Prussia was concluded in January 1756. Meanwhile Kaunitz consummated his alliance with France. One consequence was to marry the future Louis XVI to one of Maria Theresa's daughters, Marie Antoinette, the "Austrian woman" of French Revolutionary fame. The Austrian alliance was never popular in France. Some French thought that the ruin of Prussia would only enhance the Austrian control of Germany and so undo the fundamental "Westphalia system." The French progressive thinkers, known as "philosophes," believed Austria to be priest-ridden and backward and were for ideological reasons admirers of the freethinking Frederick II. Dissatisfaction with its foreign policy was one reason for the growth of internal opposition to the Bourbon government.

The Diplomatic Revolution of 1756

In any case, when the Seven Years' War broke out in 1756, though it was a continuation of the preceding war in that Prussia fought Austria, and Britain fought France, the belligerents had all changed partners. Great Britain and Prussia were now allies, as were, more remarkably, the Bourbons and the Habsburgs. In addition, Austria had concluded a treaty with the Russian empire for the annihilation of Prussia.

The Seven Years' War, 1756–1763: In Europe and America

Although the Seven Years' War began in America, let us turn first to Europe, where the war was another war of "partition." As a league of powers had but recently attempted to partition the empire of Maria Theresa, and a generation before had in fact partitioned the empires of Sweden and Spain, so now Austria, Russia, and France set out to partition the newly created kingdom of Prussia. Their aim was to relegate the Hohenzollerns to the territory of Brandenburg. Even with Silesia, Prussia had less than 6,000,000 people; each of its three principal enemies had 20,000,000 or more. But war was less an affair of peoples

Schönbrunn Palace, near Vienna, was the great palace of the Austrian Habsburgs. It was planned to compete with the vast palace of their French Bourbon rivals, but the plan was never completed because Maria Theresa (1740–1780) thought that the building seen here was adequate for her needs.

(Kunsthistoriches Museum, Vienna)

Frederick's military triumphs

than of states and standing armies, and the Prussian state and Prussian army were the most efficient in Europe. Frederick fought brilliant campaigns, won victories as at Rossbach in 1757, moved rapidly along interior lines, and eluded, surprised, and reattacked the badly coordinated armies opposed to him. He proved himself the great military genius of his day. But genius was scarcely enough. Against three such powers, reinforced by Sweden and the German states, and with no ally except Great Britain (and Hanover) whose aid was almost entirely financial, the kingdom of Prussia by any reasonable estimate had no chance of survival. There were times when Frederick believed all to be lost, yet he went on fighting, and his strength of character in these years of adversity, as much as his ultimate triumph, later made him a hero and symbol for the Germans. His subjects, Junkers and even serfs, advanced in patriotic spirit under pressure. The coalition tended to fall apart. The French lacked enthusiasm; they were fighting Britain, the Austrian alliance was unpopular, and Kaunitz would not plainly promise them Belgium. The Russians found that the more they moved westward the more they alarmed their Austrian allies. Frederick was left to deal only with the implacable Austrians, for whom he was more than a match. By the peace of Hubertusburg in 1763 not only did he lose nothing but he also retained Silesia.

The Masters of the Cloth Guild
by **Rembrandt van Rijn** (Dutch, 1606–1669)
This painting was done on commission for the guild of "clothiers" in Amsterdam; these men are
the prosperous leaders of the guild.
(Rijksmuseum, Amsterdam)

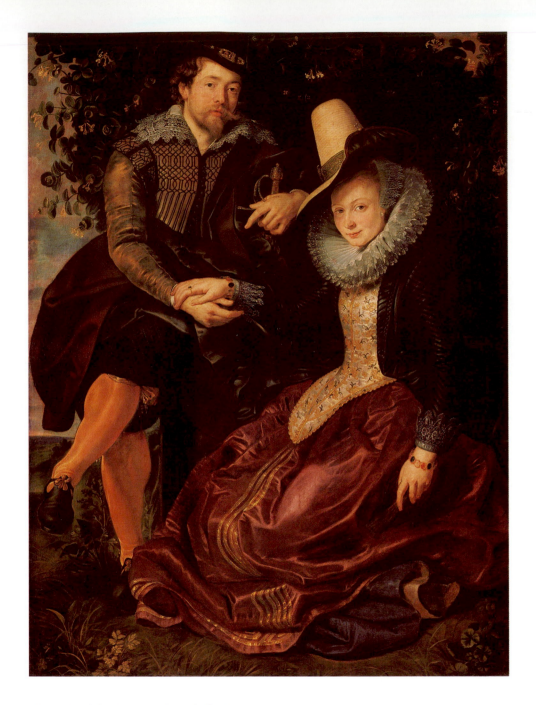

Portrait of the Artist with Isabelle Brant
by **Peter Paul Rubens** (Flemish, 1577–1640)
Isabelle Brant married Rubens about the time he painted this dual portrait, which conveys the affection in an early seventeenth-century marriage.
(Bayerische Staatsgemäldesammlungen. Alte Pinakothek, Munich, Kustdia-Archive ARTOTHEK, D-Peissenberg)

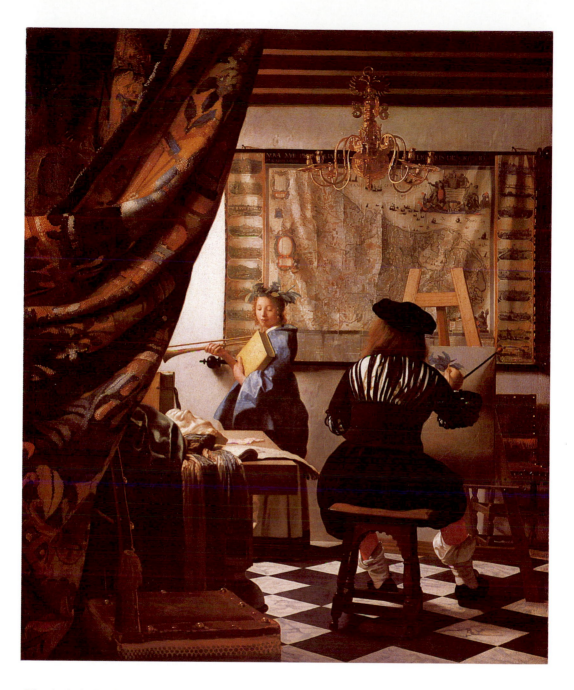

The Artist's Studio
by **Jan Vermeer** (Dutch, 1632–1675)
The shadings of light and the textures of cloth are joined with the mysteries of human character
in Vermeer's painting of the creative artist and his subject.
(Kunsthistorisches Museum, Vienna)

Old Woman Cooking Eggs
by **Diego Velásquez** (Spanish, 1559–1660)
Velásquez was best known for his portraits of people at the Spanish royal court, but he also portrayed the lives and character of the lower classes — as in this painting of an unknown woman preparing food.
(National Galleries of Scotland)

Self-Portrait
by **Elisabeth Vigée-Lebrun** (French, 1755–1842)
Vigée-Lebrun boldly represented her creative ambitions, looking directly toward the viewer and claiming her place in the mostly male world of eighteenth-century art.
(Scala/Art Resource, NY)

Mrs. Philip Thicknesse
by **Thomas Gainsborough** (English, 1727–1788)
Although eighteenth-century women could not enter politics, their role in the fine
arts became a theme in paintings such as Gainsborough's portrait of the fashionable
Mrs. Thicknesse.
(Cincinnati Art Museum, Bequest of Mary M. Emery)

A Woman of the Revolution
by **Jacques-Louis David** (French, 1748–1825)
David's portrait of a lower-class French woman in 1795 suggests the determination of the women
who joined the revolutionary Parisian crowds and clubs during the French Revolution.
(Giraudon/Art Resource, NY)

The Gleaners
by **Jean-François Millet** (French, 1814–1875)
Most French women still worked in the countryside during the nineteenth century, as Millet showed in this painting of poor peasants who gleaned the fields for a few stalks of grain.
(Art Resource, NY)

CHRONOLOGY OF NOTABLE EVENTS, 1619–1763

1619	First enslaved Africans arrive in Virginia
1720	The "Mississippi Bubble" in France and "South Sea Bubble" in Britain
1740–1748	War of Austrian Succession in Europe
1740–1780	Queen Maria Theresa rules and expands the Austrian Empire
1740–1786	Frederick II (the Great) rules and expands the kingdom of Prussia
1756–1763	The Seven Years' War; expansion of British power in India and America

For the rest, the Seven Years' War was a phase in the long dispute between France and Great Britain. Its stakes were supremacy in the growing world economy, control of colonies, and command of the sea. The two empires had been left unchanged in 1748 by the peace of Aix-la-Chapelle. Both held possessions in India, in the West Indies, and on the American mainland (see maps, pp. 187, 295). In India both British and French possessed only disconnected commercial establishments on the coast, infinitesimal specks on the giant body of India. Both also traded with China at Canton. Both occupied way stations on the route to Asia—the British in St. Helena and Ascension Island in the south Atlantic, the French in the more valuable islands of Mauritius and Reunion in the Indian Ocean. The French were active also on the coasts of Madagascar. The greatest way station, the Cape of Good Hope, belonged to the Dutch. In the West Indies the British plantations were mainly in Jamaica, Barbados, and some of the Leeward Islands; the French, in Santo Domingo, Guadeloupe, and Martinique. All were supported by the booming slave trade in Africa.

British and French colonial interests

On the American mainland the French had more territory and the British had more people. In the British colonies from Georgia to Nova Scotia lived perhaps two million Europeans, predominantly English but with strong infusions of Scots-Irish, Dutch, Germans, French, and Swedes. Philadelphia, with some 40,000 people, was as large as any city in England except London. The colonies in population bulked about a quarter as large as the mother country. But they were provincial, locally minded, and incapable of concerted action. In 1754 the British government called a congress at Albany in New York, hoping that the colonies would assume some collective responsibility for the coming war. The congress adopted an "Albany plan of union" drawn up by Benjamin Franklin, but the colonial legislatures declined to accept it, through fear of losing their separate identity. The colonials were willing, in a politically immature way, to rely on Britain for military action against France.

The French were still in possession of Louisburg on Cape Breton Island, a stronghold established by Louis XIV, located in the Gulf of St. Lawrence. It was designed for naval domination of the north Atlantic and to control access to the St. Lawrence River, the Great Lakes, and the vast region now called the Middle West. Through all this tract of country the French constantly came and went, but there were sizable French settlements only around New Orleans in the south and Quebec in the north. One source of French strength was that the French were more successful than the British in gaining the support of the Indians. This was probably because the French, being few in numbers, did not threaten to expropriate their lands and also because Catholics at this time were incomparably more active than Protestants in Christian missions among non-European peoples.

Both empires, French and British, were held together by mercantilist regulations framed mainly in the interest of the home countries. In some ways the British empire was more liberal than the French; it allowed local self-government and permitted immigration from all parts of Europe. In other ways the British system was stricter. British subjects, for example, were required by the Navigation Acts to use British ships and seamen—English, Scottish, or colonial—whereas the French were freer to use the transport services of other nations. British sugar planters had to ship raw sugar to the home country, there to be refined and sold to Europe, whereas French planters were free to refine their sugar in the islands. The mainland British colonials were forbidden to manufacture ironware and numerous other articles for sale; they were expected to buy such objects from England. Since the British sold little to the West Indies, where the slave population had no income with which to buy, the mainland colonies, though less valued as a source of wealth, were a far more important market for British goods. The colonials, though they had prospered under the restrictive system, were beginning to find much of it irksome at the time of the Seven Years' War, and indeed evaded it when they could.

Mercantilist regulations

Fighting was endemic even in the years of peace in Europe. Nova Scotia was a trouble spot. French in population, it had been annexed by Britain at the Peace of Utrecht. Its proximity to Louisburg made it a scene of perpetual agitation. The British government in 1755, foreseeing war with France, bodily removed about 7,000 of the mostly French-speaking inhabitants of Acadia, originally a French colony and part of Nova Scotia. Although they were dispersed throughout Britain's North American colonies, some of these displaced people eventually migrated to Louisiana and preserved a distinctive identity in the French Cajun culture that developed there. But the great disputed area was the Alleghenies. British colonials were beginning to feel their way westward through the mountains. French traders, soldiers, and empire builders were moving eastward toward the same mountains from points on the Mississippi and the Great Lakes. In 1749, at the request of Virginia and London capitalists, the British government chartered a land-exploitation company, the Ohio Company, to operate in territory claimed also by the French. The French built a fort at the point where the Ohio River is formed by the junction of two smaller rivers—Fort Duquesne, later called Pittsburgh. A force of colonials and British regular troops, under General Braddock, started through the wilderness to dislodge the French. It was defeated in July 1755, perhaps through its commander's unwillingness to take advice from the colonial officers, one of whom was George Washington.

A year later France and Britain declared war. The British were brilliantly led by William Pitt, subsequently the Earl of Chatham, a man of wide vision and superb confidence. "I know that I can save the country," he said, "and I know that no one else can." He concentrated British effort on the navy and colonies, while subsidizing Frederick of Prussia to fight in Europe, so that England, as he put it, might win an empire on the plains of Germany. Only the enormous financial credit of the British government made such a policy feasible. In 1758 British forces successfully took Fort Duquesne. Louisburg fell again in the same year. Gaining entry to the St. Lawrence, the British moved upstream to Quebec, and in 1759 a force under General Wolfe, stealthily scaling the heights, appeared by surprise on the Plains of Abraham outside the fortress, forcing the garrison to accept a battle, which the British won. With the fall of Quebec no further French resistance was possible on the American mainland. The British also, with superior naval power, occupied Guadeloupe and Martinique in the Caribbean and the French slave stations in Africa.

The Seven Years' War, 1756–1763: In India

Both British and French interests meanwhile profited from disturbed conditions in India. As large as Europe without Russia, India was a congested country of impoverished masses, speaking hundreds of languages and following many religions and subreligions, the two greatest being the Hindu and the Muslim. Waves of invasion through the northwest frontier since the Christian year A.D. 1001 had produced a Muslim empire, whose capital was at Delhi and which for a time held jurisdiction over most of the country. These Muslim emperors were known as Great Moguls. The greatest was Akbar, who ruled from 1556 to 1605, built roads, reformed the taxes, patronized the arts, and attempted to minimize religious differences among his peoples. The Muslim artistic culture flourished for a time after Akbar. One of his successors, Shah Jehan (1628–1658), built the beautiful Taj Mahal near Agra and at Delhi built the delicately carved alabaster palace of the Moguls, in which he placed the Peacock Throne made of solid gold and studded with gems.

But meanwhile there was restlessness among the Hindus. The Sikhs, who had originated in the fifteenth century as a reform movement in Hinduism, went to war with the Mogul emperor in the seventeenth century. They became one of the most ferociously warlike of Indian peoples. Hindu princes in central India meanwhile formed a "Mahratta confederacy" against the Muslim emperor at Delhi. Matters were made worse when Aurungzeb, the last significant Mogul emperor (1658–1707), adopted repressive measures against the Hindus. After Aurungzeb, India fell into political dissolution. Many of the modern princely states originated or became autonomous at this time. Hindu princes rebelled against the Mogul. Muslims, beginning as governors or commanders under the Mogul, set up as rulers in their own right. Thus originated Hyderabad, which included the fabulous diamond mines of Golconda and whose ruler long was called the wealthiest man in the world. Princes and would-be princes fought with each other and with the emperor. New Muslim invaders also poured across the northwest frontier. In 1739 a Persian force occupied Delhi, slaughtered 30,000 people, and departed with the Peacock Throne. Between 1747 and 1761 came a series of forays from Afghanistan, which again resulted in the looting of Delhi and the massacre of thousands.

Religious and political upheaval in India

The situation in India resembled, on a larger and more frightful scale, what had happened in Europe in the Holy Roman Empire, where irreconcilable religious differences (of Catholics and Protestants) had also torn the country asunder, ambitious princes and city-states had won a chaotic independence, and foreign armies appeared repeatedly as invaders. India, like central Europe, suffered chronically from war, intrigue, and rival pretensions to territory; and in India, as in the Holy Roman Empire, outsiders and ambitious insiders benefited together.

The instability and violence in the interior had repercussions on the Indian coasts. Here handfuls of Europeans were established in the coastal cities. By the troubles in the interior the Indian authorities along the coasts were reduced, so to speak, to a size and power with which the Europeans could deal. The Europeans—British and French—were agents of their respective East India companies. The companies built forts, maintained soldiers, coined money, and entered into treaties with surrounding Indian powers, under charter of their home governments and with no one to deny them the exercise of such sovereign rights. Agents of the companies, like Indians themselves, ignored or respected the Mogul emperor as suited their own purpose. They were, at first, only one of the many elements in the flux and reflux of Indian affairs. Their presence in India showed the international reach

The battle of Quebec, depicted here in an English illustration of the British army's surprise approach to the Plains of Abraham, allowed Britain to gain control over most of North America and to increase its power in the expanding, global system of eighteenth-century trade.
(Courtesy of the Director, National Army Museum, London)

of European companies, the worldwide competition between British and French interests, and the growing importance of India in the global economic system.

Intentions of the British and the French

Neither the British nor the French government, during the Seven Years' War, had any intention of territorial conquest in India, their policy in this respect differing radically from policy toward America. Nor were the two trading companies pushing their agents toward imperialistic political interventions. The company directors in London and Paris disapproved of fantastic schemes to intervene in Indian politics, insisted that their agents should attend to business only, and resented every penny and every sou not spent to bring in commercial profit. But it took a year or more to exchange messages between Europe and India, and company representatives in India, caught up in the Indian vortex and overcome by the chance to make personal fortunes or by dreams of empire, acted very much on their own, committing their home offices without compunction. Involvement in Indian affairs was not exactly new. We have seen how "Diamond" Pitt, in 1702, purchased the goodwill of the local ruler of the Carnatic when he threatened by military force to reduce the English traders at Madras to submission.

The first European to exploit the possibilities of the changing situation in mid-eighteenth-century India was the Frenchman Joseph-François Dupleix, who believed that the funds sent out by the company in Paris to finance the Indian trade were insufficient. His idea seems to have been not empire-building but to make the company into a local territorial power in order that, from taxes and other political revenues, it might have more capital for its commercial operations. In any case, during the years of peace in Europe after 1748, Dupleix found himself with about 2,000 French troops in the Carnatic. He lent them out to neighboring local rulers in return for territorial concessions. He also began to drill Indian soldiers by European methods, thereby creating the first regiments of "sepoys"—Indian troops who served in the military forces of the European companies. Following a program of backing claimants to various Indian thrones, he built up a clientele of local rulers under obligation to himself. He was very successful, for a few well-armed European troops or sepoys could overcome much larger, poorly armed Indian forces in pitched battle. But he was recalled to France in 1754, after the company became apprehensive of war with Britain and other trouble; and he died in disgrace.

When war came in 1756, British interests in India were advanced chiefly by Robert Clive. He had come to India many years before as a clerk for the East India Company but had shown military talents and an ability to comprehend Indian politics. He had maneuvered, with little success, against Dupleix in the Carnatic in the 1740s. In 1756, on hearing the news of war in Europe, he shifted his attention to Bengal, hoping to drive the French from their trading stations there. The French were favored in Bengal by the local Muslim ruler, Suraja Dowla, who proceeded to anticipate Clive's arrival by expelling the British from Calcutta. Capturing the city, he shut up 146 Englishmen in a small room without windows (soon known in England as the "Black Hole of Calcutta") and kept them there all night, during which most of them died of suffocation. Clive, soon appearing with a small force of British and sepoys, routed Suraja Dowla at the battle of Plassey in 1757. He put his own puppet on the Bengal throne and extorted huge reparations both for the company and for himself. Returning to England, he was received with mixed feelings; but he was given a new title (Baron Clive of Passy) and appointed the "governor" of Bengal. He strove in India to reduce the almost incredible corruption of company employees there, individuals normal enough but demoralized by irresistible chances for easy riches. Finally he committed suicide in 1774.

Robert Clive

It was British sea power, more fundamentally than Clive's tactics, that assured the triumph of British over French ambitions in the East. The British government still had no intention of conquest in India, but it could not see its East India Company forced out by agents of the French company in collaboration with Indian princes. Naval forces were therefore dispatched to the Indian Ocean, and they not only allowed Clive to shift from Madras to Calcutta at will but also gradually cut off the French posts in India from Europe and from each other. By the end of the war all the French establishments in India, as in Africa and America, were at the mercy of the British. The French overseas lay prostrate, and France itself was again detached from the overseas world on which much of its economy rested. In 1761 France made an alliance with Spain, which was alarmed for the safety of its own American empire after the British victories at Quebec and in the Caribbean. But the British also defeated Spain.

The Peace Settlement of 1763

The British armed forces had been spectacularly successful. Yet the peace treaty, signed at Paris in February 1763, five days before the Austro-Prussian peace of Hubertusburg, was by no means unfavorable to the defeated. The French Duke of Choiseul was a

Britain's imperial role in late eighteenth-century India is represented in this Indian miniature of a British officer's wife surrounded by Indian servants. The social hierarchies within the growing empire appear in this scene of domestic order and wealth, which dates from about 1785.
(Werner Forman Archive/Art Resource, NY)

French concessions

skillful and single-minded negotiator. The British, Pitt having fallen from office in 1761, were represented by a confused group of parliamentary favorites of the new king, George III. France ceded to Britain all French territory on the North American mainland east of the Mississippi. Canada thereby became British, and the colonials of the thirteen colonies were relieved of the French presence beyond the Alleghenies. To Spain, in return for aid in the last days of the war, France ceded all holdings west of the Mississippi and at its mouth. France thereby virtually abandoned the North American continent. But these almost empty regions were of minor commercial importance, and the French, in return for surrendering them, retained many economically more valuable establishments elsewhere. In the West Indies the British planters, and in England the powerful "West India interest," feared competition from the French sugar islands and wanted to exclude them from the protected economic system of

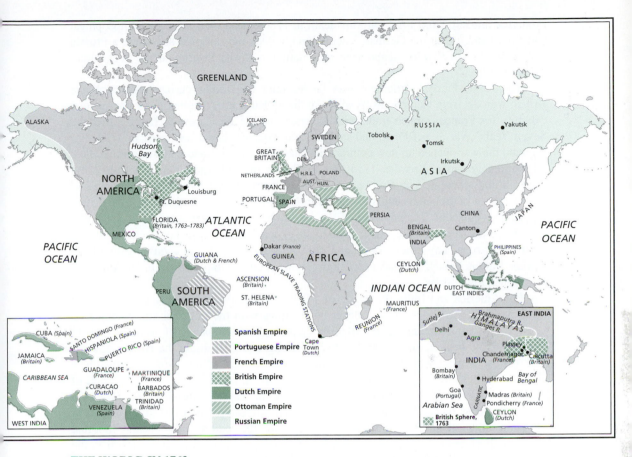

THE WORLD IN 1763

At the Peace of Paris of 1763 the British overseas empire trimphed over the French. The French ceded their holdings on the North American mainland east of the Mississippi to Britain, those west of the Mississippi to Spain. Britain also took Florida from Spain in 1763, but lost it, returning it to Spain in 1783, at the close of the War of American Independence. The French retained their sugar islands in the West Indies and their trading stations in India; they were stopped from empire-building but did not greatly suffer commercially from the Seven Years' War. The British proceeded to build their empire in India.

the British empire. France therefore received back Guadeloupe and Martinique, as well as most of its slave stations in Africa. In India, the French remained in possession of their commercial installations—offices, warehouses, and docks—at Pondicherry and other towns. They were forbidden to erect fortifications or pursue political ambitions among Indian princes—a practice which neither the French nor the British government had hitherto much favored in any case.

The treaties of Paris and Hubertusburg, closing the prolonged war of the mid-century, made the year 1763 a memorable turning point. Prussia was to remain a major power, which meant that the dualism of Germany would continue. Austria and Prussia eyed each other as rivals. Frederick's aggression of 1740 was legalized and even given a new moral status in Prussia by the heroic defense that had proved necessary to retain the plunder.

Frederick himself, from 1763 until his death in 1786, was a man of peace, philosophical and even benign. But the German crucible had boiled, and out of it had come a Prussia even more disposed by its escape from annihilation to glorify its army as the steel framework of its life.

The Anglo-French settlement was far-reaching and rather curious. Although the British won decisive victories everywhere in the global war, it resulted in no commercial calamity for France. French trade with America and the East grew as rapidly after the Seven Years' War as before it, and in 1785 was double what it had been in 1755. For England the war opened up new commercial channels. British trade with America and the East probably tripled between 1755 and 1785. But the outstanding British gains were imperial and strategic. The European balance of power was preserved, the French had been kept out of Belgium, British subjects in North America seemed secure, and Britain had again vindicated its command of the sea. British sea power implied, in turn, that British sea-borne commerce was safe in peace or war, while the seaborne commerce for the French, or of any others, depended ultimately on the political requirements of the British. But the French still had a few cards to play and were to play them in the American and French revolutions.

For America and India the peace of 1763 was decisive in pushing the peoples of these two vast territories toward closer connections with the political and commercial institutions of the British empire. America north of Mexico was to become part of an English-speaking world. In India the British government was drawn increasingly into a policy of territorial occupation; a British "paramount power" eventually emerged in place of the empire of the Moguls. British political rule in India stimulated and protected British business there, until in the greatest days of British prosperity India was one of the main pillars of the British economic system, and the road to India became in a real sense the lifeline of the British empire. But in 1763 this state of affairs was still in the future and was to be reached by many intermediate steps.

Repercussions of the settlement

For interactive exercises, glossary, chronologies, and more, go to the *Online Learning Center* at **www.mhhe.com/palmer10.**

Chapter 8

THE AGE
OF ENLIGHTENMENT

35. The Philosophes—
and Others

36. Enlightened Despotism:
France, Austria, Prussia

37. Enlightened Despotism:
Russia

38. The Partitions of Poland

39. New Stirrings: The British
Reform Movement

40. The American Revolution

The eighteenth century, or at least the years of that century preceding the French Revolution of 1789, is commonly known in European history as the Age of Enlightenment, and though that name raises some difficulties, still there is no other that describes so many features of the time so well. People strongly felt that theirs was an enlightened age, and it is from their own evaluation of themselves that our term Age of Enlightenment is derived. Everywhere there was a feeling that Europeans had at last emerged from a long twilight. The past was generally regarded as a time of barbarism and darkness. The sense of progress was all but universal among the educated classes. It was the belief both of the forward-looking thinkers and writers known as the philosophes and of the forward-looking monarchs, the "enlightened despots," together with their ministers and officials.

The leading ideas of the Enlightenment—optimistic beliefs in the historical advance of reason, science, education, social reform, tolerance, and enlightened government—have been constant themes in the modern world. The Enlightenment, in short, remains a dynamic tradition in cultural and political life. Intellectual debates since the eighteenth century have almost always returned, explicitly or implicitly, to questions about the validity and legacy of Enlightenment conceptions of truth, knowledge, and progress. The Enlightenment has often been challenged or condemned by influential cultural movements (for example, romanticism, postmodernism, religious revivals) and by modern political ideologies (for example, fascism, ethnic nationalisms). Yet the vehemence of its modern critics confirms the Enlightenment's exceptional, enduring importance in the cultures and politics of modern societies.

Eighteenth-century critiques of existing regimes and cultural traditions drew increasingly on the ideas of the Enlightenment; indeed, such ideas were contributing by

Chapter emblem: Detail from a portrait of Jean-Jacques Rousseau by Allan Ramsay (1713–1784).
(Giraudon/Art Resource, NY)

the end of the century to explosive political revolutions in America and Europe. In later centuries, Enlightenment ideas continued to generate opposition to unpopular governments or dominant cultural ideologies or hierarchical social systems, but the Enlightenment was also condemned in many cultures. For its advocates and critics alike, however, the "Age of Enlightenment" has always represented a decisive historical moment or force in the development of "modernity."

35.   THE PHILOSOPHES—AND OTHERS

The Spirit of Progress and Improvement

The spirit of the eighteenth-century Enlightenment was drawn from the scientific and intellectual revolution of the seventeenth century. The Enlightenment carried over and popularized the ideas of Bacon and Descartes, of Bayle and Spinoza, and, above all, of Locke and Newton. It carried over the philosophy of natural law and of natural right. There had never been an age in which Europeans were so skeptical toward tradition, so confident in the powers of human reason and of science, so firmly convinced of the regularity and harmony of nature, and so deeply imbued with the sense of civilization's advance and progress.

Faith in progress

The idea of progress has often been described as the dominant or characteristic idea of European civilization in the modern era, or since the late seventeenth century. It is a belief, a kind of nonreligious faith, that the conditions of human life become better as time goes on, that in general each generation is better off than its predecessors and will contribute by its labor to an even better life for generations to come, and that in the long run all humankind will share in the same advance. All the elements of this belief had been present by 1700. It was after 1700, however, that the idea of progress became explicit. In the seventeenth century it had shown itself in a more rudimentary way in the sporadic intellectual dispute in England and France known as the quarrel of Ancients and Moderns (which, as noted earlier, also became part of the challenge to official theorists in Louis XIV's academies). The Ancients held that the works of the Greeks and Romans had never been surpassed. The Moderns, pointing to science, art, literature, and invention, declared that their own time was the best, that it was natural for people of their time to do better than the ancients because they came later and built upon their predecessors' achievements. The quarrel was never exactly settled, but a great many people in 1700 were Moderns.

Far-reaching also was the faith of the age in the natural faculties of the human mind. Extreme skepticism, but not a skeptical outlook, was rejected. Nor were the educated, after 1700, likely to be superstitious, terrified by the unknown, or addicted to magic. The witchcraft mania abruptly died. Indeed all sense of the supernatural became dim for many Europeans. "Modern" people not only ceased to fear the devil but also to fear God. They thought of God less as a Father than as a First Cause of the physical universe. There was less sense of a personal God, or of the inscrutable imminence of divine Providence, or of the human need for saving grace. God was less the God of Love than the inconceivably intelligent Being who had made the amazing universe now discovered by human reason. The great symbol of the Christian God was the Cross, on which a divine being had suffered in human form. The symbol which occurred to people of scientific view was the Watchmaker. The intricacies of the physical universe were compared to the intricacies of a watch, and it was argued that just as a watch could not exist without a watchmaker, so the universe as discovered by Newton could not exist without a God who created it and set it moving by its mathematical laws. It was almighty intelligence that was thought divine.

Of course not everyone was primarily moved by such ideas. The first half of the eighteenth century was in fact also a time of continuing religious fervor. Isaac Watts wrote many hymns that are still familiar in English-speaking churches; the great church music of J. S. Bach was composed mainly in the 1720s; Handel's oratorio, *The Messiah,* was first performed in 1741; and it was at about this time that congregations first sang the *Adeste fideles* ("O Come, All Ye Faithful"), originally Catholic in inspiration but soon adopted by Protestants also. The Lutherans of Germany were stirred by the movement known as Pietism, which stressed the inner spiritual experience of ordinary persons as distinct from the doctrines taught and debated in theological faculties. The quest for an "inner light," or illumination of the soul rather than of the reason, was somewhat contrary to the main thrust of the Age of Enlightenment, and a religious urge for improvement of the individual rather than of social institutions was hardly central to the ideas of the age, but such ideas were by no means merely conservative, for they were in general highly critical of the existing order.

Religious fervor and Pietism

Within the Church of England John Wesley, while a student at Oxford, joined a group of like-minded young men for prayer and meditation. They engaged in good works to relieve the sufferings of prisoners and the poor, to whom they distributed food and clothing, while also teaching them how to read. Going outside the restrictive system of parishes, Wesley and others took to "itinerant" preaching, often to immense crowds in open fields. Wesley is said to have traveled 250,000 miles within Great Britain over a period of 50 years. He and George Whitfield, who shared his views, preached also in the English American colonies, where they helped to arouse the Great Awakening of the 1740s. Such movements had a democratizing effect in stressing individual worth and spiritual consciousness independently of the established religious authorities. Indeed, the spokesmen for older churches dismissed such movements as "enthusiasm," which was then a word of reproach. By the time he died in 1791, Wesley had about half a million followers in what were called Methodist societies. Wesley himself tried to keep them within the Church of England, but separate Methodist churches were already founded in England and the United States.

John Wesley and Methodism

In a way these expressions of religious feeling reflected differences between the popular and elite cultures that have already been described. While some of the elite joined in the new movements, it was on the whole the least comfortable classes who did so. The official churches, Anglican, Lutheran, Catholic, did not wish to be disturbed by religious revivalism. Bishops were cultivated gentlemen of the age. But the most vehement intellectual leaders pushed all churches aside.

The science and new learning in this "age of reason" did not end the popular interest in magic or mystification. A Swiss pastor, J. C. Lavater, attracted attention with his supposed science of "physiognomy," by which a person's character could be read in the play of the facial features. An Austrian physician, F. A. Mesmer, created a stir in Paris by arranging séances where people were touched by a wand, or sat in tubs, to receive "animal magnetism" in the hope of curing various ills. His "mesmerism" was an early stage in the discovery of hypnosis, but it is significant that a committee of the Royal Academy of Sciences, after investigation, concluded that Mesmer's own theories to explain these strange phenomena were without foundation.

Freemasonry

More in the mainstream was Freemasonry, which took form in England and soon spread to the Continent. The Masons were generally persons who held typical Enlightenment views, well disposed toward reason, progress, toleration, and humane reforms, and respectful toward God as architect of the universe; but they met secretly in lodges, in an atmosphere of mysterious rituals and occult knowledge. People of all walks of life, nobles, clergy, and middle classes, belonged to the lodges (a few also allowed women to join). Freemasonry thus had the effect of bringing persons of different social classes together, somewhat harmlessly for self-improvement and the improvement of others. It aroused suspicion, however, because of its secrecy; and a small deviant offshoot, the Illuminati of south Germany, was considered so dangerous that the Bavarian government suppressed it in 1786. There were later some who insisted that the French Revolution had been caused by a conspiracy of Illuminati, philosophes, and other clandestine plotters, but this idea was never any more than the belief of a few frightened conservative critics. The word *Illuminati* meant "the enlightened ones," but the notion of secrecy was foreign to the Enlightenment, which relied above all else on publicity and the reading public.

The Philosophes

Philosophe is simply French for philosopher, but to be "philosophical" in the eighteenth century meant to approach any subject in a critical and inquiring spirit. The French word is used in English to denote a group of writers who were not philosophers in the sense of treating ultimate questions of knowledge or existence. They were social or literary critics, popularizers, and publicists. Most philosophes were men, but many women also participated in Enlightenment culture. The French writer Emilie du Châtelet, for example, translated Newton and explained the significance of the new theories in her scientific essays. Though often learned, the philosophes wrote to gain attention, and it was through the philosophes that the ideas of the Enlightenment spread. Formerly authors had generally been persons of leisure, or talented protégés of aristocratic or royal patrons, or professors or clerics supported by the income from religious foundations. In the Age of Enlightenment a great many were freelancers, grub-streeters, or journalists. They wrote for "the publick."

The reading public

The reading public had greatly expanded; by the 1780s in France, literacy rates had risen to 47 percent among men and 27 percent among women. The educated middle class, commercial and professional, was much larger than ever before. Women readers formed a growing audience for novels and literary journals, country gentlemen sought new scientific advice on agriculture, and even noblemen wished to keep informed. Newspapers and magazines multiplied, and people who could not read them at home could read them in coffeehouses or in reading rooms organized for that purpose. There was a great demand also for dictionaries, encyclopedias, and surveys of all fields of knowledge. The new readers wanted matters made interesting and clear. They appreciated wit and lightness of touch. From such a public, literature itself greatly benefited.

The style of the eighteenth century became admirably fluent, clear, and exact, neither ponderous on the one hand nor frothy on the other. And from writings of this kind the readers benefited also, from the interior of Europe to the America of Benjamin Franklin. People began to talk of "public opinion" as a kind of critical tribunal that judged the significance of new books and established or destroyed the reputations of ambitious authors. This new public opinion, the French writer Malesherbes explained, was an independent social force "that all powers respect, that appreciates all talents, that pronounces on all people of merit." Critical reviews of literature, art, and music provoked debates in newspapers, journals, and coffeehouses, all of which contributed to an expanding public sphere beyond the personal world of private households and outside the official world of government institutions. The bourgeois middle class was becoming not only educated but also thoughtful and critical. But the movement was not a class movement only.

There was another way in which writings of the day were affected by social conditions. They were all written under censorship. The theory of censorship was to protect people from harmful ideas as they were protected from shoddy merchandise or dishonest weights and measures. In England the censorship was so mild as to have little effect. Other countries, such as Spain, had a powerful censorship. France, the center of the Enlightenment, had both a complicated censorship and a large reading and writing public. The church, the Parlement of Paris, the royal officials, and the printers' guilds all had a hand in the censoring of books. French censorship, however, was loosely administered, and after 1750 writers were little disturbed by it. It cannot be compared to censorship in some countries in the twentieth century. Yet in one way it had an unfavorable effect on French thought and letters. It discouraged writers from openly or explicitly addressing concrete public questions. Legally forbidden to criticize church or state, they threw their criticisms on an abstract level. Barred from attacking matters in particular, they tended to attack matters in general. Or they talked of the customs of the Persians and the Iroquois but not the French. Their works became full of double meanings, sly digs, innuendoes, and jokes by which authors, if questioned, could declare that they did not mean what all the world knew they did mean. As for readers, they developed a taste for forbidden books, which were always easy enough to obtain through illicit channels and foreign booksellers.

Censorship

Paris was the heart of the movement. Here, in the town houses of the well-to-do, literary and social celebrities gathered for literate conversation. It might occasionally happen that a notable philosophe was also wealthy; such was the case of Helvétius, who not only wrote books *On the Mind* and *On Man* but also gave grand entertainments at which such matters were discussed. Mainly, however, this mingling of people and ideas went on in salons conducted by women who became famous as hostesses, or salonnières, and who played a crucial mediating role in what came to be called the "Republic of Letters." Madame de Geoffrin, for example, for a period of 25 years beginning about 1750, organized conversations of artists and writers at dinner, sometimes helped them financially, and introduced them to persons of influence in high society or in government. She welcomed visiting foreigners also, such as Horace Walpole and David Hume from England and young Stanislas Poniatowski before he became king of Poland. Since other women held similar salons, philosophes and other writers had frequent opportunity to meet and exchange ideas.

Paris: the heart of the Enlightenment

Salons became well-organized meeting places at which authors introduced new works to critical readers, salonnières read letters from travelers or distant correspondents, and lively conversation spread the reputations of aspiring philosophes. The leading salonnières gave careful attention to the intellectual themes and social continuities of their salons. Suzanne Necker, whose salon met on Friday afternoons during the 1770s and 1780s, prepared for her weekly conversations by listing in her journal the ideas and books that she wanted to discuss. Julie de Lespinasse provided opportunities for almost constant discussion at her Parisian home, where she received visitors every evening of the week for 12 years. "Her great art," wrote one admirer, "was to show to advantage the minds of others, and she enjoyed doing that more than revealing her own." Salons and salonnières promoted the ideals of a cosmopolitan Republic of Letters in which talent and creativity counted for more than noble lineage; and though women lost much of their cultural influence after the 1780s, some salons of this kind survived the Revolution. In 1795, after the Terror, the widows of two eminent philosophes, Helvétius and Condorcet, opened or reopened their salons in Paris for people of moderate republican or liberal sentiments. Sophie Condorcet became a writer herself and a translator of Adam Smith. Her salon remained a center of liberal opposition during the years of Napoleon. More short-lived was the salon of the even more famous Germaine de Staël, who also wrote widely read books and who, among her many other ideas, deplored the subordination of women that the Revolution had done little to change. In these post-Revolutionary salons much of the French liberalism of the nineteenth century was born.

Diderot's Encyclopédie

In Paris also, in the mid–eighteenth century, the most serious of all philosophe enterprises, the *Encyclopédie,* was published in 17 large volumes and completed over the years 1751 to 1772. Edited by Denis Diderot, it was a great compendium of scientific, technical, and historical knowledge, carrying a strong undertone of criticism of existing society and institutions and epitomizing the skeptical, rational, and scientific spirit of the age. It was not the first encyclopedia, but it was the first to have a distinguished list of contributors or to be conceived as a positive force for social progress. Virtually all the French philosophes contributed—Voltaire, Montesquieu, Rousseau, d'Alembert (who assisted in the editing), Buffon, Turgot, Quesnay, and many others, all sometimes collectively called the Encyclopedists. Although edited in Paris, the *Encyclopédie* became very widely known and read. About 25,000 multivolumed sets were sold before the Revolution, about half of them outside France, since French had become an international language understood by educated persons all over Europe. Within France itself the *Encyclopédie* was read in all parts of the country and in the most influential ranks of society. At Besançon, for example, a city of about 28,000 inhabitants, 137 sets were sold to local residents, of whom 15 were members of the clergy, 53 were of the nobility, and 69 were lawyers, doctors, merchants, government officials, or others of what was called the Third Estate. The privileged groups of whom the Encyclopedists were the most critical, that is, the clergy and the nobility, read it or at least purchased it far out of proportion to their numbers in the population as a whole.

Men and women who considered themselves philosophes, or close to the philosophes in spirit, were found all over Europe. Frederick the Great was an eminent philosophe; not only was he the friend of Voltaire and host to a circle of literary and scientific men at Potsdam, but he also wrote epigrams, satires, dissertations, and histories, as well as works on military science; and he had a gift of wit, a sharp tongue, and a certain impishness toward the traditional and the pompous. Catherine the Great, empress of Russia, was also a philosophe for much the same reason. Maria Theresa, of Austria, was not a philosophe; she was too religious and too little concerned with general ideas. Her son Joseph, on the other hand, as we shall see, proved to be virtually a philosophe enthroned. In England Bishop Warburton was considered by some of his friends as a philosophe; he held that the Church of England of his day, as a social institution, was exactly what pure reason would have invented. The Scottish skeptical philosopher David Hume counted as a philosophe, as did Edward Gibbon, who shocked the pious by his attacks on Christianity in his famous *Decline and Fall of the Roman Empire*. Dr. Samuel Johnson was not a philosophe, though he was best known for a typical eighteenth-century project—the compilation of a new dictionary of the English language. Johnson worried over the supernatural, adhered to the

The salon of Madame de Geoffrin, depicted here by the artist Lemonnier, became one of the best-known meeting places for writers and artists in mid-eighteenth-century Paris. This imagined scene of an author reading from his work was painted early in the following century, but it shows the cultural reputation of famous salons and salonnières.
(Réunion des Musées Nationaux/Art Resource, NY)

established church, deflated pretentious authors, and even declared that Voltaire and Rousseau were evil men who should be sent "to the plantations." There were also Italian and German philosophes, like the Marquis di Beccaria, who sought to humanize the criminal law, or Baron Grimm, who sent a literary newsletter from Paris to his many subscribers.

Montesquieu, Voltaire, and Rousseau

Most famous of all philosophes were the French trio, Montesquieu (1689–1755), Voltaire (1694–1778), and Rousseau (1712–1778). They differed vehemently with each other. All were hailed as literary geniuses in their own day. All turned from pure literature to works of political commentary and social analysis. All thought that the existing state of society could be improved.

Montesquieu, twice a baron, was a landed aristocrat, a seigneur or manorial lord of southern France. He inherited from his uncle a seat in the Parlement of Bordeaux and sat actively in that parlement after the death of Louis XIV. He was part of the noble resurgence that began about 1715 and continued on through the eighteenth century. Although he shared many of the ideas in the stream of aristocratic and antiabsolutist thought, he went beyond a mere self-centered class philosophy. In his great work, *The Spirit of*

This portrait of Voltaire (c. 1736) by Maurice-Quentin de La Tour suggests the playful, ironic style that made his works accessible and popular, even when he was attacking religious persecutions or the suppression of controversial ideas. (Réunion des Musées Nationaux/Art Resource, NY)

Montesquieu's The Spirit of Laws

Laws, published in 1748, he developed two principal ideas. One was that forms of government varied according to climate and circumstances, for example, that despotism was suited only to large empires in hot climates, and that democracy would work only in small city-states. His other great doctrine, aimed against royal absolutism in France (which he called "despotism"), was the separation and balance of powers. In France he believed that power should be divided between the king and a great many "intermediate bodies"—parlements, provincial estates, organized nobility, chartered towns, and even the church. His position as a judge in parlement, a provincial, and a nobleman gave him good reasons to favor the first three, and his work in Bordeaux helped him to recognize the importance of the bourgeoisie in French towns; as for the church, he observed that, while he took no stock in its teachings, he thought it useful as a barrier to undue centralization of government. He greatly admired the English constitution as he understood it, believing that England carried over, more successfully than any other country, the feudal liberties of the early Middle Ages. He thought that in England the necessary separation and balance of powers was obtained by an ingenious mixture of monarchy, aristocracy, and democracy (king, lords, and commons) and by a separation of the functions of the executive, legislature, and judiciary. This doctrine had a wide influence and was well known to the Americans who in 1787 wrote the Constitution of the United States. Montesquieu's own philosophe friends thought him too conservative and even tried to dissuade him from publishing his ideas. He was, indeed, technically a reactionary, favoring a scheme of things that antedated Louis XIV, and he was unusual among contemporaries in his admiration of the "barbarous" Middle Ages.

Voltaire

Voltaire was born in 1694 into a comfortable bourgeois family and christened François-Marie Arouet; "Voltaire," an invented name, is simply the most famous of all pen names. Until he was over 40 he was known only as a clever writer of epigrams, tragedies in verse, and an epic. Thereafter he turned increasingly to philosophical and public questions. His strength throughout lay in the facility of his pen. He is the easiest of all great writers to read. He was always trenchant, logical, and incisive, sometimes scurrilous; mocking and sarcastic when he wished, equally a master of deft irony and of withering ridicule. However serious in his purpose, he achieved it by getting his readers to laugh.

In his youth Voltaire spent 11 months in the Bastille for what was considered to be impertinence to the Regent, who, however, in the next year rewarded him with a pension for one of his dramas. He was again arrested after a fracas with a nobleman, the Chevalier de Rohan. He remained an incorrigible bourgeois, while never deeply objecting to the aristocracy on principle. Through his admirer Mme. de Pompadour (another bourgeois, though the king's favorite) he became a gentleman of the bedchamber and royal historian to Louis XV. These functions he fulfilled *in absentia,* when at all, for Paris and Versailles were too unsafe for him. He was the personal friend of Frederick the Great, in whose household he lived for about two years at Potsdam. The two finally quarreled, for no stage was big enough to hold two such prima donnas for long. Voltaire made a fortune from his writings, pensions, speculations, and practical business sense. In his later years he purchased a manor at Ferney near the Swiss frontier. Here he became, as he said, the "hotel keeper of Europe," receiving the streams of distinguished admirers, favor hunters, and distressed persons who came to seek him out. He died at Paris in 1778, at the age of 84, by far the most famous man of letters in Europe. His collected writings fill over 70 volumes.

Voltaire was mainly interested in the freedom of thought. Like Montesquieu, he was an admirer of England. He spent three years in that country, where, in 1727, he witnessed the state funeral accorded to Sir Isaac Newton and his burial in Westminster Abbey. Voltaire's *Philosophical Letters on the English* (1733) and *Elements of the Philosophy of Newton* (1738) not only brought England increasingly before the consciousness of the rest of Europe but also popularized the new scientific ideas—the inductive philosophy of Bacon, the physics of Newton, and the psychology of Locke, whose doctrine that all true ideas arose from sense experience undercut the authority of religious belief. What Voltaire mainly admired in England was its religious liberty, its tolerance for diverse ideas and scientific inquiry, its relative freedom of the press, and its respect for men of letters like himself. Political liberty concerned him much less than it did Montesquieu. Louis XIV, a villain for Montesquieu and the neoaristocratic school, was a hero for Voltaire, who wrote a laudatory *Age of Louis XIV* (1751) praising the Sun King for the splendor of art and literature in his reign. Voltaire likewise continued to esteem Frederick the Great, though he quarreled with him personally. Frederick was in fact almost his ideal of the enlightened ruler, a man who sponsored the arts and sciences, recognized no religious authority, and granted toleration to all creeds, welcoming Protestants and Catholics on equal terms if only they would be socially useful.

After about 1740 Voltaire became more definitely the crusader, preaching the cause of religious toleration. He fought to clear the memory of Jean Calas, a Protestant put to death on the charge of murdering a son to prevent his conversion to Rome. He wrote also to exonerate a youth named La Barre, who had been executed for defiling a wayside cross. *Écrasez l'infâme!* became the famous Voltairean war cry—"crush the infamous thing!" The *infâme* for him was bigotry, intolerance, and superstition and behind these the power of an organized clergy. He assaulted not only the Catholic church but the whole traditional Christian view of the world as well. He argued for "natural religion" and "natural morality," holding that belief in God and the difference between good and evil arose from reason itself. This doctrine had in fact long been taught by the Catholic church. But Voltaire insisted that no supernatural revelation in addition to reason was desirable or necessary; belief in a special supernatural revelation, he argued, made people intolerant, stupid, and cruel.

Voltaire was also the first to present a purely secular conception of world history. In his *Essai sur les moeurs,* or "Universal History," he began with ancient China and surveyed the great civilizations in turn. Earlier writers of world history had put human events within a Christian framework. Following the Bible, they began with the Creation, proceeded to the Fall, recounted the rise of Israel, and so on. Voltaire put Judeo-Christian history within a much broader world history and placed religious thought in a sociological framework. He represented Christianity and all other organized religions as social phenomena or mere human inventions. Spinoza had said as much; Voltaire spread these ideas through Europe.

Voltaire on politics

In matters of politics and self-government Voltaire was neither a liberal nor a democrat. His opinion of the human race was about as low as his friend Frederick's. If only a government was enlightened, he did not care how powerful it was. By an enlightened government he meant one that fought against sloth and stupidity, kept the clergy in a subordinate place, allowed freedom of thought and religion, and advanced the cause of material and technical progress. He had no developed political theory, but his ideal for large civilized countries approached that of enlightened or rational despotism. Believing that only a few could be enlightened, he thought that these few, a king and his advisers, should have the power to carry out their program against all opposition. To overcome ignorance, credulity, and priestcraft it was necessary for the state to be strong. What Voltaire most desired was liberty for the enlightened, or for people like himself.

Jean-Jacques Rousseau

Jean-Jacques Rousseau was very different. Born in Geneva in 1712, he was a Swiss, a Protestant, and almost of lower-class origin. He never felt at ease in France or in Paris society. Neglected as a child, a runaway at 16, he lived for years by odd jobs, such as copying music, and not until the age of 40 did he have any success as a writer. He was always the little man, the outsider. In addition, his personal relations with women were difficult and unstable; he finally settled down with an uneducated woman named Thérèse Levasseur and with her mother, who kept interfering in his affairs. By Thérèse he had five children, whom he deposited at an orphanage. He had no social status, no money; and no sense of money; and after he became famous he lived largely by the generosity of his friends. He was pathetically and painfully maladjusted. He came to feel that he could trust no one, that those who tried to befriend him were deriding or betraying him behind his back. He condemned the cultural influence of French women, criticizing especially their prominent role in Parisian salons ("they do not know anything, although they judge everything"). He suffered from what would now be termed psychological complexes; possibly he was paranoid. He talked endlessly of his own virtue and innocence and complained bitterly that he was misunderstood.

But unbalanced though he was, he was possibly the most profound writer of the age and was certainly the most permanently influential. Rousseau felt, from his own experience, that in society as it existed a good person could not be happy. He therefore attacked society, declaring that it was artificial and corrupt. He even attacked reason, calling it a false guide when followed alone. He felt doubts on all the progress which gave satisfaction to his contemporaries. In two "discourses," one on the *Arts and Sciences* (1750), the other on the *Origin of Inequality Among Men* (1753), he argued that civilization was the source of much evil and that life in a "state of nature," were it only possible, would be much better. As Voltaire said, when Rousseau sent him a copy of his second discourse (Voltaire who relished civilization in every form), it made him "feel like going on all fours." To Rousseau

Rousseau's "discourses"

the best traits of human character, such as kindness, unselfishness, honesty, and true understanding, were products of nature. Deep below reason, he sensed the presence of feeling. He delighted in the warmth of sympathy, the quick flash of intuition, the clear message of conscience. He was religious by temperament, for though he believed in no church, no clergy, and no revelation, he had a respect for the Bible, a reverent awe toward the cosmos, a love of solitary meditation, and a belief in a God who was not merely a "first cause" but also a God of love and beauty. Rousseau thus made it easier for serious-minded people to slip away from orthodoxy and all forms of churchly discipline. He was feared by the churches as the most dangerous of all "infidels" and was condemned both in Catholic France and at Protestant Geneva.

In general, in most of his books, Rousseau, unlike so many of his contemporaries, gave the impression that impulse is more reliable than considered judgment, spontaneous feeling more to be trusted than critical thought. Mystical insights were for him more truthful than rational or clear ideas. He became the "man of feeling," the "child of nature," the forerunner of the coming age of romanticism, and an important source of all modern emphasis on the nonrational and the subconscious. He thus became an early, influential critic of the Enlightenment, even as he resembled other philosophes in his desire to change the existing social order.

In the *Social Contract* (1762) Rousseau seemed to contradict much of his famous sentiment for nature. In this book he held, somewhat like Hobbes, that the "state of nature" was a brutish condition without law or

The Social Contract

morality. In other works he had held that human evil was due to the evils of society. He now held that good people could be produced only by an improved society. Earlier thinkers, such as John Locke, for example, had thought of the "contract" as an agreement between a ruler and a people. Rousseau thought of it as an agreement among the people themselves. It was a social, not merely a political, contract. Organized civil society, that is, the community, rested upon it. The social contract was an understanding by which all individuals surrendered their natural liberty to each other, fused their individual wills into a combined General Will, and agreed to accept the rulings of this General Will as final. This General Will was the sovereign; and true sovereign power, rightly understood, was "absolute," "sacred," and "inviolable." Government was secondary; kings, officials, or elected representatives were only delegates of a sovereign people. Rousseau devoted many difficult and abstruse pages to explaining how the *real* General Will could be known. It was not necessarily determined by vote of a majority. "What generalizes the will," he said, "is not the number of voices but the common interest that unites them." He said little of the mechanism of government and had no admiration for parliamentary institutions. He was concerned with something deeper. Maladjusted outsider that he was, he craved a commonwealth in which every person could feel that he or she belonged. He wished a state in which all persons had a sense of membership and participation.

By these ideas Rousseau made himself the prophet of both democracy and nationalism. Indeed, in his *Considerations on Poland,* written at the request of Poles who were fighting against the partitions of their nation's territories by foreign powers, Rousseau applied the ideas of the *Social Contract* in more concrete form and became the first systematic theorist of a conscious and calculated nationalism. In writing the *Social Contract* he had in mind a small city-state like his native Geneva. But what he did, in effect, was to generalize and make applicable to large territories the psychology of small city republics—the sense of membership, of community and fellowship, of responsible citizenship and intimate participation in public affairs—in short, of common will. All modern states, democratic or undemocratic, strive to impart this sense of moral solidarity to their peoples. Whereas in democratic states the General Will can in some way be identified with the sovereignty of the people, in dictatorships it becomes possible for individuals (or parties) to arrogate to themselves the right to serve as spokesmen and interpreters of the General Will. Both totalitarians and democrats have regarded Rousseau as one of their prophets.

Rousseau's influence on his contemporaries was spread also by his other writings and especially his novels, *Émile* (1762) and the *Nouvelle Héloïse* (1760). The novels were widely read in all literate classes of society, especially by women, who made a kind of cult of Jean-Jacques. He was a literary master, able to evoke shades of thought and feeling that few writers had touched before, and by his literary writings he spread in the highest circles a new respect for the common person, a love of common things, an impulse of human pity and compassion, a sense of artifice and superficiality in aristocratic life. Women took to nursing their own babies, as Rousseau said they should. Men began describing the delicacy of their sentiments. Tears became the fashion. The queen, Marie Antoinette, built herself a village in the gardens at Versailles, where she pretended to be a simple milkmaid. In all this there was much that was ridiculous or shallow. Yet it was the wellspring of modern humanitarianism, the force leading to a new sense of human equality. Rousseau estranged the French upper classes from their own mode of life. He made many of them lose faith in their own superiority. That was his main direct contribution to the French Revolution.

Political Economists

Physiocrats

In France, somewhat apart from the philosophes, were the Physiocrats, whom their critics called "economists," a word originally thought to be mildly insulting. Many of the Physiocrats, unlike the philosophes, were close to the government as administrators or advisers. Quesnay was physician to Louis XV, Turgot was an experienced official who became minister to Louis XVI, and Dupont de Nemours, an associate of Turgot's, became the founder of the industrial family of the Du Ponts in the United States. Such men concerned themselves with fiscal and tax reform and with measures to increase the national wealth of France. They opposed guild regulations and price controls as impediments to the production and circulation of goods, and so were the first to use the term laissez-faire ("let them do as they see fit") as a principle of economic activity. They favored strong government, however, relying on it to overcome traditional obstacles and to provide inducements for the establishment of new industries.

Economics, or what was long called political economy, arose from these activities of the Physiocrats, from the somewhat similar work of "cameralists" in the German states, and from the collection and analysis of quantitative data, that is, the birth of statistics. Economic thinking flourished especially in Great Britain, and notably in Scotland, where Adam Smith's *Wealth of Nations* appeared in 1776. By 1800 the *Wealth of Nations* had been translated into every west-European language except Portuguese.

Adam Smith

Adam Smith's purpose, like that of the French Physiocrats, was to increase the national wealth by the reduction of barriers that hindered its growth. He undercut the premises of what we have called "the struggle for wealth and empire" in Chapter 7, since he argued that to build up a nation's wealth it was unnecessary to have an empire. He attacked most of the program of mercantilism that had obtained since the sixteenth century, and he expected that Britain's American colonies would soon become independent without loss to British trade. Where others

**JEAN-JACQUES ROUSSEAU
by Allan Ramsay (Scottish,
1713–1784)**

**Some hints of the complexities
of Rousseau's personality and
thought appear in this portrait
by a Scottish artist who admired the famous writers of the
French Enlightenment.**
(Giraudon/Art Resource, NY)

looked to planning by an enlightened government, Adam Smith preferred to limit the functions of government to defense, internal security, and the provision of reasonable laws and
fair law courts by which private differences could be adjudicated. For innovation and
enterprise he counted more on private persons than on the state. He became the philosopher of the free market, the prophet of free trade. If there was a shortage of a given commodity, its price would rise and so stimulate producers to produce more, while also
attracting new persons into that line of production. If there was an excess, if more was produced than purchasers would buy, both capital and labor would withdraw and gradually
move into another area where demand was stronger. Demand would increase with lower
prices, which depended on lower costs, which in turn depended on the specialization of
labor. His most famous example was that of the pin factory of his time, where each of a
dozen workers engaged in only one part of the process of manufacture, so that together
they produced far more pins than if each worker produced whole pins; the price of pins
then fell, and more pins could be used by more people. The same principle held in international trade; some countries or climates could produce an article more cheaply than others,
so that if each specialized and then exchanged with the others, all would have more. Each
nation could use its comparative advantage in certain spheres of production or trade to
compensate for economic weaknesses in other spheres and also to increase its national
wealth.

　　The motivation for all such production and exchange was to be the self-interest of the
participants. As he said, we rely for our meat not on the goodwill of the butcher but on his
concern for his own income. To those who might object that this was a system of selfish-
ness Adam Smith would reply (being a professor of moral philosophy at the University of

Glasgow) that it was at least realistic, describing how people really behaved, and that it was morally justified since it ultimately produced a maximum both of freedom and of abundance. The mutual interaction of the enlightened self-interest of millions of persons would in the end, as if by an "invisible hand," he said, result in the highest welfare of all. Among problems that Smith minimized, or accepted as lesser evils, were the insecurity of individuals and the dangers of excessive dependence of a whole country on imports of essentials, such as food; and if the visible hand of government continued to regulate the price of bread, it should not be for economic reasons, but to prevent rioting and maintain social peace.

Main Currents of Enlightenment Thought

It is clear that the currents of thought in France and Europe were divergent and inconsistent. There was a general belief in progress, reason, science, and civilization. Rousseau had his doubts and praised the imagined conditions in a precivilized state of nature. Montesquieu thought the church useful but did not believe in religion; Rousseau believed in religion but saw no need for any church. Montesquieu was concerned about practical political liberty; Voltaire would surrender political liberty in return for guarantees of intellectual freedom; Rousseau wanted emancipation from the restraints of society and sought the freedom that consists in merging with nature and with one's fellows. Most philosophes were closest to Voltaire. They favored more tolerance for intellectual differences and more equality in European societies. It was not a very far-reaching equality, but it meant equality of rights for persons of different religions, a reduction of privileges enjoyed by nobles but not by commoners, greater equality of status in law courts and in the payment of taxes, and more opportunity for middle-class persons to rise to positions of social or political importance.

France was the main center of the Enlightenment. French philosophes traveled all over Europe. Frederick II and Catherine II invited French thinkers to their courts. French was the language of the academies of St. Petersburg and Berlin. Frederick wrote his philosophical works in the French language. The upper classes of Europe shared a uniform cosmopolitan culture, and this culture was predominantly French. But Britain was important also. Hitherto somewhat on the fringes of the European consciousness, Britain now moved closer to the center. Montesquieu and Voltaire may be said to have "discovered" Britain for Europe. Through them the ideas of Bacon, Newton, and Locke, and the whole theory of British liberty and parliamentary government became matters for general discussion and comment. We have seen, too, how Adam Smith's *Wealth of Nations* was soon translated into many languages.

The main agency of progress was thought to be the state. Whether in the form of limited monarchy on the British model favored by Montesquieu, or of enlightened despotism preferred by Voltaire, or of the idealized republican commonwealth portrayed by Rousseau, the rightly ordered government was considered the best guarantee of social welfare. Even the political economists needed the state to shake people out of the habits of ages, sweep away a mass of local regulation, preserve law and order and the enforcement of contracts, and so assure the existence of a free market. But if they relied on the state,

Belief in the unity of humankind

they were not nationalists in any later sense of the word. As "universalists," they believed in the unity of humankind under a natural law of right and reason and thus they carried over the classical and Christian outlook in a secular way. They supposed that all peoples would participate eventually in the same progress. No nation was thought to have a peculiar message. French ideas enjoyed a wide currency, but no one thought of them as peculiarly French, arising from a French "national character." It was simply thought that the French at the time were in the vanguard of civilized thinking. Such was the idea of Condorcet, one of the later philosophes, a leading spokesman of the Enlightenment who became an active figure in the French Revolution, and also one of its victims, and who in 1794, while in hiding from the guillotine, wrote the great testament to the Enlightenment, his *Sketch of the Progress of the Human Mind*.

36. ENLIGHTENED DESPOTISM: FRANCE, AUSTRIA, PRUSSIA

The Meaning of Enlightened Despotism

Enlightened despotism is hard to define, because it grew out of earlier forms of absolutism that Louis XIV and Peter the Great had established in France and Russia. Characteristically, the enlightened despots drained marshes, built roads and bridges, codified the laws, repressed provincial autonomy and localism, curtailed the independence of church and nobles, and developed a trained and salaried officialdom. All these things had been done by kings before. Enlightened despots differed from their "unenlightened" predecessors mainly in attitude and tempo. They said little of a divine right to the throne. They might even not emphasize hereditary or dynastic family rights. They justified their authority on grounds of usefulness to society, calling themselves, as Frederick the Great did, the "first servant of the state."

The secular outlook

Enlightened despotism was secular; it claimed no mandate from heaven and recognized no special responsibility to God or church. The typical enlightened despot consequently favored toleration in religion, and this was an important new emphasis after about 1740; but here again there was precedent in the older absolutism, for the rulers of Prussia had been inclined toward toleration before Frederick, and even the French Bourbons had recognized a degree of religious liberty for almost a century following the Edict of Nantes in 1598. The secular outlook of the enlightened governments is again seen in the common front they adopted against the Jesuits. High papalists, affirming the authority of a universal church in Rome and asserting themselves in other ways as the strongest religious order in the Catholic world, the Jesuits were distasteful to the enlightened monarchs. In the 1760s the order was banned in almost all Catholic countries. In 1773 the pope was persuaded to dissolve the Society of Jesus entirely. Governments in France, Austria, Spain, Portugal, and Naples confiscated Jesuit property and took over the Jesuit schools. Not until 1814 was the order reconstituted.

Enlightened despotism was also rational and reformist. The typical monarch set out to reconstruct the state by the use of reason. Sharing the widespread eighteenth-century view of the past as benighted, the new monarchs were impatient of custom and of all that was imbedded in custom or claimed as a heritage from the past, such as systems of customary law and the rights and privileges of church, nobles, towns, guilds, provinces, assemblies of estates, or, in France, the judicial bodies called parlements. The complex of such institutions was disparagingly referred to as "feudalism." Monarchs had long struggled against feudalism in this sense, but in the past they had usually compromised. The enlightened despot was less willing to compromise, and herein lay the difference in tempo. The new monarchs acted abruptly, desiring quicker results.

*The roots of
enlightened despotism*
Enlightened despotism, in short, was an acceleration of the old centralizing institution of monarchy, which now put aside its quasi-sacred mantle
and undertook to justify itself in the cold light of reason and secular usefulness. In theory even the dynastic claim was awkward, for it rested on inheritance from the past. Under enlightened despotism the idea of the state itself was changing,
from the older notion of an estate belonging by a kind of sanctified property right to its
ruler, to a newer notion of an abstract and impersonal authority exercised by public officers, of whom the king was simply the highest.

The trend to enlightened despotism after 1740 owed a great deal to writers and
philosophes, but it arose also out of a very practical situation, namely, the great war of the
mid-eighteenth century. War, in modern history, has usually led to concentration and
rationalizing of government power, and the wars of 1740–1748 and 1756–1763 were no
exception. Under their impact even governments where the rulers were not considered by
philosophes to be enlightened, notably those of Louis XV and Maria Theresa, and even the
government of Great Britain, which was certainly not despotic, embarked on programs
that all bear features in common. They attempted to augment their revenues, devise new
taxes, tax persons or regions hitherto more or less tax-exempt, limit the autonomy of outlying political bodies, and centralize and renovate their respective political systems. The
workings of enlightened despotism might be seen in many states, but the new policies had
the most far-reaching influence in the larger Continental countries—France and Austria,
Prussia and Russia—and in the rather different, yet not wholly different, course of events
in the British empire.

The Failure of Enlightened Despotism in France

It was in France that enlightened despotism had the least success. Louis XV, who had
inherited the throne as a child in 1715 and lived until 1774, though by no means stupid,
was indifferent to most serious questions, absorbed in the daily rounds at Versailles, disin-
clined to make trouble for people with whom he had personal contact, and interested in
government only by fits and starts. His reputed remark, *après moi le déluge,* whether or
not he really said it, sufficiently characterizes his personal attitude to conditions in France.
Yet the French government was not unenlightened, and many capable officials carried on
its affairs all through the century. These officials generally knew what the basic trouble
was. Most of the practical difficulties of the French monarchy could be traced to its methods of raising revenue. It derived some income from the sale of offices and privileges,

Tax collection
which had the perverse effect of building up vested interests in the existing
system. Of actual taxes the most important was the *taille,* a kind of land tax,
generally paid only by peasants. Nobles were exempt from it on principle,
and officeholders and bourgeois, for one reason or another, were generally

EUROPE, 1740

**Boundaries are as of 1740. There were now three Bourbon monarchies (France, Spain, and
the Two Sicilies), while the Austrian monarchy possessed most of what is now Belgium, and in
Italy the duchy of Milan and grand duchy of Tuscany, where the Medici family had recently
died out. Prussia expanded by acquiring Silesia in the war of the 1740s. The first partition of
Poland in 1772 enlarged Prussia, Austria, and Russia. France acquired Lorraine in 1766 and
Corsica in 1768. Otherwise there were no changes until the Revolutionary-Napoleonic wars of
1792–1814.**

Bourbon Dominions

Habsburg Dominions

Boundary of Holy Roman Empire

SWEDEN

NORWAY

KINGDOM OF DENMARK AND NORWAY

St. Petersburg

Stockholm

Riga

SCOTLAND

Edinburgh

North Sea

DENMARK

Copenhagen

Baltic Sea

LITHUANIA

Memel

Minsk

IRELAND GREAT BRITAIN

SCHLESWIG

PRUSSIA

EAST PRUSSIA

Dublin Liverpool

ENGLAND

WALES

Hamburg

Bremen

HANOVER (Britain)

Danzig

Thorn

POLAND

London

Amsterdam

Utrecht

BRANDENBURG

Magdeburg

Berlin

Warsaw

Lublin

ATLANTIC OCEAN

Cape de la Hogue

AUSTRIAN NETHERLANDS

Oudenarde

Antwerp

Cologne

MINOR GERMAN STATES

Leipzig

SAXONY

Dresden

SILESIA

Breslau

Oder R.

Cracow

Lemberg

CHANNEL I. (Britain)

Malplaquet

Ramilies

Rhine R.

Frankfurt

PALATI- NATE

BOHEMIA

Prague

MORAVIA

PODOLIA

Quiberon

Rouen

Reims

Paris

Seine R.

Metz

Strasbourg

Blenheim

BAVARIA

AUSTRIA

Vienna

Pressburg

Munkacz

Orléans

LORRAINE (France 1766)

Budapest

Tours

Besançon

Munich

TYROL

AUSTRIAN MONARCHY

FRANCE

Limoges

Geneva

SWITZERLAND

KINGDOM OF HUNGARY

TRANSYLVANIA

Bordeaux

Lyons

SAVOY

MILAN

VENETIA

Venice

CROATIA

Save R.

BANAT

Belgrade

WALLACHIA

Santiago

León

Pamplona

Toulouse

Avignon

Rhône R.

Turin

Po R.

PAR- MA

Genoa

Bologna

DALMATIA (Venice)

Adriatic Sea

BOSNIA

SERBIA

Danube R.

OTTOMAN EMPIRE

Burgos

Marseille

Toulon

KINGDOM OF SARDINIA

TUSCANY

PAPAL STATES

MONTENEGRO

Sofia

PORTUGAL

SPAIN

Ebro R.

Madrid

Corsica (Genoa)

Rome

Benevento

Bari

ALBANIA

Salonica

Lisbon

Tagus R.

Toledo

Barcelona

Minorca (Britain)

Sardinia

NAPLES

Naples

IONIAN I. (Venice)

Athens

Guadalquivir R.

Almanza

Majorca (Spain)

KINGDOM OF THE TWO SICILIES

MOREA

Seville

Granada

BALEARIC I.

Cagliari

Palermo

Cadiz

Gibraltar (Britain)

Mediterranean

Algiers

SICILY

Tangier

Tunis

MALTA (Knights of St. John)

MOROCCO (Independent)

ALGERIA (Turkish)

TUNISIA (Turkish)

Sea

0   200   400 miles

exempt also. In addition, the church, which owned between five and ten percent of the land of the country, insisted that its property was not taxable by the state; it granted to the king a periodic "free gift" which, though sizable, was less than the government might expect from direct taxation. The consequence of the tax exemptions was that, although France itself was wealthy and prosperous, the government was chronically poor, because the social classes which enjoyed most of the wealth and prosperity did not pay taxes corresponding to their incomes.

Louis XIV, under pressure of war, had tried to tax everybody alike by creating new levies—the capitation or poll tax and the *dixième* or tenth, both of which were assessed in proportion to income; but these taxes had been widely evaded. A similar effort was made in 1726, but it too had failed. The propertied classes resisted taxation because they thought it degrading. France had succumbed to the appalling principle that to pay direct taxes was the sure mark of inferior status. Nobles, churchmen, and bourgeois also resisted taxation because they were kept out of policymaking functions of government and so had no sense of political responsibility or control.

In the 1740s, under pressure of heavy war costs, a new tax was introduced, the *vingtième* or twentieth, which imposed a five percent tax on income from all forms of property and was to be paid irrespective of class status, provincial liberties, or previous exemptions of any kind. In practice, the *vingtième* amounted to less than five percent and fell only upon land, but it was paid by nobles and bourgeois alike and lasted until the Revolution. During the Seven Years' War the government tried to increase it, without success. A clamor arose from the Parlement of Paris, the provincial parlements, the estates of Brittany, and the church. All these were now stronger than in the days of Louis XIV, and they could now cite Montesquieu to justify their opposition to the crown. The parlements ruled the tax increase to be incompatible with the laws of France, that is, unconstitutional; and the *pays d'états,* or provinces having assemblies of estates, declared that their historic liberties were being violated. After several years of wrangling, Louis XV decided to push the matter no further.

But after the Seven Years' War, burdened with war debts, the government sought to win effective central control by eliminating the parlements as a political force. In 1768 Louis XV called to the chancellorship a man named Maupeou, who simply abrogated the old parlements and set up new ones in their place. Maupeou had the sympathy of Voltaire and most of the philosophes. In the "Maupeou parlements" the judges had no property rights in their seats but became salaried officials appointed by the crown with assurances of secure tenure; and they were forbidden to reject government edicts or to pass on their constitutionality, being confined to purely judicial functions. Maupeou proposed to make the laws and judicial procedure more uniform throughout the whole country. Meanwhile, with the old parlements out of the way, another attempt was made to tax the privileged and exempted groups.

The "Maupeou parlements"

Louis XVI

But Louis XV died in 1774. His grandson and successor, Louis XVI, though more conscientious than his grandfather and possessed by a genuine desire to govern well, resembled Louis XV in that he lacked sustained will power and could not bear to offend the people who could get to see him personally. In any case he was only 20 in 1774. The kingdom resounded with outcries against Maupeou and his colleagues as minions of despotism and with demands for the immediate restoration of the old Parlement of Paris and the others. Louis XVI, fearful of beginning his reign as a "despot," therefore recalled the old parlements and abolished those of Maupeou. The abortive Maupeou parlements represented the farthest step taken by enlightened despotism in France. It was arbitrary, high-handed, and despotic for Louis XV to destroy the old parlements, but it was certainly "enlightened" in the sense then connoted by the word, for the old parlements were strongholds of aristocracy and privilege and had for decades blocked programs of reform.

Louis XVI, in recalling the old parlements in 1774, began his reign by pacifying the privileged classes. At the same time he appointed a reforming ministry. At its head was Turgot, a philosophe and a Physiocrat and a widely experienced government administrator. Turgot undertook to suppress the guilds and their privileged municipal monopolies in their several trades. He allowed greater freedom to the internal commerce in grain. He planned to abolish the royal *corvée* (a requirement that certain peasants labor on the roads a few days each year), replacing it by a money tax which would fall on all classes. He began to review the whole system of taxation and in religious matters was known even to favor the legal toleration of Protestants. The Parlement of Paris, supported by the Provincial Estates and the church, vociferously opposed him, and in 1776 he resigned. Louis XVI, by recalling the parlements, had made reform impossible. In 1778 France again went to war with Britain. The same cycle was repeated: war costs, debt, deficit, new projects of taxation, resistance from the parlements and other semiautonomous bodies. In the 1780s the clash led to revolution.

Austria: The Reforms of Maria Theresa (1740–1780) and of Joseph II (1780–1790)

For Maria Theresa the European war of the 1740s proved the extraordinary flimsiness of her empire and the Austrian monarchy. Her subjects did not show much inclination to remain united under her rule, even when threatened by invading armies. The empire was only a loose bundle of territories without common purpose or common will. The Pragmatic Sanction devised by Charles VI, it should be recalled, had been meant not only to guarantee the Habsburg inheritance against foreign attack but also to secure the assent of the several parts of the empire to remain united under the Habsburg dynasty.

The war of the 1740s led to internal consolidation. The reign of Maria Theresa set the course of all later development of the Austrian empire and hence of the many peoples who lived within its borders. She was aided by a notable team of ministers, whose origin illustrated the nonnational character of the Habsburg system. Her most trusted adviser in foreign relations, *Internal consolidation of the empire* the astute Kaunitz, was a Moravian; her main assistants in domestic affairs were a Silesian and a Bohemian-Czech. They worked smoothly with the German archduchess-queen and with German officials in Vienna. Their aim was to prevent dissolution of the monarchy by enlarging and guaranteeing the flow of taxes and soldiers. This involved breaking the local control of territorial nobles in their diets. Hungary, profoundly separatist, was left alone. But the Bohemian and Austrian provinces were welded together, and a unified state bureaucracy took the place of local self-government. Officials (following the form of mercantilist doctrine called "cameralism" in central Europe) planned to augment the economic strength of the empire by increasing production. They checked the local guild monopolies; suppressed brigandage on the roads; and in 1775 created a tariff union of Bohemia, Moravia, and the Austrian duchies. This region became the largest area of free trade on the European continent, since even France was still divided by internal tariffs. Bohemia, industrially the most advanced part of the empire, benefited substantially; one of its cotton manufacturing plants, at the end of Maria Theresa's reign, employed 4,000 persons.

Le Roy Louis XVI. tenant son Lit de Justice pour la 1er Fois au Palais a Paris le 12 de Novembre 1774. pour

The restoration of the traditional parlements at the beginning of the reign of Louis XVI was an important political victory for the privileged classes in French society, whose power had been challenged by the Maupeou ministry in the early 1770s. This illustration of the young king at the first session of the restored Parlement of Paris (he occupies the elevated seat on the upper left side of the assembly) offers an early example of his lifelong tendency to align himself with older elites and to oppose reformers who wanted to reduce the power or privileges of the old nobility. The caption lists the royal officials and dignitaries who accompanied the king at this meeting of the Parlement in November 1774.

(Bibliothèque Nationale de France, Paris)

The great social fact, both in the Habsburg lands and in all eastern Europe, was the serfdom into which the rural masses had progressively fallen during the past 200 years. Serfdom meant that the peasant belonged more to the landlord than to the state. The serf owed labor to the lord, often unspecified in amount or kind. The tendency, so long as the landlords ruled locally through their diets, was for the serf to do six days a week of forced labor on the lord's land. Maria Theresa, from humane motives and also from a desire to control the manpower from which her armies were recruited, launched a systematic attack on the institutions of serfdom, which meant also an attack on the landed aristocracy of the empire. With the diets reduced in power, the protests of the nobles were less effective; still, the whole agricultural labor system of her territories was involved, and Maria Theresa proceeded with caution. Laws were passed against abuse of peasants by lords or their overseers. Other laws regularized the labor obligations, requiring that they be publicly registered and usually limiting them to three days a week. The laws were often evaded. But the peasant was to some extent freed from arbitrary exactions of the lord. Maria Theresa accomplished more to alleviate serfdom than any other ruler of the eighteenth century in eastern Europe, with the single exception of her own son, Joseph II.

Attacks on serfdom

The great archduchess-queen died in 1780, having reigned for 40 years. Her son, who had been co-regent with his mother since 1765, had little patience with her methods. Maria Theresa, though steady enough in aim, had always been content with partial measures. Instead of advertising her purposes by philosophical pronouncements, she disguised or understated them, never carrying matters to the point of arousing an unmanageable reaction or of uniting against her the vested interests that she undermined. She watched and waited. Joseph II was more impatient. Though he thought the French philosophes frivolous, and Frederick of Prussia a mere clever cynic, he was himself a pure representative of the Age of Enlightenment, and it is in his brief reign of 10 years that the character and the limitations of enlightened despotism can best be seen. He was a solemn, earnest, good man, who sensed the misery and hopelessness of the lowest classes. He believed existing conditions to be bad, and he would not regulate or improve them; he would end them. Right and reason, in his mind, lay with the views which he himself adopted; upholders of the old order were self-seeking or mistaken and to yield to them would be to compromise with evil.

Joseph II: the "revolutionary emperor"

"The state," said Joseph, anticipating the later Philosophical Radicals in England, meant "the greatest good for the greatest number." He acted accordingly. His 10 years of rule passed in a quick succession of decrees. Maria Theresa had regulated serfdom. Joseph abolished it. His mother had collected taxes from nobles as well as peasants, though not equally. Joseph decreed absolute equality of taxation. He insisted on equal punishment for equal crimes whatever the class status of the offender; an aristocratic army officer, who had stolen 97,000 gulden, was exhibited in the pillory, and Count Podstacky, a forger, was made to sweep the streets of Vienna chained to common convicts. At the same time many legal punishments were made less physically cruel. Joseph granted complete liberty of the press. He ordered toleration of all religions, except for a few popular sects that he thought too ignorant to allow. He granted equal civil rights to the Jews, and equal duties, making Jews liable, for the first time in Europe, to service in the army. He even created Jewish nobles, an amazing phenomenon to those of aristocratic "blood."

Joseph clashed openly and rudely with the pope. He demanded increased powers in the appointment and supervision of Catholic bishops, and he suppressed a good many monasteries, using their property to finance secular hospitals in Vienna, and thus laying the foundations of Viennese excellence as a medical center. He attempted also to develop the empire economically and built up the port of Trieste, where he even established an East India Company, which soon failed for obvious reasons—neither capital nor naval support being forthcoming from central Europe. His attempts to reach the sea commercially through Belgium, like those of his grandfather at the time of the Ostend Company, were blocked by Dutch and British interests.

To force through his program Joseph had to centralize his state, like earlier rulers, except that he went further. Regional diets and aristocratic self-government fared even worse than under his mother. Where she had always sagaciously let Hungary go its own way, he applied most of his measures to Hungary also—what was right must be right everywhere. His ideal was a perfectly uniform and rational empire, with all irregularities smoothed out as if under a steamroller. He thought it reasonable to have a single language for administration and naturally chose German; this led to a program of Germanizing the Czechs, Poles, Magyars, and others, which in turn aroused their nationalistic resistance. Using the German language, and pushing the emperor's program against regional and class opposition, was a hard-pressed, constantly growing, and increasingly disciplined body of officials. Bureaucracy became recognizably modern, with training courses, promotion schedules, retirement pensions, efficiency reports, and visits by inspectors. The clergy likewise were employed as representatives of the state to explain new laws to their parishioners and teach due respect for the government. To watch over the whole structure Joseph created a secret police, whose agents, soliciting the confidential aid of spies and informers, reported on the performance of government employees or on the ideas and actions of nobles, clergy, or others from whom trouble might be expected. The police state, so infamous to the liberal world, was first systematically built up under Joseph as an instrument of enlightenment and reform.

Joseph II, the "revolutionary emperor," anticipated much that was done in France by the Revolution and under Napoleon. He could not abide "feudalism" or "medievalism"; he personally detested the nobility and the church. But few of his reforms proved lasting. He died prematurely in 1790, at the age of 49, disillusioned and broken-hearted. Joseph was a revolutionist without a party. He failed because he could not be everywhere and do everything himself, and because he was opposed by the most powerful social groups in his empire. His reign demonstrated the limitations of a merely despotic enlightenment. It showed that a legally absolute ruler could not really do as he pleased. It suggested that drastic and abrupt reform could perhaps come only with a true revolution, on a wave of public opinion, and under the leadership of persons who shared in a coherent body of ideas.

Limitations of Joseph's reforms

Joseph was succeeded by his brother Leopold, one of the ablest rulers of the century, who for many years as grand duke of Tuscany had given that country the best government known in Italy for generations. Now, in 1790, Leopold was plagued by outcries from his sister, Marie Antoinette, caught in the toils of a real revolution in France. He refused to interfere in French affairs; in any case, he was busy dealing with the uproar left by Joseph. He abrogated most of Joseph's edicts, but he did not yield entirely. The nobles did not win back full powers in their diets. The peasants were not wholly consigned to the old serfdom; Joseph's efforts to provide them with land and to rid them of forced labor had to be given up, but they remained legally free to migrate, marry, or choose an occupation at will. Leopold died in 1792 and was followed by his son Francis II. Under Francis the aristocratic and clerical reaction gathered strength, terrified by the memory of Joseph II and by the spectacle of revolutionary France, with which Austria went to war soon after Leopold's death.

Prussia under Frederick the Great (1740–1786)

In Prussia, Frederick the Great continued to reign for 23 years after the close of the Seven Years' War in 1763. "Old Fritz," as he was called, spent the time peaceably, writing memoirs and histories, rehabilitating his shattered country, promoting agriculture and industry, replenishing his treasury, drilling his army, and assimilating his huge conquest of Silesia, and, after 1772, the Polish lands which fell to him in the first partition of Poland. Frederick's fame as one of the most eminent of enlightened despots rests, however, not so much on his actual innovations as on his own intellectual gifts, which were considerable, and on the admiring publicity which he received from such literary friends as Voltaire. "My chief occupation," he wrote to Voltaire, "is to fight ignorance and prejudices in this country. . . . I must enlighten my people, cultivate their manners and morals, and make them as happy as human beings can be, or as happy as the means at my disposal permit." He did not conceive that sweeping changes were necessary to happiness in Prussia. The country was docile, for its Lutheran church had long been subordinate to the state, its relatively few burghers were largely dependents of the crown, and the independence of the Junker landlords, as expressed in provincial diets, had been curtailed by Frederick's predecessors. Frederick simplified and codified the many laws of the kingdom and made the law courts cheaper, more expeditious, and more honest. He kept up a wholesome and energetic tone in his civil service. He protected religious freedom, and he decreed, though he did not achieve, a modicum of elementary education for all children of all classes. Prussia under Frederick was attractive enough for some 300,000 immigrants to seek it out.

But society remained stratified in a way hardly known in western Europe. Nobles, peasants, and burghers lived side by side in a kind of segregation. Each group paid different taxes and owed different duties to the state, and no person could buy property of the type owned by one of the other two groups. Property was legally classified, as well as persons; there was little movement from one group to another. These policies served a specific military purpose. They preserved a distinct peasant class from which to draw soldiers and a distinct aristocratic class from which to draw officers. The peasants, except in the western extremities of the kingdom, were serfs holding patches of land on precarious terms with obligations to labor on the estates of the lords. They were likewise considered the lord's "hereditary subjects" and were not free to leave the lord's estate, to marry, or to learn a trade except with his permission. Frederick in his early years considered steps to relieve the burden of serfdom. He did relieve it on his own manors, those belonging to the Prussian crown domain, which comprised a quarter of the area of the kingdom. But he did nothing for serfs belonging to the private landlords or Junkers. No king of Prussia could antagonize the Junker class which commanded the army. On the other hand, even in Prussia, the existence of a monarchical state was of some advantage for the common person; the serf in Prussia was not so badly off as in adjoining areas—Poland, Livonia, Mecklenburg, or Swedish Pomerania—where the will of the landlords was the law of the land, and which therefore have been called Junker republics. In these countries cases came to light in which owners sold their serfs as movable property or gambled or gave them away, breaking up families in the process, as Russian landlords might do with their serfs or American plantation owners with their slaves. Such abuses were unknown in Prussia.

Social stratification in Prussia

Frederick's system was centralized not merely at Potsdam but in his own head. He himself attended to all business and made all important decisions. None of his ministers or generals ever achieved an independent reputation. As he said of his army, "no one reasons, everyone executes"—that is, no one reasoned except the king himself. Or again, as Frederick put it, if Newton had had to consult with Descartes he would never have discovered the law of universal gravitation. To have to take into account other people's ideas, or to entrust responsibilities to people less capable than himself, seemed to Frederick wasteful and anarchic. He died in 1786, after ruling 46 years and having trained no successors. Twenty years later Prussia was all but destroyed by Napoleon. It was not surprising that Napoleon should defeat Prussia, but Europe was amazed, in 1806, to see Prussia collapse totally and abruptly. It was then concluded in Prussia and elsewhere that government by a mastermind working in lofty and isolated superiority did not offer a viable form of state under modern conditions.

 ## 37. ENLIGHTENED DESPOTISM: RUSSIA

The Russian empire has long been out of sight in the preceding pages. There are reasons for its absence, for it played no part in the intellectual revolution of the seventeenth century, and its role in the struggle for wealth and empire, which reached a climax in the Seven Years' War, was somewhat incidental. In the Age of Enlightenment the role of Russia was passive. No Russian thinker was known to western Europe, but western European thinkers were well known in Russia. The French-dominated cosmopolitan culture of the European upper classes spread to the upper classes of Russia. The Russian court and aristocracy took over French as their common conversational language. With French (German was also known, and sometimes English, for the Russian aristocrats were remarkable linguists) all the ideas boiling up in western Europe streamed into Russia. The Enlightenment, if it did not affect Russia profoundly, affected it significantly. It continued the westernization so forcibly pushed forward by Peter and carried further the estrangement of the Russian upper classes from their own people and their own native scene.

Russia absorbs French culture

Russia after Peter the Great

Peter the Great died in 1725. To secure his revolution he had decreed that each tsar should name his successor, but he himself had named none and had put to death his own son Alexis to prevent social reaction. Peter's long reign was therefore followed by a period of political instability. Rival factions at court—a German party and a native Russian party—struggled for control over successive tsars, tsarinas, and short-lived governments until a palace revolution in 1741 brought to the throne Peter the Great's daughter, Elizabeth, who managed to hold power until her death 21 years later. In her reign the military power of Russia expanded, and she entered into European diplomacy and joined in the Seven Years' War against Prussia, fearing that the continued growth of Prussia would endanger the new Russian position on the Baltic. Her nephew, Peter III, was almost immediately dethroned, and probably assassinated, by a group acting in the name of his young wife Catherine. The victorious coterie gave it out that Peter III had been almost a half-wit, who at the age of 24 still played with paper soldiers. Catherine was proclaimed the Empress Catherine II and is called "the Great." She enjoyed a long reign from 1762 to 1796, during which she acquired a somewhat exaggerated reputation as an enlightened despot.

The names of the tsars and tsarinas between Peter I and Catherine II are of slight importance, but their violent and rapid sequence tells a story. With no principle of succession, dynastic or other, the empire fell into a lawless struggle of parties, in which plots against rulers while living alternated with palace revolutions upon their death. In all the confusion an underlying issue was always how the westernizing reform program of Peter would turn out. To most people in western Europe Russia still seemed alien or even barbaric.

Catherine the Great (1762–1796): Domestic Program

Catherine the Great was a German woman of a small princely house of the Holy Roman Empire. She had gone to Russia at the age of 15 to be married. She had immediately cultivated the goodwill of the Russians, learned the language, and embraced the Orthodox church. Early in her married life, disgusted with her husband, she foresaw the chance of becoming empress herself. Like the other prominent woman ruler of this era in Europe, Maria Theresa, she approached political issues with a strong practical sense and great energy (though she did not share Maria Theresa's devotion to family life). Catherine's intellectual powers were as remarkable as her physical vigor; even after becoming empress she often got up at five in the morning, lit her own fire, and turned to her books, making a digest, for example, of Blackstone's *Commentaries on the Laws of England,* published in 1765. She corresponded with Voltaire and invited Diderot, editor of the *Encyclopédie,* to visit her at St. Petersburg, where, she reported, he thumped her so hard on the knee in the energy of his conversation that she had to put a table between them. She bought Diderot's library, allowing him to keep it during his lifetime, and in other ways won renown by her benefactions to the philosophes, whom she regarded as useful press agents for Russia.

When she first came to power, she publicized an intention to introduce certain enlightened reforms. She summoned a great consultative assembly, called a Legislative Commission, which met in the summer of 1767. From *Catherine's reforms* its numerous proposals Catherine obtained a good deal of information on conditions in the country and concluded, from the profuse loyalty exhibited by the deputies, that though a usurper and a foreigner she possessed a strong hold upon Russia. The reforms which she subsequently enacted consisted in a measure of legal codification, restrictions on the use of torture, and a certain support of religious toleration, though she would not allow Old Believers to build their own chapels. Such innovations were enough to raise an admiring chorus from the philosophes, who saw in her, as they saw retrospectively in Peter the Great, the standard-bearer of an enlightened civilization among a backward people.

Whatever ideas Catherine may conceivably have had at first, as a thoughtful and progressive young woman, on the fundamental subject of reforming serfdom in Russia, did not last long after she became empress and dissolved with the great peasant insurrection of 1773, known as Pugachev's rebellion. The condition of the Russian serfs was deteriorating. Serf owners were increasingly selling them apart from the land, breaking up families, using them in mines or manufactures, disciplining and punishing them at will, or exiling them to Siberia. The serf population was restless, worked upon by Old Believers and cherishing distorted popular memories of the mighty hero, Stephen Razin, who a century before had led an uprising against the landlords. Class antagonism, though latent, was profound, nor was it made less when the rough muzhik, in some places, heard the lord and his family talking French so as not to be understood by the servants or saw them wearing European clothes, reading European books, and adopting the manners of a foreign way of life.

In 1773 a Don Cossack, Emelian Pugachev, a former soldier, appeared at the head of an insurrection in the Urals. Following an old Russian cus- *Pugachev's rebellion* tom, he announced himself as the true tsar, Peter III (Catherine's deceased husband), now returned after long travels in Egypt and the Holy Land. He surrounded himself with his own imperial family, courtiers, and even a secretary of state, He issued an imperial manifesto proclaiming the end of serfdom and of taxes and military conscription. Tens of hundreds of thousands, in the Urals and Volga regions, Tartars, Kirghiz, Cossacks, agricultural serfs, servile workers in the Ural mines, fishermen in the rivers and in the Caspian Sea, flocked to Pugachev's banner. The great host surged through eastern Russia, burning and pillaging, killing priests and landlords. The upper classes in Moscow were terrified; 100,000 serfs lived in the city as domestic servants or industrial workers and their

CATHERINE THE GREAT
by Alexander Roslin (Swedish,
1718–1793)

Catherine's forceful character and
slightly whimsical smile are represented
in this portrait, which was painted
shortly after the powerful tsarina sup-
pressed the great peasant rebellion of
1773–1774.

(Giraudon/Art Resource, NY)

sympathies went out to Pugachev and his militant supporters. Armies sent against him were at first unsuccessful. But famine along the Volga in 1774 dispersed the rebels. Pugachev, betrayed by some of his own followers, was brought to Moscow in an iron cage. Catherine forbade the use of torture at his trial, but he was executed by the drawing and quartering of his body, a punishment, it should perhaps be noted, used at the time in western Europe in cases of flagrant treason.

Pugachev's rebellion was the most violent peasant uprising in the history of Russia, and the most formidable mass upheaval in Europe in the century before 1789. Catherine replied to it by repression. She conceded more powers to the landlords. The nobles shook off the last vestiges of the compulsory state service to which Peter had bound them. The peasants were henceforth the only bound or unfree class. As in Prussia, the state came more than ever to rest on an understanding between ruler and gentry, by which the gentry accepted the monarchy, with its laws, officials, army, and foreign policy, and received from it, in return, the assurance of full authority over the rural masses. Government reached down through the aristocracy and the scattered towns, but it stopped short at the manor; there the lord took over and was himself a kind of government in his own person. Under these conditions the number of serfs increased, and the load on each became heavier. Catherine's reign saw the culmination of Russian serfdom, which now ceased to differ in any important respect from the chattel slavery to which blacks were subject in the Americas. One might read in the Moscow *Gazette* such advertisements as the following: "For sale, two plump coachmen; two girls 18 and 15 years, quick at manual work. Two

Emelian Pugachev, leader of the most violent, widespread peasant uprising in Russian history, was held in an iron cage before his trial and execution for treason.

barbers; one, 21, knows how to read and write and play a musical instrument; the other can do ladies' and gentlemen's hair."

Catherine the Great: Foreign Affairs

Territorially Catherine was one of the main builders of modern Russia. When she became tsarina in 1762, the empire reached to the Pacific and into central Asia, and it touched upon the Gulf of Riga and the Gulf of Finland on the Baltic, but westward from Moscow one could go only 200 miles before reaching Poland, and no one standing on Russian soil could see the waters of the Black Sea (see map, pp. 222–223). Russia was separated from central Europe by a wide band of loosely organized domains, extending from the Baltic to the Black Sea and the Mediterranean and nominally belonging to the Polish and Turkish states. Poland was an old enemy, which had once threatened Muscovy, and in both Poland and the Ottoman Empire there were many Greek Orthodox Christians with whom Russians felt an ideological tie. In western Europe the disposal of the whole Polish-Turkish tract, which stretched through Asia Minor, Syria, and Palestine into Egypt, came to be called the Eastern Question. Though the name went out of use after 1900, the question of who would control these lands remained a contentious issue in the modern history of both Europe and the Middle East.

Catherine's supreme plan was to penetrate the entire area, Polish and Turkish alike. In a war with Turkey in 1772 she developed her "Greek project," in which "Greeks," that is, members of the Greek Orthodox Church, would replace Muslims as the dominant element throughout the Middle East. She defeated the Turks in the war, but was herself checked by the diplomatic pressures of the European

Territorial expansion

balance of power. The result was the first partition of Poland—a seizure of land and people in which the monarchs of Prussia, Russia, and Austria began to divide up Polish territory between them. Frederick took Pomerelia, which he renamed West Prussia; Catherine took parts of Byelorussia; Maria Theresa, Galicia. Frederick digested his portion with relish, realizing an old dream of the Brandenburg house; Catherine swallowed hers with somewhat less appetite, since she had satisfactorily controlled the whole of Poland before; to Maria Theresa the dish was distasteful, and even shocking, but she could not see her neighbors go ahead without her, and she shared in the feast by suppressing her moral scruples. "She wept," said Frederick cynically, "but she kept on taking." Catherine, in 1774, signed a peace treaty with the defeated Turks at Kuchuk Kainarji on the Danube. The sultan ceded his rights over the Tartar principalities on the north coast of the Black Sea, where the Russians soon founded the seaport of Odessa.

Catherine had only delayed, not altered, her plans with respect to Turkey. She decided to neutralize the opposition of Austria. She invited Joseph II to visit her in Russia, and the two sovereigns proceeded together on a tour of her newly won Black Sea provinces. Her long-time adviser and lover, Grigory Potemkin, accompanied Catherine on this tour, which included visits to numerous towns and fortresses that Potemkin had established in the Crimea. Although the Russians had actually made significant progress in developing the region, Potemkin's enemies claimed that the new towns were nothing but a facade—thus creating the famous phrase "Potemkin villages" to mean bogus evidence of a nonexistent prosperity. At Kherson Catherine and Joseph II passed through a gate marked "The Road to Byzantium." "What I want is Silesia," said Joseph II, but the tsarina induced him to join in a war of conquest against Turkey.

This war with Turkey was interrupted by the French Revolution. Both governments reduced their commitments in the Balkans to await developments in western Europe. It became Catherine's policy to incite Austria and Prussia into a war with revolutionary France, in the name of monarchy and civilization, in order that she might have a free hand in the Polish-Turkish sphere. Meanwhile she contributed to killing off the nationalist and reforming movement among the Poles. In 1793 she arranged with Prussia for the second partition, and in 1795, with both Prussia and Austria, for the third. She was the only ruler who lived to take part in all three partitions of Poland (which are described later in this chapter).

Catherine's reign evaluated

Her protestations of enlightenment tempt one to an ironic judgment of her career. Her foreign policy was purely expansionist and unscrupulous, and the net effect of her domestic policy, aside from a few reforms of detail, was to favor the half-Europeanized aristocracy and to extend serfdom among the people. In her defense it may be observed that unscrupulous expansion was the accepted practice of the time, and that, domestically, probably no ruler could have corrected the social evils from which Russia suffered. If there was to be a Russian empire, it had to be with the consent of the serf-owning gentry, which was the only politically significant class. As Catherine observed to Diderot on the subject of reforms: "You write only on paper, but I have to write on human skin, which is incomparably more irritable and ticklish." She had reason to know how easily tsars and tsarinas could be unseated and even murdered and that the danger of overthrow came not from the peasants but from cliques of army officers and landlords.

Yet she remained attuned to the West. She never thought that the peculiar institutions of Russia should become a model for others. She continued to recognize the standards of the Enlightenment. In her later years she gave careful attention to her favorite grandson,

Alexander, closely supervising his education, which she planned on the Western model. She gave him as a tutor the Swiss philosophe La Harpe, who filled his mind with humane and liberal sentiments on the duties of princes. Trained by Catherine as a kind of ideal ruler, Alexander I was destined to cut a wide circle in the affairs of Europe, to help defeat Napoleon Bonaparte, preach peace and freedom, and suffer from the same internal cultural divisions and frustrations by which educated Russians seemed characteristically to be afflicted.

The Limitations of Enlightened Despotism

Enlightened despotism, seen in retrospect, foreshadowed an age of revolution and even signified a preliminary effort to revolutionize society by authoritative action from above. People were told by their own governments that reforms were needed, that many privileges, special liberties, or tax exemptions were bad, that the past was a source of confusion, injustice, or inefficiency in the present. The state rose up as more completely sovereign, whether acting frankly in its own interest or claiming to act in the interest of its people. All old and established rights were brought into question—rights of kingdoms and provinces, orders and classes, legal bodies and corporate groups. Enlightened despotism overrode or exterminated the Society of Jesus, the Parlement of Paris, the autonomy of Bohemia, and the independence of Poland. Customary and common law was pushed aside by authoritative legal codes. Governments, by opposing the special powers of the church and the feudal interests, tended to make all persons into uniform and equal subjects. To this extent enlightened despotism favored equality before the law. But it could go only a certain distance in this direction. The king was after all a hereditary aristocrat himself, and no government can be revolutionary to the point of breaking up its own foundations.

Even before the French Revolution enlightened despotism had run its course. Everywhere the "despots," for reasons of politics if not of principle, had reached a point beyond which they could not go. In France Louis XVI had appeased the privileged classes; in the Austrian empire Joseph's failure to appease them threw them into open revolt; in Prussia and in Russia the brilliant reigns of Frederick and Catherine wound up in an aggravation of landlordism for the mass of the people. Almost everywhere there was an aristocratic and even feudal revival. Religion also was renewing itself in many ways. Many were again saying that kingship was in a sense divine, and a new alliance was forming between "the throne and the altar." The French Revolution, by terrifying the old vested interests, was to accelerate and embitter a reaction which had already begun. Monarchy in Europe, ever since the Middle Ages, had generally been a centralizing but progressive institution that set itself against the feudal and ecclesiastical powers. Enlightened despotism was the culmination of the historic institution of monarchy. After the enlightened despots, and after the French Revolution, monarchy became on the whole nostalgic and backward-looking, supported most ardently by the churches and aristocracies that it had once tried to subdue and least of all by those who felt in themselves the surge of the future.

38. THE PARTITIONS OF POLAND

The fate of eighteenth-century Poland has been mentioned as a consequence of the growing power of the newer Central European monarchies, but the partitions of Polish territories also illustrate the assumptions and practices of the so-called "enlightened despots." Apart from the still somewhat non-European state of Russia, Poland in the eighteenth century was by far the largest state in Europe. It reached at the beginning of the century from the Baltic almost to the Black Sea and extended eastward for 800 miles across the north-European plain. But it was the classic example, along with the Holy Roman Empire, of an older political structure which failed to develop modern organs of government (see maps, pp. 193, 194). It fell into ever deeper anarchy and confusion. Without army, revenues, or administration and internally divided among parties forever at cross-purposes, the country was a perpetual theater for foreign diplomatic maneuvering and was finally absorbed by its growing neighbors.

The Polish kings were chosen in elections that became an object of regular international interference. A movement for reform therefore began to gather strength after the 1730s, and Polish patriots sought to do away with the *liberum veto* and other elements in the constitution that made government impossible. The reformers were repeatedly frustrated, however, by the influence of Catherine the Great and other foreign rulers who preferred a Poland in which they could intervene at will. Catherine's candidate for the Polish throne, Stanislas Poniatowski, won an election in 1763, thereby giving her new influence over Poland's domestic affairs. She declared herself protector of the Polish liberties. It was to the Russian advantage to maintain the existing state of affairs in Poland rather than to divide the country with neighbors who might exclude Russian influence from their own spheres. The Prussian government, which was eager to join the old duchy of Prussia with its other territories in the east, developed a greater interest in dividing Poland as a means to enhance its own strategic position.

Interference in Polish elections

The opportunity for Prussia presented itself in 1772, when Russia's war with Turkey destabilized the situation in eastern Europe. The Russian victories in this war were so overwhelming that both Austrians and Prussians feared an enduring Russian disruption of the balance of power. The Prussians therefore came forward with a proposal. It was a proposal to prevent an Austro-Russian war and to preserve the balance in Eastern Europe by leaving the Ottoman Empire more or less intact, but to have all three European powers annex territory from Poland instead. The proposition was accepted by all three parties.

Poland was thus sacrificed. By the first partition in 1772, its outer territories were cut away. Russia took an eastern slice around the city of Vitebsk. Austria took a southern slice, the region known as Galicia. Prussia realized its territorial ambitions by taking the Pomerelian borderland in West Prussia and creating a solid Prussian block from the Elbe to the borders of Lithuania (see map, p. 208, panel 4). The partition sobered the Poles, who renewed their efforts at a national revival, hoping to create an effective sovereignty which could secure the country against outsiders. But the Polish movement lacked deep popular strength, for it was confined mainly to nobles, whose conflicts had brought the country to ruin. The mass of the serf population and the numerous Jews did not much care at this time whether they were governed by Poles, Russians, or Germans.

Nevertheless, beginning in 1788, a reform party gathered strength. One of its members was King Stanislas Poniatowski himself, who had begun his reign as a protégé of the Russian empress. The reformers produced a new constitution in 1791. It made the Polish kingship hereditary, thus strengthening the executive government, and it reduced the powers of the great magnates while giving political rights to many burghers in the towns. By this time, however, the governments of eastern Europe were afraid of the French Revolution, which they saw as an outbreak of "Jacobinism." Denouncing the Polish reformers as Jacobins, Catherine the Great said she would "fight Jacobinism and beat it in Poland." In collusion with a few disgruntled Polish noblemen she sent an army into Poland and destroyed the constitution of 1791. In agreement with Prussia she then carried out the Second Partition in 1793. In 1794 Thaddeus Kosciusko led a more revolutionary political movement, which included even a proposed abolition of serfdom. Although it received no aid from the revolutionaries then governing France, it was crushed in the general European counterrevolution when Russian and Prussian armies again invaded Poland, defeated Kosciusko, and in a Third Partition in 1795 divided what remained of the country among themselves and Austria. Poland as a political entity ceased to exist.

Many advanced thinkers of the day praised the partitions of Poland as a triumph of enlightened rulers, putting an end to an old nuisance. The three partitioning powers justified their conduct on various grounds and even took pride in it as an enlightened diplomatic achievement by which war was prevented among them. It was argued also that the partitions of Poland put an end to an old cause of international rivalry and war, replacing anarchy with more stable governments in a large area of eastern Europe. It is a fact that Poland had been scarcely more independent before the partitions than after. It is to be noted also, though nationalist arguments were not used at the time, that on national grounds the Poles themselves had no claim to large parts of the old Poland. The regions taken by Russia were inhabited overwhelmingly by Byelorussians and Ukrainians, among whom the Poles were mainly a landlord class. Russia, even after the third partition, reached only to the true ethnic border of Poland. But later, after the fall of Napoleon, by general international agreement, the Russian sphere was extended deep into the territory inhabited by Poles.

Debate over the partitions

The partitions of Poland, however extenuated, were nevertheless a great shock to the old system of Europe. Edmund Burke, in England, prophetically saw in the first partition the crumbling of the old international order. His diagnosis was a shrewd one. The principle of the balance of power had been historically invoked to preserve the independence of European states and to secure weak or small ones against universal monarchy. It was now used to destroy the independence of a weak but ancient kingdom. Poland was not the first European kingdom to be "partitioned," but it was the first to be partitioned without war and the first to disappear totally. That Poland was partitioned without war, a source of great satisfaction to the partitioning powers, was still a very unsettling fact. It was alarming for a huge state to vanish simply by cold diplomatic calculation. It seemed that no established rights were safe even in peacetime. The partitions of Poland showed that in a world where great powers had arisen in control of a modern state apparatus it was dangerous not to be strong. They suggested that any area failing to develop a sovereign state capable of keeping out foreign infiltration, and so situated as to be within the reach of the great powers of Europe, was unlikely to retain its independence. In this way the history of eighteenth-century Poland anticipated, for example, the partitions of Africa a century later, when Africa too, lacking strong governments, was almost totally divided, without war, among half a dozen states of Europe.

Moreover the partitions of Poland, while maintaining a balance of power in eastern Europe, profoundly changed the balance of Europe as a whole. The disappearance of Poland was a blow to France, which had long used Poland, as it had used Hungary and Turkey, as an outpost of French influence in eastern Europe. The three Eastern powers expanded their territory, while France enjoyed henceforth no permanent growth. Eastern Europe bulked larger than ever before in the affairs of Europe. Prussia, Russia, and the Austrian empire became contiguous. Although they had drawn somewhat differently on western European methods of statecraft and military organization to build their power, they had a common interest and objective in eastern Europe, the repression of Polish resistance to their rule. Polish resistance, dating from before the partitions and continuing thereafter, was the earliest example of modern revolutionary nationalism in Europe.

The independence of Poland, and of other submerged nationalities, later became a popular cause in western Europe, while the three great monarchies of eastern Europe were

POLAND SINCE THE EIGHTEENTH CENTURY

The top panel shows, in simplified form, the ethnic composition of the area included in the Poland of 1772. In addition to languages shown, Yiddish was spoken by the large scattered Jewish population. The line set in 1795 as the western boundary of Russia persists through later changes. It reappears as the eastern border of Napoleon's Grand Duchy and of Congress Poland. After the First World War the victorious Allies contemplated much this same line as Poland's eastern frontier (the dotted line in the fourth panel, known as the Curzon Line); but the Poles in 1920–1921 conquered territory farther east. After the Second World War the Russians pushed the Poles back to the same basic line, but compensated Poland with territory taken from Germany, as far west as the river Oder and its tributary, the Neisse. The position of Warsaw in each panel shows how Poland has been shoved westward.

drawn together in common opposition to national liberation; this fact, plus the fact that the eastern monarchies were primarily landlord states, accentuated the political and social division of Europe in the nineteenth century between a western Europe that inclined to be liberal and an eastern Europe that inclined to be reactionary. The first great assault on the older social order and political system in eighteenth-century Europe, however, came from the "enlightened despots" who destroyed the kingdom of Poland.

39.   NEW STIRRINGS: THE BRITISH REFORM MOVEMENT

It was not only by monarchs and their ministers that the older privileged, feudal, and ecclesiastical interests were threatened. Beginning about 1760 they were challenged also in more popular quarters. Growing out of the Enlightenment, and out of the failure of governments to cope with grave social and fiscal problems, a new era of revolutionary disturbance was about to open. It was marked above all by the great French Revolution of 1789, but the American Revolution of 1776 was also of international importance. In Great Britain, too, the long-drawn-out movement for parliamentary reform that began in the 1760s was in effect revolutionary in character, though nonviolent, since it questioned the foundations of traditional English government and society. In addition, in the last third of the eighteenth century, there was revolutionary agitation in Switzerland, Belgium, and Holland, in Ireland, Poland, Hungary, Italy, and in lesser degree elsewhere. After 1800 revolutionary ferment was increasingly evident in Germany, Spain, and Latin America. This general wave of revolution may be said not to have ended until after the revolutions of 1848.

Onset of an Age of "Democratic Revolution"

For the whole period the term "Atlantic Revolution" has sometimes been used, since countries on both sides of the Atlantic were affected. It has been called also an age of "Democratic Revolution," since in all the diversity of these upheavals, from the American Revolution to those of 1848, certain principles of the modern democratic society were in one way or another affirmed. In this view, the particular revolutions, attempted revolutions, or basic reform movements are seen as aspects of one great revolutionary wave by which virtually the whole area of Western civilization was transformed. There is also another view of this revolutionary age, namely, that each country presented a special case, which can be misunderstood if specific national events are described only as part of a vague general international turmoil. Thus the American Revolution, it is argued, was essentially a movement for independence, conservative in its objectives, and entirely different from the French Revolution, in which a thorough renovation of all society and ideas was contemplated; and both were utterly different from what happened in England, where there was no revolution at all. It need only be stressed here, however, that the American revolutionaries, the French Jacobins, the United Irish, the Dutch Patriots, and similar groups, though differing from each other, shared much in common that can only be characterized as revolutionary and as contributing to a revolutionary age.

It is important to see in what ways the movement that began about 1760 was and was not "democratic." It did not generally demand universal suffrage, though a handful of persons in England did so as early as the 1770s and some of the American states practiced an almost universal male suffrage after 1776, as did the more militant French revolutionaries in 1792. It did not aim at a welfare state, nor question the right of property, though there were signs pointing in these directions in the extreme wing of the French Revolution. It was not especially directed against monarchy as such. The quarrel of the Americans was primarily with the British Parliament, not the king; the French proclaimed a republic by default in 1792, three years after their revolution began; the revolutionary Poles after 1788 tried to strengthen their king's position, not weaken it; and revolutionary groups could come into action where no monarchy existed at all, as in the Dutch provinces before the French Revolution, and the Swiss cantons, the Venetian Republic, or again in Holland, under French influence after 1795. Indeed the first revolutionary outbreak of the period occurred in 1768 at Geneva, a very nonmonarchical small city-republic, ruled by a close-knit circle of hereditary patricians. Royal power, where it existed, became the victim of revolutionaries only where it was used to support various privileged social groups.

Liberty and equality

The revolutionary movement announced itself everywhere as a demand for "liberty and equality." It favored declarations of rights and explicit written constitutions. It proclaimed the sovereignty of the people, or "nation," and it formulated the idea of national citizenship. In this context the "people" were essentially classless; it was a legal term, signifying not government but the community over which public authority was exercised and from which government itself was in principle derived. To say that citizens were equal meant originally that there was no difference between noble and commoner. To say that the people were sovereign meant that neither the king, nor the British Parliament, nor any group of nobles, patricians, regents, or other elite possessed power of government in their own right; that all public officers were removable and exercised a delegated authority within limits defined by the constitution. There must be no "magistrate" above the people, no self-perpetuation or cooptation in office, no rank derived from birth and acknowledged in the law. Social distinctions, as the French said in their Declaration of Rights of 1789, were to be based only "on common utility." Elites of talent or function there might be, but none of birth, privilege, or estate. "Aristocracy" in every form must be shunned. In representative bodies, there could be no special representation for special groups; representatives should be elected by frequent elections, not indeed by universal suffrage, but by a body of voters, however defined, in which each voter should count for one in a system of equal representation. Representation by numbers, with majority rule, replaced the older idea of representation of social classes, privileged towns, or other corporate groups.

In short, everything associated with absolutism, feudalism, or inherited right (except the right of property) was repudiated. Likewise rejected was any connection between religion and citizenship, or civil rights. The Democratic Revolution undermined the special position of the Catholic church in France, the Anglican in England and Ireland, and the Dutch Reformed in the United Provinces. This was also the great period of what has been called Jewish "emancipation," which gave Jews political and social rights that had been denied to them throughout the Middle Ages and early modern era. The whole idea that government, or any human authority, was somehow willed by God and protected by religion faded away. A general liberty of opinion on all subjects was countenanced, in the belief that it was necessary to progress. Here again the secularism of the Enlightenment was carried from science and philosophy into many of the new political and cultural institutions that emerged during this era of revolutionary change.

On the whole, the Democratic Revolution was a middle-class movement, and indeed the term "bourgeois revolution" was later invented to describe it. Many of its leaders in Europe were in fact nobles who were willing to forgo the historic privileges of nobility; and many of its supporters were of the poorer classes, especially in the great French Revolution. But the middle classes were the great beneficiaries, and it was a kind of middle-class or bourgeois society that emerged. Persons of noble ancestry continued to exist after the storm was over, but the world of noble values was gone; and they either took part in various activities on much the same terms as others or retreated into exclusive drawing rooms to enjoy their aristocratic distinctions in private. The main drive of the working classes was still to come.

The English-Speaking Countries: Parliament and Reform

If the American Revolution was the first act of a larger drama, it must be understood also in connection with the broader British world of which the American colonies formed a part. The British Empire in the middle of the century was decentralized and composite. Thirty-one governments were directly subordinate to Westminster, ranging from the separate kingdom of Ireland through all the crown and charter colonies to the various political establishments maintained in the East by the East India Company. The whole empire, with about 15,000,000 people of all colors in 1750, was less populous than France or the Austrian monarchy. The whole tract of the American mainland from Georgia to Nova Scotia compared in the number of its white population with Ireland or Scotland—or with Brittany or Bohemia—a figure of about 2,000,000 being roughly applicable in each case.

Britain had its own way of passing through the Age of Enlightenment. There was general contentment with the arrangements that followed the English Revolution of 1688—it has often been remarked that nothing is so conservative as a successful revolution. British thought generally lacked the asperity of thought on the Continent. The writers who most resembled French philosophes, such as the Scottish philosopher David Hume and the English historian Edward Gibbon, were moderate in their political ideas. The prevailing mood, however, was one of complacency, a self-satisfaction in the glories of the unwritten British constitution by which Englishmen enjoyed liberties unknown on the Continent.

In Britain, Parliament was as supreme as the monarchs in most Continental countries. It had the power, as one facetious journalist put it, to do all things except change a man into a woman. The British Parliament was indeed more sovereign than any European ruler, since less that could be called feudalism remained in England than on the Continent. Nor was there any "despotism" in England, enlightened or otherwise. The young George III, who inherited the throne in 1760, did feel himself to be a "patriot king." He did wish to heighten the influence of the crown and to overcome the factionalism of parties. But it was through Parliament that he had to work. He had to descend into the political arena himself, buy up or otherwise control votes in the Commons, grant pensions and favors, and make promises and deals with other parliamentary politicians. What he did in effect was to create a new faction, the "king's friends." This faction was in power during the ministry of Lord North from 1770 to 1782. It is worth noting that all factions were factions of Whigs, that the Tory party was practically defunct, that Britain did not yet have a two-party system, and that the word "Tory," as it came to be used by American revolutionaries, was little more than a term of abuse.

The monarchy in Great Britain

While Parliament was supreme, and constitutional questions apparently settled, there were nevertheless numerous undercurrents of discontent. These were expressed, since the press was freer in England than elsewhere, in many books and pamphlets which were read in the American colonies and helped to form the psychology of the American Revolution. There was, for example, a school of Anglo-Irish Protestant writers who argued that since Ireland was in

English discontent

any case a separate kingdom, with its own parliament, it ought to be less dependent on the central government at Westminster. The possibility of a similar separate state remaining within the British Empire, was one of the alternatives considered by Americans before they settled on independence. In England there was the considerable body of Dissenters, or Protestants not accepting the Church of England, who had enjoyed religious toleration since 1689 but continued to labor (until 1828) under various forms of political exclusion. They overlapped with two other amorphous groups, a small number of "commonwealth-men" and a larger and growing number of parliamentary reformers. The commonwealth-men, increasingly eccentric and largely ignored, looked back nostalgically to the Puritan Revolution and the republican era of Oliver Cromwell. They kept alive memories of the Levellers and ideals of equality, well mixed with a pseudo-history of a simple Anglo-Saxon England that had been crushed by the despotism of the Norman Conquest. They had less influence in England than in the American colonies and especially New England, whose origins were closely connected to the Puritan Revolution. The parliamentary reformers were a more diverse and influential group. They were condemned in the eighteenth century to repeated frustration; not until the First Reform Bill of 1832 did they begin to accomplish their goals.

Parliamentary politics

The very power of Parliament meant that political leaders had to take strong measures to assure its votes. These measures were generally denounced by their critics as "corruption," on the grounds that Parliament, whether or not truly representative, should at least be free. Control of Parliament, and especially of the House of Commons, was assured by various devices, such as patronage or the giving of government jobs (called "places"), or awarding contracts, or having infrequent general elections (every seven years after 1716); or the fact that in many constituencies there were no real elections at all. The distribution of seats in the Commons bore no relation to numbers of inhabitants. A town having the right to send members to Parliament was called a "borough," but no new borough was created after 1688 (or until 1832). Thus localities that had been important in the medieval or Tudor periods were represented, but towns that had grown up recently, such as Manchester and Birmingham, were not. A few boroughs were populous and democratic, but many had few inhabitants or none, so that influential "borough mongers" decided who should represent them in Parliament.

The reform movement

The reform movement began in England before the American Revolution, with which it was closely associated. Since complaints were diverse, it attracted people of different kinds. The first agitation centered about John Wilkes, a journalist and member of Parliament who vehemently attacked the policies of King George III. He was vindicated when the courts pronounced the arrest of his publisher illegal, but the king's supporters expelled him from the House of Commons. Wilkes became a political hero, however, and was later reelected three times to the House, which refused to seat him. A whirl of protests, public meetings, and petitions supported him against the exclusionary actions of Parliament. His followers in 1769 founded the Supporters of the Bill of Rights, the first of many societies dedicated to parliamentary reform. His case raised the question of whether the House of Commons should be dependent on the electorate and on the propriety of mass agitation "out of doors" on political questions. It was in this connection, also, that debates in Parliament for the first time came to be reported in the London press. Parliament stood on the eve of a long transition, by which it was to be converted from a select body meeting in private to a modern representative institution answerable to the public and its constituents. Wilkes himself finally

THE HON. MRS. GRAHAM
by Thomas Gainsborough (English, 1727–1788)

High social status is very evident in this portrayal of a young English gentlewoman. The wealth of her social class is apparent in the brooch, the plumes, the silks, bows and ruffles, and in the strings of pearls. Her delicate hands and the classical colonnade suggest a life of leisure and cultural importance. This is the way that English aristocrats of the eighteenth century liked to imagine themselves and to be portrayed for posterity.

(National Galleries of Scotland)

regained his parliamentary seat in 1774 and soon introduced the first of many reform bills, none of which passed for over half a century.

Meanwhile, the important Whig leaders, who had previously managed Parliament by manipulating elections in lightly populated boroughs, began to sense "corruption" in such methods after control passed to George III and his "friends." Their most eloquent spokesman was Edmund Burke. Other reformers called for more frequent elections, "annual parliaments," a wider and more equal or even universal

Edmund Burke

male suffrage, with dissolution of some boroughs in which no one was really represented. Burke favored none of these things; in fact he came strenuously to oppose them. A founder of philosophical conservatism, he was yet in his way a reformer. He was more concerned that the House of Commons should be independent and responsible than that it should be mathematically representative. He thought that the landowning interest should govern. But he pleaded for a strong sense of party in opposition to royal encroachments, and he argued that members of Parliament should follow their own best judgment of the country's interests, bound neither by the king on the one hand nor by their own constituents on the other. Like other reformers, he objected to "placemen," or jobholders dependent on their ministerial patrons, and he objected to the use made, for political purposes, of a bewildering array of pensions, sinecures, honorific appointments, and ornamental offices, ranks, and titles. In his Economical Reform of 1782, which curtailed crown patronage, he got many of these abolished.

The reform movement, though ineffectual, remained strong. Even William Pitt, as prime minister in the 1780s, gave it his sponsorship. It took on new strength at the time of the French Revolution, spreading then to more popular levels, as members of the skilled artisan class responded to events in France by demanding a more adequate "representation of the people" in England. They then had upper-class support from Charles James Fox and a minority of the Whigs. But conservatism, satisfaction with the British constitution, patriotism engendered by a new round of French wars, and reaction against the French Revolution all raised an impassable barrier. Reform was delayed for another generation.

After the American Revolution, which in a way was a civil struggle within the English-speaking world, the English reformers generally blamed the trouble with America on King George III. This was less than fair, since Parliament on the American question was never dragooned by the king. The most ardent reformers later argued that if Parliament had been truly representative of the British people, the Americans would not have been driven to independence. This seems unlikely. In any case, reformers of various kinds, from Wilkes to Burke, were sympathetic to the complaints of the American colonials after 1763. There was much busy correspondence across the Atlantic. Wilkes was a hero in Boston as well as London. Burke pleaded for conciliation with the colonies in a famous speech of 1775. His very insistence on the powers and dignity of Parliament, however, made it hard for him to find a workable solution; and after the colonies became independent, he showed no interest in the political ideas of the new American states. It was the more radical reformers in England, as in Scotland and Ireland, who most consistently favored the Americans, both before and after independence. They of course had no power. On the American side, for a decade before independence, the increasingly discontented colonials, reading English books and pamphlets and reports of speeches, heard George III denounced for despotism and Parliament accused of incorrigible corruption. All this seemed to confirm what Americans had long been reading anyway in the works of English Dissenters or old commonwealthmen, now on the fringes of English society but sure of a receptive audience in the American colonies. The result was to make Americans suspicious

Edmund Burke's insistence on the political and social value of inherited traditions made him a key figure in the emergence of modern conservatism. Although he favored an independent Parliament in Britain, he wrote a famous critique of the revolution that abolished traditional royal prerogatives in France. He appears here in an engraving from the 1770s, after a painting by Sir Joshua Reynolds.
(Getty Images)

of all actions by the British government, to sense tyranny everywhere, to magnify such things as the Stamp Act into a kind of plot against American liberties.

The real drift in England in the eighteenth century, however, despite the chronic criticism of Parliament, was for Parliament to extend its powers in a general centralization of the empire. The British government faced somewhat the same problems as governments on the Continent. All had to deal with the issues raised by the great war of the mid-century, in its two phases of the Austrian Succession and Seven Years' War. Everywhere the solution adopted by governments was to increase their own central power. We have seen how the French government, in attempting to tap new sources of revenue, tried to encroach on the liberties of Brittany and other provinces and to subordinate the bodies which in France were called parlements. We have likewise seen how the Habsburg government, also in an effort to raise more taxes, repressed local self-government in the empire and consolidated power in a more centralized bureaucracy. The same tendency showed itself in the British system. The Habsburg revocation of a constitutional charter in Bohemia in 1749 had its parallel in the revocation of the charter of Massachusetts in 1774. The disputes of the French king with the estates of Brittany or Languedoc had their parallel in the disputes of the British Parliament with the provincial assemblies of Virginia or New York.

British centralization

Scotland, Ireland, India

The British also faced problems nearer home. Scotland proved a source of weakness in the War of the Austrian Succession. The Lowlanders were loyal enough, but the Highlanders revolted with French assistance in the Jacobite rising of 1745 and by invading England threatened to attack the British government in the rear as it was locked in the struggle with France. The Highlands had never really been under any government, even under the old Scottish monarchy before

British rule in Scotland

CHRONOLOGY OF NOTABLE EVENTS, 1733–1795

1733	Voltaire publishes *Philosophical Letters on the English*
1741	Montesquieu publishes *The Spirit of Laws*
1751–1772	Publication of the *Encyclopedia* in Paris
1753	Jean-Jacques Rousseau publishes *Origin of Inequality Among Men*
1762	Rousseau publishes *The Social Contract* and *Émile*
1762–1796	Tsarina Catherine the Great reigns as "enlightened despot" in Russia
1769	Emergence of Reform Movement in British Parliament
1772	Prussia, Austria, and Russia impose the First Partition of Poland
1773	Emelian Pugachev leads a rebellion of the lower classes in Russia
1774–1792	King Louis XVI reigns in France
1776	Adam Smith publishes *The Wealth of Nations*
1776–1783	Revolutionary War achieves American independence from Britain
1780–1790	Emperor Joseph II introduces "enlightened" reforms in Austria
1784	Britain creates the India Office to manage British interests in India
1787	Written Constitution establishes new government in the United States
1793, 1795	Second and Third Partitions of Poland destroy the Polish state

the union of 1707 with England. Men in the Highlands looked to their chiefs, the heads of the clans, to tell them whom and when to fight. The chiefs had hereditary jurisdiction, often including powers of life and death, over their clans. A few leaders could throw the whole region to the Stuarts or the French. The British government, after 1745, proceeded to make its sovereignty effective in the Highlands. Troops were quartered there for years. Roads were pushed across the moors and through the glens. Law courts enforced the law of the Scottish Lowlands. Revenue officers collected funds for the treasury of Great Britain. The chiefs lost their old quasi-feudal jurisdiction. The old system of land tenure was broken up, and the holding of land from clannish chiefs was ended. Fighting High-landers were incorporated into newly formed Highland regiments of the British army, under the usual discipline imposed by the modern state on its fighting forces. For 30 years the Scots were forbidden to wear the kilt or play the bagpipes.

The British in Ireland

In Ireland the process of centralization worked itself out more slowly. How Ireland was subjected after the battle of the Boyne has already been described. It was a French army that had landed in Ireland, supported James II, and been defeated in 1690. The new English constitutional arrangements, the Hanoverian succession, the Protestant ascendancy, the church and the land settlement in Ireland, together with the prosperity of British commerce, were all secured by the subordination of the smaller island. The native or Catholic Irish remained generally pro-French. The Presbyterian Irish disliked both the French and popery, but they were alienated from England also; many in fact emigrated to America in the generation before the American Revolution. Ireland remained quiet in the mid-century wars. When the trouble began between the

British Parliament and the American colonies, the Presbyterian Irish generally took the American side. They were greatly stirred by the example of American independence. Thousands formed themselves into Volunteer Companies; they wore uniforms, armed, and drilled; they demanded both internal reform of the Irish parliament (which was even less representative than the British) and greater autonomy for the Irish parliament as against the central government at Westminster.

Faced with these demands, and fearing a French invasion of Ireland during the War of American Independence, the British government made concessions. It allowed an increase of power to the Irish parliament at Dublin. But from the English parliament Catholics were still excluded. In the next war between France and Great Britain, which began in 1793, many Irish felt a warm sympathy for the French Revolution. Catholics and Presbyterians, at last combining, formed a network of United Irish societies throughout the whole island. They sought French aid, and the French barely failed to land a sizable army. Even without French military support, the United Irish rose in 1798 to drive out the English and establish an independent republic. The British, suppressing the rebellion, now turned to centralization. The separate kingdom of Ireland, and the Irish parliament, ceased to exist. The Irish were thereafter represented in the imperial Parliament at Westminster. These provisions were incorporated in the Act of Union of 1801, creating the United Kingdom of Great Britain and Ireland, which lasted until 1922.

British establishments in India also felt the hand of Parliament increasingly upon them. At the close of the Seven Years' War the various British posts in and around Bombay, Madras, and Calcutta were unconnected with *Intervention in India* each other and subordinate only to the board of directors of the East India Company in London. Company employees interfered at will in the wars and politics of the Indian states and enriched themselves by such means as they could, not excluding graft, trickery, intimidation, rapine, and extortion. In 1773 the ministry of Lord North passed a Regulating Act, of which the main purpose was to regulate the British subjects in India, whom no Indian government could control. The company was left with its trading activities, but its political activities were brought under parliamentary supervision. The act gathered all the British establishments under a single governor general, set up a new supreme court with British judges at Calcutta, and required the company to submit its correspondence on political matters for review by the ministers of His Majesty's Government. Warren Hastings became the first British governor general in India. He was so high-handed with some of the Indian princes, and made so many enemies among jealous English residents in Bengal, that he was denounced at home, impeached, and subjected to a trial which dragged on for seven years in the House of Lords. He was finally acquitted. After Clive, whose interventions had rapidly expanded British power there during the 1750s, Hastings was the main author of British supremacy in India. Meanwhile, in 1784 an India office was created in the British ministry at home. The governor general henceforth ruled the growing British sphere in India almost as an absolute monarch but only as the agent of the ministry and Parliament of Great Britain.

Thus the trend in the British world was to centralization. Despite the flutter of royalism under George III, it was to a centralization of all British territories under the authority of Parliament. What was happening in empire affairs, as in domestic politics in England, was a continuing application of the principles of 1689. The parliamentary sovereignty established in 1689 was now, after the middle of the eighteenth century, being applied to regions where it had heretofore had little effect. And it was against the authority of the British Parliament that the Americans primarily rebelled.

40.   THE AMERICAN REVOLUTION

Background to the Revolution

The behavior of the Americans in the Seven Years' War, as viewed by the British government, left much to be desired. The several colonial legislatures rejected the Albany Plan of Union drafted by Franklin and commended to them by British officials. During the war it was the British regular army and navy, financed by taxes and loans in Great Britain, that drove the French out of America. The war effort of the Anglo-Americans was desultory at best. After the defeat of the French the colonials had still to reckon with the Indians of the interior, who preferred French rule to that of their new British and British-colonial masters. Many tribes joined in an uprising led by Pontiac, a western chief, and they carried their attacks on colonial and British outposts as far eastward as the Pennsylvania and Virginia frontiers. Again, the colonials proved unable to deal with a problem vital to their own future, and peace was brought about by officials and army units taking their orders from Great Britain.

The British government tried to make the colonials pay a larger share toward the expenses of the empire. The colonials had hitherto paid only local taxes. They were liable to customs duties, of which the proceeds went in principle to Great Britain; but these duties were levied to enforce the Acts of Trade and Navigation and to direct the flow of commerce, not to raise revenue; and they were seldom paid, because the Acts of Trade and Navigation were persistently ignored. American merchants, for example, commonly imported sugar from the French West Indies, contrary to law, and even shipped in return the iron wares which it was against the law for Americans to manufacture for export. The colonials in practice paid only such taxes as were approved by their own local legislature for local purposes. The Americans in effect enjoyed a degree of tax exemption within the empire, and it was against this form of provincial privilege that Parliament began to move.

By the Revenue Act of 1764 (the "Sugar" Act), the British ministry, while reducing and liberalizing the customs duties payable in America, entered upon a program of actual and systematic collection. In the following year the ministry attempted to extend to British subjects in America a tax peaceably accepted by those in Great Britain and commonplace in most of Europe. This imposed on all uses of paper, as in newspapers and commercial and legal documents, the payment of a fee that was certified by the affixing of a stamp. The Stamp Act aroused violent and concerted resistance in the colonies, especially among the businessmen, lawyers, and editors who were the most articulate class. It therefore was repealed in 1766. In 1767 Parliament, clumsily casting about to find a tax acceptable to the Americans, hit upon the "Townshend duties," which taxed colonial imports of paper, paint, lead, and tea. Another outcry went up, and the Townshend duties were repealed, except the one on tea, which was kept as a token of the sovereign power of Parliament to tax all persons in the empire.

Colonial resistance to new taxes

The colonials had proved stubborn, the government pliable but lacking in constructive ideas. The Americans argued that Parliament had no authority to tax them because they were not represented in it. The British replied that Parliament represented America as much as it represented Great Britain. If Philadelphia sent no actually elected deputies to the Commons, so this argument ran, neither did Manchester in England. Both places enjoyed a kind of "virtual representation," since members of the Commons did not merely speak for local constituencies but made themselves responsible for imperial interests as a whole. To this

Debate over representation

many Americans retorted that if Manchester was not "really" represented it ought to be, which was of course also the belief of the English reformers. Meanwhile the strictly Anglo-American question subsided after the repeal of the Stamp Act and the Townshend program. There had been no clarification of principle on either side. But in practice the Americans had resisted significant taxation, and Parliament had refrained from making any drastic use of its sovereign power.

The calm was shattered in 1773 by an event which proved, to the more dissatisfied Americans, the disadvantages of belonging to a global economic system in which the main policies were made on the other side of the ocean. The East India Company was in difficulties. It had a great surplus of Chinese tea, and in any case it wanted new commercial privileges in return for the political privileges which it was losing in India by the Regulating Act of 1773. In the past the company had been required to sell its wares at public auction in London; other merchants had handled distribution from that point on. Now, in 1773, Parliament granted the company the exclusive right to sell tea through its own agents in America to American local dealers. Tea was a large item of business in the commercial capitalism of the time. The colonial consumer might pay less for it, but the intermediary American merchant would be shut out. The company's tea was boycotted in all American ports. In Boston, to prevent its forcible landing, a party of disguised men invaded the tea ships and dumped the chests into the harbor. To this act of vandalism the British government replied by measures far out of proportion to the offense. It "closed" the port of Boston, thus threatening the city with economic ruin. It virtually rescinded the charter of Massachusetts, forbidding certain local elections and the holding of town meetings.

The Boston Tea Party

And at the same time, in 1774, apparently by coincidence, Parliament enacted the Quebec Act. The wisest piece of British legislation in these troubled years, the Quebec Act provided a government for the newly conquered Canadian French, granting them security in their French civil law and Catholic religion and laying foundations for the British Empire that was to come. But the act defined the boundaries of Quebec somewhat as the French themselves would have defined them, including in them all territory north of the Ohio River—the present states of Wisconsin, Michigan, Illinois, Indiana, and Ohio. In the view of British legislators these boundaries were perfectly reasonable, since the few Europeans in the area were French, and since, in the age before canals or railways, the obvious means of reaching the whole region was by way of the St. Lawrence valley and the Lakes. But to the Americans the Quebec Act was a pro-French and pro-Catholic outrage, and at a time when the powers of juries and assemblies in the old colonies were threatened, it was disquieting that the Quebec Act made no mention of such representative institutions for the new northern province. It was lumped with the closing of an American port and the destruction of the Massachusetts government as one of the "Intolerable Acts" to be resisted.

The Quebec Act

And indeed the implications of parliamentary sovereignty and centralized planning were now apparent. It was no longer merely an affair of taxation. A government that had to take account of the East India Company, the French Canadians, and the British taxpayers, even if more prudent and enlightened than Lord North's ministry of 1774, could not possibly at the same time have satisfied the Americans of the thirteen seaboard colonies. These Americans, since 1763 no longer afraid of the French empire, were less inclined to forgo their own interests in order to remain under British protection or control. British policies had aroused antagonism in the coastal towns and in the backwoods, among wealthy land speculators and poor squatter frontiersmen, among merchants and the workers who depended on the business of merchants. The freedom of Americans to determine their own

MRS. ISAAC SMITH
by John Singleton Copley (American, then English, 1737–1815)
The wife of a Boston merchant, Mrs. Smith represents the bourgeois family background of
many leaders in the American and French revolutions. In general, it was a background of substance, comfort, and hard work. Mrs. Smith's costume and surroundings (though less elegant
than those portrayed in the painting of Mrs. Graham on p. 333) suggest her high station in
New England society. Copley disliked the rising revolutionary agitation in America and emigrated permanently to England in 1774.

(Yale University Art Gallery, Gift of Maitland Fuller Griggs, B.A. 1869, LHD 1938 (1941.74), (detail)) political life was in question. Yet there were few in 1774, or even later, prepared to face the thought of independence.

The War of American Independence

After the "Intolerable Acts," self-authorized groups met in the several colonies and sent delegates to a "continental congress" in Philadelphia. This body adopted a boycott of British goods, to be enforced on unwilling Americans by local organizers of resistance. Fighting began in the next year, 1775, when the British commander at Boston sent a detachment to seize unauthorized stores of weapons at Concord. On the way, at Lexington, in a brush between soldiers and partisans, or "minute-men," someone fired the "shot heard round the world." The Second Conti- *The "shot heard round the world"* nental Congress, meeting a few weeks later, proceeded to raise an American army, appointed George Washington as the commanding general of its troops, dispatched an expedition to force Quebec into the revolutionary union, and entered into overtures with Bourbon France.

The Congress was still reluctant to repudiate the tie with Britain. But passions grew fierce in consequence of the fighting. Radicals convinced moderates that the choice now lay between independence and enslavement. It appeared that the French, naturally uninter-ested in a reconciliation of British subjects, would give help if the avowed aim of Ameri-can rebels was to dismember the British Empire. In January 1776 Thomas Paine, in his pamphlet *Common Sense,* made his debut as a kind of international revolutionary; he was to figure in the French Revolution and to work for revolution in England. He had come from England less than two years before, and he detested English society for its injustices. Eloquent and vitriolic, *Common Sense* identified the independence of the American colonies with the cause of liberty for all humankind. It pitted freedom against tyranny in the person of "the royal brute of Great Britain." It was "repugnant to reason," said Paine, "to suppose that this Continent can long remain subject to any external power. . . . There is something absurd in supposing a Continent to be perpetually governed by an island." *Common Sense* was read everywhere in the colonies, and its slashing arguments unques-tionably spread a sense of proud isolation from the Old World. Such ideas also gained wide support in the Continental Congress, where Thomas Jefferson and other members of a special committee began drafting a theoretical and historical justification for America's separation from Britain. Like Paine, the authors linked their specific grievances to broad Enlightenment claims for universal human rights, thus giving the widest possible signifi-cance to the armed rebellion of some sparsely settled colonies in Britain's far-flung eighteenth-century empire. On July 4, 1776, the Congress adopted the Declaration of Inde-pendence, by which the United States assumed its separate and equal sta-tion among the powers of the earth.

The War of American Independence thereupon turned into another *Role of the European powers* European struggle for empire. For two years more the French government remained ostensibly noninterventionist but meanwhile poured munitions into the colonies through an especially rigged-up commercial concern. Nine-tenths of the arms used by the Americans at the battle of Saratoga came from France. After the Ameri-can victory in this battle the French government concluded, in 1778, that the insurgents were a good political risk, recognized them, signed an alliance with them, and declared war on Great Britain. Spain soon followed, hoping to drive the British from Gibraltar and deciding that its overseas empire was more threatened by a restoration of British supremacy in North America than by the disturbing example of an independent American republic. The Dutch were drawn into hostilities through their trade with the Americans, which flowed mostly by way of the Dutch West Indies. Other powers—Russia, Sweden, Denmark, Prussia, Portugal, and Turkey—irked at British employment of blockade and sea power in time of war, formed an "Armed Neutrality" to protect their commerce from dictation by the British fleet. The French, in a brief revival of their own sea power, landed an expeditionary force of 6,000 men in Rhode Island. The Americans suffered from the internal differences inseparable from all revolutions and were in any case still unable to govern themselves to any effect, meeting with the old difficulties in raising both troops and money. It was therefore the participation of regiments of the French army, in conjunction with squadrons of the French fleet, that made possible the defeat of the armed forces of the British Empire and so persuaded the British government to recognize the independence of the United States. By the peace treaty of 1783, though the British were still in possession of New York and Savannah and though the governments befriending the Americans would just as soon have confined them east of the mountains, the new republic obtained territory as far west as the Mississippi. Canada remained British. It received an English-speaking population by the settlement of over 60,000 refugee Americans who remained loyal to Great Britain.

Significance of the Revolution

The upheaval in America was a revolution as well as a war of independence. The cry for liberty against Great Britain raised echoes within the colonies themselves. The Declaration of Independence was more than an announcement of secession from the empire; it was a justification of rebellion against established authority. Curiously, although the American quarrel had been with the Parliament, the Declaration arraigned no one but the king. One reason was that the Congress, not recognizing the authority of Parliament, could separate from Great Britain only by a denunciation of the British crown; another reason was that the cry of "tyrant" made a more popular and flaming issue. Boldly voicing the natural right philosophy of the age, the Declaration held as "self-evident"—that is, as evident to all reasonable people—that "all men are created equal, that they are endowed by their Creator with certain unalienable rights, that among these are life, liberty, and the pursuit of happiness." These electrifying words leaped inward into America and outward to the world.

The Declaration of Independence

In the new states democratic equality made many advances. It was subject, however, to a great limitation, in that it long applied only to white males of European origin. It was more than a century before women received the vote. American Indians were relatively few in number, but the black population at the time of the Revolution comprised about a fifth of the whole. Many American whites of the revolutionary generation were indeed troubled by the institution of slavery. It was abolished outright in Massachusetts, and all states north of Maryland took steps toward its gradual extinction. But application of the principles of liberty and equality without regard to race or gender went far beyond the political and cultural assumptions of even the most enlightened white Americans at the time. In the South, all censuses from 1790 to 1850 showed a third of the population to be slaves. In the North, free blacks found that in fact, and often in law, they were debarred from voting, from adequate schooling, and from the widening opportunities in which white Americans saw the essence of their national life and their superiority to Europe.

Equality advances and limitations

Brief, violent clashes in Massachusetts in April 1775 launched the long military struggle of the American Revolution. This picture shows the local militia exchanging fire in the village of Lexington with a detachment of the British army that had been sent from Boston to search for arms that American rebels were collecting in the area.

(Photo from the collection of the Lexington, Massachusetts, Historical Society)

For the white male population the Revolution had a democratizing effect in many ways. Lawyers, landowners, and businessmen who led the movement against England needed the support of numbers and to obtain it were willing to make promises and concessions to the lower classes. Or the popular elements, workmen and mechanics, farmers and frontiersmen, often dissidents in religion, extorted concessions by force or threats. There was a good deal of violence, as in all revolutions; the new states confiscated property from the counterrevolutionaries, called Tories, some of whom were tarred and feathered by infuriated mobs. The dissolution of the old

Democratization

colonial governments threw open all political questions. In some states more men became qualified to vote. In some, governors and senators were now popularly elected, in addition to the lower houses of the legislatures as in colonial times. The principle was adopted, still unknown to the parliamentary bodies of Europe, that each member of a legislative assembly should represent about the same number of citizens. Primogeniture and entail, which landed families aspiring to an aristocratic mode of life sometimes favored, went down before the demands of democrats and small property owners. Tithes were done away with, and the established churches—Anglican in the South, Congregationalist in New England—lost their privileged position in varying degree. But the Revolution was not socially as profound as the revolution soon to come in France, or as the revolution in Russia in 1917. Property changed hands, but the law of property was modified only in detail. There had been no such thing in British America as a native nobleman or even a bishop; clergy and aristocracy had been incomparably less ingrained in American than in European society, and the rebellion against them was less devastating in its effect.

The main importance of the American Revolution remained political and even constitutional in a strict sense. The American leaders were themselves part of the Age of Enlightenment, sharing fully in its humane and secular spirit. But probably the only non-British thinker by whom they were influenced was Montesquieu, and Montesquieu owed his popularity to his philosophizing upon English institutions. The Americans drew heavily on the writings of John Locke, but their cast of mind went back before Locke to the English Puritan movement of the first half of the seventeenth century. Their thought was formed not only by Locke's ideas of human nature and government, but, as already noted, by the dissenting literature and the neorepublican writings that had never quite died out in England. The realities of life for five generations in America had sharpened the old insistence upon personal liberty and equality. When the dispute with Britain came to a head, the Americans found themselves arguing both for the historic and chartered rights of the English and for the timeless and universal rights of man, both of which were held up as barriers against the inroads of parliamentary sovereignty. The Americans came to believe, more than any other people, that government should possess limited powers and operate only within the terms of a fixed and written constitutional document.

Influence of Enlightenment thinkers

All 13 of the new states lost no time in providing themselves with written constitutions (in Connecticut and Rhode Island merely the old charters reaffirmed), all of which enshrined virtually the same principles. All followed the thought stated in the great Declaration, that it was to protect "unalienable" rights that governments were instituted among men and that whenever government became destructive to this end the people had a right to "institute new government" for their safety and happiness. All the constitutions undertook to limit government by a separation of executive, legislative, and judicial powers. Most appended a bill of rights, stating the natural rights of the citizens and the actions which no government might justly take. None of the constitutions were as yet fully democratic; even the most liberal gave some advantage in public affairs to the owners of property.

Constitutionalism and federalism

Federalism, or the allocation of power between central and outlying governments, went along with the idea of written constitutions as a principal offering of the Americans to the world. Like constitutionalism, federalism developed in the atmosphere of protest against a centralized sovereign power. It was a hard idea for Americans to work out, since the new states carried over the old separatism which had so distracted the British. Until 1789 the states remained banded together in the

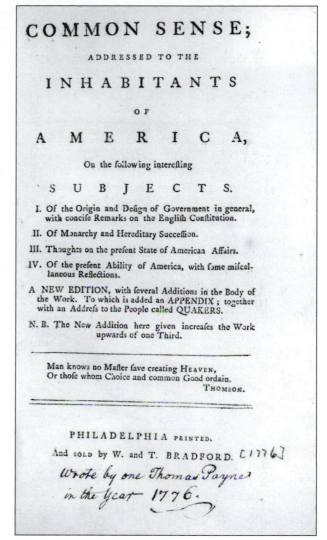

COMMON SENSE;

ADDRESSED TO THE

INHABITANTS

OF

AMERICA,

On the following interesting

SUBJECTS.

I. Of the Origin and Design of Government in general, with concise Remarks on the English Constitution.

II. Of Monarchy and Hereditary Succession.

III. Thoughts on the present State of American Affairs.

IV. Of the present Ability of America, with some miscellaneous Reflections.

A NEW EDITION, with several Additions in the Body of the Work. To which is added an APPENDIX; together with an Address to the People called QUAKERS.

N. B. The New Addition here given increases the Work upwards of one Third.

Man knows no Master save creating HEAVEN, Or those whom Choice and common Good ordain. THOMSON.

PHILADELPHIA PRINTED.

And SOLD by W. and T. BRADFORD. [1776]

Wrote by one Thomas Payne in the year — 1776.

Thomas Paine (1737–1809) lived in England until he arrived in Philadelphia in 1774. He published his *Common Sense* anonymously two years later, after the armed conflict had begun. Widely read, it helped persuade Americans to fight for complete independence from Britain.
(Library of Congress)

Articles of Confederation. The United States was a union of 13 independent republics. Disadvantages in this scheme becoming apparent, a constitutional convention met at Philadelphia in 1787 and drew up the constitution which is today the world's oldest written instrument of government still in operation. In it the United States was conceived not merely as a league of states but as a union in which individuals were citizens of the United States of America for some purposes and of their particular states for others. Persons, not states, composed the federal republic, and the laws of the United States fell not merely on the states but on the people.

The consequences of the American Revolution can hardly be overstated. By overburdening the French treasury, the American war became a direct cause of the French Revolution. Beyond that, it ushered in the age of predominantly liberal or democratic revolution which lasted through the European revolutions of 1848. The American doctrine, like most thought in the Age of Enlightenment, was expressed in universal terms of "man" and "nature." All peoples regardless of their own history could apply it to themselves, because, as Alexander Hamilton once put it in his youth, "the sacred rights of man are not to be rummaged for among old parchments or musty records. They are written, as with a sunbeam, in the whole volume of human nature, by the hand of Divinity itself, and can never be erased or obscured by mortal power." The Americans, in freeing themselves, had done what all peoples ought to do.

*Significance of
American Revolution*

The revolt in America offered a dramatic judgment on the old colonial system, convincing some, in England and elsewhere, that the empires for which they had long been struggling were hardly worth acquiring, since colonies in time, in the words of Turgot, fell away from the mother country "like ripe fruit." The idea spread, since trade between Britain and America continued to prosper, that one could do business with a country without exerting political influence or control, and this idea became fundamental to the coming movement of economic liberalism and free trade. By coincidence, the book that became the gospel of the free trade movement, Adam Smith's *Wealth of Nations,* was published in England in the year 1776. The American example was pointed to by other peoples wishing to throw off colonial status—first by the Latin Americans, then by the peoples of the older British dominions, and, finally, in the twentieth century, by those of Asia and Africa also. In Europe, the American example encouraged the type of nationalism in which subjugated nations aspire to be free. And at home the Revolution did much to determine the spirit and method by which the new nation spread across the North American continent and the ideas by which the United States, when it became a leading power a century and a half later, would explain and justify its national actions in the modern world.

More immediately, the American example was not lost on the many Europeans who sojourned in the new states during and after the war. Of these the Marquis de Lafayette was the most famous, but there were many others: Thomas Paine, who returned to Europe in 1787; the future French revolutionist Brissot; the future Polish national leader Kosciusko; the future marshals of Napoleon, Jourdan and Berthier; the future reformer of the Prussian army Gneisenau. Contrariwise various Americans went to Europe, notably the aging Benjamin Franklin, who in the 1780s was incredibly lionized in the fashionable and literary world of Paris.

*Vindication of
Enlightenment ideas*

The establishment of the United States was taken in Europe to prove that many ideas of the Enlightenment were practicable. Rationalists declared that here was a people, free of past errors and superstitions, who showed how enlightened beings could plan their affairs. Rousseauists saw in America the very paradise of natural equality, unspoiled innocence, and patriotic virtue. But nothing so much impressed Europeans, and especially the French, as the spectacle of the Americans meeting in solemn conclave to draft their state constitutions. These, along with the Declaration of Independence, were translated and published in 1778 by a French nobleman, the Duke de la Rochefoucauld. They were endlessly and excitedly discussed. Constitutionalism, federalism, and limited government were not new ideas in Europe. They came out of the Middle Ages and were currently set forth in many quarters, for example, in Hungary, the Holy Roman Empire, and the Parlement of Paris. But in their prevailing form, and even in the philosophy of Montesquieu, they were associated with feudalism and aristocracy. The American Revolution made such ideas progressive. The American influence, added to the force of developments in Europe, made the thought of the later Enlightenment more democratic. The United States replaced England as the model country of advanced thinkers. On the Continent there was less passive trust in

DECLARATION OF INDEPENDENCE
by John Trumbull (American, 1756–1843)

Trumbull's painting shows the committee that presented America's Declaration of Independence to the Continental Congress in 1776. Although Franklin and Adams are standing with the committee, Thomas Jefferson is presenting the document. Trumbull met often with Jefferson in Paris when he was at work on this painting in the late 1780s, and the picture conveys a Jeffersonian view of the event it portrays.

(Yale University Art Gallery, Trumbull Collection (1832.3))

the enlightened despotism of the official state. Confidence in self-government was aroused.

The American constitutions seemed a demonstration of the social contract. They offered a picture of men in a "state of nature," having cast off their old government, deliberately sitting down to contrive a new one, weighing and judging each branch of government on its merits, assigning due powers to legislature, executive, and judiciary, declaring that all government was created by the people and in possession of a merely delegated authority, and listing specifically the inalienable human rights—inalienable in that they could not conceivably be taken away, since all persons possessed them even if denied them by force. And these rights were the very same rights that many Europeans wanted secured for themselves—freedom of religion, freedom of press, freedom of assembly, freedom from arbitrary arrest at the discretion of officials. And they were all based on the rigorous principle of equality before the law. The American example crystallized and made tangible the ideas that were strongly blowing in Europe, and the American example was one reason why the French, in 1789, began their revolution with a declaration of human rights and with the drafting of a written constitution.

And more deeply still, America became a kind of mirage or ideal vision for Europe, land of open opportunity and of new beginnings, free from the load of history and of the past, wistfully addressed by Goethe:

> *America, thou hast it better*
> *Than has our Continent, the old one.*

It is evident that this was only part of the picture. The United States, as its later history was to show, bore a heavy load of inherited burdens and unsolved problems, especially slavery and pervasive racial discrimination. But in a general way, until new revolutionary and radical social movements set in a century later, America stood as a kind of utopian opportunity for common people, not only for the millions who emigrated to it but for other millions who stayed at home, who often wished that their own countries might become more like it, and many of whom might even agree with Abraham Lincoln in calling it the last best hope of earth.

 For interactive exercises, glossary, chronologies, and more, go to the *Online Learning Center* at **www.mhhe.com/palmer10.**

Chapter *9*

THE FRENCH REVOLUTION

41. Backgrounds

42. The Revolution and the Reorganization of France

43. The Revolution and Europe: The War and the "Second" Revolution, 1792

44. The Emergency Republic, 1792–1795: The Terror

45. The Constitutional Republic: The Directory, 1795–1799

46. The Authoritarian Republic: The Consulate, 1799–1804

In 1789 France fell into revolution, and the world has never since been the same. The French Revolution was by far the most momentous upheaval of the whole revolutionary age. It replaced the "old regime" with "modern society," and at its extreme phase it became very radical, so much so that later revolutionary movements often looked back to it as a predecessor. The ideas of the French Revolution, spreading far beyond France itself, decisively influenced the subsequent development of political parties and ideological conflicts throughout much of Europe and elsewhere; indeed, the Revolution still provokes highly charged debates about the characteristics or consequences of social reform, political radicalism, and revolutionary violence. At the time, in the age of the Democratic or Atlantic Revolution from the 1760s to 1848, the role of France was decisive. Even the Americans, without French military intervention, would hardly have won such a clear settlement from England or been so free to set up the new states and new constitutions that have just been described. And while revolutionary disturbances in Ireland and Poland, or among the Dutch, Italians, and others, were by no means caused by the French example, it was the presence or absence of French aid that usually determined whatever successes they achieved.

The French Revolution, unlike the Russian or Chinese revolutions of the twentieth century, occurred in what was in many ways the most advanced country of the day. France was the center of the intellectual movement of the Enlightenment. French science then led the world. French books were read everywhere, and the newspapers and political journals that became very numerous after 1789 carried a message that hardly needed translation.

Chapter emblem: Detail from *The Tennis Court Oath* by Jacques-Louis David (1748–1825). (Giraudon/Art Resource, NY)

French was a kind of international spoken language in the educated and aristocratic circles of many countries. France was also, potentially before 1789 and actually after 1793, the most powerful country in Europe. It may have been the wealthiest, though not per capita. With a population of 24,000,000 the French were the most numerous of all European peoples under a single government. Even Russia was hardly more populous until after the partitions of Poland. The Germans were divided, the subjects of the Habsburgs were of diverse nationalities, and the English and Scots together numbered only 10,000,000. Paris, though smaller than London, was over twice as large as Vienna or Amsterdam. French exports to Europe were larger than those of Great Britain. It is said that half the goldpieces circulating in Europe were French. Europeans in the eighteenth century were in the habit of taking ideas from France; they were therefore, depending on their social position, the more excited, encouraged, alarmed, or horrified when revolution broke out in that country.

41.   BACKGROUNDS

The Old Regime: The Three Estates

Some remarks have already been made about the Old Regime, as the prerevolutionary society came to be called after it disappeared, and about the failure of enlightened despotism in France to alter it in any fundamental way. The essential fact about the Old Regime was that it was still legally aristocratic and in some ways feudal. Everyone belonged legally to an "estate" or "order" of society. The First Estate was the clergy, the Second Estate was the nobility, and the Third Estate included everyone else—from the wealthiest business and professional classes to the poorest peasantry and city workers. These categories were important in that the individual's legal rights and personal prestige depended on the category to which he or she belonged. Politically, they were obsolescent; not since 1614 had the estates assembled in an Estates General of the whole kingdom, though in some provinces they had continued to meet as provincial bodies. Socially, they were obsolescent also, for the threefold division no longer corresponded to the real distribution of interest, influence, property, or productive activity among the French people.

The church

Conditions in the church and the position of the clergy have in the past been much exaggerated as a cause of the French Revolution. The church in France levied a tithe on all agricultural products, but so did the church in England; the French bishops often played a part in government affairs, but so did bishops in England through the House of Lords. The French bishoprics of 1789 were in reality no wealthier than those of the Church of England were found to be when investigated 40 years later. In actual numbers, in the secular atmosphere of the Age of Enlightenment, the clergy, especially the monastic orders, had greatly declined, so that by 1789 there were probably not more than 100,000 Catholic clergy of all types in the entire population. But if the importance of the clergy has been overemphasized, still it must be said that the church was deeply involved in the prevailing social system. For one thing, church bodies—bishoprics, abbeys, convents, schools, and other religious foundations— owned between 5 and 10 percent of the land of the country, which meant that collectively the church was the greatest of all landowners. Moreover, the income from church properties, like all income, was divided very unequally, and much of it found its way into the hands of the aristocratic occupants of the higher ecclesiastical offices.

This image of French peasants shows how farmers prepared their fields and planted seeds during the 1760s, when the picture was published in a French book. The agrarian system shaped property rights and social hierarchies as well as the supply of food in French cities—all of which created resentments or fears that contributed to the coming of the French Revolution.

(Ann Ronan Picture Library/HIP/ The Image Works)

The noble order, which in 1789 comprised about 400,000 persons, including women and children, had enjoyed a great resurgence since the death of Louis XIV in 1715. Distinguished government service, higher church offices, army, parlements, and most other public and semipublic honors were almost monopolized by the nobility in the time of Louis XVI, who, it will be recalled, had mounted the throne in 1774. Repeatedly, through parlements, Provincial Estates, or the assembly of the clergy dominated by the noble bishops, the aristocracy had blocked royal plans for taxation and shown a desire to control the policies of state. At the same time the bourgeoisie, or upper crust of the Third Estate, had never been so influential. Although the "bourgeoisie" was an amorphous social category (indeed, some historians argue that "bourgeois" refers to a class that never had a real social identity), the number of French merchants, lawyers, and other professional groups clearly grew over the course of the eighteenth century. The fivefold increase of French foreign trade between 1713 and 1789 suggests the growth of the merchant class and of the legal and governmental classes associated with it. As members of the bourgeoisie became stronger, more widely read, and more self-confident, they resented the distinctions enjoyed by the nobles. Some of these were financial: nobles were exempt on principle from the most important direct tax, the taille, whereas bourgeois obtained exemption with more effort; but so many bourgeois enjoyed tax privileges that purely monetary self-interest was not

The nobility

primary in their psychology. The bourgeois resented the nobleman for his superiority and his arrogance. What had formerly been customary respect was now felt as humiliation. And they felt that they were being shut out from office and honors and that the nobles were seeking more power in government as a class. The Revolution thus began in the social and political collision of two moving objects, a rising aristocracy and a rising bourgeoisie.

The Third Estate

The common people, below the commercial and professional families in the Third Estate, were probably as well off as in most countries. But they were not well off compared with the upper classes. Wage earners had by no means shared in the wave of business prosperity. Between the 1730s and the 1780s the prices of consumers' goods rose about 65 percent, whereas wages rose only 22 percent. Persons dependent on wages were therefore badly pinched, but they were less numerous than today, for in the country there were many small farmers and in the towns many small craftsmen who made a living not by wages but by selling the product of their own labor at market prices. Yet in both town and country there was a significant wage-earning population, which was to play a decisive part in the Revolution.

The Agrarian System of the Old Regime

Over four-fifths of the people were rural. The agrarian system had developed so that there was no serfdom in France as it was known in eastern Europe. The peasant owed no labor to the lord—except a few token services in some cases. The peasants worked for themselves, either on their own land or on rented land; or they worked as sharecroppers (*métayers*); or they hired themselves out to the lord or to another peasant.

Survival of feudal privileges

The manor, however, still retained certain surviving features of the feudal age. The noble owner of a manor enjoyed "hunting rights," or the privilege of keeping game preserves and of hunting on his own and the peasants' land. He usually had a monopoly over the village mill, bakeshop, or wine press, for the use of which he collected fees called *banalités*. He possessed certain vestigial powers of jurisdiction in the manorial court and certain local police powers, from which fees and fines were collected. These seigneurial privileges were of course the survivals of a day when the local manor had been a unit of government and the noble had performed the functions of government, an age that had long passed with the development of the centralized modern state.

There was another special feature to the property system of the Old Regime. Every owner of a manor (there were some bourgeois and even wealthy peasants who had purchased manors) possessed what was called a right of "eminent property" with respect to all land located in the manorial village. This meant that lesser landowners within the manor "owned" their land in that they could freely buy, sell, lease, and inherit or bequeath it; but they owed to the owner of the manor, in recognition of his "eminent property" rights, certain rents, payable annually, as well as transfer fees that were payable whenever the land changed owners by sale or death. Subject to these "eminent property" rights, landownership was fairly widespread. Peasants directly owned about two-fifths of the soil of the country; bourgeois, a little under a fifth. The nobility owned perhaps a little over a fifth and the church owned somewhat under a tenth, the remainder being crown lands, wastelands, or commons. Finally, all property rights were subject also to certain "collective" rights by which villagers might cut firewood, run their pigs in the commons, or pasture cattle on land belonging to other owners after the crops were in, which they could easily do because there were usually no fences or enclosures.

All this may seem rather complex, but it is important to realize that property is a changing institution. Even today, in industrialized countries, a high proportion of all property is in land, including natural resources in and below the soil. In the eighteenth century property meant land even more than it does today. The bourgeois class, whose wealth was so largely in ships, merchandise, or commercial paper, also invested heavily in land, and in 1789 they owned almost as much land in France as the nobility and more than the church. The Revolution was to revolutionize the law of property by freeing the private ownership of land from all the indirect encumbrances described—manorial fees, "eminent property" rights, communal village agricultural practices, and church tithes. It also was to abolish other older forms of property, such as property in public office or in masterships in the guilds, which had worked to the advantage mainly of closed and privileged groups. In final effect the Revolution defined and established the institutions of private property in the modern sense and therefore mostly benefited the landowning peasants and the bourgeoisie.

The peasants not only owned two-fifths of the soil but also worked almost all of it on their own initiative and risk. In effect, the land owned by the nobility, the church, the bourgeoisie, and the crown was divided up and leased to peasants in small parcels. France was already a country of small farmers. There was no "big agriculture" as in England, eastern Europe, or the plantations of America. The manorial lord performed no economic function. He lived (there were of course exceptions) not by managing an estate and selling his own crops and cattle but by receiving innumerable dues and fees. During the eighteenth century, in connection with the general aristocratic resurgence, there took place a phenomenon often called the "feudal reaction." Manorial lords, faced with rising living costs and acquiring higher living standards because of the general material progress, collected their dues more rigorously or revived old ones that had fallen into disuse. Leases and sharecropping arrangements also became less favorable to the peasants. The farmers, like the wage earners, were under a steadily increasing pressure. At the same time the peasants resented the "feudal dues" more than ever because they regarded themselves as in many cases the real owners of the land and viewed the lord as a gentleman of the neighborhood who for no reason enjoyed a special income and a status different from their own. The trouble was that much of the property system no longer bore any relation to real economic usefulness or activity.

The "feudal reaction"

The political unity of France, achieved over the centuries by the monarchy, was likewise a fundamental prerequisite, and even a cause, of the Revolution. Whatever social conditions might have existed, they could give rise to nationwide public opinion, nationwide agitation, nationwide policies, and nationwide legislation only in a country already politically unified as a nation. These conditions were lacking in central Europe. In France a centralized French state existed. Reformers did not have to create it but only capture and remodel it. The French in the eighteenth century already had the sense of membership in a political entity called France. The Revolution saw a tremendous stirring of this sense of membership and of fraternity, turning it into a passion for citizenship, civic rights, voting powers, and the use of the state and its sovereignty for the public advantage. At the very outbreak of the Revolution people saluted each other as *citoyen* or *citoyenne* and shouted *vive la nation!*

Political Culture and Public Opinion after 1770

The social and economic resentments that existed among ambitious people in French cities and among peasants in the French countryside could finally explode in a revolutionary upheaval because eighteenth-century writers had created a culture that encouraged political and social criticism. Educated persons in the Third Estate could draw on Enlightenment conceptions of reason, natural rights, and historical progress to complain about the irrationality of ancient privileges or the injustice of noble prerogatives. Enlightenment thought provided a language in which people could now describe their dissatisfactions with the obstacles that stymied professional or economic ambitions.

The Revolution and the Enlightenment

It has been argued that the famous works of the French philosophes led directly to the revolutionary events of 1789; it was the "fault" of Voltaire, critics explained; it was the "fault" of Rousseau. Many who supported the Revolution also made such claims for its intellectual origins, so that the history of the French Revolution has always been linked in complex ways with the legacy of the Enlightenment. Yet most historians now argue that the connections between the philosophes and the Revolution were by no means as direct as people once imagined. The philosophes themselves favored enlightened social reforms, but they were not revolutionaries and, except perhaps for Rousseau, they rarely promoted the political rights of the lower classes. Their most important publications, including the famous *Encyclopédie,* often attracted more readers among the nobility than among the middle classes. Political theory was far less popular than novels or social satires; there was an enormous audience for Rousseau's *Nouvelle Héloise,* for example, but few persons read the *Social Contract*. The notion that great Enlightenment writers "caused" the French Revolution is therefore an inadequate explanation for what happened (much as claims that bourgeois economic interests "caused" the Revolution are also inadequate). It is nevertheless true that the Enlightenment contributed widely to new forms of criticism, public debate, and "public opinion," most of which challenged the traditional authority of the French king and nobles.

The last two decades of the Old Regime were filled with intense political controversy as the monarchy sought unsuccessfully to suppress the traditional French parlements, as successive ministries sought to raise new revenues, as French journals reported on the new American state constitutions, and as pamphleteers increasingly attacked the officials and courtiers at Versailles. The critical spirit that had developed in salons, coffeehouses, and literary arguments spread rapidly into a developing public sphere of political debate. The new political pamphlets were scarcely concerned with the subtle nuances of political theory; in fact, many consisted of little more than scandalous rumors of sexual misconduct or financial corruption in the affairs of the royal family and government ministries. Stories of corruption in high places stripped away the once sacred image of the monarchy, the church, and the social hierarchy. At the same time, the reading public developed an interest in scandalous legal cases that pitted members of the aristocracy against aggrieved persons of the Third Estate or that revealed immorality and decadence among ancient noble families. Lawyers could publish their legal briefs without securing the approval of government censors, and, using this freedom, they bolstered their legal arguments with appeals to popular sentiment or natural rights. The injustice of inherited privilege thus became a recurring theme in the scandalous stories of social and personal disputes that French lawyers carried from French courtrooms to the tribunal of "public opinion."

Critical spirit

By 1789, in France, educated persons in all social classes were coming to believe what Voltaire had said after the famous Calas Affair in the 1760s: "Opinion governs the world." Campaigns to influence public opinion became a powerful political force in French society during the last decades of the Old Regime, and most such campaigns appealed for public support in the name of reason, rights, or justice. In these ways, the critical thought of Enlightenment culture entered into bitter political conflicts that led finally and unexpectedly to the Revolution.

42. THE REVOLUTION AND THE REORGANIZATION OF FRANCE

The Financial Crisis

The Revolution was precipitated by a financial collapse of the government. What overburdened the government was by no means the costly magnificence of the court of Versailles. Only five percent of public expenditures in 1788 was devoted to the upkeep of the entire royal establishment. What overburdened all governments was war costs, both current upkeep of armies and navies and the burden of public debt, which in all countries was due almost totally to the war costs of the past. In 1788 the French government devoted about a quarter of its annual expenditure to maintenance of the armed forces and about half to the payment of its debts. British expenditures showed almost the same distribution. The French debt stood at almost four billion livres. It had been greatly swollen by the War of American Independence. Yet it was only half as great as the national debt of Great Britain, and less than a fifth as heavy per capita. It was less than the debt of the Dutch Republic. It was apparently no greater than the debt left by Louis XIV three-quarters of a century before. At that time the debt had been lightened by repudiation. No responsible French official in the 1780s even considered repudiation, a sure sign of the progress in the interim of the well-to-do classes, who were the main government creditors.

Yet the debt could not be carried, for the simple reason that revenues fell short of necessary expenditures. This in turn was not due to national poverty but to the tax exemptions and tax evasions of privileged elements and to complications in the fiscal system, or lack of system, by which *Problems of taxation* much of what taxpayers paid never came into the hands of the Treasury. We have already described how the most important tax, the taille, was generally paid only by the peasants—the nobles being exempt by virtue of their class privilege, and office holders and bourgeois obtaining exemption in various ways. The church too insisted that its property was not taxable by the state; and its periodic "free gift" to the king, though substantial, was less than might have been obtained from direct taxation of the church's land. Thus, although the country itself was prosperous, the government treasury was empty. The social classes which enjoyed most of the wealth of the country did not pay taxes corresponding to their income—and, even worse, they resisted taxation as a sign of inferior status.

A long series of responsible persons—Louis XIV himself, John Law, Maupeou, Turgot—had seen the need for taxing the privileged classes. Jacques Necker, a Swiss banker made director of the finances in 1777 by Louis XVI, made moves in the same direction and, like his predecessors, was dismissed. His successor, Calonne, as the crisis mounted, came to even more revolutionary conclusions. In 1786 he produced a program in which enlightened despotism was tempered by a modest resort to representative institutions. He proposed, in place of the taille, a general tax to fall on all landowners without exemption, a lightening of indirect taxes and abolition of internal tariffs to stimulate economic production, and a confiscation of some properties of the church. He also sought to give the propertied elements a greater interest in the government by proposing the establishment of provincial assemblies in which all landowners should be represented without regard to estate or order.

Calonne's program, if carried out, might have solved the fiscal problem and averted the Revolution. But it struck not only at privileges in taxation—noble, provincial, and others—but also at the threefold hierarchic organization of society. Knowing from experience that the Parlement of Paris would never accept it, Calonne in 1787 convened an "assembly of notables," hoping to win its endorsement of his ideas. The notables insisted on concessions in return, for they wished to share in control of the government. A deadlock followed; the king dismissed Calonne and appointed as his successor Loménie de Brienne, the exceedingly worldly-wise archbishop of Toulouse. Brienne tried to push the same program through the Parlement of Paris. The Parlement rejected it, declaring that only the three estates of the realm, assembled in an Estates General, had authority to consent to new taxes. Brienne and Louis XVI at first refused, believing that the Estates General, if convened, would be dominated by the nobility. Like Maupeou and Louis XV, Brienne and Louis XVI tried to break the parlements, replacing them with a modernized judicial system in which the law courts should have no influence over policy. This led to a veritable revolt of the nobles. All the parlements and Provincial Estates resisted; army officers refused to serve; the intendants hesitated to act; and noblemen began to organize political clubs and committees of correspondence. With his government brought to a standstill, and unable to borrow money or collect taxes, Louis XVI on July 5, 1788, promised to call the Estates General for the following May. The various classes were invited to elect representatives and also to draw up lists of their grievances.

Resistance of the nobles

From Estates General to National Assembly

Since no Estates General had met in over a century and a half, the king asked for proposals on how such an assembly should be organized under modern conditions. This led to an outburst of public discussion, which soon expanded far beyond all previous campaigns to influence public opinion. Hundreds of political pamphlets appeared, many of them demanding a change in the old system by which the three estates sat in separate chambers, each chamber voting as a unit. This voting system was widely criticized because it meant, in practice, that the chamber of the Third Estate was always outnumbered. But in September 1788 the Parlement of Paris, restored to its functions, ruled that the Estates General should meet and vote as in 1614, in three separate orders.

The aims of the nobility

The nobility, through the Parlement, thus revealed its aim. It had forced the summoning of the Estates General, and in this way the French nobility initiated the Revolution. The Revolution began as another victory in the aristocratic resurgence against the absolutism of the king. The nobles actually had a liberal program: they demanded constitutional government, guarantees of personal liberty for all, freedom of speech and press, freedom from arbitrary arrest and confinement. Many now were even prepared to give up special privileges in taxation; this might have worked itself out in time. But in return they hoped to become the preponderant political element in the state. It was their idea not merely to have the Estates General meet in 1789 but for France to be henceforth governed through the Estates General, a supreme body in three chambers—one for nobles, one for a clergy in which the higher officers were also nobles, and one for the Third Estate.

This was precisely what the Third Estate wished to avoid. Lawyers, bankers, business owners, government creditors, shopkeepers, artisans, working people, and peasants had no desire to be governed by lords temporal and spiritual. Their hopes of a new era, formed by the philosophy of the Enlightenment, stirred by the revolution in America, rose to the utmost excitement when "good king Louis" called the Estates General. The ruling of the Parlement of Paris in September 1788 came to them as a slap in the face—an unprovoked class insult. The whole Third Estate turned on the nobility with detestation and distrust. The Abbé Sieyès in January 1789 launched his famous pamphlet *What Is the Third Estate?*, declaring that the nobility was a useless caste which could be abolished without loss, that the Third Estate was the one necessary element of society, that it was identical with the nation, and that the nation was absolutely and unqualifiedly sovereign. Through Sieyès the ideas of Rousseau's *Social Contract* entered the thought of the Revolution. At the same time, even before the Estates General actually met, and not from the books of philosophes so much as from actual events and conditions, nobles and commoners viewed each other with fear and suspicion. The Third Estate, which had at first supported the nobles against the "despotism" of the king's ministers, now ascribed to the former the worst possible motives. Bourgeois critics vehemently rejected the political program and ambitions of the nobility. Class antagonism poisoned the Revolution at the outset, made peaceful reform impossible, and threw many bourgeois without delay into a radical and destructive mood.

The Third Estate reacts

The Estates General met as planned in May 1789 at Versailles. The Third Estate, most of whose representatives were lawyers, would not accept the division of the orders into three separate chambers. It insisted that deputies of all three orders should sit as a single house and vote as individuals; this procedure would be of advantage to the Third Estate, since the king had granted it as many deputies as the other two orders combined. For six weeks a deadlock was maintained. On June 13 a few priests, leaving the chamber of the First Estate, came over and sat with the Third. They were greeted with jubilation. On June 17 the Third Estate declared itself the "National Assembly." Louis XVI, under pressure from the nobles, closed the hall in which it met. The members found a neighboring indoor tennis court and there, milling about in a babel of confusion and apprehension, swore and signed the Oath of the Tennis Court on June 20, 1789, affirming that wherever they foregathered the National Assembly was in existence and that they would not disband until they had drafted a constitution. This was a revolutionary step, for it assumed virtually sovereign power for a body that had no legal authority. The king ordered members of the three estates to sit in their separate houses. He now somewhat tardily presented a reforming program of his own, too late to win the confidence of the disaffected and in any case continuing the organization of French society in legal classes. The self-entitled National Assembly refused to back down. The king faltered, failed to enforce his commands promptly, and allowed the Assembly to remain in being. In the following days, at the end of June, he summoned about 18,000 soldiers to Versailles.

What had happened was that the king of France, in the dispute raging between nobles and commoners, chose the nobles. It was traditional in France for the king to oppose feudalism. For centuries the French monarchy had drawn strength from the bourgeoisie. All through the eighteenth century the royal ministers had carried on the struggle against the privileged interests. Only a year before, Louis XVI had been almost at war with his rebellious aristocracy. In 1789 he failed to assert himself. He lost control

OUVERTURE DES ÉTATS GÉNÉRAUX.
(D'après C. Monet.)

Convoked for the first time in 175 years, the Estates General met in a large hall at Versailles in May 1789. This picture shows Louis XVI seated on his throne, with deputies of the clergy seated on his right, those of the nobility on his left, and those of the Third Estate facing him at the other end of the hall.
(Culver Pictures)

over the Estates General, exerted no leadership, offered no program until it was too late, and provided no symbol behind which parties could rally. He failed to make use of the profound loyalty to himself felt by the bourgeoisie and common people, who yearned for nothing so much as a king who would stand up for them, as in days of yore, against an aristocracy of birth and status. He tried instead, at first, to compromise and postpone a crisis; then he found himself in the position of having issued orders which the Third Estate boldly defied; and in this embarrassing predicament he yielded to his wife Marie Antoinette, to his brothers, and to the court nobles with whom he lived and who told him that his dignity and authority were outraged and undermined. At the end of June Louis XVI undoubtedly intended to dissolve the Estates General by military force. But what the Third Estate most feared was not a return to the old theoretically absolute monarchy. It was a future in which the aristocracy should control the government of the country. There was now no going back; the revolt of the Third Estate had allied Louis XVI with the nobles, and the Third Estate now feared the nobles more than ever, believing with good reason that they now had the king in their hands.

Failure of royal leadership

The Lower Classes in Action

The country meanwhile was falling into dissolution. The lower classes, below the bourgeoisie, were out of hand. For them too the convocation of the Estates General had seemed to herald a new era. The grievances of ages, and those which existed equally in other countries than France, rose to the surface. Short-run conditions were bad. The harvest of 1788 had been poor; the price of bread, by July 1789, was higher than at any time since the death of Louis XIV. The year 1789 was also one of depression; the rapid growth of trade since the American war had suddenly halted, so that wages fell and unemployment spread while scarcity drove food prices up. The government, paralyzed at the center, could not take such measures of relief as were customary under the Old Regime. The masses were everywhere restless. Labor trouble broke out; in April a riot of workers devastated a wallpaper factory in Paris. In the rural districts there was much disorder. Peasants declared that they would pay no more manorial dues and were refusing to pay taxes. In the best of times the countryside was troubled by vagrants, beggars, and smugglers who flourished along the many tariff frontiers. Now the business depression reduced the income of honest peasants who engaged in weaving or other domestic industries in their homes; unemployment and indigence spread in the country; people were uprooted; and the result was to raise the number of vagrants to terrifying proportions. It was believed, since nothing was too bad to believe of the aristocrats (though it was not true), that they were secretly recruiting these "brigands" for their own purposes to intimidate the Third Estate. The economic and social crises thus became acutely political.

The towns were afraid of being swamped by beggars and desperadoes. This was true even of Paris, the largest city in Europe except London. The Parisians were also alarmed by the concentration of troops about Versailles. They began to arm in self-defense. All classes of the Third Estate took part. Crowds began to look for weapons in arsenals and public buildings. On July 14 they came to the Bastille, a stronghold built in the Middle Ages to overawe the city, like the Tower of London in England. It was used as a place of detention for persons with enough influence to escape the common jails but was otherwise in normal times considered harmless; in fact there had been talk, some years before, of tearing it down to make room for a public park. Now, in the general turbulence, the governor had placed cannon in the embrasures. The crowd requested him to remove his cannon and to furnish them with arms. He refused. Through a series of misunderstandings, reinforced by the vehemence of a few firebrands, the crowd turned into a mob, which assaulted the fortress and which, when helped by a handful of trained soldiers and five artillery pieces, persuaded the governor to surrender. The mob, enraged by the death of 98 of its members, streamed in and murdered six soldiers of the garrison in cold blood. The governor was murdered while under escort to the Town Hall. A few other officials met the same fate. Their heads were cut off, stuck on the ends of pikes, and paraded about the city. While all this happened, the regular army units on the outskirts of Paris did not stir; their reliability was open to question and the authorities were in any case unaccustomed to firing on the people.

The capture of the Bastille, though not so intended, had the effect of saving the Assembly at Versailles. The king, not knowing what to do, accepted the new situation in Paris. He recognized a citizens' committee, which had formed there, as the new municipal government. He sent away the troops that he had summoned and commanded the recalcitrants among nobles and clergy to join in the National Assembly. In Paris and other cities a

The storming of the Bastille

THE TENNIS COURT OATH
by Jacques-Louis David (French, 1748–1825)

This famous picture portrays the momentous decision by members of the Third Estate to continue meeting as the National Assembly of France until they had written a new constitution. The deputies swore their oath at an indoor tennis court because the king had closed the hall in which they had been holding their sessions.

(Giraudon/Art Resource, NY)

bourgeois or national guard was established to keep order. The Assembly appointed the Marquis de Lafayette, "the hero of two worlds," to command the guard in Paris. For insignia he combined the colors of the city of Paris, red and blue, with the white of the house of Bourbon. The French tricolor, emblem of the Revolution, thus originated in a fusion of old and new.

The Great Fear of 1789

In the rural districts matters went from bad to worse. Vague insecurity rose to the proportions of panic in the Great Fear of 1789, which spread over the country late in July in the wake of travelers, postal couriers, and others. The cry was relayed from point to point that "the brigands were coming." Peasants, armed to protect their homes and crops and gathered together and working upon each other's feelings, turned their attention to the manor houses, burning them in some cases and in others simply destroying the manorial archives in which fees and dues were recorded. The Great Fear became part of a general agrarian insurrection, in which peasants, far from being motivated by wild alarms, knew perfectly well what they were doing. They intended to destroy the manorial regime by force.

The Initial Reforms of the National Assembly

The Assembly at Versailles could restore order only by meeting the demands of the peasants. To wipe out all manorial payments would deprive the landed aristocracy of much of its income. Many bourgeois also owned manors. There was therefore much perplexity. A small group of deputies prepared a surprise move in the Assembly, choosing an evening session from which many would be absent. Hence came the "night of August 4." A few liberal noblemen, by prearrangement, arose and surrendered their hunting rights, their *banalités,* their rights in manorial courts, and feudal and seigneurial privileges generally. What was left of serfdom and all personal servitude was declared ended. Tithes were abolished. Other deputies repudiated the special privileges of their provinces. All personal tax privileges were given up. On the main matter, the dues arising from "eminent property" in the manors, a compromise was adopted. These dues were all abolished but compensation was to be paid by the peasants to the former owners. The compensation was in most cases never paid. Eventually, in 1793, in the radical phase of the Revolution, the provision for compensation was repealed. In the end French peasant landowners rid themselves of their manorial obligations without cost to themselves. This was in contrast to what later happened in most other countries, where peasants, when liberated from manorial obligations, either lost part of their land or were burdened with installment payments lasting many years.

In a decree summarizing the resolutions of August 4 the Assembly declared flatly that "feudalism is abolished." With legal privilege replaced by legal equality, it proceeded to map the principles of the new order. On August 26, 1789, it issued the Declaration of the Rights of Man and Citizen.

The Declaration of 1789 was meant to affirm the principles of the new state, which were essentially the rule of law, equal individual citizenship, and collective sovereignty of the people. "Men are born and remain," declared Article I, "free and equal in rights." Man's natural rights were held to be "liberty, property, security, and resistance to oppression." Freedom of thought and religion was guaranteed; no one might be arrested or punished except by process of law; all persons were declared eligible for any public office for which they met the requirements. Liberty was defined as the freedom to do anything not injurious to others, which in turn was to be determined only by law. Law must fall equally upon all persons. Law was the expression of the general will, to be made by all citizens or their representatives. The only sovereign was the nation itself, and all public officials and armed forces acted only in its name. Taxes might be raised only by common consent, all public servants were accountable for their conduct in office, and the powers of government were to be separated among different branches. Finally, the state might for public purposes, and under law, confiscate the property of private persons, but only with fair compensation. The Declaration, printed in thousands of leaflets, pamphlets, and books, read aloud in public places, or framed and hung on walls, became the catechism of the Revolution in France. When translated into other languages it soon carried the same message to all of Europe. Thomas Paine's book *The Rights of Man,* published in 1791 to defend the French Revolution, gave the phrase a powerful impact in English.

The "rights of man" had become a motto or watchword for potentially revolutionary ideas well before 1789. The thinkers of the Enlightenment had used it, and during the American Revolution even Alexander Hamilton had spoken of "the sacred rights of man" with enthusiasm. "Man" in this sense was meant to apply abstractly, regardless of nationality, race, or sex. In French as in English the word "man" was used to designate all human beings, and the Declaration of 1789 was not intended to refer to males alone. In German,

The Declaration of the Rights of Man and Citizen

The capture of the Bastille—the prison-fortress that became a symbol of Old Regime repression—marked the dramatic entry of the Parisian crowd into the rapidly evolving Revolution. Violence in the streets of Paris in July 1789 saved the National Assembly from the king's intention to dissolve it.

(Bibliothèque Nationale de France, Paris)

for example, where a distinction is made between *Mensch* as a human being and *Mann* as an adult male, the "rights of man" was always translated as *Menschenrechte*. Similarly the word "citizen" in its general sense applied to women, as is shown by the frequency of the feminine *citoyenne* during the Revolution, in which a great many women were very active. But when it came to the exercise of specific legal rights the Revolutionaries went no farther than contemporary opinion. Thus they assigned the right to vote and hold office only to men, and in most matters of property, family law, and education it was the boys and men who benefited most. Very few persons at the time argued for legal equality between the sexes.

The Rights of Woman

One of them, however, was Olympe de Gouges, a woman who had gained prominence as a writer for the theater and who in 1791 published *The Rights of Woman*. Following the official Declaration in each of its 17 articles, she applied them to women explicitly in each case, and she asserted also, in addition, the right of women to divorce under certain conditions, to the control of property in marriage, and for equal access with men to higher education and to civilian careers and public employment. Mary Wollstonecraft in England published a similar *Vindication of the Rights of Woman* in 1792. In France some of the secondary figures in the Revolution, and some of the teachers in boys' schools, thought that women should have greater opportunities at least in education. And there were in fact a few reforms that improved the social rights of women. The revolutionary government redefined marriage as a civil contract and legalized divorce in 1792, thereby enabling women to leave abusive or unhappy marriages (until divorce was banned again in 1816). Inheritance laws were also changed in ways that gave women the legal right to equal inheritance of their family's property.

But among the leaders of the Revolution, only Condorcet argued for legal equality of the sexes. Intent on political change, the Revolutionaries thought that politics, government, law, and war were a masculine business, for which only boys and young men needed to be educated or prepared. The Revolution generally reduced or restricted the cultural and political influence that some women had exercised in the elite circles of Old Regime society. The new political order, as most revolutionaries defined it, was to develop through "manly" opposition to the "feminine" corruptions of the Old Regime court and social hierarchies. "Women are disposed . . . to an over-excitation which would be deadly in public affairs," one revolutionary deputy argued in a typical justification for excluding women from government institutions. Such assumptions led to restrictions on the rights of women to petition or gather in political meetings; finally, in 1793, the revolutionary government closed all women's political clubs.

Shortly after adoption of the Declaration of the Rights of Man the Revolutionary leadership fell apart. In September 1789 the Assembly began the actual planning of the new government. Some wanted a strong veto power for the king and a legislative body in two houses, as in England. Others, the "patriots," wanted only a delaying veto for the king and a legislative body of one chamber. Here again, it was suspicion of the aristocracy that proved decisive. The "patriots" were afraid that an upper chamber would bring back the nobility as a collective force, and they were afraid to make the king constitutionally strong by giving him a full veto, because they believed him to be in sympathy with the nobles. He was, at the moment, hesitating to accept both the August 4th decrees and the Declaration of Rights. His brother, the Count of Artois, followed by many aristocrats, had already emigrated to foreign parts and, along with these other émigrés, was preparing to agitate against the Revolution with all the governments of Europe. The patriot party would concede nothing; the more conservative party could gain nothing. The debate was interrupted again, as in July, by insurrection and violence. On October 4, a crowd of market women and revolutionary militants, followed by the revolutionary Paris national guard, took the road from Paris to Versailles. Besieging and invading the château, they obliged Louis XVI to take up his residence in Paris, where he could be watched. The National Assembly also shifted itself to Paris, where it too soon fell under the influence of radical elements in the city. The champions of a one-chamber legislative body and of a suspensive veto for the king won out.

The more conservative revolutionaries, if such they may be called, disillusioned at seeing constitutional questions settled by mobs, began to drop out of the Assembly. Men who on June 20 had bravely sworn the Oath of the Tennis Court now felt that the Revolution was falling into unworthy hands. Some even emigrated, forming a second wave of émigrés that would have nothing to do with the first. The counterrevolution gathered strength.

But those who wanted still to go forward, and they were many, began to organize in clubs. Most important of all was the Society of Friends of the Constitution, called the Jacobin club for short, since it met in an old Jacobin monastery in Paris. The dues were at first so high that only substantial bourgeois belonged; the dues were later lowered but never enough to include persons of the poorest classes, who therefore formed clubs of their own. The most advanced members of the Assembly were Jacobins, who used the club as a caucus in which to discuss their policies and

The Jacobins

lay their plans. They remained a middle-class group even during the later and more radical phase of the Revolution. Madame Rosalie Jullien, for example, who was as dedicated a revolutionary as her husband and son, attended a meeting of the Paris Jacobin club on August 5, 1792. Tell your friends in the provinces, she wrote to her husband, that these Jacobins are "the flower of the Paris bourgeoisie, to judge by the fancy jackets they wear. There were also two or three hundred women present, dressed as if for the theater, who made an impression by their proud attitude and forceful speech."

Constitutional Changes

In the two years from October 1789 to September 1791 the National Assembly (or the Constituent Assembly, as it had come to be called because it was preparing a constitution) continued its work of simultaneously governing the country, devising a written constitution, and destroying in detail the institutions of the Old Regime. The Assembly soon discarded most of the political and legal institutions that had governed French affairs for centuries—the old monarchical ministries, the organization of government bureaus, the taxes, the property in office, the titles of nobility, the parlements, the hundreds of regional systems of law, the internal tariffs, the provinces, and the urban municipalities. Contemporaries, like Edmund Burke, were appalled at the thoroughness with which the French seemed determined to eradicate their national institutions. Why, asked Burke, should the French fanatics cut to pieces the living body of Normandy or Provence? The truth is that the provinces, like everything else, formed part of the whole system of special privilege and unequal rights. All had to disappear if the hope of equal citizenship under national sovereignty was to be attained. In place of the provinces the Constituent Assembly divided France into 83 equal "departments." In place of the old towns, with their quaint old magistrates, it introduced a uniform municipal organization, all towns henceforth having the same form of government, varying only according to size. All local officials, even prosecuting attorneys and tax collectors, were elected locally. Administratively the country was decentralized in reaction against the bureaucracy of the Old Regime. No one outside Paris now really acted for the central government, and local communities enforced the national legislation, or declined to enforce it, as they chose. This proved ruinous when the war came, and although the "departments" created by the Constituent Assembly still exist, it became traditional in France after the Revolution, as it was before, to keep local officials under strong control by ministers in Paris.

The Constitution of 1791

Under the constitution that was prepared, sometimes called the Constitution of 1791 because it went into effect at that date, the sovereign power of the nation was to be exercised by a unicameral elected assembly called the Legislative Assembly. The king was given only a suspensive veto power by which legislation desired by the Assembly could be postponed. In general, the executive branch, that is, king and ministers, was kept weak, partly in reaction against "ministerial despotism," partly from a well-founded distrust of Louis XVI. In June 1791 Louis attempted to escape from the kingdom, join with émigré noblemen, and seek help from foreign powers. He left behind him a written message in which he explicitly repudiated the Revolution. Arrested at Varennes in eastern France, he was brought back to Paris and forced to accept his status as a constitutional monarch. The hostile attitude of Louis XVI greatly disoriented the Revolution, for it made impossible the creation of a strong executive power and left the country to be ruled by a debating society which under revolutionary conditions contained more than the usual number of hotheads.

Not all this machinery of state was democratic. As noted above, women did not receive the right to vote or hold public office; and in the granting of political rights to men

The three men at an anvil are a noble, a cleric, and a commoner hammering out a new constitution together. At the beginning of the Revolution, most people expected the three estates to fraternize in the redefined French nation.
(Bibliothèque Nationale de France, Paris)

the abstract principles of the great Declaration were seriously modified for practical reasons. Since most people were illiterate, it was thought that they could have no reasonable political views. Since the small man was often a domestic servant or shop assistant, it was assumed that in politics he would merely follow the views of his employer. The Constituent Assembly therefore distinguished in the new constitution between "active" and "passive" citizens. Both had the same civil rights, but only active citizens had the right to vote. These active citizens chose "electors" on the basis of one elector for every hundred active citizens. The electors convened in the chief town of their new "department" and there chose deputies to the national legislature as well as certain local officials. Males over 25 years of age, and wealthy enough to pay a small direct tax, qualified as "active" citizens; well over half the adult male population could so qualify. Of these, men paying a somewhat higher tax qualified as "electors"; even so, almost half the adult males qualified for this role. In practice, what limited the number of available electors was that, to function as such, a man had to have enough education, interest, and leisure to attend an electoral assembly at a distance from home and remain in attendance for several days. In any case, only about 50,000 persons served as electors in 1790–1791 because a proportion of one for every hundred active citizens yielded that figure.

Economic and Cultural Policies

Economic policies favored the middle rather than the lowest classes. The public debt had precipitated the Revolution, but the revolutionary leaders, even the most extreme Jacobins, never disowned the debt of the Old Regime. The reason is that the bourgeois class, on the whole, were the people to whom the money was owed. To secure the debt, and to pay current expenses of government, since tax collections had become very sporadic, the Constituent Assembly as early as November 1789 resorted to a device by no means new in Europe, though never before used on so extensive a scale. It confiscated all the property of the church. Against this property, it issued negotiable instruments

Assignats

called *assignats,* first regarded as bonds and issued only in large denominations, later regarded as currency and issued in small bills. Holders of *assignats* could use them, or any money, to buy parcels of the former church lands. None of the confiscated land was given away; all was in fact sold, since the interest of the government was fiscal rather than social. The peasants, even when they had the money, could not easily buy land because the lands were sold at distant auctions or in large undivided blocks. The peasants were disgruntled, though they did acquire a good deal of the former church lands through middlemen. Peasant landowners were likewise expected, until 1793, to pay compensation for many of their old manorial fees. And the landless peasants were aroused when the government, with its modern ideas, encouraged the dividing up of the village commons and extinction of various collective village rights in the interest of individual private property.

The revolutionary leadership favored free economic individualism. It had had enough, under the Old Regime, of government regulation over the sale or quality of goods and of privileged companies and other economic monopolies. Reforming economic thought at the time in France and in Britain, where Adam Smith had published his epoch-making *Wealth of Nations* in 1776, held that organized special interests were bad for society and that all prices and wages should be determined by free arrangement between the individuals concerned. The more prominent leaders of the French Revolution believed firmly in this freedom from control. The Constituent Assembly thus abolished the guilds, which were mainly monopolistic organizations of small businessmen or master craftsmen, interested in keeping up prices and averse to new machinery or new methods.

There was also in France what we would now call an organized labor movement. Since the masterships in the guilds were practically hereditary (as a form of property and privilege), the journeymen had formed their own associations, or trade unions, called *compagnonnages,* outside the guilds. Many trades were so organized—the carpenters, plasterers, paper workers, hatters, saddlers, cutlers, nail makers, carters, tanners, locksmiths, and glassworkers. Some were organized nationally; some, only locally. All these journeymen's unions had been illegal under the Old Regime, but they had flourished nevertheless. They collected dues and maintained officers. They often dealt collectively with the guild masters or other employers, requiring the payment of a stipulated wage or change of working conditions. Sometimes they even imposed closed shops. Organized strikes were quite common. The labor troubles of 1789 continued on into the Revolution. Business fell off in the atmosphere of disorder. In 1791 there was another wave of strikes. The Assembly, in the Le Chapelier law of that year, renewed the old prohibitions of the *compagnonnages.* The same law restated the abolition of the guilds and forbade the organization of special economic interests of any kind. All trades, it declared, were free for all to enter. All persons, without belonging to any organization, had the right to work at any occupation or business they might choose. All wages were to be settled privately by the worker and his or her employer. This was not at all what the workers, at that time or any other, really wanted. Nevertheless the provisions of the Le Chapelier law remained a part of French law for three-quarters of a century. The embryonic trade unions continued to exist secretly, though with more difficulty than under the hit-and-miss law enforcement of the Old Regime.

Banning labor organizations

Meanwhile, revolutionary activists set about transforming the symbols, rituals, dress, and holidays of Old Regime society. Seeking to break from the hierarchies and privileges of the past, they developed a new political culture that would be symbolized by a new flag,

The revolutionary government used paper money to finance its policies. The notes were called *assignats* because they were assigned to, or secured by, real estate confiscated during the Revolution, mostly from the church. Inflation rose rapidly after 1794, so that even notes with denominations as high as 10,000 livres, as shown in this picture, became worthless. The assignats were therefore abolished, and a new, more stable French currency came into use in 1796. (Bibliothèque Nationale de France, Paris)

new forms of democratic language, new clothing, new festivals, and new public monuments. The art and imagery of the traditional monarchy and church rapidly disappeared from public life. Great festivals of national unity were organized, beginning with the famous "Festival of the Federation," which brought together a vast crowd in Paris to mark the first anniversary of the assault on the Bastille (July 14, 1790), to celebrate the new liberties of the French people and to begin creating rituals for what would eventually become the French national holiday.

A revolutionary political culture

Supporters of the Revolution planted "liberty trees" in towns throughout France, and they began to wear "liberty caps" and tricolor cockades to show their political allegiances. Later revolutionary governments encouraged new artwork in which the nation came to be represented by a female symbol of liberty, Marianne. Statues of Marianne offered alternatives to traditional Catholic icons of the Virgin Mary and gave illiterate persons new visual images by which they could understand that national sovereignty and liberty had replaced the king and church at the symbolic center of French political life. A profusion of revolutionary plays, novels, and songs conveyed the same message. By promoting the new political ideas and symbols in every sphere of daily life, the French Revolution created a new national identity and "nationalized" the French people through the use of cultural rituals that would later become common in other national movements of the modern world.

The Quarrel with the Church

Most fatefully of all, the Constituent Assembly quarreled with the Catholic church. The confiscation of church properties naturally came as a shock to the clergy. The village priests, whose support had made possible the revolt of the Third Estate, now found that the very buildings in which they worshipped with their parishioners on Sunday belonged to the "nation." The loss of income-producing properties undercut the religious orders and ruined the schools, in which thousands of boys had received free education before the Revolution. Yet it was not on the question of material wealth that the church and the Revolution came to blows. Members of the Constituent Assembly took the view of the church that the great monarchies had taken before them. The idea of separation of church and state was far from their minds. They regarded the church as a form of public authority and as such subordinate to the sovereign power. They frankly argued that the poor needed religion if they were to respect the property of the more wealthy. In any case, having deprived the church of its own income, they had to provide for its maintenance. For the schools many generous and democratic projects of state-sponsored education were drawn up, though under the troubled conditions of the time little was accomplished.

The Civil Constitution of the Clergy

For the clergy the new program was mapped out in the Civil Constitution of the Clergy of 1790.

This document went far toward setting up a French national church. Under its provisions the parish priests and bishops were elected, the latter by the same 50,000 electors who chose other important officials. Protestants, Jews, and agnostics could legally take part in the elections, purely on the ground of citizenship and property qualifications. Archbishoprics were abolished, and all the borders of existing bishoprics were redrawn. The number of dioceses was reduced from over 130 to 83, so that one would be coterminous with each department. Bishops were allowed merely to notify the pope of their elevation; they were forbidden to acknowledge any papal authority on their assumption of office, and no papal letter or decree was to be published or enforced in France except with government permission. All clergy received salaries from the state; the average income of bishops was somewhat reduced and that of parish clergymen was raised. Sinecures, plural holdings, and other abuses by which the church had supported noble families were done away with. The Constituent Assembly (independently of the Civil Constitution) also prohibited the taking of religious vows and dissolved all monastic houses.

Some of all this was not in principle alarmingly new, since before the Revolution the civil authority of the king had designated the French bishops and passed judgement on the admission of papal documents into France. French bishops, in the old spirit of the "Gallican liberties," were traditionally jealous of papal power in France. Many were now willing to accept something like the Civil Constitution if allowed to produce it on their own authority. The Assembly refused to concede so much jurisdiction to the Gallican church and applied instead to the pope, hoping to force its plans upon the French clergy by invoking the authority of the Vatican. But the Vatican pronounced the Civil Constitution a wanton usurpation of power over the Catholic church. Unfortunately, the pope also went further, condemning the whole Revolution and all its works. The Constituent Assembly retorted by requiring all French clergy to swear an oath of loyalty to the constitution, including the Civil Constitution of the Clergy. Half took the oath and half refused it, the latter half including all but seven of the bishops. One of the seven willing to accept the new arrangements was Talleyrand, soon to be famous as foreign minister of numerous French governments.

There were now two churches in France, one clandestine, the other official, one maintained by voluntary offerings or by funds smuggled in from abroad, the other financed and sponsored by the government. The former, comprising the nonjuring, unsworn, or "refractory" clergy, turned violently counterrevolutionary. To protect themselves from the Revolution they insisted, with an emphasis quite new in France, on the universal religious supremacy of the Roman pontiff. They denounced the "constitutional" clergy as schismatics who spurned the pope and as mere careerists willing to hold jobs on the government's

The revolutionaries created rituals and symbols to celebrate the new nation they were trying to establish. The great festival of the Federation in Paris on July 14, 1790, assembled the king, the National Guard, and a huge crowd in a symbolic expression of the national unity and national liberties that the new political institutions were supposed to protect.
(Giraudon/Art Resource, NY)

terms. The constitutional clergy, those taking the oath and upholding the Civil Constitution, considered themselves to be patriots and defenders of the rights of man; and they insisted that the Gallican church had always enjoyed a degree of liberty from Rome. The Catholic laity were terrified and puzzled. Many were sufficiently attached to the Revolution to prefer the constitutional clergy but to do so meant to defy the pope, and Catholics who persisted in defying the pope were on the whole those least zealous in their religion. The constitutional clergy therefore stood on shaky foundations. Many of their followers, under stress of the times, eventually turned against Christianity itself.

"Constitutional" and "refractory" clergy

Good Catholics tended to favor the "refractory" clergy. The outstanding example was the king himself. He personally used the services of refractory priests, and thus gave a new reason for the revolutionaries to distrust him. Whatever chance there was that Louis XVI might go along with the Revolution was exploded, for he concluded that he could do so only by endangering his immortal soul. Former aristocrats also naturally preferred the refractory clergy. They now put aside the Voltairean levities of the Age of Enlightenment, and the "best people" began to exhibit a new piety in religious matters. The peasants, who found little in the Revolution to interest them after their own insurrection of 1789 and the consequent abolition of the manorial regime, also favored the old-fashioned or refractory clergy. Much the same was true of the urban working-class families, in which both men and women might shout against priests and yet want to be sure that their marriages were valid and their children were properly baptized. The Constituent Assembly, and its successors, could never finally decide what to do. Sometimes they shut their eyes at the intrigues of refractory clergy, in which case the constitutional clergy then became fearful. Sometimes they hunted out and persecuted the refractories; in that case they only stirred up religious fanaticism.

The Civil Constitution of the Clergy has been called the greatest tactical blunder of the Revolution. Certainly its consequences were unfortunate in the extreme, and they spread to much of Europe. In the nineteenth century the church was to be officially antidemocratic and antiliberal; and democrats and liberals in most cases became outspokenly anticlerical. The main beneficiary was the papacy. The French church, which had clung for ages to its Gallican liberties, was thrown by the Revolution into the arms of the pope. Even Napoleon, when he healed the schism a decade later, acknowledged powers in the papacy that had never been acknowledged by the French kings. These were steps in the process, leading through the proclamation of papal infallibility in 1870, by which the affairs of the modern Catholic church became increasingly centralized at the Vatican.

With the proclamation of the constitution in September 1791, the Constituent Assembly disbanded. Before dissolving, it ruled that none of its members might sit in the forthcoming Legislative Assembly. This body was therefore made up of men who still wished to make their mark in the Revolution. The new regime went into effect in October 1791. It was a constitutional monarchy in which a unicameral Legislative Assembly confronted a king unconverted to the new order. Designed as the permanent solution to France's problems, it was to collapse in 10 months, in August 1792, as a result of popular insurrection four months after France became involved in war. A group of Jacobins, known as Girondins, for a time became the left or advanced party of the Revolution and in the Legislative Assembly led France into war.

43.   THE REVOLUTION AND EUROPE: THE WAR AND THE "SECOND" REVOLUTION, 1792

The International Impact of the Revolution

The European governments were long reluctant to become involved with France. They were under considerable pressure. On the one hand, pro-French and pro-revolutionary groups appeared immediately in many quarters. The doctrines of the French Revolution, as of the American, were highly exportable: they took the form of a universal philosophy, proclaiming the rights of man regardless of time or place, race or nation. Moreover, depending on what one was looking for, one might see in the first disturbances in France a revolt of either the nobility, the bourgeoisie, the common people, or the entire nation. In Poland those who were trying to reorganize the country against further partition hailed the French example. The Hungarian landlords pointed to it in their reaction against Joseph II. In England, for a time, those who controlled Parliament complacently believed that the French were attempting to imitate them.

Inspiration of the Revolution

But it was the excluded classes of European society who were most inspired. The hard-pressed Silesian weavers were said to hope that "the French would come." Strikes broke out at Hamburg, and peasants rebelled elsewhere. One English diplomat found that even the Prussian army had "a strong taint of democracy among officers and men." In Belgium, where the privileged elements were already in revolt against the Austrian emperor, a second revolt broke out, inspired by events in France and aimed at the privileged elements. In England the newly developing "radicals," men like Thomas Paine and Dr. Richard Price, who wished a thorough overhauling of Parliament and the established church, entered into correspondence with the Assembly in Paris. Business leaders of importance, including Watt and Boulton, the pioneers of the steam engine, were likewise pro-French since they had no representation in the House of Commons. The Irish too were excited and presently revolted. Everywhere the young were aroused, the young Hegel in Germany or in England the young Wordsworth, who later recalled the sense of a new era that had captivated so many spirits in 1789:

Bliss was it in that dawn to be alive,
But to be young was very heaven!

On the other hand the anti-Revolutionary movement gathered strength. Edmund Burke, frightened by the French proclivities of English radicals, published as early as 1790 his *Reflections on the Revolution in France*. For France, he predicted anarchy and dictatorship. For England, he sternly advised the English to accept a slow adaptation of their own English liberties. For all the world, he denounced a political philosophy that rested on abstract principles of right and wrong, declaring that every people must be shaped by its own national circumstances, national history, and national character. He drew an eloquent reply and a defense of France from Thomas Paine in the *Rights of Man*. Burke soon began to preach the necessity of war, urging a kind of ideological struggle against French barbarism and violence. His *Reflections* was translated and widely read, becoming in the long run an influential work in the emergence of modern conservative thought. In the short run it fell on willing ears. The king of Sweden, Gustavus III, offered to lead a monarchist crusade. In Russia Empress Catherine was appalled; she forbade further translations of her erstwhile friend Voltaire, she called the French "vile riffraff" and "brutish cannibals," and she packed off to Siberia a Russian named Radischev, who in his *Voyage from St. Petersburg to Moscow* pointed out the evils of serfdom. The terrors were heightened by plaintive messages from Louis XVI and Marie Antoinette and by the émigrés who kept bursting out of France, led as early as July 1789 by the king's own brother, the Count of Artois. The émigrés, who at first were nobles, settled in various parts of Europe and began using their international aristocratic connections. They preached a kind of holy war against the evils of revolution. They bemoaned the sad plight of the king, but what they most wanted was to get back their manorial incomes and other rights. Extremists among the émigrés even hinted that Louis XVI himself was a dangerous revolutionary and much preferred his brother, the unyielding Count of Artois.

In short, Europe was soon split by a division that overran all frontiers. The same was true of America also. In the United States the rising party of Jefferson was branded as Jacobin and pro-French, that of Hamilton as aristocratic and pro-British, while in colonial Latin America there was new interest in ideas of independence, and the Venezuelan Miranda became a general in the French army. In all countries of the European world, though least of all in eastern and southern Europe, there were revolutionary or pro-French elements that were feared by their own governments. In all countries, including France, there were implacable enemies of the French Revolution. In all countries were people whose loyalties or sympathies lay abroad. There had been no such situation since the Protestant Reformation, nor was there anything like it again until after the Russian Revolution of the twentieth century.

The Coming of the War, April 1792

Yet the European governments were slow to move. Catherine had no intention of becoming involved in western Europe. She only wished to involve her neighbors. William Pitt, the British prime minister, resisted the war cries of Burke. Pitt had tried and failed to carry a plan for reform of Parliament and was now concentrating on a policy of orderly finance and systematic economy. His domestic program would be ruined by war. He insisted that the internal affairs of France were of no concern to the British government. The key position was occupied by the Habsburg emperor, Leopold II, brother to the French queen.

Anti-Revolutionary sentiment

Leopold at first answered Marie Antoinette's pleas for help by telling her to adjust herself to conditions in France. He resisted the furious demands of the émigrés, whom he understood perfectly, having inherited from Joseph II a fractious aristocracy himself.

Still, the new French government was a disturbing phenomenon. It openly encouraged malcontents all over Europe. It showed a tendency to settle international affairs by unilateral action. For example, it annexed Avignon at the request of local revolutionaries but without the consent of its historic sovereign, the pope. Or again, in Alsace there had been much overlapping jurisdiction between France and Germany ever since the Peace of Westphalia in 1648 (see maps, pp. 142–143, 180, 313). The Constituent Assembly abolished feudalism and manorial dues in Alsace as elsewhere in France. To German princes who had feudal rights in Alsace the Assembly offered compensation, but it did not ask their consent. Moreover, after the arrest of Louis XVI at Varennes, after his attempted flight in June 1791, it became impossible to deny that the French king and queen were prisoners of the revolutionaries.

The Declaration of Pillnitz

In August Leopold met with the king of Prussia at Pillnitz in Saxony. The resulting Declaration of Pillnitz rested on a famous *if:* Leopold would take military steps to restore order in France if all the other powers would join him. Knowing the attitude of Pitt, he believed that this could never materialize. His aim was mainly to rid himself of the French émigrés, but the émigrés perversely received the Declaration with delight. They used it as an open threat to their enemies in France, announcing that they would soon return alongside the forces of civilized Europe to punish the guilty and right the wrongs that had been done to them.

In France the upholders of the Revolution were alarmed. They were ignorant of what Leopold really meant and took the dire menaces of the émigrés at their face value. The Declaration of Pillnitz, far from cowing the French, enraged them against all the crowned heads of Europe. It gave a political advantage to the then dominant faction of Jacobins, known to history as the Girondins. These included the philosophe Condorcet, the humanitarian lawyer Brissot, and the civil servant Roland and his more famous wife, Madame Roland, whose house became a kind of headquarters of the group. They attracted many foreigners also, such as Thomas Paine and the German Anacharsis Cloots, the "representative of the human race." In December 1791 a deputation of English radicals, led by James Watt, son of the inventor of the steam engine, received a wild ovation at the Paris Jacobin club.

The Girondins became the party of international revolution. They declared that the Revolution could never be secure in France until it spread to the world. In their view, once war had come, the peoples of states at war with France would not support their own governments. There was reason for this belief, since revolutionary elements antedating the French Revolution already existed in both the Dutch and the Austrian Netherlands, and to a lesser degree in parts of Switzerland, Poland, and elsewhere. Some Girondins therefore contemplated a war in which French armies should enter neighboring countries, unite with local revolutionaries, overthrow the established governments, and set up a federation of republics. War was also favored by a very different group, led by Lafayette, which wished to curb the Revolution by holding it at the line of constitutional monarchy. This group mistakenly believed that war might restore the much damaged popularity of Louis XVI, unite the country under the new government, and make it possible to put down the continuing Jacobin agitation. As the war spirit boiled up in France, the Emperor Leopold II died. He was succeeded by Francis II, a man much more inclined than Leopold to yield to the clamors of the old aristocracy. Francis resumed negotiations with Prussia. In France all who dreaded a return of

France goes to war

the Old Regime listened more readily to the Girondins. Among the Jacobins as a whole, only a few, generally a handful of radical democrats, opposed the war. On April 20, 1792, without serious opposition, the Assembly declared war on "the king of Hungary and Bohemia," that is, the Austrian monarchy.

The "Second" Revolution: August 10, 1792

The war intensified the existing unrest and dissatisfaction of the unpropertied classes. Both peasants and urban workers felt that the Constituent and the Legislative Assembly had served the propertied interests and had done little for them. Peasants were dissatisfied with the inadequate measures taken to facilitate land distribution; workers felt especially the pinch of soaring prices, which by 1792 had greatly risen. Gold had been taken out of the country by the émigrés; paper money, the *assignats,* was almost the sole currency, and the future of the government was so uncertain that it steadily lost value. Peasants concealed their food products rather than sell them for depreciating paper. Actual scarcity combined with the falling value of money to drive up the cost of living. The lowest income groups suffered the most. But dissatisfied though they were, when the war began they were threatened with a return of the émigrés and a vindictive restoration of the Old Regime, which at least for the peasants would be the worst of all possible eventualities. The working classes—peasants, artisans, mechanics, shopkeepers, wage workers—rallied to the Revolution but not to the revolutionary government in power. The Legislative Assembly and the constitutional monarchy lacked the confidence of large elements of the population.

In addition, the war at first went very unfavorably for the French. Prussia joined immediately with Austria, and by the summer of 1792 the two powers were on the point of invading France. They issued a proclamation to the French people, the Brunswick Manifesto of July 25 declaring that if any harm befell the French king and queen the Austro-Prussian forces, upon their arrival in Paris, would exact the most severe retribution from the inhabitants of that city. Such menaces, compounding the military emergency, only played into the hands of the most violent activists. Masses of the French people, roused and guided by bourgeois Jacobin leaders, notably Robespierre, Danton, and the vitriolic journalist Marat, burst out in a passion of patriotic excitement. They turned against the king because he was identified with powers at war with France and also because, in France itself, those who still supported him were using the monarchy as defense against the lower classes. Republicanism in France was partly a rather sudden historical accident, in that France was at war under a king who could not be trusted, and partly a kind of popular lower-class movement, in which, however, many bourgeois revolutionaries shared.

Feeling ran high during the summer of 1792. Recruits streamed into Paris from all quarters on their way to the frontiers. One detachment, from Marseilles, brought with them a new marching song, known ever since as the *Marseillaise,* a fierce call to war upon tyranny. The transient provincials stirred up the agitation in Paris. On August 10, 1792, the working-class quarters of the city rose in revolt, supported by the recruits from Marseilles and elsewhere. They stormed the Tuileries against resistance by the Swiss Guard, many of whom were massacred, and seized and imprisoned the king and the royal family. A revolutionary municipal government, or "Commune," was set up in Paris. Usurping the powers of the Legislative Assembly, it forced the abrogation of the constitution and the election, by universal male suffrage, of a Constitutional Convention that was to govern France and prepare a new and more democratic constitution. The very word Convention was used in

Agitation and violence in Paris

recollection of the American Constitutional Convention in 1787. Meanwhile hysteria, anarchy, and terror reigned in Paris; mobs of insurrectionary volunteers, declaring that they would not fight enemies on the frontiers until they had disposed of enemies in Paris, dragged about 1,100 persons—refractory priests and other counterrevolutionaries—from the prisons of the city and killed them after drumhead trials, in brutal executions known as the "September massacres."

For nearly three years, since October 1789, there had been an abatement of popular violence. Now the coming of the war and the dissatisfaction of the lower classes with the course of events so far had led to new explosions. The insurrection of August 10, 1792, the "second" French Revolution, initiated the most advanced phase of the Revolution.

44.   THE EMERGENCY REPUBLIC, 1792–1795: THE TERROR

The National Convention

The National Convention met on September 20, 1792; it was to sit for three years. It immediately proclaimed the Year One of the French Republic. The disorganized French armies, also on September 20, won a great moral victory in the "cannonade of Valmy," a battle that was hardly more than an artillery duel, but which induced the Prussian commander to give up his march on Paris. The French soon occupied Belgium (the Austrian Netherlands), the Savoy region near the Swiss-Italian border (which belonged to the king of Sardinia who had joined with the Austrians), and Mainz and other cities on the German Left Bank of the Rhine. Revolutionary sympathizers in these places appealed for French aid. The National Convention decreed assistance to "all peoples wishing to recover their liberty." It also ordered that French generals, in the occupied areas, should dissolve the old governments; confiscate government and church property; abolish tithes, hunting rights, and seigneurial dues; and set up provisional administrations. Thus revolution spread in the wake of the successful French armies.

Spread of the Revolution

The British and Dutch now prepared to resist. Pitt, still insisting that the French might have any domestic regime that they chose, declared that Great Britain could not tolerate the French occupation of Belgium. The British and Dutch began conversations with Prussia and Austria, and the French declared war on them on February 1, 1793. Within a few weeks the Republic had annexed Savoy and Nice, as well as Belgium, and had much of the German Rhineland under its military government (see map, p. 388). Meanwhile, in eastern Europe, while denouncing the rapacity of the French savages, the rulers of Russia and Prussia, as we have seen, came to an arrangement of their own, each appropriating a portion of Poland in the second partition in January 1793. The Austrians, excluded from the second partition, became anxious about their interests in eastern Europe. The infant French Republic, now at war with all Europe, was saved by the weakness of the Coalition, for Britain and Holland had no land forces of consequence and Prussia and Austria were too jealous of each other, and too preoccupied with Poland, to commit the bulk of their armies against France.

The Jacobins split

In the Convention all the leaders were Jacobins, but the Jacobins were again splitting. The Girondins were no longer the most advanced revolutionary group as they had been in the Legislative Assembly. Beside the Girondins appeared a new group, whose members preferred to sit in the highest seats in the hall, and therefore were dubbed the "Mountain" in the political language of the day. The leading Girondins came from the great provincial cities; the leading Montagnards, though mostly of provincial birth, represented Paris and owed most of their political strength to the radical and popular elements in that city.

These popular revolutionists, outside the Convention, proudly called themselves "sans-culottes," since they wore the workingman's long trousers, not the knee breeches or *culottes* of the middle and upper classes. They were the working class of a preindustrial age, shopkeepers and shop assistants, skilled artisans in various trades, including some who were owners of small manufacturing or handicraft enterprises. For two years their militancy and their activism pressed the Revolution forward. They demanded an equality that should be meaningful for people like themselves, they called for a mighty effort against foreign powers that presumed to intervene in the French Revolution, and they denounced the now deposed king and queen (correctly enough) for collusion with the Austrian enemy. The sans-culottes feared that the Convention might be too moderate. They favored direct democracy in their neighborhood clubs and assemblies, together with a mass rising if necessary against the Convention itself. The Girondins in the Convention began to dismiss these popular militants as anarchists. The group known as the Mountain was more willing to work with them, so long at least as the emergency lasted.

The Convention put Louis XVI on trial for treason in December 1792. On January 15 it unanimously pronounced him guilty, but on the next day, out of 721 deputies present, only 361 voted for immediate execution, a majority of one. Louis XVI died on the guillotine forthwith. The 361 deputies were henceforth branded for life as regicides; never could they allow, in safety to themselves, a restoration of the Bourbon monarchy in France. The other 360 deputies were not similarly compromised; their rivals called them Girondins, "moderatists," counterrevolutionaries. All who still wanted more from the Revolution, or who feared that the slightest wavering would bring the Allies and the émigrés into France, now looked to the Mountain wing of the Jacobins.

The execution of the king

Background to the Terror

In April 1793 the most prominent French general, Dumouriez, who had won the victories in Belgium five months before, defected to Austria. The Allied armies now drove the French from Belgium and again threatened to invade France. Counterrevolutionaries in France exulted. From the revolutionaries went up the cry, "We are betrayed!" Prices continued to rise, the currency fell, food was harder to obtain, and the working classes were increasingly restless. The sans-culottes demanded price controls, currency controls, rationing, legislation against the hoarding of food, and requisitioning to enforce the circulation of goods. They denounced bourgeois traders as profiteers and exploiters of the people. While the Girondins resisted, the Mountain went along with the sans-culottes, partly from sympathy with their ideas, partly to win mass support for the war, and partly as a maneuver against the Girondins. On May 31, 1793, the Commune of Paris, under pressure from the sans-culottes assembled a host of demonstrators and insurrectionists who invaded the Convention and forced the arrest of the Girondin leaders. Other Girondins fled to the provinces, including Condorcet, who, while in hiding, and before his death, found occasion to write his famous book on the *Progress of the Human Mind*.

The Mountain now ruled in the Convention, but the Convention itself ruled very little. Not only were the foreign armies and the émigrés at the gates bent on destroying the Convention as a band of regicides and social incendiaries, but the authority of the Convention

A wave of popular violence in Paris in 1792 led to the fall of the monarchy and the proclamation of a new French republic. Angry crowds pulled down the symbols of the old regime, including this statue of Louis XIV.
(Stock Montage, Inc.)

was also widely repudiated in France itself. In the west, in the Vendée, the peasants had revolted against military conscription; they were worked upon by refractory priests, British agents, and royalist emissaries of the Count of Artois. The great provincial cities, Lyons, Bordeaux, Marseilles, and others, had also rebelled, especially after the fugitive Girondins reached them. These "federalist" rebels demanded a more "federal" or decentralized republic. Like the Vendéans, with whom they had no connection, they objected to the ascendancy of Paris, having been accustomed to more regional independence under the Old Regime. These rebellions became counterrevolutionary, since all sorts of foreigners, royalists, émigrés, and clericals streamed in to assist them.

The Convention under attack

The Convention had to defend itself against extremists of the Left as well. To the genuine mass action of the sans-culottes were now added the voices of even more excited militants called *enragés*. Various organizers, enthusiasts, agitators, and neighborhood politicians declared that parliamentary methods were useless. Generally they were men outside the Convention—and also women, for women were particularly sensitive to the crisis of food shortage and soaring prices, and an organization of Revolutionary Republican Women helped to mobilize the sans-culottes in 1793 (until the suppression of women's political clubs). All such activists worked through units of local government in Paris and elsewhere as well as in thousands of "popular societies" and provincial clubs throughout the whole country. They also formed "revolutionary armies," semimilitary bands that scoured the rural areas for food, searched the barns of peasants, denounced suspects, and preached revolution.

As for the Convention, while it cannot be said ever to have had any commanding leaders, the program it followed for about a year was on the whole that of Maximilien Robespierre, himself a Jacobin but not one to go along forever with popular revolution or anarchy. Robespierre is one of the most argued about and least understood figures in history. Persons accustomed to stable conditions dismiss him with a shudder as a bloodthirsty fanatic, dictator, and demagogue. Others have considered him an idealist, a visionary, and an ardent patriot whose goals and ideals were at least avowedly democratic. All agree on his personal honesty and integrity and on his revolutionary zeal. He was by origin a lawyer from northern France, educated with the aid of scholarships in Paris. He had been elected in 1789 to sit for the Third Estate in the Estates General, and in the ensuing Constituent Assembly played a minor role, though calling attention to himself by his views against capital punishment and in favor of universal suffrage. During the time of the Legislative Assembly, in 1791–1792, he continued to agitate for democracy and vainly pleaded against the declaration of war. In the Convention, elected in September 1792, he sat for a Paris constituency. He became a prominent member of the Mountain and welcomed the purge of the Girondins. He had always kept free of the bribery and graft in which some others became involved and for this reason was known as the Incorruptible. He was a great believer in the importance of "virtue," a term that the philosophes had used in a specialized way. Both Montesquieu and Rousseau, for example, had held that republics depended upon "virtue," or unselfish public spirit and civic zeal, to which was added, under Rousseauist influence, a somewhat sentimentalized idea of personal uprightness and purity of life. Robespierre was determined, in 1793 and 1794, to bring about a democratic republic made up of good, virtuous, and honest citizens.

Robespierre

The Program of the Convention, 1793–1794: The Terror

The program of the Convention, which Robespierre helped to form, was to repress anarchy, civil strife, and counterrevolution at home and to win the war by a great national mobilization of the country's people and resources. It would prepare a democratic constitution and initiate legislation for the lower classes, but it would not yield to the Paris Commune and other agencies of direct revolutionary action. To conduct the government, the Convention granted wide powers to a Committee of Public Safety, a group of 12 members of the Convention who were reelected every month. Robespierre was an influential member; others were the youthful St. Just, the militant lawyer Couthon, and the army officer Carnot, "organizer of victory."

To repress the "counterrevolution," the Convention and the Committee of Public Safety set up what is popularly known as the "Reign of Terror." Revolutionary courts were instituted as an alternative to the lynch law of the September massacres. A Committee of General Security was created as a kind of supreme political police. Designed to protect the Revolutionary Republic from its internal enemies, the Terror struck at those who were in league against the Republic and

The "Reign of Terror"

at those who were merely suspected of hostile activities. Its victims ranged from Marie Antoinette and other royalists to the former revolutionary colleagues of the Mountain, the Girondin leaders; and before the year 1793–1794 was over, some of the old Jacobins of the Mountain who had helped inaugurate the program also went to the guillotine.

Many thousands of people died in France at the height of the Revolution. Most deaths were in places in open revolt against the Convention, as in the Vendée in western France. Some resulted from acts of private vengeance. But if the Terror is understood to mean the official program of the government, which at one time decreed "terror the order of the day," the number who died in it was not large by the brutal standards of the twentieth century, in which dictatorial governments attempted to wipe out not only their political opponents but whole social classes or ethnic groups. About 40,000 persons perished in the Terror thus defined, and many others were temporarily imprisoned. About 8 percent of the

Victims of the "Terror"

victims of the "official" Terror were nobles, but nobles as a class were not molested unless suspected of political agitation; 14 percent of the victims were classifiable as bourgeois, mainly of the rebellious southern cities; 6 percent were clergy, while no less than 70 percent were of the peasant and laboring classes. A democratic republic, founded on the Declaration of the Rights of Man, was in principle to follow the Terror once the war and the emergency were over, but meanwhile, the Terror was inhuman at best and in some places atrocious, as at Nantes where 2,000 persons were loaded on barges and deliberately drowned. The Terror left long memories in France and created much of the enduring antipathy to the Revolution and to republicanism.

The Committee of Public Safety

To conduct the government in the midst of the war emergency the Committee of Public Safety operated as a joint dictatorship and war cabinet. It prepared and guided legislation through the Convention. It gained control over the "representatives on mission," who were members of the Convention on duty with the armies and in the insurgent areas of France. It established the *Bulletin des loix,* so that all persons might know what laws they were supposed to enforce or to obey. It centralized the administration, converting the swarm of locally elected officials left over from the Constituent Assembly (who were royalists in some places, wild extremists, in others) into centrally appointed "national agents" named by the Committee of Public Safety.

To win the war the Committee proclaimed the *levée en masse,* calling on all able-bodied men to rally to the colors. It recruited scientists to work on armaments and munitions. The most prominent French scientists of the day, including Lagrange and Lamarck, worked for or were protected by the government of the Terror, though one, Lavoisier, "father of modern chemistry," was guillotined in 1794 because he had been involved in tax farming before 1789. For military reasons also the Committee instituted economic controls, which at the same time met the demands of the *enragés* and other working-class spokesmen. The value of the *assignats* ceased to fall during the year of the Terror. Thus the government protected both its own purchasing power and that of the masses. It did so by controlling the export of gold, by confiscating specie and foreign currency from French citizens, to whom it paid assignats in return, and by legislation against hoarding or the withholding of goods from the market. Food and supplies for the armies, and for civilians in the towns, were raised and allocated by a system of requisitions, centralized in a Subsistence Commission under the Committee of Public Safety. A "general maximum" set ceilings for prices and wages. It helped to check inflation during the crisis, but it did not work very well; the Committee believed, in principle, in a free market economy and lacked the technical and administrative machinery to enforce thorough controls. By 1794 it was giving freer rein to private enterprise and to the peasants to encourage production. It tried also to hold down wages and in that respect lost the adherence of many working-class leaders.

In June 1793 the Committee produced, and the Convention adopted, a republican constitution which provided for universal male suffrage. But the new constitution was suspended indefinitely, and the government was declared "revolutionary until the peace," "revolutionary" meaning extraconstitutional or of an emergency character. In other ways the Committee showed intentions of legislating on behalf of the lower economic classes. The price controls and other economic regulations answered the demands of the sans-culottes. The last of the manorial regime was done away with; the peasants were relieved of having to pay compensation for the obligations that had been abolished at the opening of the Revolution. The Committee busied itself also with social services and measures of public improvement. It issued pamphlets to teach farmers to improve their crops, selected promising youths to receive instruction in useful trades, opened a military school for boys of all classes, even the humblest, and certainly intended to introduce universal elementary education.

It was also at this time, in 1794, that the National Convention decreed the abolition of slavery in the French colonies, meaning chiefly Saint-Domingue, the modern Haiti, the richest of all the sugar islands in the Caribbean. Free blacks in the colonies had already received civic rights earlier in the Revolution. The black slaves had in fact already liberated themselves in a massive rebellion in 1791. They had produced a leader in Toussaint L'Ouverture, born a slave, who after the French abolished slavery served as a general in the French army against the Spanish and British who had ambitions in Haiti. Amid the ensuing political and military conflicts Toussaint became France's governor-general in Haiti, but his new government soon broke away from all French control. Under pressure from the slave-owning and commercial interests (and the European demand for sugar) the government of Napoleon in 1802 reestablished slavery in the French colonies, sent troops to reassert French authority in Haiti, captured Toussaint, and took him to France, where he died in prison. Unable in any case to defeat the armed rebellion of the black population, most of the French army sent out in this operation perished of yellow fever. Haitian leaders, in 1804, established an independent Republic of Haiti. An unexpected consequence of the French defeat in Haiti was that Napoleon sold the remaining French possessions on the North American mainland ("Louisiana") to the United States in 1803. Slavery was not effectively abolished in the French colonies until 1848.

Slavery abolished in French colonies

At the climax of the Revolution, in 1793–1794, the Committee of Public Safety was determined to concentrate revolutionary initiative in itself. It had no patience with unauthorized revolutionary violence. With a democratic program of its own, it disapproved of the turbulent democracy of popular clubs and local assemblies. In the fall of 1793, at the time of its prohibition of revolutionary women's organizations, the Committee arrested the leading *enragés*. Extreme revolutionary demands were expressed by Jacques Hébert, a journalist and officer of the Paris Commune. Robespierre called such people "ultra revolutionaries." They were a large and indefinable group and included many members of the Convention. They indiscriminately denounced merchants and bourgeoisie. They were the party of extreme Terror; an Hébertist brought about the drownings at Nantes. Believing all religion to be counterrevolutionary, they launched the movement of Dechristianization and strongly supported the creation of a new republican calendar. The Convention adopted this calendar as part of its campaign to strengthen popular allegiance to the republic and to establish a new national organization of daily life that would replace the Christian cycle of Sundays, saints' days, and holidays such as Christmas and Easter. The new calendar thus counted years from the founding of the French Republic, divided each year into new months of 30 days each, and even abolished the week, which it replaced with the 10-day *décade*.[1]

The Revolution and religion

Dechristianization also contributed to the development of the cult of reason, which sprang up all over France at the end of 1793. In Paris the bishop resigned his office, declaring that he had been deluded; and the Commune put on ceremonies in the cathedral of Notre Dame, in which Reason was impersonated by an actress who was the wife of one of the city officials. But Dechristianization was severely frowned upon by Robespierre. He believed that it would alienate the masses from the Republic and ruin such sympathy as was still felt for the Revolution abroad. The Committee of Public Safety, therefore, ordered the toleration of peaceable Catholics, and in June 1794 Robespierre introduced the cult of the Supreme Being, a deistic natural religion, in which the Republic was declared to recognize the existence of God and the immortality of the soul. Robespierre hoped that both Catholics and agnostic anticlericals could become reconciled on this ground. But Catholics were now beyond reconciliation, and the freethinkers, appealing to the tradition of Voltaire, regarded Robespierre as a reactionary mystery monger and were instrumental in bringing about his fall.

Meanwhile the Committee proceeded relentlessly against the Hébertists, whose main champions it sent to the guillotine in March 1794. The paramilitary "revolutionary armies" were suppressed. The extreme Terrorists were recalled from the provinces. The revolutionary Paris Commune was destroyed. Robespierre filled the municipal offices of Paris with his own appointees. This Robespierrist commune disapproved of strikes and tried to hold down wages, on the plea of military necessity; it failed to win over the ex-Hébertists and working-class leaders, who became disillusioned with the Revolution and dismissed it as a bourgeois movement. Probably to prevent just such a conclusion, and to avoid the appearance of deviation to the Right, Robespierre and the Committee, after liquidating the left-wing Hébertists, also liquidated certain right-wing members of the Mountain who were known as Dantonists. Danton and his followers were accused of financial dishonesty and of dealing with counterrevolutionaries; the charges contained some truth but were not the main reason for the executions.

By the spring of 1794 the French Republic possessed an army of 800,000 men, the largest ever raised up to that time by a European power. It was a national army representing a people in arms, commanded by officers who had been promoted rapidly on grounds of merit and composed of troops who felt themselves to be citizens fighting for their own cause. Its intense political-mindedness made it the more formidable and contrasted strongly with the indifference of the opposing troops, some of whom were in fact serfs and none of whom had any sense of membership in their own political systems. The Allied governments, each pursuing its own ends and still distracted by their ambitions in Poland, where the third partition was impending, could not combine their forces against France. In

Revolutionary military victories

June 1794 the French won the battle of Fleurus in Belgium. The Republican hosts again streamed into the Low Countries; in six months their calvary rode into Amsterdam on the ice. A revolutionary Batavian Republic soon replaced the old Dutch provinces. The opposite occurred at this time

---

[1]Though not adopted until October 1793, the revolutionary calendar dated the Year I of the French Republic from September 22, 1792. The names of the months, in order and corresponding to the seasons of the year, were Vendémiaire, Brumaire, Frimaire (autumn); Nivôse, Pluviôse, Ventôse (winter); Germinal, Floréal, Prairial (spring); Messidor, Thermidor, Fructidor (summer).

The French army won a great victory at the battle of Fleurus in June 1794, thus opening the way for republican troops to enter the Low Countries and easing the external threats that had pushed the Revolution toward internal repression and the Terror. This picture shows how the French used a balloon to observe enemy forces during the battle, but the results must have been disappointing, since balloons were not thereafter used by either side.
(Picture Collection, The New York Public Library, Astor, Lenox and Tilden Foundations)

in eastern Europe, where Russian and Prussian armies stamped out the attempted revolution that Kosciusko led in Poland. All Polish lands and people were finally merged into the east-European empires in 1795.

Military success made the French less willing to put up with the dictatorial rule and economic regimentation of the Terror. Robespierre and the Committee of Public Safety had antagonized all significant parties. The working-class radicals of Paris would no longer support him, and after the death of Danton the National Convention was afraid of its own ruling committee. A group in the Convention obtained the "outlawing" of Robespierre on 9 Thermidor (July 27, 1794); he was guillotined with some of his associates on the following day. Many who turned against Robespierre believed they were pushing the Revolution farther forward, as

Fall of Robespierre

The guillotine was used during the most radical phase of the Revolution to execute persons judged to be enemies of the republic. First adopted as a more humane way of inflicting capital punishment, it became a permanent symbol of revolutionary violence and it claimed victims from every part of the Revolution itself. This picture illustrates the execution of Robespierre and four others who were denounced as conspirators against liberty and sent to the guillotine in July 1794.
(Bettmann/Corbis)

in destroying the Girondins the year before. Others thought, or said, that they were stopping a dictator and a tyrant. All agreed, to absolve themselves, in heaping all blame upon Robespierre. The idea that Robespierre was an ogre originated more with his former colleagues than with conservatives of the time.

The Thermidorian Reaction

The fall of Robespierre stunned the country, but its effects manifested themselves during the following months as the "Thermidorian reaction." The Terror subsided. The Convention reduced the powers of the Committee of Public Safety, and it closed the Jacobin club. Price controls and other regulations were removed. Inflation resumed its course, prices again rose, and the disoriented and leaderless working classes suffered more than ever. Sporadic uprisings broke out, of which the greatest was the insurrection of Prairial in the Year III (May 1795), when a mob all but dispersed the Convention by force. Troops were called to Paris for the first time since 1789. Insurrectionists in the working-class quarters threw up barricades in the streets. The army prevailed without much bloodshed, but the Convention arrested, imprisoned, or deported 10,000 of the insurgents. A few organizers were guillotined. The affair of Prairial gave a foretaste of modern social revolution.

The triumphant element consisted mostly of the bourgeois class which had guided the Revolution since the Constituent Assembly and had not been really unseated even during the Terror. It was not mainly a bourgeoisie of modern capitalists, eager to make a financial profit by developing new factories or machinery. The political victors after Thermidor were "bourgeois" in an older social sense, those who had not been noble or aristocratic before 1789 yet had held a secure position under the Old Regime, many of them lawyers or officeholders and often drawing income from the ownership of land. To them were now added new elements produced by the Revolution itself, parvenus and *nouveaux riches,* who had made money by wartime government contracts or had profited by inflation or by buying up former church lands at bargain prices. Such people, often joined by former aristocrats, and in reaction against Robespierrist virtue, set an extravagant and ostentatious style of living that gave a bad name to the new order. They also unleashed a "white terror" in which many ex-Jacobins were simply murdered.

Politics and society after Thermidor

But the Thermidorians, disreputable though a few of them were, had not lost faith in the Revolution. Democracy they associated with red terror and mob rule, but they still believed in individual legal rights and in a written constitution. Conditions were rather adverse, for the country was still unsettled, and although the Convention made a separate peace with Spain and Prussia, France still remained at war with Great Britain and the Habsburg empire. But the men of the Convention were determined to make another attempt at constitutional government. They set aside the democratic constitution written in 1793 (and never used) and produced the Constitution of the Year III, which went into effect at the end of 1795.

45. THE CONSTITUTIONAL REPUBLIC: THE DIRECTORY, 1795–1799

The Weakness of the Directory

The first formally constituted French Republic, known as the Directory, lasted only four years. Its weakness was that it rested on an extremely narrow social base and that it presupposed certain military conquests. The new constitution applied not only to France but also to Belgium, which was now regarded as incorporated constitutionally into France, though the Habsburgs had not yet ceded these "Austrian Netherlands," nor had the British yielded in their refusal to accept French occupation. The constitution of 1795 thus committed the republic to a program of successful expansion. At the same time it restricted the politically active class. It gave almost all adult males the vote, but they voted only for "electors." Persons chosen as electors were usually men of some means, able to give their time and willing to take part in public life; this in effect meant men of the upper middle class, since the old aristocracy was disaffected. The electors chose all important department officials and also the members of the national Legislative Assembly, which this time was divided

The constitution of 1795

into two chambers. The lower chamber was called the Council of Five Hundred; the upper, composed of 250 members, the Council of Ancients—"ancients" being those over 40. The chambers chose the executive, which was called the Directory (from which the whole regime took its name) and was made up of five Directors.

The government was thus constitutionally in the hands of substantial property owners, rural and urban, but its real base was narrower still. In the reaction after Thermidor many people began to consider restoring the monarchy. The Convention, to protect its own members, had ruled that two-thirds of the men initially elected to the Council of Five Hundred and Council of Ancients must be ex-members of the Convention. This interference with the freedom of the elections provoked serious disturbances in Paris, instigated mainly by royalists. The Convention, having now accustomed itself to using the army, instructed a young general named Bonaparte, who happened to be in Paris, to put down the royalist mob. He did so with a "whiff of grapeshot." The constitutional republic thus made itself dependent on military protection at the outset.

The regime had enemies to both Right and Left. On the Right, undisguised royalists agitated in Paris and even in the two councils; and they were in continuous touch with the late king's brother, the Count of Provence, whom they regarded as Louis XVIII (Louis XVI's son, who died in prison, was counted as Louis XVII). Louis XVIII had installed himself at Verona in Italy, where he headed a propaganda agency financed largely by British money. The worst obstacle to the resurgence of royalism in France was Louis XVIII himself. In 1795, on assuming the title, he had issued a Declaration of Verona, in which he announced his intention to restore the Old Regime and punish all involved in the Revolution back to 1789. It has been said, correctly enough in this connection, that the Bourbons "learned nothing and forgot nothing." Had Louis XVIII offered in 1795 what he offered in 1814, it is quite conceivable that his partisans in France might have brought about his restoration and terminated the war. As it was, the bulk of the French adhered not exactly to the republic as set up in 1795, but more negatively to any system that would shut out the Bourbons and privileged nobility, prevent a reimposition of the manorial system, and secure the new landowners, peasant and bourgeois, in the possession of the church properties which they had purchased.

The Left was made up of persons from various levels of society who still favored the more democratic ideas expressed earlier in the Revolution. Some of them thought that the fall of Robespierre had been a great misfortune. A tiny group of extremists formed the Conspiracy of Equals, organized in 1796 by "Gracchus" Babeuf. His intention was to overthrow the Directory and replace it with a dictatorial government which he called "democratic," in which private property would be abolished and equality would be decreed. For these ideas, and for his activist program, he has been regarded as a political precursor to modern communism. The Directory repressed the Conspiracy of Equals without difficulty and guillotined Babeuf and one other. Meanwhile it did nothing to relieve the distress of the lower classes, who showed little inclination to follow Babeuf even though they suffered from the ravages of scarcity and inflation.

The Political Crisis of 1797

In March 1797 occurred the first really free election ever held in France under republican auspices. The successful candidates were for the most part constitutional monarchists or at least vaguely royalist. A change of the balance within the Five Hundred and the Ancients, in favor of royalism, seemed to be impending. This was precisely what most of the republicans of 1793, including the regicides, could not endure, even though they had to violate the constitution to prevent it. Nor was it endurable, for other reasons, to General Napoleon Bonaparte.

Bonaparte had been born in 1769 into the minor nobility of Corsica, shortly after the annexation of Corsica to France. He had studied in French military schools and been commissioned in the Bourbon army but would   *Napoleon Bonaparte* never have reached high rank under the conditions of the Old Regime. In 1793 he was a fervent young Jacobin officer, who had been useful in driving the British from Toulon and who was consequently made a brigadier general by the government of the Terror. In 1795, as noted, he rendered service to the Convention by breaking up a demonstration of royalists. In 1796 he received command of an army, with which, in two brilliant campaigns, he crossed the Alps and drove the Austrians from north Italy. Like other generals he soon became independent from the government in Paris, which was financially too harassed to pay his troops or to supply him. He lived by local requisitions in Italy, became self-supporting, and in fact made the civilian government in Paris dependent on him.

He developed a foreign policy of his own. Many Italians had become dissatisfied with their old governments, so that the arrival of the French republican armies threw north Italy into a turmoil. The Venetian cities revolted against Venice, Bologna against the pope, Milan against Austria, and in Piedmont the Savoy monarchy was threatened by uprisings of its own subjects. Combining with some of these revolutionaries, while rejecting others, Bonaparte established a "Cisalpine" Republic in the Po valley, modeled on the French system, with Milan as its capital. Where the Directory, on the whole, had originally meant to return Milan to the Austrians in compensation for Austrian recognition of the French conquest of Belgium, Bonaparte insisted that France hold its position in both Belgium and Italy. He therefore needed expansionist republicans in the government in Paris and was perturbed by the royalist victories in the elections of 1797.

The Austrians negotiated with Bonaparte because they had been beaten by him in battle. The British also, in conferences with the French at Lille, discussed peace in 1796 and 1797. The war had gone badly for England; a party of Whigs led by Charles James Fox had always openly disapproved it, and the pro-French and republican radicals were so active that the government suspended habeas corpus in 1794, and thereafter imprisoned political agitators at its discretion. Crops were bad and bread was scarce and costly. England too suffered from inflation, for Pitt at first financed the war by extensive loans, and a good deal of gold was shipped to the Continent to finance the Allied armies. In February 1797 the Bank of England suspended gold payments to private citizens. Famine threatened, the populace was restless, and there were even mutinies in the fleet. Ireland was in rebellion; the French came close to landing a republican army there, and it could be supposed that the next attempt might be more successful. The Austrians, Britain's only remaining ally, had been routed by Bonaparte, and at the moment the British could subsidize them no   *Prospects for peace* further. The British had every reason to make peace.

Prospects for peace therefore seemed good in the summer of 1797, but, as always, it would be peace upon certain conditions. It was the royalists in France that were the peace party, since a restored king could easily return the conquests of the republic and would in any case abandon the new republics in Holland and the Po valley. The republicans in the French government could make peace with difficulty, if at all. They were constitutionally bound to retain Belgium. They were losing control of their own generals. Nor could the supreme question be evaded: Was peace dear enough to purchase by a return of the Old Regime, such as Louis XVIII had himself promised?

CHRONOLOGY OF NOTABLE EVENTS, 1789–1804

May 1789	Estates General convenes at Versailles
June 1789	The Third Estate declares itself to be the National Assembly
July 1789	Crowd assaults and captures the Bastille fortress in Paris
August 1789	National Assembly issues "Declaration of the Rights of Man and Citizen" and abolishes "feudal privileges"
September 1791	New French Constitution establishes a constitutional monarchy
April 1791	France declares war on Austria and Prussia
September 1792	New National Convention meets in Paris; France becomes a republic
January 1793	King Louis XVI is executed in Paris
1793–1794	The Radical Revolution and the "Reign of Terror"
July 1794	Robespierre and his Jacobin allies are executed
1795–1799	Republic called "the Directory" governs France and sends armies to spread revolutionary republicanism in Europe
November 1799	Napoleon Bonaparte seizes power in a coup d'état
1799–1804	Napoleon is "First Consul" in French government called the Consulate; laws are codified in Napoleonic Code
1801	Napoleon's Concordat with the Roman Catholic Church
1804	France becomes an empire under Emperor Napoleon I

The coup d'état of Fructidor

The coup d'état of Fructidor (September 4, 1797) resolved all these many issues. It was the turning point of the constitutional republic and was decisive for all Europe. The Directory asked for help from Bonaparte, who sent one of his generals, Augereau, to Paris. While Augereau stood by with a force of soldiers, the councils annulled most of the elections of the preceding spring. On the whole, it was the old republicans of the Convention who secured themselves in power. Their justification was that they were defending the revolution, keeping out Louis XVIII and the Old Regime. But to do so they had violated their own constitution and quashed the first free election ever held in a constitutional French republic. And they had become more than ever dependent on the army.

After the coup d'état the "Fructidorian" government broke off negotiations with England. With Austria it signed the treaty of Campo Formio on October 17, 1797, incorporating Bonaparte's ideas. By the new treaty Austria recognized the French annexation of Belgium (the former Austrian Netherlands), the French right to incorporate the Left Bank of the Rhine, and the French-dominated Cisalpine Republic in Italy. In return, Bonaparte allowed the Austrians to annex Venice and most of mainland Venetia.

Revolutionary republicanism spreads

In the following months, under French auspices, revolutionary republicanism spread rapidly through much of Italy, creating new republics with classical names. The old patrician republic of Genoa turned into a Ligurian Republic on the French model. At Rome the pope was deposed from his temporal power and a Roman Republic was established. In southern Italy a Neapolitan Republic, also called Parthenopean, was set up. In Switzerland at the same time, Swiss reformers cooperated with the French to create a new Helvetic Republic.

The Left Bank of the Rhine, in the atomistic Holy Roman Empire, was occupied by a great many German princes who now had to vacate. The treaty of Campo Formio provided that they be compensated by church territories in Germany east of the Rhine and that France have a hand in the redistribution. The German princes turned greedy eyes on the German bishops and abbots, and the almost 1,000-year-old empire, hardly more than a solemn form since the Peace of Westphalia, sank to the level of a land rush or real estate speculation, while France became involved in the territorial reconstruction of Germany.

The Coup d'État of 1799: Bonaparte

After Fructidor the idea of maintaining the republic as a free or constitutional government was given up. There were more uprisings, more quashed elections, more purgings both to Left and Right. The Directory turned into an ineffective dictatorship. It repudiated most of the assignats and the debt but failed to restore financial confidence or stability. Guerrilla activity flared up again in the Vendée and other parts of western France. The religious schism became more acute; the Directory had to take severe measures toward the refractory clergy.

Meanwhile Bonaparte waited for the situation to ripen. Returning from Italy a conquering hero, he was assigned to command the army in training to invade England. He concluded that invasion was premature and decided to strike indirectly at England, by threatening India in a spectacular invasion of Egypt. In 1798, outwitting the British fleet, he landed a French army at the mouth of the Nile. Egypt was part of the Ottoman Empire, and the French occupation of it alarmed the Russians, who had their own designs on the Middle East. The Austrians objected to the French rearrangement of Germany. A year and a half after the treaty of Campo Formio, Austria, Russia, and Great Britain formed an alliance known as the Second Coalition. The French Republic was again involved in a general war. And the war went unfavorably, for in August 1798 the British fleet had cut off the French army in Egypt by winning the battle of the Nile (or Aboukir), and in 1799 Russian forces, under Marshal Suvorov, were operating as far west as Switzerland and north Italy, where the Cisalpine Republic went down in ruin.

General Bonaparte's opportunity had now come. He left his army in Egypt and, slipping through the British fleet, reappeared unexpectedly in France. He found that certain civilian leaders in the Directory were planning a change. They included Sieyès, of whom little had been heard since he wrote *What Is the Third Estate?* in 1789, but who had sat in the Convention and voted for the death of Louis XVI. Sieyès' formula was now "confidence from below, authority from above"—what he now wanted of the people was acquiescence, and of the government, power to act. This group was looking about for a general, and their choice fell on the sensational young Bonaparte, who was still only 30. Dictatorship by an army officer was repugnant to most republicans of the Five Hundred and the Ancients. Bonaparte, Sieyès, and their followers resorted to force, executing the coup d'état of Brumaire (November 9, 1799), in which armed soldiers drove the legislators from the chambers. They proclaimed a new form of the republic, which Bonaparte entitled the Consulate. It was headed by three consuls, with Bonaparte as the First Consul.

The Directory turns to Bonaparte

THE FRENCH REPUBLIC AND ITS SATELLITES, 1798–1799

By 1799 the French Republic had annexed Belgium (the Austrian Netherlands) and the small German bishoprics and principalities west of the Rhine, and had created, with the aid of native sympathizers, a string of lesser revolutionary republics in the Dutch Netherlands, Switzerland, and most of Italy. With the treaty of Campo Formio between France and Austria in 1797, the Holy Roman Empire began to disintegrate, for the German princes of the Left Bank of the Rhine, who were dispossessed when their territories went to France, began to be compensated with territory of the church-states of the Holy Roman Empire. These developments were carried further by Napoleon (see map, p. 430).

46.   THE AUTHORITARIAN REPUBLIC: THE CONSULATE, 1799–1804

The next chapter takes up the affairs of Europe as a whole in the time of Napoleon Bonaparte, the purpose at present being only to tell how he closed, in a way, the Revolution in France.

It happened that the French Republic, in falling into the hands of a general, fell also to a man of such remarkable talents as are often denominated genius. Bonaparte was a short man who would never have looked

Napoleon's genius

impressive in civilian clothing. His manners were rather coarse; he lost his temper, cheated at cards, and pinched people by the ear in a kind of formidable play—he was no "gentleman." A child of the Enlightenment and the Revolution, he was entirely emancipated not only from customary ideas but from moral scruples as well. He regarded the world as a flux to be formed by his own mind. He had an exalted belief in his own destinies, which became more mystical and exaggerated as the years went on. He claimed to follow his "star." His ideas of the good and the beautiful were rather blunt, but he was a man of extraordinary intellectual capacity, which impressed all with whom he came in contact. "Never speak unless you know you are the ablest man in the room," he once advised his stepson, on making him viceroy of Italy, a maxim which, if he followed it himself, still allowed him to do most of the talking. His interests ran to solid subjects, history, law, military science, public administration. His mind was tenacious and perfectly orderly; he once declared that it was like a chest of drawers, which he could open or close at will, forgetting any subject when its drawer was closed and finding it ready with all necessary detail when its drawer was opened. He had all the masterful qualities associated with leadership; he could dazzle and captivate those who had any inclination to follow him at all. Some of the most humane men of the day, including Goethe and Beethoven in Germany, and Lazare Carnot among the former revolutionary leaders, at first looked on him with high approval. He inspired confidence by his crisp speech, rapid decisions, and quick grasp of complex problems when they were newly presented to him. He was, or seemed, just what many people in France were looking for after ten years of upheaval.

Under the Consulate France reverted to a form of enlightened despotism, and Bonaparte may be thought of as the last and most eminent of the enlightened despots. Despotic the new regime undoubtedly was from the start. Self-government through elected bodies was ruthlessly pushed aside. Bonaparte delighted in affirming the sovereignty of the people; but to his mind the people were a sovereign, like Voltaire's God, who somehow created the world but never thereafter interfered in it. He clearly saw that a government's authority was greater when it was held to represent the entire nation. In the weeks after Brumaire he assured himself of a popular mandate by devising a written constitution and submitting it to a general referendum or "plebiscite." The voters could take it—or nothing. They took it by a majority officially reported as 3,011,007 to 1,562.

Bonaparte as First Consul

The new constitution set up a make-believe of parliamentary institutions. It provided for universal male suffrage, but the citizens merely chose "notables"; men on the lists of notables were then appointed by the government itself to public position. The notables had no powers of their own. They were merely available for appointment to office. They might sit in a Legislative Body, where they could neither initiate nor discuss legislation but only mutely reject or enact it. There was also a Tribunate which discussed public policies but had no enacting powers. There was a Conservative Senate, which had rights of appointment of notables to office ("patronage" in American terms) and in which numerous storm-tossed regicides found a haven. The main agency in the new government was the Council of State, imitated from the Old Regime; it prepared the significant legislation, often under the presidency of the First Consul himself, who always gave the impression that he understood everything. The First Consul made all the decisions and ran the state. The regime did not openly represent anybody, and that was its strength, for it provoked the less opposition. In any case, the political machinery just described fell rapidly into disuse.

Bonaparte entrenched himself also by promising and obtaining peace. The military problem at the close of 1799 was much simplified by the attitude of the Russians, who in effect withdrew from the war with France. In the Italian theater Bonaparte had to deal only with the Austrians, whom he again defeated, by again crossing the Alps, at the battle of Marengo in June 1800. In February 1801 the Austrians signed the treaty of Lunéville, in which the terms of Campo Formio were confirmed. A year later, in March 1802, peace was made even with Britain.

Peace was made also at home. Bonaparte kept internal order, partly by a secret political police but more especially through a powerful and centralized administrative machine in which a "prefect," under direct orders of the minister of the interior, ruled firmly over each of the regional departments created by the Constituent Assembly. The new government put down the guerrillas in the west. Its laws and taxes were imposed on Brittany and the Vendée. Peasants there were no longer terrorized by marauding partisans. A new peace settled down on the factions left by the Revolution. Bonaparte offered a general amnesty and invited back to France, with a few exceptions, exiles of all stripes, from the first aristocratic émigrés to the refugees and deportees of the republican coups d'état. Requiring only that they work for him and stop quarreling with each other, he picked reasonable men from all camps. His Second Consul was Cambacérès, a regicide of the Terror; his Third Consul was Lebrun, who had been Maupeou's colleague in the days of Louis XV. Fouché emerged as minister of police; he had been an Hébertist and extreme terrorist in 1793 and had done as much as anyone to bring about the fall of Robespierre. Before 1789 he had been an obscure bourgeois professor of physics. Talleyrand appeared as minister of foreign affairs; he had spent the Terror in safe seclusion in the United States, and his principles, if he had any, were those of constitutional monarchy. Before 1789 he had been a bishop, and he descended from an old and famous aristocratic lineage—no one who had not known the Old Regime, he once said, could realize how pleasant it had been. Men of this kind were now willing, for a few years beginning in 1800, to forget the past and work in common toward the future.

Disturbers of the new order the First Consul ruthlessly put down. Indeed, he concocted alarms to make himself more welcome as a pillar of order. On Christmas Eve, 1800, on the way to the opera, he was nearly killed by a bomb, or "infernal machine," as people then called such bombs. It had been set by royalists, but Bonaparte represented it as the work of Jacobin conspiracy, being most afraid at the moment of some of the old republicans; and over 100 former Jacobins were deported. Contrariwise, in 1804, he greatly exaggerated certain royalist plots against him, invaded the independent state of Baden, and there arrested the Duke of Enghien, who was related to the Bourbons. Though he knew Enghien to be innocent, he had him shot. His purpose now was to please the old Jacobins by staining his own hands with Bourbon blood; Fouché and the regicides concluded that they were secure so long as Bonaparte was in power.

After repeatedly winning battles against all the powers of Europe, Napoleon developed even more grandiose ideas of himself and the imperial power of France. This painting was completed in 1806 by Jacques-Louis David, the aging revolutionary whose work had once portrayed the Tennis Court Oath and the faces of common people in Paris. Here he presents an idealized image of Napoleon as a young republican hero who crossed the Alps in 1800 to win the battle of Marengo.
(Giraudon/Art Resource, NY)

The Settlement with the Church; Other Reforms

For all but the most convinced royalists and republicans, reconciliation was made easier by the establishment of peace with the church. Bonaparte himself was a pure eighteenth-century rationalist. He regarded religion as a convenience. He advertised himself as a Muslim in Egypt, as a Catholic in France, and as a freethinker among the professors at the Institute in Paris. But a Catholic revival was in full swing and he saw its importance. The refractory clergy were the spiritual force animating all forms of counter-revolution. "Fifty émigré bishops, paid by England," he once said, "lead the French clergy today. Their influence must be destroyed. For this we need the authority of the pope." Ignoring the horrified outcries of the old Jacobins, in 1801 he signed a concordat with the Vatican.

Concordat with the Vatican

Both parties gained from the settlement. The autonomy of the prerevolutionary Gallican church came to an end. The pope received the right to depose French bishops, since before the schism could be healed both constitutional and refractory bishops had to be obliged to resign. The constitutional or pro-revolutionary clergy came under the discipline of the Holy See. Publicity of Catholic worship, in such forms as processions in the streets, was again allowed. Church seminaries were again permitted. But Bonaparte and the heirs of the Revolution gained even more. The pope, by signing the concordat, virtually recognized the Republic. The Vatican agreed to raise no question over the former tithes and the former church lands. The new owners of former church properties thus obtained clear titles. Nor was there any further question of Avignon, an enclave within France, formerly papal, annexed to France in 1791. Nor were the papal negotiators able to undermine religious toleration; all that Bonaparte would concede was a clause that was purely factual, and hence harmless, stating that Catholicism was the religion of the majority of the French people. The clergy, in compensation for loss of their tithes and property, were assured of receiving salaries from the state. But Bonaparte, to dispel the notion of an established church, put Protestant ministers of all denominations on the state payroll also. He thus checkmated the Vatican on important points. At the same time, simply by signing an agreement with Rome, he disarmed the counterrevolution. It could no longer be said that the Republic was godless. Good relations did not, indeed, last very long, for Bonaparte and the papacy were soon at odds. But the terms of the concordat proved lasting.

With peace and order established, the constructive work of the Consulate turned to the fields of law and administration. The First Consul and his advisers combined what they conceived to be the best of the Revolution and of the Old Regime. The modern state took on clearer form. It was the reverse of everything feudal. All public authority was concentrated in officially employed agents of government, no person was held to be under any legal authority except that of the state, and the authority of government fell on all persons alike. There were no more estates, legal classes, privileges, local liberties, hereditary offices, guilds, or manors. Judges, officials, and army officers received specified salaries. Neither military commissions nor civil offices could be bought and sold. Citizens were to rise in government service according to their abilities rather than their wealth or privileged birth.

Consulate reforms

"Careers open to talent"

This was the doctrine of "careers open to talent"; it was what the bourgeoisie had wanted before the Revolution, and a few persons of quite humble birth profited also. For sons of the old aristocracy, it meant that pedigree was not enough; they must also show individual capacity to obtain employment. Qualification came to depend increasingly on education, and the secondary and higher schools were reorganized in these years, with a view to preparing young men for government service and the learned professions. Scholarships were provided, but it was mainly the upper middle class that benefited. Education, in fact, in France and in Europe generally, came to be an important determinant of social standing, with one system for those who could spend a dozen or more years at school, and another for those who were to enter the workforce at the age of 12 or 14. Meanwhile, French intellectual life was strictly regulated and censored. When a few professors at the National Institute began to question certain government policies, for example, Bonaparte suppressed both their writings and the section of the Institute in which they worked; and when the liberal critic Germaine de Staël published books that displeased the First Consul, she was sent off to exile in Switzerland. Creative, critical intellectual debate thus became impossible in France during these years, though Bonaparte satisfied many of the popular demands for education and professional advancement.

Another deep demand of the French people, deeper than the demand for the vote, was for more reason, order, and economy in public finance and taxation. The Consulate gave these also. There were no tax exemptions because of birth, status, or special arrangement. Everyone was supposed to pay, so that no disgrace attached to payment, and there was less evasion. In principle these changes had been introduced in 1789; after 1799 they began to work. For the first time in ten years the government really collected the taxes that it levied and so could rationally plan its financial affairs. Order was introduced also into expenditure, and accounting methods were improved. There was no longer a haphazard assortment of different "funds" on which various officials drew independently and confidentially as they needed money, but a concentration of financial management in the treasury and even in a kind of budget. The revolutionary uncertainties over the value of money were also ended. Because the Directory had shouldered the odium of repudiating the paper money and government debt, the Consulate was able to establish a sound currency and public credit. To assist in government financing, one of the banks of the Old Regime was revived and established as the Bank of France.

Like all enlightened despots, Bonaparte codified the laws, and of all law codes since the Romans the Napoleonic codes are the most famous. To the 300 legal systems of the Old Regime and the mass of royal ordinances were now added the thousands of laws enacted but seldom implemented by the revolutionary assemblies. Five codes emerged—the Civil Code (often called simply the Code Napoleon), the codes of civil and of criminal procedure, and the commercial and penal codes. The codes made France legally and judicially uniform. They assured legal equality; all French citizens had the same civil rights. They formulated the new law of property and set forth the law of contracts, debts, leases, stock companies, and similar matters in such a way as to create the legal framework for an economy of private enterprise. They repeated the ban of all previous regimes on organized labor unions and were severe with individual workers, their word not being acceptable in court against that of the employer—a significant departure from equality before the law. The criminal code was somewhat freer in giving the government the means to detect crime than in granting the individual the means of defense against legal charges. As for the family, the codes recognized civil marriage and divorce but left the wife with very restricted powers over property and the father with extensive authority over minor children; the legal system codified a paternalistic view of all family relations. The codes reflected much of French life under the Old Regime. They also set the character of France as it has been ever since, socially bourgeois, legally egalitarian, and administratively bureaucratic.

The Napoleonic Codes

In France, with the Consulate, the Revolution was over. If its highest hopes had not been accomplished, the worst evils of the Old Regime had at least been cured. The beneficiaries of the Revolution felt secure. Even former aristocrats were rallying. The working-class movement, repeatedly frustrated under all the revolutionary regimes, now vanished from the political scene to reappear as socialism 30 years later. What the Third Estate had most wanted in 1789 was now both codified and enforced, with the exception of parliamentary government, which after ten years of turmoil many people were temporarily willing to forgo. Moreover, in 1802, the French Republic was at peace with the papacy, Great Britain, and all Continental powers. It reached to the Rhine and had dependent republics in Holland and Italy. So popular was the First Consul that in 1802, by another plebiscite, he had himself elected consul for life. A new constitution, in 1804, again ratified by plebiscite, declared that "the government of the republic is entrusted to an emperor." The Consulate became the Empire, and Bonaparte emerged as Napoleon I, Emperor of the French.

From Consulate to Empire

But France, no longer revolutionary at home, was revolutionary outside its borders. Napoleon became a terror to the patricians of Europe. They called him the "Jacobin." And the France which he ruled, and used as his arsenal, was an incomparably formidable state. Even before the Revolution it had been the most populous in Europe, perhaps the most wealthy, in the front rank of scientific enterprise and intellectual leadership. Now all the old barriers of privilege, tax exemption, localism, and caste exclusiveness had disappeared. The new France could tap the wealth of its citizens and put able men into positions without inquiring into their origins. Every private, boasted Napoleon, carried a marshal's baton in his knapsack. The French looked with disdain on their caste-ridden adversaries. The principle of civic equality proved not only to have the appeal of justice, but also to be politically useful, and the resources of France were hurled against Europe with a force which for many years nothing could check.

 For interactive exercises, glossary, chronologies, and more, go to the *Online Learning Center* at **www.mhhe.com/palmer10.**

Chapter 10

NAPOLEONIC EUROPE

47. The Formation of the French Imperial System

48. The Grand Empire: Spread of the Revolution

49. The Continental System: Britain and Europe

50. The National Movements: Germany

51. The Overthrow of Napoleon: The Congress of Vienna

The repercussions of the French Revolution had been felt throughout Europe since the fall of the Bastille, and even more definitely after the outbreak of war in 1792 and the ensuing victories of the republican armies. They became even more evident after the republican General Bonaparte turned into Napoleon I, Emperor of the French, King of Italy, and Protector of the Confederation of the Rhine. Napoleon surpassed all previous European rulers in imposing a broad political unity on the European continent. Although his imperial power collapsed in less than fifteen years, his military campaigns and political ascendancy transformed both international relations in Europe and the internal development of the various European peoples. The French impact on other nations, though based on military success, represented more than mere forcible subjugation. Innovations of a kind made in France by revolution were brought to other countries by administrative decree. There were for several years Germans, Italians, Dutch, and Poles who worked with the French emperor to introduce the changes that he demanded, and which they themselves often desired. In Prussia it was resistance to Napoleon that gave the incentive to internal reorganization and fostered the emergence of a new German nationalism. Whether by collaboration or resistance, Europe was transformed.

It is convenient to think of the fighting from 1792 to 1814 as a "world war," as indeed it was, affecting not only all of Europe but also places as far away as Latin America, where the wars of independence began, or the interior of North America, where the United States purchased Louisiana in 1803 and attempted a conquest of Canada in the War of 1812. But it is important to realize that this world war was actually a series of wars, most of them quite short and distinct. Only Great Britain remained continually at war with France, except for about a year of peace in 1802–1803. Never were the four

Chapter emblem: Detail from a nineteenth-century illustration of Napoleon and Tsar Alexander I meeting on the Niemen River in 1807. (Rare Book Collection, University of North Carolina–Chapel Hill (Hoyt IC-187))

great European powers, Britain, Austria, Russia, and Prussia, simultaneously in the field against France until 1813.

The history of the Napoleonic period would be much simpler if the European governments had fought merely to protect themselves against the aggressive French. Each, however, in its way, was as dynamic and expansive as Napoleon himself. For some generations Great Britain had been building a commercial empire, Russia had been pushing upon Poland and Turkey, and Prussia had been consolidating its territories and striving for leadership in north Germany. Austria was less aggressive, but the Austrians were not without their own dreams of ascendancy in Germany, the Balkans, and the Adriatic. None of these ambitions ceased during the Napoleonic years. Governments, in pursuit of their own aims, were quite as willing to ally with Napoleon as to fight him. Only gradually, and under repeated provocation, did they conclude that their main interest was to dispose of the French emperor entirely.

47. THE FORMATION OF THE FRENCH IMPERIAL SYSTEM

The Dissolution of the First and Second Coalitions, 1792–1802

The conflicting purposes of the powers had been apparent from almost the beginning of the French Revolution. Leopold of Austria, in issuing the Declaration of Pillnitz in 1791, had believed a general European coalition against France to be impossible. When war began in 1792, the Austrians and Prussians kept their main forces in eastern Europe, more afraid of each other and of Russia, in the matter of Poland, than of the French revolutionary republic. Indeed, the main accomplishment of the First Coalition was the partition of Poland and the dissolution of the Polish state.

The First Coalition disintegrates

In 1795 the French broke up the coalition. The British withdrew their army from the Continent. Prussia and Spain each made a separate peace with France. Indeed, Bourbon Spain—acting for reasons of strategic self-interest that ignored all ideology or principle—formed an alliance with the French republic that had guillotined Louis XVI and kept Louis XVIII from his monarchic rights. Spain simply reverted to the eighteenth-century pattern in allying with France because of hostility to Great Britain, whose possession of Gibraltar, naval influence in the Mediterranean, and attitude toward the Spanish empire were disquieting to the Spanish government. When Austria signed the peace of Campo Formio in 1797, the First Coalition was totally dissipated, only British naval forces remaining engaged with the French.

The Second Coalition of 1799 fared no better. After the British fleet defeated the French at the battle of the Nile, cutting off the French army in Egypt, the Russians saw their ambitions in the Mediterranean blocked mainly by the British and withdrew Suvorov's army from western Europe. Austria's acceptance of the peace of Lunéville in 1801 dissolved the Second Coalition, and in 1802 Great Britain signed the peace of Amiens. For the only time between 1792 and 1814 no European power was at war with another.

Peace Interim, 1802–1803

Never had a peace been so advantageous to France as the peace of 1802. But Bonaparte gave it no chance. He used peace as he did war to advance his interests. He dispatched a sizable army to Haiti, ostensibly to suppress Toussaint L'Ouverture and the Haitian military campaign to establish an independent republic. But he also sent this army with the further thought (since Louisiana had been ceded back by Spain to France in 1800) of reviving the French colonial empire in America. He reorganized the Cisalpine Republic into an "Italian" Republic with himself as president. He reorganized the Helvetic Republic, making himself "mediator" of the Confederation of Switzerland. He reorganized Germany; that is to say, he and his agents closely watched the rearrangement of territory which the Germans themselves had been carrying out since 1797.

By the treaty of Campo Formio, it will be recalled, German princes of the Left Bank of the Rhine, expropriated by the annexation of their dominions to the French Republic, were to receive new territories on the Right Bank. The result was a scramble called by patriotic German historians the "shame of the princes." The German rulers, far from opposing Bonaparte or upholding any national interests, competed desperately for the absorption of German territory, each bribing and fawning upon the French (Talleyrand made over 10,000,000 francs in the process) to win French support against other Germans. The Holy Roman Empire was fatally mauled by the Germans themselves. Most of its ecclesiastical principalities and 45 out of its 51 free cities disappeared, annexed by their larger neighbors. The number of states in the Holy Empire was greatly reduced, but Prussia, Bavaria, Württemberg, and Baden consolidated and enlarged themselves. These arrangements were ratified in February 1803 by the diet of the Empire. The enlarged German states now depended on Bonaparte for the maintenance of their new position.

The "shame of the princes"

Formation of the Third Coalition in 1805

Britain and France went to war again in 1803. Bonaparte, his communications with America menaced by the British navy, and his army in Haiti decimated by disease and by the military campaigns of the Haitian independence movement, suspended his ideas for recreating an American empire and sold Louisiana to the United States. Great Britain began to seek allies for a Third Coalition. In May 1804 Napoleon pronounced himself Emperor of the French to ensure the hereditary permanency of his system, though at the time he had no heir. Francis II of Austria, seeing the Holy Roman Empire in ruins, promulgated the Austrian Empire in August 1804. He thus advanced the long process of integrating the Danubian monarchy. In 1805 Austria signed an alliance with Great Britain. The Third Coalition was completed by the accession of the Russian Tsar Alexander I, who, after Napoleon himself, was to become the most considerable figure on the European stage.

Tsar Alexander I

Alexander was the grandson of Catherine the Great, educated by her to be a kind of enlightened despot on the eighteenth-century model. The Swiss tutor of his boyhood, La Harpe, later turned up as a pro-French revolutionary in the Helvetic Republic of 1798. Alexander became tsar in 1801, at the age of 24, through a palace revolution which implicated him in the murder of his father Paul. He still corresponded with La Harpe, and he surrounded himself with a circle of liberal and zealous young men of various nationalities, of whom the most prominent was a Polish youth, Czartoryski. Alexander regarded the still recent partitions of Poland as a crime. He wished to restore the unity of Poland with himself as a constitutional king. In Germany many who had first warmed to the French Revolution, but had been disillusioned, began to hail the new liberal tsar as the protector of Germany and hope of the future. Alexander conceived of himself as a rival to Napoleon in

Toussaint L'Ouverture, pictured here with a sword and documents to symbolize his independence, led the political and military movement that created a new Republic of Haiti. Although Toussaint himself was captured and sent to a prison in France (where he died in 1803), the French defeat in Haiti made Napoleon abandon his plans for an American empire and sell Louisiana to the United States.
(Library of Congress)

guiding the destinies of Europe in an age of change. Moralistic and self-righteous, he puzzled and disturbed the statesmen of Europe, who generally saw, behind his humane and republican utterances, either an enthroned leader of all the "Jacobins" of Europe or the familiar specter of Russian aggrandizement.

Yet Alexander, more than his contemporaries, formed a conception of international collective security and the indivisibility of peace. He was shocked when Napoleon in 1804, in order to seize the duke of Enghien, rudely violated the sovereignty of Baden. He declared that the issue in Europe was clearly between law and force—between an international society in which the rights of each member were secured by international agreement and organization and a society in which all trembled before the rule of cynicism and conquest embodied in the French usurper.

Alexander was therefore ready to enter a Third Coalition with Great Britain. Picturing himself as a future arbiter of central Europe, and with secret designs on the Ottoman Empire and the Mediterranean, he signed a treaty with England in April 1805. The British agreed to pay Russia £1,250,000 for each 100,000 soldiers that the Russians raised.

The Third Coalition, 1805–1807: *The Peace of Tilsit*

Napoleon meanwhile, since the resumption of hostilities in 1803, had been making preparations to invade England. He concentrated large forces on the Channel coast, together with thousands of boats and barges in which he gave the troops amphibious training in embarkation and debarkation. He reasoned that if his own fleet could divert or cripple the British fleet for a few days he could place enough soldiers on the defenseless island to force its capitulation. The British, sensing mortal danger, lined their coasts with lookouts and signal beacons and set to drilling a home guard. Their main defense was twofold: the Austro-Russian armies and the British fleet under Lord Nelson. The Russian and Austrian armies moved westward in the summer of 1805. In August Napoleon relieved the pressure upon England, shifting seven army corps from the Channel to the upper Danube. On October 15 he surrounded an Austrian force of 50,000 men at Ulm in Bavaria, forcing it to surrender without resistance. On October 21 Lord Nelson, off Cape Trafalgar on the Spanish coast, caught and annihilated the main body of the combined fleets of France and Spain.

The battle of Trafalgar established the supremacy of the British navy for over a century—but only on the proviso that Napoleon be prevented from controlling the bulk of Europe, which would furnish an ample base for eventual construction of a greater navy than the British. And to control Europe was precisely what Napoleon proceeded to do. Moving east from Ulm he came upon the Russian and Austrian armies in Moravia, where on December 2 he won the great victory of Austerlitz. The broken Russian army withdrew into Poland, and Austria made peace. By the treaty of Pressburg Napoleon took Venetia from the Austrians, to whom he had given it in 1797, and annexed it to his kingdom of Italy (the former Cisalpine and Italian Republic), which now included a good deal of Italy north of Rome. Venice and Trieste soon resounded with the hammers of shipwrights rebuilding the Napoleonic fleet. In Germany, early in 1806, the French emperor raised Bavaria and Württemberg to the stature of kingdoms and Baden to a grand duchy. The Holy Roman Empire was finally, formally, and irrevocably dissolved. In its place Napoleon began to gather his German client states into a new kind of Germanic federation, the Confederation of the Rhine, of which he made himself the "protector."

British victory at Trafalgar

Prussia, at peace with France for ten years, had declined to join the Third Coalition. But as Napoleon's program for controlling Germany became clear after Austerlitz, the war party in Prussia became irresistible, and the Prussian government, outwitted and distraught, went to war with the French unaided and alone. The French smashed the famous Prussian army at the battles of Jena and Auerstädt in October 1806. The French cavalry galloped all over north Germany unopposed. The Prussian king and his government took refuge in the east, at Königsberg, where the tsar and the re-forming Russian army might protect them. But the terrible Corsican pursued the Russians also. Marching through western Poland and into East Prussia, he met the Russian army first at the sanguinary but indecisive battle of Eylau and then defeated it on June 14, 1807, at Friedland. Alexander I was unwilling to retreat into Russia. He was unsure of his own resources; if the country were invaded, there might be a revolt of the nobles or even of the serfs—for people still remembered the great serf rebellion of the 1770s. Alexander feared also merely playing the game of the British. He put aside his war aims of 1804 and signified his willingness to negotiate with Napoleon. The Third Coalition had gone the way of the two before it.

The Third Coalition collapses

The Emperor of the French and the Autocrat of All the Russias met privately on a raft in the Niemen River, not far from the border between Prussia and Russia, the very easternmost frontier of civilized Europe, as the triumphant Napoleon gleefully imagined it. The hapless Prussian king, Frederick William III, paced nervously on the bank. Bonaparte turned all his charm upon Alexander, denouncing England as the author of all the troubles of Europe and captivating him by flights of Latin imagination, in which he set before Alexander a boundless destiny as Emperor of the East, intimating that Russia's future lay toward Turkey, Persia, Afghanistan, and India. The result of their conversations was the treaty of Tilsit of July 1807, in many ways the high point of Napoleon's success. The French and Russian empires became allies, mainly against Great Britain. Ostensibly this alliance lasted for five years. Alexander accepted Napoleon as a kind of Emperor of the West. As for Prussia, Napoleon continued to occupy Berlin with his troops, and he took away all Prussian territories west of the Elbe, combining them with others taken from Hanover to make a new kingdom of Westphalia, which became part of his Confederation of the Rhine.

The Treaty of Tilsit

The Continental System and the War in Spain

Hardly had the "peace of the continent" been reestablished on the foundation of a Franco-Russian alliance when Napoleon began to have serious trouble. He was bent on subduing the British who, secure on their island, seemed beyond his reach. Since the French naval disaster at Trafalgar, there was no possibility of invading England in the foreseeable future. Napoleon therefore turned to economic warfare. He would fight sea power with land power, using his political control of the Continent to shut out British goods and shipping from all European ports. He would destroy the British trade in exports to Europe, both exports of British products and the profitable British reexport of goods from America and Asia. Thereby, he hoped, he would ruin British commercial firms and cause a violent business depression, marked by overloaded warehouses, unemployment, runs on the banks, a fall of the currency, rising prices, and revolutionary agitation. The British government, which would simultaneously be losing revenues from its customs duties, would thus find itself unable to carry the enormous national debt, or to borrow additional funds from its subjects, or to continue its financial subsidies to the military powers of Europe. At Berlin, in 1806, after the battle of Jena, Napoleon issued the Berlin Decree, forbidding the importation of British goods into any part of Europe allied with or dependent on himself. He in that way formally established the Continental System.

Economic warfare

To make the Continental System effective Napoleon believed that it must extend to all continental Europe without exception. By the treaty of Tilsit, in 1807, he required both Russia and Prussia to adhere to it. They agreed to exclude all British goods; in fact, in the following months Russia, Prussia, and Austria all declared war on Great Britain. Napoleon then ordered two neutral states, Denmark and Portugal, to adhere. Denmark was an important entrepôt for all central Europe, and the British, fearing Danish compliance, dispatched a fleet to Copenhagen, bombarded the city for four days, and took captive the Danish fleet. The outraged Danes allied with Napoleon and joined the Continental System. Portugal, long a satellite of Britain, refused compliance; Napoleon invaded it. To control the whole European coastline from St. Petersburg around to Trieste he now had only to control the ports of Spain. By a series of deceptions he got both the Bourbon Charles IV and his son Ferdinand to abdicate the Spanish throne. He made his brother Joseph king of Spain in 1808 and reinforced him with a large French army.

He thus involved himself in an entanglement from which he never escaped. The Spanish regarded the Napoleonic soldiers as godless villians who desecrated churches. Fierce guerrillas took the field. Cruelties of one side were answered by atrocities of the

This meeting between Napoleon and Russia's Alexander I on the Niemen River produced an alliance and the Continental System. The new system was aimed against the British, but Alexander soon disliked the restrictions on Anglo-Russian commerce. His withdrawal from the Continental System provoked Napoleon's disastrous invasion of Russia in 1812.
(Rare Book Collection, University of North Carolina–Chapel Hill (Hoyt IC-187))

other. The British sent an expeditionary force of their small regular army, eventually under the Duke of Wellington, to sustain the Spanish guerrillas; the resulting Peninsular War dragged on for five years. But from the beginning the affair went badly for Napoleon. In July 1808 a French general, for the first time since the Revolution, surrendered an army corps, without fighting, by the capitulation at Baylen. In August another French force surrendered to the British army in Portugal. And these events raised hopes in the rest of Europe. An anti-French movement swept over Germany. It was felt strongly in Austria, where the Habsburg government, undaunted by three defeats and hoping to lead a general German national resistance, prepared for a fourth time since 1792 to go to war with France.

The Peninsular War in Spain

The Austrian War of Liberation, 1809

Napoleon summoned a general congress which met at Erfurt in Saxony in September 1808. His main purpose was to talk with his ally of a year, Alexander; but he assembled numerous dependent monarchs as well, by whose presence he hoped to overawe the tsar. He even had Talma, the leading actor of the day, play in the theater of Erfurt before "a parterre of kings." Alexander was unimpressed. He was hurt in a sensitive spot because Napoleon, a few months before, had made moves to re-create a Polish state, setting up what was called the Grand Duchy of Warsaw. He had found Napoleon unwilling, despite the grandiose language of Tilsit, really to support his expansion into the Balkans. In addition, Alexander was taken aside by Talleyrand, Napoleon's foreign minister. Talleyrand had concluded that Napoleon was overreaching himself and said so confidentially to the tsar, advising him to wait. Talleyrand thus betrayed the man whom he ostensibly served and prepared a safe place for himself in the event of Napoleon's fall; but he acted also as an aristocrat of the prenationalistic Old Regime, seeing his own country as only one part of the whole of Europe, believing a balance among the several parts to be necessary and holding that peace would be possible only when the exaggerated reach of French power would be reduced. For France and Russia, the two strongest states, to combine against all other states was contrary to all principles of the older diplomacy.

Talleyrand

Austria proclaimed a war of liberation in April 1809. Napoleon advanced rapidly along the familiar route to Vienna. The German princes, indebted to the French, declined to join in a general German war against him. Alexander stood watchfully on the sidelines. Napoleon won the battle of Wagram in July. In October Austria made peace. The short war of 1809 was over. The Danubian monarchy, by no means as fragile as it seemed, survived a fourth defeat at the hands of the French without internal revolution or disloyalty to the Habsburg house. From it, in punishment, Napoleon took considerable portions of its territory. Part of Austrian Poland was used to enlarge Napoleon's Grand Duchy of Warsaw, and parts of Dalmatia, Slovenia, and Croatia, on the south, were erected into a new creation which Napoleon called the Illyrian Provinces (see map, p. 407).

Napoleon at His Peak, 1809–1811

The next two years saw the Napoleonic empire at its peak. In Austria after the defeat of 1809 the conduct of foreign affairs fell to Clemens von Metternich, who was to remain the Austrian foreign minister for 40 years. He was a German from west of the Rhine, whose ancestral territories had been annexed to the French Republic, but he had entered the Austrian service and even married the granddaughter of Kaunitz, the old model of diplomatic savoir-faire, of which Metternich now became a model himself. Austria had been repeatedly humiliated and even partitioned by Napoleon, most of all in the treaty of 1809. But Metternich was not a man to conduct diplomacy by grudges. Believing that Russia was the really permanent problem for a state situated in the Danube valley, Metternich thought it wise to renew good relations with France. He was quite willing to go along with Napoleon, whom he knew personally, having been Austrian ambassador to Paris before the short war of 1809.

Metternich

The French emperor, who in 1809 was exactly 40, was increasingly concerned by the fact that he was childless. He had made an empire which he pronounced hereditary. Yet he had no heir. Between him and his wife Josephine whom he had married in youth, and who

THE THIRD OF MAY 1808
by Francisco de Goya (Spanish, 1746–1808)
Facing steadfast resistance to their military occupation of Spain, the French army committed atrocities such as the brutal scene that Goya portrayed in this image of the Peninsular War.
(Erich Lessing/Art Resource, NY)

was six years his senior, there had long since ceased to be affection or even fidelity on either side. He divorced her in 1809, though since she had two children by a first husband she naturally protested that Napoleon's childlessness was not her fault. He intended to marry a younger woman who might bear him offspring. He intended also to make a spectacular marriage, to extort for himself, a self-made Corsican army officer, the highest and most exclusive recognition that aristocratic Europe could bestow. He debated between Habsburgs and Romanovs, between an archduchess and a grand duchess. Tactful inquiries at St. Petersburg concerning the availability of Alexander's sister were tactfully rebuffed; the tsar intimated that his mother would never allow it. The Russian alliance again showed its limitations. Napoleon was thrown into the arms of Metternich—and of Marie Louise, the 18-year-old daughter of the Austrian emperor and niece of another "Austrian woman," Marie Antoinette. They were married in 1810. In a year she bore him a son, whom he entitled the King of Rome.

Napoleon assumed ever more pompous airs of imperial majesty. He was now, by marriage, the nephew of Louis XVI. He showed more consideration to French noblemen of the Old Regime—only they, he said, knew really how to serve. He surrounded himself with a newly made hereditary Napoleonic nobility, hoping that the new families, as time went on, would bind their own fortunes to the house of Bonaparte. The marshals became dukes and princes; Talleyrand became the Prince of Benevento; and the bourgeois Fouché, an Hébertist radical in 1793 and more latterly a police official, was now solemnly addressed as the Duke of Otranto. In foreign affairs also the cycle had been run. With one significant exception, all the powers of the successive coalitions were allied with the French, and the Son of the Revolution now gravely referred to the emperor of Austria as "my father."

48.   THE GRAND EMPIRE: SPREAD OF THE REVOLUTION

The Organization of the Napoleonic Empire

The empire at its height

Territorially Napoleon's influence enjoyed its farthest reach in 1810 and 1811, when it included the entire European mainland except the Balkan peninsula. The Napoleonic domain was in two parts. Its core was the French empire; then came thick layers of dependent states, which together with France comprised the Grand Empire. In addition, to the north and east were the "allied states" under their traditional governments—the three great powers, Prussia, Austria, and Russia, and also Denmark and Sweden. The allied states were at war with Great Britain, though not engaged in positive hostilities; their populations were supposed to do without British goods under the Continental System, but otherwise Napoleon had no direct lawful influence upon their internal affairs.

The French empire, as successor to the French Republic, included Belgium and the Left Bank of the Rhine. In addition, by 1810, it had developed two appendages which on a map looked like tentacles outstretched from it (see the map on p. 407). When he proclaimed France an empire and turned its dependent republics into kingdoms, Napoleon had set up his brother Louis as king of Holland; but Louis had shown such a tendency to ingratiate himself with the Dutch, and such a willingness to let Dutch businessmen trade secretly with the British, that Napoleon dethroned him and incorporated Holland into the French empire. In his endless war upon British goods he found it useful to exert more direct control over the ports of Bremen, Hamburg, Lübeck, Genoa, and Leghorn; he therefore annexed directly to the French empire the German coast as far as the western Baltic, and the Italian coast far enough to include Rome, which he desired for its imperial rather that its commercial value. Harking back to traditions as old as Charlemagne, he considered Rome the second city of his empire and entitled his son the "King of Rome." When Pope Pius VII protested, Napoleon took him prisoner and interned him in France. The whole French empire, from Lübeck to Rome, was governed directly by departmental prefects who reported to Paris, and the 83 departments of France, created by the Constituent Assembly, had risen in 1810 to 130.

The dependent states, forming with France the Grand Empire, were of different kinds. The Swiss federation remained republican in form. The Illyrian Provinces, which included Trieste and the Dalmatian coast, were administered in their brief two years almost like departments of France. In Poland, since the Russians objected to a revived kingdom of Poland, Napoleon called his creation the Grand Duchy of Warsaw. Among the most important of the dependent states in the Grand Empire were the German states organized into the

Confederation of the Rhine. Too modestly named, the Confederation included all Germany between what the French annexed on the west and what Prussia and Austria retained on the east. It was a league of all the German princes in this region who were regarded as sovereign and who now numbered only about 20, the most important being the four newly made kings of Saxony, Bavaria, Württemberg, and Westphalia. Westphalia was an entirely new and synthetic state, made up of Hanoverian and Prussian territories and of various small parts of the old Germany. Its king was Napoleon's youngest brother, Jerome.

Napoleon liked to use his family as a means of rule. The Corsican clan became the Bonaparte dynasty. His brother Joseph from 1804 to 1808 functioned as king of Naples and after 1808 as king of Spain. Louis Bonaparte was for six years king of Holland; Jerome was king of Westphalia. Sister Caroline became queen of Naples after brother Joseph's transfer to Spain; for Napoleon, running out of brothers (having quarreled with his remaining brother, Lucien), gave the throne of Naples to his brother-in-law, Joachim Murat, a cavalry officer who was Caroline's husband. In the "Kingdom of Italy," which in 1810 included Lombardy, Venetia, and most of the former papal states, Napoleon himself retained the title of king, but set up his stepson, Eugène Beauharnais (Josephine's son) as viceroy. The mother of the Bonapartes, Letitia, who had brought up all these children under very different circumstances in Corsica, was suitably installed at the imperial court as Madame Mère. According to legend she kept repeating to herself, "If only it lasts!"; she outlived Napoleon by 15 years.

Napoleon and the Spread of the Revolution

In all the states of the Grand Empire the same course of events tended to repeat itself. First came the stage of military conquest and occupation by French troops. Then came the establishment of a native satellite government with the support of local persons who were willing to collaborate with the French and who helped in the drafting of a constitution specifying the powers of the new government and regularizing its relationships with France. In some areas these two stages had been accomplished under the republican governments before Napoleon came to power. In some regions no more than these two stages really occurred, notably in Spain and the Grand Duchy of Warsaw.

Stages of French occupation

The third stage of French influence was one of sweeping internal reform and reorganization, modeled on Bonaparte's program for France and hence derivatively on the French Revolution. Belgium and the German territories west of the Rhine underwent this stage most thoroughly, since they were annexed directly to France for 20 years. Italy and the main bulk of Germany west of Prussia and Austria also experienced the third stage.

Napoleon considered himself a great reformer and man of the Enlightenment. He called his system "liberal," and though the word to him meant almost the reverse of what it meant later to liberals, he was possibly the first to use it in a political sense. He believed also in "constitutions"; not that he favored representative assemblies or limited government, but he wanted government to be rationally "constituted," that is, deliberately mapped out and planned, not merely inherited from the jumble of the past. Man on horseback though he was, he believed firmly in the rule of law. He insisted with the zeal of conviction on transplanting his Civil Code to the dependent states. He assumed that this code was based on the very nature of justice and human relationships, and he believed that it must therefore be applicable to all countries with no more than minor adaptation. The idea that a country's laws must mirror its peculiar

Napoleon as reformer

national character and history was foreign to his mind, for he carried over the rationalist and universalist outlook of the Age of Enlightenment. He thought that people everywhere wanted, and deserved, much the same thing. As he wrote to his brother Jerome, on making him king of Westphalia, "the peoples of Germany, as of France, Italy and Spain, want equality and liberal ideas. For some years now I have been managing the affairs of Europe, and I am convinced that the crowing of the privileged classes was everywhere disliked. Be a constitutional king."

The same plan of reform was initiated, with some variation, in all the dependent states from Spain to Poland and from the mouth of the Elbe to the Straits of Messina. The reforms were directed, in a word, against everything feudal. They established the legal equality of individual persons and gave governments more complete authority over their individual subjects. Legal classes were wiped out, as in France in 1789; the theory of a society made up of "estates of the realm" gave way to the theory of a society made up of legally equal individuals. The nobility lost its privileges in taxation, officeholding, and military command. Careers were "opened to talent."

The manorial system, bulwark of the old aristocracy, was virtually liquidated. Lords lost all legal jurisdiction over their peasants; peasants became subjects of the state, personally free to move, migrate, or marry, and able to bring suit in the courts of law. The manorial fees, along with tithes, were generally abolished, as in France in 1789. In France the peasants escaped from these burdens without having to pay compensation, in part because they had themselves risen in rebellion in 1789 and in part because France passed through a radical popular revolution in 1793. In other parts of the Grand Empire, however, the peasants were committed to payment of indemnities, and the former feudal class continued to receive income from its abolished rights. Only in Belgium and the Rhineland, incorporated into France under the republic, did the manorial regime disappear without compensation as in France, leaving a numerous entrenched class of small landowning farmers. East of the Rhine Napoleon had to compromise with the aristocracy that he assailed. In Poland, the only country in the Grand Empire where a thoroughgoing serfdom had prevailed, the peasants received legal freedom during the French occupation; but the Polish landlords remained economically unharmed, since they owned all the land. Napoleon had to conciliate them, for there was no other effective class in Poland to which he could look for support. In general, outside of France, the assault upon feudal traditions was not socially as revolutionary as it had been in France. The lord was gone, but the landlord remained.

Everywhere in the Grand Empire the church lost its position as a public authority alongside the state. Church courts were abolished or restricted; the Inquisition was outlawed in Spain. Tithes were done away with, church property was confiscated, and monastic orders were dissolved or severely regulated. Toleration became the law; Catholics, Protestants, Jews, and unbelievers received the same civil rights. The state was to be based not on the idea of religious community but on the idea of territorial residence. With the nobility, or on

NAPOLEONIC EUROPE, 1810

Napoleon extended the sphere of French power well beyond the earlier expansion of the French Republic. By 1810 he dominated the whole continent except Portugal and the Balkan peninsula. Russia, Prussia, and Austria had been forced into alliance with him, and he had made his brothers kings of Spain, Holland, and Westphalia; his brother-in-law king of Naples; and his stepson viceroy of Italy. The old Holy Roman Empire disappeared into other states, including Napoleon's Confederation of the Rhine. In Poland, Napoleon undid the partitions of the 1770s by setting up the Grand Duchy of Warsaw.

Baltic Sea

0 100 200 miles

Moscow
Riga
Vitebsk
Borodino
Vilna
Smolensk
Tilsit
Kovno
Borisov
Königsberg

RUSSIAN EMPIRE

Warsaw
Brest-Litovsk

**Napoleon's Russian Campaign
June to December, 1812**

NORWAY

SWEDEN

FINLAND

St. Petersburg

SCOTLAND

ESTONIA

LIVONIA

IRELAND

North Sea

Baltic Sea

COURLAND

KINGDOM OF DENMARK AND NORWAY

Copenhagen

Memel

Tilsit
Nieman R.
Vilna

Königsberg
Friedland
Eylau

GREAT BRITAIN

Edinburgh

DENMARK

SWEDISH POMERANIA

Danzig

ENGLAND

HELIGOLAND (Britain)

Lübeck
Hamburg

MECKLEN-BURG

PRUSSIA

Vistula R.

Posen
Warsaw

Brest-Litovsk

London
Amsterdam

KINGDOM OF HOLLAND

Bremen

Berlin

Oder R.

Plymouth
Dover
Antwerp

Rhine R.

BERG

K. OF WESTPHALIA

K. OF SAXONY

Breslau

GRAND DUCHY OF WARSAW

English Channel

CHANNEL I. (Britain)

Cherbourg
Brussels
Cologne
Auerstaadt

Leipzig
Dresden

Cracow

GALICIA

Tarnapol

ATLANTIC OCEAN

Amiens

Seine R.

Erfurt
Jena

Mainz

CONFEDERATION OF THE RHINE

Prague

BOHEMIA

Austerlitz

Versailles
Paris
Valmy

Metz

Austerlitz

Nantes

Loire R.

Orléans

Strasbourg

BADEN

WÜRTTEMBERG
Ulm

Danube R.

Wagram

Fontainebleau

Munich
Hohenlinden

Vienna

AUSTRIA

FRENCH EMPIRE

Basel

K. OF BAVARIA

Budapest

CAPE FINISTERRE

La Coruña

Bordeaux

Lyons

SWITZERLAND

AUSTRIA

HUNGARY

SAVOY

LOMBARDY
Milan

VENETIA
Trieste

ILLYRIAN PROVINCES

SLOVENIA

Drave R.

Oporto

Burgos

Ebro R.

Rhone R.

PIEDMONT

Po R.

KINGDOM OF ITALY

Genoa

Save R.

Belgrade

WALLACHIA

Danube R.

Douro R.

Toulouse
Avignon

CROATIA

Almeida
Ciudad Rodrigo

Saragossa

Marseille
Nice
Toulon

LUCCA
Leghorn

Florence

BOSNIA

SERBIA

OTTOMAN EMPIRE

PORTUGAL

Tagus R.

Talavera

SPAIN
Madrid

Ocaña

Barcelona

CORSICA

Elba

MONTENEGRO

Lisbon
Elvas

Guadiana R.

Valencia

Rome

Bari

Salonica

Albuera

BALEARIC IS. (Spain)

MINORCA

KINGDOM OF SARDINIA

Naples

KINGDOM OF NAPLES

Taranto

CORFU

ALBANIA

Seville
Baylen

ANDALUSIA

IVIZA

MAJORCA

Cagliari

CORFU

IONIAN I. (Britain)

MOREA

Cadiz

TRAFALGAR

Gibraltar (Britain)

Palermo

Tangier

Algiers

KINGDOM OF SICILY

CERIGO

MOROCCO

Tunis

ALGERIA (Turkish)

TUNISIA (Turkish)

MALTA (Britain)

Mediterranean Sea

	French Empire
	Grand Empire
	Allied with Napoleon

0 100 200 300 miles

economic matters, Napoleon would compromise; but he would not compromise with the Catholic clergy on the principle of a secular state. Even in Spain he insisted on these fundamentals of his system, a sure indication that he was not motivated by expediency only, since it was largely his antireligious program that provoked the Spanish populace to rebellion.

Guilds were generally abolished or reduced to empty forms, and the individual's right to work was generally proclaimed. Peasants, gaining legal freedom, might learn and enter any trade they chose. The old town oligarchies and bourgeois patriciates were broken up. Towns and provinces lost their antique liberties and came under general legislation. Internal tariffs were removed, and free trade within state frontiers was encouraged. Some countries shifted to a decimal system of money; and the heterogeneous weights and measures which had originated in the Middle Ages, and of which the Anglo-American bushels, yards, ounces, and pints are living survivals, yielded to the Cartesian regularities of the metric system. Ancient and diverse legal systems gave way to the Napoleonic codes. Law courts were separated from the administration. Hereditary office and the sale of office were done away with. Officials received salaries large enough to shield them from the temptations of corruption. Kings were put on civil lists, with their personal expenses separated from those of the government. Taxes and finances were modernized. The common tax became a land tax, paid by every landowner; and governments knew how much land each owner really possessed, for they developed systematic methods of appraisal and assessment. Tax farming was replaced by direct collection. New methods of accounting and of collecting statistics were introduced.

In general, in all countries of the Grand Empire, some of the main principles of the French Revolution were introduced under Napoleon, with the notable exception that there was no self-government through elected legislative bodies. In all countries Napoleon found numerous natives willing to support him, mainly among *Support for Napoleon* people in the commercial and professional classes, who were generally aware of Enlightenment writers, often anticlerical, desirous of more equality with the nobility, and eager to break down the old localisms that interfered with trade and the exchange of ideas. He found supporters also among many progressive nobles and, in the Confederation of the Rhine, among the German rulers. His program appealed to some people everywhere and in all parts of the Grand Empire was executed mainly by local leaders. Repression went with it, though hardly on the same scale as the repressions of later dictatorships. There were no vast internment camps, and Fouché's police were engaged more in spying and submitting reports than in the brutalizing of the disaffected. The execution of a single Bavarian bookseller, named Palm, became a famous outrage.

In short, there was at first a good deal of pro-Napoleonic feeling in the Grand Empire. The French influence (outside Belgium and the Rhineland) struck deepest in north Italy, where there were no native monarchist traditions and where the old Italian city-states had produced a strong and often anticlerical burgher class. In south Germany also the French influence was profound. The French system had the least appeal in Spain, where Catholic royalist sentiment produced a kind of counterrevolutionary movement of independence. Nor did it appeal to agrarian eastern Europe, the land of lord and serf. Yet even in Prussia, as will be seen, the state was remodeled along French lines. In Russia, during the Tilsit alliance, Alexander gave his backing to a pro-French reforming minister, Speranski. The Napoleonic influence was pervasive because it carried over the older movement of enlightened despotism and seemed to confer the advantages of the French Revolution without the violence and the disorder. Napoleon, it seemed to Goethe, "was the expression of all that was reasonable, legitimate and European in the revolutionary movement."

But the Napoleonic reforms were also weapons of war. All the dependent states were required by Napoleon to supply him with money and soldiers. Germans, Dutch, Belgians,

NAPOLEONIC GERMANY

In the panel at the left are shown, by shading, territories of the Duchy of Württemberg in 1800. Note how Württemberg had "islands" of territory unconnected with its main mass, and "holes" or enclaves formed by smaller states enclosed within the mass of Württemberg. Note, too, how Württemberg, itself only 50 miles wide, was surrounded by a mosaic of tiny jurisdictions—free cities, counties, duchies, principalities, abbacies, commanderies, bishoprics, archbishoprics, etc.—all "independent" within the Holy Roman Empire. The right-hand panel shows the Kingdom of Württemberg as consolidated and enlarged in the time of Napoleon. Similar consolidations all over Germany greatly reduced the number of states and added to the efficiency of law and government.

Italians, Poles, and even Spaniards fought in his armies. In addition, the dependent states defrayed much of the cost of the French army, most of which was stationed outside France. This meant that taxes in France could remain low, to the general satisfaction of the propertied interests that had issued from the Revolution.

49.   THE CONTINENTAL SYSTEM: BRITAIN AND EUROPE

Beyond the tributary states of the Grand Empire lay the countries nominally independent, joined under Napoleon in the Continental System. Napoleon thought of his allies as at best subordinate partners in a common project. The great project was to crush Great Britain, and it was for this purpose that the Continental System had been established. But the crushing of Britain became in Napoleon's mind a means to a further end, the unification and mastery of all of Europe. This in turn, had he achieved it, would doubtless have merely opened the way to further conquests.

Germaine de Staël was an influential leader of the liberal opposition to Napoleon's repressive cultural policies. She was forced to live in exile in Switzerland, but both her Swiss home and her writings provided crucial support for Napoleon's critics.
(Ken Welsh/Bridgeman Art Library)

Continental unity

At the point where he stood in 1807 or 1810 the unification of continental Europe seemed a not impossible objective. He cast about for an ideology to inspire both his Grand Empire and his allies. He held out the cosmopolitan doctrines of the eighteenth century, spoke endlessly of the enlightenment of the age, and urged all peoples to work with him against the medievalism, ignorance, and obscurantism by which they were surrounded. Although he disliked and even suppressed the creative work of writers such as his vehement critic Germaine de Staël, Napoleon encouraged innovative scientific research and rewarded the scientists who pursued it. He viewed science as the essential, rational foundation of modern knowledge. And while appealing to ideas of modernity or progress he dwelt also on the grandeur of Roman times. The Roman inspiration appeared in the arts of the day and in the architecture that expressed Napoleon's conception of imperial glory. The massive "empire" furniture, the heroic canvases of David, the church of the Madeleine in Paris (resembling a classical temple and converted to a Temple of Glory); and the Arch of Triumph in the same city (begun in 1806) all evoked the atmosphere of far-spreading majesty in which Napoleon would have liked the peoples of Europe to live. In addition, to arouse an all-European feeling, Napoleon worked upon the latent hostility to Great Britain. The British, in winning out in the eighteenth-century struggle for wealth and empire, had made themselves disliked in many quarters. There was the natural jealousy felt toward the successful, and resentment against the high-handedness by which success had been won and maintained. Such feelings were present among almost all Europeans. It was believed that the British were really using their sea power to win a larger permanent share of the world's seaborne commerce for themselves. Nor, in truth, was this belief mistaken.

British Blockade and Napoleon's Continental System

The British, in the Revolutionary and Napoleonic wars, when they declared France and its allies in a state of blockade, did not expect either to starve them or to deprive them of necessary materials of war. Western Europe was still self-sufficient in food, and armaments were to a large extent produced locally from simple materials like iron, copper, and saltpeter. Europe required almost nothing indispensable from overseas. The chief aim of the British blockade was not, therefore, to keep imports out of enemy countries; it was to keep the trade in such imports out of enemy hands. It was to kill off enemy commerce and shipping, in the short run to weaken the war-making powers of the enemy government by undermining its revenues and its navy and in the long run to weaken the enemy's position in the markets of the world. Economic warfare was trade warfare. The British were willing enough to have British goods pass through to the enemy either by smuggling or by the mediation of neutrals.

As early as 1793 the French republicans had denounced England as the "modern Carthage," a ruthless mercantile and profit-seeking power which aspired to enslave Europe to its financial and commercial system. With the wars, the British in fact obtained a monopoly over the shipment of overseas commodities into Europe. At the same time, being relatively advanced in the new techniques of industrial production, they could produce cotton cloth and certain other articles, by power machinery, more cheaply than other peoples of Europe and so threatened to monopolize the European market for such manufactured goods. There was much feeling in Europe against the modern Carthage, especially among the bourgeois and commercial classes who were in competition with it. The upper classes were perhaps less hostile, not caring where the goods that they consumed had originated, but aristocracies and governments were susceptible to the argument that Britain was a money power, a "nation of shopkeepers" as Napoleon put it, which fought its wars with pounds sterling instead of blood and was always in search of dupes in Europe.

Anti-British sentiments

It was on all these feelings that Napoleon played, reiterating time and again that England was the real enemy of all Europe, and that Europe would never be prosperous or independent until relieved of the incubus of British "monopoly." To prevent the flow of goods into Britain was no more the purpose of the Continental System than to prevent the flow of goods into France was the purpose of the British blockade. The purpose of each was to destroy the enemy's commerce, credit, and public revenues by the destruction of its exports—and also to build up markets for oneself.

To destroy British exports Napoleon prohibited, by the Berlin Decree of 1806, the importation of British goods into the continent of Europe. Counted as British, if of British or British colonial origin, were goods brought to Europe in neutral ships as the property of neutrals. The British, in response, ruled by an "order in council" of November 1807 that neutrals might enter Napoleonic ports only if they first stopped in Great Britain, where the regulations were such as to encourage their loading with British goods. The British thus tried to move their exports into enemy territory through neutral channels, which was precisely what Napoleon intended to prevent. He announced, by the Milan Decree of December 1807, that any neutral vessel that had stopped at a British port, or submitted to search by a British warship at sea, would be confiscated upon its appearance in a Continental harbor.

Trade warfare

With all Europe at war, virtually the only major trading neutral nation was the United States, which could now trade with neither England nor Europe except by violating the regulations of one belligerent or the other. It would thus become liable to reprisals, and hence to involvement in war. President Jefferson, to avoid war, attempted a self-imposed policy of commercial isolation which proved so ruinous to American foreign trade that the United States government took steps to renew trade relations with whichever belligerent first removed its controls over neutral commerce. Napoleon offered to do so, on condition that the United States would defend itself against the enforcement of British controls. At the same time an expansionist party among the Americans, ambitious to annex Canada, considered that with the British army engaged in Spain the time was ripe to complete the

The War of 1812

War of Independence by driving Britain from the North American mainland. The result was the Anglo-American War of 1812, which had few results, except to demonstrate the distressing inefficiency of military institutions in the new republic.

But the Continental System was more than a device for destroying the export trade of Great Britain. It was also a scheme for developing the economy of continental Europe, around France as its main center. The Continental System, if successful, would replace the national economies with an integrated economy for the Continent as a whole. It would create the framework for a European civilization. And it would ruin the British sea power and commercial monopoly; for a unified Europe, Napoleon thought, would itself soon take to the sea.

The Failure of the Continental System

But the Continental System failed; it was worse than a failure, for it caused widespread antagonism to the Napoleonic regime. The dream of a united Europe, under French rule, was not sufficiently attractive to inspire the necessary sacrifice—even a sacrifice more of comforts than of necessities. As Napoleon impatiently said, one would suppose that the destinies of Europe turned upon a barrel of sugar. It was true, as he and his propagandists insisted, that Britain monopolized the sale of sugar, tobacco, and other overseas goods, but people preferred to deal clandestinely with the British rather than go without them. The charms of America destroyed the Continental System.

British manufactures were somewhat easier than colonial goods to replace. Raw cotton was brought by land from the Middle East through the Balkans, and the cotton manufacturers of France, Saxony, Switzerland, and north Italy were stimulated by the relief from British competition. There was a great expansion of Danish woolens and German hardware. The cultivation of sugar beets, to replace cane sugar, spread in France, central Europe, Holland, and even Russia. Thus infant industries and investments were built up which, after Napoleon's fall, clamored for tariff protection. In general, the European industrial interests were well disposed toward the Continental System.

Consequences of the Continental System

Yet they could never adequately replace the British in supplying the market. One obstacle was transportation. Much trading between parts of the Continent had always been by sea; this coastal traffic was now blocked by the British. Land routes were increasingly used, even in the faraway Balkans and Illyrian Provinces, through which raw cotton was brought; and improved roads were built through the Simplon and Mont Cenis passes in the Alps. No less than 17,000 wheeled vehicles crossed the Mont Cenis pass in 1810. But land transport, at best, was no substitute for the sea. Without railroads, introduced some 30 years later, a purely Continental modern economy was impossible to maintain.

Construction on the Arch of Triumph began in 1806, but it was not completed until 1836. It became a monument of French nationalism, symbolizing both the Republic and the Empire. The continuous band of bas reliefs above the curve of the arch represented 172 battles since Valmy in 1792.
(Culver Pictures)

Another obstacle was tariffs. The idea of a Continental tariff union was put forward by some of his subordinates, but Napoleon never adopted it. The dependent states remained insistent on their ostensible sovereignty. Each had widened its trading area by demolishing former internal tariffs, but each kept a tariff against the others. The kingdoms of Italy and Naples enjoyed no free trade with each other nor did the German states of the Confederation of the Rhine. France remained protectionist; and when Napoleon annexed Holland and parts of Italy to France, he kept them outside the French customs. At the same time Napoleon forbade the satellite states to raise high tariffs against France. France was his base, and he meant to favor French industry, which was much crippled by its loss of its Middle Eastern and American markets.

Shippers, shipbuilders, and dealers in overseas goods, a powerful element of the older bourgeoisie, were ruined by the Continental System. The French ports were idle and their populations were distressed and disgruntled. The same problems befell all ports of Europe where the blockade was *Economic stagnation* strictly enforced; at Trieste, total annual tonnage fell from 208,000 in 1807 to 60,000 in 1812. Eastern Europe was especially hard hit. In the West there was the stimulus to new manufactures. Eastern Europe, long dependent on western Europe for manufactured goods, could no longer obtain them from England legally, nor from France, Germany, or Bohemia because of the difficulties of land transport and the British control of the Baltic.

Napoleon used architecture to show that Paris was the capital of modern Europe and that his empire replicated the imperial grandeur of ancient Rome. He built the multicolumned Madeleine to be a temple of glory, but after his fall from power it became a church.
(Bettmann/Corbis)

Nor could the landowners of Prussia, Poland, and Russia market their produce. The aristocracy of eastern Europe, which was the principal spending and importing class, had additional reason to dislike the French and to sympathize with the British.

As a war measure against Britain the Continental System also failed. British trade with Europe was significantly reduced, but the loss was made up elsewhere because of British control of the sea. Exports to Latin America rose from £300,000 in 1805 to £6,300,000 in 1809. Here again the existence of the overseas world frustrated the Continental System. Despite the System, export of British cotton goods, rising on a continuous tide of the rapidly developing Industrial Revolution, more than doubled in four years from 1805 to 1809. And while part of the increase was due to mere inflation and rising prices, it is estimated that the annual income of the British people more than doubled in the Revolutionary and Napoleonic wars, growing from £140,000,000 in 1792 to £335,000,000 in 1814.

 ## 50.   THE NATIONAL MOVEMENTS: GERMANY

The Resistance to Napoleon: Nationalism

From the beginning, as far back as 1792, the French met with resistance as well as collaboration in the countries they occupied. There was resentment when the invading armies plundered and laid requisitions upon the occupied countries, which were required to pay tribute in men and money, and whose policies were dictated by French residents or ambassadors. The Continental System was also resented because it was used for the benefit of French manufacturers. Europeans began to feel that Napoleon was employing them merely as tools against England. And in all countries, including France itself, people grew tired of the peace that was no peace, the wars and rumors of war, the conscription and the taxes, the loss of lives and local liberties, the aloof bureaucratic government, and the obviously growing and insatiable appetite of Napoleon for power and self-exaltation. Movements of protest and independence showed themselves even within the Napoleonic structure. We have seen how the dependent states protected themselves by tariffs. Even the emperor's proconsuls tried to root themselves in local opinion, as when Louis Bonaparte, king of Holland, tried to defend Dutch interests against Napoleon's demands, or when Murat, king of Naples, appealed to Italian sentiment to secure his own throne.

Nationalism developed as a movement of resistance against the forcible internationalism of the Napoleonic empire. Since the international system was essentially French, the nationalistic movements were anti-French; and since Napoleon was an autocrat, they were antiautocratic. The nationalism of the period was a mixture of the conservative and the liberal. Some nationalists, predominantly conservative, insisted on the value of their own peculiar institutions, customs, folkways, and historical development, which they feared might be obliterated under the French and Napoleonic system. Others, or indeed the same persons, insisted on more self-determination, more participation in government, more representative institutions, more freedom for the individual against the bureaucratic interference of the state. Both conservatism and liberalism rose up against Napoleon, destroyed him, outlasted him, and shaped the history of the following generations.

Anti-French nationalism

Nationalism was thus very complex and appeared in different countries in different ways. In England the profound solidarity of the country exhibited itself; all classes rallied and stood shoulder to shoulder against "Boney"; and ideas of reforming Parliament or tampering with historic English liberties were resolutely put aside. It is possible that the Napoleonic wars helped England through a very difficult social crisis, for the Industrial Revolution was causing dislocation, misery, unemployment, and even revolutionary agitation among a small minority, all of which were eclipsed by the patriotic need for resistance to Bonaparte. In Spain, nationalism took the form of implacable resistance to the French armies that desolated the land. Some Spanish nationalists were liberal; a bourgeois group at Cádiz, rebelling against the French regime, proclaimed the Spanish constitution of 1812, modeled on the French constitution of 1791. But Spanish nationalism drew its greatest strength from sentiments that were counterrevolutionary, aiming to restore the clergy and the Bourbons. In Italy the Napoleonic regime was better liked and national feeling was less anti-French than in Spain. Bourgeois of the Italian cities generally prized the efficiency and enlightenment of French methods and often shared in the anticlericalism of the French Revolution. The French regime, which lasted in Italy from 1796 to 1814, broke the habit of loyalty to the various duchies, oligarchic republics, papal states, and foreign dynasties by which Italy had long been ruled. Napoleon never unified Italy, but he consolidated it into only three parts, and the French influence brought the notion of a politically united Italy within the bounds of reasonable aspiration. With the Poles, Napoleon positively encouraged national feeling. He repeatedly told them that they might win a restored and united Poland by faithfully fighting in his cause. A few Polish nationalists, like the aging patriot Kosciusko, never trusted Napoleon, and some others, like Czartoryski, looked rather to the Russian tsar for a restoration of the Polish kingdom; but in general the

Poles, for their own national reasons, were exceptionally devoted to the emperor of the French and lamented his passing.

The Movement of Thought in Napoleonic Germany

The national movement in Germany

By far the most momentous new national movement developed in Germany. The Germans rebelled not only against the Napoleonic rule but also against the century-old ascendancy of French civilization. They rebelled not only against the French armies but also against much of the philosophy of the Age of Enlightenment. The years of the French Revolution and Napoleon were for Germany the years of great cultural efflorescence, the years of Beethoven, Goethe, and Schiller, of Herder, Kant, Fichte, Hegel, Schleiermacher, and many others. German ideas fell in with all the ferment of the new cultural movement known as "romanticism," which was everywhere challenging the "dry abstractions" of the Age of Reason and shaping the new themes of literature, music, art, and historical research. Germany became the most "romantic" of all countries, and German influence spread throughout Europe. In the nineteenth century the Germans came to be widely regarded as intellectual leaders, somewhat as the French had been in the century before. And most of the distinctive features of German thought were somehow connected with nationalism in a broad sense.

Formerly, especially in the century following the Peace of Westphalia, the Germans had been the least nationally minded of all the larger European peoples. They prided themselves on their world citizenship or cosmopolitan outlook. Looking out from the tiny states in which they lived, they were conscious of Europe, conscious of other countries, but hardly conscious of Germany. The Holy Roman Empire was neither a forceful political power nor the public embodiment of a well-defined national culture. The German world had no tangible frontiers; the area of German speech simply faded out into Alsace or the Austrian Netherlands, or into Poland, Bohemia, or the upper Balkans. That "Germany" ever did, thought, or hoped anything never crossed the German mind. The upper classes, becoming contemptuous of much that was German, took over French fashions, dress, etiquette, manners, ideas, and language, regarding them as an international norm of civilized living. Frederick the Great hired French tax collectors and wrote his own books in French.

About 1780 signs of a change set in. Even Frederick, in his later years, predicted a golden age of German literature, proudly declaring that Germans could do what other nations had done. In 1784 appeared a book by J. G. Herder called *Ideas on the Philosophy of the History of Mankind*. Herder was an earnest soul, a Protestant pastor and theologian who thought the French somewhat frivolous. He concluded that imitation of foreign ways made people

Herder's cultural nationalism

shallow and artificial. He declared that German ways were indeed different from French but not for that reason the less worthy of respect. All true culture or civilization, he held, must arise from native roots. It must arise also from the life of the common people, the *Volk,* not from the cosmopolitan and artificial life of the upper classes. Each people, he thought, meaning by a people a group sharing the same language, had its own attitudes, spirit, or genius. A sound civilization must express a national character or *Volksgeist*. And the character of each people was special to itself. Herder did not believe the nations to be in conflict; quite the contrary, he simply insisted that they were different. He did not believe German culture to be the best; many other peoples, notably the Slavs, later found his ideas applicable to their own needs. His philosophy of history was very different from that of Voltaire and the philosophes, who had

BRITANNIA
Blowing up the
Corsican Bottle Conjurer

Nationalism grew rapidly in all the European countries that resisted Napoleon's expansionist military policies. This image of Britannia "blowing up the Corsican Bottle Conjurer" expressed British national pride during this era. The bottle's label says "British spirits, composed of True Liberty, Courage, Loyalty and Religion."
(Rare Book Collection, University of North Carolina–Chapel Hill (Hoyt 11-192))

expected all people to progress along the same path of reason and enlightenment toward a similar civilization. Herder thought that all peoples should develop their own genius in their own way, each slowly unfolding with the inevitability of plantlike growth, avoiding sudden change or distortion by outside influence, and all ultimately reflecting, in their endless diversity, the infinite richness of humanity and of God.

The idea of the *Volksgeist* was reinforced from other and non-German sources and soon passed to other countries in the general movement of romantic thought. Like much else in romanticism, it emphasized genius or intuition rather than reason. It stressed the differences rather than the similarity of mankind. It broke down that sense of human similarity or universality which had been characteristic of the Age of Enlightenment, and which revealed itself in French and American doctrines of the rights of man, or again in the law codes of Napoleon. In the past it had been usually thought that what was good was good for all peoples. Good poetry was poetry written according to certain classical principles or "rules" of composition, which were the same for all writers from the Greeks on down. Now, according to Herder and to romantics in all countries, good poetry was poetry that expressed an inner genius, either an individual genius or the genius of a people—there were no more rigid, classical "rules." Good and just laws, according to the older philosophy of natural law, somehow corresponded to a standard of justice that was the same for all people. But now, according to Herder and the romantic school of jurisprudence, good laws were those that reflected local conditions or national idiosyncrasies. Here again there were no "rules," except possibly the rule that each nation should follow its own path.

Herder's philosophy set forth a cultural nationalism, without a political message. The Germans had long been a nonpolitical people. In the microscopic states of the Holy Roman Empire they had had no significant political questions to think about; in the more sizable ones they had been excluded from public affairs. The French Revolution made the Germans acutely conscious of the state. It showed what a people could do with a state, once they took it over and used it for their own purposes. For one thing, the French had raised themselves to the dignity of citizenship; they had become free individuals, responsible for themselves, taking part in the affairs of their country. For another, because they had a unified state which included all French people, and one in which a whole nation surged with a new sense of freedom, they were able to rise above all the other nations of Europe. Many in Germany were beginning to feel humiliation at the paternalism of their governments. The futilities of the Holy Roman Empire, which had made Germany for centuries the battlefield of Europe, now filled them with shame and indignation. They saw with disgust how their German princes, forever squabbling with each other for control over German subjects, disgraced themselves before the French to promote their own interests. The national awakening in Germany, which set in strongly after 1800, was therefore directed not only against Napoleon and the French but also against the German rulers and many of the half-Frenchified German upper classes. It was democratic in that it stressed the superior virtue of the common people.

Germans became fascinated by the idea of political and national greatness, precisely because they had neither. A great national German state, expressing the deep moral will and distinctive culture of the German people, seemed to them the solution to all their problems. It would give moral dignity to the individual German, solve the vexatious question of the selfish petty princes, protect the deep German *Volksgeist* from violation, and secure the Germans from subjection to outside powers. The nationalist philosophy remained somewhat vague, because in practice there was little that one could do. "Father" Jahn organized a kind of youth movement, had his young men do calisthenics for the Fatherland and led them on open-air expeditions into the country, where they made fun of aristocrats in French costume. He taught them to be suspicious of foreigners, Jews, and internationalists, and indeed of everything that might corrupt the purity of the German *Volk*. Most Germans thought him too extreme. Others collected wonderful stories of the rich medieval German past. There was an anonymous anti-French work, *Germany in Its Deep Humiliation,* for selling which the publisher Palm was put to death. Others founded the Moral and Scientific Union, generally known as the *Tugendbund* or league of virtue or manliness, whose members, by developing their own moral character, were to contribute to the future of Germany.

Fichte and the German national spirit

The career of J. G. Fichte illustrates the course of German thought in these years. Fichte was a moral and metaphysical philosopher, a professor at the University of Jena. His doctrine that the inner spirit of the individual creates its own moral universe was much admired in many countries. In America, for example, it entered into the transcendental philosophy of Ralph Waldo Emerson. Fichte at first was practically without national feeling. He enthusiastically approved of the French Revolution, as did many other German intellectuals at the time. In 1793, with the Revolution at its height, Fichte published a laudatory tract on the French Republic. He saw it as an emancipation of the human spirit, a step upward in the elevation of human dignity and moral stature. He accepted the idea of the Terror, that of "forcing men to be free," and he shared Rousseau's conception of the state as the embodiment of the sovereign will of a people. He came to see the state as the means of human salvation. In 1800, in his *Closed Commercial State,* he sketched a kind of totalitarian system in which the state planned and operated the whole economy of the country, shutting itself off from the rest of the world in order that, at home, it might freely develop the character of its own citizens. When the French conquered Germany Fichte became intensely and self-consciously German. He took over the idea of the *Volksgeist:* not only did the individual spirit create its own moral universe, but the spirit of a people created a kind of moral universe as well, manifested in its language, history, arts, folkways, customs, institutions, and ideas.

At Berlin, in 1808, Fichte delivered a series of *Addresses to the German Nation,* declaring that there was an ineradicable German spirit, a primordial and immutable national character, more noble than that of other peoples (thus going beyond Herder), to be kept pure at all costs from all outside influence, either international or French. The German spirit, he held, had always been profoundly different from that of France and western Europe; it had never yet really been heard from but would be some day. The French army commander then occupying the city thought the lectures too academic to be worth suppression. They attracted only small audiences; but his published lectures provided an enduring philosophical argument for German nationalism, and many Germans later regarded him as a national hero.

Reforms in Prussia

Politically, the revolt against the French led to major transformations in Prussia and the Prussian state. After the death of Frederick the Great in 1786 Prussia had fallen into a period of satisfied inertia, such as is likely to follow upon rapid growth or spectacular success. Then in 1806, at Jena-Auerstädt, the kingdom collapsed in a single battle. Its western and most of its Polish territories were taken away. It was relegated by Napoleon to its old holdings east of the Elbe River. Even here the French remained in occupation, for Napoleon stationed his Ninth Corps in Berlin. But in the eyes of German nationalists Prussia had a moral advantage. Of all the German states it was the least compromised by collaboration with the French. Toward Prussia, as toward a haven, German patriots therefore made their way. Prussia, east of the Elbe, formerly the least German of German lands, became the center of an all-German movement for national freedom. The years after Jena contributed to the "Prussianizing" of Germany; but it is to be observed that neither Fichte nor Hegel, Gneisenau nor Scharnhorst, Stein nor Hardenberg, all rebuilders of Prussia, was a native Prussian.

The reform movement in Prussia

The main problem for Prussia was military, since Napoleon could be overthrown only by military force. And as always in Prussia, the requirements of the army shaped the form taken by the state. The problem was conceived to be one of morale and personnel. The old Prussia of Frederick, which had fallen ingloriously, had been mechanical, arbitrary, soulless. Its people had lacked the sense of membership in the state, and in the army its soldiers had held no hope of promotion and felt no patriotism or spirit. To produce this spirit was the aim of the army reformers Scharnhorst and Gneisenau. Gneisenau, a Saxon, had served in one of the British "Hessian" regiments in the War of American Independence, during which he had observed the military value of patriotic feeling in the American soldiers. He was a close observer also of the consequences of the French Revolution, which, he said, had "set in action the national energy of the entire French people, putting the different classes on an equal social and fiscal basis." If Prussia was to strengthen itself against France, or indeed to avoid revolution in the long run in Prussia

CHRONOLOGY OF NOTABLE EVENTS, 1799–1815

1799–1801	Second Coalition (Austria, Russia, Britain) wages war with France
1803	Napoleon's army is defeated in Haiti and France sells Louisiana to the United States
1805–1807	Third Coalition (Austria, Russia, Britain) wages war with France
1806	Napoleon defeats Prussian armies and occupies Berlin
1806–1825	Latin American countries pursue successful campaigns for national independence from Spain and Portugal
1807	Treaty of Tilsit creates French-Russian alliance; Napoleon proclaims "Continental System" to exclude trade with Britain
1808–1814	Peninsular War leads to French defeats in Spain
1810	Napoleon marries Marie Louise, daughter of Austrian Emperor
1812	Napoleon's "Grand Army" invades Russia and is destroyed in winter retreat
1813	French army loses decisive battle of Leipzig in Germany
1814	Abdication of Napoleon and restoration of Bourbon Monarchy in France
1814–1815	Congress of Vienna reorganizes the political order in Europe
1815	Napoleon returns to power for "100 Days"; final defeat at the battle of Waterloo

itself, it must find a means to inspire a similar feeling of equal participation in its own people and to allow capable individuals to fill important positions in the army and government without regard to their social status.

The reconstruction of the state, prerequisite to the reconstruction of the army, was initiated by Baron Stein and continued by his successor, Hardenberg. Like Metternich, Stein came from western Germany, and he was long hostile to what he considered a barely civilized Prussia, but he finally turned to the Prussian state as the best hope to lead Germany as a whole into the future. Deeply committed to the philosophy of Kant and Fichte, he dwelt on the concepts of duty, service, moral character, and responsibility. He thought that the common people must be awakened to moral life and raised from a brutalized servility to the level of self-determination and membership in the community. This, he believed, required an equality more of duties than of rights.

Under Stein the old caste structure of Prussia became somewhat less rigid. Property became interchangeable between social classes, and soldiers of all classes could now serve as officers in the army. The burghers, to develop a sense of citizenship and participation in the state, were given extensive freedom of self-government in the cities; the municipal systems of Prussia, and later of Germany, became a model for much of Europe in the following century.

Stein's most famous work was the "abolition of serfdom." It was naturally impossible, since the whole reform program was aimed at strengthening Prussia for a war of liberation against the French, to antagonize the Junkers who commanded the army. Stein's ordinance of 1807 abolished serfdom only in that it abolished the "hereditary subjection" of peasants to their manorial lords. It gave peasants the right to move and migrate, marry, and take up trades without the lord's approval. If, however, they remained on the land, they were still subject to all the old services of forced labor in the fields of the lord. Peasants enjoying small tenures of their own continued to be liable for the old dues and fees. By an edict of 1810, they might convert their tenure into private property, getting rid of the manorial obligations, but only on condition that one-third of the land held should become the private property of the lord. In the following decades many such conversions took place; as a result, the estates of the Junkers grew considerably larger. The reforms in Prussia somewhat reduced the old patriarchal powers of the lords and gave legal status and freedom of movement to the mass of the population, thus laying the foundation for a modern state and modern economy. But the peasants tended to become mere hired agricultural laborers and the position of the Junkers was heightened, not reduced. Prussia avoided the Revolution. Stein himself, because Napoleon feared him, was obliged to go into exile in 1808, but his reforms endured.

51.   THE OVERTHROW OF NAPOLEON: THE CONGRESS OF VIENNA

The situation at the close of 1811 may be summarized as follows. Napoleon had the mainland of Europe in his grip. Russia and Turkey were at war on the Danube, but otherwise there was no war except in Spain, where four

Europe in 1811

years of fighting remained inconclusive. The Continental System was working badly. Britain was hurt by it only in that, without it, British exports to Europe would have risen rapidly in these years. Well launched in the economic growth of the Industrial Revolution, Britain was amassing a vast store of national wealth that could be used to assist European governments financially against Napoleon. The peoples of Europe were growing restless, dreaming increasingly of national freedom. In Germany especially, many awaited the opportunity to rise in a war of independence. But Napoleon could be overthrown only by the destruction of his army, over which neither British wealth nor British sea power, nor the European patriots and nationalists, nor the Prussian nor the Austrian armed forces were able to prevail. All eyes turned to Russia. Alexander I had long been dissatisfied with his French alliance. He had obtained from it nothing but the annexation of Finland in 1809. He received no assistance from France in his war with Turkey; he saw Napoleon marry into the Austrian house; he had to tolerate the existence of a French-oriented Poland at his very door. The articulate classes in Russia, namely, the landowners and serf owners, loudly denounced the French alliance and demanded a resumption of open trade relations with England. An international clientele of émigrés and anti-Bonapartists, including Baron Stein, also gradually congregated at St. Petersburg, where they poured into the tsar's ears the welcome message that Europe looked to him for its salvation.

The Russian Campaign and the War of Liberation

On December 31, 1810, Russia formally withdrew from the Continental System. Anglo-Russian commercial relations were resumed. Napoleon resolved to crush the tsar. He concentrated the Grand Army in eastern Germany and Poland, a vast force of 700,000 men, the largest ever assembled up to that time for a single military operation. It was an all-European host. Hardly more than a third was French; another third was German, from German regions annexed to France, from the states of the Confederation of the Rhine, and with token forces from Prussia and Austria; and the remaining third was drawn from all other nationalities of the Grand Empire, including 90,000 Poles.

Napoleon at first hoped to meet the Russians in Poland or Prussia. This time, however, they decided to fight on their own ground, and they needed in any case to delay until their forces on the lower Danube could be recalled. In June 1812 Napoleon led the Grand Army into Russia.

He intended a short, sharp war, such as most of his wars had been in the past, and carried with him only three weeks' supplies. But from the beginning everything went wrong. It was Napoleon's principle to force a decisive battle; but the Russian army simply melted away. It was his principle to live on the country, so as to reduce the need for supply trains; but the Russians destroyed as they retreated, and in any case, in Russia, even in the summer, it was hard to find sustenance for so many men and horses. Finally, not far from Moscow, Napoleon was able to join battle with the main Russian force at Borodino. Here again everything miscarried. It was his principle always to outnumber the enemy at the decisive spot, but the Grand Army had left so many detachments along its line of march that at Borodino the Russians outnumbered it. It was Napoleon's principle to concentrate his artillery, but here he scattered it instead. His principle was to throw in his last reserves at the critical moment, but at Borodino, so far from home, he refused the risk of ordering the Old Guard into action. Napoleon won the battle, at a cost of 30,000 men, as against 50,000 lost by the Russians; but the Russian army was able to withdraw in good order.

On September 14, 1812, the French emperor entered Moscow. Almost immediately the city broke into flames. Napoleon found himself camping in a ruin, with troops strewn along a long line all the way back to Poland, and with a hostile army maneuvering near at hand. Baffled, he tried to negotiate with Alexander, who refused all overtures. After five weeks, not knowing what to do and fearful of remaining isolated in Moscow over the winter, Napoleon ordered a retreat. Prevented by the Russians from taking a more southerly route, the Grand Army retired by the same way it had come, but it could no longer live off the land. The cold weather set in early and was unusually severe. For a century after 1812 the retreat from Moscow remained the last word in military horror. Men froze and starved, horses slipped and died, vehicles could not be moved, and equipment was abandoned. Discipline broke down toward the end; the army dissolved into a horde of individual fugitives, speaking a babel of languages, harassed by bands of Russian irregulars, picking their way on foot over ice and snow, most of the time in the dark, for the nights are long in these latitudes in December. Of 611,000 who entered Russia 400,000 died of battle casualties, starvation, and exposure, and 100,000 were taken prisoner. The Grand Army no longer existed.

The retreat from Moscow

Now at last all the anti-Napoleon forces rushed together. The Russians pushed westward into central Europe. The Prussian and Austrian governments, which in 1812 had halfheartedly supplied troops for the invasion of Russia, switched over in 1813 and joined the tsar. Throughout Germany, the patriots, often half-trained boys, marched off in the War of Liberation, though it was the professional armies of the German states that made the difference. Anti-French riots broke out in Italy. In Spain Wellington at last pushed rapidly forward; in June 1813 he crossed the Pyrenees into France. The British government, in three years from 1813 to 1815, poured £32,000,000 as subsidies into Europe, more than half of all the funds granted during the 22 years of the wars. An incongruous alliance of British capitalism and east-European agrarian feudalism, of the British navy and the Russian army, of Spanish clericalism and German nationalism, of divine-right monarchies and newly aroused democrats and liberals, combined at last to bring the Man of Destiny to the ground.

Napoleon, who had left his army in Russia in December 1812 and rushed across Europe to Paris by sleigh and coach in the remarkable time of 13 days, raised a new army in France in the early months of 1813. But it was untrained and unsteady, and he himself had lost some of his genius for command. His new army was smashed in October at the battle of Leipzig, known to the Germans as the Battle of the Nations, the greatest battle in number of men engaged ever fought until the twentieth century. The allies drove Napoleon back upon France. But the closer they came to defeating him the more they began to fear and distrust each other.

The "Battle of the Nations"

The Restoration of the Bourbons

The coalition already showed signs of splitting. Should the allies, together or singly, negotiate with Napoleon? How strong should the France of the future be? What should be its new frontiers? What form of government should it have? There was no agreement on these questions. Alexander wanted to dethrone Napoleon and dictate peace in Paris, in dramatic retribution for the destruction of Moscow. He had a scheme for giving the French throne to Bernadotte, a former French marshal, now crown prince of Sweden, who as king of France would depend on Russian support. Metternich preferred to keep Napoleon or his son as French emperor, after clearing the French out of central Europe; for a Bonaparte dynasty in a reduced France would be dependent on Austria. The Prussian counsels were divided. The British, with an eye to one of their main strategic concerns, declared that the French must get out of Belgium and that Napoleon must go; they held that the French might then choose their own government but believed a restoration of the Bourbons to be the best solution. The three Continental monarchies had no concern for the Bourbons, and both Alexander and Metternich, if they could make France dependent respectively on themselves, were willing to see it remain strong to the extent of including Belgium.

The British foreign minister, Viscount Castlereagh, arrived on the Continent for consultations in January 1814. He held a number of strong cards. For one thing, Napoleon continued to fight, and the allies therefore continued to ask for British financial aid. Castlereagh skillfully used the promise of British subsidies to win acceptance of the British war aims, which included France's expulsion from Belgium. In addition, he found a common ground for agreement with Metternich, both Britain and Austria fearing the domination of Europe by Russia. Castlereagh's first great problem was to hold the alliance together, for without Continental allies the British could not defeat France. He succeeded, on March 9, 1814, in getting Russia, Prussia, Austria, and Great Britain to sign the treaty of Chaumont. Each power bound itself for 20 years to a Quadruple Alliance against France, and each agreed to provide 150,000 soldiers to enforce such peace terms as might be arrived at. For the first time since 1792 a solid coalition of the four great powers now existed against France. Three weeks later the allies entered Paris, and on April 4 Napoleon abdicated at Fontainebleau.

The Quadruple Alliance

He was forced to this step by lack of support in France itself. Twenty years before, in 1793 and 1794, France had fought off the combined powers of Europe—minus Russia. It could not and would not do so in 1814. The country cried for peace. Even the imperial marshals advised the emperor's abdication. But what was to follow him? For over 25 years the French had had one regime after another. Now they were divided. Some wanted a republic; other wished to retain the empire under Napoleon's infant son; still others desired

The French army's retreat from Russia in 1812 shattered Napoleon's image of military invincibility and brought the anti-Napoleonic forces together for a decisive victory in the following year. This French painting portrays the misery that gave the retreat of 1812 its lasting reputation for military horror.
(Alinari/Art Resource, NY)

a constitutional monarchy; and there were even those who longed for the old regime. Talleyrand stepped into the breach. The "legitimate" king, he said, Louis XVIII, was the man who would provoke the least factionalism and opposition. The powers, likewise, had by this time concluded in favor of the Bourbons. A Bourbon king would be peaceable, under no impulse to win back the conquests of the republic and empire. He would also, as the native and rightful king of France, need no foreign support to bolster him, so that the control of France would not arise as an issue to divide the victorious powers.

The Bourbons restored

The Bourbon dynasty was thus restored. Louis XVIII, ignored and disregarded for a whole generation, both by most people in France and by the governments of Europe, returned to the throne of his brother and his fathers. He issued a "constitutional charter," partly at the insistence of the liberal tsar and partly because, having actually learned from his long exile, he sought the support of influential people in France. The charter of 1814 made no concession to the principle of popular or national sovereignty. It was represented as the gracious gift of a theoretically absolute king. But in practice it granted what most of the French wanted. It promised legal equality, eligibility of all to public office without regard to class, and a parliamentary government in two chambers. It recognized the Napoleonic law codes, the Napoleonic settlement with the church, and the redistribution of property effected during the Revolution. It carried over the abolition of all feudal privileges and manorial rights. It confined the vote, to be sure, to a very few large landowners; but for the time being, except for a few irreconcilables, France settled down to enjoy the blessings of a chastened revolution—and peace.

The Settlement before the Vienna Congress

It was with the government of the restored Bourbons that the powers, on May 30, 1814, signed a treaty. This document, the "first" Treaty of Paris, confined France to its boundaries of 1792, those obtaining before the wars. The allied statesmen disregarded cries for vengeance and punishment, imposed no indemnity or reparations, and even allowed the works of art gathered from Europe during the wars to remain in Paris. It was not the desire of the victors to handicap the new French government on which they placed their hopes. Napoleon meanwhile was exiled to the island of Elba on the Italian coast.

To deal with other questions, the powers had agreed, before signing the Alliance of Chaumont, to hold an international congress at Vienna after defeating Napoleon. The recession of the French flood left the future of much of Europe fluid and uncertain. Both Russia and Great Britain, however, before consenting to a general conference, specified certain matters that they would decide for themselves as not susceptible to international consideration. The Russians refused to discuss Turkey and the Balkans; they retained Bessarabia as the prize of their recent war with the Turks. They also kept Finland, as an autonomous constitutional grand duchy, as well as certain conquests in the Caucasus almost unknown to Europe, namely Georgia and Azerbaijan. The British refused any discussion of the freedom of the seas. They also barred all colonial and overseas questions. The British government simply announced which of its colonial and insular conquests it would keep and which it would return. The revolts in Latin America were left to run their course.

In Europe, the British remained in possession of Malta, the Ionian Islands, and Heligoland; in America, they kept St. Lucia, Trinidad, and Tobago in the West Indies. Of former French possessions, the British kept the island of Mauritius in the Indian Ocean. Of former Dutch territories, they kept the Cape of Good Hope and Ceylon, but returned the Netherlands Indies. During the Revolutionary and Napoleonic wars in Europe the British had also made extensive conquests in India, bringing much of the Deccan and the upper Ganges valley under their rule. The British emerged, in 1814, as the controlling power in both India and the Indian Ocean.

British supremacy

Indeed, of all the colonial empires founded by Europeans in the sixteenth and seventeenth centuries, only the British now remained as a growing and dynamic system. The old French, Spanish, and Portuguese empires were reduced to mere scraps of their former selves; the Dutch still held vast establishments in the East Indies, but all the intermediate positions—the Cape, Ceylon, Mauritius, Singapore—were now British. Nor, in 1814, did any people except the British have a significant navy. With Napoleon and the Continental System defeated, with the Industrial Revolution bringing power machinery to the manufacturers of England, with no rival left in the contest for overseas dominion, and with a virtual monopoly of naval power, whose use they studiously kept free from international regulation, the British embarked on their century of world leadership, which may be said to have lasted from 1814 to 1914.

The Congress of Vienna, 1814–1815

The Congress of Vienna assembled in September 1814. Never had such a brilliant gathering been seen. All the states of Europe sent representatives; and many defunct states, such as the formerly sovereign princes and ecclesiastics of the late Holy Roman Empire, sent lobbyists to urge their restoration. But procedure was so arranged that all important matters were decided by the four triumphant Great Powers. Indeed it was at the Congress of Vienna that the terms great and small powers entered clearly into the diplomatic vocabulary. Europe was at peace, a treaty having been signed with the late enemy, but France was represented at the Congress, by none other than Talleyrand, now minister to Louis XVIII. Castlereagh, Metternich, and Alexander spoke for their respective countries; Prussia was represented by Hardenberg. The Prussians hoped, as always, to enlarge the kingdom of Prussia. Alexander was a question mark, but it could be surmised that he wanted Poland, that he favored constitutional governments in Europe, and that he sought some kind of international system of collective security. Castlereagh and Metternich, with support from Talleyrand, were most especially concerned to produce a balance of power on the Continent. Aristocrats of the Old Regime, they applied eighteenth-century diplomatic principles to the existing problem. They by no means desired to restore the territorial boundaries obtaining before the wars. They did desire, as they put it, to restore the "liberties of Europe," meaning the freedom of European states from domination by a single power; and it was hoped that a proper balance of power would also produce a lasting peace.

Containing France

The chief menace to peace, and most likely claimant for the domination of Europe, naturally seemed to be the late troublemaker, France. The Congress of Vienna, without much disagreement, erected a barrier of strong states along the French eastern frontier. The historic Dutch Republic, extinct since 1795, was revived as the kingdom of the Netherlands, with the house of Orange as a hereditary monarchy; to it was added Belgium, the old Austrian Netherlands with which Austria had long been willing to part. It was hoped that the combined Dutch-Belgian kingdom would be strong enough to discourage the perennial French drive into the Low Countries. On the south, the kingdom of Sardinia (or Piedmont) was restored and strengthened by the incorporation of Genoa. Behind the Netherlands and Piedmont, and further to discourage a renewal of French pressure upon Germany and Italy, two great powers were installed. Almost all the German left bank of the Rhine was ceded to Prussia, which was to be, in Castlereagh's words, a kind of "bridge" spanning central Europe, a bulwark against both France in the West and Russia in the East. In Italy, again as a kind of secondary barrier against France, the Austrians were firmly installed. They not only took back Tuscany and the Milanese, which they had held before 1796, but also annexed the extinct republic of Venice. The Austrian empire now included a Lombardo-Venetian kingdom in north Italy, which lasted for almost half a century. In the rest of Italy the Congress recognized the restoration of the pope in the papal states and of former rulers in the smaller duchies; but it did not insist on a restoration of the Bourbons in the kingdom of Naples. There Napoleon's brother-in-law Murat, with support from Metternich, managed for a time to retain his throne. The Bourbon and Braganza rulers restored themselves in Spain and Portugal, respectively, and were recognized by the Congress.

Germany remains divided

As for Germany, the Congress made no attempt to put together again the Humpty Dumpty of the Holy Roman Empire. The French and Napoleonic reorganization of Germany was substantially confirmed, and the kings of Bavaria, Württemberg, and Saxony kept the royal crowns that Napoleon had bestowed on them. The king of England, George III, was now recognized as

The Congress of Vienna combined complex diplomatic negotiations with the cultural elegance of traditional elites. This picture shows the social status of the diplomats who sought to establish peace and order in Europe after 25 years of revolution and warfare.
(akg-images)

king, not "elector," of Hanover. The German states, 39 in number, including Prussia and Austria, were joined in a loose confederation in which the members remained virtually sovereign. The Congress ignored the yearnings of German nationalists for a great unified Fatherland; Metternich especially feared nationalistic agitation; and in any case the nationalists themselves had no practical answer to concrete questions, such as the government and frontiers that a united Germany should have.

The Polish-Saxon Question

The question of Poland, reopened by the fall of Napoleon's Grand Duchy of Warsaw, brought the Congress almost to disaster. Alexander still insisted on undoing the crime of the partitions, which to his mind meant reconstituting the Polish kingdom with himself as constitutional king, in a merely personal union with the Russian empire. To reunite Poland required that Austria and Prussia surrender their respective segments of the old Poland, most of which they had lost to Napoleon. The Prussians were willing, with the proviso, which Alexander supported, that Prussia receive instead the whole of the kingdom of Saxony, which was considered available because the king of Saxony had been the last German ruler to abandon Napoleon. The issue presented itself as the Polish-Saxon question, with

Russia and Prussia standing together to demand all Poland for Russia and all Saxony for Prussia.

Such a prospect horrified Metternich. For Prussia to absorb Saxony would raise Prussia prodigiously in the eyes of all Germans, and it would greatly lengthen the common frontier between Prussia and the Austrian Empire. Furthermore, for Alexander to become king of all Poland, and incidentally the protector of an extended Prussia, would incalculably augment the influence of Russia in the affairs of Europe. Metternich found that

Diplomatic maneuvers

Castlereagh shared these views. To Castlereagh it seemed that the main problem at Vienna was to restrain Russia. The British had not fought the French emperor only to have Europe fall to the Russian tsar. For months the Polish-Saxon question was debated, Metternich and Castlereagh exploring every device of argument to dissuade the Russo-Prussian combination from its expansionist designs.

Finally they accepted the proffered assistance of Talleyrand, who shrewdly used the rift between the victors to bring France back into the diplomatic circle as a power in its own right. On January 3, 1815, Castlereagh, Metternich, and Talleyrand signed a secret treaty, pledging themselves to go to war if necessary against Russia and Prussia. So, in the very midst of the peace conference, war again reared its head.

No sooner had news of the secret treaty leaked out than Alexander offered to compromise. In his complicated nature he was, among other things, a man of peace, and he agreed to content himself with a reduced Polish kingdom. The Congress therefore created a new

"Congress Poland"

Poland (called "Congress Poland," which lasted for 15 years); Alexander became its king, and he gave it a constitution. It comprised much the same area as Napoleon's Grand Duchy, representing in effect a transfer of this region from French to Russian control. It reached 250 miles farther west into Europe than had the Russian segment of the third partition of 1795. Some Poles still remained in Prussia and some remained in the Austrian Empire; Poland was not reunited. With the tsar thus content, Prussia too had to back down. It received about two-fifths of Saxony, the rest remaining to the Saxon king. The addition of both Saxon and Rhineland territories brought the Prussian monarchy into the most advanced parts of Germany. The net effect of the peace settlement, and of the Napoleonic wars, in this connection, was to shift the center of gravity of both Russia and Prussia farther west—Russia almost to the Oder River and Prussia to the borders of France (see maps, pp. 208–209, 222–223).

With the solution of the Polish-Saxon question the main political work of the Congress was completed, and various committees of the Congress set to work to draft the Final Act. But at this point the whole settlement was unexpectedly brought into jeopardy.

The Hundred Days and Their Aftermath

Napoleon escaped from Elba, landed in France on March 1, 1815, and again proclaimed the empire. In the year since the return of the Bourbons discontent had been spreading in France. Louis XVIII proved to be a sensible man, but a swarm of unreasonable and vindictive émigrés had come back with him. Reaction and a "white terror" were raging through the country. Adherents of the Revolution rallied to the emperor on his dramatic reappearance. Napoleon reached Paris, took over the government and army, and headed for Belgium. He would, if he could, disperse the pompous assemblage at Vienna. To the victors of the year before, and to most of Europe, it seemed that the Revolution was again stirring, that the old horror of toppling thrones and recurring warfare might not after all be ended. The opposing forces met in Belgium at Waterloo, where the Duke of Wellington, commanding an allied force, won a great victory. Napoleon again abdicated and was again exiled, this time to distant St. Helena in the south Atlantic. A new peace treaty was made with France, the "second" Treaty of Paris. It was more severe than the first, since the French seemed to have shown themselves incorrigible and unrepentant. The new treaty imposed minor changes of the frontiers, an indemnity of 700,000,000 francs, and an army of occupation.

The effect of the Hundred Days, as the episode following Napoleon's return from Elba is called, was to renew the dread of revolution, war, and aggression. Britain, Russia, Austria, and Prussia, after being almost at war with each other in January, again joined forces to get rid of the apparition from Elba, and in November 1815 they solemnly reconfirmed the Quadruple Alliance of Chaumont, adding a provision that no Bonaparte should ever govern France. They agreed also to hold future congresses to review the political situation and enforce the peace. No change was made in the arrangements agreed to at Vienna, except that Murat, who fought for Napoleon during the Hundred Days, was captured and shot, and an extremely unenlightened Bourbon monarchy was restored in Naples. In addition to the Quadruple Alliance of the Great Powers, bound specifically to enforce or amend the terms of the peace treaty by international action, Alexander devised a vaguer scheme which he called the Holy Alliance. Long attracted to the idea of an international order, appalled by the return of Napoleon, and influenced at the moment by the pious Baroness von Krüdener, the tsar proposed, for all monarchs to sign, a statement by which they promised to uphold Christian principles of charity and peace. All signed except the pope, the sultan of the Ottoman Empire, and the prince regent of Great Britain. The Holy Alliance, probably sincerely meant by Alexander as a condemnation of violence, and at first not taken seriously by the others who signed it and who thought it absurd to mix Christianity with politics, soon came to signify, in the minds of liberals, a kind of unholy alliance of monarchies against liberty and progress.

Alliances against Napoleon

The Peace of Vienna, including generally the Treaty of Vienna itself, the treaties of Paris, and the British and colonial settlement, was the most far-reaching diplomatic agreement between the Peace of Westphalia of 1648 and the Peace of Paris, which closed the First World War in 1919. It had its strong points and its weak ones. It produced a minimum of resentment in France; the late enemy accepted the new arrangements. It ended almost two centuries of European conflicts over the control of colonial territories in Asia and the Americas; for 60 or 70 years no colonial empire seriously challenged the British. Two other causes of friction in the eighteenth century—the control of Poland and the Austro-Prussian dualism in Germany—were smoothed over for 50 years. With past issues the peace of 1815 dealt rather effectively; with future issues, not unnaturally, it was less successful. The Vienna treaty was not illiberal in its day; it was by no means entirely reactionary, for the Congress showed little desire to restore the state of affairs in existence before the wars. The reaction that gathered strength after 1815 was not written into the treaty itself.

The Peace of Vienna

But the treaty gave no satisfaction to nationalists and democrats. It was a disappointment even to many liberals, especially in Germany. The transfer of peoples from government to government without consultation of their wishes opened the way under nineteenth-century conditions to a good deal of subsequent trouble. The peacemakers were in fact hostile both to nationalism and to democracy, the potent forces of the coming age; they regarded them, with reason, as leading to revolution and war. The problem to which they addressed themselves was to restore the balance of power, the "liberties of Europe," and to make a lasting peace. In this they were successful. They restored the European state system, a system in which a number of sovereign and independent states existed without

KINGDOM OF NORWAY
AND SWEDEN

FINLAND
(Russia, 1808)

St. Petersburg

Oslo

Reval

Stockholm

Baltic Sea

Riga

SCOTLAND

Edinburgh

*North
Sea*

DENMARK

Copenhagen

Nieman R.

EAST
PRUSSIA

LITHUANIA

UNITED KINGDOM
OF GREAT BRITAIN AND IRELAND

IRELAND   Dublin

*HELIGOLAND
(Britain)*

SCHLESWIG

HOLSTEIN

Hamburg

Danzig

RUSSIAN
EMPIRE

ENGLAND

KINGDOM OF THE
NETHERLANDS

HANOVER

Elbe R.

Rhine R.

P R U S S I A

Berlin

Oder R.

Vistula R.

Warsaw

London

English Channel

BELGIUM
(Ind. 1831)

Cologne

KINGDOM OF
POLAND-
(1815–1831)

Breslau

Cracow

GALICIA

ATLANTIC
OCEAN

Rouen

Seine R.

Paris

LUX.

HESSE

SAXON
STATES

SAXONY

Prague

Austerlitz

Metz

LORRAINE

WÜRT-
TEMBERG

BAVARIA

Pressburg

Loire R.

Strasbourg

ALSACE

BADEN

Munich

AUSTRIA

Vienna

AUSTRIAN EMPIRE

Budapest

HUNGARY

*BESSARABIA
(Russia 1812)*

FRANCE

Bern

SWITZERLAND

TYROL

ILLYRIAN

*MOLDAVIA
(Autonomous 1829)*

Bordeaux

Garonne R.

Lyon

Rhone R.

SAVOY

PIEDMONT

LOM-
BARDY

Milan

Po R.

VENETIA

CROATIA

Danube R.

WALLACHIA
(Autonomous 1829)

Burgos

Toulouse

PYRENEES

Marseille

Nice

Genoa

PARMA

MODENA

DALMATIA

BOSNIA

Belgrade

SERBIA
*(Autonomous
1829)*

Douro R.

Ebro R.

Toulon

LUCCA

TUSCANY

Adriatic Sea

OTTOMAN EMPIRE

BULGARIA

PORTUGAL

SPAIN

Madrid

Guadiana R.

Tagus R.

Lisbon

Barcelona

KINGDOM OF SARDINIA

Elba

*CORSICA
(France)*

Rome

PAPAL
STATES

MONTENEGRO

Sofia

Salonica

Valencia

*BALEARIC IS.
(Spain)*

Naples

*Aegean
Sea*

Seville

Cadiz

Gibraltar *(Britain)*

KINGDOM OF THE
TWO SICILIES

*IONIAN I.
(Britain)*

GREECE
(Independent 1829)

Athens

Palermo

SICILY

MOROCCO

Algiers

ALGERIA
(France, 1830)

TUNISIA
(Turkish)

*MALTA
(Britain)*

CRETE

Mediterranean Sea

TRIPOLI

TRIPOLI

■ Ottoman Empire   ▨ Prussia
▨ Austrian Empire   ▨ Kingdom of Sardinia
□ Bavaria

0   100   200   300 miles

fear of conquest or domination. And the peace they made, though some details broke down in 1830 and others in 1848, on the whole subsisted for half a century; and not for a full century, not until 1914, was there a war in Europe that lasted longer than a few months or in which all the great powers were involved.

The Peace of Vienna thus brought to a close the great political and military upheavals that had spread across Europe in the wake of the French Revolution. Yet even the most conservative diplomats at Vienna recognized that the revolutionary events and legacy would not simply vanish from European culture or history; indeed the Holy Alliance and the vigilance of the conservative European states after 1815 showed how deeply the French Revolution had affected all of Europe and those places outside Europe where revolutionary ideas had become popular and influential. The Latin American struggle for independence from Spain, *Legacy of the Revolution* for example, continued to draw on the new conceptions of national sovereignty and continued to spread across the New World while diplomats in Vienna were working to restore stability and order in Europe.

The French Revolution and the Napoleonic empire had demonstrated how a new, more open system of social and professional advancement enabled a nation to exercise power more effectively than any of the traditional, monarchical states. The revolutionary regimes had introduced new methods for mobilizing national economic resources, military forces, and large populations, all of which would reappear in the national mobilizations of other modern states. The Revolution and Napoleon, in short, gave the modern world new models of political organization and authoritarian rule. At the same time, however, the famous revolutionary events also helped to spread new conceptions of human rights, political participation, democratic government, and economic organization that would remain powerful cultural ideals throughout much of the modern world; and the popular ideology of nationalism, which developed among both supporters and opponents of the French Revolution and Napoleon, rapidly became one of the most pervasive political and cultural forces in modern world history.

All of these ideas helped to produce and reshape the characteristic institutions of modern societies. They continued to attract fervent supporters after the Congress of Vienna and after all other attempts to defend or revive the old order. The French Revolution and the Napoleonic wars, for all their turmoil and terrible destructive violence, created a lasting political and cultural legacy that has influenced modern nations almost everywhere, down to our own time.

For interactive exercises, glossary, chronologies, and more, go to the *Online Learning Center* at **www.mhhe.com/palmer10.**

EUROPE, 1815

Boundaries are those set by the Congress of Vienna. France was reduced to the borders it had in 1789. Prussia was firmly installed on both banks of the Rhine, but South Germany remained as reorganized by Napoleon. Poland was again partitioned, with a larger share than in 1795 going to Russia—which also acquired Finland and Bessarabia. The Austrians added Venetia to what they had held before 1796. The union of the Dutch and Belgian Netherlands lasted only until 1831, when the kingdom of Belgium was established. Otherwise, the boundaries of 1815 lasted until the Italian war of 1859, which led to the unification of Italy.

APPENDIX, SUGGESTIONS FOR FURTHER READING, INDEX

RULERS AND REGIMES
In Principal European Countries since 1500

HOLY ROMAN EMPIRE

Habsburg Line

Maximilian I, 1493–1519

Charles V, 1519–1556

Ferdinand I, 1556–1564

Maximilian II, 1564–1576

Rudolph II, 1576–1612

Matthias, 1612–1619

Ferdinand II, 1619–1637

Ferdinand III, 1637–1657

Leopold I, 1658–1705

Joseph I, 1705–1711

Charles VI, 1711–1740

Charles VI was succeeded by a daughter, Maria Theresa, who as a woman could not be elected Holy Roman Emperor. French influence in 1742 secured the election of

Bavarian Line

Charles VII, 1742–1745

On Charles VII's death the Habsburg control of the emperorship was resumed.

Lorraine Line

Francis I, 1745–1765 (husband of Maria Theresa)

Habsburg-Lorraine Line

Joseph II, 1765–1790 (son of Francis I and Maria Theresa)

Leopold II, 1790–1792

Francis II, 1792–1806

The Holy Roman Empire became extinct in 1806.

AUSTRIAN DOMINIONS

The rulers of Austria from 1438 to 1740, and at least titular kings of Hungary from 1526 to 1740, were the same as the Holy Roman Emperors. After 1740:

Habsburg Line (through female heir)

Maria Theresa, 1740–1780

Joseph II, 1780–1790

Leopold II, 1790–1792

Francis II, 1792–1835

In 1804 Francis II took the title of Emperor, as Francis I of the Austrian Empire. Austria was declared an "empire" because Napoleon proclaimed France an empire in that year, and because the demise of the Holy Roman Empire could be foreseen.

Ferdinand I, 1835–1848

Francis Joseph, 1848–1916

Charles I, 1916–1918

The Austrian Empire became extinct in 1918.

BRITISH ISLES

Tudor Line

Kings of England and Ireland

Henry VII, 1485–1509

Henry VIII, 1509–1547

Edward VI, 1547–1553

Mary I, 1553–1558

Elizabeth I, 1558–1603

In 1603 James VI of Scotland, a great-great-grandson of Henry VII, succeeded to the English throne.

Stuart Line

Kings of England and Ireland, and of Scotland

James I, 1603–1625

Charles I, 1625–1649

Republican Interregnum

The Commonwealth, 1649–1653

The Protectorate

Oliver Cromwell, 1653–1658, Lord Protector

Richard Cromwell, 1658–1660

Restored Stuart Line

Charles II, 1660–1685

James II, 1685–1688

In 1688 James II was forced out of the country, but Parliament kept the crown in a female branch of the Stuart family, calling in Mary, the daughter of James II, and her husband William III of the Netherlands. Mary died in 1694.

William III and Mary II, 1689–1702/1694

Anne, 1702–1714

In 1707, through the Union of England and Scotland, the royal title became King (or Queen) of Great Britain and Ireland. The Stuart family having no direct Protestant heirs, the throne passed in 1714 to the German George I, Elector of Hanover, a great-grandson of James I.

Hanoverian Line

Kings of Great Britain and Ireland

George I, 1714–1727

George II, 1727–1760

George III, 1760–1820

George IV, 1820–1830

William IV, 1830–1837

William IV having no heirs, the British throne passed in 1837 to Victoria, a granddaughter of George III. Though the British family has continued in direct descent from George I, it has dropped the Hanoverian designation and is now known as the House of Windsor. From 1877 to 1947 the British rulers bore the additional title of Emperor (or Empress) of India.

Victoria, 1837–1901

Edward VII, 1901–1910

George V, 1910–1936

Edward VIII, 1936

George VI, 1936–1952

Elizabeth II, 1952–

FRANCE

Valois Line

Louis XI, 1461–1483

Charles VIII, 1483–1498

Louis XII, 1498–1515

Francis I, 1515–1547

Henry II, 1547–1559

Francis II, 1559–1560

Charles IX, 1560–1574

Henry III, 1574–1589

In 1589 the Valois line became extinct, and the throne passed to Henry of Bourbon, a remote descendant of French kings of the fourteenth century.

Bourbon Line

Henry IV, 1589–1610

Louis XIII, 1610–1643

Louis XIV, 1643–1715

Louis XV, 1715–1774

Louis XVI, 1774–1792

The Republic

Convention, 1792–1795

Directory, 1795–1799

Consulate, 1799–1804

The Empire

Napoleon I, 1804–1814, Emperor of the French and King of Italy

Restored Bourbon Line

Louis XVIII, 1814–1824

(Royalists count a Louis XVII, 1793–1795, and date the reign of Louis XVIII from 1795.)

Charles X, 1824–1830

The Revolution of 1830 gave the throne to the Duke of Orleans, descendant of Louis XIII.

Orleans Line

Louis-Philippe, 1830–1848

Second Republic

1848–1852

Second Empire

Napoleon III, 1852–1870, Emperor of the French

Third Republic

1870–1940

Vichy Regime

1940–1944

Provisional Government

1944–1946

Fourth Republic

1946–1958

Fifth Republic

1958–

PRUSSIA (AND GERMANY)

A continuous Hohenzollern line ruled until 1918.

Electors of Brandenburg and Dukes of Prussia

George William, 1619–1640
Frederick William, 1640–1688, the "Great Elector"
Frederick III, 1688–1713

In 1701 Frederick III was permitted by the Holy Roman Emperor to entitle himself King in Prussia, as Frederick I.

Kings of Prussia

Frederick I, 1701–1713
Frederick William I, 1713–1740
Frederick II, the "Great," 1740–1786
Frederick William II, 1786–1797
Frederick William III, 1797–1840
Frederick William IV, 1840–1861
William I, 1861–1888

In 1871 William I took the title of German Emperor.

German Emperors

William I, 1871–1888
Frederick III, 1888
William II, 1888–1918

The German Empire became extinct in 1918. It was succeeded by the

Weimar Republic

1919–1933

(The Weimar Republic is an unofficial title for what was still called the Deutsches Reich, a phrase not easy to translate accurately.)

The Third Reich

1933–1945

(The Third Reich is an unofficial title for the Deutsches Reich under Adolf Hitler.)
Allied Military Government in 1945 was followed by

German Federal Republic (West Germany)

1949–1990

German Democratic Republic (East Germany)

1949–1990

The two Germanys were united in 1990.

German Federal Republic

1990–

SARDINIA (AND ITALY)

In 1720 Victor Amadeus II, Duke of Savoy, took the title of King of Sardinia, having acquired the island of that name. The kingdom was often called Piedmont because of the king's older mainland domain.

Kings of Sardinia

Victor Amadeus II, 1720–1730
Charles Emmanuel III, 1730–1773
Victor Amadeus III, 1773–1796
Charles Emmanuel IV, 1796–1802
Victor Emmanuel I, 1802–1821
Charles Felix, 1821–1831
Charles Albert, 1831–1849
Victor Emmanuel II, 1849–1878

In 1861 Victor Emmanuel II took the title of King of Italy.

Kings of Italy

Victor Emmanuel II, 1861–1878
Humbert I, 1878–1900

Victor Emmanuel III, 1900–1946

Humbert II, 1946

In 1946 the Kingdom of Italy became extinct and was succeeded by the

Italian Republic

1946–

SPAIN

Ferdinand and Isabella, 1479–1504/1516

Isabella died in 1504, but Ferdinand lived until 1516, whereupon the Spanish thrones were inherited by their grandson Charles, who became Charles V of the Holy Roman Empire, but was known in Spain as Charles I.

Habsburg Line

Charles I, 1516–1556

Philip II, 1556–1598

Philip III, 1598–1621

Philip IV, 1621–1665

Charles II, 1665–1700

With Charles II the Spanish Habsburg line became extinct, and the throne passed to the French Bourbon grandson of Louis XIV of France and great-grandson of Philip IV of Spain.

Bourbon Line

Philip V, 1700–1746

Ferdinand VI, 1746–1759

Charles III, 1759–1788

Charles IV, 1788–1808

Bonaparte Line

Joseph, 1808–1813 (brother of Napoleon)

Restored Bourbon Line

Ferdinand VII, 1813–1833

Isabella II, 1833–1868

In 1868 Isabella abdicated; after a regency, and a brief reign by Amadeus I (Savoy), 1871–1873, there was a short-lived First Republic, 1873–1874, succeeded by

Alfonso XII, 1874–1885

Alfonso XIII, 1885–1931

In 1931 a republican revolution unseated Alfonso XIII.

Second Spanish Republic

1931–1936

Spanish Civil War

1936–1939

Regime of General Francisco Franco

1939–1975

Upon the death of Franco the Bourbon family was restored.

Juan Carlos I, 1975–

RUSSIA (AND U.S.S.R.)

Grand Dukes of Moscow

Ivan III, the "Great," 1462–1505

Basil III, 1505–1533

Ivan IV, the "Terrible," 1533–1584

In 1547 Ivan IV took the title of Tsar of Russia.

Tsars of Russia

Ivan IV, the "Terrible," 1547–1584

Theodore I, 1584–1598

Boris Godunov, 1598–1605

Time of Troubles

1604–1613

Romanov Line

Michael, 1613–1645

Alexis, 1645–1676

Theodore II, 1676–1682

Ivan V and Peter I, 1682–1689

Peter I, the "Great," 1689–1725

Catherine I, 1725–1727

Peter II, 1727–1730

Anna, 1730–1740

Ivan VI, 1740–1741

Elizabeth, 1741–1762

Peter III, 1762

Catherine II, the "Great," 1762–1796

Paul, 1796–1801

Alexander I, 1801–1825

Nicholas I, 1825–1855

Alexander II, 1855–1881

Alexander III, 1881–1894

Nicholas II, 1894–1917

In 1917 the tsardom became extinct.

Provisional Government
1917

Communist Revolution
1917

Union of Soviet Socialist Republics
1922–1991

In 1991 the Communist regime ended and the U.S.S.R. dissolved into its component republics (Russia, Ukraine, Belarus, etc.), loosely associated with each other in a Commonwealth of Independent States.

Russian Federation
1991–

Suggestions for Further Reading

The following bibliographical guide is intended for the convenience of students, teachers, and general readers. Although professional students of history may also find it useful, no attempt has been made to provide comprehensive coverage of special areas or topics or to include specialized monographs. Although many older volumes have been included, the aim throughout has been to call attention to recent historical works to which the reader may turn for additional bibliographical guidance. Classification follows the plan of chapters in the present book. For reasons of space, untranslated works in foreign languages have been excluded, as have been general textbooks, articles in periodicals, and (with a few exceptions) primary source materials. When a second date of publication for a book is given without further specification, it is generally the date of the most recent reprinting or reissue. We have also included up-to-date information on useful Web sites that may be consulted for additional information or sources on the themes of each chapter. Such sites often change and evolve, but the Web addresses were all "active" when this book went to press.

Many of the book titles are available in paperback; up-to-date listings may be found in *Books in Print* and in the *Paperback Book Guide for Colleges.*

INTRODUCTION
Guides, Reference Works, and Special Topics
An invaluable bibliographical tool for historical works published prior to 1992 is the American Historical Association's *Guide to Historical Literature* (3rd ed., 2 vols., 1995). Much expanded since its second edition in 1961, the *Guide* consists of 48 sections organized into regional, national, chronological, and topical categories, with coverage from prehistory to the present. It provides annotated entries for thousands of books and articles as well as an introductory essay for each section, all carefully indexed. The *Guide*'s first section, "Theory and Practice in Historical Study," provides a convenient introduction to historical method, historiography, philosophy of history, demography, the many varieties of history, and other important subjects. To keep up with the outpouring of historical books, however, it is important to read the book reviews and listings of new books in the *American Historical Review,* the *Journal of Modern History, The Journal of World History,* the (London) *Times Literary Supplement,* the *New York Review of Books,* and other periodicals, and the book reviews in the daily and weekend press. A valuable source of information on relevant articles is *Historical Abstracts,* which is also available in an electronic database. Many historical resources are now accessible on the Internet, though readers must use such materials with careful assessments of their reliability. For a helpful guide to history on the Internet, organized by thematic categories, readers may consult D. A. Trinkle and S. A. Merriman (eds.), *The History Highway: A 21st-Century Guide to Internet Resources* (rev. 2006).

Brief descriptions of major events and historical figures as well as a chronology of world history may be found in the *Oxford Encyclopedia of World History* (1998); there are also useful chronologies in J. Paxton and E. W. Knappman (eds.), *The Wilson Calendar of World History* (1999), and in P. N. Stearns (ed.), *Encyclopedia of World History: Ancient, Medieval, and Modern* (2001), the most recent edition of an invaluable reference for chronology. Of the many multivolume encyclopedias, the *Encyclopedia Britannica* (rev. 2005, with CD-ROM) remains the most valuable, and articles may also be found electronically at www.britannica.com. Convenient one-volume reference tools are the *Cambridge Encyclopedia* (rev. 2000), and the *Columbia Encyclopedia* (6th ed., 2000), which is now updated regularly in an electronic edition.

Several encyclopedias provide excellent up-to-date articles on themes and events in both world history and European history. See, for example, W. H. McNeill, et al. (eds.), *Berkshire Encyclopedia of World History* (5 vols., 2005), and J. Dewald (ed.), *Europe, 1450–1789: Encyclopedia of the Early Modern World* (6 vols., 2004).

Among historical atlases that place European history in its world setting, G. Parker (ed.), the (London) *Times Atlas of World History* (rev. 1993) and N. Grove (ed.), *National Geographic Society Atlas of World History* (1997) are impressive. Also useful, and periodically updated, are the *Rand McNally Atlas of World History,* Hammond's *Historical Atlas of the World,* and the Penguin Historical Atlas series. Of many geographical atlases one of the best is the *National Geographic Atlas of the World* (8th ed., 2005).

Of multivolume historical series, the New *Cambridge Modern History* (14 vols., 1957–1979) remains useful, though it is no longer "new." The volumes, which will be referred to in the chapters below, contain outstanding contributions by specialists from all over the world. There are other series, to which reference will be made below, under the auspices of various publishers.

Geographical influences on European history are discussed in N. J. G. Pounds, *An Historical Geography of Europe* (3 vols., 1973– 1985) and in the essays in E. Genovese and L. Hochberg (eds.), *Geographic Perspectives in History* (1989). The case for new conceptualizations in geography is made in M. W. Lewis and K. E. Wigen, The *Myth of Continents: A Critique of Metageography* (1997). I. G. Simmons, *Changing the Face of the Earth: Culture, Environment, and History* (rev. 1996) traces the human impact on the planet over the centuries; E. Le Roy Ladurie examines an important subject in *Times of Feast, Times of Famine: A History of Climate since the Year 1000* (trans. 1971).

For the impact of famine, disease, and the movement of peoples, one may read W. H. McNeill, *Plagues and Peoples* (1976) and *The Global Condition: Conquerors, Catastrophes, and Community* (1992); T. McKeown, *The Origins of Human Disease* (1988); A. Crosby, *Germs, Seeds and Animals: Studies in Ecological History* (1994); and K. F. Kiple (ed.), *The Cambridge World History of Human Disease* (1993), a valuable reference work. On cultural advantages and disadvantages in the encounters between peoples, J. Diamond, *Guns, Germs, and Steel: The Fate of Human Societies* (rev. 2005), is rewarding; the same author examines various cultural responses to changing environmental conditions in *Collapse: How Societies Choose to Fail or Succeed* (2005).

Of the many books on military history treating war as a social and human phenomenon, three outstanding studies ranging from earliest times to the present are A. Jones, *The Art of War in the Western World* (1989); R. L. O'Connell, *Of Arms and Men: A History of War, Weapons, and Aggression* (1990); and J. Keegan, *A History of Warfare* (1993); the latter, like others of Keegan's books, is especially noteworthy. Of interest in a related category is M. Walzer, *Just and Unjust Wars* (rev. 1992). The importance of technology is stressed in B. Brodie and F. Brodie, *From Crossbow to H-Bomb* (rev. 1973); W. H. McNeill, *The Pursuit of Power: Technology, Armed Force, and Society since A.D. 1000* (1982); and M. van Creveld, *Technology and War: From 2000 B.C. to the Present* (1988).

A few books of special interest deserve mention here: W. H. McNeill, *The Rise of the West: A History of the Human Community* (rev. 1991), a notable effort to recount the human experience in a global setting,

which has been continued in J. R. McNeill and W. H. McNeill, *The Human Web: A Bird's-eye View of Human History* (2003); E. R. Wolf, *Europe and the People without History* (1982), by an anthropologist, which portrays Western history as seen by non-Western societies in Asia, Africa, and the Americas; P. Kennedy, *The Rise and Fall of the Great Powers: Economic Change and Military Conflict from 1500 to 2000* (1987), which examines the political and economic fortunes of the European nations that successively played the leading role in world affairs in the modern centuries; and J. Barzun, *From Dawn to Decadence: 500 Years of Cultural Life, 1500 to the Present* (2000), a provocative study of Western thought since the sixteenth century. Two wide-ranging efforts at a synthesis of European history are N. Davies, *Europe: A History* (1996), a highly idiosyncratic but challenging work; and J. M. Roberts, *A History of Europe* (1996), a more conventional, thoughtful account. F. Fernández-Armesto, *Millennium: A History of the Last Thousand Years* (1995), is an ambitious attempt at global history. K. A. Appiah and H. L. Gates, Jr., *The Dictionary of Global Culture* (1998) is a pioneer effort to integrate the contributions of Western and non-Western cultures.

Changing Directions in Historical Writings

For a sampling of insights into contemporary trends in historical writing, one may turn to M. Kammen (ed.), The *Past before Us: Contemporary Historical Writing in the United States* (1980); T. K. Rabb and R. I. Rotberg (eds.), *The New History: The 1980s and Beyond* (1982); P. Burke (ed.), *New Perspectives on Historical Writing* (rev. 2001); J. Appleby, L. Hunt, and M. Jacob, *Telling the Truth about History* (1994); G. Iggers, *Historiography in the Twentieth Century: From Scientific Objectivity to the Postmodern Challenge* (1997); L. Kramer and S. Maza, *A Companion to Western Historical Thought* (2002); M. T. Gilderhus, *History and Historians: A Historiographical Introduction* (rev. 2003); and two challenging books by B. Southgate, *History: What and Why? Ancient, Modern, and Postmodern Perspectives* (rev. 2001), and *What Is History For?* (2005).

One of the major contemporary interests of historians has been social history. Stimulated by the *Annales* school of historical writing in France (the name derived from the French periodical *Annales: économies, sociétés, civilisations,* which in 1994 was renamed *Annales: histoire, sciences sociales*), and by newer kinds of working-class history in England, in which E. P. Thompson, *The Making of the English Working Class* (1963), was a pioneer, historians have concerned themselves with a social history distinct from traditional interests in social classes and labor and laboring conditions. They have been examining such subjects as the history of the family, women, sexuality, marriage, the everyday lives and outlook (or *mentalité*) of the urban and rural poor, and popular culture—all studied as history "from the bottom up." Many such works are listed below in the appropriate chapters. An introduction to the newer social history and to popular culture is provided in O. Zung (ed.), *Reliving the Past: The Worlds of Social History* (1985); P. Burke, *Popular Culture in Early Modern Europe* (rev. 1994); C. Mukerjee and M. Schudson (eds.), *Rethinking Popular Culture* (1990); and L. Berlanstein (ed.), *Rethinking Labor History: Essays on Discourse and Class Analysis* (1993). A useful collection of recent contributions to the newer social history is available in R. M. Goldin (ed.), *The Social Dimension of Western Civilization* (4th ed., 1999).

Although the *Annales* historians have contributed a good deal to the newer social history, they have also been important for their emphasis, often quantitative and interdisciplinary, on long-term factors that influence the course of historical change, such as geography, environment, resources, climate, population, diet, and disease, which in their view often merit closer attention than "events." Here F. Braudel, *The Mediterranean and the Mediterranean World in the Age of Philip II* (2 vols., 1949; trans. 1974; rev. and abridged 1 vol. ed., 1992), was a pioneering work; his other books are described in the chapters below.

There has been much attention in recent decades to the history of women. Many of the writings call for reassessments of various historical eras from the viewpoint of women's status in the era and for the fuller integration of the history of women into general history. Contributions to the history of women in Europe and the West may be sampled in R. Bridenthal, S. Stuard, and M. Wiesner (eds.), *Becoming Visible: Women in European History* (rev. 1998), with essays covering ancient times to the twentieth century; M. J. Boxer and J. H. Quataert (eds.), *Connecting Spheres: European Women in a Globalizing World, 1500 to the Present* (rev. 2000), case studies with informative overview chapters; B. S. Anderson and J. P. Zinsser, *A History of Their Own: Women in Europe from Prehistory to the Present* (2 vols.; rev. 2000), thematically organized; and B. G. Smith, *Changing Lives: Women in European History since 1700* (1989), a helpful narrative account. G. Duby and M. Perrot (gen. eds.), *A History of Women in the West* (trans. 1992–1994), is a multivolume history from ancient times to the present. Important theoretical perspectives on the role of gender in historical understanding can be found in *Women, History and Theory: The Essays of Joan Kelly* (1984); J. W. Scott, *Gender and the Poltics of History* (rev. 1999); and B. G. Smith, *The Gender of History: Men, Women, and Historical Practice* (1998). The role of gender in both ancient and modern global history is examined in B. G. Smith (ed.), *Women's History in Global Perspective* (2004). G. Lerner provides many insights into women and history in *The Creation of Patriarchy* (1986) and *The Creation of Feminist Con-*

sciousness: From the Middle Ages to 1870 (1993). Diverse collections of documents on women's history can be found in J. C. Fout and E. Reimer (eds.), *European Women: A Documentary History, 1789–1945* (1980); J. O'Faolain and L. Martines (eds.), *Not in God's Image: Women in History from the Greeks to the Victorians* (1973); E. O. Hillerstein, L. P. Hume, and K. M. Offen (eds.), *Victorian Women: Women's Lives in England, France, and the United States* (1981); and S. G. Bell and K. M. Offen (eds.), *Women, the Family, and Freedom: The Debate in Documents* (2 vols.; 1983).

Psychological approaches to the writing of history are explored in S. Friedländer, *History and Psychoanalysis* (trans. 1978); P. Loewenberg, *Decoding the Past: The Psychohistorical Approach* (1982); P. Gay, *Freud for Historians* (1985); and the more theoretical work of D. LaCapra, *History in Transit: Experience, Identity, Critical Theory* (2004). For an introduction to the quantitative analysis of historical data, one may turn to K. H. Jarausch and K. A. Hardy, *Quantitative Methods for Historians: A Guide to Research, Data, and Statistics* (1991). Two useful introductions to a crucial component of contemporary historical work are J. L. Reiff, *Structuring the Past: The Use of Computers in History* (1991) and D. I. Greenstein, *A Historian's Guide to Computing* (1994). There is much practical information on historical research and writing in J. Barzun and H. F. Graff, *The Modern Researcher* (rev. 2004).

The tapping of neglected sources through the methods of oral history is examined in P. Thompson, *The Voice of the Past: Oral History* (1978); D. Henige, *Oral Historiography* (1982); D. K. Dunaway and W. K. Baum (eds.), *Oral History: An Interdisciplinary Anthology* (1984); and K. Howarth, *Oral History* (1999). A contemporary medium is explored in J. E. O'Connor (ed.), *Image as Artifact: The Historical Analysis of Film and Television* (1990); R. Rosenstone (ed.), *Revisioning History: Film and the Construction of a New Past* (1995) and *Visions of the Past: The Challenge of Film to Our Idea of History* (1995).

Changing assessments of cultural and intellectual history, borrowing from philosophy, linguistics, anthropology, and literary criticism, which may remain elusive for many readers, may be sampled in L. Hunt (ed.), *The New Cultural History* (1989); V. E. Bonnell and L. Hunt (eds.), *Beyond the Cultural Turn: New Directions in the Study of Society and Culture* (1999); D. LaCapra, *Rethinking Intellectual History: Texts, Contexts, Language* (1983); C. Ginzburg, *Clues, Myths, and the Historical Method* (trans. 1992); D. R. Kelley, *The Descent of Ideas: The History of Intellectual History* (2002); and two helpful books by P. Burke, *Varieties of Cultural History* (1997) and *What Is Cultural History?* (2004).

Some books critical of the trends in historical writing that have emerged since the 1970s include

J. Barzun, *Clio and the Doctors: Psychohistory, Quantohistory, and History* (1974); J. H. Hexter, *On Historians: Some of the Makers of Modern History* (1979); T. S. Hamerow, *Reflections on History and Historians* (1987); G. R. Elton, *Return to Essentials: Some Reflections on the Present State of Historical Study* (1993); G. Himmelfarb, *The New History and the Old* (1987) and *On Looking into the Abyss: Untimely Thoughts on Culture and Society* (1994); and E. Fox-Genovese and E. Lasch-Quinn (eds.), *Reconstructing History: The Emergence of a New Historical Society* (1999). Two probing accounts of the historical profession in the United States, with insights into past and present historiographical debates, are J. Higham, *History: Professional Scholarship in America* (rev. 1989); and P. Novick, *That Noble Dream: The "Objectivity Question" and the American Historical Profession* (1988).

On the relationship of history to other disciplines and its own distinctive role, one may turn to such varied explorations as E. H. Carr, *What Is History?* (1962); P. Gay, *Style in History* (1974); L. Gottschalk, *Understanding History* (rev. 1969); A. Marwick, *The Nature of History* (rev. 1989); L. Gossman, *Between History and Literature* (1990); D. LaCapra, *History and Criticism* (1985); and H. V. White, *Metahistory: The Historical Imagination in Nineteenth-Century Europe* (1973). Of special interest for the relationship of the discipline to the social sciences are P. Burke, *History and Social Theory* (1993); T. J. McDonald (ed.), *The Historic Turn in the Human Sciences* (1996); J. Elster, *The Cement of Society: A Study of Social Order* (1991) and *Nuts and Bolts from the Social Sciences* (1991); and J. Gaddis, *The Landscape of History: How Historians Map the Past* (2002).

Among thoughtful reflections by historians who have themselves made notable contributions to the writing of history, the following may be suggested: F. Gilbert, *History: Choice and Commitment* (1977); W. H. McNeill, *Mythistory and Other Essays* (1986); C. Vann Woodward, *Thinking Back: The Perils of Writing History* (1986) and *The Future of the Past* (1989); L. Stone, *The Past and the Present Revisited* (1987); D. Cannadine, *The Pleasures of the Past* (1989); W. J. Bouwsma, *A Usable Past* (1990); M. Beloff, *An Historian in the Twentieth Century* (1992); G. Lerner, *Why History Matters: Life and Thought* (1997); C. E. Schorske, *Thinking with History* (1998); and E. J. Hobsbawm, *Interesting Times: A Twentieth-Century Life* (2002). An insightful study of how historians write about themselves can be found in J. D. Popkin, *History, Historians, and Autobiography* (2005). Other interesting historical reflections appear in two collections of interviews with contemporary historians: H. Abelove (ed.), *Visions of History* (1984), and R. Adelson (ed.), *Speaking of History: Conversations with Historians* (1997).

Useful Web Sites

For interactive historical maps, readers might consult *Mapping History: The Darkwing Atlas Project* at http://darkwing.uoregon.edu/~atlas/, a well-designed site that includes maps and images of Europe, the Americas, and global history. Useful chronological information can be found at the *WebChron Project*, http://campus.northpark.edu/history/WebChron/, and at *World History: Hyper History*, www.hyperhistory .com/online_n2/History_n2/a.html. An accessible, general introduction to historical timelines, maps, and images is also available through the site of the *History Channel* at www.historychannel.com/. Readers might also visit the site of the *American Historical Association* for reports on developments in contemporary historical scholarship and teaching, www.historians.org.

1. THE RISE OF EUROPE
Prehistoric and Ancient Times

For prehistory, the reader may wish to consult B. Fagan, *People of the Earth: An Introduction to World Prehistory* (rev. 2004); P. Phillips, *The Prehistory of Europe* (1980); T. Champion et al., *Prehistoric Europe* (1984); and B. Cunliffe (ed.), *The Oxford Illustrated Prehistory of Europe* (1994). Of special interest are M. R. Ehrenberg, *Women in Prehistory* (1989) and W. W. Barber, *Women's Work: The First 20,000 Years: Women, Cloth, and Society in Early Times* (1994).

Informative accounts for the ancient world include T. B. Jones, *From the Tigris to the Tiber* (rev. 1983); C. G. Starr, *A History of the Ancient World* (rev. 1991); and H. Howe and R. T. Howe, *The Ancient World* (1987). For Mesopotamia and Egypt one may read J. Hawkes, *The First Great Civilizations* (1973); H. Saggs, *The Greatness That Was Babylon* (1991); M. A. Murray, *The Splendor That Was Egypt* (rev. 2004); and C. Freeman, *Egypt, Greece, and Rome: Civilizations of the Ancient Mediterranean* (1999).

Excellent summaries of Greek and Roman antiquity, from the eighth century B.C. through the second century A.D., are found in J. Boardman, J. Griffin, and O. Murray (eds.), *The Oxford History of the Classical World* (1986); other valuable accounts of the ancient world include L. de Blois and R. J. van der Spek, *An Introduction to the Ancient World* (1997) and M. Grant, *The Founders of the Western World: A History of Greece and Rome* (1991). There are rewarding insights in M. I. Finley's many writings on Greece and Rome, among them *The Legacy of Greece: A New Appraisal* (1981) and *Politics in the Ancient World* (1983). An outstanding study of women in Greece and Rome is S. B. Pomeroy, *Goddesses, Whores, Wives, and Slaves: Women in Classical Antiquity* (1975, 1995); one may also read S. Blundell, *Women in Ancient Greece* (1995).

In addition to numerous surveys of classical Greece, the reader will profit from S. B. Pomeroy et al., *Ancient Greece: A Political, Social, and Cultural History* (1999). For Alexander the Great, one should read P. Green, *Alexander of Macedon, 356–323 B.C.* (1974, 1991). On the rise and fall of the Hellenistic civilization that Alexander helped create, one may read E. S. Gruen, *The Hellenistic World and the Coming of Rome* (2 vols., 1984); P. Green's critical *Alexander to Actium: The Historical Evolution of the Hellenistic Age* (1991); and G. W. Bowersock, *Hellenism in Late Antiquity* (1990), a more sympathetic brief assessment.

Among many surveys of Rome and Roman civilization, one may suggest H. H. Scullard, *A History of the Roman World, 753–146 B.C.* (rev. 2002); and for all aspects of Roman society, see K. Christ, *The Romans: An Introduction to Their History and Civilization* (trans. 1984) and M. T. Boatwright, D. J. Gargola, and R. J. A. Talbert, *The Romans: From Village to Empire* (2004). Earlier Roman history is examined in H. MacDonald, *Republican Rome* (1966) and C. Nicolet, *The World of the Citizen in Republican Rome* (trans. 1980). Books on the Empire include P. Garnsey and R. Saller, *The Roman Empire: Economy, Society and Culture* (1987) and C. M. Wells, *The Roman Empire* (rev. 1992). There is also an important account of Rome's relations with other ancient cultures in P. Wells, *The Barbarians Speak: How the Conquered Peoples Shaped Roman Europe* (1999).

For the coming of Christianity, comprehensive introductions may be found in W. H. C. Frend, *The Rise of Christianity* (1984) and in R. A. Fletcher, *The Barbarian Conversion: From Paganism to Christianity* (1998). Early Christianity's interaction with both the politics and philosophy of the ancient world is examined in C. Freeman, *The Closing of the Western Mind: The Rise of Faith and the Fall of Reason* (2002). The many efforts to reconstruct the historical Jesus include A. N. Wilson, *Jesus* (1992) and J. D. Crossan, *Jesus: A Revolutionary Biography* (1994). On St. Augustine and his times, there is a sensitive account by P. Brown, *Augustine of Hippo* (rev. 2000) and a lively appraisal by G. Wills, *Saint Augustine* (1999). For all aspects of theology there is the magisterial work of J. Pelikan, *The Christian Tradition* (5 vols., 1971–1989), the first three volumes of which relate to the Middle Ages.

The Middle Ages: The Formation of Europe

Among many surveys of the medieval era as a whole, B. Tierney and S. Painter, *Western Europe in the Middle Ages, 300–1475* (rev. 1999); and C. W. Hollister and J. M. Bennett, *Medieval Europe: A Short History* (rev. 2006) are excellent. A successful effort emphasizing social history is E. Peters, *Europe and The Middle Ages* (rev. 1997). G. Holmes (ed.), *The Oxford Illustrated History of Medieval Europe* (1988), available also in abridged form (1992), is a collaborative work of distinction and J. Le Goff, *Medieval Civiliza-*

tion, 400–1500 (trans. 1988), is a remarkable synthesis by a leading French historian of the *Annales* school. Historians who have reshaped our understanding of the medieval era are examined in N. Cantor, *Reinventing the Middle Ages* (1992).

Fundamental to the reassessment of Europe's emergence in the early medieval centuries is R. W. Southern, *The Making of the Middle Ages* (1953, 1993). Another important work of synthesis is P. Brown, *The Rise of Western Christendom: Triumph and Diversity, A.D. 200–1000* (rev. 2003), building on the author's numerous other works on late antiquity. Also available are D. Hay, *Europe: The Emergence of an Idea* (rev. 1968); G. Barraclough, *The Crucible of Europe: The Ninth and Tenth Centuries in European History* (1976); C. Brooks, *Europe in the Central Middle Ages, 916–1154* (rev. 2000); and G. Duby, *The Making of the Christian West, 980–1140* (trans. 1968). For the era of Charlemagne one may read P. Geary, *Before France and Germany: The Creation and Transformation of the Merovingian Empire* (1988); R. Collins, *Charlemagne* (1998); M. Becker, *Charlemagne* (trans. 2003); and P. Riché, *Daily Life in the World of Charlemagne* (trans. 1978).

The Byzantine Empire and the Islamic World

There are many books on the two civilizations in the Middle East that flourished while Europe in the early medieval centuries was in the so-called Dark Ages. For the Byzantine, or Eastern Roman, Empire, one may read the comprehensive, scholarly account by W. Treadgold, *A History of the Byzantine State and Society* (1998), and a shorter work by the same author, *A Concise History of Byzantium* (2001); T. E. Gregory, *A History of Byzantium* (2005); and J. J. Norwich, *A Short History of Byzantium* (1997). The essence of Byzantine culture is captured in H. C. Evans (ed.), *The Glory of Byzantine Art and Culture of the Byzantine Medieval Era, A.D. 893–1261* (1997). The end of the empire is graphically described in S. Runciman, *The Fall of Constantinople, 1453* (1965). Valuable for all aspects of Byzantine civilization is A. P. Kazhdan (ed.), *The Oxford Dictionary of Byzantium* (3 vols., 1991).

Good starting points for the study of Islam include B. Lewis, *Islam in History: Ideas, People and Events in the Middle East* (rev. 1993), *Islam and the West* (1993), and his many other writings; W. M. Watt, *The Majesty That Was Islam: The Islamic World, 661–1100* (rev. 1990); and M. G. S. Hodgson, *The Venture of Islam: Conscience and History in a World Civilization* (3 vols., 1974), from the beginnings to the mid-twentieth century. Accounts of the founder of Islam include T. W. M. Watt, *Muhammad: Prophet and Statesman* (1961), a condensation of a detailed two-volume study; M. H. Haykal, *The Life of Muhammad* (trans. 1976); M. Rodinson, *Muhammad* (trans.

1971, 2002); and K. Armstrong, *Muhammad: A Biography of the Prophet* (1993). The historical legacy of early Islam is examined in R. Asian, *No God but God: The Evolution of Islam* (2005). The best introduction to Arab history is A. Hourani, *A History of the Arab Peoples* (rev. 2002); other informative accounts include B. Lewis, *The Arabs in History* (rev. 1993); P. Mansfield, *The Arabs* (rev. 1985); and M. Rodinson, *The Arabs* (1981). There are many interesting cultural insights in R. Bulliett, *The Camel and the Wheel* (1975), while S. N. Fisher and W. Ochsenwal, *The Middle East: A History* (rev. 1997) studies the region from pre-Islamic times on. D. J. Geanakoplos focuses on the interrelationships of the three civilizations *in Medieval Western Civilization and the Byzantine and Islamic Worlds: Interaction of Three Cultures* (1979), while M. L. Colish, *Medieval Foundations of the Western Intellectual Tradition, 400–1400* (1998), provides a valuable comparative survey of the three cultures.

Readers can find contrasting accounts of European views of Islamic societies in E. Said, *Orientalism* (1978, 1995), and M. Rodinson, *Europe and the Mystique of Islam* (trans. 1987); and a helpful, brief overview is available in R. M. Easton, *Islamic History as Global History* (1990).

The Middle Ages: Economy, Politics, Society

For economic development, the pioneering books by H. Pirenne on the origins of the cities, revival of trade, and other social and economic developments still merit reading, but they have been superseded by more recent research. Among useful histories are R. S. Lopez, *The Commercial Revolution of the Middle Ages, 950–1350* (rev. 1976); G. Duby, *The Growth of the European Economy* (1974); and J. L. Bolton, *The Medieval Economy, 1150–1500* (1980). Also informative are N. J. G. Pounds, *An Economic History of Medieval Europe* (rev. 1994); C. M. Cipolla, *Before the Industrial Revolution: European Society and Economy, 1000–1700* (rev. 1980); and J. Day, *Medieval Market Economy* (1987). The volumes in the collaborative *Cambridge Economic History of Europe* (1941 ff.) provide authoritative but highly specialized accounts. The second volume, M. M. Postan and E. Miller (eds.), *Trade and Industry in the Middle Ages* (1952, 1987), was thoroughly revised for its new edition. L. White, Jr., *Medieval Technology and Social Change* (1962) and *Medieval Religion and Technology* (1978) illustrate some of the scholarship which has dispelled the image of the early medieval years as technologically stagnant.

E. Ennen, *The Medieval Town* (trans. 1979), incorporates the considerable research since Pirenne, but it may be supplemented by D. Nichols, *The Growth of the Medieval City* (1997); and K. D. Lilley, *Urban Life in the Middle Ages, 1000–1450* (2002). On feudalism and manorialism, useful introductions are available in F. L. Ganshof, *Feudalism* (rev. 1964), and J. S. Critch-

ley, *Feudalism* (1978). An imaginative effort at comparing ideal models and material realities is G. Duby, *The Three Orders: Feudal Society Imagined* (trans. 1980). M. Bloch's classic contributions include *Feudal Society* (1938–40; trans. 1961) and *Slavery and Serfdom in the Middle Ages* (trans. 1975).

Studies of the emergent monarchical states include B. Guenée, *States and Rulers in Later Medieval Europe* (trans. 1985), and S. Reynolds, *Kingdoms and Communities in Western Europe, 900–1300* (rev. 1997), which stresses cultural bonds. An important collaborative work is C. Tilley (ed.), *The Formation of National States in Western Europe* (1975). Of the many books available for the national formations the following are a sampling. For Germany: G. Barraclough, *Origins of Modern Germany* (rev. 1984); and T. Reuter, *Germany in the Early Middle Ages, c. 800–1056* (1991); For England: M. T. Clanchy, *England and Its Rulers, 1066–1272* (rev. 1998); and T. Rowley, *The High Middle Ages, 1200–1540* (1986) in the *Making of Britain* series. For Spain: A. MacKay, *Spain in the Middle Ages: From Frontier to Empire 100–1500* (1989); and there is valuable information in L. P. Harvey, *Islamic Spain, 1250 to 1500* (1990). For France: J. Dunbabin, *France in the Making, 843–1180* (rev. 2000); E. M. Hallam, *Capetian France, 987–1328* (1983); and E. James, *The Origins of France: From Clovis to the Capetians, 500–1000* (1980). For the Italian city-states one may read D. Waley, *The Italian City Republics* (rev. 1988) and P. J. Jones, *The Italian City-State: From Commune to Signoria* (1997).

Social History

The first two volumes of *A History of Private Life*, P. Veyne (ed.), *From Pagan Rome to Byzantium* (1987) and G. Duby (ed.), *Revelations of the Medieval World* (1988), explore aspects of social history, as do R. Fossier, *Peasant Life in the Medieval West* (trans. 1988) and H. W. Goetz, *Life in the Middle Ages: From the Seventh to the Thirteenth Century* (1993). For women in the Middle Ages, their constraints and opportunities, one may read A. Lucas, *Women in the Middle Ages: Religion, Marriage, and Letters* (1984); S. Shahar, *The Fourth Estate: A History of Women in the Middle Ages* (1984); D. Herlihy, *Opera Muliebria: Women at Work in Medieval Europe* (1990); E. Ennen, *The Medieval Woman* (1990); and a useful, concise summary by J. M. Bennett, *Medieval Women in Modern Perspective* (2000). Informative collections of essays include J. M. Bennett et al. (eds.), *Sisters and Workers in the Middle Ages* (1989); M. Erler and M. Kowaleski (eds.), *Women and Power in the Middle Ages* (1988); M. Erler and M. Kowaleski (eds.), *Gendering the Master Narrative: Women and Power in the Middle Ages* (2003); and J. M. Bennett and A. M. Froide (eds.), *Single Women in the European Past* (1999). The transformation of the household is masterfully explored in D. Herlihy, *Medieval Households* (1985), which may be supplemented by the important works of B. A. Hanawalt, *The Ties That Bound: Peasant Families in Medieval England* (1986) and *Of Good and Ill Repute: Gender and Social Control in Medieval England* (1998). Special subjects are explored in C. Brooke, *The Medieval Idea of Marriage* (1989), in J. A. Brundage, *Law, Sex, and Christian Society in Medieval Europe* (1990), and in N. Orme, *Medieval Children* (2001).

The Middle Ages: Intellect and Piety

Intellectual developments and scholasticism are discussed in many of the books already cited but are also examined with insight in R. C. Dales, *The Intellectual Life of Western Europe* (rev. 1992); B. B. Price, *Medieval Thought: An Introduction* (1992); M. L. Colish, *Medieval Foundations of the Western Intellectual Tradition, 400–1400* (1997); and J. Pelikan, *The Growth of Medieval Theology, 600–1300* (1981), Vol. III of his *The Christian Tradition* referred to earlier. For political thought and philosophy one may also turn to J. B. Morrall, *Political Thought in Medieval Times* (rev. 1980); and W. Ullman, *A History of Political Thought in the Middle Ages* (1965).

For the universities one may read C. H. Haskins, The *Rise of the Universities* (1923, 1979); H. Rashdall's monumental *The Universities of Europe in the Middle Ages* (3 vols., 1895; revised and reissued 1936, 1987); and H. de Ridder-Symoens (ed.), *Universities in the Middle Ages* (1992). For ancient and medieval scientific activities as background to the emergence of modern science, an excellent synthesis is D. C. Lindberg, *The Beginnings of Western Science: The European Scientific Tradition in Philosophical, Religious, and Institutional Context, 600 B.C. to A.D. 1450* (1992).

Valuable introductions to the church as an institution are M. Deanesley, *A History of the Medieval Church, 590–1500* (rev. 1969); C. Morris, *The Papal Monarchy: The Western Church from 1050 to 1250* (1989); J. Lynch. *The Medieval Church: A Brief History* (1992); and I. W. Frank, *A History of the Medieval Church* (trans. 1995). For the popes from the earliest times on, a wealth of information is available in J. N. D. Kelly (ed.), *The Oxford Dictionary of Popes* (1986); and in E. Duffy, *Saints and Sinners: A History of the Popes* (rev. 2002); and for all aspects of church history one may turn to J. McManners, *The Oxford Illustrated History of Christianity* (1990). Of special interest is J. Sayers, *Innocent III: Leader of Europe, 1198–1216* (1994).

For the lives of the saints and the society in which they lived, one may read D. Weinstein and R. M. Bell, *Saints and Society: The Two Worlds of Western Christendom, 1000–1700* (1983). Other insights into religious life may be obtained from C. Brooke, *The Monastic World, 1000–1300* (1974), and C. H. Laurence, *Medieval Monasticism* (1989).

For the treatment of heresy in medieval society one may read E. Le Roy Ladurie, *Montaillou: The Promised Land of Error* (trans. 1978); and E. Peters, *Inquisition* (1988). Peters has also written a broad study, *Torture* (rev. 1996), which includes its incorporation into medieval law and practice. A sweeping indictment of medieval intolerance toward "outside" groups is presented in R. I. Moore, *The Formation of a Persecuting Society: Power and Deviance in Western Europe, 950–1250* (1987), while scholarly explorations of medieval attitudes toward such groups can be found in J. Boswell, *Christianity, Sexual Tolerance, and Homosexuality: Gay People in Western Europe from the Beginning of the Christian Era to the Fourteenth Century* (1980). On medieval Jewry one may turn to K. R. Stow, *Alienated Minority: The Jews of Medieval Latin Europe* (1992); L. B. Glick, *Abraham's Heirs: Jews and Christians in Medieval Europe* (1999); and R. Chazan, *Fashioning Jewish Identity in Medieval Western Christendom* (2004). The roots of anti-Semitism are explored in R. S. Wistrich, *Anti-Semitism: The Longest Hatred* (1992).

The Crusades

The expansion and conquests of medieval Europeans are described in J. R. S. Phillips, *The Medieval Expansion of Europe* (rev. 1998), and in R. Bartlett, *The Making of Europe: Conquest, Colonization, and Cultural Change, 950–1350* (1993), an important synthesis. The Crusades may be approached through J. R. Smith, *The Crusades: A Short History* (1987); T. F. Madden, *The New Concise History of the Crusades* (rev. 2005); T. Asbridge, *The First Crusade: A New History: The Roots of Conflict between Christianity and Islam* (2005); the detailed, colorful S. Runciman, *A History of the Crusades* (3 vols., 1951–54, 1987); H. E. Mayer, *The Crusades* (rev. and trans. 1988); and the collaborative multivolume K. M. Setton (ed.), *History of the Crusades* (6 vols., 1955–90). The assault on Jewish communities in the Rhineland as a consequence of the First Crusade is carefully examined in R. Chazan, *European Jewry and the First Crusade* (1987), while the twelfth-century Muslim foe of the Crusaders is studied in A. S. Ehrenkrentz, *Saladin* (1978).

Useful Web Sites

A vast range of documents and modern scholarly works on the ancient and medieval world can be found at numerous university-sponsored Web sites; see, for example, the *Ancient World Mapping Center* at the University of North Carolina, www.unc.edu/awmc/; the *Perseus Digital Library* at Tufts University, www.perseus.tufts.edu/cache/perscoll_Greco-Roman.html; and the *Internet Ancient History Sourcebook* at Fordham University, www.fordham.edu/halsall/ancient/asbook2.html, where readers will also find an excellent *Internet Medieval Sourcebook*, www.fordham.edu/

halsall/sbook.html. Other comprehensive sites focusing on the medieval era include *The Labyrinth* at Georgetown University, http://labyrinth.georgetown.edu/, which provides helpful information on Islam and Byzantium as well as every aspect of medieval Europe; and valuable resources on medieval women are available at the Haverford College library site, *Feminae: Medieval Women and Gender Index*, www.haverford.edu/library/reference/mshcaus/mfi/mfi.html.

2. THE UPHEAVAL IN WESTERN CHRISTENDOM, 1300–1560

Two books by J. R. Hale, *The Civilization of Europe in the Renaissance* (1993) and *Renaissance Europe, 1480–1520* (rev. 2000), are outstanding. Other helpful overviews for these years encompassing the later Middle Ages, the Renaissance, and the Reformation include S. E. Ozment, *The Age of Reform, 1250–1550: An Intellectual and Religious History of Late Medieval and Reformation Europe* (1980); H. F. Koenigsberger, *Early Modern Europe, 1500–1789* (1987); E. F. Rice, Jr., and A. Grafton, *The Foundations of Early Modern Europe* (rev. 1993); and D. Nicholas, *The Transformation of Europe, 1300–1600* (1999). There are informative chapters in G. R. Potter (ed.), *The Renaissance, 1493–1520* (rev. 1991) and G. R. Elton (ed.), *The Reformation, 1520–1599* (rev. 1990), Vols. I and II of the *New Cambridge Modern History*. T. K. Rabb, *Renaissance Lives: Portraits of an Age* (rev. 2001) provides vivid accounts of notable figures. War and diplomacy are explored in G. Mattingly, *Renaissance Diplomacy* (1971); M. S. Anderson, *The Rise of Modern Diplomacy, 1450–1919* (1993); and J. R. Hale, *War and Society in Renaissance Europe, 1450–1620* (1985, 1998); while E. L. Eisenstein explores the printing press as a direct and indirect agent of cultural change in *The Printing Revolution in Early Modern Europe* (1984).

Much newer social history has centered on the early modern centuries. Here P. Burke, *Popular Culture in Early Modern Europe* (rev. 1994), ranging in time from 1500 to 1800, is a fundamental analysis. C. Ginzburg, *The Cheese and the Worms: The Cosmos of a Sixteenth-Century Miller* (trans. 1980) reconstructs the mentality of an obscure Italian miller of the age. N. Z. Davis, *Society and Culture in Early Modern France* (1975) illuminates the religious and other beliefs of nonliterate peasants and *The Return of Martin Guerre* (1983) recounts a fascinating episode in village life. R. Chartier (ed.), *Passions of the Renaissance* (1988), the third volume of the *History of Private Life* series, opens the door to aspects of life among all classes in this era. G. Huppert, *After the Black Death: A Social History of Early Modern Europe* (rev. 1998) is a valuable study. Other aspects of social history are examined in K. von Greyerz (ed.), *Religion and Society in Early Modern Europe,*

1500–1800 (1984) and in R. Jütte, *Poverty and Deviance in Early Modern Europe* (1994), a volume in the *New Approaches to European History* series. The ambivalent position of women in the Renaissance is ably conveyed in M. L. King, *Women of the Renaissance* (1991), an outstanding study; I. Maclean, *The Renaissance Notion of Women* (1980); O. Hufton, *The Prospect Before Her: A History of Women in Western Europe, 1500–1800* (1995), and M. E. Wiesner, *Women and Gender in Early Modern Europe* (rev. 2000), also a volume in the *New Approaches to European History* series.

Disasters of the Fourteenth Century

Two brief surveys of the era are R. E. Lerner, *The Age of Adversity: The Fourteenth Century* (1968) and M. McKisack, *The Fourteenth Century, 1307–1399* (1959, 1991). B. W. Tuchman, *A Distant Mirror: The Calamitous Fourteenth Century* (1978) is a vivid account of war, disease, and religious schism written for the general reader. G. Leff, *The Dissolution of the Medieval Outlook: An Essay on Intellectual Change in the Fourteenth Century* (1976), despite the title, stresses the continuity of medieval thought. J. Kaye, *Economy and Nature in the Fourteenth Century: Money, Market Exchange, and the Emergence of Scientific Thought* (1998) explores the influence of economic life on early scientific thought. The growing restlessness within the church before the Reformation is described in F. Oakley, *The Western Church in the Later Middle Ages* (1979) and R. N. Swanson, *Church and Society in Late Medieval England* (1989). Heresies of the period may be examined in H. Kaminsky, *A History of the Hussite Revolution* (1967); in R. Rex, *The Lollards* (2002); and in M. Lambert, *Medieval Heresy: Popular Movements From the Gregorian Reform to the Reformation* (rev. 2002).

The devastating fourteenth-century plague that swept Europe and other parts of the globe from 1347 to 1351 is examined in W. H. McNeill, *Plagues and Peoples* (1976), cited earlier; R. S. Gottfried, *The Black Death: Natural and Human Disaster in Medieval Europe* (1983); D. Herlihy, *The Black Death and the Transformation of the West* (1997); N. F. Cantor, *In the Wake of the Plague* (2001); J. Kelley, *The Great Mortality: An Intimate History of the Black Death* (2005); and S. K. Cohn, *The Black Death Transformed: Disease and Culture in Early Renaissance Europe* (2002), which challenges the usual physiological explanations for the plague. A useful work, which includes documents from the era, is J. Alberth, *The Black Death: The Great Mortality of 1348–1350: A Brief History with Documents* (2005). The long war between France and England over the years 1337 to 1453 may be studied in A. Curry, *The Hundred Years War* (rev. 2003). The works by D. Seward, *The Hundred Years War: The English in France, 1337–1453* (rev. 1999) and C. Allmand, *The Hundred Years' War: England and France at War, c. 1300–c. 1450* (1988) explore the war's impact on both countries. Of the large literature on the "Maid of Orléans" a recent brief account with fresh interpretations is M. Gordon, *Joan of Arc* (2000) in the *Penguin Lives* series.

For the *jacqueries* and other popular revolts one may read M. Mollat and P. Wolff, *The Popular Revolutions of the Late Middle Ages* (trans. 1972) and G. Fourquin, *The Anatomy of Popular Rebellion in the Middle Ages* (trans. 1978).

The phenomenon of witchcraft in the early modern centuries between 1450 and 1750 has understandably attracted a good deal of attention. During those years more than 100,000 people, mainly but not exclusively women, were prosecuted in secular and ecclesiastical courts, and many were put to death. To understand the phenomenon, K. Thomas, *Religion and the Decline of Magic* (1971) is of fundamental importance, but one may also turn to J. Klaits, *Servants of Satan: The Age of the Witch Hunts* (1985); C. Larner, *Witchcraft and Religion: The Politics of Popular Belief* (1985); C. Ginzburg, *Ecstasies: Deciphering the Witches' Sabbath* (1991); and B. P. Levack, *The Witch-Hunt in Early Modern Europe* (rev. 1995), which synthesizes the literature. Available also are M. D. Bailey, *Battling Demons: Witchcraft, Heresy, and Reform in the Later Middle Ages* (2003); G. K. Waite, *Heresy, Magic, and Witchcraft in Early Modern Europe* (2003); W. Behringer, *Witches and Witch-Hunts: A Global History* (2004); and R. Briggs, *Witches and Neighbors: The Social and Cultural Context of European Witchcraft* (1997), based on a wide range of materials from all parts of Europe.

The Renaissance in Italy

In addition to the general accounts already cited, one may turn for all aspects of the Renaissance to the now-classic study by M. P. Gilmore, *The World of Humanism, 1453–1517* (1952, 1983). The concept of the "Renaissance" itself, which is still debated, was skillfully explored in classic works by J. Burckhardt, *The Civilization of the Renaissance in Italy* (1860, 1990) and W. K. Ferguson, *The Renaissance in Historical Thought: Five Centuries of Interpretation* (1948). Readers will also find important interpretations of Renaissance culture and its enduring influence in W. J. Bouwsma, *The Waning of the Renaissance* (2000). For the quickening of activities in the Italian city-states one turns to D. Hay and J. Law, *Italy in the Age of the Renaissance, 1380–1530* (1989); P. Burke, *The Italian Renaissance: Culture and Society in Italy* (rev. 1999); F. Braudel, *Out of Italy, 1450–1650* (trans. 1992), by the *Annales* historian; J. Najemy (ed.), *Italy in the Renaissance, 1300–1550* (2004); E. Welch, *Art and Society in Italy, 1350–1500* (1997); and I. Rowland, *From Heaven to Arcadia: The Sacred and the Profane in the Renaissance* (2004). The revived interest in the classics is examined in R. Weiss, *The Renaissance Discov-*

ery of Classical Antiquity (1969, 1988), and the philosophical debates of the time are examined in B. P. Copenhaver and C. B. Schmitt, *Renaissance Philosophy* (1992), and in A. Levi, *Renaissance and Reformation: The Intellectual Genesis* (2002). Some additional insights into Renaissance culture are offered in L. Jardine, *Worldly Goods: A New History of the Renaissance* (1997). The fusion of politics and humanism (or "civic humanism") is traced in a pioneering work by H. Baron, *The Crisis of the Early Italian Renaissance: Civic Humanism and Republican Liberty in an Age of Classicism and Tyranny* (1955, 1966). The relationship of politics and cultural life is also graphically portrayed in L. Martines, *Power and Imagination: City States in Renaissance Italy* (1979); and the interaction between commercial and intellectual life is explored in T. Parks, *Medici Money: Banking, Metaphysics, and Art in Fifteenth-Century Florence* (2005). A famous Renaissance prelate is portrayed in C. Shaw, *Julius II: The Warrior Pope* (1993).

Of the large literature on Machiavelli, there is a brief, insightful study by J. R. Hale, *Machiavelli and Renaissance Italy* (1960) and a more recent study by the intellectual historian Q. Skinner, *Machiavelli: A Very Short Introduction* (2000); S. de Grazia, *Machiavelli in Hell* (1989), an intriguing intellectual biography; A. J. Parel, *The Machiavellian Cosmos* (1992); and M. Viroli, *Machiavelli* (1998). A provocative study of political thought and discourse as influenced by the Renaissance from the fifteenth to the eighteenth centuries is J. G. A. Pocock, *The Machiavellian Moment: Florentine Political Thought and the Atlantic Republican Tradition* (rev. 2003). J. R. Hale (ed.), *A Concise Encyclopedia of the Italian Renaissance* (1981) is a convenient reference tool.

Numerous studies focusing on each of the Italian city-states have helped illuminate the world of humanism, of which only a few titles can be cited here. Much of the focus has been on Florence, for which G. Brucker, *Renaissance Florence* (rev. 1983) and G. Holmes, *The Florentine Enlightenment, 1400–50* (1992) are the most helpful. Other informative studies include J. R. Hale, *Florence and the Medici: The Pattern of Control* (1978), an especially insightful account; R. A. Goldthwaite, *The Building of Renaissance Florence: An Economic and Social History* (1980); M. Becker, *Florence in Transition* (2 vols., 1967–69); D. Weinstein, *Savanorola and Florence* (1970); and C. Fusero, *The Borgias* (trans. 1973). A colorful popular account is C. Hibbert, *Florence: The Biography of a City* (1993).

Outstanding studies of Venice with varying perspectives include F. C. Lane, *Venice: A Maritime Republic* (1973); W. H. McNeill, *Venice, The Hinge of Europe, 1081–1797* (1974); R. Finlay, *Politics in Renaissance Venice* (1980); and E. Muir, *Civic Ritual in Renaissance Venice* (1981). Valuable studies in social and cultural history include the books by G. Ruggiero,

The Boundaries of Eros: Sex Crime, and Sexuality in Renaissance Venice (1985); S. Chojnacki, *Women and Men in Renaissance Venice* (2000); and P. F. Brown, *Private Lives in Renaissance Venice: Art, Architecture, and the Family* (2004). For Rome one may read P. Partner, *Renaissance Rome, 1500–1559: A Portrait of a Society* (1976) and C. L. Stinger, *The Renaissance in Rome* (reissued 1998).

The Renaissance outside Italy

One of the best introductions to the northern Renaissance can still be found in the classic work by J. Huizinga, *The Autumn of the Middle Ages* (1924; new trans., 1996); one should also read the same author's *Erasmus and the Age of Reformation* (1924,1984). For the Dutch humanist one may also read R. M. Bainton, *Erasmus of Christendom* (1969, 1988); E. Rummel, *Erasmus* (2004); J. McConica, *Erasmus* (1991); and L. Halkin, *Erasmus: A Critical Biography* (trans. 1993). For Christian humanism in general and its contribution to the religious changes of the age, one turns to J. H. Overfield, *Humanism and Scholasticism in Late Medieval Germany* (1984).

The New Monarchies

A good overview is provided in R. Bonney, *The European Dynastic States, 1494–1660* (1991). For England, J. Youings, *Sixteenth-Century England* (1984) examines all aspects of the age. J. R. Lander, *Government and Community: England, 1450–1509* (1980) describes in detail the curbing of feudal power and the evolution of the modern state. Also helpful for England are E. F. Jacob, *The Fifteenth Century* (1961, 1993) and A. Goodman, *The New Monarchy: England, 1471–1534* (1988). For France several books are illuminating: L. Febvre, *Life in Renaissance France* (trans. 1977); and H. A. Lloyd, *The State, France, and the Sixteenth Century* (1983). Two good biographies of "new monarchs" are J. M. Tyrell, *Louis XI* (1980) and R. J. Knecht, *Renaissance Warrior and Patron: The Reign of Francis I* (1982, rev. 1994), the latter a biography of distinction.

General Works on the Reformation

Syntheses of the sixteenth-century upheaval in church and society may be found in L. W. Spitz, *The Protestant Reformation, 1517–1559* (1985) and in M. Gray, *The Protestant Reformation: Belief, Practice, and Tradition* (2003). Other informative accounts are available in E. Cameron, *The European Reformation* (1991); D. MacCulloch, *The Reformation: A History* (2004); and P. Collinson, *The Reformation: A History* (2004).

For political and social background one may turn to H. Holborn, *A History of Modern Germany: The Reformation* (1959), the first volume of his three-volume history of Germany; R. P. Hsia (ed.), *The German People and the Reformation* (1988); and R. W. Scribner, *Popular Culture and Popular Movements in Reformation Germany* (1987). Recent accounts of the leading ruler of the age are available in W. S. Maltby, *The Reign of Charles V* (2002) and H. Kleinschmidt, *Charles V: The World Emperor* (2004).

Biographical accounts of Luther include R. H. Bainton, *Here I Stand: A Life of Martin Luther* (1950, 1994); H. Oberman, *Luther: Man Between God and the Devil* (trans. 1990); M. Brecht, *Martin Luther* (2 vols., trans. 1985, 1990); and M. Marty, *Martin Luther* (2004), an interesting analysis by a noted American historian of religion. E. H. Erikson offers psychoanalytic insights into the religious leader's identity crisis in *Young Man Luther: A Study in Psychoanalysis and History* (1962). Among other studies are H. G. Haile, *Luther: An Experiment in Biography* (1980); M. U. Edwards, Jr., *Luther's Last Battles: Politics and Polemics, 1531–1546* (1983); and G. Brendler, *Martin Luther: Theology and Revolution* (1989). The appeal of Lutheran ideas is skillfully analyzed in R. W. Scribner, *For the Sake of Simple Folk: Popular Propaganda in the German Reformation* (1981); in P. Blickle, *The Revolution of 1525: The German Peasants' War from a New Perspective* (trans. 1981); and in B. Scribner and G. Benecke (eds.), *The German Peasant War, 1525: New Viewpoints* (1979).

An admirable biography of Calvin, capturing the spirit of the man and his times, is W. J. Bouwsma, *John Calvin: A Sixteenth Century Portrait* (1987). Studies of the reformer's thought and influence include F. Wendel, *Calvin: The Origins and Development of His Religious Thought* (trans. 1963, reissued 1987) and P. Helm, *John Calvin's Ideas* (2004). The wider development of the Calvinist movement is examined in P. Benedict, *Christ's Churches Purely Reformed: A Social History of Calvinism* (2002). An outstanding biography of another reformer is G. R. Potter, *Zwingli* (1977), on whom W. P. Stephens has also written *Zwingli: An Introduction to His Thought* (1992). R. H. Bainton, *Hunted Heretic: The Life and Death of Michael Servetus* (1960) may be compared with J. Friedman, *Michael Servetus: A Case Study in Total Heresy* (1978). Studies of another important religious reformer can be found in W. S. Reid, *Trumpeter of God: A Biography of John Knox* (1975) and R. K. Marshall, *John Knox* (2000).

The cities in which the major events of the Reformation occurred are examined in W. Monter, *Calvin's Geneva* (1967) and S. E. Ozment, *The Reformation in the Cities: The Appeal of Protestantism to Sixteenth Century Germany and Switzerland* (1975). S. E. Ozment, *When Fathers Ruled: Family Life in Reformation Europe* (1983) describes the patriarchal household as less tyrannical than traditionally portrayed. R. H. Bainton, *Women of the Reformation* (3 vols., 1971–77) studies the contributions of women to the religious changes of the era; and S. Marshall (ed.), *Women in Reformation and Counter-Reformation Europe: Public and Private Worlds* (1989) provides informative essays on women of the time in various social contexts.

The Reformation in England

The course of the Reformation in England may be approached through a number of helpful syntheses: A. G. Dickens, *The English Reformation* (rev. 1989); J. J. Scarisbrick, *The Reformation and the English People* (1986); and R. Rex, *Henry VIII and the English Reformation* (1993). Recent scholarship is also communicated in P. Marshall and A. Ryrie (eds.), *The Beginnings of English Protestantism* (2002); in W. I. P. Hazlett, *The Reformation in Britain and Ireland: An Introduction* (2003); and in S. Doran and C. Durston, *Princes, Pastors, and People: The Church and Religion in England, 1529–1689* (rev. 2003).

The influential English scholar, statesman, and martyr is studied in R. Marius, *Thomas More: A Biography* (1985), a somewhat critical and unsympathetic account; while P. Ackroyd, *The Life of Thomas More* (1998) and J. A. Guy, *Thomas More* (2000) create a more balanced appraisal of a complex personality. Also available is L. L. Martz, *Thomas More: The Search for the Inner Man* (1990). The conflicts between English Catholics and Protestants are examined in E. Duffy, *The Stripping of the Altars* (rev. 2005) and in A. F. Marotti, *Religious Ideology and Cultural Fantasy: Catholic and Anti-Catholic Discourses in Early Modern England* (2005).

Three older but still provocative books dealing with the social and economic implications of the Reformation for the future course of England are R. H. Tawney, *Religion and the Rise of Capitalism* (1926, 1962), insightful even if modified by later research; C. Hill, *Reformation to Industrial Revolution: The Making of Modern English Society* (1967), also emphasizing class interests; and H. R. Trevor-Roper, *Religion, the Reformation, and Social Change* (rev. 1984), which is less persuaded by the connection between religion and class.

A distinguished biography focusing on the king as well as the events of his reign is J. J. Scarisbrick, *Henry VIII* (1968, 1986); also thoughtful is L. B. Smith, *Henry VIII: The Mask of Royalty* (1971), which may be supplemented by the more recent work of M. A. R. Graves, *Henry VIII, A Study in Kingship* (2000) and A. Weir, *Henry VIII: The King and His Court* (2001). On the history of Henry's wives, in addition to several individual biographies for each, one may read A. Fraser, *The Wives of Henry VIII* (1992); A. Weir, *Six Wives of Henry VIII* (1992); and D. Starkey, *Six Wives: The Queens of Henry VIII* (2003). Henry VIII's two immediate successors and their brief reigns are described in S. Alford, *Kingship and Politics in the Reign of Edward VI* (2002); D. M. Loades, *Mary Tudor* (1989); and C. Erickson, *Bloody Mary: The Life of Mary Tudor* (1993). Books on Elizabeth will be described in the next chapter, but for studies of religion in all or part of her reign one may turn to A. Morey, *The Catholic Subjects of Elizabeth I* (1978) and P. Collinson's two books, *The Elizabethan Puritan Movement* (1967, 1990) and *The Religion of Protestants: The Church in English Society, 1559–1625* (1983).

Other Reformation Themes

The various forms of Protestantism are placed in doctrinal perspective in B. M. G. Reardon, *Religious Thought in the Reformation* (rev. 1995) and A. McGrath, *Reformation Thought* (1988), while the radical movements of the era may be studied in G. H. Williams, *The Radical Reformation* (rev. 1992); N. Cohn, *The Pursuit of the Millennium: Revolutionary Messianism in Medieval and Reformation Europe* (rev. 1970); and M. A. Mullett, *Radical Religious Movements in Early Modern Europe* (1980). An important subject is explored in H. Kamen, *The Rise of Toleration* (1967).

On the relation between economic change and Protestant religious doctrine, especially Calvinism, a debate that was opened by Max Weber in *The Protestant Ethic and the Spirit of Capitalism* (1904, 1985) and further developed by R. H. Tawney in the 1920s, one may read G. Marshall, *In Search of the Spirit of Capitalism: An Essay on Max Weber's Protestant Ethic Thesis* (1982), a balanced review; and the essays in H. Lehmann and G. Roth (eds.), *Weber's Protestant Ethic* (1993) and in W. H. Swatos Jr. and L. Kaelber (eds.), *The Protestant Ethic Turns 100: Essays on the Centenary of the Weber Thesis* (2005), which add many new insights.

The Catholic response to the Reformation is studied in N. S. Davidson, *The Counter Reformation* (1987), which provides a brief overview, and in M. D. W. Jones, *The Counter Reformation: Religion and Society in Early Modern Europe* (1995). Important for the Catholic response and other matters is J. Pelikan, *Reformation of Church and Dogma, 1300–1700* (1983), Vol. IV of his *The Christian Tradition*. H. Jedin, *The Council of Trent* (2 vols., 1957–61) presents the fullest account of the important council and its reforms. Introductions to the literature on the Society of Jesus are provided in W. B. Bangert, *A History of the Society of Jesus* (1972) and J. P. Donnelly, *Ignatius of Loyola: Founder of the Jesuits* (2004). A masterful review of the early Jesuits is J. O'Malley, *The First Jesuits* (1999). There are also biographies of Loyola by P. Caramon (1990) and W. Meissner (1992), the latter a psychoanalytical study.

Useful Web Sites

Several Web sites provide access to information on the crisis of the later middle ages; see, for example, information about the plague in Britain at the useful site of the British radio network, *BBC-History*, www.bbc.co.uk/history/society_culture/welfare/black_01.shtml; the excellent *Internet Medieval Sourcebook* at

Fordham University, cited earlier, includes materials on the disasters of the fourteenth century at www.fordham.edu/halsall/sbook1w.html. For sources on the history of witchcraft, one may visit *The Witch Hunts* at http://history.hanover.edu/early/wh.html. There are helpful links to diverse themes in the history of both the Renaissance and Reformation at the Web site of the *History Department, University of Colorado, Colorado Springs*, http://web.uccs.edu/history/globalhistory/renaissance.htm. More links to the history of all European countries in the Renaissance era can be found at *Medieval and Renaissance Europe: Primary Historical Documents*, www.lib.byu.edu/~rdh/eurodocs/, where readers can also locate helpful material on the early monarchical states. The evolution of the French state is examined with useful documents and images at a Library of Congress site called *Creating French Culture*, which is available at www.loc.gov/exhibits/bnf/bnf0001.html. The Reformation can be explored through Fordham University's *Internet Modern History Sourcebook* at www.fordham.edu/halsall/mod/modsbook.html; and see also the excellent links at the Web site of *The Centre for Reformation and Renaissance Studies*, affiliated with the University of Toronto, at www.crrs.ca/library/webresources/webresources.htm.

3. ECONOMIC RENEWAL AND WARS OF RELIGION, 1560–1648

Of general treatments for these years, covering institutional and international developments, the best guides are G. Parker, *Europe in Crisis, 1598–1648* (rev. 2001); H. Kamen, *Early Modern European Society* (2000), which describes the evolving social history of the era; V. G. Kiernan, *State and Society in Europe, 1550–1650* (1987); and J. H. Elliott, *Europe Divided, 1559–1598* (rev. 2000). F. Braudel's magisterial work stressing broad geographic, demographic, and economic developments, *The Mediterranean and the Mediterranean World in the Age of Philip II* (rev. and abr. ed., 1992), has been cited in the introductory section.

Analytical treatments focusing on the concept of crisis in the seventeenth century (and useful for this and the following chapter) include T. Aston (ed.), *Crisis in Europe, 1560–1660: Essays from Past and Present* (1966); G. Parker and L. M. Smith, *The General Crisis of the Seventeenth Century* (1978); T. K. Rabb, *The Struggle for Stability in Early Modern Europe* (1976); and T. Munck, *Seventeenth-Century Europe: State, Conflict, and the Social Order in Europe, 1598–1700* (rev. 2005). Agrarian and urban unrest is studied in P. Zagorin, *Rebels and Rulers, 1500–1660* (2 vols., 1982); J. A. Goldstone's sociological study, *Revolution and Rebellion in the Early Modern World* (1991); and C. Tilly, *European Revolutions, 1492–*

1992 (1992). The impact on society of military change is examined in G. Parker, *The Military Revolution: Military Innovation and the Rise of the West, 1500–1800* (rev. 1996) and in J. Black, *A Military Revolution? Military Change and European Society, 1550–1800* (1991). B. M. Downing, *The Military Revolution and Political Change: The Origins of Democracy and Autocracy in Early Modern Europe* (1992) is intended to revise and supplement B. Moore, *The Social Origins of Dictatorship and Democracy: Lord and Peasant in the Making of the Modern World* (1966, reissued 1993).

The Opening of the Atlantic

Good introductions to European exploration and settlement, beginning in the pre-Columbian age, are F. Fernández-Armesto, *Before Columbus: Exploration and Colonization from the Mediterranean to the Atlantic, 1229–1492* (1987); J. H. Parry, *The Age of Reconnaissance: Discovery, Exploration, and Settlement, 1450–1650* (rev. 1981); and G. Scammell, *The First Imperial Age: European Overseas Expansion, 1400–1715* (1989). Still interesting is S. E. Morison, *The European Discovery of America* (2 vols., 1971–74, 1993), but a more analytical overview of European imperial expansion is available in D. B. Abernethy, *The Dynamics of Global Dominance: European Overseas Empires, 1415–1980* (2000); and there is a helpful survey of European expansion throughout the world in D. R. Ringrose, *Expansion and Global Interaction* (2001). C. M. Cipolla stresses the importance of technology for the European explorations in *Guns, Sails, and Empires: 1400–1700* (1965, reissued 1985), as does A. W. Crosby in a far-ranging study, *The Measure of Reality: Quantification and Western Society, 1250–1600* (1997). China's naval exploits in the early 15th century are described in L. E. Leviathes, *When China Ruled the Seas* (1994).

The 500th anniversary of Columbus's first voyage stimulated the appearance of numerous books, many vehemently critical of the European impact on the New World and seeing the voyages less as discovery than intrusion or conquest, or at best as an encounter between very different peoples and cultures. Three examples of this critical literature are K. Sale, *Christopher Columbus and the Conquest of Paradise* (rev. 2006); T. Todorov, *The Conquest of America: The Question of the Other* (trans. 1984, reissued 1999); and D. E. Stannard, *American Holocaust: Columbus and the Conquest of the New World* (1993). Two balanced accounts placing Columbus in the context of his time without overlooking the consequences of the European arrival are W. D. Phillips, Jr., and C. R. Phillips, *The Worlds of Christopher Columbus* (1991) and F. Fernández-Armesto, *Columbus* (1991); the latter author provides additional assessments in *Columbus and the Conquest of the Impossible* (rev. 2000), ambitious but not as satisfactory as some of his other books. Other scholarly efforts to examine much that remains obscure about the explorer are D. Heinge, *In Search of Columbus: The Sources for the First Voyage* (1991) and V. Flint, *The Imaginative Landscape of Christopher Columbus* (1992). P. K. Liss, *Isabel the Queen* (1992) is a thoughtful biography of his patron.

A splendidly illustrated catalog prepared for an exhibition to commemorate the quincentenary, J. A. Levenson (ed.), *Circa 1492: Art in the Age of Exploration* (1991), presents the impressive art and artifacts of people from all over the globe in this age, including the New World. In two thoughtful books A. W. Crosby demonstrates that European plants, animals, and diseases had as much to do with the success of European expansion and the consequent devastation of the indigenous peoples as military conquest: *The Columbian Exchange: Biological and Cultural Consequences of 1492* (rev. 2003) and *Ecological Imperialism: The Biological Expansion of Europe, 900–1900* (1986), a broader study. C. C. Mann describes the diversity of Native American societies before the arrival of Europeans in *1491: New Revelations of the Americas before Columbus* (2005). For the impact of the discoveries on European thought, one may turn to W. Brandon, *New Worlds for Old: Reports from the New World and Their Effect on the Development of Social Thought in Europe, 1500–1800* (1986); J. H. Elliott, *The Old World and the New, 1492–1650* (1970, 1992); and A. Pagden's two books, *European Encounters with the New World: From Renaissance to Romanticism* (1992) and *Lords of All the World: Ideologies of Empire in Spain, Britain, and France, c. 1500–c. 1850* (1995). The latter may be compared with the two works of P. Seed, *Ceremonies of Possession in Europe's Conquest of the New World, 1492–1640* (1995) and *American Pentimento: The Invention of Indians and the Pursuit of Riches* (2001). On European interactions with native peoples in the years after the initial explorations, see the important books of J. Axtell, *Beyond 1492: Encounters in Colonial North America* (1993) and *Natives and Newcomers: The Cultural Origins of North America* (2001).

Portugal and Spain in Europe and Overseas

The best introduction to the overseas exploits of both countries is L. N. McAlister, *Spain and Portugal in the New World, 1492–1700* (1983). Portuguese maritime and colonial enterprises are recounted in C. R. Boxer, *The Portuguese Seaborne Empire: 1415–1825* (rev. 1991); one may also read B. W. Diffie and G. D. Winius, *Foundations of the Portuguese Empire, 1415–1580* (1977). On Portugal, there are sound histories by J. M. Anderson, *The History of Portugal* (2000) and D. Birmingham, *A Concise History of Portugal* (rev. 2003); and on the Iberian peninsula as a whole, S. G. Payne, *A History of Spain and Portugal* (2 vols., 1973).

The best accounts for Spain in the early modern centuries are J. H. Elliott, *Imperial Spain, 1469–1714*

(1964, reissued, 2002), which may be supplemented by his *Spain and Its World, 1500–1700* (1986); J. Lynch, *Spain under the Habsburgs, 1516–1700* (2 vols.; rev. 1992); and H. Kamen, *Empire: How Spain Became a World Power, 1492–1763* (2003). Social trends in Spanish society are discussed in J. Casey, *Early Modern Spain: A Social History* (1999). For the Spanish monarch one may read P. Pierson, *Philip II of Spain* (1975) and G. Parker, *Philip II* (rev. 1995) and *The Grand Strategy of Philip II* (1998). H. Kamen, *Philip of Spain* (1997) is more sympathetic than other biographical accounts. On the Spanish arm of the Counter-Reformation H. Kamen, *The Spanish Inquisition: A Historical Revision* (1997) attempts to redress the balance in favor of a less harsh judgment, to which even his own earlier writings contributed. However, the works of B. Netanyahu, *The Origins of the Inquisition in Fifteenth-Century Spain* (rev. 2001) and J. Perez, *The Spanish Inquistion: A History* (trans. 2005) stress the human costs of religious persecutions.

Although G. Mattingly, *The Armada* (1959, 1989) remains the classic study of this dramatic episode in its diplomatic and ideological setting, readers will wish to turn also to C. Martin and G. Parker, *The Spanish Armada* (rev. 1999); F. Fernández-Armesto, *The Spanish Armada: The Experience of War in 1588* (1989); and the more recent works of J. McDermott, *England and the Spanish Armada: The Necessary Quarrel* (2005) and N. Hanson, *The Confident Hope of A Miracle: The True History of the Spanish Armada* (2005).

Books examining Spain after the age of Philip II include R. A. Stradling, *Philip IV and the Government of Spain, 1621–1665* (1988) and two outstanding studies by J. H. Elliott: *The Revolt of the Catalans: A Study in the Decline of Spain, 1598–1640* (1963, 1984) and *The Count-Duke of Olivares: The Statesman in an Age of Decline* (1986), on Philip IV's principal adviser from 1621 to 1643.

For the Spanish empire in the new world one may read C. Gibson, *Spain in America* (1966, 1990); J. H. Parry, *The Spanish Seaborne Empire* (1966); S. J. Stein and B. H. Stein, *Silver, Trade, and War: Spain and America in the Making of Early Modern Europe* (2000); D. J. Weber, *The Spanish Frontier in North America* (1995); and C. M. MacLachlan, *Spain's Empire in the New World: The Role of Ideas in Institutional and Social Change* (1988). A pioneer inquiry into the impact of the discovery of silver upon economic changes in Europe was E. J. Hamilton, *American Treasure and the Price Revolution in Spain, 1501–1650* (1934, 1965), although some of its conclusions have been modified. The subject is also examined in P. Vila, *A History of Gold and Money, 1450–1920* (trans. 1976) and in J. N. Ball, *Merchants and Merchandise: The Expansion of Trade in Europe, 1500–1630* (1977). For the Spanish conquest, readers may turn to M. Wood, *Conquistadors* (2000), the work of a writer who has also produced a documentary film on the subject. Modern historical scholarship is reflected in R. L. Marks, *Cortés: The Great Adventurer and the Fate of Aztec Mexico* (1993) and in H. Thomas, *Conquest: Montezuma, Cortés, and the Fall of Old Mexico* (1994). On attempts by the church and others to mitigate the evils of the conquest one still turns to L. Hanke, *The Spanish Struggle for Justice in the Conquest of America* (1949, reissued 2002). The best scholarly accounts of the enforced labor and demographic consequences of the conquest may be found in the chapters contributed to L. Bethell (ed.), *The Cambridge History of Latin America*, Vols. I and II: *Colonial Latin America* (1988). An informative survey for all aspects of Latin America in the colonial era is M. A. Burkholder and L. L. Johnson, *Colonial Latin America* (rev. 2003).

The Atlantic slave trade and slavery, which launched the massive migrations of people that historians now call the African Diaspora, can be studied in numerous important historical works. Among the most informative are H. S. Klein, *African Slavery in Latin America and the Caribbean* (1987); V. B. Thompson, *The Making of the African Diaspora in the Americas, 1441–1900* (1988); R. Blackburn, *The Making of New World Slavery* (1997); D. Eltis, *The Rise of African Slavery in the Americas* (2000); and W. Klooster and A. Padula (eds.), *The Atlantic World: Essays on Slavery, Migration, and Imagination* (2005). The writings of D. B. Davis, *Slavery and Human Progress* (1984) and *The Problem of Slavery in Western Culture* (1988), as well as his other volumes cited in later chapters, offer penetrating insights, as do O. Patterson's books *Slavery and Social Death: A Comparative Study* (1982) and *Freedom in the Making of Western Culture* (1991). The historical background is presented in W. D. Phillips, *Slavery from Roman Times to the Early Transatlantic Trade* (1985), carrying the story to 1650, and in B. Lewis, *Race and Slavery in the Middle East* (1990). E. Williams, *Capitalism and Slavery* (1944, reissued 1994) early emphasized that the emerging Atlantic economy was supported by African slavery, a theme on which there are informative essays in B. L. Solow (ed.), *Slavery and the Rise of the Atlantic System* (1991). The grim story of the slave trade is recounted in many books, among them J. Pope-Hennessy, *Sins of the Fathers: A Study of the Atlantic Slave Traders 1441–1807* (1968); P. D. Curtin, *The Atlantic Slave Trade* (1969); H. S. Klein, *The Middle Passage* (1978); J. A. Rawley, *The Transatlantic Slave Trade* (1981); and C. A. Palmer, *Human Cargoes: The British Slave Trade to Spanish America, 1700–1739* (1981). H. Thomas, *The Slave Trade: The Story of the Atlantic Slave Trade, 1440–1870* (1997) graphically conveys its multinational character. A case study of slavery on a Caribbean plantation is available in T. Burnard, *Mastery, Tyranny, and Desire: Thomas Thistlewood and His Slaves in the Anglo-Jamaican World* (2004). Two valuable syntheses of historical writings on slavery in its North American setting are P. Kolchin, *American Slavery, 1619–1877* (1993) and I. Berlin, *Many Thousands Gone: The First Two Centuries of Slavery in North America* (1998).

Changing Social Structures, Early Capitalism, Mercantilism

A key study of early economic history is J. De Vries, *The Economy of Europe in an Age of Crisis, 1600–1750* (1976). One will wish to consult also R. Davis, *The Rise of the Atlantic Economies* (1973); C. M. Cipolla, *Before the Industrial Revolution: European Society and Economy, 1000–1700* (rev. 1994); P. Kriedte, *Peasants, Landlords, and Merchant Capitalists: Europe and the World Economy 1500–1800* (1983); and A. K. Smith, *Creating a World Economy: Merchant Capital, Colonialism, and World Trade, 1400–1825* (1991). The reasons why rapid economic change took place in western Europe rather than elsewhere are explored in E. L. Jones, *The European Miracle: Environments, Economics, and Geopolitics in the History of Europe and Asia* (rev. 2003) and in J. Baechler et al. (eds.), *Europe and the Rise of Capitalism* (1988).

A remarkable though often impressionistic account of social and economic change in the early modern centuries is the three-volume work of F. Braudel, *Civilization and Capitalism, 15th–18th Century* (trans. 1981–84; reissued 1992): Vol. I, *The Structures of Everyday Life;* Vol. II, *The Wheels of Commerce;* and Vol. III, *The Perspective of the World*. The broad themes of the work are summarized in *Afterthoughts on Material Civilization and Capitalism* (trans. 1977). Another large-scale study, reflecting the influence of Braudel and focusing on the shifting of economic power is I. Wallerstein, *The Modern World-System* (3 vols. 1974), analyzing the origins of the world economy, mercantilism, and the expansion of the global economy from 1730 to the 1840s. The development of a capitalist economy is also traced in W. N. Parker, *Europe, America, and the Wider World: Essays on the Economic History of Western Capitalism* (2 vols., 1984, 1991); and important intercultural dimensions are added in P. D. Curtin, *Cross-Cultural Trade in World History* (1984).

Much of the debate on the early modern centuries focuses on the continuity of European economic history since the Middle Ages and on early industrialization. The debate on "protoindustrialization" is examined in P. Kriedte (ed.), *Industrialization before Industrialization: Rural Industry and the Genesis of Capitalism* (1981) and in M. P. Gutmann, *Toward the Modern Economy: Early Industry in Europe, 1500–1800* (1988).

For demography one may turn to M. W. Flynn, *The European Demographic System, 1500–1820*

(1981); and for the growth of cities one may consult P. M. Hohenberg and L. H. Lees, *The Making of Urban Europe, 1000–1994* (rev. 1995) and J. De Vries, *European Urbanization, 1500–1800* (1984). There are valuable chapters in C. M. Cipolla (ed.), *The Fontana Economic History of Europe: The Sixteenth and Seventeenth Centuries* (1974) and in E. E. Rich and C. H. Wilson (eds.), *Cambridge Economic History of Europe,* Vol. IV (1976) and Vol. V (1977).

Revolt of the Netherlands

G. Parker, *The Dutch Revolt* (1977), an admirable comprehensive study, may be compared with P. Geyl's masterful older account, *The Revolt of the Netherlands, 1555–1609* (1932; trans. 1958) and *The Netherlands in the Seventeenth Century, 1609–1715* (2 vols.; trans. 1961–64). Dutch political culture is examined in H. H. Rowen, *The Princes of Orange: the Stadholders in the Dutch Republic* (1988); and W. S. Maltby, *Alba: A Biography* (1983) studies the Duke of Alba, the Spanish governor sent to suppress the Dutch in the mid-sixteenth century and who thereby helped to create the Dutch nation.

The Tudor Age: Elizabethan England

The best syntheses for the Tudor monarchs are G. R. Elton, *England under the Tudors* (rev. 1991); and J. Guy, *Tudor England* (1988); a useful collection of articles is available in J. Guy (ed.), *The Tudor Monarchy* (1997). Informative for the Tudors and their successors are D. M. Loades, *Politics and Nation: England, 1450–1660* (rev. 1999) and J. Guy and J. Morrill, *The Tudors and Stuarts* (1993), a volume in the *Oxford History of Britain.*

For the Elizabethan era one may read W. T. MacCaffrey's trilogy of distinction—*The Shaping of the Elizabethan Regime* (1968), *Queen Elizabeth and the Making of Policy, 1572–1588* (1981), and *Elizabeth I: War and Politics, 1588–1603* (1992). For the religious question in these years one may turn to D. MacCulloch, *The Later Reformation in England, 1547–1603* (rev. 2001). A survey of foreign affairs is available in R. B. Wernham, *The Making of Elizabethan Foreign Policy* (1980). On the naval and imperial side one may also read D. B. Quinn and A. N. Ryan, *England's Sea Empire, 1550–1642* (1983) and K. R. Andrews, *Trade, Plunder, and Settlement: Maritime Enterprise and the Genesis of the British Empire, 1480–1630* (1985).

Of the numerous biographies of Elizabeth one may read A. Somerset, *Elizabeth I* (1992, 2003), a lively volume; S. Bassnett, *Elizabeth I: A Feminist Perspective* (1988); D. M. Loades, *Elizabeth I* (2003); and the concise account in S. Doran, *Queen Elizabeth I* (2003). There are other commendable studies by L. B. Smith (1976), E. Erickson (1983), A. Weir (1998), and C. Haigh (rev. 2001). A. Fraser, among her many notable volumes, has written *Mary Queen of Scots* (1969, 1993). On Elizabeth's devoted courtier,

H. Kelsey, *Sir Francis Drake: The Queen's Pirate* (1998) is a scholarly account.

An overview of society and economy is helpfully presented in D. M. Palliser, *The Age of Elizabeth: England under the Later Tudors, 1547–1603* (rev. 1992). Social and economic changes of the age, or that take their start in this age, are masterfully explored in L. Stone, *The Crisis of the Aristocracy, 1558–1641* (1965; abr. ed., 1967) and in L. Stone and J. C. Stone, *An Open Elite?: England, 1540–1880* (1984; abr. ed., 1986), which questions upward social mobility in England. Other important studies are G. E. Mingay, *The Gentry: The Rise and Fall of a Ruling Class* (1976); A. Macfarlane, *The Origins of English Individualism: The Family, Property, and Social Transition* (1978); and I. W. Archer, *The Pursuit of Stability: Social Relations in Elizabethan London* (1991).

Historical research to reconstruct the history of the family is brilliantly exemplified in L. Stone's several works: *The Family, Sex, and Marriage in England, 1500–1800* (1977; abr. ed., 1979), *Road to Divorce: England, 1530–1987* (1990), and in a volume of revealing case studies, *Uncertain Unions and Broken Lives: Marriage and Divorce in England, 1660–1857* (1995). Other recommended studies are R. A. Houlbrooke, *The English Family, 1450–1700* (1984); J. R. Gillis, *For Better, For Worse: British Marriages, 1600 to the Present* (1985); A. Macfarlane, *Marriage and Love in England: Modes of Reproduction, 1300–1840* (1987); and B. J. Harris, *English Aristocratic Women 1450–1550: Marriage and Family, Property and Careers* (2002). R. A. Houlbrooke's *Death, Religion, and the Family in England, 1480–1750* (1998) examines views of death in this era.

Two important books are P. Laslett, *The World We Have Lost: England before the Industrial Age* (1965, rev. 2004), a pioneering work that presents a somewhat overly stable picture of these years, and E. A. Wrigley and R. S. Schofield, *The Population History of England, 1541–1871* (1981), a model of demographic research.

Disintegration and Reconstruction of France

Informative introductions to the religious and dynastic turmoil in sixteenth-century France include R. Briggs, *Early Modern France, 1560–1715* (rev. 1998); H. A. Lloyd, *The State, France, and the Sixteenth Century* (1983); and R. J. Knecht, *French Renaissance Monarchy: Francis I and Henry II* (rev. 1996). J. H. M. Salmon's two books are of special value: *Society in Crisis: France in the Sixteenth Century* (rev. 1979) and *Renaissance and Revolt: Essays in the Intellectual and Social History of Early France* (1987). Major French works available in translation are R. Mandrou, *Introduction to Modern France, 1500–1640: An Essay in Historical Psychology* (trans. 1976); E. Le Roy Ladurie's two studies *The French Peasantry, 1450–1660* (rev. and trans. 1986) and *Early Modern*

France, 1460–1610 (trans. 1993); and R. Mousnier, *The Institutions of France under the Absolute Monarchy, 1598–1789* (2 vols., trans. 1979–84), an exhaustive study of society and the state.

The religious wars are also explored in N. M. Sutherland's *The Massacre of St. Bartholemew and the European Conflict, 1559–1572* (1973) and *The Huguenot Struggle for Recognition* (1980); B. B. Diefendorf, *Beneath the Cross: Catholics and Huguenots in Sixteenth-Century Paris* (1991); H. Heller, *Iron and Blood: Civil Wars in Sixteenth-Century France* (1991); M. P. Holt, *The French Wars of Religion, 1562–1629* (1996); and R. J. Knecht, *The French Civil Wars, 1562–1598* (2000). The intellectual dimension is examined in D. R. Kelley, *The Beginning of Ideology: Consciousness and Society in the French Reformation* (1981). An illuminating biography of the first Bourbon king, D. Buisseret, *Henri IV* (1984) may be supplemented by M. Greengrass, *France in the Age of Henri IV: The Struggle for Stability* (rev. 1995); R. S. Love, *Blood and Religion: The Conscience of Henry IV, 1553–1593* (2001); and the comprehensive work of N. M. Sutherland, *Henry IV of France and the Politics of Religion: 1572–1596* (2 vols., 2002)

Constitutional developments are comprehensively explored in J. R. Major, *Representative Government in Early Modern France* (1980), stressing the vitality of the early representative bodies; in P. Anderson, *Lineages of the Absolutist State* (1974); in H. H. Rowen, *The King's State: Proprietary Dynasticism in Early Modern France* (1980), examining the state as royal property; and in E. Le Roy Ladurie, *The Royal French State, 1460–1610* (trans. 1994), describing the changing public functions of the royal government. The cultural values of the early modern nobility are examined in E. Schalk, *From Valor to Pedigree: Ideas of Nobility in France in the Sixteenth and Seventeenth Centuries* (1986) and K. B. Neuschel, *Word of Honor: Interpreting Noble Culture in Sixteenth-Century France* (1989).

For the era of Louis XIII and the minister who overshadowed him one reads V. L. Tapié, *France in the Age of Louis XIII and Richelieu* (trans. 1974; reissued 1984). The king himself is studied in A. Lloyd Moote, *Louis XIII, The Just* (1989). The scholarship on Richelieu includes W. F. Church, *Richelieu and Reason of State* (1972); J. Bergin, *Cardinal Richelieu: Power and the Pursuit of Wealth* (1985) and *The Rise of Richelieu* (1991); R. J. Knecht, *Richelieu* (1991); D. Parrott, *Richelieu's Army: War, Government, and Society In France, 1624–1642* (2001); and A. Levi, *Cardinal Richelieu and the Making of France* (2000). The strengthening of royal power under Richelieu and his successor is examined in R. Bonney, *Society and Government in France under Richelieu and Mazarin, 1624–1661* (1988) and in J. Bergin and L. Brockless (eds.), *Richelieu and His Age* (1992). An important work by J. B. Collins, *The State in Early Modern France* (1995), stresses the close connection between the monarchy and social elites; and a penetrating comparative study of Richelieu and of his Spanish contemporary and rival, the Count-Duke of Olivares, can be found in J. H. Elliott, *Richelieu and Olivares* (1984).

The Thirty Years' War, 1618–1648

The most up-to-date authoritative account is G. Parker (ed.), *The Thirty Years' War* (rev. 1997), which includes chapters on all phases of the war. A useful, brief survey is available in P. Limm, *The Thirty Years' War* (1984). Other accounts include the classic work by C. V. Wedgwood (1938, reissued 2005), and other accounts by G. Pagès (trans. 1971), and J. V. Polisensky (trans. 1971). Biographical accounts of key leaders can be found in G. Mann, *Wallenstein: His Life Narrated* (trans. 1976) and M. Roberts, *Gustavus Adolphus* (1992). A detailed treatment of all aspects of Swedish history is to be found in the books of M. Roberts: *The Early Vasas: A History of Sweden, 1523–1611* (1968, 1986); *Gustavus Adolphus and the Rise of Sweden* (1973); *The Swedish Imperial Experience, 1560–1718* (1979); and *The Age of Liberty: Sweden, 1719–1772* (1986). The conversion to Catholicism of Gustavus Adolphus's daughter and her abdication is told in G. Masson, *Queen Christina* (1968) and in S. Svolpe, *Christina of Sweden* (trans. and abr. 1966), by a Swedish historian.

Useful Web Sites

Print and artistic resources on European exploration in the Atlantic world are available at an excellent Web site, *American Journeys*, at the Wisconsin Historical Society, www.americanjourneys.org. There are additional sources on the age of explorations at *European Voyages of Exploration*, which may be found at www.ucalgary.ca/applied_history/tutor/eurvoya/, and at a site maintained by the Library of Congress, *1492 Exhibit*, www.ibiblio.org/expo/1492.exhibit/intro.html. A helpful collection of links is available at the *African Diaspora in Latin America*, which is part of a comprehensive site on Latin American history at the University of Texas, http://lanic.utexas.edu/la/region/african/. For a well-organized site on all aspects of Tudor England, readers may visit *Tudor History* at http://tudorhistory.org/; and there is a useful Web site for current research on this era in French history at *Historians of Early Modern France*, www.history.emory.edu/BEIK/index.htm. Helpful material on an important conflict may be found at *The Thirty Years War,* www.pipeline.com/~cwa/tywhome.htm. Readers will also find numerous other sites on early modern European history by visiting *Best of History Web Sites* at www.besthistorysites.net/EarlyModernEurope.shtml.

4. THE GROWING POWER OF WESTERN EUROPE, 1640–1715

General accounts of the seventeenth century overlap with many of the books described in the preceding chapter. Informative general works include D. H. Pennington, *Europe in the Seventeenth Century* (rev. 1989) and J. Bergin (ed.) *The Seventeenth Century: Europe, 1598–1715* (2001). Two commendable general histories that begin with these years are W. Doyle, *The Old European Order, 1660–1800* (rev. 1992) and G. R. R. Treasure, *The Making of Modern Europe, 1648–1780* (1985). For international affairs, diplomacy, and war, two thoughtful accounts are D. McKay and H. M. Scott, *The Rise of the Great Powers, 1648–1815* (1983) and J. Black, *The Rise of the European Powers, 1679–1793* (1990). The diplomatic practices and institutions of the age are described in W. J. Roosen, *The Age of Louis XIV: The Rise of Modern Diplomacy* (1976), while the nature of warfare is examined in J. Childs, *Armies and Warfare in Europe, 1648–1789* (1982) and in M. S. Anderson, *War and Society in Europe of the Old Regime, 1618–1789* (rev. 1998).

The Dutch Republic

For the Netherlands in the seventeenth century one may read C. Wilson, *The Dutch Republic and the Civilization of the Seventeenth Century* (1968), an excellent brief introduction, and S. Schama, *The Embarrassment of Riches: An Interpretation of Dutch Culture in the Golden Age* (1988), an exemplary synthesis of art history and social history. Of special interest are three books by J. I. Israel: *The Dutch Republic: Its Rise, Greatness, and Fall, 1477–1806* (1995), *The Dutch Republic and the Hispanic World, 1606–1661* (1982), and *Dutch Primacy in World Trade, 1585–1740* (1989). Colonial expansion is described in C. R. Boxer, *The Dutch Seaborne Empire, 1600–1800* (1965); the Dutch economy is examined in J. A. van Houtte, *An Economic History of the Low Countries, 800–1800* (1977) and J. De Vries, *The Dutch Rural Economy in the Golden Age, 1500–1700* (1974).

For William of Orange, the best study is S. B. Baxter, *William III and the Defense of European Liberty, 1650–1702* (1966). A comprehensive biography of a leading Dutch statesman is H. H. Rowen, *Jan de Witt: Statesman of "True Freedom"* (1978; abr. 1986). Rowen also examines the later stadholders in a book that was noted earlier, *The Princes of Orange: The Stadholders in the Dutch Republic* (1988).

Seventeenth-Century England

Three judicious accounts of the seventeenth-century political and religious conflicts are D. Hirst, *Authority and Conflict: England, 1603–1658* (1986); D. Hirst, *England in Conflict, 1603–1660: Kingdom, Community, Commonwealth* (1999); and G. E. Aylmer, *Rebellion or Revolution?: England, 1640–1660* (1986). Other recommended general works include A. Stroud, *Stuart England* (1999); R. Lockyer, *The Early Stuarts: A Political History of England, 1603–1642* (rev. 1999) and, by the same author, *Tudor and Stuart Britain, 1485–1714* (rev. 2005); B. Coward, *The Stuart Age:*

England 1603–1714 (rev. 2003); and R. Bucholz and N. Key, *Early Modern England, 1485–1714* (2004).

For social and economic developments, illuminating studies include C. Wilson, *England's Apprenticeship, 1603–1763* (rev. 1984); K. Wrightson, *English Society, 1580–1680* (1982); and J. A. Sharpe, *Early Modern England: A Social History, 1550–1760* (rev. 1997). Books on the gentry and aristocracy have been cited in Chapter 3; to them should be added J. V. Beckett, *The Aristocracy in England, 1660–1914* (1988).

Few subjects have been as debated as the political and religious conflicts in seventeenth-century England. Some historians stress class and ideological conflict and interpret the events as the first modern European revolution. Others downplay what they see as anachronistic ideological interpretations, emphasize local rivalries, and insist on the importance of day-to-day contingencies. As an introduction to divergent interpretations one may compare L. Stone, *The Causes of the English Revolution, 1629–1642* (rev. 2002) and three books with much the same title by C. Russell (1990), A. Hughes (rev. 1998), and N. Carlin (1999).

For the general reader, the narrative excitement of the events is captured in C. V. Wedgwood's trilogy *The King's Peace, 1637–1641* (1955, reissued 1983), *The King's War, 1641–1647* (1959), and *A Coffin for King Charles: The Trial and Execution of Charles I* (1964), in which she demonstrates that the "why" (the analysis) must flow from the "how" (the narrative). A dramatic account, with considerable attention to military aspects, is C. Hibbert, *Cavaliers and Roundheads: The English Civil War, 1642–1649* (1993). For the opening episodes of these years A. Fletcher, *The Outbreak of the English Civil War* (1981) and K. Sharpe, *The Personal Rule of Charles I* (1992), both of which tend to minimize long-term social and economic causes, may be compared with L. J. Reeve, *Charles I and the Road to Personal Rule* (1989); R. Cust, *The Forced Loan and English Politics* (1986); and R. Brenner, *Merchants and Revolution* (1992). Of special interest also is C. Carlton, *Going to the Wars: The Experience of the British Civil Wars, 1638–1651* (1992).

Studies that downplay broader ideological interpretations but provide detailed narrative and analysis include C. Russell's books, *The Crisis of Parliaments* (1971), *Parliaments and English Politics, 1621–1629* (1979), and *The Fall of the British Monarchies, 1637–1742* (1991), which may be read along with J. Morrill, *The Revolt of the Provinces: Conservatism and Revolution in the English Civil War, 1630–1650* (1980) and *The Nature of the English Revolution* (1993), a collection of essays.

Studies of the first Stuart king in England include R. Lockyer, *James VI and I* (1998) and W. B. Patterson, *King James VI and I and the Reunion of Christendom* (1997). Assessments of his ill-fated successor appear in C. Carlton, *Charles I: The Personal*

Monarch (rev. 1995) and P. Gregg, *King Charles I* (1984). On the prelate who reinforced the king's persecution of the Puritans, H. R. Trevor-Roper's impressive *Archbishop Laud, 1573–1645* (rev. 1988) has not been superseded but should be read along with C. Carlton, *Archbishop William Laud* (1988).

For Cromwell many maintain that C. Firth, *Oliver Cromwell and the Rule of the Puritans in England* (1900; reissued many times) remains the best biographical account, but more recent studies include A. Fraser, *Cromwell, The Lord Protector* (1973); C. Hill, *God's Englishman* (1972); J. Morrill, *Oliver Cromwell and the English Revolution* (1990), generally unsympathetic; B. Coward, *Oliver Cromwell* (1991); and D. L. Smith, *Oliver Cromwell: Politics and Religion in the English Revolution, 1640–1658* (1991). Cromwell's military leadership is examined in A. Marshall, *Oliver Cromwell: Soldier: The Military Life of a Revolutionary at War* (2004), while an impressive study of Cromwell's army is available in I. Gentles, *The New Model Army in England, Ireland, and Scotland, 1645–1653* (1992). A good introduction to the Cromwellian era and the interregnum is R. Hutton, *The British Republic, 1649–1660* (1990), while a more detailed study is A. Woodrych, *Commonwealth to Protectorate* (1982).

Christopher Hill has done much to influence class and ideological interpretations of seventeenth-century events. His several Marxist-inspired but not dogmatic studies emphasize that the ideas of the age reflected economic class interests and that many contemporary political and social issues first emerged in the radicalism of the period. Among his books are *Puritanism and Revolution* (1958), *The Century of Revolution, 1603–1714* (1961, 1980), *Intellectual Origins of the English Revolution* (rev. 1997), *The World Turned Upside Down: Radical Ideas during the English Revolution* (1972), *Change and Continuity in Seventeenth-Century England* (rev. 1991), and *England's Turning Point: Essays on 17th-Century English History* (1998). Additional examples of inquiries into the radicalism of the age are M. Walzer, *The Revolution of the Saints: A Study in the Origins of Radical Politics* (1965); P. G. Rogers, *The Fifth Monarchy Men* (1966); G. E. Aylmer, *The Levelers in the English Revolution* (1975); and B. Manning, *The English People and the English Revolution, 1640–1649* (1976). An important assessment is J. O. Appleby, *Economic Thought and Ideology in Seventeenth Century England* (1978, reissued 2004), while an intriguing study in social history relating popular culture to the political ferment of the age is D. Underdown, *Revel, Riot, and Rebellion: Popular Politics and Culture in England, 1603–1660* (1985). The same author has also written *Pride's Purge: Politics and the Puritan Revolution* (1971, 1985), *Fire from Heaven: Life in an English Town in the Seventeenth Century* (1992), and *A Freeborn People: Politics and the Nation in Seventeenth-Century England* (1996).

Class and ideological interpretations may also be sampled in R. Cust and A. Hughes (eds.), *Conflict in Early Stuart England: Studies in Religion and Politics, 1603–1642* (1991); J. P. Somerville, *Politics and Ideology in England, 1603–1642* (1986); and T. Cogswell, *The Blessed Revolution: English Politics and the Coming of War, 1621–1624* (1989).

For Ireland good introductions beginning with this age are provided in J. C. Beckett, *The Making of Modern Ireland, 1603–1921* (rev. 1981) and R. F. Foster, *Modern Ireland, 1600–1972* (1988); for the Cromwellian years there are several important studies: P. B. Ellis, *Ireland, 1652–1660* (1975); T. C. Barnard, *Cromwellian Ireland: English Government and Reform in Ireland, 1649–1660* (1975); and J. S. Wheeler, *Cromwell in Ireland* (1999). Many other aspects of Irish history are explored in R. F. Foster (ed.), *The Oxford Illustrated History of Ireland* (1989).

The Restoration: Charles II; James II; The Revolution of 1688

Two of the best accounts of this and the age that followed are J. R. Jones, *Country and Court: England, 1658–1714* (1978) and G. Holmes, *The Making of a Great Power: Late Stuart and Early Georgian Britain, 1660–1722* (1993). For the end of the Protectorate and the restoration of the monarchy, one also turns to P. Seaward, *The Restoration, 1660–1688* (1991) and R. Hutton, *The Restoration: A Political and Religious History of England and Wales, 1658–1667* (1985, 1993). The king's abilities are assessed in A. Fraser, *Royal Charles: Charles II and the Restoration* (1971), perhaps the best of her many biographies; in J. R. Jones, *Charles II: Royal Politician* (1987); and in R. Hutton, *Charles II: King of England, Scotland, and Ireland* (1990). For his successor M. Ashley, *James II* (1977) is fair and factual, as is J. Miller, *James II: A Study of Kingship* (1977, 1989), which stresses the monarch's personal integrity but failure as a king.

For the background to the Revolution of 1688 and subsequent events one may read, among other accounts, D. Ogg, *England in the Reign of James II and William III* (1955, 1984); S. Prall, *The Bloodless Revolution: England, 1688* (1972); J. R. Jones, *The Revolution of 1688 in England* (1972); and J. Childs, *The Army, James II, and the Glorious Revolution* (1980). Brief surveys are available in J. Miller, *The Glorious Revolution* (rev. 1997) and in M. Mullett, *James II and English Politics, 1678–1688* (1994). A special subject is admirably studied in L. G. Schwoerer, *The Declaration of Rights, 1689* (1981). G. M. Trevelyan, *The English Revolution 1688–1989* (1939, 1965), a classic defense of the revolution, argues that the revolution strengthened conservatism for the eighteenth century but that the long-run consequences made it a turning point in history. The Whig historian is himself studied in D. Cannadine, *G. M. Trevelyan: A Life in History* (1993). Another assessment of the revolution, W. A.

Speck, *Reluctant Revolutionaries: Englishmen and the Revolution of 1688* (1988) sees the events as a decisive though not inevitable step toward parliamentary government. A more recent work by E. Cruickshanks, *The Glorious Revolution* (2000) challenges the Whig interpretation and portrays James II as an enlightened advocate of religious toleration. Evolving historical interpretations are discussed in J. I. Israel (ed.), *The Anglo-Dutch Movement: Essays on the Glorious Revolution and Its World Impact* (1991); in L. G. Schwoerer (ed.), *The Revolution of 1688–1689: Changing Perspectives* (1992); and in S. C. A. Pincus (ed.), *England's Glorious Revolution: A Brief History with Documents* (2005); and there are additional insights in H. R. Trevor-Roper's essays, *From Counter Reformation to Glorious Revolution* (1992).

For the role played in international affairs by William of Orange after he took the English throne in 1689, one may read D. W. Jones, *War and Economy in the Age of William III and Marlborough* (1988). Winston Churchill's detailed biography of John Churchill, the military commander who was his ancestor, is available as W. S. Churchill, *Marlborough: His Life and Times* (4 vols., 1933–38; abr. ed., 1968). G. M. Trevelyan, *England under Queen Anne* (3 vols., 1930–34) vividly portrays the succeeding age; and on the sovereign herself, E. Gregg, *Queen Anne* (1980) is excellent. The background to the Act of Union of 1707 joining England and Scotland is explored in B. P. Levack, *The Formation of the British State: England, Scotland, and the Union, 1603–1707* (1987).

For women in seventeenth-century England one may turn to A. Fraser, *The Weaker Vessel: Woman's Lot in Seventeenth Century England* (1985), a series of portraits, mostly of upper-class women. The scholarly essays in M. Prior (ed.), *Women in English Society, 1500–1800* (1985) relate to women of all classes. A pioneering work in social history of continuing value is A. Clark, *Working Life of Women in the Seventeenth Century* (1919, 1993), and R. Thompson, *Women in Stuart England and America* (1974) is a successful comparative study. More recent works, with an emphasis on social history, include S. D. Amussen, *An Ordered Society: Gender and Class in Early Modern England* (1988); A. Hughes, *English Revolution and Gender* (2006); and A. Lawrence, *Women in England, 1500–1760* (1994). L. G. Schwoerer illuminates the independent life of a seventeenth-century woman in *Lady Rachel Russell: "One of the Best of Women"* (1987), while S. Rowbotham ranges across a much wider historical era in *Hidden from History: Rediscovering Women in History, from the 17th Century to the Present* (1974, 1989).

The France of Louis XIV

Many of the general accounts cited at the beginning of this chapter focus on the French predominance in this age. In addition, the following books explore various aspects of Louis XIV and his reign: J. B. Wolf, *Louis XIV* (1968), a comprehensive biography, may be supplemented by I. Dunlap, *Louis XIV* (2000), and by A. Levi, *Louis XIV* (2004). Readers may also turn to A. Lossky, *Louis XIV and the French Monarchy* (1994); and F. Bluche, *Louis XIV* (1990), a detailed narrative. Available also are the essays in P. Sonnino et al. (eds.), *The Reign of Louis XIV* (1991), while P. Burke, *The Fabrication of Louis XIV* (1992) examines the molding of the king's image over his long reign. A broader study of the whole era can be found in W. Doyle (ed.), *Old Regime France, 1648–1789* (2001).

Other interpretive volumes include V. L. Tapié, *The Age of Grandeur* (rev. 1966), and O. Ranum, *Paris in the Age of Absolutism* (rev. 2002). Three studies by P. Goubert—*Louis XIV and Twenty Million Frenchmen* (trans. 1970), his more detailed *The Ancien Regime: French Society, 1600–1750* (trans. and abr. 1974), and *The French Peasantry in the Seventeenth Century* (trans. 1986)—are invaluable studies of French society and the people of the time. C. Tilly, *The Contentious French: Four Centuries of Popular Struggle* (1986), an incisive study of popular restlessness and collective action, begins with these years; and W. Beik, *Urban Protest in Seventeenth-Century France: The Culture of Retribution* (1997) examines popular resistance to authority. A comprehensive study of the mid-century challenge to royal authority is O. Ranum, *The Fronde: A French Revolution, 1648–1652* (1993).

Three books focusing on provincial institutions and other limitations of royal authority, and providing added insights into the methods by which Louis XIV ruled, are W. Beik, *Absolutism and Society in Seventeenth-Century France: State Power and Provincial Aristocracy in Languedoc* (1985); R. Mettam, *Power and Faction in Louis XIV's France* (1988); and S. Kettering, *Patrons, Brokers, and Clients in Seventeenth-Century France* (1986). J. M. Smith, *The Culture of Merit: Nobility, Royal Service, and the Making of Absolute Monarchy in France, 1600–1789* (1996) describes the king's response to noble aspirations for recognition and glory. Two older books that examine constraints on royal authority are A. L. Moote, *The Revolt of the Judges: The Parlement of Paris and the Fronde, 1643–1652* (1971) and L. Rothkrug, *Opposition to Louis XIV: The Political and Social Origins of the Enlightenment* (1965).

A biography of the French finance minister is available in A. Trout, *Jean-Baptiste Colbert* (1978). Financial matters are examined on a broad scale in J. Dent, *Crisis in France: Crown, Financiers, and Society in Seventeenth-Century France* (1973) and in R. Bonney, *The King's Debts: Finance and Politics in France, 1589–1661* (1981). The global expansion of French trade is discussed in C. J. Ames, *Colbert, Mercantilism, and the French Quest for Asian Trade* (1996).

Religious matters are explored in E. I. Perry, *From Theology to History: French Religious Controversy and the Revocation of the Edict of Nantes* (1973); A. Sedgwick, *Jansenism in Seventeenth-Century France* (1977); W. Doyle, *Jansenism: Catholic Resistance to Authority from the Reformation to the French Revolution* (2000); and in a special way in W. Scoville, *The Persecution of the Huguenots and French Economic Development, 1680–1720* (1960). On the colonial empire one may read W. J. Eccles, *The French in North America, 1500–1783* (rev. 1998); and various religious aspects of French expansion in the new world are examined in A. Greer, *Mohawk Saint: Catherine Tekakwitha and the Jesuits* (2005) and in N. Z. Davis, *Women on the Margins: Three Seventeenth-Century Lives* (1995).

C. C. Lougee, *Le Paradis des Femmes: Women, Salons, and Social Stratification in Seventeenth Century France* (1976) examines the evolving cultural influence of French women, a theme also explored in E. C. Goldsmith (ed.), *Going Public: Women and Publishing in Early Modern France* (1995); a more general work is W. Gibson, *Women in Seventeenth-Century France* (1989); and an outstanding woman of letters is studied in J. A. Ojala and W. T. Ojala, *Madame de Sévigné: A Seventeenth-Century Life* (1990). An important cultural theme is treated in J. De-Jean, *Ancients Against Moderns: Culture Wars and the Making of a Fin de Siècle* (1997).

On Louis XIV's military policies one may read an excellent survey, J. A. Lynn, *The Wars of Louis XIV, 1667–1714* (1999). Other works on the subject include P. Sonnino, *Louis XIV and the Origins of the Dutch War* (1988) and H. Kamen, *The War of Succession in Spain, 1700–1715* (1969). Two books about the final stages of Habsburg rule in Spain are H. Kamen, *Spain in the Later Seventeenth Century, 1665–1700* (1980), in which he sees revival rather than decline on the eve of the French attack, and R. A. Stradling, *Europe and the Decline of Spain, 1580–1720* (1981). For Spain in the century after the Habsburgs, an outstanding account is J. Lynch, *Bourbon Spain, 1700–1808* (1989).

Useful Web Sites

For an introduction to the Dutch republic, one may visit *The Williamite Universe,* http://let.uu.nl/ogc/William/, a site that provides information on William III and other aspects of Dutch history. Readers will find useful information on Cromwell and the wider history of the English Civil wars by visiting *The Oliver Cromwell Website,* http://olivercromwell.org/index/htm; and *BBC-History* provides additional resources for research on all majors events of the seventeenth century through the links at www.bbc.co/uk/history/. *The Official Web Site of the British Monarchy* provides information about the history of every British king, including those who faced opposition in the seventeenth century at http://royal.gov.uk/output/page5

.asp. Valuable materials on France and wider European developments can be located through *The Society for Seventeenth Century French Studies* in Britain, at http://solinuxbrookes/ac.uk/mark/17/webres.html.

Interesting images and information about Louis XIV's great palace are available in English; see the *Chateau de Versailles,* www.chateauversailles.fr/en/index.php; and there are very helpful links to Web sites on the history of early modern European women at *Early Modern Resources,* www.earlymodernweb.org.uk/emr/index.php/category/themes/gender/.

5. THE TRANSFORMATION OF EASTERN EUROPE, 1648–1740

J. H. Shennan, *Liberty and Order in Early Modern Europe: The Subject and the State, 1650–1800* (1986), focusing on France and Russia, highlights differences in the development of western and eastern Europe. Informative books that explain the complexities of central and eastern Europe, carrying their accounts toward the present, are L. C. Tihany, *A History of Middle Europe: From the Earliest Times to the Age of the World Wars* (1976); P. Wandycz, *The Price of Freedom: A History of East Central Europe from the Middle Ages to the Present* (rev. 2001); P. D. Longworth, *The Making of Eastern Europe: From Prehistory to Postcommunism* (rev. 1997); R. Bideleux and Ian Jeffries, *A History of Eastern Europe: Crisis and Change* (1998); and E. Niederhauser, *A History of Eastern Europe Since the Middle Ages* (trans. 2003). P. R. Magocsi, *Historical Atlas of East Central Europe* (1993), Vol. I of the series *A History of Central Europe,* is an impressive work of reference. J. W. Sedlar, *East Central Europe in the Middle Ages, 1000–1500* (1994) synthesizes the medieval period, while A. Maczak et al., *East Central Europe in Transition* (1985) focuses on the seventeenth to the seventeenth centuries. For the Balkans, valuable studies are L. S. Stavrianos, *The Balkans since 1453* (1958, 2000); B. Jelavich and C. Jelavich, *The Balkans* (1965); R. Ristelheuber, *A History of the Balkan Peoples* (trans. 1971); and P. F. Sugar, *Southeastern Europe under Ottoman Rule, 1354–1804* (1977), in the series on Central Europe cited above.

The Ottoman Empire

Readers will find informative accounts of the Ottoman empire in a number of recent works, including J. McCarthy, *The Ottoman Turks: An Introductory History to 1923* (1997); C. Imber, *The Ottoman Empire, 1300–1650: The Structure of Power* (2002); and S. Turnbull, *The Ottoman Empire, 1326-1699* (2003), which is a concise survey. Important coverage of Ottoman history is also found in J. Goodwin, *Lords of the Horizon: A History of the Ottoman Empire* (1999); and in D. Quataert, *The Ottoman Empire, 1700–1922* (2000). The social foundations of Ottoman power are described in H. Inalcik and D. Quataert (eds.), *An Eco-*

nomic and Social History of the Ottoman Empire, 1300–1914 (1994), while L. P. Peirce, *The Imperial Harem: Women and Sovereignty in the Ottoman Empire* (1993) describes the political role and influence of women. Ottoman relations and interactions with Europe, which are currently attracting historical attention, are explored in K. M. Setton, *Venice, Austria, and the Turks in the Seventeenth Century* (1991); R. Schwoebel, *The Shadow of the Crescent: The Renaissance Image of the Turk, 1453–1517* (1967); N. Bisaha, *Creating East and West: Renaissance Humanists and the Ottoman Turks* (2004); and D. Goffman, *The Ottoman Empire and Early Modern Europe* (2002). C. E. Bosworth, *The New Islamic Dynasties: A Chronological and Genealogical Manual* (1996) is a useful reference tool.

Austria and the Habsburgs: To 1740

Basic for these years are R. A. Kann, *A History of the Habsburg Empire, 1526–1918* (1974); R. J. Evans, *The Making of the Habsburg Empire, 1550–1770* (1979); C. Ingrao, *The Habsburg Monarchy, 1618–1815* (rev. 2000); J. Bérenger, *The History of the Habsburg Empire, 1273–1700* (trans. 1994); and P. S. Fichtner, *The Habsburg Monarchy, 1490–1848: Attributes of Empire* (2003). A number of important essays on social and political history have been collected in C. Ingrao (ed.), *State and Society in Early Modern Austria* (1994). J. P. Spielman has written *Leopold I of Austria* (1977), a balanced treatment of the seventeenth-century emperor; and for Eugene of Savoy, an outstanding biography is D. McKay, *Prince Eugene of Savoy* (1977). A vivid account of the Turkish siege of 1683 is available in J. Stoye, *The Siege of Vienna* (rev. 2000).

The Holy Roman Empire: The German States

A good introductory survey of German history is M. Fulbrook, *A Concise History of Germany* (rev. 2004). H. Holborn, in his *History of Modern Germany, Vol. II: 1648–1840* (1975), covers the fluid situation in the Holy Roman Empire after the Thirty Years' War, as does J. Gagliardo, *Germany under the Old Regime, 1600–1790* (1991). A useful, brief survey is P. H. Wilson, *The Holy Roman Empire, 1495–1806* (1999), which summarizes recent historical challenges to older assumptions about the Empire's flaws and failures. One will also wish to read E. Sagorra, *A Social History of Germany, 1648–1914* (1977), with many fascinating insights, and R. Vierhaus, *Germany in the Age of Absolutism* (1988), which studies the years 1618–1763. G. Benecke, *Society and Politics in Germany, 1500–1750* (1974) presents the case for the Empire as a viable constitutional entity, while two important contributions to understanding the formation of the German political tradition are F. L. Carsten, *Princes and Parliaments in Germany* (1959) and M. Walker, *German Home Towns: Community, State,*

and General Estate, 1648–1871 (1971). J. A. Vann thoroughly explores the evolving social structure and institutions of a key principality in *The Making of a State: Württemberg, 1593–1793* (1984).

For Prussia, convenient introductions are F. L. Carsten, *The Origins of Prussia* (1954) and H. W. Koch, *A History of Prussia* (1978). A thoughtful evocation of the state (dissolved after the Second World War) is T. von Thadden, *Prussia: The History of a Lost State* (1986). An invaluable study going well beyond the scope of this chapter is G. A. Craig, *The Politics of the Prussian Army, 1640–1945* (1956, 1964). Important also is H. Rosenberg, *Bureaucracy, Aristocracy, and Autocracy: The Prussian Experience, 1660–1815* (1958), which may be supplemented by the essays in P. G. Dwyer, *The Rise of Prussia, 1700–1830* (2002). On the early Hohenzollerns, one may read F. Schevill, *The Great Elector* (1974) and R. Ergang, *The Potsdam Führer: Frederick William I, Father of Prussian Militarism* (1941, 1972). Books on Frederick the Great are cited in Chapter 8.

Russia: To 1725

There are many excellent narrative accounts of Russian history with good coverage of the early years; for example, one may read N. V. Riasanovsky and M. D. Steinberg, *A History of Russia* (rev. 2004); R. Bartlett, *A History of Russia* (2005); and P. Dukes, *A History of Russia, c. 882–1996* (1998). For the early years and the expansion and transformation of Muscovy, one may turn to R. O. Crummey, *The Formation of Muscovy, 1304–1613* (1987), while P. Dukes, *The Making of Russian Absolutism, 1613–1801* (rev. 1990) traces the tsardom from the beginning of the Romanov dynasty over the next two centuries. The military side to Russian society and the "service state" are ably examined in J. L. H. Keep, *Soldiers of the Tsar: Army and Society in Russia, 1462–1874* (1985) and the rural scene is studied in J. Blum, *Lord and Peasant in Russia from the Ninth to the Nineteenth Century* (1961). P. Avrich examines social upheavals in *Russian Rebels, 1600–1800* (1972), while R. Mousnier treats agrarian unrest comparatively in *Peasant Uprisings in Seventeenth-Century France, Russia, and China* (trans. 1970).

The early rulers are studied in A. Pavlov and M. Perrie, *Ivan the Terrible* (2003); and in I. de Madariaga, *Ivan the Terrible: First Tsar of Russia* (2005), an outstanding study of the brutal ruler. W. B. Lincoln, *Autocrats of All the Russias* (1981) is a remarkable large-scale study of the Romanovs, the 15 tsars and 4 tsarinas who ruled Russia between 1613 and 1917. A more recent study of the changes in the early modern period can be found in S. Dixon, *The Modernisation of Russia, 1676–1825* (1999); and Russia's early imperial expansion is examined in the important work by J. P. LeDonne, *The Grand Strategy of the Russian Empire, 1650–1831* (2004). An absorbing impressionistic cultural history is J. H. Billington, *The*

Icon and the Axe: An Interpretive History of Russian Culture (1966), while a provocative reassessment of Russia's relationship to European intellectual and cultural history is M. Malia, *Russia under Western Eyes: From the Bronze Horseman to the Lenin Mausoleum* (1999).

On Peter and the reforms of his reign, an older outstanding biography, M. Klyuchevsky, *Peter the Great* (trans. 1958), may be compared with the briefer, more recent accounts by S. J. Lee, *Peter the Great* (1993); M. S. Anderson, *Peter the Great* (rev. 1995); and L Hughes, *Peter the Great, A Biography* (2002). Peter's interest in western Europe is discussed in L. Hughes (ed.), *Peter the Great and the West: New Perspectives* (2001). An excellent account of Russian society, culture, and government in this era appears in the comprehensive, insightful study by L. Hughes, *Russia in the Age of Peter the Great* (1998), in which she neglects no aspect of Peter's rule. R. K. Massie, *Peter the Great: His Life and World* (1980) is a long, vivid, and colorful popular account, less critical of Peter than other studies. N. V. Riasanovsky, *The Image of Peter the Great in Russian History and Thought* (1985) examines the ruler's long-range cultural impact, while one aspect of his cultural revolution is examined in J. Cracraft, *The Petrine Revolution in Russian Architecture* (1988). An admirable study in comparative cultural history is D. W. Treadgold, *The West in Russia and China: Religious and Secular Thought in Modern Times* (2 vols., 1973), the first volume of which covers Russia for the years 1472–1917. For Sweden, and for Peter's great Swedish rival, an outstanding biography is R. N. Hatton, *Charles XII of Sweden* (1969). A number of important studies by M. Roberts and others have been cited in Chapter 3; for these years M. Roberts, *The Swedish Imperial Experience, 1560–1718* (1979) deserves mention. The Baltic shore is explored in S. P. Oakley, *War and Peace in the Baltic, 1560–1790* (1992).

Useful Web Sites

Resources on Ottoman history can be found at *World Civilizations*, www.wsu.edu:8080/~dee/OTTOMAN/ OTTOMAN1.HTM, which is part of an excellent Web site at Washington State University, and at *Internet Islamic History Sourcebook*, www.fordham.edu/halsall/ islam/islamsbook.html, where readers may locate links to Ottoman materials from the outstanding internet resources at Fordham University. On the Habsburgs and the Austrian empire, readers will find useful resources at *The Imperial House of Hapsburg*, www .hapsburg.com/home.htm, and at the helpful links from this site. There is concise, well-organized information on early modern Prussia, Poland, Russia, and other European states at the wide-ranging British Web site, *History World,* www.historyworld.net/, where readers will find valuable timelines as well as other interactive materials. On Russian imperial history in the age of Peter the Great, one may consult the materials pertaining to the *History and Culture of Russia* at www.geographica.com/russia.rushis.01.htm; and readers will find excellent links to a wide range of resources on the early history of Russia at Bucknell University's *Russian Studies Program*, www.bucknell .edu/Russian.

6. THE SCIENTIFIC VIEW OF THE WORLD

Histories of Science

An outstanding, broad-ranging study is B. L. Silver, *The Ascent of Science* (1998). A valuable new series on the history of modern science is available in D. C. Lindberg and R. Numbers (eds.), *The Cambridge History of Science* (2003–06), a collaborative project that will eventually include eight volumes. An older, but still useful collaborative survey is L. P. Williams and H. J. Steffens (eds.), *The History of Science in Western Civilization* (3 vols., 1977–78), from antiquity to the twentieth century. Other excellent historical accounts include R. Olson, *Science Deified and Science Defied: The Historical Significance of Science in Western Culture* (2 vols., 1982–91), a far-reaching study ranging from prehistory to 1820. Ancient and medieval science is also explored in D. C. Lindberg, *The Beginnings of Western Science* (1992), cited in Chapter 2. Other important perspectives on the long history of science appear in M. Serres (ed.), *A History of Scientific Thought: Elements of a History of Thought* (trans. 1995) and in the comprehensive analysis of the historical study of science by H. F. Cohen, *The Scientific Revolution: A Historiographical Inquiry* (1994). For individual scientists one may consult the *Dictionary of Scientific Biography* (8 vols., 1970–80) and for new works in the history of science, the annual bibliographies published in *Isis*.

The Scientific Revolution

For the fundamental reorientation of thinking about nature and the universe in early modern times, three older but still valuable introductions are H. Butterfield, *The Origins of Modern Science* (rev. 1965); A. Koyré, *From the Closed World to the Infinite Universe* (1968); and A. R. Hall, *The Revolution in Science, 1500–1750: The Formation of the Modern Scientific Attitude* (rev. 1983). These works may now be supplemented by K. Park and L. Daston, *Early Modern Science* (2006), which is the third volume in *The Cambridge History of Science*. Other informative accounts include A. G. Debus, *Man and Nature in the Renaissance* (1978) and R. S. Westfall, *The Construction of Modern Science* (1971). Of special interest are I. B. Cohen's *The Newtonian Revolution* (1980) and *Revolution in Science* (1985), an encyclopedic study of the transformation of scientific ideas. Useful shorter surveys of this era may be found in J. R. Jacob, *The Scientific Revolution: Aspirations and Achievements, 1500–1700* (1998);

J. Henry, *The Scientific Revolution and the Origins of Modern Science* (rev. 2002); and S. Shapin, *The Scientific Revolution* (1996), which examines the cultural dimensions of scientific knowledge. On the nature of revolutionary breakthroughs in science a highly influential work has been T. S. Kuhn, *The Structure of Scientific Revolution* (1962, rev. 1970, reissued 1989), which challenges the belief in progressive, cumulative scientific advance and emphasizes the role of shifting cultural assumptions in the development of scientific knowledge. Kuhn has also written *The Copernican Revolution* (1957, 1985). Some historians of science have questioned traditional views of the scientific revolution, arguing that the changes in thought proceeded slowly and that most early modern scientists retained decidedly unmodern views of human knowledge. For discussion of these issues, readers may turn to M. J. Osler (ed.), *Rethinking the Scientific Revolution* (2000). P. B. Medawar, *Pluto's Republic* (1982), humorously entitled but a serious book, explores the persistence of pseudo- and quasi-scientific thinking from Bacon to the present.

For all aspects of technology and the practical application of science, one may consult C. Singer et al., *A History of Technology* (8 vols., 1954–84). Three related books are A. Pacey, *The Maze of Ingenuity* (1976); S. Shapin and S. Schaffer, *Leviathan and the Air Pump* (1985); and L. Jardine, *Ingenious Pursuits: Building the Scientific Revolution* (2000). Technology as a social force is explored in the classic study of L. Mumford, *Technics and Civilization* (1934, reissued 1963) and in O. Mayr, *Authority, Liberty, and Automatic Machinery in Early Modern Europe* (1986). A brief, informative survey appears in E. D. Brose, *Technology and Science in the Industrializing Nations, 1500–1914* (1998).

A number of provocative studies relate the scientific revolution to the political and social ferment and economic developments in seventeenth-century England and stress the practical implications for a commercial society. Here two pioneer studies were R. K. Merton, *Science, Technology, and Society in Seventeenth Century England* (1970) and C. Webster, *The Great Instauration: Science, Medicine, and Reform, 1626–1660* (1975). An admirable synthesis is M. C. Jacob, *The Cultural Meaning of the Scientific Revolution* (1988), a work that has been revised and expanded in *Scientific Culture and the Making of the Industrial West* (1997). The applications of Newtonian science are examined in M. C. Jacob and L. C. Stewart, *Practical Matter: Newton's Science in the Service of Industry and Empire, 1687–1851* (2004). Connections between early scientific writing and early modern literature are analyzed in E. Spiller, *Science, Reading, and Renaissance Literature: The Art of Making Knowledge, 1580–1670* (2004).

Biographically Oriented Accounts

The contributions of the pioneer astronomers are described in many of the books already cited and in

A. Armitage, *The World of Copernicus* (1972); J. M. Caspar, *Kepler* (reissued 1993); and K. Ferguson, *Tycho and Kepler: The Unlikely Partnership that Forever Changed Our Understanding of the Heavens* (2002), an accessible double biography of two major scientists and their times . For Galileo one may read A. Koyré, *Galileo Studies* (1978); while a study of his scientific activities is available in S. Drake, *Galileo at Work: His Scientific Biography* (1978), in which the author has reconstructed the scientist's instruments and examined his notebooks; the same author has written a concise biographical study, *Galileo* (2001). The condemnation that Galileo aroused from the Church and other authorities is described in J. J. Langford, *Galileo, Science, and the Church* (rev. 1992), while P. Redondi, *Galileo: Heretic* (trans. 1987) is a provocative, not entirely convincing, revisionist account. Galileo's links to the culture of patronage are examined in M. Biagioli, *Galileo, Courtier* (1993); and helpful accounts of the wider culture in which he worked can be found in J. Renn (ed.), *Galileo in Context* (2001). For Newton, R. S. Westfall, *Never at Rest: A Biography of Isaac Newton* (1982, 1993) is a biography of distinction; D. Berlinski, *Newton's Gift: How Sir Isaac Newton Unlocked the System of the World* (2000) is illuminating on the man and his accomplishments; and there are also notable biographies by G. E. Christianson (1984), A. R. Hall (1992), and J. Gleick (2003). Newton's fascination with other forms of thought is described in the influential revisionist work of B. J. T. Dobbs, *The Janus Face of Genius: The Role of Alchemy in Newton's Thought* (1991).

Science and Thought

Three informative studies of a key figure in the new science are P. Zagorin, *Francis Bacon* (1998), which is especially strong on Bacon's intellectual contributions; L. Jardine and A. Stewart, *Hostage to Fortune: The Troubled Life of Francis Bacon* (1998), which describes in detail all aspects of his complex career; and C. Whitney, *Francis Bacon and Modernity* (1986). B. H. G. Wormald, *Francis Bacon: History, Politics, and Science, 1561–1626* (1993) remains a major appraisal. Descartes and his influence are described in T. Sorell, *Descartes* (1987), and in P. A. Schouls, *Descartes and the Enlightenment* (1989). Readers may turn to H. M. Bracken, *Descartes* (2002) for a concise account of his life and ideas. The complexities of Cartesian thought are examined from new perspectives in S. Bordo (ed.), *Feminist Interpretations of René Descartes* (1999).

The role played by women in the scientific revolution is skillfully explored in L. Schiebinger, *The Mind Has No Sex? Women in the Origins of Modern Science* (1989), the title derived from Descartes. It may be read along with the same author's *Nature's Body: Gender in the Making of Modern Science* (1993, reissued 2004), focusing on eighteenth-century studies of plants and animals. An important book by

E. Harth, *Cartesian Women: Versions and Subversions of Rational Discourse in the Old Regime* (1992), compares the role of women intellectuals in the seventeenth and eighteenth centuries.

For Pascal one may read A. Krailsheimer, *Pascal* (1980); H. M. Davidson, *Blaise Pascal* (1983); and J. R. Cole, *Pascal: The Man and His Two Loves* (1995), which offers debatable psychological interpretations of the writer's life and work. There is a perceptive, brief study of Pierre Bayle by E. Labrousse, *Bayle* (trans. 1983). Skepticism is further explored in F. L. Baumer, *Religion and the Rise of Skepticism* (1960) and in R. H. Popkin, *The History of Skepticism from Savonarola to Spinoza* (rev. 2003); Montaigne, its sixteenth-century exemplar, is studied in excellent biographies by D. M. Frame (1965) and H. Friedrich (trans. 1991), which may be compared with G. Hoffmann, *Montaigne's Career* (1998). A judicious, balanced biography of the seventeeth-century Dutch philosopher is S. Nadler, *Spinoza: A Life* (1999). The cultural influence of Spinoza and other skeptical thinkers is analyzed in the wide-ranging work of J. I. Israel, *The Radical Enlightenment: Philosophy and the Making of Modernity 1650–1750* (2002). A provocative book exploring the relationship of rationalism to Western thought from the seventeenth century on is E. Gellner, *Reason and Rationalism* (1990).

For the political thought of the period an overview is provided in F. L. Baumer, *Modern European Thought: Continuity and Change in Ideas, 1600–1950* (1977). On Locke one may read J. Dunn, *The Political Thought of John Locke* (1969), and the same author's *Locke: A Very Short Introduction* (rev. 2003); R. Ashcraft, *Locke's Two Treatises of Government* (1986); and E. J. Lowe, *Locke* (2005). There are also useful accounts of Locke's life and work in W. M. Spellman, *John Locke* (1997) and in K. L. Cope, *John Locke Revisited* (1999). Hobbes is studied in two notable books by A. Martinich, *Hobbes, A Biography* (1999), and *Hobbes* (2005); in A. A. Rogow, *Thomas Hobbes: Radical in the Service of Reaction* (1986); and in R. Tuck, *Hobbes* (1989), a brief appraisal. Useful for French thinkers in these years is N. O. Koehane, *Philosophy and the State in France: The Renaissance to the Enlightenment* (1980). Two important studies of modern conceptions of individual identity also discuss the intellectual history of this era: C. Taylor, *Sources of the Self: The Making of the Modern Identity* (1989) and J. Seigel, *The Idea of the Self: Thought and Experience in Western Europe Since the Seventeenth Century* (2005).

Useful Web Sites

Resources on European science in the sixteenth and seventeenth centuries can be found at Rice University's *Galileo Project* at http://galileo.rice.edu/index .html, an excellent site that focuses on Galileo but includes many other valuable materials and links. Additional information on early astronomy and other sciences is available at *History of Astronomy,* www .astro.uni-bonn.de/%Epbrosche/astoria.html. There are useful materials and helpful links on seventeenth–century science at the Web site of the *Newton Project,* at Imperial College, London, http://newtonproject.ic.ac.uk/. The history of early modern philosophy, including bibliographic materials and links to sites on Bacon, Descartes, Spinoza, Bayle and others, can be explored through the excellent *Stanford Encyclopedia of Philosophy* at http://plato .stanford.edu/.

7. THE STRUGGLE FOR WEALTH AND EMPIRE

For the years covered in this chapter, helpful syntheses include T. C. W. Blanning (ed.), *The Eighteenth Century* (2000) and Blanning's more recent book, *The Culture of Power and the Power of Culture: Old Regime Europe, 1660–1789* (2002); I. Woloch, *Eighteenth Century Europe: Tradition and Progress, 1715–1798* (1982); M. S. Anderson, *Europe in the Eighteenth Century, 1713–1783* (rev. 2000); J. Black, *Eighteenth-Century Europe* (rev. 1999); and W. Doyle, *The Old European Order, 1660–1800* (rev. 1992). Europe's colonial empires and the new global trading system are examined in J. Black, *Europe and the World, 1650–1830* (2002). A useful reference work is J. Black and R. Porter (eds.), *A Dictionary of Eighteenth-Century World History* (1993).

Popular Culture and Everyday Life

The differences between elite and popular culture emerge from three books mentioned earlier: P. Burke, *Popular Culture in Early Modern Europe* (rev. 1994); K. Thomas, *Religion and the Decline of Magic* (1971); and F. Braudel, *The Structures of Everyday Life* (trans. 1981, 1991), the first volume of his three-volume study. They may be supplemented by the essays in A. Mitchell and I. Deák (eds.), *Everyman in Europe: Essays in Social History* (2 vols., rev. 1997). There are also studies of English social mores in K. Olsen, *Daily Life in 18th-Century England* (1999) and in P. Langford, *Englishness Identified: Manners and Character, 1650–1850* (2000). The role of language in shaping social identities is examined in an insightful work by P. Burke, *Languages and Communities in Early Modern Europe* (2004).

The Global Economy and the Colonial Empires

The final two volumes of Braudel's work, *The Wheels of Commerce* (trans. 1983) and *The Perspectives of the World* (both reissued in 1991), offer remarkable accounts of the global economy. A far-ranging study relevant for the years after 1650 is S. W. Mintz, *Sweetness and Power: The Place of Sugar in Modern History* (1985). The celebrated speculative ventures of the age are graphically described in J. Carswell, *The South Sea Bubble* (1960); in the relevant chapters of C. P. Kindleberger, *Manias, Panics, and Crashes: A History of Financial Crises* (1978); in J. K. Galbraith, *A Short History of Financial Euphoria: A Hymn of Caution* (1993); and in R. Dale, *The First Crash: Lessons from the South Sea Bubble* (2004).

Several books on European overseas expansion listed for Chapters 3 and 4 also discuss the eighteenth century. To these must be added H. Furber's excellent synthesis, *Rival Empires of Trade in the Orient, 1600–1800* (1976); J. H. Parry, *Trade and Dominion: The European Overseas Empires in the Eighteenth Century* (1971); two works by G. Williams, *The Expansion of Europe in the Eighteenth Century: Overseas Rivalry, Discovery, and Exploitation* (1966) and *The Great South Sea: English Voyages and Encounters, 1570–1750* (1997); P. K. Liss, *Atlantic Empires: The Network of Trade and Revolution, 1713–1826* (1983); P. D. Curtin, *Cross-Cultural Trade in World History* (1984), cited earlier; and A. K. Smith, *Creating a World Economy: Merchant Capital, Colonialism, and World Trade, 1400–1825* (1991). One may also read the relevant chapters of D. K. Fieldhouse, *The Colonial Empires: A Comparative Survey from the Eighteenth Century* (rev. 1982). A valuable, collaborative work under the general editorship of W. R. Louis, *The Oxford History of the British Empire* (5 vols., 1998–1999), offers up-to-date research by specialists and includes two volumes on the early era of global expansion: N. Canny (ed.), *British Overseas Enterprise to the Close of the Seventeenth Century* and P. J. Marshall (ed.), *The Eighteenth Century*.

The impact of Asia on Europe in the early modern centuries from the sixteenth century on is studied in great detail in D. F. Lach, *Asia in the Making of Europe* (3 vols., 1965–93), of which E. J. Van Kley is coauthor of volume 3. A useful collaborative work is A. T. Embree and C. Gluck (eds.), *Asia in Western and World History: A Guide for Teaching* (1997).

P. Lawson, *The East India Company: A History* (1993) describes its activities from its beginnings in 1603 to its demise in 1857; a wide-ranging collection of early and recent historical writings on the same subject has been brought together in P. Tuck, *The East India Company, 1600–1858* (6 vols., 1998). The eighteenth-century impact on India is further explored in P. Woodruff [Mason], *The Men Who Ruled India* (2 vols., 1954–57) and in P. J. Marshall, *The Making and Unmaking of Empires: Britian, India, and America, c. 1750–1783* (2005), which examines how Britain expanded its imperial role in India while it was losing imperial control of its American colonies. A recent study of the controversial British governor general is available in J. Bernstein, *Dawning of the Raj: The Life and Trials of Warren Hastings* (2000). For India itself the best introductions appear in P. Spear, *The Oxford History of Modern India, 1740–1975* (rev.

1978); S. Wolpert, *A New History of India* (rev. 2000); J. Keay, *India: A History* (2000); and H. Kulke and D. Rothermund, *A History of India* (rev. 2004), and P. Robb, *A History of India* (2002). J. E. Schwartzberg (ed.), *A Historical Atlas of South Asia* (rev. 1992) is a superb atlas.

For the French in North America one may read W. J. Eccles, *The French in North America, 1500–1783* (rev. 1998), cited earlier, and *The Canadian Frontier, 1534–1760* (1974); P. Boucher, *Les Nouvelles Frances: France in America, 1500–1815* (1989), a brief illustrated account; and D. H. Usner, Jr., *Indians, Settlers, & Slaves in a Frontier Exchange Economy: The Lower Mississippi Valley Before 1783* (1992). The importance of the West Indies for the Atlantic economy emerges from N. F. Crouse, *The French Struggle for the West Indies, 1665–1713* (1944); R. S. Dunn, *Sugar and Slaves* (1972); and S. W. Mintz's *Sweetness and Power* (1985), cited above.

British Politics and Society in the Eighteenth Century

Books on eighteenth-century France are listed below in Chapter 8, but two works should be mentioned here: C. Pevitt, *The Man Who Would be King: The Life of Philippe, Duc d'Orléans: Regent of France* (1998); and R. Butler, *Choiseul* (1980).

There is a growing literature on eighteenth-century British politics and society after the settlement of 1688–1689. L. B. Namier, who wrote with precision and depth but insisted on narrow political and parliamentary history, long had an enormous influence. His most important books were *The Structure of Politics at the Accession of George III* (2 vols., 1920; 1957) and *England in the Age of the American Revolution* (rev. 1961). He also launched a large-scale collaborative project in prosopography, or collective biography, seeking to reconstruct in minute detail the composition of the modern British parliaments. His approach, adopted by other historians, downplayed the importance of ideology in the seventeenth-century revolutions, as discussed in Chapter 4, and even the triumph of Parliament over crown in 1688. His continuing influence is demonstrated in J. P. Kenyon, *Revolution Principles: The Politics of Party, 1689–1720* (1977, 1990) as well as in J. C. D. Clark's two books: *English Society, 1688–1832* (1985) and *Revolution and Rebellion* (1986).

J. Brewer has widened the political arena in two innovative works, *Party Ideology and Popular Politics at the Accession of George III* (1976) and *The Sinews of Power: War, Money, and the English State, 1688–1783* (1989). At the same time E. P. Thompson's interest in social history has influenced eighteenth-century studies. Thompson's own work on this era includes *Whigs and Hunters: The Origin of the Black Act* (1976). For other books affording broad insights into eighteenth-century British politics and society one may turn to G. S. Holmes, *British Politics in the Age of Anne* (1967, 1987) and *The Age of Oligarchy: Pre-Industrial Britain, 1722–1783* (1993); N. Rogers, *Whigs and Cities: Popular Politics in the Age of Walpole and Pitt* (1989); W. A. Speck, *The Birth of Britain: A New Nation, 1700–1710* (1994) and *Stability and Strife: England, 1714–1760* (1977); and J. Black, *Eighteenth-Century Britain, 1688–1783* (2001).

For the economy and society one may read three informative accounts: N. McKendrick, J. Brewer, and J. H. Plumb, *The Birth of a Consumer Society: The Commercialization of Eighteenth-Century England* (1982); P. Langford, *A Polite and Commercial People: England, 1727–1783* (1989); and R. Porter, *English Society in the Eighteenth Century* (rev. 1990). One may also read P. Mathias, *The First Industrial Nation: An Economic History of Britain, 1700–1914* (rev. 1983); C. P. Hill, *British Economic and Social History, 1700–1982* (rev. 1985); and P. Langford and C. Harvie, *The Eighteenth Century and the Age of Industry* (1992), in the *Oxford History of Britain*. F. M. L. Thompson, *The Cambridge Social History of Britain, 1750–1950* (rev. 1993) begins with these years. For an excellent, wide-ranging study of the era's cultural history, one may turn to J. Brewer, *The Pleasures of the Imagination: English Culture in the Eighteenth Century* (1997).

Biographical accounts include R. N. Hatton, *George I, Elector and King* (1979); J. H. Plumb, *Sir Robert Walpole* (2 vols., 1951–56), a biography of distinction, and *The First Four Georges* (1956); H. T. Dickinson, *Walpole and the Whig Supremacy* (1973); and J. Black, *Robert Walpole and the Nature of Politics in Early Eighteenth-Century England* (1990). There are biographies of the elder Pitt by S. Ayling (1976), P. D. Brown (1978), and J. Black (rev. 1999). The Jacobite uprisings are discussed in books by B. Lenman (1995), P. K. Monod (1983), J. L. Roberts (2002), C. Duffy (2003), and F. McLynn (1981). McLynn has also written a biography of the Young Pretender, *Bonnie Prince Charlie: Charles Edward Stuart* (1991) as well as *Crime and Punishment in Eighteenth-Century England* (1989), which traces the prevailing insecurity to the Jacobite threat. The latter may be supplemented by P. Linebaugh, *The London Hanged: Crime and Punishment in the Eighteenth Century* (1992), an impressive study.

Especially insightful on the formation of the British national identity in these years is L. Colley, *Britons: Forging the Nation, 1707–1837* (1992), which may be supplemented by H. F. Kearney, *The British Isles: A History of Four Nations* (1989). W. A. Speck's informative survey, *A Concise History of Britain, 1707–1975* (1993) begins with these years.

The Great War of the Mid-Eighteenth Century, 1740–1763

R. Browning, *The War of the Austrian Succession* (1993) is an outstanding wide-ranging study of the first phase of the mid-eighteenth century conflict; and there is an excellent comprehensive account of the second important war in F. Anderson, *Crucible of War: The Seven Years' War and the Fate of Empire in British North America, 1754–1766* (2000); a briefer account is available from the same author in *The War that Made America: A Short History of the French and Indian War* (2005); and in D. Marston, *The Seven Years' War* (2001). The latter subject is studied also in J. Keegan in *Fields of Battle: The Wars for North America* (1996).

J. Brewer, *The Sinews of Power: War, Money, and the English State, 1688–1783* (1989), noted earlier, persuasively demonstrates that it was the fiscal strength and war-making capacities of the British parliamentary government after 1688 that made possible Britain's ascent as a global power. For the crisis created by the mid-century wars, in addition to the biographical accounts of Pitt already cited, one may read M. Peters, *Pitt and Popularity: The Patriot Minister and London Opinion during the Seven Years' War* (1980) and R. Middleton, *The Pitt-Newcastle Ministry and the Conduct of the Seven Years' War, 1757–1762* (1985).

C. Duffy, *The Army of Maria Theresa: The Armed Forces of Imperial Austria, 1740–1780* (1977) ably explores the nature of the Habsburg army, and the same author examines Frederick's skill in statecraft and military prowess in *Frederick the Great: A Military Life* (1985). Other aspects of Frederick's military and foreign policies are discussed with perceptive insights in T. Schieder, *Frederick the Great* (trans. 2000). Additional works on Frederick are listed below in Chapter 8.

Some Useful Web Sites

For information and links on the finanical panics of the era, see the *Bubble Project* at Dalhousie University, http://myweb.dal.ca/dmcneil/bubble.html. There are useful materials and links on the early British empire at *BBC-History*, hhtp.bbc.co.uk/history/state/empire. The history of France's role in early America can be explored through the links at the *Virtual Museum of New France*, http://www.vmnf.civilization.ca/vmnf/vmnf.asp. The Web site of *The Royal Historical Society*, at http://www.rhs/ac/uk/bibl/bibwel.asp, offers links to numerous resources on eighteenth-century history and culture. The themes of both early modern and modern global history are addressed regularly at *World History Connected*, http://worldhistoryconnected.press.uiuc.edu/, the site of an excellent "e-journal" that offers up-to-date information and analysis of the transnational exchanges in world history.

8. THE AGE OF ENLIGHTENMENT

For background, the eighteenth-century accounts listed at the beginning of Chapter 7 should be consulted and to them should be added A. Goodwin (ed.), *The American and French Revolutions, 1763–1793*

(1965), Vol. VIII of *The New Cambridge Modern History*. There are helpful essays in D. E. D. Beales, *Enlightenment and Reform in Eighteenth-Century Europe* (2005) and a valuable overview in O. Hufton, *Europe: Privilege and Protest: 1730–1789* (rev. 2000). Readers will also find an intriguing, comprehensive account of the later eighteenth century in F. Venturi, *The End of the Old Regime in Europe, 1776–1789* (2 vols., trans. 1991).

Enlightenment Thought

The most wide-ranging survey of the thought of the era is P. Gay, *The Enlightenment: An Interpretation* (2 vols., 1966–69), a comprehensive work that praises the rationalist themes of many eighteenth-century writers; the author also explores some of his theses in *The Party of Humanity: Essays on the French Enlightenment* (1964). Other influential, older interpretations are to be found in E. Cassirer, *The Philosophy of the Enlightenment* (1932; trans. 1951); A Cobban, *In Search of Humanity: The Role of the Enlightenment in Modern History* (1960); N. Hampson, *A Cultural History of the Enlightenment* (1969); and I. O. Wade, *The Structure and Form of the French Enlightenment* (2 vols., 1977). An informative concise introduction is M. Cranston, *Philosophers and Pamphleteers: Political Theorists of the Enlightenment* (1986), while two useful, brief surveys entitled *The Enlightenment* are available by R. Porter (rev. 2001) and D. Outram (1995). G. Himmelfarb, *The Roads to Modernity: The British, French, and American Enlightenments* (2004) is provocative but not always convincing when it elevates British and American contributions above those of the French. Readers may also turn to M. C. Jacob (ed.), *The Enlightenment: A Brief History with Documents* (2001).

Many recent works on the Enlightenment stress the role of social and cultural institutions that promoted the circulation of ideas and new forms of intellectual debate. This approach to the Enlightenment has been influenced by the challenging work of J. Habermas, *The Structural Transformation of the Public Sphere* (trans. 1989). Among the many recent studies that examine institutions of the Enlightenment "public sphere," readers will find valuable insights in D. Goodman, *The Republic of Letters: A Cultural History of the French Enlightenment* (1994), which discusses the role of women in French salons; D. Gordon, *Citizens Without Sovereignty: Equality and Sociability in French Thought, 1670–1789* (1994); A. Goldgar, *Impolite Learning: Conduct and Community in the Republic of Letters* (1995); and T. Munck, *The Enlightenment: A Comparative Social History, 1721–1794* (2000), which argues that the new ideas spread widely beyond the elite centers of intellectual life. Other important books include U. Im Hof, *The Enlightenment* (trans. 1994) and D. Roche, *France in the Enlightenment* (1993, trans. 1998), a balanced, informative, and entertaining work by a leading French historian. Interesting work on more specific topics may be found in M. C. Jacob, *Living the Enlightenment: Freemasonary and Politics in Eighteenth-Century Europe* (1991) as well as in O. P. Grell and R. Porter (eds.), *Toleration in Enlightenment Europe* (2000). M. Vovelle (ed.), *Enlightenment Portraits* (1997) brings to life many of the people of the age; and D. M. McMahon examines the critics of Enlightenment thought in *Enemies of the Enlightenment: The French Counter-Enlightenment and the Making of Modernity* (2001).

On the theme of progress, readers may consult the classic work by J. B. Bury, *The Idea of Progress: An Inquiry into Its Origin and Growth* (1920, 1955) and R. Nisbet, *History of the Idea of Progress* (rev. 1994), which treats the concept on a broad time scale. The idea has also been examined in A. M. Melzer, J. Weinberger, and M. R. Zinman (eds.), *History and the Idea of Progress* (1995). On economic thought and the early advocates of free trade, there is E. Fox-Genovese, *The Origins of Physiocracy: Economic Revolution and Social Order in Eighteenth-Century France* (1976) and the important work of P. Groenwegen, *Eighteenth-Century Economics: Turgot, Beccaria and Smith and Their Contemporaries* (2002).

The Philosophes

There are numerous books on the leading thinkers of the Enlightenment. On Voltaire, P. Gay, *Voltaire's Politics: The Poet as Realist* (rev. 1988) reveals Voltaire's pragmatic reactions to the events of his day; H. Mason, *Voltaire: A Biography* (1981) is a concise authoritative account; J. Gray, *Voltaire* (1999) offers a brief introduction; and A. J. Ayer, *Voltaire* (1986) stresses Voltaire as crusader. More recent studies include R. Pearson, *Voltaire Almighty: A Life in Pursuit of Freedom* (2005) and I. Davidson, *Voltaire in Exile* (2005), which focuses on the philosophe's later life and career. For Montesquieu one may read an outstanding study by R. Shackleton, *Montesquieu: A Critical Biography* (1961) and an illuminating brief examination of his thought in J. N. Shklar, *Montesquieu* (1987). On Diderot, A. M. Wilson's biography (2 vols., 1957, 1972) is admirable and P. N. Furbank, *Diderot: A Critical Biography* (1992) is equally impressive and adds new materials.

For the elusive Rousseau, a comprehensive introduction is L. G. Crocker, *Jean-Jacques Rousseau* (2 vols., 1968), while E. Cassirer, *The Question of Jean-Jacques Rousseau* (trans. 1963) remains fundamental. In addition to many other studies, readers may turn to J. H. Huizinga, *Rousseau: The Self-Made Man* (1975); R. Grimsley, *Jean-Jacques Rousseau* (1983); and M. Cranston's important reassessment, *Jean-Jacques: The Early Life and Works of Jean-Jacques Rousseau, 1712–1754* (1982), with a sequel, *The Noble Savage: Jean-Jacques Rousseau, 1754–1762* (1991). Two challenging books are J. Miller, *Rousseau: Dreamer of Democracy* (1984) and J. N. Shklar, *Men and Citizens: A Study of Rousseau's Social Theory* (1985). The work of M. Hulliung, *The Autocritique of Enlightenment: Rousseau and the Philosophes* (1994), describes Rousseau's critical analysis of his own era's intellectual culture. Rousseau's life and thought are also examined in L. Damrosch, *Jean-Jacques Rousseau, Restless Genius* (2005), an excellent biography.

On Condorcet, K. M. Baker has written the exhaustive *Condorcet: From Natural Philosophy to Social Mathematics* (1975), while D. Williams, *Condorcet and Modernity* (2005) discusses both the ideas and political vision of a philosophe who also participated in the French Revolution. On the leading biologist or "natural historian" of the age, one may read J. Roger, *Buffon* (trans. 1998). On a lesser known philosophe sympathetic to the poorer classes, an excellent account is D. G. Levy, *The Ideas and Careers of Simon-Nicholas-Henri Linguet* (1980). H. G. Payne, *The Philosophes and the People* (1971) traces the divergent views of the famous writers toward the lower classes, as does H. Chisick, *The Limits of Reform in the Enlightenment* (1981).

For the connection between the ideas of the Enlightenment and the Revolution one still reads the classic work of D. Mornet, *Intellectual Origins of the French Revolution* (trans. 1933), which saw a more direct link than some contemporary scholars would concede. Three major reassessments are F. Furet, *Interpreting the French Revolution* (trans. 1981); K. M. Baker, *Inventing the French Revolution: Essays in the Political Culture of the Eighteenth Century* (1990); and R. Chartier, *The Cultural Origins of the French Revolution* (trans. 1991). Two books on the use and abuse of the ideas of the philosophes by the later revolutionaries are N. Hampson, *Will and Circumstance: Montesquieu, Rousseau, and the French Revolution* (1984) and C. Blum, *Rousseau and the Republic of Virtue: The Language of Politics in the French Revolution* (1986).

Intellectual ties between France and America are discussed in L. Gottschalk and D. F. Lach, *Toward the French Revolution: Europe and America in the Eighteenth-Century World* (1973) and in S. Schiff, *A Great Improvisation: Franklin, France, and the Birth of America* (2005). On Franklin one may also read C. A. Lopez, *Mon Cher Papa: Franklin and the Ladies of Paris* (rev. 1990) and two excellent biographies by E. S. Morgan (2002) and W. Isaacson (2005). Books that explore the significance of the Americas for European life and thought include A. Gerbi, *The Dispute of the New World, 1750–1900* (1973); S. Brandon, *New Worlds for Old* (1986), cited in Chapter 3; and C. Vann Woodward, *The Old World's New World* (1991), on changing European perceptions of America. An outstanding effort to explore the most important collaborative work of the French Enlightenment is R. Darnton, *The Business of Enlightenment: A Publishing History of the Encyclopédie, 1775–1800* (1979). The same author's other books, among them

Mesmerism and the End of the Enlightenment in France (1968), *The Literary Underground of the Old Regime* (1985), and *The Great Cat Massacre and Other Episodes in French Cultural History* (1984) help explain popular culture and radical political thought among ordinary men and women of the age. An engaging recent study of the philosophes' cultural and political ambitions is available in P. Blom, *Enlightening the World: Encyclopédie, the Book that Changed the Course of History* (2005). The growth of literacy is explored, especially for the years after 1680, in F. Furet and J. Ozouf, *Reading and Writing: Literacy in France from Calvin to Jules Ferry* (trans. 1983); the history of reading is also examined in R. Chartier, *The Cultural Uses of Print in Early Modern France* (trans. 1987). W. Roberts, *Morality and Social Class: Eighteenth-Century French Literature and Painting* (1974) links the creative arts to political and social life, as do A. Boime, *Art in an Age of Revolution, 1750–1800* (1987) and M. Craske, *Art in Europe, 1700–1830* (1997).

The Enlightenment: Scotland, England, Italy, Germany

An informative introduction to Scotland in this age is D. Allan, *Scotland in the Eighteenth Century* (2001), and valuable assessments of the important Scottish thinkers are available in A. C. Chitnis, *The Scottish Enlightenment: A Social History* (1976) and in G. Davie, *The Scotch Metaphysics: A Century of Enlightenment in Scotland* (2001), which also describes the influence of Scottish philosophy in the nineteenth century. Other helpful books are K. Haakonssen, *The Science of a Legislator: The Natural Jurisprudence of David Hume and Adam Smith* (1981); D. Forbes, *Hume's Philosophical Politics* (1984); A. Fitzgibbons, *Adam Smith's System of Liberty, Wealth, and Virtue: the Moral and Political Foundations of the Wealth of Nations* (1995); and J. Dwyer, *The Age of the Passions: An Interpretation of Adam Smith and Scottish Enlightenment Culture* (1998). The essays in three collaborative volumes are rewarding: I. Hont and M. Ignatieff (eds.), *Wealth and Virtue in the Shaping of the Political Economy in the Scottish Enlightenment* (1984); D. Daiches et al. (eds.), *A Hotbed of Genius: The Scottish Enlightenment, 1730–1790* (1987); and J. Dwyer and R. B. Sher (eds.), *Sociability and Society in Eighteenth-Century Scotland* (1993).

For the Enlightenment in its British setting, one may read J. Redwood, *Reason, Ridicule, and Religion: The Age of Enlightenment in England, 1660–1750* (1976) and R. Porter, *The Creation of the Modern World: The Untold Story of the British Enlightenment* (2000), a wide-ranging work that stresses Britain's distinctive contributions to Enlightenment culture. The relation between religion and new democratic movements is examined in B. Semmel, *The Methodist Revolution* (1973), which sees Wesleyan evangelicalism as the English counterpart to democratic stirrings in Europe and America; and R. Hattersley, *A Brand from the Burning: The Life of John Wesley* (2002) examines a key leader. J. G. A. Pocock subtly reexamines a number of British thinkers, including Hume, Gibbon, and Burke, in *Virtue, Commerce, and History: Essays in Political Thought and History* (1985). For Gibbon the brief J. W. Burrow, *Gibbon* (1985) and P. B. Craddock's admirable two-volume biography (1982–88) are available, but readers should also turn to the monumental work of J. G. A. Pocock, *Barbarism and Religion* (4 vols., 1999–2005), which examines Gibbon's work and places it in a wider context of Enlightenment historical writing. For the German poet-philosopher Goethe, one may turn to N. Boyle, *Goethe: The Poet and the Age* (2 vols., 1991, 2000).

H. Maestro has written a comprehensive biography of the Italian jurist and reformer who served the Austrian state, *Cesare Beccaria and the Origins of Penal Reform* (1973). For the Italian city-states in this age there are available D. Carpanetto and G. Ricuperati, *Italy in the Age of Reason, 1685–1789* (1987) and F. Venturi, *Italy and the Enlightenment: Studies in a Cosmopolitan Century* (1972). The leading Italian philosopher of the Enlightenment, little known in his own time but increasingly influential in recent years, is studied in L. Pompa, *Vico: A Study of the "New Science"* (1975); P. Burke's brief *Vico* (1985); M. Lilla, *G. B. Vico: The Making of an Anti-Modern* (1993); G. Mazzotta, *The New Map of the World: The Poetic Philosophy of Giambattista Vico* (1999); and R. C. Miner, *Vico, Genealogist of Modernity* (2002).

Other Enlightenment Themes

Religion and related themes are examined in R. R. Palmer, *Catholics and Unbelievers in Eighteenth Century France* (1939); F. E. Manuel, *The Changing of the Gods* (1983); J. M. McManners, *Death and Enlightenment: Changing Attitudes to Death among Christians and Unbelievers in Eighteenth Century France* (1982); J. M. Byrne, *Religion and the Enlightenment: From Descartes to Kant* (1997); and the wide-ranging survey by W. R. Ward, *Christianity Under the Ancien Régime, 1648–1789* (1999). An important episode is studied in D. D. Bien, *The Calas Affair: Persecution, Toleration, and Heresy in Eighteenth Century Toulouse* (1960), while M. C. Jacob, *The Radical Enlightenment: Pantheists, Freemasons, and Republicans* (1981) explores radical ideas that flourished in Dutch literary circles. J. Riskin, *Science in the Age of Sensibility: The Sentimental Empiricists of the French Enlightenment* (2002) challenges older assumptions about the era's pervasive rationalism; and there is an intriguing study of the philosophes' conception of truth and falsehood in D. W. Bates, *Enlightenment Aberrations: Error and Revolution in France* (2002).

For an introduction to women in the Enlightenment, their accomplishments and the constraints upon them, one may turn to K. Rogers, *Feminism in Eighteenth-Century England* (1976); the essays in S. I. Spencer (ed.), *French Women and the Age of Enlightenment* (1985); the important work on the salons by D. Goodman (1994), cited earlier; N. R. Gelbart, *Feminine and Opposition Journalism in Old Regime France: Le Journal des dames* (1987); and S. C. Maza, *Private Lives and Public Affairs: The Causes Célèbres of Prerevolutionary France* (1993), which discusses the images of women in late eighteenth-century legal disputes. The life of the marquise who headed the best known of the many salons in France is recounted in B. Craveri, *Madame du Deffand and Her World* (trans. 1994).

On a special subject, A. Hertzberg, *The French Enlightenment and the Jews* (1968) contends that by downgrading all religions the philosophes (and especially Voltaire) contributed to anti-Semitism; also critical of the Enlightenment is J. Katz, *Out of the Ghetto: The Social Background of Jewish Emancipation, 1770–1870* (1973). But Jewish integration into European society in these years is explored in R. Mahler, *A History of Modern Jewry, 1780–1815* (1971); J. Israel, *European Jewry in the Age of Mercantilism, 1550–1750* (rev. 1998); and F. Malino and D. Sorkin (eds.), *From East to West: Jews in a Changing Europe* (1990), which focuses on the years 1750 to 1870. The views of eighteenth-century intellectuals are examined in excellent recent books by A. Sutcliffe, *Judaism and the Enlightenment* (2003) and J. M. Hess, *Germans, Jews, and the Claims of Modernity* (2002). H. Sachar, *A History of the Jews in the Modern World* (2005) provides a scholarly, highly readable account focusing on the years from the Enlightenment to the present.

France in the Old Regime

Several books on modern France examine developments in the eighteenth century; among them are C. Jones, *The Great Nation: France from Louis XV to Napoleon, 1715–99* (2002) and R. Price, *An Economic History of Modern France 1730–1914* (1981). Price has also written *A Concise History of France* (rev. 2005). A. Moulin, *Peasantry and Society in France since 1789* (1991) examines important social themes.

Books that study the era for its own sake and not merely as a prologue to the Revolution include P. R. Campbell, *The Ancien Regime in France* (1988) and E. Le Roy Ladurie, *The Ancien Regime: A History of France, 1610–1774* (trans. 1996). The financial crisis is explored in depth in J. F. Bosher, *French Finances, 1770–1795: From Business to Bureaucracy* (1970).

The changing role of the nobility may be studied in older works by F. L. Ford, *Robe and Sword: The Regrouping of the French Aristocracy after Louis XIV* (1953) and R. Forster, *The Nobility of Toulouse in the Eighteenth Century* (1960), as well as in Forster's other books. G. Chaussinand-Nogaret, *The French Nobility in the Eighteenth Century* (1985) portrays the prerevolutionary nobility as socially productive; and J. M. Smith examines the nobility's contribution to conceptions of French nationhood in *Nobility Reimagined: The Patriotic Nation in Eighteenth-Century France* (2005). The response to problems of poverty and hunger in eighteenth-century France may be examined in O. Hufton, *The Poor of Eighteenth-Century France, 1750–1789* (1974); in S. L. Kaplan's detailed and impressive *Bread, Politics, and Political Economy in the Reign of Louis XV* (2 vols., 1976) and his two later volumes on related themes (1994, 1996); and in S. M. Adams, *Bureaucrats and Beggars: French Social Policy in the Age of Enlightenment* (1990). Parisian life at the time is graphically reconstructed in D. Roche, *The People of Paris* (trans. 1987). The status of domestic servants as a key to broader social relations is examined in S. C. Maza, *Servants and Masters in Eighteenth Century France: The Uses of Loyalty* (1983) and in C. Fairchilds, *Domestic Enemies: Servants and Their Masters in Old Regime France* (1984). Maza also discusses French conceptions of social class in *The Myth of the French Bourgeoise: An Essay on the Social Imaginary, 1750–1850* (2003), which argues that the bourgeoisie did not exist as the coherent social group that its critics imagined.

Enlightened Despotism in Europe

A thoughtful brief introduction is J. G. Gagliardo, *Enlightened Despotism* (1967), while L. Krieger, *An Essay on the Theory of Enlightenment and Despotism* (1975) is a difficult but rewarding analysis.

German political fragmentation and cultural stirrings are examined in J. G. Gagliardo's *Reich and Nation: The Holy Roman Empire as Idea and Reality, 1763–1806* (1980) and *Germany under the Old Regime, 1600–1790* (1991). R. Vierhaus, *Germany in the Age of Absolutism* (1988) is a brief survey, while J. J. Sheehan, *Germany, 1770–1866* (1989) is an outstanding larger history that begins with this period. For Prussia and Frederick the Great, one may turn to D. B. Horn, *Frederick the Great and the Rise of Prussia* (1969) and R. B. Asprey, *Frederick the Great: The Great Enigma* (1986) as well as to the recent biographies by G. MacDonogh, *Frederick the Great: A Life in Deed and Letters* (1999) and D. Fraser, *Frederick the Great* (2000). His bureaucracy is examined in H. C. Johnson, *Frederick the Great and His Officials* (1975).

A concise introduction to eighteenth-century Austria is E. Wangermann, *The Austrian Achievement, 1700–1800* (1973). D. F. Good, *The Economic Rise of the Habsburg Empire, 1750–1914* (1984) begins with these years, while P. G. M. Dickson, *Finance and Government under Maria Theresa, 1740–1780* (2 vols., 1988) is an in-depth economic study. The Habsburg empress may be studied in E. Crankshaw, *Maria Theresa* (1969); her son may be studied in P. P. Bernard, *Joseph II* (1968), a brief, balanced account;

in T. C. W. Blanning, *Joseph II* (1994); and in D. Beales, *Joseph II,* Vol. I: *In the Shadow of Maria Theresa, 1741–1780* (1987), which shows in detail how Joseph attempted to shape policy even before his own reign began in 1780.

Enlightened despotism in Russia is examined in a judicious large-scale study by I. de Madariaga, *Russia in the Age of Catherine the Great* (1981), available in abridged form as *Catherine the Great: A Short History* (1990), and in her *Politics and Culture in Eighteenth-Century Russia: Collected Essays* (1998). For a somewhat different appraisal, one may read J. T. Alexander, *Catherine the Great: Life and Legend* (1988). There are also biographies of Catherine by C. Erickson (1995) and S. Dixon (2001). Other valuable studies of eighteenth-century Russia include two works by M. Raeff, *Origins of the Russian Intelligentsia: The Eighteenth-Century Nobility* (1966) and *Political Ideas and Institutions in Imperial Russia* (1994), as well as D. Ransel, *The Politics of Catherinean Russia* (1975). Additional insights are provided in J. Burbank and D. L. Ransel (eds.), *Imperial Russia: New Histories for the Empire* (1998). Economic developments are traced in A. Kahan, *The Plow, the Hammer, and the Knout: An Economic History of Eighteenth-Century Russia* (1985), and revolts and social stirrings may be studied in P. Avrich, *Russian Rebels, 1600–1800* (1972), cited earlier, and in two books by J. T. Alexander on the Pugachev uprising: *Autocratic Politics in a National Crisis* (1969) and *Emperor of the Cossacks* (1973).

Poland: The Partitions

For Poland in these years one may turn to N. Davies, *A History of Poland: God's Playground* (2 vols., rev. 2005), Vol. I: *The Origins to 1795* and *Heart of Europe: A Short History of Poland* (1984) as well as the accounts in J. Lukowski and H. Zawadzki, *A Concise History of Poland* (2001) and A. J. Prazmowska, *A History of Poland* (2004). The quarrel over the succession to the Polish throne is recounted in J. L. Sutton, *The King's Honor and the King's Cardinal* [*Fleury*]: *The War of the Polish Succession* (1980). On the eighteenth-century partitions, J. Lukowski, *The Partitions of Poland, 1772, 1793, 1795* (1999) updates and expands upon older studies. For the years that followed the partitions, one turns to P. Wandycz, *The Lands of Partitioned Poland, 1795–1918* (1974), Vol. VII of *A History of East Central Europe*. A special subject is treated in B. D. Weinryb, *The Jews of Poland: A Social and Economic History of the Jewish Community in Poland from 1100 to 1800* (rev. 1976), and in the essays in C. Abramsky et al. (eds.), *The Jews in Poland* (1986). K. Friedrich, *The Other Prussia: Royal Prussia, Poland, and Liberty, 1569–1772* (2000) examines the history of Polish-Prussian relations.

The American Revolution and Britain

Major works by R. R. Palmer, J. Godechot, and others exploring the American and French Revolutions in a broader eighteenth-century revolutionary setting are described in the next chapter. H. F. May, *The Enlightenment in America* (1976) and H. S. Commager, *The Empire of Reason: How Europe Imagined and America Realized the Enlightenment* (1977) are both challenging books. For background to the revolution one should read B. Bailyn, *The Ideological Origins of the American Revolution* (1967; 1992). The link with events and ideas in seventeenth-century England is stressed in E. S. Morgan, *Inventing the People: The Rise of Popular Sovereignty in England and America* (1988); and the influence of Enlightenment ideas on American leaders is discussed in D. Staloff, *Hamilton, Adams, Jefferson: The Politics of Enlightenment and the American Founding* (2005).

For a sampling of interpretive studies one may turn to I. R. Christie and B. W. Labaree, *Empire or Independence, 1760–1776: A British-American Dialogue on the Coming of the American Revolution* (1976); B. Bailyn, *Faces of Revolution: Personalities and Themes in the Struggle for American Independence* (1990); J. P. Greene, *Understanding the American Revolution: Issues and Actors* (1995); and two books by G. S. Wood, *The Radicalism of the American Revolution* (1991) and *The American Revolution: A History* (2002). Important examples of the expanding research on the history of women in this era may be found in L. K. Kerber, *Women of the Republic: Intellect and Ideology in Revolutionary America* (1980); in M. B. Norton, *Liberty's Daughters: The Revolutionary Experience of American Women* (1980, 1996); and in C. Berkin, *Revolutionary Mothers: Women in the Struggle for America's Independence* (2005). British responses to the revolutionary events in America are discussed in K. Perry, *British Politics and the American Revolution* (1990); in H. T. Dickinson (ed.), *Britain and the American Revolution* (1998); and in S. Conway, *The British Isles and the War of American Independence* (2000).

For the military aspects of the war one may turn to J. Shy, *A People Numerous and Armed: Reflections on the Military Struggle for American Independence* (rev. 1990) and S. Conway, *The War of American Independence* (1995). The French contribution is examined in J. Dull, *The French Navy and American Independence* (1975); in L. Kennett, *The French Forces in America, 1780–1783* (1978); and in S. F. Scott, *From Yorktown to Valmy: The Transformation of the French Army in an Age of Revolution* (1998).

For diplomacy and international affairs there are F. W. Brecher, *Securing American Independence: John Jay and the French Alliance* (2003) and H. M. Scott, *British Foreign Policy in the Age of the American Revolution* (1991); and on the peace negotiations, R. B. Morris, *The Peacemakers: The Great Powers and American Independence* (1965) is an outstanding study.

For Britain in the eighteenth century one should also consult the books described in Chapter 7. In addition, on movements for parliamentary reform informative studies include J. R. Pole, *Political Representation in England and the Origins of the American Revolution* (1967); P. D. G. Thomas, *John Wilkes: A Friend to Liberty* (1996); M. Turner, *British Politics in an Age of Reform* (1999); and E. H. Gould, *The Persistence of Empire: British Political Culture in the Age of the American Revolution* (2000). Two books by I. R. Christie, *Wars and Revolutions: Britain, 1760–1815* (1982) and *Stress and Stability in Late Eighteenth-Century Britain: Reflections on the British Avoidance of Revolution* (1984) are rewarding.

Useful Web Sites

The *International Centre for Eighteenth-Century Studies* maintains a comprehensive Web site at www.c18.org, where readers will find links to diverse materials on all aspects of eighteenth-century history and culture; and there are more useful links at the *International Society for Eighteenth-Century Studies*, www.isecs.org. The *Voltaire Foundation*, www.voltaire.ox.ac.uk, is another good starting point for further research on the Enlightenment as well as the life and work of France's best-known philosophe. Two valuable sites for resources on early American history and the American Revolution are maintained by the *Gilder Lehrman Institute of American History* at www.gilderlehrman.org and by the *History Matters* project at George Mason University, www.historymatters.gmu.org, both of which have outstanding links to other materials. The collection of electronic sources at Fordham Univeristy, *Internet Modern History Sourcebook*, includes links to many valuable eighteenth-century materials at www.fordham.edu/halsall/mod/modsbook2.html.

9. THE FRENCH REVOLUTION

Still useful works on the revolutionary era include A. Goodwin (ed.), *The American and French Revolutions, 1763–1793* (1965), Vol. VIII of the *New Cambridge Modern History,* and its sequel volume, C. W. Crawley (ed.), *War and Peace in an Age of Upheaval, 1793–1830* (1965). Books encompassing the revolutionary era as a whole include E. J. Hobsbawm, *The Age of Revolution: Europe, 1789–1848* (1962, reissued 1996); N. Hampson, *The First European Revolution, 1776–1850* (1969); and C. Breunig and M. Levinger, *The Revolutionary Era, 1789–1850* (rev. 2002); of special value is G. Best, *War and Society in Revolutionary Europe, 1770–1870* (1982).

The French Revolution

As the bicentennial in 1989 of the French Revolution demonstrated, the French themselves are less divided than formerly over the legacy of 1789, but wide differences in scholarly interpretation, emphasis, and conceptualization persist. The reader may assess current scholarship through F. Furet and M. Ozouf (eds.), *A Critical Dictionary of the French Revolution* (trans. 1989), which consists of 99 encyclopedia-type articles covering events, institutions, persons, and ideas, as well as historians of the Revolution. Another informative compendium is S. F. Scott and B. Rothaus, *Historical Dictionary of the French Revolution, 1787–1799* (2 vols., 1985). Four impressive volumes incorporating the contributions of many international scholars have been published as *The French Revolution and the Creation of Modern Political Culture:* Vol. I, K. M. Baker (ed.), *The Political Culture of the Old Regime* (1987); Vol. II, C. Lucas (ed.), *The Political Culture of the French Revolution* (1989); Vol. III, F. Furet (ed.), *The Influence of the French Revolution on Nineteenth-Century Europe* (1989); and Vol. IV, K. M. Baker (ed.), *The Terror* (1994). The Revolution is viewed in thoughtful perspective for the general reader by eight scholars in G. Best (ed.), *The Permanent Revolution: The French Revolution and Its Legacy, 1789–1989* (1989); in depth by specialists in C. Lucas (ed.), *Rewriting the French Revolution* (1991); and in E. J. Hobsbawm, *Echoes from the Marseillaise: Two Centuries Look Back on the French Revolution* (1990), an insightful examination of liberal, Marxist, and revisionist interpretations.

Of narrative histories S. Schama, *Citizens: A Chronicle of the French Revolution* (1989), carrying the events to 1794, effectively captures their color and drama. Comprehensive political narratives are available in W. Doyle, *The Oxford History of the French Revolution* (rev. 2002); J. F. Bosher, *The French Revolution* (1988); D. G. M. Sutherland, *France, 1789–1815: Revolution and Counterrevolution* (1986), and by the same author, *The French Revolution and Empire, the Quest for a Civic Order* (2003) ; and A. Forrest, *The French Revolution* (1995). Other useful recent surveys include J. Popkin, *A Short History of the French Revolution* (rev. 2002); P. McPhee, *The French Revolution, 1789–1799* (2002); and D. Andress, *French Society in Revolution, 1789–1799* (1999). One still reads with profit the older work of C. Brinton, *A Decade of Revolution, 1789–1799* (1934, 1962); and the wider meaning of the Revolution is discussed in the influential work of F. Furet, *Revolutionary France, 1770–1880* (trans. 1992).

For special aspects the reader may turn to E. Kennedy, *A Cultural History of the French Revolution* (1989), which ably communicates the cultural effervescence of the age; F. Aftalion, *The French Revolution: An Economic Interpretation* (trans. 1990); and R. Cobb, *The French and Their Revolution* (1998), a collection of writings by an English historian interested in the history of the lower classes. The popular response to revolutionary events is examined in

D. Andress, *The French Revolution and the People* (2004); and D. Bell discusses the emergence of French nationalism before and during the Revolution in *The Cult of the Nation in France: Inventing Nationalism, 1680–1800* (2001). The art of the era comes alive in R. Paulson, *Representations of Revolution, 1750–1800* (1987), cited in the previous chapter, while architectural design is explored imaginatively in J. A. Leith, *Space and Revolution* (1991). In another area R. R. Palmer, *The Improvement of Humanity: Education and the French Revolution* (1985) examines the educational institutions which sought to disseminate revolutionary ideals.

There is a helpful introduction to the wide range of historical interpretations of the French Revolution in M. R. Cox (ed.), *The Place of the French Revolution in History* (1998). Recent debates among historians may be sampled in T. C. W. Blanning (ed.), *The Rise and Fall of the French Revolution* (1996) and in G. Kates (ed.), *The French Revolution: Recent Debates and New Controversies* (1998). A comprehensive summary of French views during the Revolution's bicentennial is available in S. L. Kaplan, *Farewell Revolution* (2 vols., 1995). There are numerous older volumes, now more important to historiography than to history, by writers of such vastly differing viewpoints as Jules Michelet, Jean Jaurès, Hippolyte Taine, Thomas Carlyle, Louis Madelin, Pierre Gaxotte, Alphonse Aulard, and Albert Mathiez.

Many twentieth-century scholars emphasized the class basis of the Revolution and saw political differences emerging from the economic self-interest of groups and factions. A classical synthesis of this approach, which nonetheless retains a judicious balance, is G. Lefebvre, *The French Revolution* (1951; 2 vols. in trans. 1962–64). A more extreme example, stressing class struggle, is A. Soboul, *The French Revolution, 1789–1799: From the Storming of the Bastille to Napoleon* (trans. 1977). The class struggle is also highlighted in G. Rudé, *The French Revolution* (1988). Two books by A. Cobban, *The Myth of the French Revolution* (1953) and *The Social Interpretation of The French Revolution* (1964), vigorously rejected the notion of a "bourgeois revolution."

New ways to study the Revolution as a cultural phenomenon rather than as a revolution of social classes are explored in F. Furet, *Interpreting the French Revolution* (1978; trans. 1981), cited earlier. The new methodology is exemplified in two books by L. Hunt: *Politics, Culture, and Class in the French Revolution* (1984) and *The Family Romance of the French Revolution* (1992), which approaches the questions of legitimacy and authority by examining the wide use of family metaphors during the Revolution. Cultural aspects of the Revolution are also explored in J. R. Censor and L. Hunt, *Liberty, Equality, Fraternity: Exploring the French Revolution* (2001), an innovative book that includes a CD-ROM disk with images and songs from the revolutionary era. The emphasis on symbolic meanings appears also in M. Ozouf, *Festivals and the French Revolution* (1988) and in H. J. Lesebrink, *The Bastille: A History of a Symbol of Despotism and Freedom* (trans. 1997).

The Events of the Revolution

For the immediate background of the Revolution, including the financial crisis, one may read M. Vovelle, *The Fall of the French Monarchy, 1787–1792* (trans. 1984); W. Doyle, *Origins of the French Revolution* (rev. 1999); J. Egret, *The French Pre-Revolution, 1787–1788* (trans. 1977); and the two older volumes by G. Lefebvre: *The Coming of the French Revolution* (trans. 1947) and *The Great Fear of 1789: Rural Panic in Revolutionary France* (trans. 1982). The final effort at financial reconstruction is recounted in R. D. Harris, *Necker: Reform Statesman of the Ancien Regime* (1979) and *Necker and the Revolution of 1789* (1988). J. Hardman's two books, *Louis XVI* (1992) and *Louis XVI: The Silent King* (2000), provide thoughtful accounts of the king and his reputation. The famous queen is described in E. Lever, *Marie Antoinette: The Last Queen of France* (trans. 2000) and in a biography by A. Fraser, *Marie Antoinette: The Journey* (2002). The fate of the royal family is also examined in M. Price, *Louis XVI, Marie Antoinette, and the Fall of the French Monarchy* (2004); and the king's attempted escape from France is the subject of an excellent book by T. Tackett, *When the King Took Flight* (2003).

The reform phase of the Revolution under the first two legislative bodies is studied in N. Hampson, *Prelude to Terror: The Constituent Assembly and the Failure of Consensus, 1789–1791* (1989) and C. J. Mitchell, *The French Legislative Assembly of 1791* (1988). The coming of the war in 1792 and the radicalization of the Revolution may be studied in M. Bouloiseau, *The Jacobin Republic, 1792–1794* (trans. 1984), and in M. J. Sydenham, *The First French Republic 1792–1804* (1974). Other studies of the Jacobins and their ideas may be found in M. Kennedy, *The Jacobin Clubs in the French Revolution, 1793–1795* (2000) and in P. Higonnet, *Goodness Beyond Virtue: Jacobins during the French Revolution* (1998), which offers a more sympathetic view of the Jacobins than most recent works.

For the year of the Terror the reader may turn to A. Soboul, *The Parisian Sans-Culottes and the French Revolution, 1793–1794* (trans. 1964); R. R. Palmer, *Twelve Who Ruled: The Year of the Terror in the French Revolution* (1941; reissued 2005); C. Lucas, *The Structure of the Terror* (1973); and D. Andress, *The Terror: The Merciless War for Freedom in Revolutionary France* (2006). A dramatic episode foreshadowing the Terror is recounted in D. J. Jordan, *The King's Trial: Louis XVI vs. The French Revolution* (1979).

Different aspects of the Revolution are explored in M. Vovelle, *The Revolution Against the Church: From Reason to the Supreme Being* (trans. 1991); P. Jones, *The Peasantry in the French Revolution* (1988); and J. Markoff, *The Abolition of Feudalism: Peasants, Lords and Legislators in the French Revolution* (1996). A. Forrest, *The French Revolution and the Poor* (1981) examines the welfare legislation adopted in the revolutionary decade. Changes in family life and gender relations are discussed in S. Desan, *The Family on Trial in Revolutionary France* (2004). For a summary of how the revolutionaries conceived of human rights, one may turn to the analysis and documents in L. Hunt (ed.), *The French Revolution and Human Rights* (1996); and an important study of social changes across the entire revolutionary and Napoleonic era appears in I. Woloch, *The New Regime: Transformations of the French Civic Order: 1789–1820s* (1994).

The role of women in this era is explored in J. B. Landes, *Women and the Public Sphere in the Age of the French Revolution* (1988), which argues that the Revolution reduced the rights of women in France; L. Kelly, *Women of the French Revolution* (1989); S. E. Meltzerand and L. W. Rabine (eds.), *Rebel Daughters: Women and the French Revolution* (1992); and J. Heuer, *The Family and the Nation: Gender and Citizenship in Revolutionary France, 1789–1830* (2005). The essays in D. G. Levy and H. B. Applewhite (eds.), *Women and Politics in the Age of the Democratic Revolution* (1990) study women activists in revolutionary Europe and America; and the work by M. Yalom, *Blood Sisters: The French Revolution in Women's Memory* (1993) examines accounts by women who participated in the revolutionary events. The expansion of women's writing during the revolutionary decade is the subject of C. Hesse, *The Other Enlightenment: How French Women Became Modern* (2001); and the relation between gender and the new French nationalism is analyzed in J. B. Landes, *Visualizing the Nation: Gender, Representation, and Revolution in Eighteenth-Century France* (2001).

Among R. Cobb's illuminating books about the life and activism of the lower classes are *The Police and the People: French Popular Protest, 1789–1820* (1970); *Paris and Its Provinces, 1792–1802* (1975); and *The People's Armies* (1961, 1987), an impressive study of the armed groups that scoured the countryside for food and other military needs of the revolutionary government. For the counterrevolution one turns to the broader narratives cited above and to J. Godechot, *The Counter-Revolution* (trans. 1971); J. Roberts, *The Counter-Revolution in France, 1787–1830* (1990); C. Tilly, *The Vendée* (1964); and M. Hutt, *Chouannerie and the Counter-Revolution* (1984).

For the reaction after Robespierre's downfall and the regime that followed, one may turn to D. Woronoff, *The Thermidorean Regime and the Directory, 1794–1799* (trans. 1984) and to M. Lyons, *France under the Directory* (1975). The crushing of the Babeuf uprising is described in R. B. Rose, *Gracchus Babeuf: The First Revolutionary Communist* (1978); Babeuf's ideas are also discussed in I. H. Birchall, *The Spectre of Babeuf* (1997).

War and Diplomacy

On the coming of the war in 1792 and the first two coalitions one may read T. C. W. Blanning, *The Origins of the French Revolutionary Wars* (1989) and the same author's *The French Revolutionary Wars, 1781–1802* (1996); there is also a useful, brief account in G. Fremont-Barnes, *The French Revolutionary Wars* (2001). The French army that fought the war is described in impressive detail in J. P. Bertaud, *The Army of the French Revolution: From Citizen-Soldiers to Instrument of Power* (trans. 1988); it may be supplemented by A. Forrest, *Conscripts and Deserters: The Army and French Society during the Revolution and Empire* (1989). Military technologies are discussed in K. Alder, *Engineering the Revolution: Arms and Enlightenment in France, 1763–1815* (1997). On the emergence of Bonaparte one may turn to M. Crook, *Napoleon Comes to Power: Democracy and Dictatorship in Revolutionary France, 1795–1804* (1998). Additional books on Napoleon are listed in the following chapter.

Biographical Accounts

J. M. Thomson, *Leaders of the French Revolution* (1929, 1988), sketching 11 outstanding personalities, is a classic account that still merits reading. Specific biographical accounts include B. Luttrell, *Mirabeau* (1990); M. Forsyth, *Reason and Revolution: The Political Thought of the Abbé Sieyès* (1987); W. H. Sewell, *A Rhetoric of Revolution: The Abbé Sieyès and "What is the Third Estate?"* (1994); L. Gottschalk's two volumes on Lafayette in the French Revolution (1969, 1973); and C. D. Connor, *Jean Paul Marat: Scientist and Revolutionary* (1997), sympathetic to Marat's radicalism. N. Hampson has written the most fair-minded account of a controversial political leader in *Danton* (1978, 1988), while G. May, *Madame Roland and the Age of Revolution* (1970) sympathetically portrays a Girondist leader who fell victim to the Terror. A. G. Sepinwall examines the ideas and actions of another influential leader in *The Abbé Grégoire and the French Revolution: The Making of Modern Universalism* (2005).

A balanced biography of the most prominent figure on the Committee of Public Safety is J. M. Thompson, *Robespierre* (1935, 1988). One also may read M. Gallo, *Robespierre, the Incorruptible: A Psychobiography* (trans. 1971), provocative but not completely convincing; G. Rudé, *Robespierre: Portrait of a Revolutionary Democrat* (1975), which makes the best possible case for the Jacobin leader; N. Hampson, *The Life and Opinions of Maximilien Robespierre* (1974, 1988), which asks observers to react to the often contradictory evidence; D. P. Jordan, *The Revolutionary Career of Maximilien Robespierre* (1985); and J. Hardman, *Robespierre* (1999). A useful collection of recent scholarship is available in C. Haydon and W. Doyle (eds.), *Robespierre* (1999). Robespierre's associates are studied in N. Hampson, *Saint-Just* (1991) and in L. Gershoy, *Bertrand Barère: A Reluctant Terrorist* (1962).

The Revolution outside France

For the view of the French Revolution as part of a broader European and Atlantic movement, one may turn to R. R. Palmer, *The Age of the Democratic Revolution: A Political History of Europe and America, 1760–1800* (2 vols., 1959–64); the first volume, *The Challenge,* carries the account to 1792 and the second, *The Struggle,* to 1800; see also by the same author *The World of the French Revolution* (1970). The conclusions of the French scholar J. Godechot are available in summary form as *France and the Atlantic Revolution, 1770–1799* (1975). Along related lines P. Higonnet traces the genesis of the republican idea in *Sister Republics: The Origins of French and American Republicanism* (1988), while M. Durey, *Transatlantic Radicals and the Early American Republic* (1997) looks at British political activists who migrated to America during the era of the French Revolution. There is a useful survey of the Revolution's enduring international influence in J. Klaits and M. H. Haltzel (eds.), *The Global Ramifications of the French Revolution* (1994). The German states are studied in T. C. W. Blanning, *The French Revolution in Germany: Occupation and Resistance in the Rhineland, 1792–1802* (1983); and in J. M. Diefendorf, *Businessmen and Politics in the Rhineland, 1789–1834* (1980).

Events in the Netherlands are examined in S. Schama, *Patriots and Liberators: Revolution and Government in the Netherlands, 1780–1813* (1977) and in northern Europe in H. A. Barton, *Scandinavia in the Revolutionary Era, 1760–1815* (1986). The Irish rebellion of 1798 is placed in its European setting in M. Elliott, *Partners in Revolution: The United Irishmen in France* (1982) and *Wolfe Tone: Prophet of Irish Independence* (1989); and in the wide-ranging work of R. B. McDowell, *Ireland in the Age of Imperialism and Revolution, 1760–1801* (1979).

For repercussions in Haiti and the African-American world, one may read the classic work of C. L. R. James, *The Black Jacobins: Toussaint L'Ouverture and the San Domingo Revolution* (1938, 1963), which should be supplemented by D. P. Geggus, *Slavery, War, and Revolution: The British Occupation of Saint Domingue, 1793–1798* (1982), and by the same author, *Haitian Revolutionary Studies* (2002); M. Duffy, *Soldiers, Sugar, and Seapower: The British Expeditions to the West Indies and the War against Revolutionary France* (1987); and L. Dubois, *Avengers of the New World: The Story of the Haitian Revolution* (2004), an excellent recent account. The struggle against slavery in Haiti and elsewhere is also the subject of A. Hochschild, *Bury the Chains: Prophets and Rebels in the Fight to Free an Empire's Slaves* (2005). There are helpful essays in D. B. Gaspar and D. P. Geggus (eds.), *A Turbulent Time: The French Revolution and the Greater Caribbean* (1997), and in D. P. Geggus (ed.), *The Impact of the Haitian Revolution in the Atlantic World* (2001).

An outstanding study of British reaction to the Revolution is A. Goodwin, *The Friends of Liberty: The English Democratic Movement in the Age of the French Revolution* (1979), while an informative brief essay is H. T. Dickinson, *British Radicalism and the French Revolution, 1789–1815* (1985). A more recent brief survey appears in C. Emsley, *Britain and the French Revolution* (2000); longer discussions of the era's political debates and conflicts can be found in M. Morris, *The British Monarchy and the French Revolution* (1998) and in J. Mori, *Britain in the Age of the French Revolution* (2000). An informative older book that focuses on popular unrest in both France and England is G. Rudé, *The Crowd in History: A Study of Popular Disturbances in France and England, 1730–1848* (1964).

The revolutionary career in England, America, and France of a leading revolutionist of the age is studied in J. Keane, *Tom Paine: A Political Life* (1995) and in E. Foner, *Tom Paine and Revolutionary America* (rev. 2005). Paine's political thought is examined in A. J. Ayer, *Thomas Paine* (1989) and in M. Philip, *Paine* (1989). For the thought and career of a leading Englishwoman of the age, a pioneer feminist sympathetic to the Revolution, one may read J. Todd, *Mary Wollstonecraft: A Revolutionary Life* (2000); C. Franklin, *Mary Wollstonecraft: A Literary Life* (2004); and L. Gordon, *Vindication: A Life of Mary Wollstonecraft* (2005).

In a comparative study C. B. A. Behrens, *Society, Government, and the Enlightenment: The Experiences of Eighteenth-Century France and Prussia* (1985) seeks to explain the different responses to the challenges of the age, while J. C. Lamberti, *Tocqueville and the Two Democracies* (trans. 1989) grapples with Tocqueville's explanations of why revolution led to an era of instability in France and to stable constitutional government in the United States.

Early efforts to study the phenomenon of revolution on a comparative basis include C. Brinton, *The Anatomy of Revolution* (1935, 1965) and H. Arendt, *On Revolution* (1963). J. Talmon in *The Origins of Totalitarian Democracy* (1952) and his other books saw the roots of twentieth-century dictatorship in the radical phase of the French Revolution—a controversial theme that has attracted strong criticism as well as some new support in recent scholarship. There is also a stimulating comparative analysis in A. J. Mayer, *The Furies: Violence and Terror in the French and Russian Revolutions* (2000).

Useful Web Sites

Readers will find an excellent collection of documents, images, and accounts of the French Revolution by visiting a Web site at George Mason University, *Liberty, Equality, Fraternity: Exploring the French Revolution*, which is located at http://chnm.gmu.edu/revolution/. There are additional sources to explore in the *Internet Modern History Sourcebook*, www.fordham.edu/halsall/mod/modsbook13.html, and there is a helpful site called *Links on the French Revolution* at the University of Portsmouth in Britain, http://userwww.port.ac.uk/andressd/frlinks.htm.

10. NAPOLEONIC EUROPE

Many of the books on the Revolution cited in the previous chapter continue on into the Napoleonic age. Informative surveys of Europe in the age of Napoleon are available in O. Connelly, *The French Revolution and Napoleonic Era* (rev.1991) and M. Broers, *Europe Under Napoleon, 1799–1815* (1996); and the latter author also examines Napoleon's imperial policies in *The Napoleonic Empire in Italy, 1796–1814: Cultural Imperialism in a European Context?* (2005). Other useful accounts include S. J. Woolf, *Napoleon's Integration of Europe* (1991); M. Lyons, *Napoleon Bonaparte and the Legacy of the French Revolution* (1994); O. Bernier, *The World in 1800* (2000); and A. Grab, *Napoleon and the Transformation of Europe* (2003). Two reference works for the age are O. Connelly et al. (eds.), *Historical Dictionary of Napoleonic France* (1985) and C. Emsley, *The Longman Companion to Napoleonic Europe* (1993).

Napoleon and Napoleonic France

For Napoleonic France a valuable synthesis of French society is L. Bergeron, *France under Napoleon* (trans. 1981), while R. Holtman, *The Napoleonic Revolution* (1967) is a brief judicious assessment. A more recent account may be found in A. Horne, *The Age of Napoleon* (2004). A. Boime continues his *Social History of Modern Art* with Vol. II: *Art in the Age of Bonapartism, 1800–1815* (1992).

Of the many biographies and biographically oriented studies of Napoleon, several may be singled out: J. M. Thompson, *Napoleon Bonaparte: His Rise and Fall* (1952); G. Lefebvre, *Napoleon* (2 vols., 1935; trans. 1969), a work of distinction; F. M. Markham, *Napoleon* (1964); and the comprehensive A. Schom, *Napoleon Bonaparte* (1997). Other accounts—all entitled *Napoleon*—by R. Dufraisse (trans. 1990), G. Ellis (1997), and R. S. Alexander (2001) may also be recommended. I. Woloch, *Napoleon and His Collaborators: The Making of a Dictatorship* (2001) shows how Napoleon rose to power and controlled his empire. The empire that Napoleon governed is studied in O. Connelly, *Napoleon's Satellite Kingdoms* (1965, 1990); G. Ellis, *The Napoleonic Empire* (rev. 2003); and C. Emsley, *Napoleonic Europe* (1993). Napoleon as a military leader is appraised in G. E. Rothenberg, *The Art of Warfare in the Age of Napoleon* (1978) and in the same author's *The Napoleonic Wars* (1999);

O. Connelly, *Blundering to Glory: Napoleon's Military Campaigns* (1987); and J. R. Elting, *Swords around a Throne: Napoleon's Grande Armée* (1988); D. Gates, *The Napoleonic Wars, 1803–1815* (1997); and A. Horne, *How Far from Austerlitz? Napoleon, 1805–1815* (1997).

The Continental blockade is studied in G. Ellis, *Napoleon's Continental Blockade* (1991). The Spanish military effort, along with popular resistance, is studied in books on the Peninsular War by D. Gates (1986) and C. J. Esdaile (1988). On the campaign in Russia, readers may consult N. Nicolson, *Napoleon: 1812* (1986). Britain's role in the later Napoleonic wars is described in R. Muir, *Britain and the Defeat of Napoleon, 1807–1815* (1996). On the final phase of the emperor's career one may read N. MacKenzie, *The Escape from Elba: The Fall and Flight of Napoleon, 1814–1815* (1982) and A. Schom, *One Hundred Days: Napoleon's Road to Waterloo* (1992).

The career of Napoleon's famous diplomat is examined in P. Dwyer, *Talleyrand* (2002). Studies of prominent women in this era include A Stuart, *The Rose of Martinique: A Life of Napoleon's Josephine* (2004); E. Bruce, *Napoleon and Josephine: The Improbable Marriage* (1995); J. C. Herold's older biography of Madame de Staël, *Mistress to an Age* (1958, 1979); R. Winegarten, *Mme de Staël* (1985); G. R. Besser, *Germaine de Staël Revisited* (1994); M. Fairweather, *Madame de Staël*; and M. Gutwirth et al. (eds.), *Germaine de Staël: Crossing the Borders* (1991). Napoleon's family is studied in F. Markham, *The Bonapartes* (1975).

Britain in the Time of Napoleon

The war era receives special attention in J. Ehrmann, *William Pitt the Younger* (2 vols., 1969–84) and in P. Mackesy, *War without Victory: The Downfall of Pitt, 1799–1802* (1984). There are biographies of Lord Nelson by B. Lavery (2003), and by R. Knight (2005), the latter providing perhaps the best scholarly study to date. Other accounts of the famous naval commander include the excellent works of J. Sugden, *Nelson: A Dream of Glory, 1758–1797* (2004) and J. S. A. Hayward, *For God and Glory: Lord Nelson and His Way of War* (2003). For Wellington one may turn to J. Strawson, *The Duke and the Emperor: Wellington and Napoleon* (1994) and R. Holmes, *Wellington: The Iron Duke* (2002). The impact of the war and other economic changes of the age are explored in C. Emsley, *British Society and the French Wars, 1973–1814* (1980) and in A. D. Harvey, *Britain in the Early Nineteenth Century* (1978). British expansion overseas is examined in C. A. Bayly, *Imperial Meridian: The British Empire and the World, 1780–1830* (1989). Important books on the slave trade in this era are D. B. Davis, *The Problem of Slavery in the Age of Revolution, 1770–1823* (1975, reissued 1999); J. Walvin, *Making the Black Atlantic: Britain and the African Di-* aspora (2000); and R. Anstey, *The Atlantic Slave Trade and British Abolition, 1760–1810* (1975).

Other Countries in Napoleonic Times

For Anglo-American relations in the decades from 1795 to 1823, there are the three volumes of B. Perkins: *The First Rapprochement* (1955), *Prologue to War* (1961), and *Castlereagh and Adams* (1964). American developments during this era are examined in M. Smelser, *The Democratic Republic, 1801–1815* (1986) and in R. Horsman, *The New Republic: The United States of America 1789–1815* (2000). D. R. Hickey, *The War of 1812: A Forgotten Conflict* (1989) provides a useful description of the war; and a more recent military history is available in W. R. Borneman, *1812, The War that Forged a Nation* (2004).

For the German states, in addition to books cited in the two previous chapters, one may read H. Kohn, *Prelude to Nation-States: The French and German Experience, 1789–1815* (1967); H. Brunschwig, *Enlightenment and Romanticism in Eighteenth Century Prussia* (trans. 1974); and B. Giesen, *Intellectuals and the German Nation: Collective Identity in an Axial Age* (1998), a sociological account of German national identity in the Napoleonic era. For the reactions in Prussia there is the older, but still valuable, assessment of W. M. Simon, *The Failure of the Prussian Reform Movement, 1807–1819* (1955); one may also read W. O. Shanahan, *Prussian Military Reforms, 1786–1813* (1966). On the Prussian military theorist, P. Paret has written a comprehensive biography, *Clausewitz and the State* (1976, reissued 1985) and has edited the famous tract *On War* written in 1832 (ed. 1989).

For Russia in this era one may read the early sections of D. Saunders, *Russia in the Age of Reaction and Reform, 1801–1881* (1992); and for Alexander, one may consult A. McConnell, *Tsar Alexander I: Paternalistic Reformer* (1970); A. Palmer, *Alexander I, Tsar of War and Peace* (1975); and J. M. Hartley, *Alexander I* (1994).

The best account of Spain in the Napoleonic era is G. H. Lovett, *Napoleon and the Birth of Modern Spain* (2 vols., 1965), which may be supplemented by C. J. Esdaile, *Fighting Napoleon: Guerillas, Bandits and Adventurers in Spain, 1808–1814* (2004). The revolutionary events in the Western Hemisphere ignited by Napoleon's invasion of Spain are recounted in J. Lynch, *The Spanish American Revolutions, 1808–1820* (rev. 1986); in J. E. Rodríguez, *The Independence of Spanish America* (1998); in the wide-ranging, detailed account of L. D. Langley, *The Americas in the Age of Revolution 1750–1850* (1996); and in the relevant sections of L. Bethell (ed.), *The Cambridge History of Latin America, Vol. II: Colonial Latin America* (1988).

Wartime Diplomacy and the Congress of Vienna

An informative study of the era's decisive diplomatic event can be found in T. Chapman, *The Congress of Vienna: Origins, Processes and Results* (1998). Detailed accounts of Metternich's role are available in E. E. Kraehe, *Metternich's German Policy, Vol. I: The Contest with Napoleon, 1799–1814* (1963) and Vol. II: *The Congress of Vienna, 1814–1815* (1983). H. Kissinger, *A World Restored: Metternich, Castlereagh and the Problem of Peace, 1812–1822* (1957, 1973) is a penetrating study by a scholar who later turned diplomat; it should now be supplemented with P. W. Schroeder, *The Transformation of European Politics, 1763–1848* (1994).

Useful Web Sites

A wide-ranging commercial site, *The Napoleonic Guide*, offers a valuable collection of sources, helpful links, and many other materials on the Napoleonic era at www.napoleonguide.com/. Readers will find other useful information at the site of *The Institute on Napoleon and the French Revolution*, www.fsu.edu/~napoleon/, which is maintained at Florida State University, and at the site of the *Napoleon Series*, www.napoleon-series.org, which is a comprehensive, well-maintained resource on all aspects of Napoleon's career and empire.

Dates given after names of rulers and popes are the years of reigns or pontificates; those given for all others are the years of birth and death.

Pronunciation is indicated where it is not obvious. With foreign words the purpose is not to show their exact pronunciation in their own language but to suggest how they may be acceptably pronounced in English. Fully Anglicized pronunciations are indicated by the abbreviation *Angl*. Pronunciation is shown by respelling, not by symbols, except that the following symbols are used for vowel sounds not found in English:

ø   indicates the sound of ö as in Göttingen. To form this sound, purse the lips as if to say *o,* and then say *ay* as in *ate*.

U   indicates the sound of the French *u,* or of German *ü*. To form this sound, purse the lips as if to say *oo,* and then say *ee* as in *eat*.

aN, oN, uN, iN indicate the sounds of the French nasal vowels. Once learned, these are easily pronounced, roughly as follows: For aN, begin to pronounce the English word *on,* but avoid saying the consonant *n* and "nasalize" the *ah* sound instead. For oN do the same with the English *own;* for uN, with the English prefix *un-*; for iN, with the English word *an*.

The sound of *s* as in the word *treasure* is indicated by *zh*. This sound is common in English, though never found at the beginning or end of a word. *igh* always indicates the so-called long *i* as in *high*. The vowel sound of *hoot* is indicated by *oo,* that of *hood* by *ŏo*.

Compared with English, the European languages are highly regular in their spelling, in that the same letters or combinations of letters are generally pronounced in the same way.

Index

Abelard, Peter (1079–1142), 42

Absolutism, 134–135, 159; of James I of England, 157–158; in France, 172, 174–175, 356–357; definition, 175; in Russia, 215, 220; and natural law, 251–252

Acadia (Nova Scotia), 185

Act of Settlement of 1662, 163

Act of Settlement of 1701, 167, 276

Act of Supremacy, 88

A.D. (anno Domini), use of term, 16

Adriatic Sea, 189

Afghanistan, 291;

Africa: Dutch Republic, 150, 151; economy, eighteenth century, 268

African Americans: post–Revolutionary War, 342

Africans: slavery and slave trade, 103, 104, 105, 186, 187–188, 253, 268–270, 289; in Europe, 110

Agriculture: and technology, 7, 29–30; and population growth, 28–29, 31; eighteenth century, 265–266, 269–270, 271, 352–353; France, 352–353

Akbar, Emperor of India (1556–1605), 291

Albania, 198

Albany Plan of Union, 338

Albert of Brandenburg, 83

Alcohol, distillation of, 260

Alexander I, Tsar of Russia (1801–1825), 222, 325, 397–398, 399–400, 402, 421

Alexander the Great (356–323 B.C.), 13

Alexander VI, Pope (1492–1503), 55

Alexis (son of Peter the Great), 223

Algebra, 22

Almanacs, 262–263

Alsace, 182, 186

Alva, Duke of (1508–1583), 122, 124–125

American Revolution, 329, 331, 331–332, 338–348; British reaction, 334; taxation without representation, 338–339; Boston Tea Party, 339; and France, 341–342, 345; War of Independence, 341–348; and Enlightenment thinkers, 344; influence of, in Europe, 346, 347–348

Americas: Spanish empire in, 75, 102–105; discovery of, 102–104; British colonies, 155–156, 186, 187–188, 227, 269–270, 294–295, 296; French colonies, 185–186, 294–295, 296; and Eighteenth Century economy, 269–270; Seven Years' War, 287–290. See also Canada; Latin America; United States

Amsterdam, 124, 129, 152

Anabaptists, 77, 82

Anatomy, study of, 231–232

Anglican Church (Church of England), 88, 90–91, 97; threatened, by James II, 165; Age of Enlightenment, 299, 330

Anglo-Saxons, 25

Anne, Queen of England (1702–1714), 188, 276

Anselm, Saint (1033–1109), 42

Anthony, Saint (1195–1231), 43

Antisemitism, 52, 75

Antwerp, 124, 128, 129

Aquinas, Thomas (a-kwine'-us) (1225–1274), 42, 252; *Summa Theologica,* 42, 44

Arabic numerals, 214

Arabic world: early Middle Ages, 20–22; influence of, 42

Aragon, 74–75

Arch of Triumph, Paris, 410, 413

Archangel, port of, 213, 217

Architecture, England, seventeenth century, 156

Aristotle (384–322 B.C.), 12, 13, 42, 228–229; *Politics,* 12

Arithmetic, Russian, 214

Armies: technological limitations of, 203; standing, 206

Arminius, Jacobus (1560–1609), 150

Art: Renaissance, 60–61, 62, 70; seventeenth century, 149–150, 151, 153, 170–171; Baroque style, 150

Artists, Dutch masters, 110

Artois, Count (later Charles X of France) (ar-twah') (1757–1836), 371

Asia, 100, 101; economy, eighteenth century, 268. *See also under individual countries*

Asiento (ah-syen'-to), 186, 187–188

Assignats (sh-see-nyah'), 366, 367

Astrology, 227

Astronomy, 149, 214, 232, 232–236

Atheism, 248

Atlantic Ocean, opening of, 99–106

Atlantic Revolution, 329–337

Atlantic World after the Peace of Utrecht (map), 187

Attila the Hun (att-i'-la) (406?–453), 20

Augustine, Saint (aw'gus-teen or aw-gus'-t'n) (354–430), 17, 18; *City of God,* 17

Aurungzeb, Emperor of India (aw'-rung-zeb) (1658–1707), 291

Austrian Empire, 199–203; and War of Spanish Succession, 184; rise of, 194; dominions of, 199–200, 200, 201; diets, 201–202; growth of (map), 202; religious oppression, 202; War of Austrian Succession, 282, 283–287; and enlightened despotism, 315, 316–318; serfs, eighteenth century, 316–317; centralization attempted,

317–318; and partition of Poland, 324, 326; and
the French Revolution, 371–374, 374, 396; and
Napoleonic Europe, 396, 397, 402. *See also*
Habsburg, House of
Austrian Succession, War of, 282, 283–287; Peace of
Aix-la-Chapelle, 285
Austrian War of Liberation, 402
Aztecs, 103

Babylonian Captivity, 52
Bach family, 191
Bach, J. S. (1685–1750), 299
Bacon, Francis (1561–1626), 228–230, 239–240; *Advancement of Learning, The,* 229; *New Atlantis, The,* 229; *NovumOrganum,* 229
Bahia, Brazil, 150
Balance of power, 148, 154
Balkans: 1600s, 198, 200. *See also* Albania; Croatia;
Bosnia and Herzegovina
Baltic states. *See* Lithuania
Bank of Amsterdam, 152
Bank of England, 169, 184
Banking industry: interest payments and, 112–113;
seventeenth century, 152, 169; eighteenth century, 277–279
Baptists, 77
Barbados, 155
Barbary pirates, 127, 129, 462, 463
Baroque style, 150
Bastille, storming of (*Angl.* Bass-teel'), 359–360;
commemoration, 367
Batavia (Jakarta), 150
Bayle, Pierre (1647–1706), 170, 241; *Historical and
Critical Dictionary,* 242; *Thoughts on the Comet,*
242
B.C. (before Christ), use of term, 16
B.C.E. (before the Common Era), use of term, 16
Beauty, Greek concept of, 16
Beccaria, Marquis de (beck-a-ree'-a) (1738–1794),
303
Behaim's globe (be-hime'), 102, 244
Bekker, Balthasar (1634–1698), 149
Belgium, 128, 284, 374, 383
Bellini, Giovanni (bell-lee'-nee) (1430–1516), 62
Benedict, Saint (480–543), 23
Bering Strait, 2
Bernard of Saxe-Weimar (sakse-vihmar)
(1604–1639), 139
Bible, 25, 79, 252; and chronology, 246
Biblical criticism, 247
Bill of Rights, English, of 1689, 167, 254
Black Death, 50, 52
Black Hole of Calcutta, 293
Blenheim, battle of, 184, 185
Bodin, Jean (1530–1596), 133
Bohemia, 135, 136, 199; War of Austrian Succession,
284, 285, 287. *See also* Czechoslovakia

Bohemian Mountains, 189
Bohemian War, 137–139
Bohr, Nils (1885–1962), 1081
Boileau, Nicolas (bwah-lo', nee-ko-la') (1636–1711),
171
Boleyn, Anne (bo-lin') (1507–1536), 87, 88
Bonaparte, Napoleon. *See* Napoleon I
Boniface VIII, Pope (1294–1363), 52
Bonnie Prince Charlie, 277
Books, popular: eighteenth century Europe, 262–263;
Age of Enlightenment, 300–301
Borgia, Cesare (bor'-ja) (1475–1507), 55
Borgia, Lucretia (1480–1519), 55
Bosnia and Herzegovina, 198
Bossuet, Bishop (boss-way') (1627–1704), 174–175
Boston Tea Party, 339
Botany, study of, 231
Bourbon kings (*Angl.* Boor-bn), 133–134, 179; War
of Spanish Succession, 184; rule Spain, 274; War
of Austrian Succession, 285; restoration of,
423–425. *See also under individual monarchs*
Bourgeois revolution, 330–331
Bourgeosie, 116–117; eighteenth century Europe,
272; and the French Revolution, 351–352,
357–358, 364, 365–366. *See also* Middle class
Boyle, Robert (1627–1691), 237
Brahe, Tycho (1546–1601), 234
Brandenburg, 204–205; and Thirty Years' War, 206.
See also Prussia
Brandenburg house. *See* Hohenzollerns
Brazil: discovered, 104; Dutch Republic in, 150
Brienne, Loménie de (Archbishop of Toulouse), 356
Brissot, Jacques-Pierre (bree-so') (1754–1793), 372
British colonies, 155–156, 253, 289–290, 425; in the
Americas, 186, 187–188; in India, 291–293, 296.
See also East India Trading Companies
British East India Company, 114, 157, 268–269, 337,
339
British Empire: and the Mediterranean, 6; War of
Spanish Succession, 185; and overthrow of
Napoleon, 422; as world power, 425
British reform movement, 329–337; principles of,
329–330
Bronze Age, 11
Bruegel, Pieter (1564–1638), *Carnival on the Feast
Day of Saint George,* 264
Bubbles, South Sea and Mississippi, 277
Buddha, 15
Buffon, Georges, comte de (1707–1788), 302
Bulls, papal, 52
Bureaucracy, Austrian monarchy, 318
Burke, Edmund (1729–1797), 327, 333–334, 364; *Reflections on the Revolution in France,* 371
Byelorussians, 213
Byzantine Empire, 19, 20, 49

Cabinet Government, in Great Britain, 281

Cabot, John, 104

Cabot, Sebastian (?1474–?1557), 104

Cabral, Pedro (ka-brahl') (1468–1520), 104

Caesaropapism, 17

Calas, Jean (ka-lass', zhaN) (1698–1762), 305

Calculus, invented, 232

Calcutta, 293

Calendars, various, 191, 214

Calonne (French director of finances) (ka-lunn')
    (1734–1802), 355–356

Calvin, John (1509–1564), 70, 84, 85, 112; *Institutes
    of the Christian Religion,* 85

Calvinism, 79, 84–87, 122; doctrines of, 85; spread
    of, 86, 130, 136; and democracy, 86–87; in the
    Netherlands, 124, 128; opposition to, 131–132;
    in Germany, 136; in the Dutch Republic, 150.
    See also Huguenots

Cambacérès, Marquis de (kaN-ba-say-ress')
    (1753–1824), 390

Cambridge University, 41, 90, 118, 163

Campion, Thomas (1567–1620), 156

Canada: French, 170, 290, 292; British, 294

Canossa, 40

Canton system, of recruitment, 210–211

Cape Horn, 151

Cape of Good Hope, 150, 151

Capet, Hugh (ka-pay') (987–996), 30

Capitalism: advent of, 110, 111–114; eighteenth cen-
    tury, 270–272, 277–278. *See also* Laissez-faire
    economics

Capitulations, in Turkey, 196,

Caribbean Islands: Dutch Republic in, 150

Carinthia, 199

Carniola, 199

Carnival, eighteenth century Europe, 263–265

Carolina colonies, 156

Cartier, Jacques (1491–1557), 104

Cartography, 2–3, 70

Caspian Sea, 213

Castile, 74–75

Catalonia, Catalan war, 129–130, 139, 184

Catherine II (The Great), Tsarina of Russia
    (1762–1796), 222, 302, 320–325; domestic pro-
    gram, 320–322; foreign policies, 322–325, 326,
    326–327; and the French Revolution, 371

Catherine of Aragon (1485–1536), 88

Catholic Church (Roman Catholic Church): role, in
    Middle Ages, 37–38, 39–41, 51, 52–55; celibacy,
    39–40, 94; Babylonian Captivity, 52; Great
    Schism of the West, 53–55; corruption, 55; Re-
    naissance, 67, 75; in Spain, 75, 121–122; women
    in, 92; Catholic Reformation, 92–98, 106; educa-
    tional institutions, 96, 118; Index of Prohibited
    Books, 97; Age of Enlightenment, 317; and
    Democratic Revolution, 330; and the French
    Revolution, 350, 365–366, 367–370; and
    Napoleon's Empire, 408–409. *See also* French

Revolution of 1789–1799; Gallican Church;
    Holy Roman Empire; Papacy

Catholics: repression of, 168–169, 337

C.E. (Common Era), use of term, 16

Censorship, 97; Age of Enlightenment, 301, 354

Central and Eastern Europe, 1660–1795 (map),
    192–193

Cervantes, Miguel de (*Angl.* ser-van'-teez)
    (1547–1616): *Don Quixote,* 121

Chancellor, Richard (d. 1556), 213

Charlemagne (768–814), 25, 26–27

Charles I, King of England (1635–1649), 158–161;
    defeated, 159–160; executed, 160, 161

Charles I, King of Spain (Charles V, Holy Roman
    Emperor) (1516–1556), 76, 81, 83, 87, 93, 109,
    121

Charles II, King of England (1660–1685), 162,
    162–165; alliance with Louis XIV, 163, 182; fa-
    vors Catholicism, 163–164

Charles II, King of Spain (1665–1700), 146

Charles IX of France (1560–1574), 131

Charles X of France (1757–1836): as Count of Artois,
    371

Charles of Lorraine, Duke, 200

Charles V, Holy Roman Emperor (Charles I of Spain)
    (1500–1558), 76, 78, 81, 83, 93, 109, 121

Charles VI of Austria (1711–1740), 202–203, 211

Charles XII, King of Sweden (1697–1718), 204, 218

Châtelet, Emilie du (sha-tuh-lay', ay-muh-lee' dU)
    (1706–1749), 300

Children, born out of wedlock, 260

China, 46, 47, 100, 101; thirteenth century, 46, 47;
    trade with, 106; chronology, 246

Christian calendar, 246

Christianity, 15–18; emergence and spread of, 15–16;
    monasteries, 23, 25; Papacy, 23, 25; conversion,
    of barbarians, 25; in Middle Ages, 37–38, 39–41;
    Crusades, 44–46; and humanists, 70; in the En-
    lightenment, 298–299; and the French Revolu-
    tion, 379–380. *See also* Catholic Church; Greek
    Orthodox church; Protestant Reformation; Rus-
    sian Orthodox church

Christians, persecution of, 17

Christina, Queen of Sweden (1632–1654), 163, 204

Chronology: definition, 246; differing, by culture, 246

Church of England, 88, 90–91, 97; seventeenth cen-
    tury, 158, 159

Church of Ireland, 90–91

Churchill, John, Duke of Marlborough (1650–1722),
    184, 185

City-states, of Italy, 56–57, 67

Civil Constitution of the Clergy, 368–370

Classes, social, 114–120; and education, 118; and
    government regulation, 118–119; nobility, 119;
    eastern vs. western Europe, 119–120; and lan-
    guage, 258–259; eighteenth century Europe,
    258–265; living standards, 259–260; and

religion, 260, 299; and etiquette, 262; and health, 262; and social mobility, 272–273; Age of Enlightenment, 299, 300; Prussia, 319–320; and British reform movement, 330; and the French Revolution, 351–352; and Napoleonic Europe, 406; Germany, 420

Clement VII, Pope (1478–1574), 87

Clergy: as First Estate, 350; post-Reformation, 118

Climate, 6, 7

Clive, Robert (1725–1774), 293

Clocks, 214

Cloots, Anacharsis (kloats) (1755–1794), 372

Cloth industry, 110, 111, 112, 113–114; English woolens, 157

Clovis, King of Franks (466–511), 25

Cluniac reform movement, 38

Coffee, 260

Coffeehouses, 260, 261

Coins, minting, 51, 152; study of, 245

Colbert, Jean-Baptiste (kole-bair') (1619–1683), 179, 180

Colbert's commercial code, 179

Coligny, Gaspard de (ko-lee-nyee') (1519–1672), 132

Colonies. See under individual countries

Columbus, Christopher (1446–1506), 102–103

Comets, 241, 242

Commercial capitalism, 113

Commonwealthmen, 332

Communists, Russian Revolution. See Bolsheviks

Conciliar movement, for Church reform, 54–55

Concordat of Bologna (kon-kor'-dt of bol-lo'-nya) (1516–), 74, 93

Condorcet, Marquis de (koN-dor-say') (1743–1794): Progress of the Human Mind, 375

Condorcet, Madame de (1764–1822), 372

Confucius (551–479 B.C.), 15

Congress of Vienna, 426–427

Constantine, Emperor of Roman Empire (306–337), 19

Constantinople, 19, 20, 49

Constitution, United States, 253

Constitutionalism, 251, 252–254, 330; and American Revolution, 344–345; and French Revolution, 364–365

Consulate, French (1799–1804), 389–394; and religion, 391–392

Continental System, 409–414; failure of, 412–414, 421

Copernicus, Nicholas (1473–1543), 70, 233–234, 235; On the Revolutions of the Heavenly Orbs, 233–234

Copley, John Singleton (1738–1815), 340

Corneille, Pierre (kor-nay') (1606–1684), 170

Corporate liberties, 33–34

Cortés, Hernando (kor-tez', er-nan'-do) (1485–1547), 103

Cossacks, 213, 215

Cottage industry, 109, 111, 265, 266

Cotton cloth industry, 268–269

Council of Blood, 124–125

Council of Constance, 54–55, 81

Council of Trent, 93–95, 96

Council of Troubles, 122, 124–125

Counter Reformation (Catholic Reformation), 92–98, 136–137, 138–139, 140; financing, 106

Craft unions, 34–35

Cranach, Lucas, the Elder (1472–1553), 80

Critical methods, literary, 64–65

Croatia, 199

Cromwell, Oliver (1599–1658), 159–160, 161, 162, 332

Crusades, 44–46, 75

Culture: and geography, 2; and globalization, 100, 107, 240–241, 246; seventeenth century, 170–172; and custom, 241; and chronology, of civilization, 246; and natural law, 250–251; elite vs. popular, eighteenth century Europe, 258–265; material, 259; and written language, 259; elite vs. popular, Age of Enlightenment, 299; political, 354–355; German, 416

Currency, 51

Cusa, Nicholas of (?1400–1464), 70, 71

Customs, cultural, 241

Czechoslovakia (Bohemia), 135, 136, 137–138

Da Gama, Vasco (?1469–1524), 101–102

D'Alembert, Jean le Rond (dal-laN-bair') (1717–1783), 302

Dating, chronological, 246

David, Jacques-Louis (dah-veed') (1748–1825), 197

Da Vinci, Leonardo (1452–1519), 61, 70, 226–227

Debts, national: England, eighteenth century, 279, 281; France, eighteenth century, 279, 281, 365–366

Declaration of Independence, 253, 342; adopted, 341

Declaration of Pillnitz, 372, 396

Declaration of the Rights of Man and Citizens, 330, 361

Deductive reasoning, 228–229, 230

Democracy: and Calvinism, 86–87; and Rousseau, 307–308

Democratic Revolution, 329, 329–337; and religion, 330; and social class, 330–331; and women, 361–363

Denmark, 84; alliance with Russia, 218

Deportment, social, Renaissance, 65–67

Descartes, René (day-kart') (1596–1650), 170, 228, 229, 230–231, 232, 239, 240; portrait, 230; Discourse on Method, 231

Devis, Arthur, The Duet, 273

Diderot, Denis (dee-de-ro') (1713–1784), Encyclopédie, 302, 321, 354

Diggers, 161

Diplomatic Revolution of 1756, 287

Directory (1795–1799), 383–384, 386, 387

Disease, eighteenth century Europe, 262

Dissenters, 163–164, 167

Divine right of kings, 157, 251, 252

Divorce, legalized in France, 363

Don Juan, 125

Donation of Constantine, 25

Doubt, principle of systematic, 231

Dover, Treaty of, 163

Drake, Sir Francis (1540–1696), 127

Drang nach Osten (drahng nach ohst'-en), 205

Dualism, Cartesian, 231, 240

Duality, of religion and state, 17–18

Dublin University (Trinity College), 168

DuCange, Carolus (dU-kaNzh') (1610–1688), 245

Dupleix, Joseph-François (du-play') (1697–1763), 292–293

Dutch Barrier, 186

Dutch East India Company, 115, 129, 151

Dutch painters, 110, 149–150, 151, 153

Dutch Republic, 124, 128, 129, 148–155; and Thirty Years' War, 139; religion, 150; explorations and settlements, 150, 151; wars with France, 154; allied with England, 154–155, 169; wars with England, 154; eighteenth century, 266; after the Peace of Utrecht, 274. *See also* Holland; Netherlands

Dutch West India Company, 150

Earth, planet, 1

East India Trading Companies, 128, 151, 266; Great Britain, 114; England, 157; France, 179; and Seven Years' War, 291–293; Austria, 317

Eastern Europe, 189–224; weaknesses, of empires, 190; social stratification, 319–320

Ecclesiastical Reservation, 84

Eckhart, Meister (1260–1327), 71

Economists, 308, 309–310; and laissez-faire economics, 366

Economy: medieval, 31–34; commercial revolution, 106–114; government regulation, 118–119. *See also* Global economy

Edict of Nantes (naNt), 134; revocation of, 180–181

Edict of Restitution, 138, 139

Education: early Middle Ages, 26–27; first universities, 41–42; Renaissance, 65; for women, 65, 118, 149; and the Catholic Church, 96; later sixteenth century, 117–119; and religious discrimination, 168; in the arts, 170–171; state of, in Russia, 214

Edward I, King of England (1239–1307), 52

Edward VI, King of England (1547–1553), 88

Egypt, ancient, 10–11

El Greco (1541–1614), 121

Elector of Brandenburg, 205

Elites, social, 258–265; defining, 258; eighteenth century Asia, 268; Age of Enlightenment, 299, 308, 317, 330. *See also* Nobility

Elizabeth I, Queen of England (1558–1603), 88, 90, 97, 122, 123, 132; aid to the Netherlands, 125–128, 127; and Huguenots, 135; dies, 157

Elizabeth, Tsarina of Russia (1741–1762), 320

Emerson, Ralph Waldo (1803–1882), 418

Eminent property rights, 352, 361

Encomiendas, 104

Encyclopédie (Diderot and others) (aN-see-klo-pay-dee'), 302, 354

England. *See* British colonies; Great Britain; United Kingdom of Great Britain

English Bill of Rights, of 1689, 167, 254

English constitution, 254

English law of evidence, 243

English Poor Laws, 113, 117, 163

Enlightened Despotism, 311–329; definition of, 311; roots of, 312; failures of, 312, 314, 318; of Maria Theresa, 315, 316–317; Austria, 315, 316–318; of Joseph II, 317–318; of Frederick the Great, 318–320; Russia, 320–325; limitations of, 325; of Napoleon, 389

Enlightenment, Age of, 226, 297–348; religion and, 298–299, 305–306, 307; women in, 300, 301–302, 308; literacy, 300–301; Philosophes, 300–302; social mobilty and, 319; Great Britain, 331; and American Revolution, 344, 346; and revolution, 354

Entertainment, eighteenth century Europe, 262, 263–264

Entrepreneurs, 109

Equality, principle of, 330

Erasmus of Rotterdam, Desiderius (1466–1536), 72, 74

Escorial (ess-kor'-i-al), 122

Estates General, 172, 173, 358; and the French Revolution, 358

Estates, three, 36–37, 350–353

Ethnocentrism, 2–3

Etiquette: Renaissance, 65–67; eighteenth century Europe, 262

Eugene of Savoy, Prince (1662–1736), 184, 200

Europe, 31; influence of, 3, 6, 9–10; boundaries of, 6; climate, 6, 7; bodies of water, 6–7; Middle Ages, 9–48; Indo-Europeans, 11; prehistoric, 11; early Middle Ages, 22–28; rise of, 46–47; 1529 (map), 78; population distribution, 137; 1648 (map), 142; post-Wars of Religion, 141–142; eastern, 189–224; wealth and knowledge, 257–258; social class, eighteenth century, 258–265; 1740 (map), 312–313; 1815 (map), 431. *See also individual countries*; Western Europe

European discoveries, 1450–1600 (map), 101

Evidence: definition, 243; English law of, 243; and historical scholarship, 243, 244–245

Evil, and good, 16
Exploding the diet, 195

Fairfax, Thomas (1612–1671), 159
Faust (fowst), 71
Federalism, and American Revolution, 344–345
Ferdinand, King of Aragon and Spain (1474–1516), 74
Ferdinand I, Holy Roman Emperor (1556–1564), 76, 121
Feudalism, 30–31; decline of, 35; eastern Europe, 120, 189, 210, 316–317, 319; postmedieval, 130, 172, 173, 210; dissolution of, 162, 406, 420–421; Russian, 215, 219–220, 223–224; eighteenth century, 316–318, 319, 350, 351; France, 350, 352–353
Fichte, J. G. (fik'-tuh) (1762–1814), 418; *Addresses to the German Nation,* 419; *Closed Commercial State,* 419
Fifteen, The (Scottish Uprising), 277
Fifth Monarchy Men, 161
First Coalition, disintegrates, 396
First World War, 194
Five Great Farms, 179, 180
Flagellants, Order of (fla-jell'-nts), 52, 54
Flanders galleys, 100
Fleury, Cardinal (flur-ree') (1653–1743), 275, 279, 281, 284
Florence, Italy, 57–58, 63
Forty-Five, The (Scottish Uprising), 277
Forum, 14
Fossils, 2
Fouché, Joseph, Marquis de (foo-shay') (1759–1820), 390
Fox, Charles James (1749–1806), 334, 385
Fox, George (1624–1691), 161
France: medieval, 30, 33, 35, 41, 51; University of Paris, 41; Hundred Years' War, 51; Protestant Reformation, 83; Huguenots, 122–123, 131–132; opposition to Spain, 125, 136–137, 138–139; postmedieval feudalism, 130, 172, 173; Wars of Religion, 130–135; Spain invades, 132, 139; civil wars, 132–134, 135–136; in Thirty Years' War, 135, 138–139; under Louis XIV, 146–148, 154–155, 169–188; expansion of, 1661–1713 (map), 147; arts and culture, 169–172; seventeenth century, 169–172; colonies of, 170, 289–290, 292, 294–295, 296, 379; absolutism, 172, 174–175; the Fronde, 172, 173–174; *parlements,* 172, 180; government, of Louis XIV, 175–176, 176–177; army, under Louis XIV, 176; economy, under Louis XIV, 177, 179, 180; from last years of Louis XIV – 1789 (map), 180; wars, under Louis XIV, 181–188; Dutch War, of 1672, 182; invades Spanish Netherlands, 182; and War of Spanish Succession, 185–186; economy, eighteenth century, 266, 267–268, 277–279; popula-

tion, eighteenth century, 266, 350; universal monarchy, 274; after the Peace of Utrecht, 274–282; and War of Austrian Succession, 284, 285, 286; Seven Years' War, 289–290, 291–293, 294–296; East India Trading Companies, 291–292, 292–293; in India, 291–293; enlightened despotism, 312, 314; and the American Revolution, 341–342, 345; Age of Enlightenment, 349–350; dominates Europe, 349–350; Revolution of 1789, 349–392; feudalism, 350, 351; public debt, 355; Directory, 383–384, 386, 387; Consulate, 387, 389–394; Napoleonic, 393–394; after Napoleon, 423–425
Franche-Comté (fraNsh-con-tay'), 146, 147, 182, 186
Francis I, King of France (1515–1547), 74, 83, 93, 131
Francis II, Emperor of Austrian Empire (1792–1835), 318, 372–373
Franklin, Benjamin (1706–1790), 300
Franks, 25
Frederick I, King of Prussia (1701–1713), 206
Frederick II (the Great), King of Prussia (1740–1786), 210, 283, 302; military triumphs, 211, 288, 295–296; and Voltaire, 305, 319; enlightened despotism, 318–320
Frederick III, Elector of Brandenburg (1688–1701), 206
Frederick V, King of Bohemia (1596–1532), 137
Frederick William (the Great Elector) (1640–1688), 206, 207
Frederick William I, King of Prussia (1713–1740), 210–211, 283
Freeholders, 115
Freemasonry (Masons), 300,
French and Indian Wars, 282, 338
French Calvinists. *See* Huguenots
French East India Company, 179
French Imperial System (Napoleonic), formation of, 396–404
French Republic and its satellites, 1798–1799 (map), 388
French Revolution of 1789–1799, 308, 318, 330, 349–392; and the Church, 350, 367–370, 391–392; and religion, 350, 367–370, 379–380, 391–392; and the middle class, 351–352, 357–358, 363, 365–366; nobility and, 351–352, 356–357, 363, 372, 373; and the Enlightenment, 354; political culture, 354–355, 366–367; and taxation, 355–356; storming of the Bastille, 359, 360; and the lower class, 359, 373, 375, 376; Great Fear of 1789, 360–361; Declaration of the Rights of Man and Citizens, 361; Jacobins, 363–364, 372–373, 374; constitution, 364–366; and labor unions, 366; Girondins, 370, 372–373, 374, 375; impact on Europe, 370–374, 395; violence, 373–374; National Convention, 374–378; *sans-culottes,* 375; Reign of Terror, 377–378,

379, 380; Committee of Public Safety, 378–379; military triumphs, 380–381; Thermidorian Reaction, 382–383; and Huguenots, 392; legacy of, 431

Frisians, 207

Fronde (frond), 172, 173–174

Fructidor, coup d'etat, 386

Fugger family (foo-gr), 109

Fugger, Johann, 109

Galen (c. 130–c. 200), 13, 232

Galicia, 324, 326

Galileo (1564–1642), 225, 234, 235–236

Gallican Church, 79, 93; alienation from international Catholicism, 130–131; under Louis XIV, 180

Gama, Vasco da (?1469–1524), 101–102

Geneva, Switzerland: Calvin in, 86

Geoffrin, Madame de (1699–1777), 301

Geographical determinism, 7

Geographical knowledge, growth of (maps), 244

Geography: and history, 1; and culture, 2; and politics, 7–8, 130

Geometry: coordinate, 230–231, 232

George I, King of Great Britain and Ireland (1714–1727), 192, 276, 277

George III, King of Great Britain and Ireland (1760–1820), 331, 333, 334, 427–428

Georgia (United States), 156

Germanic liberties, 191

Germany: early Middle Ages, 22–23, 25, 26; medieval, 30–31, 33, 40, 54; Renaissance, 70–71, 76–77; early commercialism, 120; religious divisions, 135–137; decline, sixteenth century, 136; fragmented, after Thirty Years' War, 140–141, 190–192; nationalism, 416–419, 420; class, social, 420; and defeat of Napoleon, 422; post-Napoleonic, 426–427. *See also* Thirty Years' War; Weimar Republic

Germany in Its Deep Humiliation (anonymous), 418

Ghent, 129

Gibbon, Edward (1737–1794), *Decline and Fall of the Roman Empire,* 302–303

Gibraltar, Strait of, 6, 184, 186, 274

Girondins (ji-ron-dins), 370, 372–373, 374, 375

Glanville, Joseph (1636–1680), 240

Global economy, eighteenth century, 265–273; and Dutch Republic, 266; and Great Britain, 267, 268; and France, 267–268; Africa in, 268; India in, 268–269; and the Americas, 269–270; and marriage, 272

Globalization, 9–10, 49; and culture, 100, 240–241; and common calendar, 246

Glorious Revolution, 169

Gneisenau, August (gnigh'-se-now) (1760–1831), 419, 420

Goethe, Johann Wolfgang von (gø'-tuh) (1749–1832), 71, 408

Gouges, Olympe de (1755–1793); *The Rights of Woman,* 362

Government, 157–158; seventeenth century, 157; separation of powers, 304; by representation, 330; and centralization of power, 335. *See also* Absolutism; Constitutionalism

Goya, Francisco de (1746–1828), 403

Graaf, Régnier de (grahf, ray-nee-ay' de) (1641–1673), 232

Grammar schools, 118

Gravity, 236–237

Great Britain: Norman invasion, 31; medieval, 31, 33, 35, 36, 37, 51; Hundred Years' War, 51; Wars of the Roses, 51; Protestant Reformation, 87–91; rule of Ireland, 90–91, 155, 160, 167–169, 331–332; East India Trading Company, 114, 157, 268–269, 337, 339; religious rebellions, 122, 123; supports Netherlands, 125–128; as Protestant bulwark, 127, 163; wars with Spain, 127, 128, 160, 185, 281–282; supports Huguenots, 132, 135; Navigation Act of 1651, 153, 160; allied with Dutch Republic, 154, 154–155, 169; population, 155; seventeenth century, 155–169; economy, seventeenth century, 156–157; civil war, 157–162; Restoration, 1660–1688, 162–165; Revolution of 1688 (Glorious Revolution), 165–169, 254–255; seventeenth century (map), 166; national debt, 169; ascendancy, 186, 187–188; industry, eighteenth century, 265–266; economy, eighteenth century, 265–273; population, eighteenth century, 266; after the Peace of Utrecht, 274–282; Seven Years' War, 289–290, 291–293, 294–295, 296; reform movement, 329; centralization, of government, 335–338; in India, 337–338; and the French Revolution, 371, 374; Napoleonic Wars, 397–398, 398–399; and Napoleonic Europe, 409–414; nationalism, 415; Industrial Revolution, 415, 421. *See also* American Revolution; British colonies; Parliament, English

Great Elector (Frederick William), 206, 207

Great Fear of 1789, 360–361

Great Moguls, 291

Great Schism of East and West, 27–28

Great Schism of the West, 53–55

Greece, ancient, 11–13; politics, 12; written language, 13; influence of, 13, 42; love, concept of, 16; religion, 16

Greek language, use of, 63

Greek Orthodox church, 49, 198, 211, 214

Gregorian calendar, 246

Gregory VII (Hildebrand), Pope (1073–1085), 39–40

Gregory XII, Pope (?1327–1417), 191

Gregory XIII, Pope (1572–1585): Gregorian calendar, 246

Grimm, Baron (1723–1807), 303

Groote, Gerard (grote) (1340–1384), 71–72

Grotius, Hugo (gro'-shus) (1583–1645): *Law of War and Peace,* 251
Guadeloupe, 295
Guelph family, 192
Guiana, 150
Guilds, 34–35, 109, 111; opposition to, 113; abolished, 366, 408
Guillotine, 382
Guise family (gheez), 132
Guise, Henry (1550–1588), 132, 133
Guns, eighteenth century, 282
Gustavus Adolphus, King of Sweden (1771–1792), 139, 204
Gutenberg, Johannes (?1394–1468), 70

Habsburg, House of (*Angl.* Haps'-burg): and the Holy Roman Empire, 76; branches, 76, 78; dominions (map), 78; and Thirty Years' War, 135, 136–139; French opposition, 136–137; infirmities of, 146; and universal monarchy, 147–148; alliance with Dutch Republic, 154; and Austrian monarchy, 184, 199–203, 274, 284–285. *See also under individual monarchs*
Haiti, 379, 397
Halley, Edmond (1656–1742), 241, 242
Halley's Comet, 241, 242
Hals, Frans (1580–1666), 149, 230
Hamilton, Alexander (1755–1804), 361, 371
Handel, George Frederick (1685–1759): *The Messiah,* 299
Hanse league, 33
Harvard College, 106
Harvey, William (1578–1657), 239–240; *On the Movement of the Heart and Blood,* 232
Hastings, Warren (1732–1818), 337
Health: eighteenth century Europe, 262, 263. *See also* Medicine
Hébert, Jacques (1757–1794), 379
Hébertists (*Angl.* hay'-bair'-tists), 379, 380
Helvetic Body (Switzerland), 140
Helvétius, Claude Adrien (1715–1771), 301; *On Man,* 301; *On the Mind,* 301
Henry II, King of France (1547–1559), 131
Henry III, King of France (1574–1589), 131, 133
Henry of Navarre (Henry IV, King of France) (1589–1610), 40, 132, 133–134
Henry VII, King of England (1485–1509), 73, 114
Henry VIII, King of England (1509–1547), 87–88
Herder, J. G. (1744–1803), 416–417, 418; *Ideas on the Philosophy of the History of Mankind,* 416
Hereditary subjection, 189
Herodotus (484–425 B.C.), 12
Herzegovina. *See* Bosnia and Herzegovina
High Commission (England), 158, 159
Hildebrand (Pope Gregory VII) (1073–1085), 39–40
Hilliard, Nathan, 90
Hindus: and Seven Years' War, 291

Historical scholarship, 243, 244–246; and Biblical criticism, 247; Age of Enlightenment, 306
Hitler, Adolf (1889–1945), 207
Hobbes, Thomas (1588–1679), 251–252; *Leviathan,* 252
Hogarth, William (1697–1764), 261; *Gin Lane,* 261
Hohenheim (Paracelsus) (?1490–1541), 70–71, 227
Hohenzollerns (*Angl.* ho-hn-zoll-rn), 192, 205–206; territorial acquisitions, 205; and Seven Years' War, 287–288
Holbein, Hans, The Younger (1465–1524), 74
Holland, 124, 125, 126. *See also* Dutch Republic; Netherlands
Holy Alliance, 429
Holy Roman Empire, 30–31, 83, 121, 135–136; proclaimed, 38; Renaissance, 76–77; dissolution of, 140–141; after the Peace of Westphalia, 182; decline of, 189; boundaries of, 190–191; after 1648, 190–192; after 1648 (map), 194
Holy Synod, Russian Orthodox church, 216–217, 220
Homer: *Iliad,* 11; *Odyssey,* 11
Homo erectus, 1
Homo sapiens, 2
House of Commons, 158, 169, 188, 276, 333
House of Lords, 158, 188, 276
Hubertusberg, Treaty of (*Angl.* hyoo-bur'-tus-burg), 293–296
Hudson Bay territory, 185–186, 274
Huguenots (*Angl.* hyoo'-ge-notts), 122–123, 131–132; Edict of Nantes, 133–134; rebellion of, 135; under Louis XIV, 180–181, 238; and the French Revolution, 392
Human nature, views of, 252, 253
Humanism, 61–63
Humanists, 63–64, 72; Christian, 70
Humanitarianism: origins of, 308
Humans, origins of, 1
Hume, David (1711–1776), 301, 302
Hundred Years' War, 51
Hungarians, 27
Hungary, 199; battle of Mohacs, 76; under Ottoman Turks, 198, 199; and War of Austrian Succession, 284–285, 287
Huns, 19–20
Huss, John (1369–1415), 54, 55
Hussites, 54
Huyghens, Christian (*Angl.* high'-gnz) (1629–1695), 149, 236
Hyderabad, India, 291

Ice Age, 1–2
Illuminati, 300
Incas, 103
India, 269; economy, eighteenth century, 268–269; Great Moguls, 291; Seven Years' War, 291–293, 296, 337; Great Britain in, 291–293, 296, 337–338

Indians (Native Americans), 338
Individualism, 58–59
Indo-Europeans, 11
Inductive reasoning, 228–229, 230
Indulgences, 80–81
Inflation, price, 107–108, 115–116
Innocent III, Pope (1198–1216), 40–41
Innocent VIII, Pope (1488–1492), 55
Innocent XI, Pope (1676–1689), 200
Inquisition, Papal (Roman), 97
Inquisition, Spanish, 75, 97, 406
Instrument of Government, 162
Ireland: English rule, 90–91, 155, 160, 167–169,
    331–332; and American Revolution, 336–337
Iron Age, 11
Isabella of Castile (1474–1504), 74, 102
Islam, 20–22, 75, 241
Italy: medieval, 33, 41; Renaissance, 56–69, 226; Flo-
    rence, 57–58, 63
Ivan III, Duke of Muscovy (1462–1505), 211
Ivan the Terrible, Tsar of Russia (1547–1584), 213,
    214

Jacobins, 363–364, 370, 372–373, 374
Jacobites, 276, 277
Jakarta (Batavia), 150
Jamaica, 156, 160
James I, King of England (1603–1625), 157–158
James II, King of England (1685–1688), 163–164,
    164–165, 165–169, 254–255; returns to Catholi-
    cism, 165; loses throne to William of Orange,
    165, 166, 167; allies with Louis XIV, 166–167
James III (the Pretender), 276–277
James VI, King of Scotland (1566–1625), 157
Jamestown settlement, 155
Janisaries, 196
Jansenism, 180
Japan: Dutch Republic in, 150; Western contact, 213
Jefferson, Thomas (1743–1826), 341, 371
Jehan, Shah (1628–1658), 291
Jesuits, 95–97; missionary work, 241; and natural
    law, 251
Jesus Christ, birth of, 15
Jews, Judaism, 15, 42; antisemitism, 52, 75;
    Sephardic, 75; in Dutch Republic, 149, 150; mi-
    gration to Poland, 195; in Ottoman Empire, 198;
    civil rights for, 317, 330. See also Hitler, Adolf;
    Marranos
Joan of Arc (1412–1431), 51
John of Leyden (1509–1536), 82
Johnson, Samuel (1709–1784), 302–303
Joseph II, Holy Roman Emperor (1765–1790), 285,
    317–318
Josephine, Empress of France (1804–1809), 402, 403
Julian calendar, 246
Julius II, Pope (1503–1513), 55
Junkers (joong'-krz), 120, 209, 210, 319, 420–421

Justification by faith, 79–80

Kaiser, etymology of, 214
Kempis, Thomas à (1370–1471), 71
Kepler, Johannes (1571–1630), 234
King George's War, 282
Kingdom of the Serbs, Croats, and Slovenes
Kings in medieval Europe, 30–31, 51
Knights, 46, 205
Knowledge, and wealth, 257–258
Köprülu family, 199
Kosciusko, Thaddeus (Angl. kosky-os'-ko)
    (1747–1817), 327, 415

Labor strikes, 366
Labor unions, 34–35, 366
Laborde, Jean Joseph (la-bord') (1724–1794), 273
Lafayette, Marquis de (la-fay-et') (1757–1834), 360,
    372
La Fontaine, Jean de (la foN-tenn') (1621–1695), 170
Lagrange, Joseph-Louis (la-graNzh') (1736–1813),
    378
Laissez-faire economics (less-say fair'), 366
Lamarck, Jean-Baptiste de Monet de (la-mark')
    (1744–1829), 378
Land rights: private property, 162–163, 169, 253, 366;
    eminent property, 352, 361; France, 352–353.
    See also Feudalism
Langland, William: Piers Plowman, 53
Language: written, 259; and dialect, 258–259; na-
    tional vs. regional, 258–259
Languages: written, 10–11, 13, 26–27, 62–63; Indo-
    European, 11; Romance, 14. See also Books,
    popular; Literature
La Rochefoucauld, Duke of (la rush-foo-co')
    (1613–1680), 170
Latin America, 75, 102–105, 371
Latin Christendom, 22–23
Latin, use of, 62–63
Lavater, J. C. (1741–1801), 299
Lavoisier, Antoine-Laurent (la-vwah-zuyay')
    (1743–1794), 378
Law, John (1671–1729), 274, 278–279
Law of nations, 251
Lawrence, Saint (? –258), 122
Lay investiture, 40
Lay religion, 71–72
Le Nain, Louis (?1593–1648), 186
League of Schmalkald, 83
Lebrun, Marquis de (luh-bruN') (1739–1824), 390
Leeuwenhoek, Antony van (lay-vn-hook)
    (1632–1723), 149, 232
Legal system: Roman Empire, 15; Middle Ages,
    32–33, 35–37, 51; Renaissance, 73–74; England,
    seventeenth century, 158, 243; evidentiary laws,
    243; use of torture, 243; international law,
    250–251; Napoleonic Codes, 393

Leibniz, Gottfried Wilhelm (1646–1716), 191, 232
Leicester, Earl of (les-ter) (1532–1588), 126
Leningrad, 219
Leo X, Pope (1513–1521), 55, 74, 80–81
Leonardo da Vinci (1452–1519), 61, 226–227
Leopold II, Holy Roman Emperor (1790–1792), 318, 371–372, 396
Lespinasse, Julie de (1732–1776), 301–302
Levellers, 161
Liberum veto (lee'-b-rom vee'-to), 195
Libraries, early, 244
Liège (map), 126
Lilburne, John (1614–1657), 161
Literacy, 118, 300, 302
Literary critical methods. See Critical methods, literary
Literature: Renaissance, 61–65, 71; Spanish, 121; Dutch Republic, 149; English, 156; seventeenth century, 170; eighteenth century Europe, 262–263; popular books, 262–263; witchcraft and magic in, 263; Age of Enlightenment, 300–301, 302, 308; German, 416
Lithuania, 195
Little Russians, 213
Living standards, and culture, 259–260
Locke, John (1632–1704), 169, 248, 277, 305; Essay Concerning the Human Understanding, 248; Letter of Toleration, 248; Reasonableness of Christianity, 248; Two Treatises of Government, 249, 252; defense of constitutionalism, 252–254; portrait, 254
Logarithms, 232
Lollards, 53–54
Long Parliament, 159, 160
Lope de Vega (1562–1635), 121
Lorrain, Claude (lo-riN') (1600–1682), 170
Lorraine, 182
Lorraine, Cardinal of, 132
Louis XI, King of France (1461–1483), 74
Louis XIII, King of France (1610–1643), 135
Louis XIV, King of France (1643–1715), 145, 146, 147–148, 169–188; ambitions of, 146–148; invades Dutch Republic, 154; invades Spanish Netherlands, 154; allies with Charles II, 163; allies with James II, 166–167; and absolutism, 172, 174–175; as personification of state, 174; government of, 175–176; religious intolerance, 180–181; wars of, 181–188; and War of Spanish Succession, 185–186; alliance with Ottoman Turks, 199–200; visits Royal Academy of Sciences, 238
Louis XV, King of France (1715–1774), 275; enlightened despotism, 312
Louis XVI, King of France (1774–1774), 287, 314–315, 316; and the French Revolution, 355, 356, 357–358, 359, 360, 364, 371; attempts escape, 364; imprisoned, 373; executed, 375

Louis XVIII of France (1814–1824), 424–425, 428
L'Ouverture, Toussaint (?1743–1803), 379, 397, 398
Love, concept of, 16
Low Countries, 1648 (Netherlands) (map), 126
Loyola, Ignatius, Saint (1491–1556): Spiritual Exercises, 95
Luther, Katherina (von Bora) (1499–1552), 80
Luther, Martin (1483–1546), 70, 71, 79–83, 112
Lutheranism, 79–83, 136

Mabillon, Jean (ma-bee-yoN') (1632–1707): On Diplomatics, 244
Machiavelli, Niccolò (ma-kee-a-vell'-lee) (1469–1527), 67, 69, 249–250; Prince, The, 67, 249–250
Magellan, Ferdinand (1480–1521), 103, 104
Magic, magicians: eighteenth century Europe, 263; in literature, 263; Age of Enlightenment, 299
Magna Carta, 36
Magyars, 27, 285
Malpighi, Marcello (mal-pee'-ghee) (1628–1694), 232
Manhattan Island, 150, 154
Manila Galleons, 106
Manners, social: Renaissance, 65–67; eighteenth century Europe, 262
Mapmaking, 2–3, 70
Mardi Gras, eighteenth century Europe, 263
Maria Theresa of Austria (ma-ree'-a te-ress'-a) (1717–1780), 203, 211, 284–286; Schönbrunn Palace, 288; and enlightened despotism, 312, 315, 316–317
Marie Antoinette (1755–1793), 287, 308, 318, 371, 372, 378
Marlowe, Christopher (1564–1593), 71
Marranos, 75
Marriage: Renaissance, 67; Protestant ideal, 92; eighteenth century Europe, 272; as civil contract, 363; and divorce, 363
Marseillaise, The (mar-say-yez') (song), 373
Martin V, Pope (1368–1431), 55
Martinique (mar-ti-neek'), 295
Marx, Karl (1818–1883), 116
Mary I, Queen of England (1553–1558), 88
Mary II, Queen of England (1689–1694), 165, 166
Mary Queen of Scots (Mary Stuart) (1542–1568), 125, 152, 165–166
Maryland, 155
Masons (Freemasons), 300
Massachusetts: witch trials, 227; abolishes slavery, 342
Material culture, 259
Mathematics: Russian, 214; and the scientific method, 230–231, 232; advances in, 232; and astronomy, 233, 234, 235–236, 236; and technological advances, 237; and chronology, 246
Mathmatics, 13, 22
Maupeou parlements (mo-poo'), 314–315, 316

Maximilian I, Emperor of Holy Roman Empire (1493–1519), 76

Mazarin, Cardinal (ma-za-riN') (1602–1661), 172, 173, 174

Medici, Catherine de' (med-i-chee) (1519–1589), 131, 132, 260

Medici family, 57–58, 109

Medici, Marie de' (1573–1642), 134, 135

Medicine, 70–71; eighteenth century Europe, 262, 263, 265

Mediterranean Sea, 6; and Philip II of Spain, 121, 122, 127; pirates, piracy, 127, 129; Great Britain in, 186, 187–188; port of Trieste, 200

Mediterranean World, A.D. 400, 800, and 1250 (map), 24

Mennonites, 77, 150

Mercantilism, 113; Russia, under Peter the Great, 220

Mercantilist regulations, and Seven Years' War, 290

Mercenaries, 138, 141; Russian army, 219; eighteenth century, 282; sepoys, 293

Merchant class, 31–34, 35

Mesmer, F. A. (1734–1815), 299

Mestizos, 104, 106

Methodists, 299

Metternich, Clemens von (mett'-ter-nick) (1773–1859), 402

Mexico, 106

Microscope: invented, 149; use of, 232

Middle Ages, 9, 18–48; timespan of, 10; early, 18–28; population growth, 28–29, 31, 32–33, 34; high, 28–48; agriculture, 29–30; feudalism, 30–31, 35; trade, 31–32; towns, 32–34, 35; guild system, 34–35; legal system, 35–37; taxation, 36; Crusades, 44–46

Middle class, 116–117; eighteenth century Europe, 272. See also Bourgeosie

Middle East, 11; economy, eighteenth century, 268. See also under individual countries

Milan, 184

Milan Decree of 1807, 411

Militarism: definition, 204; of Prussia, 206–207

Military forces: technology and, 203; cost of maintaining, 355. See also Armies; Weaponry

Milton, John (1608–1674), 156; Paradise Lost, 156; Paradise Regained, 156

Mining, of precious metals, 106, 108, 121

Minorca, 184, 187–188, 274

Mississippi bubble, 277–279

Mississippi Company, 278–279

Modern, modernity, 10

Mogul empire, 291

Moldavia, 198

Molière (mull-yair') (1622–1673), 171

Monarchies, 35–37; Renaissance, 69–70, 73–74; English, 73–74; French, 74, 130; and the Protestant Reformation, 83, 84; new, 111, 130; and sover-eignty, 133; and absolutism, 134–135; and centralization of power, 335, 353. See also Enlightened Despotism

Monasteries, 23, 38; abolished, in French Revolution, 368

Money, 51, 152. See also Currency

Mongols, 49

Montagnards, 375

Montaigne, Michel de (moN-tenn') (1533–1592), 227, 241, 310

Montesquieu (moN-tes-kyuh') (1689–1755), 302, 303–304; The Spirit of Laws, 303–304

Moors, 75

Moral and Scientific Union (Tugendbund), 418

Moravia, 199

Moravian Brothers, 77

More, Sir Thomas (1478–1535): Utopia, 88

Moreelse, Willem (1620–1666), 233

Moriscos, 75, 122, 123, 129

Moscow, 219

Mostaert, Jan, 103

Mountebanks, 263

Muhammad (c. 570–c. 632), 15, 20–21

Muratori, Luigi Antonio (1672–1750), 244, 245

Murillo, Bartolome (moo-reel'-yo) (1617–1683), 121

Muscovy, Muscovites, 196, 211, 213

Music, 191; England, seventeenth century, 156; Age of Enlightenment, 299

Muslim faith. See Islam

Muslim lands, in Eastern Europe, 190

Muslims: in India, 291. See also Islam; Moriscos

Mysticism, 71

Mythology, 13

Napier, John (nay'-pur) (1550–1617), 232

Naples, 184

Napoleon I (Napoleon Bonaparte), Emperor of the French (1804–1814), 385, 386, 387–394; takes control, 387; genius of, 389; and the Church, 391–392; and taxation, 392–393; and hereditary succession, 402–403; and Josephine, 402, 403; invades Russia, 421–423; overthrown, 421–431; abdicates, 423; exiled, 425; at Waterloo, 428–429. See also Napoleonic Codes; Napoleonic Empire; Napoleonic Europe;

Napoleonic Codes, 393, 405–406

Napoleonic Empire, 404–409, 414–421; organization, of states, 404–405; and Bonaparte family, 405; religion and, 408–409; and Great Britain, 409–414; resistance, 414–421; Grand Army, 421–422; overthrow, 421–431

Napoleonic Europe: coalitions, 396–398; stages, of French occupation, 405–406; 1810 (map), 406–407; Germany (map), 409; anti-British sentiments, 410–411

Napoleonic wars, 222, 319–320

National Assembly, France, 357

Nationalism, 283; and Rousseau, 307–308; and revolution, 308, 353, 367; anti-French, 414–421; German, 416–419, 420
Native Americans, 338
Natural law, philosophy of, 239, 250–254, 417
Natural right. *See* Natural law, philosophy of
Navigation Act of 1651, 153, 160, 163
Necker, Jacques (neck'-r, zhak) (1732–1804), 355
Nelson, Lord Horatio (1758–1805), 399
Netherlands, 71–72, 123–128; under Philip II, 122; revolt, 123–126, 128; Antwerp, 124; Protestant Reformation, 124; Union of Utrecht, 125, 126, 128; Twelve Years' Truce, 128; partition of, 128–129. *See also* Dutch Republic
New England colonies, 155; slavery in, 269–270
New Model Army, 160
New World: discovery of, 99–106, 108; Dutch Republic in, 150; England in, 155–156; France in, 170. *See* Americas
New York: settled, by Dutch, 129; England conquers, 156
Newcomen, Thomas (1663–1729), 237
Newfoundland, 185
Newton, Sir Isaac (1642–1727), 225, 232, 236, 239, 240, 305; *Mathematical Principles of Natural Philosophy,* 236
Newtonian system, 239–240
Nicholas II, Pope (1058–1061), 39
Nicholas V, Pope (1447–1455), 55
Nimwegen, Treaty of (nigh'-me-gn), 154, 182
Nobility, 51; and Calvinism, 131, 134, 136; seventeenth century, 162–163; eighteenth century, 271–272, 275–276; Age of Democratic Revolution, 330; and the French Revolution, 351–352, 356–357, 372, 373; and Napoleonic Europe, 406
Non-Jurors, 276
Nonconformists, 261
Norfolk, Duke of (1536–1572), 302–303
Normans, 31
Northern War (1700–1721), 218–219
Nostradamus (1503–1566), 227
Nova Scotia (Acadia), 185, 274, 290
Numbers, systems of, 214
Numismatics, 245
Nystadt, Treaty of (nU'-stah or *Angl.* nigh'-staht), 219

Oath of the Tennis Court, 357, 360
Old Believers (in Russia), 216, 219, 321
Old Regime. *See* Bourbon kings
Olivares, Count (1587–1645), 129
Oral history, 11
Orbis terrarum, 14
Ordeal, trial by, 22
Orleans, Duke of (1747–1793), 275
Ostend Company, 274
Ottoman Empire, 196–199; religions of, 49; in the Mediterranean, 122, 123; decline of, 189; geographical boundaries, 190, 196–199; map, 194; military forces, 196; commerce and trade, 198; defeated in Vienna, 199–201
Oudry, Jean-Baptiste, *M. Bachelier, director of the Lyons Farms,* 280
Oxenstierna (oks'-n-steer-nuh) (1583–1654), 139
Oxford University, 41, 90, 118, 163, 241

Paine, Thomas (1737–1809), 372; *Common Sense,* 341, 345; *The Rights of Man,* 361, 371
Palatinate, 136, 137–138
Paleography, 244
Pantheism, 248
Papacy, 23, 25, 38, 39–41, 55; Babylonian Captivity, 52–53; and the Council of Trent, 94; and the French Revolution, 368–369, 370; infallibility of, 370
Papal Inquisition (Roman Inquisition), 97
Papin, Denis (pa-piN') (1647–1712), 237
Paracelsus (par-a-sel-sus) (Hohenheim) (1493–1541), 70–71, 227
Paris: salons, 171–172, 301–302, 306; Age of Enlightenment, 301
Paris, Treaty of (first), 293–296, 425
Paris, Treaty of (second), 429
Parlements, France, 172, 180, 314–315; eighteenth century, 275; and enlightened despotism, 314–315, 316
Parliament, English, 37, 51, 188; seventeenth century, 157–160, 162–163, 167; houses of, 158; ship-money dispute, 158–159; Solemn League and Covenant, 159; Long Parliament, 159, 160; Pride's Purge, 160; eighteenth century, 275–276, 331–332, 333–334; reform, 331–332, 333–334
Parliaments, origin of, 36
Parma, prince of (Alexander Farnese) (1546–1592), 125, 126
Parthenon, 12; damaged, 200
Pascal, Blaise (1623–1662), 170, 232, 239, 247
Patronage, 333
Paul III, Pope (1534–1549), 93, 95
Paul the Apostle (Saint Paul) (died c. A.D. 67), 15, 16, 43, 79
Pax Romana, 15
Peace of Aix-la-Chapelle, 285
Peace of Alais, 135
Peace of Augsburg, 83, 84, 121, 136
Peace of Belgrade, 200
Peace of Karlowitz, 200
Peace of Prague, 139
Peace of Utrecht, 184, 185–186, 188; sequelae, 274–282
Peace of Vienna, 429, 431
Peace of Westphalia, 99, 147–148, 188; sequelae, 152, 182, 188, 204; Alsace Lorraine, 182
Peacock Throne, 291

Peasants, 115; rebellion of, 31, 35, 50–51, 77, 81–82, 215, 216, 219; and the French Revolution, 359, 360–361, 366, 373, 376. *See also* Feudalism; Serfs

Pennsylvania colony, 156

Peru, 106

Peter the Apostle (Saint Peter) (died c. A.D. 67), 16, 23, 25

Peter the Great, Tsar of Russia (1682–1725), 210, 211, 216–224; and Church reform, 216–217; exposure to Western culture, 217; portrait, 218; secularism, 222; executes son, 223; death, 223, 320

Petrarch, Francesco (pee'-trark) (1304–1374), 63

Philip II, King of Spain (1556–1598), 88, 121–123; invasion of England, 127, 128; dies, 128

Philip IV, King of Spain (1621–1665), 129

Philip of Macedon (359–336 B.C.), 13

Philip the Fair, King of France (1284–1314), 52

Philip V, King of Spain (1700–1746), 184, 274

Philippines, 104

Philosophes (fee-lo-zuff), 300–303; and the French Revolution, 354, 377

Philosophy: inductive vs. deductive reasoning, 228–229, 229, 230; and mathematics, 230–231; of natural law, 239; and religious faith, 248–249

Physics, 232

Physiocrats, 308, 309–310

Physiology, study of, 232

Piedmont. *See* Sardinia (Savoy, Piedmont)

Pirates, piracy, 127, 129

Pitt, Thomas (1653–1726), 272, 273, 292, 294

Pitt, William (1708–1778), 290, 334, 371, 374

Pius II, Pope (1458–1464), 55

Pizarro, Gonzalo (pi-zah'-ro) (1506–1548), 103

Plague, 50, 52

Plantation system, 269, 271

Plato (427–347 B.C.), 12; *Republic,* 12

Poland, 213; alliance with Russia, 217–218; partition of, 319, 324, 325–329; geographical territory, 326; since the eighteenth century (map), 328; nationalism, 415–416; post-Napoleonic, 428–429

Polish Republic, 6, 194–196; early commercialism, 120; decline of, 189; boundaries of, 190; (map), 194; classes, 195; government, 195–196; as decline of, 217

Political theory, 249–255; definition, 249

Politiques, 132–133

Pomerania, 205, 218

Pompadour, Madame de (1721–1750), 305

Poniatowski, Stanislas (po-nee-a-toff-skee) (Stanislaus II, King of Poland) (1764–1795), 301, 326

Poor Laws, 113, 117, 163

Poor, working, 117–118

Pope, Alexander (1688–1744), 239

Popes, Roman Catholic. *See* Papacy

Population distribution: of Europe, 137, 170; seventeenth century, 155, 170

Population growth, 28–29, 31, 32–33, 34, 107; and the Plague, 50, 52

Portugal: regains independence, 129, 139

Portuguese colonies: in Asia, 100, 101–102

Potemkin, Grigory (po-tyom'-kin) (1739–1791), 324

Potosí silver mines (po-to-see'), 106, 108, 121

Poussin, Nicholas (poo-siN') (1594–1665), 170, 173

Pragmatic Sanction of 1438, 74

Pragmatic Sanction of 1713, 203, 284

Predestination, 85

Prehistory, 1–2, 11

Presbyterians, 159, 336–337

Pretenders, to English throne, 167, 276–277

Pride's Purge, 160

Printing industry, 111

Printing press, first, 70

Private property, 162–163, 169, 253, 270, 271, 366

Probability theory, 232

Procurator of the Holy Synod, 216–217, 220

Progress, concept of, 257, 258

Progress, faith in, 298–299

Property rights, 162–163, 169, 253; Prussia, eighteenth century, 319. *See also* Feudalism

Protestant, origin of term, 79

Protestant Reformation, 70, 77, 79–92; and social revolution, 81–83; Geneva, Switzerland, 86; in England, 87–91; and economic development, 91–92; and education, 117–118

Protestant wind, 128

Protestantism, 91–92; marriage and family, 92; and women, 92; England as bulwark, 127. *See also* Calvinism; Huguenots; Lutheranism

Protestants: return to Catholicism, 163–164, 165; repression, by Austrian monarchy, 202; in Ireland, 336–337. *See also* Calvinists; Huguenots; Lutherans

Prussia, 186, 194, 195; and Pragmatic Sanction, 203; geography, 204–205; formation of, 204–211; taxation, 207; economy, 207, 209; growth of, 1415–1918 (map), 208–209; class system, 210; parallels with Russia, 212–213; and Seven Years' War, 288, 295–296; under Frederick the Great, 318–320, 324, 326; militarism, 319; social stratification, 319–320; Napoleon conquers, 319–320, 419; and partition of Poland, 324, 326; and the French Revolution, 374; reaction to Napoleon, 395; and Napoleonic Europe, 399; and German nationalism, 419, 420

Prussian army, 206–207, 209–210; recruitment, 210–211; uniforms, 212

Ptolemy, 13; Ptolemaic system, 232, 233

Pufendorf, Samuel (poo-fn-dorf) (1632–1694): *Law of Nature and of Nations,* 251

Pugachev, Emelian (poo-ga-choff) (1726–1775), 321, 323

Purcell, Henry (1659–1695), 156
Puritan Revolution, in England, 159–161; and American Revolution, 332
Puritans, 155
Putting out system, 109, 111, 157
Pythagoras (pi-tha'-grus) (?569–?475 B.C.), 13

Quadruple Alliance, 423, 429
Quakers (Society of Friends), 161, 164
Quebec, Canada, 292
Quesnay, François (kay-náy) (1694–1774), 302
Qur'an (Koran), 20, 21, 970

Rabelais, François (?1490–1553), 70
Race: as cultural concept, 2; and equality, 10
Racine, Jean (ra-seen') (1639–1699), 170
Racism, 253
Radiocarbon dating, 2
Radischev, Alexandr Nikolaevich (1749–1802): *Voyage from St. Petersburg to Moscow,* 371
Rastadt, Treaty of (*Angl.* rah'-stat), 184, 200
Razin, Stephen (d. 1671), 215, 216, 321
Reading public, 300
Realism, 60–61, 62
Reason, and natural law, 250, 251
Reasoning, inductive vs. deductive, 228–229, 230
Recusants, 88, 97
Reformation. *See* Counter Reformation (Catholic Reformation); Protestant Reformation
Refractory clergy, 368–369, 374
Regiomontanus (John Müller) (re'-jee-o-mon-tay'-nus) (1436–1476), 70, 71
Religion: mysticism and lay religion, 71–72; and scientific thought, 238–240, 247–248; and philosophy, 248–249; and natural law, 251; eighteenth century Europe, 261, 262–263; and the Enlightenment, 298–299, 307; and Age of the Democratic Revolution, 330; and the French Revolution, 379–380. *See also* Catholic Church; Christianity; Islam; Jews, Judaism; Muslims; Witchcraft
Religions, state, in Europe about 1560 (map), 89
Religious toleration: Dutch Republic, 150; Ottoman Empire, 197–198; and cultural relativism, 241, 242; Age of Enlightenment, 305–306, 311; Great Britain, 332
Religious wars. *See* Wars of Religion
Rembrandt (1606–1669), 110, 149
Renaissance, 56–72; Italy, 56–69, 226; art, 60–61, 62; literature, 61–65; education, 65; etiquette, 65–67; Catholic Church, 67; marriage and family, 67; politics, 67–69; monarchies, 69–70, 73–74; outside Italy, 69–72; Germany, 70–71, 76–77; Universities, 70–72; religion, 71–72; Holy Roman Empire, 76–77
Revenue Act of 1764 (Sugar Act), 338
Revolution of 1688 (Glorious Revolution), 165–169, 254–255

Richard II, King of England (1367–1400), 51
Richelieu, Cardinal (re-she-lyuh') (1585–1642), 135, 138–139
Rigaud, Hyacinthe (1659–1743), 145, 176
Rights, natural, 253
Robespierre, Maximilien (ro-bes-pyair') (1758–1794), 377, 380, 480; fall of, 381–382
Robot (forced labor), 120
Rochefoucauld, Duke de la (1747–1827), 346
Rohan, Duke of (1579–1638), 135
Roi de Soleil (Sun King). *See* Louis XIV, King of France
Roland, Madame (ro-laN') (1754–1793), 372
Roman Catholic Church. *See* Catholic Church
Roman Empire, 13–15; boundaries of, 14–15, 19; and religion, 17; disintegration of, 19–20; later, 20, 24
Roman Inquisition, 97
Romance languages, 14
Romania, 198, 200
Romanov, Michael, Tsar of Russia (*Angl.* ro'ma-noff) (1613–1645), 214
Romanovs, 214–215
Romanticism, 307, 308, 416, 417
Rome, sacked, 69
Roundheads, 159–160
Rousseau, Jean-Jacques (roo-so') (1712–1778), 302, 303, 306–308, 310; *Discourse on Arts and Sciences,* 306; *Discourse on the Origin of Inequality Among Men,* 306; *Considerations on Poland,* 307; *Social Contract,* 307, 354, 357; *Emile,* 308; and French Revolution, 308, 354; *Nouvelle Héloïse,* 308, 354; portrait, 309
Royal Academy of Sciences, 299
Royal Academy of Sciences, France, 236–237, 238
Royal African Company, 253
Royal Society of London, 236
Rubens, Peter Paul (1577–1640), 96, 150
Rump Parliament, 160, 162
Russia: geographical territory, 6; medieval, 49; international trade, 111; early commercialism, 120; expansion of, 189; before Peter the Great, 213–214; peasants in, 215, 219–220, 223–224, 320–321; enlightened despotism, 320–325; territorial expansion, 323–324; and partition of Poland, 324, 326–327; and Napoleonic Europe, 397–398, 399–400, 402; defeats Napoleon, 421–422
Russia, under Peter the Great, 216–224; under Ottoman Turks, 198; westernization of, 211–224; parallels with Prussia, 212–213; commerce and trade, 213, 220; early contact, with Europe, 213–214; Time of Troubles (1604–1613), 214, 215; government, 214, 220–221; Romanov dynasty, 214–215; absolutism, 215, 220; peasant rebellion, 215, 216, 219; alliance with Poland and Denmark, 217–218; defeats Sweden, 218;

invades Europe, 218–219; taxation, 219–220; social classes, 220–221; social graces taught, 221, 222; peasants, disenfranchised, 223–224. *See also* peasants

Russian army, under Peter the Great, 218–219

Russian Orthodox church, 215–216, 220

Ruthenians, 213

Sacrament, definition, 41

Sahara Desert, 6

Salons, Paris, 171–172, 301–302, 306

Sanitation, eighteenth-century Europe, 262

Sans-culottes (saN-cUl-ut'), 375

Sardinia (Savoy, Piedmont), 186

Savoy (Sardinia, Piedmont). *See* Sardinia (Savoy, Piedmont)

Saxons, 26

Saxony, 139

Scharnhorst, General von (1775–1813), 420

Scholasticism, 44

Schönbrunn Palace, 288

Schöner, Johannes (shU-nr) (1477–1547), 244

Science: advent of, 13; Renaissance, 70–71; seventeenth century, 149, 170; importance of, 225–226; before the seventeenth century, 226–227

Scientific method, 228–229; mathematics and, 230–231, 232

Scientific revolution: and religious faith, 238–240, 247–248; and politics, 239, 240; and sense of evidence, 243, 247

Scientific societies, 236–237

Scotland: conflict with England, 155, 159, 160, 335, 336; joins with England, 167, 186; witch trials, 227; population, eighteenth century, 266

Second World War, 207

Secularization, 49–50, 56, 58–60, 69, 140; and scientific thought, 239; Age of Enlightenment, 306, 317; and enlightened despotism, 311–312; and Age of Democratic Revolution, 330

Separation of powers, 304

Sephardic Jews, 75

Sepoys, 293

Serfs, 31, 35; rebellion of, 50–51, 321–322; eastern Europe, 120, 316–318, 319; Russian, 215, 219–220, 223–224, 321–323. *See also* Feudalism

Servetus, Michael (ser-vee'-tus) (1511–1553), 86

Seven Years' War, 273, 282, 287–293; in Europe, 287–290; and Colonial America, 287–290, 338–348; in India, 291–293; Peace Settlement of 1763, 293–296

Seymour, Jane (1509–1537), 88

Shakespeare, William (1564–1616), 156, 262; *Hamlet,* 156; *King* Lear, 156; Macbeth, 263

Shiite Muslims (shee-ite), 21

Ship money dispute, 158–159

Siam (Thailand), delegations to Europe, 241, 242

Siberia, 213

Sicily, 184

Sieyès, Abbé (syay-ess') (1748–1836), 387; *What is the Third Estate?,* 357

Sikhs, 291

Silesia, 199, 211, 282–283, 318

Silesian wars, 282, 283–287

Silk industry, 113–114

Silver mines, 106, 108, 121

Silverware, origins of, 260

Simon, Richard (see-moN') (1638–1712): *Critical History of the Old Testament,* 247

Sisters and Brothers of the Common Life, 72

Skepticism, 241–242; definition, 241; rejected, in Age of Enlightenment, 298

Slave trade: eighteenth century, 269–270

Slavery: ancient Greece, 12; Middle Ages, 30; Americas, 103, 104, 105, 186, 187–188, 253; Eighteenth Century, 269–270; United States, 342; abolished, in French colonies, 379

Smith, Adam (1723–1790), 308, 309–310; *Wealth of Nations,* 308, 310, 346, 366

Sobieski, John, King of Poland (1674–1696), 195

Social mobility: eighteenth century Europe, 272–273; Age of Enlightenment, 319; Napoleonic Europe, 408; Germany, 420

Social movements, 10

Social stratification. *See* Classes, social

Social structure, definition, 114

Society of Friends (Quakers), 161, 164

Society of Jesus (Jesuits), 95–97

Socrates (469–399 B.C.), 12

Soldiers: eighteenth century, 282. *See also* Mercenaries

Solemn League and Covenant, 159

South Sea bubble, 277–279

South Sea Company, 278–279

Sovereignty, modern theory of, 133, 141

Soviet Union, dissolution of, 219

Spain: Renaissance, 74–75; in the Americas, 75, 102–105; Golden Age, 121; under Philip II, 121–122; revolt of the Netherlands, 123–128, 136; wars with Great Britain, 127, 128, 160, 281–282; Twelve Years' Truce, 128, 136; Catalan war, 129–130; decline of, 129–130, 146, 148; invades France, 132, 139; in the Mediterranean, 184; after the Peace of Utrecht, 274; and War of Jenkins's Ear, 281–282; and Napoleonic Europe, 400, 401, 409; nationalism, 415

Spanish Armada, 127, 128

Spanish Inquisition, 75, 97; in the Netherlands, 124–125

Spanish Main, 282

Spanish Netherlands, 184; Louis XIV invades, 154; become Austrian Netherlands, 184

Spanish Succession, War of, 148, 183–186, 200

Spice trade, 268
Spinoza, Baruch (spi-no'-zuh, ba-rook') (1632–1677), 149, 248; portrait, 249
St. Bartholomew's Day massacre, 132
St. Petersburg, founded, 219, 221
St. Stephen, crown of, 199
Staël, Germaine de (stahl) (1766–1817), 410
Stamp Act, 335, 338
Star Chamber, 73–74, 158, 159
State, definition, 174
Statute of Artificers of 1563, 113
Steam engine, 237
Stein, Baron (1757–1831), 420–421
Stock markets, established, 191
Stonehenge, 11
Strabo (63 B.C.–A.D. 21), 13
Streltsi, rebellion of, 219
Strikes, labor, 366
Stuart monarchs, 157–158, 167, 184, 276–277. *See also under individual monarchs*
Styria, 199
Suarez, Francisco (soo-ah'-rez) (1548–1617), 121
Suez Canal, 6
Suffrage, 329–330, 330; demands for, 334; post-Revolutionary War, 344; Revolutionary France, 364–365
Sugar, 260, 269
Suleiman the Magnificent (1520–1566), 196
Sunni Muslims, 21
Suraja Dowla (soo-rah-ja dow'-la) (d. 1757), 293
Swammerdam, Jan (1637–1680), 149
Sweden, 84; and Thirty Years' War, 138–139; allied with Dutch Republic, 154; territorial victories, 204; Thirty Years' War, 204; invades Russia, 218–219
Switzerland, 140, 182
Szlachta (shlahk'-ta) (Polish aristocracy), 195

Taille (tie) (land tax), 312, 314, 355
Taj Mahal, 291
Talleyrand, Charles Maurice de (1754–1838), 368, 390, 402, 403, 424, 427
Tartars, 46, 190, 198–199, 213
Tax farmers, 177, 179
Taxation: Middle Ages, 36, 51, 52; seventeenth century, 158–159, 162–163; of Louis XIV, 177, 179, 180, 314, 355; Prussia, 207; Russia, under Peter the Great, 219–220; eighteenth century, 279, 281; France of Louis XV, 312, 314, 355; of British colonies, 338–339; France of Louis XVI, 355–356; and French Revolution, 355–356, 361, 392–393
Tea, 260
Technology: agricultural, 7, 29–30; scientific, 149; military, 203, 237; early Russia, 214; advances in, and mathematics, 237; advances in, and wealth, 257

Telescope, invented, 149, 234–235
Tennis Court Oath, 357, 360
Teresa of Avila (1515–1582), 95
Test Act of 1673, 164
Testelin, Henri (1616–1695): *Founding of the Academy of Sciences,* 238
Teutonic Order, 46, 83, 205
Textile industry: eighteenth century, 265, 266, 268–269
Theology, early, 42
Third Estate, and the French Revolution, 352, 357–358
Thirty-Nine Articles, 90
Thirty Years' War, 79, 135–142; background, 136–137; Bohemian war, 137–138; Swedish-French phase, 139–140, 204; Peace of Westphalia, 140–141; sequelae, 147–148, 190–192, 199, 227; Dutch Republic, 149; armies, 203; Brandenburg, 206
Three-field system, 30
Thucydides (471–401 B.C.), 12
Tilsit, Treaty of, 400
Time of Troubles (1604–1613), 214, 215, 217
Timekeeping, 214
Tobacco, 260
Toleration Act, 167
Tories, 165, 188, 276, 331
Torture, and legal system, 243
Totalitarianism, 252
Towns, growth of, 35; medieval, 32–34
Townshend duties, 338
Trade warfare, 411–413
Trafalgar, Battle of (tra-fal'-gar), 399
Transylvania, 136, 137, 199; 1600s, 198
Treaty of Paris (first), 293–296, 425
Treaty of Paris (second), 429
Trinity College (Dublin University), 168
Triple Alliance, 154, 182
Trumbull, John (1756–1843): *Declaration of Independence,* 347
Tsar, etymology of, 214
Tudor monarchs, 73–74, 87–88, 90
Tugenbund (Moral and Scientific Union) (too'-gnt-boont), 418–419
Turgot, Anne Robert Jacques (1727–1781), 302
Twelve Years' Truce, 128, 136
Tyrol, 199

Ukraine (Kiev) (yoo-krane'), 213
Ulfilas (ul'-fi-lus), 25
Ulster, plantation of, 155, 160, 167
Union of Utrecht, 125, 126, 128
Unitarians, 160
United Kingdom of Great Britain: created, 167
United Nations, 10
United Provinces. *See* Dutch Republic

United States: and Napoleonic Europe, 412. *See also* Americas

United States Constitution, 253

Universal monarchy, 93, 147–148; demise, with Peace of Utrecht, 274

Universities: early, 41–42; Renaissance, 70–72; later sixteenth century, 118, 119; religious toleration at, 241

University of Basel, 70–71

University of Dublin (Trinity College), 168

University of Heidelberg, 248

University of Jena, 418

University of Lima, 106

University of Mexico, 106

University of Paris, 41, 112, 241

University of Salamanca, 119

University of Utrecht, 241

Ural Mountains, 6, 213

Urban II, Pope (1088–1099), 45

Urbanization: eighteenth century, 265

Ursuline sisters, 118

Usher, James, Archbishop (1581–1656), 246

Usury, 112

Utrecht, Treaty of, 184, 185, 186

Valois kings, 74

Van Hoogstraten, Samuel (1627–1678), 249

Van Schurman, Anna Maria (1607–1678), 149

Vatican: authority of, 368–369, 370; concordat with Napoleon, 391–392. *See also* Papacy

Vatican Council, Second (Vatican II), 93, 94

Velázquez, Diego (vay-lass'-kayth) (1599–1660), 121

Vermeer, Jan (1632–1675), 149, 150, 151, 153; *Geographer, The,* 150, 153; *Girl Reading a Letter at an Open Window,* 150–151

Versailles (vair-sigh'), 176, 178, 179; Siamese delegation at, 242; and the French Revolution, 363

Vesalius (ve-zay'-lee-us) (1514–1564): *The Structure of the Human Body,* 231–232

Vienna, 190; besieged by Turks, 200, 201

Vikings, 100

Vincent de Paul, Saint (1581–1660), 95

Virginia colonies: first established, 129; Jamestown settlement, 155; slavery in, 269

Virtú, 59

Virtues, classical, 12–13

Volga River, 213

Voltaire (1694–1778), 190, 277, 302, 303, 304–306, 310, 354–355; *Age of Louis XIV,* 305; *Elements of the Philosophy of Newton,* 305; and Frederick the Great, 305, 319; *Philosophical Letters on the English,* 305; *Essai sur les moeurs,* 306; and Catherine the Great, 321

Voting rights. *See* Suffrage

Wallachia (wa-lake'-i-uh), 198

Wallenstein, Albert of (1583–1634), 138, 139

Walpole, Horace (1717–1797), 301

Walpole, Robert (1676–1745), 275, 279, 281, 282

War of 1812, 412

War of Austrian Succession, 282, 283–287; Peace of Aix-la-Chapelle, 285

War of Jenkins's Ear, 281–282

War of the Polish Succession, 281

War of the Pragmatic Sanction, 282

Warburton, Bishop (1698–1779), 302

Warfare: eighteenth century, 282–283; trade, 411–413

Wars of Religion, 121, 122–143; Spain, 122–130; France, 130–135

Wars of the Roses, 51, 73

Wat Tyler's rebellion, 50

Waterloo, 428–429

Watt, James (1736–1819), 237

Watts, Isaac (1674–1748), 299

Wealth, of Europe, 257–258

Weaponry: seventeenth century, 203; scientific improvements in, 237; eighteenth century, 282

Weimar Republic (vigh-mar), 206, 207

Wenceslas, Saint (d. 935), 199

Wesley, John (1703–1791), 299

West Indies: and Eighteenth Century economy, 269; and Seven Years' War, 289, 294–295

Western Europe, 145–188; capitalism, 270–272; after the Peace of Utrecht, 274–282

Whigs, 165, 188, 276, 331, 334

White Russians, 213

White Sea, 213

Whitfield, George (1714–1770), 299

Wilkes, John (1727–1797), 333, 334

William I, German Emperor (1797–1888): King of Prussia (1861–1888), 211

William III: as Stadtholder of the Netherlands (1672–1689), 152; as King of England (1689–1702), 154–155, 165–166, 169, 182, 185

William the Conqueror, King of England (1066–1087), 31

William the Silent (William of Orange) (1578–1584), 125, 126, 148, 152

Witchcraft: persecution of witches, 52, 136, 227, 228; debunked, 149, 298; and evidence, 243; in literature, 263

Wollstonecraft, Mary (1759–1797): *Vindication of the Rights of Woman,* 362

Women: and gender inequality, 10, 16; and early Christianity, 16; as guild members, 34; persecution, as witches, 52, 136, 227, 228; Renaissance, 59, 61–62, 65, 67; education for, 65, 118, 149; Protestant, 92; and Catholic Church, 92; in domestic service, 117; Dutch Republic, seventeenth century, 149; Age of Enlightenment, 300, 301–302, 306, 308; in the Age of the Democratic Revolution, 361–363

Wordsworth, William (1770–1850), 370–371

Working class, 117–118, 366

World, in 1763 (map), 295
Wren, Christopher (1632–1723), 156
Written language, 10–11; and cultural change, 259;
    popular books, 262–263
Wyclif, John (wik'-liff) (1320–1384), 54

Yeomen, 115

Zeeland, 124
Zenta, battle of, 200